Springer Proceedings in Business and Economics

More information about this series at http://www.springernature.com/series/11960

Silvia Cristina Mărginean • Claudia Ogrean
Ramona Orăştean
Editors

Emerging Issues in the Global Economy

2017 International Economics Conference in Sibiu (IECS)

Springer

Editors
Silvia Cristina Mărginean
Faculty of Economic Sciences
Lucian Blaga University of Sibiu
Sibiu, Romania

Claudia Ogrean
Faculty of Economic Sciences
Lucian Blaga University of Sibiu
Sibiu, Romania

Ramona Orăştean
Faculty of Economic Sciences
Lucian Blaga University of Sibiu
Sibiu, Romania

ISSN 2198-7246 ISSN 2198-7254 (electronic)
Springer Proceedings in Business and Economics
ISBN 978-3-319-71875-0 ISBN 978-3-319-71876-7 (eBook)
https://doi.org/10.1007/978-3-319-71876-7

Library of Congress Control Number: 2017963361

Printed on acid-free paper

This Springer imprint is published by Springer Nature
The registered company is Springer International Publishing AG
The registered company address is: Gewerbestrasse 11, 6330 Cham, Switzerland

Contents

Chapter 1
Flattening Phillips Curve, "Passive" Policy, and Incidence of the Self-fulfilling Prophecy in a Standard New-Keynesian Model with Financial Accelerator

Alexie Alupoaiei

Abstract Post-crisis period is described by several stylized facts with a significant impact on the business cycles. Examples of such stylized facts consist in the Phillips curve flattening, very low inflation levels, or a "passive" stance of the monetary policy. Thus, it was contoured the so-called new normal era, which raises a series of caveats for the macroeconomic modeling. In this regard, the present paper comes to address the issue on the incidence of self-fulfilling prophecy in a New-Keynesian model extended with financial sector. This extension consists in defining an additional equation which introduces the financial accelerator related to lending conditions. Basically, calibrating the model for Romanian and Euro Area economies, the underlying work aims to investigate the operational circumstances in which the benchmark New-Keynesian framework can to be resorted for policy analysis, given the new stylized facts. By considering the condition for multiple rational expectations equilibria underlined by Bullard and Mitra (J Monet Econ 49:1105–1129, 2002), we analyzed the emergence of a unique bounded stationary equilibrium in the specified context. Preliminary results underline that under a "passive" monetary policy, flattening of the Phillips curve facilitates the occurrence of multiple rational expectations equilibria. Obtained results reveal also a nonlinear relation between interest rate spread elasticity with respect to the output-gap and the incidence of self-fulfilling prophecy. This work is normative, so further investigations have to be made on the appropriateness of a sunspot-based approach in order to study the business cycle mechanics within the present framework.

Keywords Determinacy • Financial Accelerator • New-Keynesian • Phillips Curve • "Passive" Policy

---

A. Alupoaiei (✉)
The Romanian – American University, Bucharest, Romania
e-mail: alex.alupoaiei@gmail.com

S.C. Mărginean et al. (eds.), *Emerging Issues in the Global Economy*, Springer Proceedings in Business and Economics,
https://doi.org/10.1007/978-3-319-71876-7_1

1.1 Introduction[1]

Occurrence of the 2008 financial crisis brought several major changes on the macroeconomic thinking and modeling. One of the first conclusions which appeared after 2008 episode was that developments within financial sector can have the potential to affect seriously the economic stability, being thus necessary to consider them endogenously when concerns on the general equilibrium topic are addressed. Therefore a process similar to a revolution in terms of models' revision was observed in post-crisis period. A lot of efforts were focused on the introduction of financial side in the workhorse approaches for business cycle analysis. On the other hand, the new stylized facts in the after of 2008 brought again the necessity of new changes in macroeconomic modeling. Some of these new stylized facts, which contoured the so-called new normal, consist in the sudden increase of public debt, precautionary savings, low interest rate environment (but with a strong focus of the policy makers to avoid zero and even negative rates), rapid disinflation and defilation in some cases, etc. Putting together all these mentions, several caveats have been contoured for the macroeconomic modeling activity. Given the recent episodes of deflation or near-zero inflation in several economies, sustained efforts from the policy makers to maintain positive interest rates can be observed. This means implicitly the adoption of a passive monetary policy, with potential super-inertial effects. On the other side, the Phillips curve flattening affects further the well-known macro mechanic. In this regard, under these considerations, a reexamination of the basic New-Keynesian model is necessary. For this purpose, the underlying work aims to investigate, through the use of several indicative experiments, the effects of the so-called new normal on the New-Keynesian mechanics. More exactly, we called the basic forward-looking New-Keynesian model with a standard policy rule, which was further expanded to incorporate the financial accelerator. Basically, we focused on the incidence of self-fulfilling prophecy property given the new normal environment. Having in mind the condition for multiple multiple rational expectations equilibria underlined by Bullard and Mitra (2002), we analyzed the emergence of a unique bounded stationary equilibrium in the current context. Therefore, the underlying approach aims to treat the indeterminacy topic in a normative way. The background of this paper is based on a standard New-Keynesian model with financial accelerator, which comes in line with approaches of Cecchetti and Li (2008), Cecchetti and Kohler (2012), and Poutineau and Vermandel (2014). Singh et al. (2015) expanded a BGG model to allow for a policy response to financial developments, for which they investigated the premise for self-fulfilling prophecy.

[1] Opinions expressed in this paper are those of the author and should not be associated with the institutions to which he belongs.

1.2 Methodology

Clarida et al. (1999) elaborated in a seminal paper the fundamental form of New-Keynesian science that is used today by academia as well as policy makers to form conclusion about wide economy's dynamics. In fact, the underlined model became quickly the workhorse within the monetary policy management. Of course, the primitive form of the CGG (1999) model (Clarida, Gali, and Gertler) suffered some changes in order to adjust to recent research findings. On the other hand, projection lines behind the CGG (1999) model have been introduced within the more complex DSGE models, which have been designed for policy analysis and forecasting. Even that, the original CGG (1999) model remains a benchmark reference for different topics related to monetary policy field. Here, in the spirit of Bernanke et al. (1999), the standard CGG model was expanded to allow for a financial accelerator. The resulting model is:

$$y_t^{gap} = E_t\left[y_{t+1}^{gap}\right] - \frac{1}{\gamma}\left(i_t - E_t\left[\pi_{t+1}\right]\right) - \alpha l_t \tag{1.1}$$

$$\pi_t = \beta E_t\left[\pi_{t+1}\right] + (\gamma + \Psi)\frac{(1-\theta)(1-\theta\beta)}{\theta} y_t^{gap} \tag{1.2}$$

$$i_t = \bar{i} + \phi_y y_t^{gap} + \phi_\pi \pi_t \tag{1.3}$$

$$l_t = i_t - \lambda y_t^{gap} \tag{1.4}$$

More exactly, the core CGG (1999) approach is recognized in the literature as being the basic New-Keynesian model (BNKM). Two important mentions have to be made on the model (1.1), (1.2), (1.3), and (1.4), described above. Firstly, it's important to note that the difference in comparison with the BNKM doesn't consist only in relation no. (1.4). Another important difference is the presence of loan rate in the IS relation. This idea related to demand block is not relatively new as Bernanke and Blinder (1989) used such an IS relation. Instead, the recent financial crisis underlined the high importance of a financial sector for the business cycle fluctuations. Secondly, the model (1.1), (1.2), (1.3), and (1.4) or the NK-FA model has no stochastic items, as we limited only to the study of equilibria. The four equations are presented under a log-linear form at equilibrium, being derived from optimal problems faced by representative agents that postulate a closed economy. The first equation of the above model is known as the Euler equation for output (output-gap) or the dynamic IS equation, and it is used to model the aggregate demand. In fact it is derived from consumption theory as being the optimal solution under rational expectation of a consumer's planning problem. This equation states that output-gap, y_t^{gap}, is directly influenced by expectations of its future outcomes, and it is inversely related to the real interest rate, respectively, the loan rate l_t. γ is the risk aversion parameter under CRRA preferences, mentioning the optimal consumption-saving problem used in the derivation of the above model, by supposing the severability feature of the utility function in consumption and work. The other parameter from the representative agent's utility Ψ is the inverse elasticity of work in respect with its marginal disutility, while β is the subjective discount factor. Real interest rate is computed according to rational expectations $(i_t - E_t[\pi_t])$. α denotes the output-gap elasticity in respect to the loan rate. The second equation is known as New-Keynesian Phillips curve (NKPC) and links the evolution of inflation by its future expected values and the output-gap. $(\gamma+\Psi)\frac{(1-\theta)(1-\theta\beta)}{\theta}$ represents the transformed markup, where $(1 - \theta)$ is the probability according to which the intermediate firms, within a monopolistic market, adjust their prices to new developments. The way, mentioned before, through which firms change their prices is known as *a la* Calvo setup. The policy action is defined through the use of a standard Taylor reaction function, without a preference for smoothing interest rate fluctuations. In fact, CGG (1999) addressed several options for central bank's reaction function, but here we stop to the standard form of Taylor equation for interest rate dynamics. This equation states that central bank's reaction function changes in respect with developments in the real sector ϕ_y, respectively, in prices ϕ_π, while $\bar{i}$ denotes the interest rate long mean. The last relation shows the inversely relation between the interest rate spread and the output-gap, with a related elasticity λ.

By doing a bit algebra, the following state space representation is obtained:

$$\begin{pmatrix} y_t^{gap} \\ \pi_t \end{pmatrix} = \frac{1}{\Omega}\begin{pmatrix} \gamma & 1-\beta\phi_\pi(1+\gamma\alpha) \\ \gamma\kappa & \Gamma \end{pmatrix} E_t \begin{pmatrix} y_{t+1}^{gap} \\ \pi_{t+1} \end{pmatrix} + \Upsilon \tag{1.5}$$

where $\Omega = \gamma(1 - \gamma\alpha) + (\phi_y + \phi_\pi\kappa)(1 + \gamma\alpha)$, $\kappa = (\gamma+\Psi)\frac{(1-\theta)(1-\theta\beta)}{\theta}$ is the Phillips curve slope, and $\Gamma = \Omega\beta + \kappa[1 - \beta\phi_\pi(1 + \gamma\alpha)]$, while Υ contains the other elements. In order to investigate the incidents of the self-fulfilling prophecy property, the Blanchard-Kahn conditions were studied. More exactly, according to Blanchard-Kahn conditions, a unique equilibrium of the model is obtained if and only if the two roots of the $\frac{1}{\Omega}\begin{pmatrix} \gamma & 1-\beta\phi_\pi(1+\gamma\alpha) \\ \gamma\kappa & \Gamma \end{pmatrix}$ are inside the unit circle.

1.3 Calibration and Results

There are several ways to put in practice the basic New-Keynesian model. Examples in that sense are the use of SVAR model on the base of rational econometrics and the use of GMM or 3SLS by calling instrumental variables or directly calling the form defined by (1.1), (1.2), (1.3), and (1.4). Here the last option has been chosen, and the NK-FA model was calibrated afterward for Romanian and Euro Area

Table 1.1 Calibrated parameters for the NK-FA model

	β	γ	Ψ	θ	α	λ	ϕ_y	ϕ_π
Romania	0.992	2.5	1.5	0.7	$1/\gamma$	0.3	(0,1.5)	(0,1.5)
EA	0.998	1.61	1	0.7	$1/\gamma$	0.2	(0,1.5)	(0,1.5)

economies. For calibration purposes, we used posterior estimates from several benchmark working papers, elaborated for each of the two economies. For Romanian economy, we referred to the papers written by Alupoaiei (2015) and Copaciu et al. (2016), mentioning the lack of bibliographic references in this case. Instead for Euro Area exist many references, but here we called the seminal paper of Smets and Wouters (2005) (Table 1.1).

Above can be seen the parameters that we used in calibration for the two involved economies. A few observations have to be made here. First of all, it is important to note that reported figures were chosen in such a manner to ensure as much robustness as possible, given the economies we used as reference have different structures. In that sense, we took figures in order to ensure a trade-off between the model's structure and the empirical observations on the business cycle. Perhaps many specialists consider that a better idea would be to directly estimate the model on empirical observations, but even the posterior estimates depend on a prior setup. This situation is usually met in small samples. Given that, we consider that our option is pretty robust if we take into account that we used the mean tendency provided by posterior estimates from different papers. The idea that we have to insert before is that we don't consider that our approach endows for sure a lower accuracy. More than that, as it is mentioned at the beginning of the paper, this work is a normative one and should be viewed accordingly.

Secondly, we have to note that some of the parameters we used in calibration were adapted a little bit given the specific context. More exactly, owing to different models' structures from the reference papers, we also called other evidences from case to case (econometric exercises, considerations, etc.). Therefore, somehow, our approach includes also an ad hoc component, having in mind the idea underlined by Robert Solow according to which he would “rather be ad hoc than wrong.” But this ad hoc component was only marginal, given that the most part of calibration came from posterior estimates obtained in the papers we cited. For example, some parameters, such as λ or α, were not calibrated by considering only targeted estimates, additionally taking into account the link between model and real mechanics, as well as other papers or specific stylized facts. For example, the new developments in financial markets showed that a financial crisis generates a strong tightening in credit markets. This stylized fact is captured in our model (enough or not) by the increase of real costs of financing. More than that, because our model has no link with the credit policy, λ has to cover the recent developments in banking regulation and macroprudential policy. According to Cecchetti and Li (2008), the elasticity of output-gap with respect to the loan rate was set in order to have the same importance as the real interest rate does. The parameters in the policy rates were set to take values in the usual space, given the main focus here is on the determinacy aspect.

Incidence of multiple rational expectations equilibria was analyzed on the base of computation of relation (1.5). Obtained results are reported in Appendix. Given the new context described by Phillips curve flattening, the problem of indeterminacy was separately analyzed for a standard calibration of the slope (case I), respectively, for a second scenario (case II), where the slope was calibrated at a half value as compared with case I. Figures 1.1 and 1.2 show that for Euro Area, determinacy region (in green) is highly bigger than for the BNK model. More exactly, in the NK-FA model, a unique equilibrium is assumed even with a "passive" monetary policy and implicitly out of the Taylor principle. On the other hand, for calibration related to case II, we can observe that indeterminacy region increases a little bit for low levels of ϕ_y. A similar situation can be seen also for Romania in the two scenarios. The difference observed in obtained results for Romania and Euro Area consists in a slightly bigger determinacy region for the former one, this situation being in each of the two cases regarding the Phillips curve' slope calibration (Figs. 1.3 and 1.4).

Results presented before suggest that in NK-FA model, determinacy could emerge even with a "passive" monetary policy. Therefore, the second part of the analysis addresses the problem of a "passive" monetary policy under different stances related to the importance of financial sector. In this regard, we considered a "passive" monetary action described by the following policy parameters: $\phi_y = 0.5$ and $\phi_\pi = 0.4$. Calibration of the policy parameters under a "passive" stance was set on the base of different works with Markov switching rational expectations equilibria, mentioning here Mavromatis (2011) or Foerster (2014).

Obtained results for the two economies show that even in such a "passive" policy scenario, which fairly deviates from the determinacy condition derived by Bullard and Mitra (2002) for the basic New-Keynesian model, the emergence of a unique bounded equilibrium is still possible. Figures 1.5 and 1.8 underline that indeterminacy is inversely related to the output-gap elasticity with respect to the loan rate and directly related to the interest rate spread elasticity with respect to the output-gap. In any case, we can observe a nonlinear relationship, as for high levels of interest rate spread elasticity with respect to the output-gap, the self-fulfilling prophecy is met everywhere. In the same time, we can observe that, under a "passive" monetary policy, flattening of the Phillips curve facilities the incidence of multiple rational expectations equilibria. In this case, the determinacy regions determined for Romania are significantly higher as compared with those ones obtained for the Euro Area (Figs. 1.6, 1.7, and 1.8).

1.4 Conclusions

Present work aimed to investigate the emergence of potential multiple rational expectations equilibria in a standard New-Keynesian model extended with financial sector. It's important to note that the current paper represents a normative work, so the main goal was to raise attention about the underlying topic, given the so-called *new normal* era. Thus, rigorous analysis has to be made further for a positive outcome on this issue. The underlying subject is very important, because in the presence of the self-fulfilling prophecy, specific tools have to be used in order to solve for the optimal policy in models with rational expectations. On the other hand, the emergence of self-fulfilling prophecy determines different significant implications for the model's mechanics.

Acknowledgment This work was supported by a grant of the Romanian National Authority for Scientific Research, CNCS – UEFISCDI, project number PN-II-RU-TE-2014-2499 entitled "Coordinating Monetary and Macroprudential Policies."

Appendix

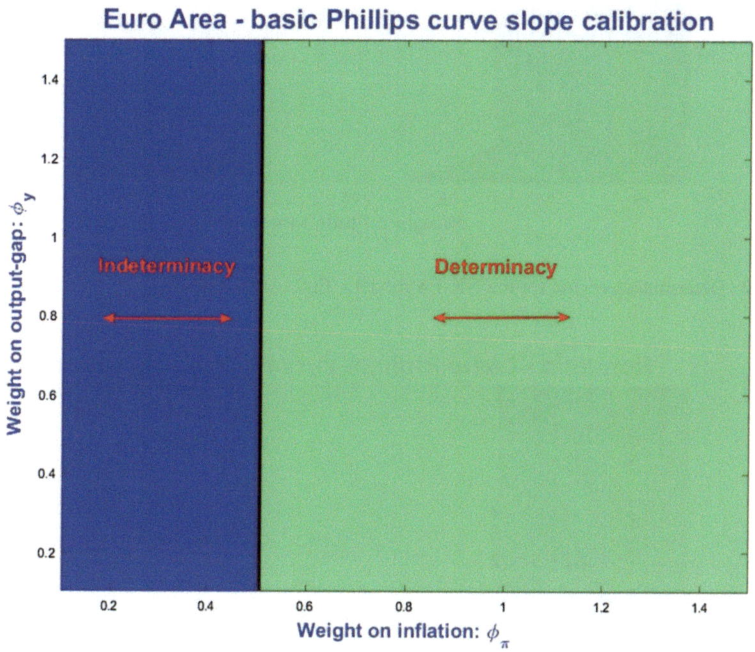

Fig. 1.1 Determinacy region for the NK-FA model – Euro Area, case I

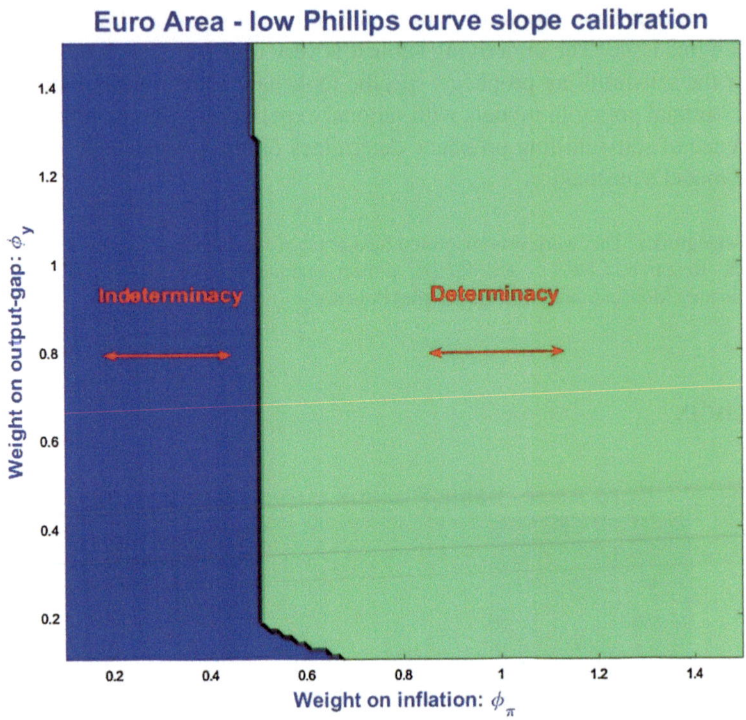

Fig. 1.2 Determinacy region for the NK-FA model – Euro Area, case II

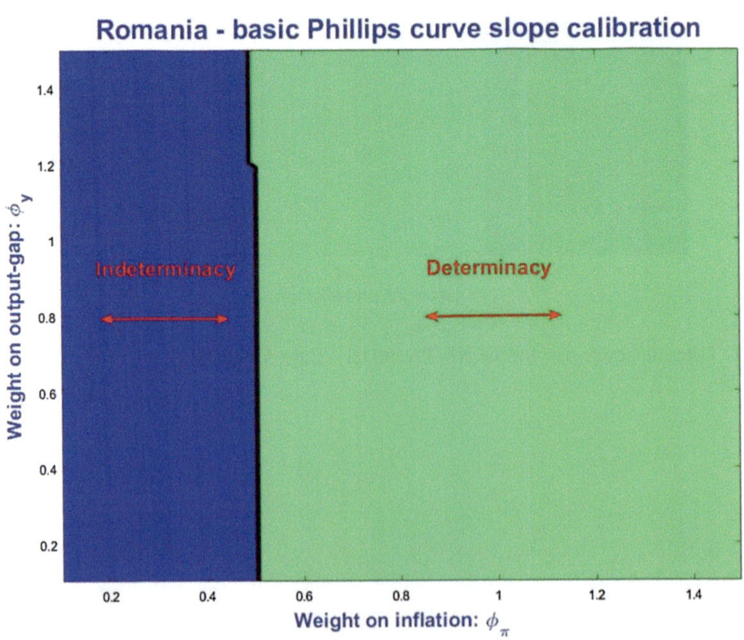

Fig. 1.3 Determinacy region for the NK-FA model – Romania, case I

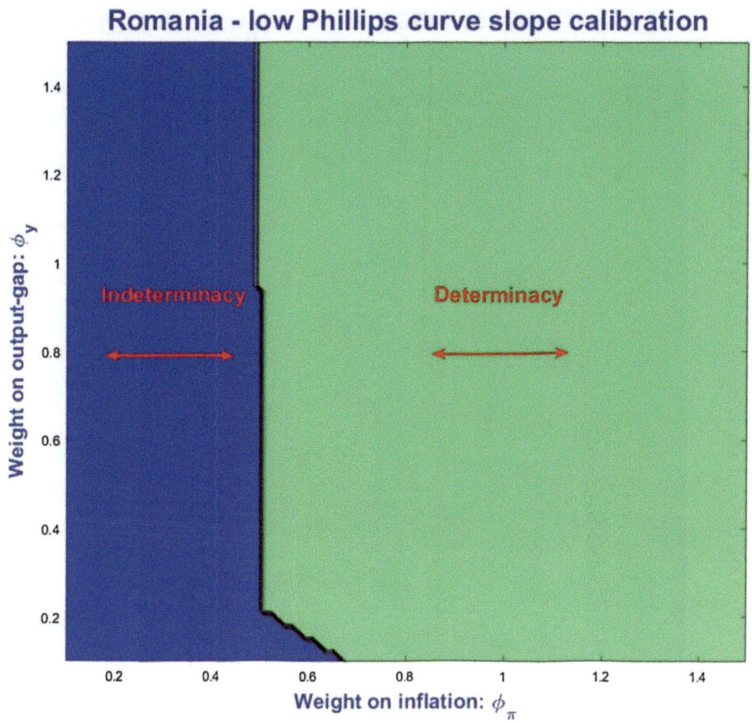

Fig. 1.4 Determinacy region for the NK-FA model – Romania, case II

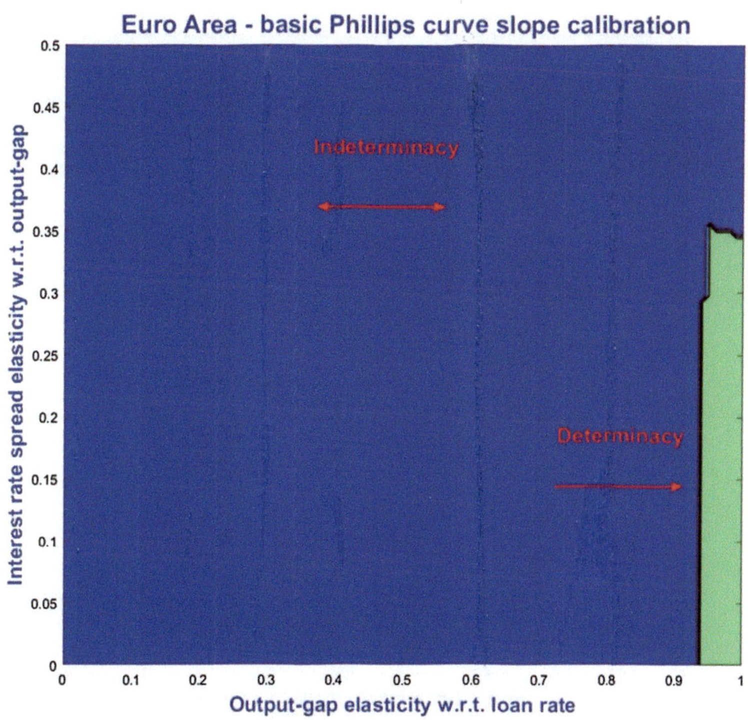

Fig. 1.5 Determinacy region for the NK-FA model with a "passive" policy – Euro Area, case I

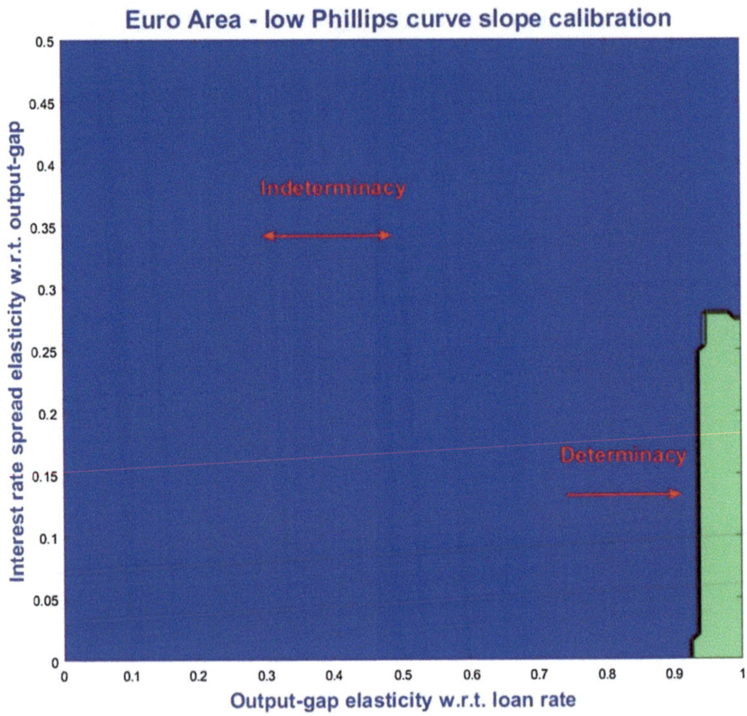

Fig. 1.6 Determinacy region for the NK-FA model with a "passive" policy – Euro Area, case II

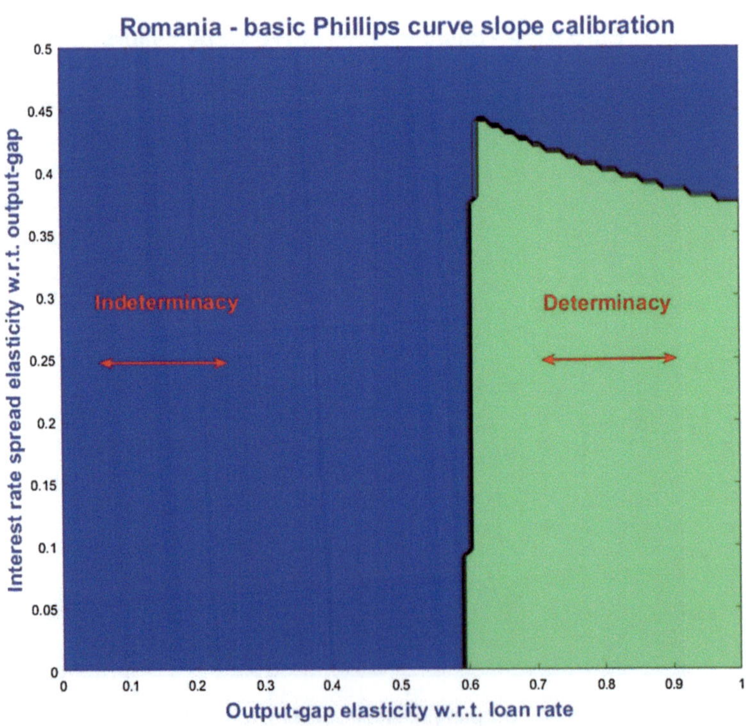

Fig. 1.7 Determinacy region for the NK-FA model with a "passive" policy – Romania, case I

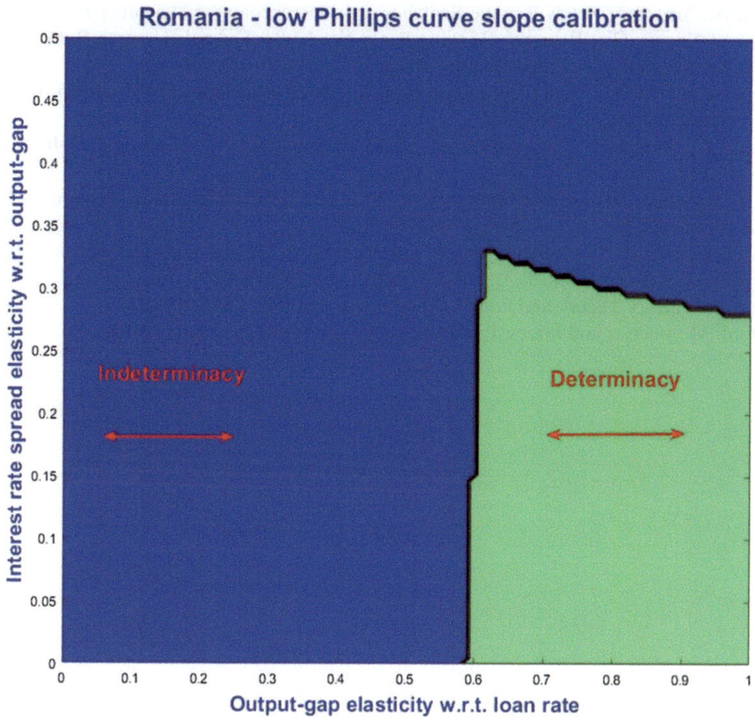

Fig. 1.8 Determinacy region for the NK-FA model with a "passive" policy – Romania, case II

References

Alupoaiei, A.: Effects of Knightian uncertainty on the term-structure of interest rates. J. Business Manag. Appl. Econ. **IV(3)**, (2015)

Bernanke, B. and Blinder, A.: Credit, money, and aggregate demand. National Bureau of Economic Research Cambridge (1989)

Bernanke, B., Gertler, M., Gilchrist, S.: The financial accelerator in a quantitative business cycle framework. Handb. Macroecon. 1341–1393 (1999)

Bullard, J., Mitra, K.: Learning about monetary policy rules. J. Monet. Econ. **49**, 1105–1129 (2002)

Copaciu, M., Bulete, C., Nalban, V.: R.E.M. 2.0 A DSGE Model with Partial Euroization Estimated for Romania National Bank of Romania Occasional Papers No. 21. National Bank of Romania, Bucureşti (2016)

Clarida, R., Galí, J., Gertler, M.: The science of monetary policy: a new Keynesian perspective. J. Econ. Lit. **37**, 1661–1707 (1999)

Cecchetti, S., Kohler, M.: When Capital Adequacy and Interest Rate Policy Are Substitutes (And When They Are Not) Bank for International Settlements, Working Paper No. 379. Bank for International Settlements, Monetary and Economic Department, Basel (2012)

Cecchetti, S., Li, L.: Do capital adequacy requirements matter for monetary policy? Econ. Inq. **46**(4), 643–659 (2008)

Foerster, A.: Monetary Policy Regime Switches and Macroeconomic Dynamics Federal Reserve Bank of Kansan City Research Working Paper No. 13-04. Federal Research Bank of Kansas City, Research Division, Kansas City (2014)
Mavromatis, K.: Markov switching monetary policy in a two-country DSGE model. In: Dynare Conference Working Papers (2011)
Poutineau, J., Vermandel, G.: A primer on macroprudential policy. J. Econ. Educ. **46**(1), 68–82 (2014)
Singh, S., Stone, S. and Suda, J.: Monetary Policy and the Financial Sector. Economics Letters. 132, 82–86 (2015)
Smets, F., Wouters, R.: Comparing shocks and frictions in US and euro area business cycles: a Bayesian DSGE approach. J. Appl. Econ. **20**(2), 161–183 (2005)
Walsh, C.: Monetary Theory and Policy. MIT Press, Cambridge, MA (1998)
Woodford, M.: Interest and Prices. Princeton University Press, Princeton (2003)

Chapter 2
European Union at a Crossroads: What Could the Next 60 Years Bring About?

Lia-Alexandra Baltador

Abstract This paper aims to synthetize some of the challenges that the European Union faces during these troubled times and also to suggest some of the possible scenarios that might actually unfold in order to address them. Symbolically, this year should have highlighted the biggest achievements of the EU and its Member States, as it celebrates 60 years of joint commitment for a better Europe. Yet, the uncertainty regarding Europe's future is at an all-time high, due to internal and external factors. On the one hand, internal challenges, such as the Brexit process and the refugee crises, led to the reevaluation of the EU's current organization and structure, which, in turn, might lead to a Europe of concentric circles or a Europe doing less more efficiently. On the other hand, there are external factors that will impose new approaches on important aspects such as the economic and political relations with the United States, negotiations with Turkey or the Republic of Moldavia in connection to their accession to the EU, and other global problems, such as tackling climate change, reducing poverty, promoting peace, and others. In order to project some of EU's possible future steps, a critical analysis of reports and statements of the EU's most important institutions and representative will be carried out, as a fundament for possible scenarios.

Keywords Future of the European Union • Challenges • Uncertainty

2.1 Introduction

The European Union has been considered to be the best example of how progressive economic and political integration between countries can lead to peace and prosperity for all citizens. This aim was pursuit and insured for more than half a century. The cooperation among the Member States wasn't always easy, but, in the end, a

L.-A. Baltador (✉)
Lucian Blaga University of Sibiu, Sibiu, Romania
e-mail: lia.baltador@ulbsibiu.ro

S.C. Mărginean et al. (eds.), *Emerging Issues in the Global Economy*, Springer Proceedings in Business and Economics,
https://doi.org/10.1007/978-3-319-71876-7_2

compromise could be reached. The UK achieved, after its accession, in 1973, the inclusion of the Regional Development Policy as an important counterbalance to the Common Agricultural Policy, to be excepted from participating to the European Monetary Union, and obtained extensive derogatory clauses with regard to the labor market, to name but a few. Still, after a referendum, "Brexit" (Britain's exit from the EU) became a reality, and now the negotiations are unfolding, with no predictable outcome.

"Unity in diversity" was hardly ever on debate, at least for the first 50 years or so. Still, in 2010 Angela Merkel was among the first to state "multiculturalism has failed," as she referred to the guest workers that came to Germany in the 1960s and are still not well integrated in the German society. Currently, by the addition of more than 1.2 million refugees in Europe, with different cultural backgrounds, the situation is even more problematic. Terrorist attacks in European cities made the situation worse and thus brought more arguments to those Member States opposing quotas of (mostly Islamic) refugees.

Troubled waters also with regard to External Relations. The new president of the United States, Donald Trump, announced from the first days in office that he is not a supporter of global free trade. Thus, the Transatlantic Trade and Investment Partnership, problematic even before Trump, is now indefinitely on hold. Other issues, such as climate change, are also handled in an "original" manner by the US president.

Turkey, once a serious and determined candidate for the EU Accession, is now undergoing a profound political transformation. In July 2016, the government survived an attempted coup which saw clashes on the streets of Istanbul and Ankara. Subsequently, the authorities detained thousands of people, mostly soldiers and judges on suspicion of involvement in the attempt coup. Hereon, Turkey's parliament approved a new draft constitution paving the way for a presidential system of government in January 2017, in a move which would significantly increase President Erdogan's powers. How will all this affect the relations with the EU, in general, but more stringent, what implications will it have on the EU-Turkey joint action plan to support Syrian refugees?

2.2 The Main Internal Challenges

Great Britain's option to withdraw from the European Union was a consequence of a referendum held on 23 June 2016, to decide whether the UK should leave or remain in the EU. Leave won by 51.9% to 48.1%. The referendum turnout was 71.8%, with more than 30 million people voting. This unexpected outcome determined the new Prime Minister, Theresa May, to trigger the Brexit negotiation, by activating Article 50 of the Lisbon Treaty, on 29 March 2017, around the celebrations of the 60th anniversary of the signing of the Treaties of Rome. The named article refers to the possibility a state has to leave the EU, after explicitly notifying the European Council. The country would officially exit the EU on the date the withdrawal agreement came into effect, or, if no agreement is reached, it could leave 2 years after the date of notification (Poptcheva 2016).

In her letter addressed to the EU Council president, Donald Tusk, May argues that the vote "was no rejection of the values we share as fellow Europeans. Nor was it an attempt to do harm to the European Union or any of the remaining Member States" (May 2017). The representatives of the two parts, David Davis, UK's Brexit secretary, and Michel Barnier for the EU, are settling the conditions of this separation, after 44 years of common living. And because it's for the first time this article is triggered, there are many uncertainties. A first unknown was regarding who should lead the negotiations for the EU, the European Commission or Member States' governments. Further, what will happen if no deal will be reached until the 2-year deadline. Thirdly, Article 50 does not include specific references to what negotiations should be about, only that it should include also the framework of future relations. Additionally, the possibility for the UK to change its mind and revoke the "exit" is also not so clear (Gostynska-Jakubowska 2017).

Now that "the dice have been thrown," the discussions evolve around a "hard" or a "soft" Brexit. But what do these two options imply? A "hard" exit would mean that the free movement of goods, services, capital, and persons between the EU and the UK will no longer be assured. Leaving the Single Market and all bodies that come under the jurisdiction of the European Court of Justice will bring the UK political sovereignty and self-determination, just as it required and, thus, more control over money, regulations, and frontiers. According to this scenario, trade will be organized over World Trade Organization rules. The Centre for Economic Performance at the London School of Economics has remodeled the trade consequences. It concludes that the hardest form of Brexit, a reversion to WTO terms, would cut trade by 40% over 10 years and reduce annual income per person by 2.6%. Applying the most favored nation principle would raise the cost of exporting to the EU for UK firms (Ottaviano et al. 2016). Other costs might arise from non-tariff barriers, as well as from services trade regulations of the WTO, less liberalized than in the Single Market. "But free movement of capital between the UK and EU would probably continue, as the EU prohibits restrictions on capital mobility not only within the EU, but also with countries outside the EU" (Dhingra and Sampson 2015). On the other hand, the UK would no longer be bound by the EU's Common External Tariff, which would lead to greater autonomy in trade negotiations, but if it would outweigh the costs from reduced bargaining, power is hard to predict, ever more since the average tariff charged on imports to the EU is only around 1%.

Other sectors that will lose from this "split" are farmers, who receive EU funding through the Common Agricultural Policy or researchers. Also many adjacent topics remain problematic, among these leaving the Euratom Treaty, which "would jeopardize not only the UK nuclear industry, but also the supply of medical isotopes for cancer treatment" (Kellner 2017). Further, Kellner indicates other implications like the fact that some UK airlines would need to set up in the EU 27 or might be forced to move its planes to EU 27 countries due to the UK leaving the Open Skies Agreement. Other aspects that might arise refer to Emissions Trading System,

Patents and Intellectual Property Rights, Europol, Food Standards, and, probably, many more.

Even if Theresa May affirmed that "no deal is better than a bad deal," the current situation indicates a softer version might be more realistic. A comprehensive analysis of future relations has been carried out by Dhingra and Sampson in 2015. One option would be to opt for the Norwegian model, namely, accessing the European Economic Area. This would minimize the trade costs of Brexit, but it would mean paying about 83% as much into the EU budget as the UK currently does. It would also require keeping current EU regulations, but without having a seat at the table when the rules are decided. According to the previous cited study, such an arrangement would cut trade by 20–25% and reduce annual incomes by 1.3%. Another possible scenario includes the Swiss model, opting for negotiating bilateral deals with the EU. Switzerland still faces regulation without representation and pays about 40% as much as the UK to be part of the Single Market for Goods. But the Swiss have no agreement with the EU on free trade in services, an area where the UK is a major exporter.

On the other side, the EU officials aim to keep Brexit as a onetime incident and to discourage anti-EU sentiments in other Member States. In order to do so, no "cherry picking" or "have the cake and eat it" from the UK will be accepted. During the first two negotiation meetings, the two parts have been discussing citizen's rights and the Irish border and separation issues, including UK financial liabilities. According to EU officials, long-term trade issues won't be addressed until there's been "adequate progress" on these issues. The UK and EU have made separate offers on residency rights, each side saying they want an early agreement to give certainty to the three million EU nationals in the UK and the 1.2 million British expats on the continent. There have been hints of progress in talks on citizen's rights accompanied by stronger hints that there's still a long way to go, for example, with regard to the EU insistence on a future oversight role for the European Court of Justice, which remains a stumbling block.

The UK has said it will honor its membership obligations and pay what it is lawfully due but has rejected talk of paying "extortionate" sums of up to 100bn euros. According to Kellner "if neither a compromise nor a transitional arrangement is possible, then the UK will be left with a stark choice: crash out of the EU in a way that could crucify the UK's economy and disrupt daily life to an alarming degree—or stay in the EU" (Kellner 2017).

Another difficult task of the EU is addressing the refugee crisis. It is intrinsically difficult to handle such complex issues of integrating people with different cultural backgrounds, because tolerance imposed by law does not create viable multicultural societies. The scale of the phenomena, starting in 2014–2015, as well as the lack of solidarity and unity between Member States on this subject brings additional challenges. The European Commission President, Jean-Claude Juncker, included migration as one of the ten political priorities of his mandate (Juncker 2014). According to the data, in the last years, there have been more displacements in Europe than during the Second World War. Over 1.2 million people have arrived in the European Union, the large majority of them fleeing from war and terror in Syria, Libya, and other troubled countries. Many asylum seekers, but also economic migrants, risk their lives by resorting to illegal smugglers to get them across borders, thus becoming "irregular" migrants. In order to tackle the refugee crises, the EU developed some measures which aim to resolve the root causes of the crisis, as well as greatly increasing aid to more than ten billion euros for people in need of humanitarian assistance both inside and outside the EU. "A European Agenda on Migration" comprises short- and long-term objectives and was elaborated in order "to restore confidence in our ability to bring together European and national efforts to address migration, to meet our international and ethical obligations and to work together in an effective way, in accordance with the principles of solidarity and shared responsibility... This requires using all policies and tools at our disposal – combining internal and external policies to best effect" (European Commission 2015). The four pillars the Agenda is built upon refer to reducing the incentives for irregular migration, thus addressing the root causes behind this phenomena, saving lives and securing the external borders, strengthening the common asylum policy, and developing a new policy on legal migration.

While immediate actions, such as saving lives at sea and targeting criminal smuggling networks, have shown significant progress, relocation and resettlement between the Member States still remain problematic, as some countries refuse to accept the distribution key or "quotas" proposed by the European Commission. The integrated European response was founded on the idea of "sharing solidarity, the basis for international credibility," but that was not the case. Poland, the Czech Republic, and Hungary have not fulfilled their responsibilities, so the Commission has decided to launch infringement procedures against these three Member States. According to a Communicate of the EC, "the total number of relocations stands at 20,869 (13,973 from Greece, 6,896 from Italy)." With almost all Member States now relocating from Italy and Greece, it is feasible to relocate all those eligible (currently around 11,000 registered in Greece and around 2000 registered in Italy, with arrivals in 2016 and 2017 still to be registered) by September 2017. An efficient solution for this crisis can't come from one single country or group of countries (European Commission 2017a). It represents a global problem, so the answer lies in an international approach. The EU's high representative for foreign affairs and security policy stated that "we are proposing a new approach for strong partnerships with key countries. Our goal is to support the countries that host so many people and foster growth in our partner countries. We are ready to increase financial and operational support and to invest in long-term economic and social development, security, rule of law and human rights, improving people's life and tacking the drivers of migration" (European Commission 2016). The current situations that some of these countries face at the moment seem to predict an uncertain and rather gloomy future. And critics state that this approach of the EU is problematic, as "their currently preferred method seems to be 'externalization'. This involves recruiting countries which refugees and migrants come from or travel through, to tighten border control, or shifting protection responsibilities to other countries" (de Bellis 2017).

2.3 Some External Challenges

Globalization implies that the world became "hot, flat, and overcrowded," according to some authors. But even if the focus wouldn't be on the negative, the increasing interdependencies between countries are no longer on debate. Global problems require a global response. So, in order to tackle the refugee crises or climate change, the need for international cooperation appears clearly. But what if the willingness to cooperate is not there? What if the values that should fundament actions are not common? What if priorities are considered to be within one's country? Nowadays, the global landscape looks quite unusual, if we compare it to what it looked like only some years before. The West, or North, from the economic perspective has had a more or less unique voice. The United States, Western Europe, Canada, and Australia, to name a few, were leading the international Agenda. Economic sanctions, even military interventions, were put in place in order to bring order. The US elections in 2016 resulted in Donald Trump occupying the Oval Office at the White House. Even if the president of the most powerful nation promised to "solve the problem in the Middle East" and to improve relations with Russia, no real progress has been made. As for the relations with the EU, Federica Mogherini said "From the economy to security, to the big work we're doing to stabilize places in the Middle East and in Africa, there is a common interest to work together." The motto "America first" used during Trump's campaign and after indicates at least two scenarios. According to Elvire Fabry, actions might evolve between "aggressive economic nationalism" and a "protectionist megaphone with limited disruption" (Fabry 2017). What would this mean for the EU, as the United States is their largest export market (20.7% of EU 28 exports in 2016) and they are themselves the United States' second largest importer ($384 billion in 2016) after China ($434 billion) (EC DG for Trade 2016)? One possible solution might be Brussels' decision to accelerate bilateral trade negotiations throughout the world in order to occupy the place abandoned by the US demand. To support this, on the 6th of July, the EU and Japan reached an agreement in principle on the main elements of the EU-Japan Economic Partnership Agreement, while some months earlier the Comprehensive Economic and Trade Agreement (CETA) with Canada was voted by the European Parliament. Another important, but at times, difficult partner of the EU is Turkey. Even if it is a candidate for EU accession since 1999 and has had closed links since the 1960s, the current political situation brings about uncertainty. In November 2016 members of the European Parliament adopted a resolution asking for the negotiations to be temporarily suspended while repression continues in Turkey: "Turkey is not showing this political will as the government's actions are further diverting Turkey from its European path" (European Parliament 2017). President Erdogan seems to be determined to provoke even more disruption of Turkey's way to the EU, and the referendum organized on 16 April 2017 that gives the president additional powers indicates a possible distance from European values. European Parliament President Antonio Tajani urged Turkey to respect fundamental rights, which are the basis of Europe. He stressed that "Europe is not an Islamophobic continent and is not closing the door on the Turkish people." The ideology is one, but there are also important economic and political aspects to be considered. The EU is by far Turkey's largest export market (44.5%), while Turkey is the EU's fourth largest export market (4.4%). Additionally, as mentioned before, Turkey is a key player in mitigating the refugee crises, after the EU and Turkey concluded an agreement in March 2016. The deal led to significantly fewer migrants reaching Europe illegally; however Turkey has threatened several times to suspend it, accusing the EU of not living up to its commitments.

2.4 Conclusions

The European Union faces numerous challenges, internal and external. Nothing new, some will say. "The Union has often been built on the back of crises and false starts. From the European Defence Community that never got off the ground in the 1950s, to the exchange rate shocks of the 1970s, through to aborted accessions and rejections in referenda in recent decades, Europe has always been at a crossroads and has always adapted and evolved" states the White Paper on the Future of Europe (European Commission 2017b). Still, the response to these challenges might affect how, or if, the European Union will exist for the next 60 years. In order to make Brexit a onetime "incident," the process has to be concluded in such a manner that other Member States will think twice before initiating such an option, primarily by indicating the net benefits of membership.

In order to go further than the binary approach of more or less Europe, the European Commission launched the White Paper on the Future of Europe – Scenarios for 2025 – which include five possible scenarios, which are on debate. The first scenario implies carrying on as before, which would determine a joint agenda for actions, but which will not overcome the perpetual discussions about who should intervene in certain issues: Member States or EU institutions. As previously stated, there are still lots of unknown regarding Brexit, such as who's in charge with the negotiations, what will happen if no deal will be reached in the foreseen period, is there a possibility to revoke the process, etc. In this scenario decision-making remains complex to grasp and the capacity to deliver does not always match expectations. The refugee crises represent another such example. As for External Relations, progress will continue toward speaking with one voice, as well as a closer defense cooperation and improved coordination on security matters between Member States. The cooperation in the management of external borders would be gradually stepped up while making progress toward a common asylum system. The second scenario would restrict common policies to those that support the functioning of the Single Market and not much more. Even with regard to the four main liberties, only free movements for goods and capital would be strengthened, while free movement of people and services will not be fully guaranteed. In the Brexit context, this outcome would represent the best achievement for all those opting out. It would leave the economic benefits, but would provide more sovereignty and power to address issues in a bilateral manner. Migration wouldn't be a common concern, as no single migration or asylum policy will be developed and further coordination on security would be dealt with bilaterally, while internal border controls would become more systematic. Bilateral negotiations would be carried out with regard to many aspects which today are being managed by Europe's one voice. Another scenario is quite similar with the first one, with the exception that in this case not all Member States have to participate in further integrative measures. "Those who want more do more" scenario implies the creation of "coalitions of the willing" who would choose to deepen cooperation in fields such as taxation, social standards, security, etc. It will create an EU of multiple speed, in which citizens' rights derived from EU law start to vary depending on whether or not they live in a country that has chosen to do more. This scenario would prevent other Member States from wanting to leave the EU, as there would be no reason for it. They would be able to choose the fields in which they stand to benefit from while opting out to deeper integration on the ones they don't. How this scenario would be implemented remains to be seen. As part of the Single Market, with free movements of persons, would there be a possibility to control migration? What about External Affairs? Will there be different decision-making levels, in order to respond to American or Turkish measures? The fourth scenario would lead to restraining the areas of common regulation, "doing less more efficiently." But what would be a priority and how will 27 states agree upon them? Would migration be of concern to all, but more so, will all Member States accept imposed decision about quotas? The trade relations would be such a common regulated field, as the Single Market will continue to function, but what about unforeseen political evolutions, such as now happening in Turkey? It's debatable if a mechanism can be put in place in order to select if emergencies or unexpected developments should become or not a common priority.

The last scenario proposed by the EC implies "doing much more together." This would have been probably the most accepted scenario, 3–4 years ago. Without such major challenges such as Brexit, refugee crises, and unprecedented political evolutions in the world, this would have been the path for an ever more integrated Europe – united in diversity. It might have been what EU's founding fathers have hoped to achieve. In Robert Schuman's words, "Europe will not be made all at once, or according to a single plan. It will be built through concrete achievements which first create a de facto solidarity." In this complex and ever-changing world, the European Union has to be more flexible in order to provide effective solutions to the challenges it faces. Probably the future will not be shaped entirely and completely by one of these scenarios. Still, they might indicate some reference points. Let's hope that in another 60 years, today's situation will be just one of many hurdles that the European has overcome, together.

References

de Bellis, M.: A radical change is needed to failing EU migration policy. https://www.amnesty.org/en/latest/news/2017/06/a-radical-change-is-needed-to-failing-eu-migration-policy/. Accessed 29 June 2017

Dhingra, S., Sampson, T.: Life after BREXIT: what are the UK's options outside the European Union? Centre for Economic Performance (2015). http://cep.lse.ac.uk/pubs/download/brexit01.pdf. Accessed 7 May 2017

European Commission – Communication from the Commission to the European Parliament, the Council, the European Economic and Social Committee and the Committee of the Regions: A European Agenda On Migration (2015). https://ec.europa.eu/home-affairs/sites/homeaffairs/files/what-we-do/policies/european-agenda-migration/background-information/docs/communication_on_the_european_agenda_on_migration_en.pdf. Accessed 2 Mar 2017

European Commission – Press release: Commission announces New Migration Partnership Framework: reinforced cooperation with third countries to better manage migration (2016). http://europa.eu/rapid/press-release_IP-16-2072_en.htm. Accessed 14 June 2017

European Commission, Directorate-General for Trade: European Union Trade with USA (2016). http://trade.ec.europa.eu/doclib/docs/2006/september/tradoc_113465.pdf. Accessed 29 June 2017

European Commission – Press release: European Agenda on Migration: Commission calls on all parties to sustain progress and make further efforts (2017a). http://europa.eu/rapid/press-release_IP-17-1587_en.htm. Accessed 14 June 2017

European Commission: White Paper on the Future of Europe (2017b). https://ec.europa.eu/commission/white-paper-future-europe_en. Accessed 25 May 2017

European Parliament: EU-Turkey: anatomy of a difficult relationship (2017). http://www.europarl.europa.eu/news/en/headlines/world/20170320STO67729/eu-turkey-anatomy-of-a-difficult-relationship. Accessed 29 Mar 2017

Fabry, E.: Tump Trade: More Bark Than Bite?, Policy Paper 193, pp. 8–12 (2017). http://www.institutdelors.eu/media/trumptradeandeurope-elvirefabry-april17.pdf?pdf=ok. Accessed 29 June 2017

Gostyńska-Jakubowska, A.: Brexit maze: The Role of EU Institutions in the Negotiations, Center for European Reform (2017). http://www.cer.eu/sites/default/files/pb_brexit_institutions_5.7.17.pdf. Accessed 15 July 2017

Juncker, J.-C.: A New Start for Europe: My Agenda for Jobs, Growth, Fairness and Democratic Change (2014). https://ec.europa.eu/commission/publications/summary-president-junckers-political-guidelines_en. Accessed 2 Mar 2017

Kellner, P.: When Brexit meets logic (2017). http://carnegieeurope.eu/strategiceurope/71558. Accessed 9 July 2017

May, T.: Prime Minister's letter to Donald Tusk triggering Article 50. UK Government (2017). https://www.gov.uk/government/publications/prime-ministers-letter-to-donald-tusk-triggering-article-50/prime-ministers-letter-to-donald-tusk-triggering-article-50. Accessed 18 June 2017

Ottaviano, G., Pessoa, J. P., Sampson, T., Van Reenen, J.: The Costs and Benefits of Leaving the EU', Centre for Economic Performance Policy Analysis (2016). http://cep.lse.ac.uk/pubs/download/pa016.pdf. Accessed 8 May 2017

Poptcheva, E.M.: Article 50 TEU: Withdrawal of a Member State from the EU. European Parliamentary Research Service Briefing (2016). http://www.europarl.europa.eu/RegData/etudes/BRIE/2016/577971/EPRS_BRI(2016)577971_EN.pdf. Accessed 21 May 2017

Chapter 3
The Development of Methodology for Innovative Project Effectiveness Parameter Estimation in Direction of Fuzzy Set Application

Alexander Baranov, Elena Muzyko, and Victor Pavlov

Abstract The purpose of the paper is to develop methodology of sustainability and reliability estimation of innovative project effectiveness' parameters with application of fuzzy sets, as well as the procedure of computation of reliability and sustainability of its fuzzy parameters. The method of fuzzy sets allows to estimate the fluctuation range of innovative project parameters depending on "swinging" its main input (exogenous) parameters, such as market prices of the product, investments expenditures, raw materials costs, etc. In the same time, it becomes possible to assess sustainability of the project effectiveness parameters to variations of its main input parameters, as well as their reliability. The use of fuzzy sets extends the capabilities of real options method's application to analysis of the effectiveness of investments in innovative projects and also allows to take into account the factor of uncertainty much better, which is especially important in the case of innovations implementation. Fuzzy set assessment of sustainability of forecasted financial flows and financial parameters generated by innovative project is carried out in three directions: for assessment of an innovative project effectiveness in a whole using discounted cash flows method, for assessment of innovative project effectiveness using the NPV method from venture fund's position, and for assessment of innovative project effectiveness using the NPV method from position of a venture fund with application of real options. The developed methodology and computing procedures are tested on a real innovative project in the pharmaceutical industry.

A. Baranov
Novosibirsk State University, Novosibirsk, Russia
e-mail: baranov@ieie.nsc.ru

E. Muzyko (✉)
Novosibirsk State Technical University, Novosibirsk, Russia
e-mail: mei927@mail.ru

V. Pavlov
Peter the Great Saint Petersburg Polytechnic University, Saint Petersburg, Russia
e-mail: victor_n_pavlov@mail.ru

S.C. Mărginean et al. (eds.), *Emerging Issues in the Global Economy*, Springer Proceedings in Business and Economics,
https://doi.org/10.1007/978-3-319-71876-7_3

Keywords Real options method • Venture financing • Fuzzy sets • Innovative project • Uncertainty

3.1 Introduction

The problem of research could be formulated in the following way: how a venture fund could assess a new fast-growing innovative company on an intensively growing market with a high degree of uncertainty. This problem is quite actual for newly created high-technology companies which require financing for their development.

Investments made by the venture funds are known for their high levels of uncertainty and risks, and quite often they show staged nature. Therefore the traditional method of discounted cash flows (NPV method) should be coupled with other approaches able to count flexibility in decision-making, particularly through the estimation of innovative project effectiveness with the help of methods used in global practice but not widely applied in Russia for now. One of them is the real options method.

The concept of real options emerged as a result of the transfer of the newly created risk management toolset into the real sector of economy. A real option is a tool of innovative project uncertainty decrease through creation of options with basic asset presented by revenues generated by the innovative project with management possessing managerial flexibility in making decisions on its further realization.

Traditional analysis of innovative project effectiveness could also be accompanied with research of how uncertainty of future financial flows generated by the project influences effectiveness parameters. This could be done with the use of fuzzy set method. In our opinion, application of real options method along with fuzzy set toolset is a perfection way for existing methods of innovative project effectiveness estimation.

The authors of the paper have made the following contribution to the study of the problem under consideration:

1. Fuzzy set assessment of sustainability of financial flows generated by an innovative project and indicators of its effectiveness with the inclusion of the compound call option when financing by venture fund has been proposed.
2. The methodology of fuzzy parameter reliability and sustainability assessment was developed.
3. The proposed approach was tested on the real innovative project. As a result of performed analysis, answers to the following questions were obtained:

    (a) Fuzzy assessment of the riskiness degree of the venture project
    (b) Fuzzy assessment of the sustainability of the financial flows generated by the innovative project
    (c) Fuzzy assessment of the level of price volatility of the underlying asset of the real option (market value of investee company's shares) depending on the variation of important input parameters of the innovative project

3.2 Literature Review

Today in Russia, the problems of fuzzy set method application to analysis of venture financing of innovative projects and to real options value assessment are actively researched, which is confirmed by a large number of defended dissertations on this problem. The majority of these research works are based on the results of the doctoral dissertation by Nedosekin (2003) in which he elaborated the main approaches to fuzzy set analysis of financial processes. The efforts of Akinina (2011) are directed to application of neural networks and fuzzy clusterization to the analysis of financial solvency. In the paper by Gareyev (2009), fuzzy set methods of venture financing multicriteriality analysis are suggested.

The comparative analysis of application of fuzzy set theory and classic probabilistic approach to the assessment of possibility of venture investments unfavorable outcome is done in Trifinov (2009). Application of fuzzy logic models to risk analysis is shown in Abdullaeva's (2013) dissertation. Nedosekin et al.'s (2016) paper considers a fuzzy set assessment of a real options value basing on Dubois-Prade arithmetics. Various aspects and properties of real options and venture financing of innovations are studied with the use of fuzzy set theory in Mednikov (2008), Klementyeva (2006), Ilyin (2009), and Kalchenko (2012).

Let's mention briefly foreign publications on the researched problematics. Uchal and Kahraman's (2009) paper suggests the model of real options assessment with the use of fuzzy set approach in oil and gas sector. In Xubo (2012) the model with fuzzy parameters for venture investment effectiveness is developed. In Yihua and Wenjing (2011), the fuzzy set approach combined with the real options approach is applied to assessment of realty investment risk assessment. Carlsson et al.'s paper (2007) develops the assessment methodology of real options which are typical for R&D projects when future cash flow is assessed with the real options approach.

The model of real options value with fuzzy parameters for assessment of investments in the construction sphere is suggested in Wang et al. (2015). In Wu (2007) the fuzzy set theory is applied to define the borders of value variation of European financial options "put" and "call." It uses fuzzy interest rate, fuzzy volatility, and fuzzy value of option basic asset. In Carlsson and Fuller (2003), the present value of expected cash flow and expected costs for an investment project is estimated with the use of fuzzy sets.

The specific feature of our approach is the synthesis of approaches from probabilistic and fuzzy set nature to analysis of venture financing of innovative projects based on real options.

3.3 The Methodology

Value of a compound call option at the present moment of time t, which is owned by a venture fund, would be (the modified Geske formula (Hsu 2002; Geske 1979)):

$$C^v = V^v N_2\left(h+\sqrt{\sigma_1^2\tau_1},;l+\sqrt{\sigma_1^2\tau_1+\sigma_2^2\tau_2},;\rho\right)-I_2^v e^{-r\tau}N_2\left(h,;l,;\rho\right)-I_1^v e^{-r\tau_1}N_1\left(h\right), \tag{3.1}$$

where C^v is value of a compound call option at the present moment of time t, which is owned by a venture fund; V^v is the present value of investee company shares belonging to the venture fund;

$$h=\frac{\ln\frac{V^v}{\overline{V}^v}+r\tau_1-\frac{1}{2}\sigma_1^2\tau_1}{\sqrt{\sigma_1^2\tau_1}};\ l=\frac{\ln\frac{V^v}{I_2^v}+r\tau-\frac{1}{2}\left(\sigma_1^2\tau_1+\sigma_2^2\tau_2\right)}{\sqrt{\sigma_1^2\tau_1+\sigma_2^2\tau_2}};\rho=\sqrt{\frac{\sigma_1^2\tau_1}{\sigma_1^2\tau_1+\sigma_2^2\tau_2}};$$

I_1^v is the exercise price of compound (external) call option (investments of the venture fund at the time moment T_1, proportional to investee company's shares);

I_2^v is the exercise price of internal call option (the value of implicit costs of a venture fund); r is risk-free interest rate; $\tau_1 = T_1 - t$, $\tau_2 = T_2 - T_1$, $\tau = T_2 - t = \tau_1 + \tau_2$; $N_2(h, l; \rho)$ is the function of two-dimensional standard normal distribution; $N_1(\cdot)$ is the function of one-dimensional standard normal distribution; and $\overline{V}^v$ is such value of investee company shares at the moment of time T_1 (V_{T_1}), for which the following equation is valid:

$$V_{T_1} N_1\left(l^*+\sqrt{\sigma_2^2\tau_2}\right)-I_2^v e^{-r\tau_2}N_1\left(l^*\right)=I_1^v, \tag{3.2}$$

where 1* is value of l at the moment of time T_1:

$$l^*=\frac{\ln\frac{V_{T_1}}{I_2^v}+r\tau_2-\frac{1}{2}\sigma_2^2\tau_2}{\sqrt{\sigma_2^2\tau_2}}. \tag{3.3}$$

3.3.1 Fuzzy Set Assessment of Sustainability of Financial Flows Generated by an Innovative Project and Indicators of Its Effectiveness

Fuzzy set assessment of sustainability of forecasted financial flows and financial indicators will be conducted in the following directions: (1) to assess effectiveness of an innovative project in a whole using the method of discounted cash flows, (2) to assess effectiveness of an innovative project using NPV method from a venture fund point of view, and (3) to assess effectiveness of an innovative project using NPV method from a venture fund point of view and with application of real options method.

The concept of experimental computations is in Monte Carlo method application to "wandering" exogenous indicators of the project financial model and in analysis of consequences of such fluctuations for the mail endogenous parameters of the financial model, which characterize the effectiveness of the innovative project.

In the first of mentioned above directions, we could "wander" the following exogenous indicators: market prices on products; prices on main raw materials, electric energy; and investments in fixed assets (e.g., there could be changes in prices on equipment or building and installation works, making therefore "investments" a fuzzy parameter as well).

Output endogenous parameters, which sustainability is to be assessed, are the following: net present value of the whole project ($NPV_{\text{whole project}}$) and internal rate of return of the whole project ($IRR_{\text{whole project}}$).

In the second direction, the following parameters could be "wandered": share of a venture fund in the stock capital of an investee company, amount of direct investments of the venture fund, dividends received by the venture fund as a share of net profit (net profit of the investee company is fuzzy), and discount rate acceptable for the fund.

We are going to assess sustainability of net present value of the venture fund ($NPV^{v}_{\text{vent.fund}}$) and internal rate of return of the venture fund ($IRR_{\text{vent.fund}}$).

In the third direction of research, the following input parameters could be used as fuzzy: I_0^v is the acquisition costs of a compound call option at the moment T_0, I_1^v is the execution price of the compound (external) call option (investments of the venture fund at the moment T_1 into acquisition of part of a risky company shares), r is the risk-free interest rate, σ_1 is the risk level of venture company operations within the time interval (0, T_1), and σ_2 is the risk level of venture company operations within the time interval (0, T_2).

Fuzzy "output" parameters, which sustainability is to be assessed, are the following: $NPV^{v}_{\text{with option}}$ and $IRR^{v}_{\text{with option}}$.

3.3.2 *The Methodology of Fuzzy Parameter Reliability and Sustainability Assessment*

Main Notations

Let *R* be a real straight line, *F*(*R*) be a populations of fuzzy sets in the space *R*, $D \in F(R)$ be a fuzzy set in *R*, and $\chi_D : R \to [0; 1]$ be a membership function of the set *D*. Let's denote *I*(*D*) as a carrier of the fuzzy set *D*:

$$I(D) = \{x \in R | \chi_D(x) > 0|\},$$

where *N*(*D*) is the smallest segment containing *I*(*D*) and $S(a, b) \in F(R)$ is the symmetric triangular number *a* with length bearer *b*.

Now let R^m be a *m*-dimensional arithmetic space and $F(R^m)$ be a population of fuzzy sets in the space R^m. Let's consider some mapping:

$$G : F\left(R^m\right) \to F\left(R\right).$$

In applications the line $R$is usually interpreted as a space of values of explored economic parameter, while the space R^m – as a space of values of parameters influencing on explored parameter. The mapping G represents a mathematical model aimed to compute value of parameter $G(D) \in F(R)$under the given values of influencing parameters $D \in F(R^m)$.

Let's define a fuzzy value of the parameter D. In this article, a stochastic algorithm is used to build the mapping G. It includes the following sequence of procedures.

1. The fuzzy set D is converted into a random mapping:

$$\xi : \Omega \to R^m,$$

   where Ω is probabilistic space with probabilistic measure p.
2. A sample of random elements $\{\omega_1, \omega_2, \ldots, \omega_n\}$ is done. For each value of a parameter $\xi(\omega_k)$, the value of resulting parameter $r_k \in R$ is computed according to the Geske model.
3. An interval conversion is applied to the sample $\{r_1, r_2, \ldots, r_n\}$ which results in the fuzzy set $G(D)$.

As a resulting value of a parameter from the fuzzy set $G(D)$, its most reasonable value $\bar{g}$, is usually chosen, it is computed in the following way:

$$\chi_{G(D)}\left(\bar{g}\right) = \max_{g \in R}\left\{\chi_{G(D)}\left(g\right)\right\}.$$

Procedures of Fuzzy Parameter Reliability and Sustainability Computation

ssess reliability of the most reasonable value of a fuzzy parameter, let's introduce the term parameter standard value. We suggest that the standard value has the highest reliability level which is equal to one. If computed value of fuzzy parameter deviates from the standard one, then its reliability could be less than one. For being a standard, one such fuzzy parameter is usually taken which complies with requirements of researchers. As a standard let's choose a symmetric triangular number $S\left(\bar{g},b\right)$, where the bearer length is $b \leq |N(G(D))|$. Then the reliability measure $H\left(G\left(D\right),S\left(\bar{g},b\right)\right)$ is computed according to the following formula:

$$H\left(G(D),S(\overline{g},b)\right)=\min\left\{\begin{array}{l}\dfrac{\int_{-\infty}^{\infty}\min\left\{\chi_{G(D)}(t),\chi_{S(\overline{g},b)}(t)\right\}dt}{\int_{-\infty}^{\infty}\chi_{G(D)}(t)\,dt},\\ \dfrac{\int_{-\infty}^{\infty}\min\left\{\chi_{G(D)}(t),\chi_{S(\overline{g},b)}(t)\right\}dt}{\int_{-\infty}^{\infty}\chi_{S(\overline{g},b)}(t)\,dt}\end{array}\right\}. \tag{3.4}$$

It is clear that absolute value of reliability measure depends on the chosen standard. This certainly decreases attractiveness of the methodology. However, if we would compute reliability ratios of two parameters $G_1(D)$ and $G_2(D)$ under the same standard, then the repeated computation of each parameter reliability after standard change shows that both ratios change proportionally and in the way that lesser of them always remains the lesser one.

Sustainability parameter is used for exploration of the parameter $G(D)$ dependence on the parameter D and characterizes speed of $G(D)$ value change after changing the parameter D. Usually sustainability parameter is used in analysis according to the following methodology. Let there be given two values of the parameter D_1 and D_2. $H(G(D_1), G(D_2))$ is computed.

Conclusion on the sustainability level of the parameter $G(D)$ when $D = D_1$ is made in the following way: the higher is reasonability of $H(G(D_1), G(D_2))$ of sets $G(D_1)$ and $G(D_2)$ coincidence, the higher is the parameter $G(D)$ sustainability. In this case sustainability ratio is declared to be equal $H(G(D_1), G(D_2))$.

3.4 The Analysis of Calculation Results

Since the size of the paper is limited, let us briefly review the most important calculation result.

The computations were conducted in relation to the real innovative project in the pharmaceutical industry in Russia (due to confidentiality of commercial data, we could not disclose the name of the company, which initiated the project, as well as the place of the plant construction). The purpose of the project is in construction of the owned plant for output of pharmaceutical oral hygiene products. It is possible to engage a venture fund in this project financing.

Figure 3.1 shows the graph of the venture fund IRR reasonability degree function depending on variations of its share in the equity capital of the investee company. It is assumed that the venture fund considers unsatisfactory the results of its investments when IRR of these investments would be less than 15% after exit. In computations the basic share of the venture fund in the stock capital of investee company is assumed to be equal to 49%. In other words, the venture fund initially does not claim on the controlling share in investee company. The fund's share in the equity capital of investee company is "wandered" within ±10%, i.e., from 44.1% to 53.9%. Computation results show that the risk of IRR <15% occurrence for the venture

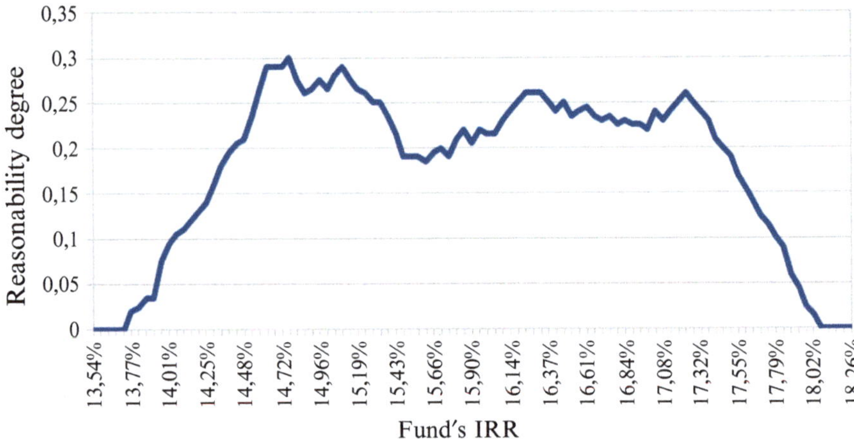

Fig. 3.1 Assessment of the venture fund's risk to get unsatisfactory IRR value depending on variation of its share in equity capital of investee company

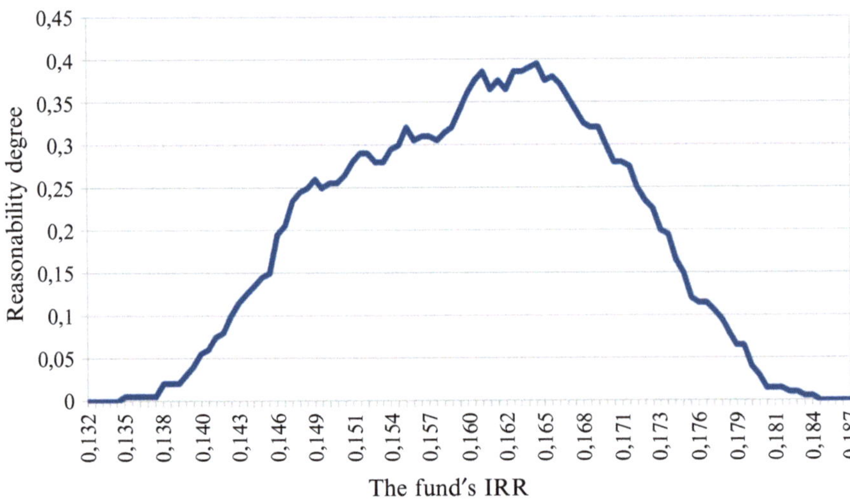

Fig. 3.2 Assessment of the venture fund's risk to get unsatisfactory IRR value depending on variations of prices on products of investee company

fund is approximately 26%. This value is defined as the ratio of subgraph to the left of the dashed line (see Fig. 3.1) to the whole square of subgraph of the reasonability degree function.

Figure 3.2 depicts the graph of the venture fund's IRR reasonability degree function depending on variations of prices on products of investee company.

Prices are "wandered" randomly (by the Monte Carlo method) for the whole computation period within ±10%. Computation results show that risk of getting IRR <15% for the venture fund is approximately 15.5%. This value is also defined

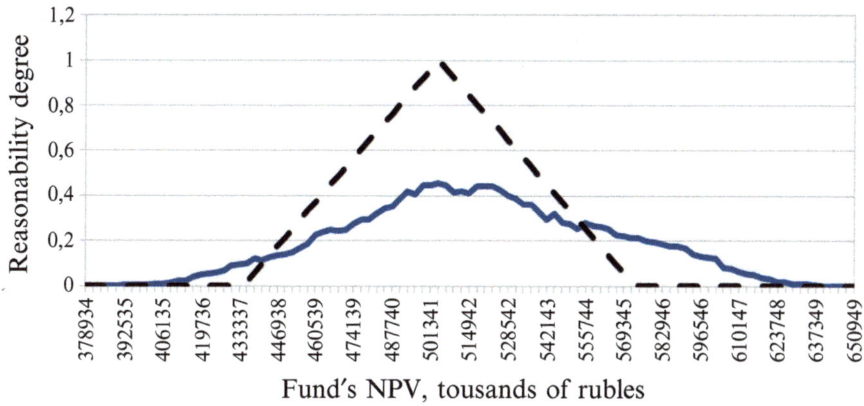

Fig. 3.3 Characteristics of reliability of the most reasonable value of the venture fund's NPV in case of changes in prices on production of investee company

as a ratio of subgraph to the left of the dashed line (see Fig. 3.2) to the whole square of the reasonability degree function subgraph. Therefore the influence of variations of venture fund's share in the equity capital on the risk level of getting unsatisfactory IRR value of the venture fund as a result of a venture project carrying out is significantly greater than the influence of variations of prices on products of investee company.

From the substantial point of view, the important thing is reliability of the most reasonable parameter of the innovative project effectiveness. In order to identify it, we use the so-called standard value of the most reasonable effectiveness indicator value, for instance, IRR and NPV of the whole project or venture fund's effectiveness indicators. In the given research, we consider a symmetric triangular representation of the most reasonable value of the effectiveness indicator (e.g., the fund's NPV) with the bearer equal to 0.7 of the range of sample of explored indicator (NPV of the fund or the whole project) to be a standard.

Figure 3.3 shows that reliability of the computed most reasonable venture fund's NPV value (512 mln rubles) in case of change in prices on investee company production is 56.4%. This reliability value is obtained as a result of production prices variation within the interval ±10% of their factual values in the basic year of the forecast. Geometrically reliability is characterized by a ratio of reasonability degree function subgraph intersecting with standard subgraph square (hatched area on the graph) to the whole square of the reasonability degree function subgraph.

On Fig. 3.4, the share of hatched square of the subgraph of reasonability degree function to the whole subgraph square (0.311) represents the probability of liquidation value V^{ν} surpassing a venture fund's threshold value, which is the value which triggers positive decision on investments in the amount of I_1^{ν}. This value equals to 219.1 mln rubles and is computed as the sum of investments at the time T_0 in the amount of I_0^{ν} = 35 mln rubles and discounted to the zero year (2009) investments at the time T_1 in the amount of I_1^{ν} = 184.1 mln rubles (197/1.07 = 184.1).

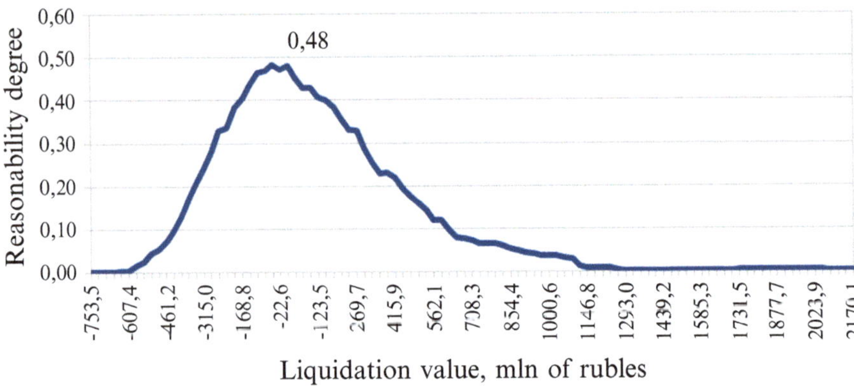

Fig. 3.4 Reasonability degree of getting various values of liquidation values of investee company V^v

Probability of positive decision on the internal option, i.e., decision-making on main investments in the amount of 197 mln rubles, is defined according to the Geske formula and is equal to 0.25. Then the overall probability of successful execution of the compound call option is 0,311•0.25 = 0,109.

Reasonability degree of reaching threshold value 219.1 mln rubles by the liquidation value is approximately 0.35. For even higher values, reasonability degree is less than 0.35 (values to the right of 219.1 mln rubles on Fig. 3.4).

3.5 Summary

Application of fuzzy set approach to the assessment of a compound call option value widens analytic possibilities of practicing financiers. The following additional possibilities appear: (1) assessment of probability of successful execution of a compound call option; (2) assessment of reasonability degree of reaching threshold value of a project liquidation value for a venture fund, which triggers positive decision on main investments I_1^v ; (3) quantitative assessment of uncertainty caused by not only the whole set of influencing parameters, as done in the Geske-Hsu model (see Fig. 3.4), but also by separate groups of parameters (see Figs. 3.1, 3.2, and 3.3), which richens the results of analytic research.

Acknowledgment This research was financially supported by the Russian Foundation for Basic Research (RFBR) (Grant NO. 15–06-06914).

References

Abdullaeva, Z.I.: Development of methods of innovative activity risks management. Dissertation, Saint-Petersburg (2013)
Akinina, V.P.: Innovative reformation of national economy in the context of modern financial and economic transformations and global turbulence: theory, methodology, practice. Dissertation, Stavropol (2011)
Carlsson, C., Fuller, R.: A fuzzy approach to real option valuation. Fuzzy Sets Syst. **139**, 29–312 (2003)
Carlsson, C., et al.: A fuzzy approach to R&D project portfolio selection. Int. J. Approx. Reason. **44**, 9–105 (2007)
Gareyev, T.F.: Formation of innovations complex assessment on the base of fuzzy interval descriptions. Dissertation, Kazan' (2009)
Geske, R.: The valuation of compound options. J. Financ. Econ. **7**(1), 63–81 (1979)
Hsu, Y.-W.: Staging of Venture Capital Investment: A Real Options Analysis. University of Cambridge. JIMS, May, pp. 1–47 (2002)
Ilyin, I.V.: Development of the methodology of evaluation of investment projects on the basis of the real options method and fuzzy sets theory. Scientific and technical sheets of SPbSPU. Econ. Sci. **6**, 114–119 (2009)
Kalchenko, O.A.: Principles and methods of evaluation of the effectiveness of industrial innovative projects under uncertainty and risk. Dissertation St. Petersburg (2012)
Klementyeva, S.V.: Application of fuzzy set theory to measure and evaluation of the effectiveness of the implementation of high-tech product innovations. Factory laboratory. Diagn. Mater. **11**, 65–69 (2006)
Mednikov, M.D.: Fuzzy-sets analysis in the crisis management. Scientific and technical sheets of SPbSPU. Econ. Sci. **2**, 315–321 (2008)
Nedosekin, A.O.: Methodological basics of financial activity modelling with the use of fuzzy set descriptions. Dissertation, Saint-Petersburg (2003)
Nedosekin, A.O., Abdullaeva, Z.I., Naryshkina, E.I.: Analysis of "relational" real options price. International Fuzzy Economics. Laboratory Russia. http://www.ifel.ru/docs/Opt_AZN.doc (2016). Accessed 28 Mar 2016
Trifinov, E.S.: Assessment of economic efficiency of venture investments. Dissertation, Moscow (2009)
Uchal, I., Kahraman, C.: Fuzzy real options valuation for oil investments. Technol. Econ. Dev. Econ. **15**(4), 646–669 (2009)
Wang, Q., Kilgour, D.M., Hipel, K.W.: Facilitating risky project negotiation: an integrated approach using fuzzy real options, multicriteria analysis, and conflict analysis. Inf. Sci. **295**, 544–557 (2015)
Wu, H.-C.: Using fuzzy sets theory and Black-Scholes formula to generate pricing boundaries of European options. Appl. Math. Comput. **185**, 13–146 (2007)
Xubo, Z.: Venture capital investment selection decision-making base on fuzzy theory. Paper presented at the International Conference on Solid State Devices and Materials School of Economics and Management, Wuhan Polytechnic University, Wuhan, China, 2012
Yihua, M., Wenjing, W.: Fuzzy real option evaluation of real estate project based on risk analysis. Syst. Eng. Procedia. **1**, 228–235 (2011)

Chapter 4
Foreign Direct Investments and Economic Growth in Central and Eastern Europe: A Panel-Based Analysis

Lucian Belaşcu, Oana Popovici, and Alexandra Horobeţ

Abstract One of the most discussed issues related to foreign direct investments (FDI) refers to the impact they have on the economic and social welfare of a country. Moreover, if these effects are positive, the question is to what extent and by what instruments they can be enhanced by host country governments. In recent decades, the general political opinion on FDI changed, as they are rather understood as generating competitiveness and growth for host countries and less in terms of their negative effects on the economy. Our paper investigates the relationship between FDI flows and economic growth in countries from Central and Eastern Europe that are also EU members using the panel methodology and implementing various panel specifications that shed light on the particularities of this relationship among the five countries. We find that FDI have a positive contribution to economic growth in these economies, together with capital and, to some extent, international trade size, but also that country and period idiosyncrasies matter for a better understanding of economic growth determination.

Keywords Foreign direct investments • Central and Eastern Europe • Panel analysis

---

L. Belaşcu (✉)
Lucian Blaga University of Sibiu, Sibiu, Romania
e-mail: lucian.belascu@ulbsibiu.ro

O. Popovici • A. Horobeţ
Bucharest University of Economic Studies, Bucharest, Romania
e-mail: popovici.oana@yahoo.com; alexandra.horobet@rei.ase.ro

S.C. Mărginean et al. (eds.), *Emerging Issues in the Global Economy*, Springer Proceedings in Business and Economics,
https://doi.org/10.1007/978-3-319-71876-7_4

4.1 Introduction

The influence of foreign direct investments (FDI) on economic growth has received the attention of both academia and policymakers in the past decades, with a particular focus on its attributes for emerging economies, including the ones from Central and Eastern Europe (CEE). These latter countries have taken into account FDI as a healthy source on which economic growth can be based, including in times when economic stability is at risk and growth is under pressure, but their experiences after the fall of communism have not been homogeneous when FDI were at stake.

Our paper's objective resides in investigating and formalizing the relationship between economic growth and FDI in CEE economies in a panel framework, through the implementation of various panel specifications that shed light on the particularities of this relationship for the five countries in our sample – Bulgaria, Czech Republic, Hungary, Poland, and Romania. Our choice of panel methodology is based on two reasons: first, it is able to capture the evolving country-specific differences, thus eliminating many of the difficulties encountered in other types of estimations; and second, it helps mitigate the low data frequency available for FDI flows observations, which limits the application of other methodologies. The paper is structured as follows: Sect. 4.2 presents the existing research background on the topic, Sect. 4.3 introduces data and research methodology, Sect. 4.4 shows the most important results and discusses them, and the last section concludes and points out the main directions for intended research on the topic.

4.2 Literature Review

Empirical studies generally agree on the positive impact of FDI on the economic development of the CEE countries (see, e.g., Acarvaci and Ozturk 2012). In the struggle of economic transformation from planned to market economy during the 1990s, FDI are seen as a "key agent" (Hanousek et al. 2011, p. 304) for providing the needed modernization and economic restructuring, under the limited national capabilities and resources (Demekas et al. 2007). When testing the impact of FDI on economic growth, studies in the literature mainly focus on examining both direct and indirect effects of FDI, namely, FDI spillovers or channels through which growth is influenced. The direct effect regards the enhancement of productivity in the company where FDI is contributing, while the indirect effects, or spillovers, could be assessed at the local companies' level, according to Hanousek et al. (2011). Tiwari and Mutascu (2010) propose three types of channels through which FDI influence economic growth: the direct channel is generated by greenfield investments, the indirect one is determined by ownership participations, and there is a "second-round transmission" channel, which is enhanced by the technology spillovers. More detailed, Moura and Forte (2010) identify in the literature six main channels through which FDI spread its effects in the economy of the host country:

the transfer of new technologies, the human capital, the integration in international networks and production chains, the increased competition, the development of firms, and the implementation of economic policies.

As compared to other transition economies, the CEE countries had the advantage of improving their legal and institutional frameworks as a requirement for joining the European Union. In this way, they continuously ameliorated their advantages for attracting foreign investors and developed their absorptive capacity – described as "the ability of the domestic economy to absorb spillovers from FDI" (Lall and Narula 2004, p. 454). Therefore, a positive and significant impact of FDI on growth is expected.

Borensztein et al. (1998) estimate a panel data using the seemingly unrelated regressions technique (SUR) for testing the impact of FDI on the economic growth and identifying the main channel through which growth is influenced. The investigation is focused on 69 host developing countries in two periods – 1970–1979 and 1980–1989. The main result generally indicates to a positive and significant impact of FDI on economic growth, while the stock of human capital is the key element that positively or negatively influences the effects of FDI. Also, the authors indicate that the main channel through which growth is influenced when attracting FDI is the transfer of advanced technology in the host country. A similar result is obtained by Johnson (2006), who tests the relationship between FDI and economic growth on 90 developed and developing economies from 1980 to 2002, using cross-section and panel data analysis. Its main result points to a significant impact of FDI on economic growth in developing countries but not in the developed ones, potentially due to the increasing returns to investment generated by the per capita stocks of physical capital. Tiwari and Mutascu (2010) use several panel specifications and prove that both FDI and exports are responsible for enhancing economic growth in 23 Asian countries during 1986–2008.

Hanousek et al. (2011) develop a meta-analysis comprising 21 studies that use both cross-section and panel data. The authors' results support the existence of forward and backward spillovers, stating that there is an increase in efficiency if the foreign companies are implied in the supply industries or are providers for domestic firms. Another similar methodology is employed by Irsova and Havranek (2013), who provide a meta-analysis for examining the horizontal spillovers from FDI using Bayesian model averaging, based on 52 empirical studies in 45 countries. The extent of FDI spillovers depends on the country and the methodology used, but generally, human capital is responsible for generating large spillovers, while an important technological gap, large trade openness, and high protection through intellectual property rights diminish the effects of FDI on domestic companies in the same sector.

Moving the empirical analysis to the CEE countries, Prochniak (2011) shows the important role of FDI in stimulating economic growth in ten such countries between 1993 and 2009. For Damijan and Rojec (2007), FDI contributed to bridging the development gap for the countries in CEE, while Badinger and Tondl (2002) assign this evolution to the capital accumulation and technology transfer, also due to foreign investors. Still, the impact of FDI on economic growth is influenced by the initial conditions of the host country and its absorptive capacity. For example, for Blomstrom et al. (2000), the positive impact of FDI is strengthened only in an environment characterized by trade openness and macroeconomic stability. Moreover, some studies argue that the positive impact of FDI occurs only on the short term, but in the long run, growth and prosperity are reduced because investors' main interest is the profit in the most lucrative industries, such as banking, pharmaceutics, and telecommunications (Zykovic et al. 2014). In this respect, the same authors demonstrate that, while for three countries in CEE there is a positive influence of FDI in the long run on the GDP, for Croatia the positive relationship is available only in the short run, due to the type of foreign investment. In Croatia's case, the predominance of brownfield investments risks to induce a negative impact on GDP. The authors use a VECM model, which allows for the comparison of FDI impact in the long and short run.

Demekas et al. (2007) even propose an economic development threshold level – established at per capita PPP GDP of US $5887 – which influences the absorption capacity of host countries for FDI and cause a change in FDI determinants. Therefore, for a less developed country or a newly opened one to foreign investments, FDI are attracted by geographical and cultural proximity and cheap labor force and infrastructure, while, as the level of income increases, there are other determinants that grow in importance, such as the market dimension and the quality of the business environment. Once at this point, literature provide divergent conclusions: either that FDI is not influencing growth in developed countries (Johnson 2006) or that there is a positive relationship between FDI and economic growth in developed countries, while the relationship is inconclusive for developing countries (Beugelsdijk et al. 2008). Still, the result of Demekas et al. (2007) should be carefully interpreted, as the authors are using the non-privatization FDI in their empirical analysis, which diminishes the real volume of FDI in host countries.

Concerning the initial conditions that favored or not the FDI presence, Estrin et al. (2009) draw attention to the privatization process in several regions and conclude that foreign owners implied in such processes significantly improved the performance of privatized firms, especially in the transition countries in CEE. Not only it enhanced a rapid growth in performance but also had a better evolution than domestic counterparts involved in privatization. The authors explain this result through some of the advantages of the foreign companies, such as the access to the global production and distribution networks and the implementation of new and efficient management practices.

Apergis et al. (2008) use a dataset for the period from 1991 to 2004 in order to test the impact of FDI on GDP in 27 transition economies using panel methodology – cointegration and causality. The study provides a robust result confirming the hypothesis of a significant and positive relationship, but more detailed analysis certifies that this is available only for high-income host countries and those in which there were successful privatization programs. The author emphasizes that FDI will not enhance the economic growth in the host country if, at their turn, it has nothing to offer to foreign investors, such as high investments rates and quality of labor, infrastructure, etc.

Acarvaci and Ozturk (2012) investigate the causal relationship between economic growth, exports, and FDI in ten new European Union member states that have undergone a transition process. The authors use the ARDL model and Granger causality test based on the quarterly time series from 1994 to 2008. The long- and short-term relationships between the three variables are confirmed for only four out of the ten countries in the sample. FDI influences growth in the Czech Republic and in Slovakia, while there is no long-term or equilibrium relationship between these variables in Bulgaria, Estonia, Hungary, Lithuania, Romania, and Slovenia. The authors recommend – as a strategy for improving the economic growth – an increased capacity of public policy in attracting FDI and several methods, among which granting tax incentives and developing the human capital, the financial system, and the infrastructure quality.

A lack of homogeneous results could also be seen in the study of Gallova (2012), who analyzes the relationship among FDI, economic growth, and exports in eight CEE countries. The time period covers the years from 1993 to 2010 in a quarterly recording of data, and the VECM and cointegration method are used. The author finds a long-term causal relationship between the three variables only in five out of the eight investigated countries.

Generally, the macroeconomic analyses suggest a positive relationship between FDI and economic growth. Still, Carkovic and Levine (2002), citing several previous studies, conclude that, when the analysis is undertaken at the firm level, there is no evident impact of FDI on economic growth or performance improvements of the domestic companies following the presence of the foreign companies. The authors use the GMM estimation for a panel analysis formed by 72 countries for testing the abovementioned hypothesis during 1960 to 1995. In this way, several econometric biases are corrected. The results indicate that the exogenous component of FDI does not significantly affect economic growth, and there are no robust results for considering that such a relationship is enhanced by the level of financial development or by trade openness. Still, the paper agrees with the beneficial influence of FDI on the growth of the host countries in the long run. A similar result at the macroeconomic level is obtained by Curwin and Mahutga (2014) who focus their panel regression analysis on 25 countries in transition from CEE and Asia, in the period from 1990 to 2010. Their finding suggests that FDI penetration is reducing economic growth and the absorptive capacity of a country, expressed through the human capital stock and its quality in the host country, as suggested in the literature.

4.3 Data and Research Methodology

Our analysis is undertaken for the period 1999–2013, and it includes five CEE countries with similar economic and political background – Bulgaria, Czech Republic, Hungary, Poland, and Romania – as they are all former communist countries that are now European Union members. Also, their evolutions in terms of FDI flows starting with the 1990s were to a high extent rather similar.

The choice of variables is based on the aggregate production function, whereby labor and capital determine the level of output in an economy, as follows:

$$Y = f\left(L,K\right) \tag{4.1}$$

where Y is the level of output, measured by GDP or GDP per capita, L is the amount of labor measured by the total labor force in a country, and K is the amount of capital, measured by the gross capital formation (GCF). In this production function, the labor and capital coefficients are positive, i.e., any increase in the amount of labor and/or capital will lead to the increase of the output level in the economy, if one assumes that the technological level remains constant.

The traditional production function is expanded according to the new theory of growth proposed by Barro and Salla-i-Martin (2003) that introduces technological progress and diffusion as endogenous factors for economic growth. Specifically, the size of the country's international trade (measured by the level of exports) is added to the aggregate production function, taking into account existing research that proves the influence of international trade on growth, seeing it as a type of technology that transforms non-specialized forms of production into more specialized forms or promotes the transmission of technical knowledge, such as Mankiw (2015) or Grossman and Helpman (1994).

Furthermore, foreign direct investments (FDI) flows are added to the production function, since these are complex flows that include financial, technological, managerial, and organizational expertise that is transmitted to the host economy either directly or indirectly. As shown in Sect. 4.2, the literature is not convergent in terms of a decisive result regarding the FDI-economic growth relationship for CEE economies, so we are interested in investigating this relationship. Therefore, the final form of the aggregate production function used in our research is the following:

$$Y = f\left(L,,,K,,,FDI,,,X\right) \tag{4.2}$$

where Y, L, and K are defined as in Eq. 4.1, FDI is the foreign direct investment flow, and X is the level of exports.

Taking into account Eq. 4.2, we specify a panel in the following general form:

$$Y_{it} = \alpha + \beta_{it} X_{it}^{'} + \delta_{it} + \gamma_{it} + \varepsilon_{it} \tag{4.3}$$

where Y_{it} is the dependent variable (gross domestic product (GDP) or gross domestic product per capita (GDPC)), X_{it}' is a k-vector of regressors (foreign direct investment flows (FDI), level of exports (X), gross capital formation (GCF), and total labor force (L)), δ_{it} and γ_{it} capture the cross-section or period specific fixed effects, α is the overall constant of the model, and ε_{it} is the error terms for i = 1,2,…, M cross-sectional units observed for periods t = 1,2,..,T; $\varepsilon_{it} \sim N(0, \sigma_\varepsilon^2)$, where M = 7 and t = 13. X_{it}' has two different compositions: one that includes L and another one that excludes L, given the low significance of this independent variable for economic growth.

Panels were estimated in two main specifications, i.e., no effects (NE) and fixed effects (FE). Since NE is a highly restrictive specification that ignores the possible presence of differences in coefficients across countries and time, we have allowed the intercept to vary across countries and time (in cross or/and period FE specification), which permits the existence of heterogeneity at sample level, induced by different macroeconomic structure for the countries included in our analysis. Coefficients were estimated using panel least squares, after applying Durbin-Wu-Hausman test for endogenity/heterogeneity, with white diagonal standard errors and covariance (d.f. corrected). Overall, 16 panels with linear specifications were estimated, and the results are presented in the next section.

Data for each country was collected from the World Bank database with annual frequency between 1999 and 2013, as follows: GDP and GDP per capita, FDI flows, total labor force, and gross capital formation in current US dollars. Data series used in our panels are constructed using the first difference in the natural logarithm of raw data.

4.4 Results and Discussion

The first step in conducting the panel data analysis consisted in performing stationarity tests. We have used the Levin et al. (2002), Im et al. (2003), ADF Fisher test, and PP Fisher test proposed by Maddala and Wu (1999) and Choi (2001). The tests performed indicated that panels are stationary in all specifications, regardless of the independent variable and dependent variables.[1]

The results of our estimations are presented in Table 4.1 for panels where GDP is the dependent variable and in Table 4.2 for panels with GDP per capita as the dependent variable. In both tables, the upper part presents estimations for panels with all independent variables, while the lower part shows estimations for panels where labor was excluded, given the lack of statistical significance of this variable in the first panels.

The relationship between FDI, GCF and economic growth is robust, as indicated by the positive and strongly statistically significant coefficients for FDI and GCF in all panel specifications. At the same time, our results suggest that capital, through GCF, contributes more to economic growth than FDI, which might be explained by rather small FDI flows and stocks in some CEE countries included in our sample – particularly Romania and Bulgaria – compared to the size of the economy. Moreover, the relationship between exports and economic growth is rather confusing, as panel regression coefficients vary across speficications and are either positive or negative, while in some specifications (period FE), there is no link identified between exports and GDP or GDP per capita. This might suggest that the specificities of the period under scrutiny, which includes the global financial crisis and the EU debt sovereign

[1] Results are available from authors.

Table 4.1 Panel least squares results for GDP as dependent variable

Panel specification	α	FDI	X	GCF	L	Adj. R^2	Akaike criterion	Log likelihood	S.E. regression
NE	0.015*	0.009**	0.062***	0.094*	0.043	0.678	−5.074	182.59	0.018
Cross FE	0.015*	0.010*	0.055***	0.097*	0.028	0.686	−5.047	185.65	0.018
Period FE	0.023*	0.009**	−0.001	0.089*	0.042	0.705	−5.014	193.51	0.017
Cross and period FE	0.037*	0.010**	−0.103***	0.080*	0.032	0.741	−5.111	200.88	0.016
No effects	0.015*	0.009**	0.062**	0.094*		0.682	−5.101	182.54	0.018
Cross FE	0.015*	0.010*	0.055***	0.097*		0.690	−5.075	185.63	0.018
Period FE	0.024*	0.009**	−0.005	0.087*		0.711	−5.041	193.46	0.017
Cross and period FE	0.037*	0.010**	−0.105***	0.080*		0.746	−5.138	200.86	0.016

Note: *, **, and *** denote statistical significance at 1%, 5%, and 10% level, respectively. Adj. R2 is the R2 penalized for the number of regressors; the Akaike criterion value is calculated as 2(l/T) 2(k/T), where l is the log likelihood function value with the k parameters estimated using T observation. We use the outputs of panel estimations as provided by E-views

Table 4.2 Panel least squares results for GDP per capita as dependent variable

Panel specification	α	FDI	X	GCF	L	Adj. R^2	Akaike criterion	Log likelihood	S.E. regression
NE	0.018*	0.010**	0.060***	0.099*	−0.026	0.674	−5.004	180.16	0.019
Cross FE	0.018*	0.010*	0.056***	0.097*	0.042	0.696	−5.022	184.77	0.018
Period FE	0.022*	0.010**	0.025	0.100*	−0.015	0.694	−4.917	190.13	0.018
Cross and period FE	0.041*	0.010**	−0.107***	0.080*	0.065	0.754	−5.105	200.69	0.016
No effects	0.018*	0.010**	0.060***	0.099*		0.679	−5.032	180.14	0.019
Cross FE	0.018*	0.010**	0.056***	0.097*		0.700	−5.049	184.73	0.018
Period FE	0.022*	0.010**	0.027	0.101*		0.699	−4.946	190.12	0.018
Cross and period FE	0.041*	0.010**	−0.111***	0.081*		0.759	−5.130	200.57	0.016

Note: *, **, and *** denote statistical significance at 1%, 5%, and 10% level, respectively. Adj. R2 is the R2 penalized for the number of regressors; the Akaike criterion value is calculated as 2(l/T) 2(k/T), where l is the log likelihood function value with the k parameters estimated using T observation. We use the outputs of panel estimations as provided by E-views

crisis, have undermined the documented positive relationship between X and economic growth.

An interesting and to some extent surprising result is the lack of a relationship between labor and economic growth, as no statistically significant coefficients (not even at 10%) in any panel specification that includes labor have been identified. This might either indicate that is not necessarily the size of the labor force that is a determinant of economic growth, but its level of education and training that contribute more, or that labor is dominated in terms of influence on economic growth by capital and foreign openess for the economies in the region.

When one compares the results for various panel specifications, a number of observations are noteworthy. First, panels with period and cross-effects are best specified for both GDP and GDP per capita as dependent variables, as they have the highest adj. R-squared, the lowest Akaike criterion value, the highest log likelihood, and the lowest standard error of regressions. This suggests that country idyosincrasies are important in terms of economic growth determinants, as well as period specificities, for the countries included in our sample.

At the same time, GDP panels are better specified compared to GDP per capita panels, while panel specifications that exclude labor are slightly better estimated than panels that include it. This supports the previous finding that for CEE economies, labor is a marginal variable that influences economic growth, at least in terms of size (as it was considered in our panels), and is dominated in terms of influence on economic growth by the other variables.

4.5 Conclusions

Our research aimed at shedding light on the relationship between foreign direct investments and economic growth in five countries from Central and Eastern Europe that are EU members, using the panel methodology with various panel specifications that are able to capture the particularities of this relationship. This research adds to the existing debate in the literature on the impact of FDI on economic growth. Based on our results, it is clear that the most important variables that determine economic growth for CEE economies are gross capital formation and foreign direct investments, and the latter have clearly a role for economic growth, measured either as GDP or GDP per capita. At the same time, CEE countries exhibit specificities in terms of the FDI-GDP relationship, and these are visible between countries, but also when time is taken into account. Certainly, more insight into this multifaceted relationship is needed, for example, taking into account more variables – such as the technological level of FDI or technological gap between the origin and host countries of FDI, domestic investments, or educational level of the labor force. Also, it is worthy to investigate further this relationship by exploring the two-way link between FDI and economic growth, as well as considering potential nonlinearities that might shape it.

References

Acarvaci, A., Ozturk, I.: Foreign direct investment, export and economic growth: empirical evidence from new EU countries. Roman. J Econ. Forecast. **2**, 52–67 (2012)

Apergis, N.: The relationship between foreign direct investment and economic growth: evidence from transition countries. Transit. Stud. Rev. **15**(1), 37–51 (2008)

Badinger, H., Tondl, G.: Trade, Human Capital and Innovation: The Engines of European Regional Growth in the 1990s. ERSA conference papers No. ERSA02P043 (2002)

Barro, R.J., Salla-i-Martin, X.: Economic Growth, 2nd edn. The MIT Press, Boston (2003)

Beugelsdijk, S., Smeets, R., Zwinkels, R.: The impact of horizontal and vertical FDI on host's country economic growth. Int. Bus. Rev. **17**, 452–472 (2008)

Blomstrom, M., Globerman, S., Kokko, A.: The determinants of host country spillovers from foreign direct investment. CEPR Discussion Paper No. 2350 (2000)

Borensztein, E., De Gregoria, J., Lee, J.W.: How does foreign direct investment affect economic growth? J. Int. Econ. **45**(1), 115–135 (1998)

Carkovic, M.V., Levine, R.: Does foreign direct investment accelerate economic growth? University of Minnesota Department of Finance Working Paper, Minneapolis (2002)

Choi, I.: Unit root tests for panel data. J. Int. Money Financ. **20**(2), 249–272 (2001)

Curwin, K.D., Mahutga, M.C.: Foreign direct investment and economic growth: new evidence from post-socialist transition countries. Soc. Forces. **92**(3), 1159–1187 (2014)

Damijan, J.P., Rojec, M.: Foreign direct investment and catching up of new EU member states: is there a flying geese pattern? Appl. Econ. Q. **53**(2), 91–118 (2007)

Demekas, D.G., Horváth, B., Ribakova, E., Wu, Y.: Foreign direct investment in European transition economies — the role of policies. J. Comp. Econ. **35**, 369–386 (2007)

Estrin, S., Hanousek, J., Kocenda, E., Svejnar, J.: The effects of privatization and ownership in transition economies. J. Econ. Lit. **47**(3), 1–30 (2009)

Gallova, Z.: A causal relationship between foreign direct investment, economic growth and export for Central and Eastern Europe. In: Proceedings of 30th International Conference Mathematical Methods in Economics, pp. 201–206 (2012)

Grossman, G.M., Helpman, E.: Endogenous innovation in the theory of growth. J. Econ. Perspect. **8**(1), 23–44 (1994)

Hanousek, J., Kočenda, E., Maurel, M.: Direct and indirect effects of FDI in emerging European markets: a survey and meta-analysis. Econ. Syst. **35**(3), 301–322 (2011)

Im, K.S., Pesaran, M.H., Shin, Y.: Testing for unit roots in heterogeneous panels. J. Econ. **115**(1), 53–74 (2003)

Iršová, Z., Havránek, T.: Determinants of horizontal spillovers from FDI: evidence from a large meta-analysis. World Dev. **42**, 1–15 (2013)

Johnson, A.: The Effects of FDI Inflows on Host Country Economic Growth CESIS Working Paper Series, Paper No. 58. Royal Institute of Technology, Sweden (2006)

Lall, S., Narula, R.: Foreign direct investment and its role in economic development: do we need a new agenda? Eur. J. Dev. Res. **16**(3), 447–464 (2004)

Levin, A., Lin, C.-F., Chu, C.-S.: Unit root tests in panel data: asymptotic and finite-sample properties. J. Econ. **108**(1), 1–24 (2002)

Maddala, G.S., Wu, S.: A comparative study of unit root tests with panel data and a new simple test. Oxf. Bull. Econ. Stat. **61**(S1), 631–652 (1999)

Mankiw, N.G.: Principles of Economics, 7th edn. South-Western Cengage Learning, Stamford (2015)

Moura, R., Forte, R.: The Effects of Foreign Direct Investment on the Host Country Economic Growth – Theory and Empirical Evidence, FEP Working Papers 390. Universidade do Porto, Faculdade de Economia do Porto (2010)

Prochniak, M.: Determinants of economic growth in Central and Eastern Europe: the global crisis perspective. Post-Communist Econ. **23**(4), 449–468 (2011)
Tiwari, A.K., Mutascu, M.: Economic growth and FDI in Asia: a panel-data approach. Econ. Anal. Policy. **41**(2), 173–187 (2010)
Zykovic, S., Zykovic, I.T., Grdinic, M.: A VECM approach to detangling growth, exports, imports and FDI knot in selected CEE countries. Croat. Oper. Res. Rev. **5**, 161–175 (2014)

Chapter 5
Returns on the Capital Market: A Challenge for Investment

Dorel Berceanu, Nicolae Sichigea, and George-Daniel Popa

Abstract At the end of 2016, only the deposits in RON of households exceeded 103 billion RON, and those of nonfinancial companies exceeded 73 billion RON; this is why we consider that the approach of the return of investments on the capital market, as an alternative to investments on the monetary market, is a highly actual issue. In order to ensure the relevance of our approach, we have calculated and interpreted total return for the seven companies in the energy sector corresponding to the BET index (TGN, TEL, COTE, SNG, SNP, SNN, EL). In conclusion, the action of two "vectors," i.e., low financial education and the fear of risk, is obvious in terms of both population and companies (seen not as an abstract notion but as entities managed by decision markers). For these reasons, many Romanian citizens and companies choose bank deposits as a way of investment money. This is why, in this context, we can talk of poverty generated by the fear of taking risks. It is very clear that, in order to achieve higher profitability, the risk one has to take is also higher.

Keywords Return • Dividend • Share • Net profit • Shareholders

5.1 Introduction

The effect of the decision of investing money under one form or another should meet, above all, the expectations of investors. Such expectations are measured in terms of profitability and risk, as these notions represent the very essence of the rationale for investment decisions.

D. Berceanu (✉) • N. Sichigea
University of Craiova, Craiova, Romania
e-mail: dorelberceanu@yahoo.com; nicolaesichigea@yahoo.com

G.-D. Popa
Financial Investment Service Company Estinvest, Focşani, Romania
e-mail: jorginho_bull@yahoo.com

S.C. Mărginean et al. (eds.), *Emerging Issues in the Global Economy*, Springer Proceedings in Business and Economics,
https://doi.org/10.1007/978-3-319-71876-7_5

Analyzing the Romanian capital market, the returns provided by investment money in shares have lately proven to be much higher than the interest obtained for a bank deposit.

The future is extremely unpredictable, which is why an investment decision also implies a "risk" that should be measured and integrated in the investment process. It is already known that investments on the capital market are more risky than, for instance, a deposit set up with a bank, within the limits of the bank guarantee threshold. At the same time, it is our opinion that, since interests for deposits are less than 1%, other forms of investment are worthy to be analyzed.

In the last 10–12 years, public listings on the Bucharest Stock Exchange mainly referred to the sectors of energy and utilities. Thus, after Transelectrica was listed in 2006, Transgaz followed in 2007. After a longer pause, the state lists Nuclearelectrica and Romgaz in 2013, with Electrica being the last listing in 2014. These listings being made by the Romanian state in the last 10 years resulted in the transfer of the investors' interest toward the field of energy and utilities, away from the field of finance and banking that dominated the period 1997–2007. In this context, we only remind the five SIF companies (literally, in Romanian: Financial Investment Companies), along with BRD and Banca Transilvania.

Investors focus on the energy sector due to the high share of distribution of net profits as dividends, i.e., 90% imposed by the state through a memorandum as of the beginning of the year, but especially due to the possibility that national companies and companies with fully or mostly public capital might award additional dividends from reserves and not allocated profits of previous years (Government OG 29/ March 30, 2017).

5.2 Determining the Total Return of the Shares of Companies in the Energy Sector Listed on the Bucharest Stock Exchange, Included in the BET Index

5.2.1 Short Theoretical Considerations on the Determination of Total Return

Any investor (a natural person or a legal entity) is said to consider, when purchasing a share, above all, the *return* resulting from the dividends and the increase in added value; the latter is determined as a favorable difference between the price of the security as it is sold and the price when it is purchased.

Return (profitability) may be defined as the gain obtained from the ownership of a security (share, bond, etc.) for a certain time. This is the return calculated in absolute terms (monetary units).

The return rate (relative return) shall be determined as a ratio between the obtained results (absolute return) and the investors' financial effort (the purchase price for the security).

Return is determined after the share is bought, i.e., based on already recorded values.

Thus, practically, an investor will find what results were obtained after the share has been owned.

The total return of a share may be decomposed as follows:

$$\text{Total return} = \text{Return from dividends} + \text{Return from capital increases}\left(\text{added value}\right) \quad (5.1)$$

In the general case, for a share purchased at moment t_0 and sold at moment t_1, returns per components shall be determined as follows:

$$\text{Return from dividends} = \frac{\text{Div}}{P_0} \quad (5.2)$$

where:
Div = net dividends collected during the ownership period (from moment t_0 to moment t_1)
P_0 = the price of the share when purchased

$$\text{Return from capital increases} = \frac{P_1 - P_0}{P_0} \quad (5.3)$$

where:
P_1 = the price of the share when sold
Hence:

$$\text{Total return} = \frac{\text{Div} + \left(P_1 - P_0\right)}{P_0} \quad (5.4)$$

In order to determine *annual returns*, we shall use the following formula:

$$\text{Return from dividends t year} = \frac{\text{Div}_t}{P_{t-1}} \quad (5.5)$$

where:
Div_t = net dividends collected for year t
P_{t-1} = closing price of the share in year t-1 (closing price of the previous year, i.e., the reference price for the first day of the current year)

$$\text{Return from capital increases t year} = \frac{P_t - P_{t-1}}{P_{t-1}} \quad (5.6)$$

where:
P_t = closing price of the share in year t

$$\text{Total return t year} = \frac{Div_t + (P_t - P_{t-1})}{P_{t-1}} \quad (5.7)$$

5.2.2 *Determining the Total Return of Shares of Companies in the Energy Sector*

Along the times, the interest of investors for the energy sector resulted in an increased liquidity of issuers in the field, which was seen from the fact that seven companies in this sector *(TGN, TEL, COTE, SNG, SNP, SNN, EL)* were included in the BET index (as of March 2017, the BET index includes 12 companies). The other five companies belong to the finance sector (FP, BVB), banking (BRD, TLV), and medicine (Medlife).

Total return was calculated and interpreted for the seven companies in the field of energy.

Thus, for three of them (TGN, TEL, and SNP), which had been listed before 2008 as well, an analysis was performed for the 2008–2015 period; for the other companies, we covered the period from their first listing to 2015 inclusively. At the moment when our study was developed, the General Ordinary Meetings of Shareholders to establish the allocation of net profits for 2016 had not been called yet.

Thus, for each share, we determined both an increase in the added value and the net dividend. The total return was calculated accordingly.

Based on the previously presented formulae, we first determined total return for each of the seven energy companies listed on the BVB, included in the BET index (Table 5.1, Fig. 5.1).

Table 5.1 Determining total return in S.N.T.G.N. Transgaz S.A

Name of the company	Years	Total net profit (thousand RON)	Total dividends (thousand RON)	Distri bution rate (3:2) (%)	Closing price – prev. year (RON)	Closing price – curr. year (RON)	Increase in added value (6–5) (RON)	Gross divi dends (RON)	Net divi dends 8×(1−T) (RON)	Total output $\frac{7+9}{5}$ (%)
0	**1**	**2**	**3**	**4**	**5**	**6**	**7**	**8**	**9**	**10**
TGN	2008	239,007.09	123,272.14	51.58	280.00	122.00	−158.00	10.47	8.79	−53.20
	2009	298,631.54	153,295.44	51.33	122.00	157.00	+35.00	13.02	10.94	+37.65
	2010	376,352.99	338,733.49	90.00	157.00	280.00	+123.00	28.77	24.17	+93.74
	2011	379,571.47	350,389.60	92.31	280.00	223.35	−56.65	29.76	25.00	−11.30
	2012	329,305.24	250,665.14	76.12	223.35	218.00	−5.35	21.29	17.88	+5.61
	2013	334,491.42	206,984.18	61.88	218.00	185.25	−32.75	17.58	14.77	−8.25
	2014	502,516.06	256,669.80	51.08	185.25	262.90	+77.65	21.80	18.31	+51.80
	2015	488,729.02	325,075.83	66.51	262.90	277.00	+14.10	27.61	26.23	+15.34

where T the tax rate is 16%, except 2015, with 5%

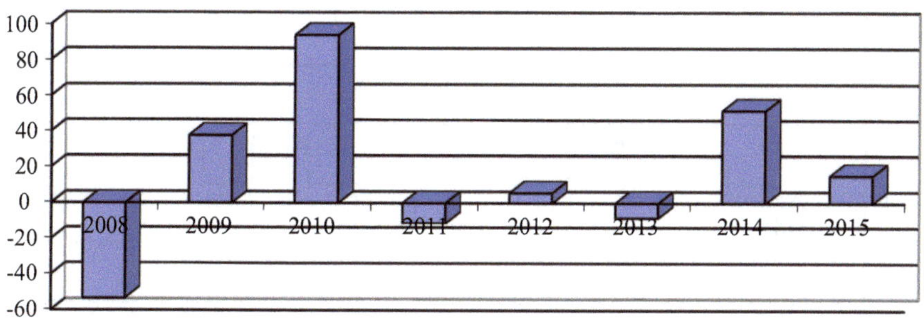

Fig. 5.1 Total return Transgaz

S.N.T.G.N. Transgaz S.A.

$$\text{Total return TGN}_{2008-2015} = \frac{146,09 + (277 - 280)}{280} = 51,10\%$$

Transgaz is a stock exchange-listed company that went through the crisis period very well compared to other listed companies in the same period. It went through a difficult 2008, like most listed shares, and had small negative returns in 2011 and 2013. This last year with a negative return was influenced by the sale of the Transgaz package owned by Fondul Proprietatea; it is known that the sale of packages held by FP in public companies resulted in "pressure" and lower quotations of the concerned shares.

The total return of the share during 2008–2015 was higher than 50%; in our opinion, this is good, since the period also included the financial crisis (Table 5.2, Fig. 5.2).

Table 5.2 Determining total return in C.N.T.E.E. Transelectrica S.A

Name of the company	Years	Total net profit (thousand RON)	Total dividends (thousand RON)	Distri bution rate (3:2) (%)	Closing price – prev. year (RON)	Closing price – curr. year (RON)	Increase in added value (6–5) (RON)	Gross divi dends (RON)	Net divi dends 8×(1−T) (RON)	Total output $(\frac{7+9}{5})$ (%)
0	**1**	**2**	**3**	**4**	**5**	**6**	**7**	**8**	**9**	**10**
TEL	2008	41,943.08	21,990.94	52.43	40.00	11.00	−29.00	0.30	0.25	−71.87
	2009	6135.59	3665.18	59.74	11.00	13.50	+2.50	0.05	0.04	+23.09
	2010	9557.42	8503.16	88.97	13.50	19.35	+5.85	0.116	0.10	+44.07
	2011	90,913.32	80,633.46	88.69	19.35	17.40	−1.95	1.10	0.92	−5.32
	2012	34,487.97	29,321.26	85.02	17.40	12.69	−4.71	0.40	0.34	−25.11
	2013	200,927.86	163,466.00	81.35	12.69	15.79	+3.10	2.23	1.87	+39.16
	2014	357,616.48	205,248.80	57.39	15.79	29.27	+13.48	2.80	2.35	+100.25
	2015	360,054.47	194,253.33	53.95	29.27	29.15	−0.12	2.65	2.52	+8.20

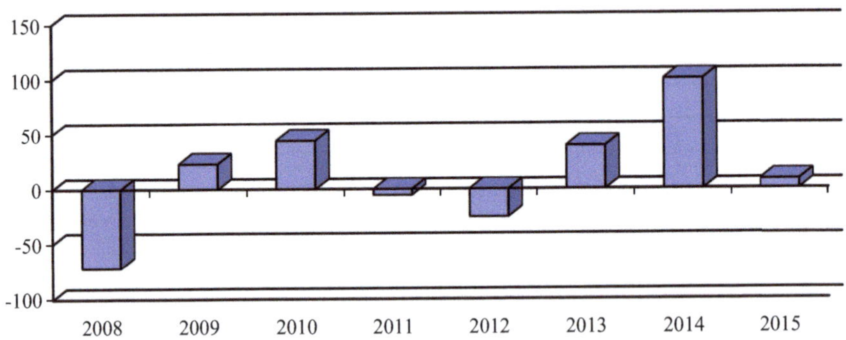

Fig. 5.2 Total return Transelectrica

C.N.T.E.E. Transelectrica S.A.

$$\text{Total return TEL}_{2008-2015} = \frac{8{,}39 + (29{,}15 - 40)}{40} = -6{,}15\%$$

Transelectrica went through a very difficult period during 2008–2012, and it had modest results in these years. After 2013, it managed to solve its issues, with higher and higher profits; in the last 2 years analyzed, net profit exceeded 350 million RON. This was also seen in the ascending evolution of its quotation on the BVB. Hence, we have a difficult first part of the analyzed period. Its second part was profitable for who invested when due (Table 5.3, Fig. 5.3).

Table 5.3 Determining total return in OMV Petrom S.A

Name of the company	Years	Total net profit (thousand RON)	Total dividends (thousand RON)	Distri bution rate (3:2) (%)	Closing price – prev. year (RON)	Closing price – curr. year (RON)	Increase in added value (6–5) (RON)	Gross divi dends (RON)	Net divi dends 8× (1–T) (RON)	Total output $(\frac{7+9}{5})$ (%)
0	**1**	**2**	**3**	**4**	**5**	**6**	**7**	**8**	**9**	**10**
SNP	2008	1,022,387.00	0	0	0.4970	0.1810	−0.3160	0	0	−63.58
	2009	1,368,127.00	0	0	0.1810	0.2490	+0.0680	0	0	+37.57
	2010	1,799,154.00	962,950.00	53.52	0.2490	0.3350	+0.0860	0.017	0.0140	+40.16
	2011	3,685,607.00	1,755,967.00	47.64	0.3350	0.2900	−0.0450	0.031	0.0260	−5.67
	2012	3,850,620.00	1,586,035.00	41.19	0.2900	0.4281	+0.1381	0.028	0.0235	+55.72
	2013	4,839,327.00	1,755,967.00	36.28	0.4281	0.4698	+0.0417	0.031	0.0260	+15.81
	2014	1,837,149.00	623,085.20	33.92	0.4698	0.4080	−0.0618	0.011	0.0090	−11.24
	2015	−630,646.62	0	0	0.4080	0.2900	−0.1180	0	0	−28.92

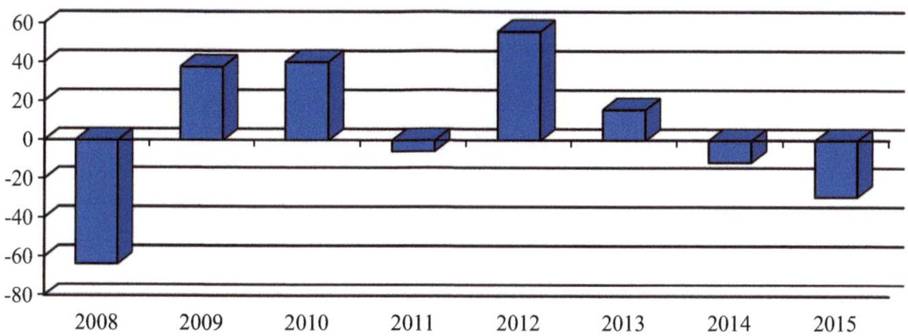

Fig. 5.3 Total return Petrom

OMV Petrom S.A.

$$\text{Total return SNP}_{2008-2015} = \frac{0{,}095 + \left(0,{,}29 - 0,{,}497\right)}{0{,}497} = -21{,}83\%$$

OMV Petrom is one of the largest BVB-listed companies. Its activity and stock exchange price are strongly influenced by the evolution of oil price on large American stock exchanges. Even though oil price had fluctuated over 100 \$/barrel at the beginning of the analyzed period, for various years, it has lately undergone a marked decrease, reaching a minimum of about 28 \$/barrel. Thus, the first part we analyzed, except for 2008, was profitable for SNP, as the issues appeared in the last years. In 2015, the company had a loss of more than 630 million RON. Under these conditions, the price of the share also decreased in the latest years, reaching 0.29 RON at the end of 2015. For the period 2008–2015, we may talk of a total loss of more than 20%, due to the low return in 2013–2015 (Table 5.4, Fig. 5.4).

Table 5.4 Determining total return in S.N. Nuclearelectrica S.A

Name of the company	Years	Total net profit (thousand RON)	Total divi dends (thousand RON)	Distri bution rate (3:2) (%)	Closing price – prev. year (RON)	Closing price – curr. year (RON)	Increase in added value (6–5) (RON)	Gross divi dends (RON)	Net divi dends 8× (1−T) (RON)	Total output $(\frac{7+9}{5})$ (%)
0	**1**	**2**	**3**	**4**	**5**	**6**	**7**	**8**	**9**	**10**
SNN	Sept 2013	423,391.49	340,957.13	80.53	11.55	11.19	−0.36	1.21	1.02	+5.70
	2014	133,064.66	84,534.83	63.53	11.19	7.74	−3.45	0.30	0.25	−28.60
	2015	149,143.73	99,499.57	66.71	7.74	6.42	−1.32	0.33	0.28	−13.44

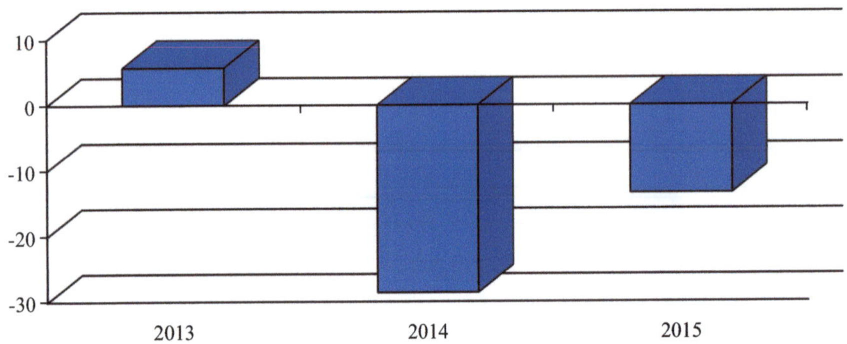

Fig. 5.4 Total return Nuclearelectrica

S.N. Nuclearelectrica S.A.

$$\text{Total return SNN}_{2013-2015} = \frac{1,65 + (6,,42 - 11,,55)}{11,55} = -30,12\%$$

Unfortunately, after being listed, Nuclearelectrica had worse and worse results, due to the unfavorable conjuncture. The fee for special constructions or for posts, of 1.5%, came into force in 2014, resulting in a decrease in the company's profit. The latter was well known for its tangible assets, and no solutions were found to fight the impact of the fee for posts. The total output for the analyzed period is negative, of more than 30%, mostly due to the decrease in the share price, at almost one half of its stock exchange entry value (Table 5.5, Fig. 5.5).

Table 5.5 Determining total return in S.N.G.N. Romgaz S.A

Name of the company	Years	Total net profit (thousand RON)	Total divi dends (thousand RON)	Distri bution rate (3:2) (%)	Closing price – prev. year (RON)	Closing price – curr. year (RON)	Increase in added value (6–5) (RON)	Gross divi dends (RON)	Net divi dends 8×(1−T) (RON)	Total output $(\frac{7+9}{5})$ (%)
0	**1**	**2**	**3**	**4**	**5**	**6**	**7**	**8**	**9**	**10**
SNG	Nov 2013	995,554.37	990,535.57	99.50	34.40	34.19	−0.21	2.57	2.1588	+5.66
	2014	1,409,881.2	1,214,080.0	86.11	34.19	35.36	+1.17	3.15	2.646	+11.16
	2015	1,194,284.2	1,040,640.0	87.13	35.36	27.20	−8.16	2.70	2.565	−15.82

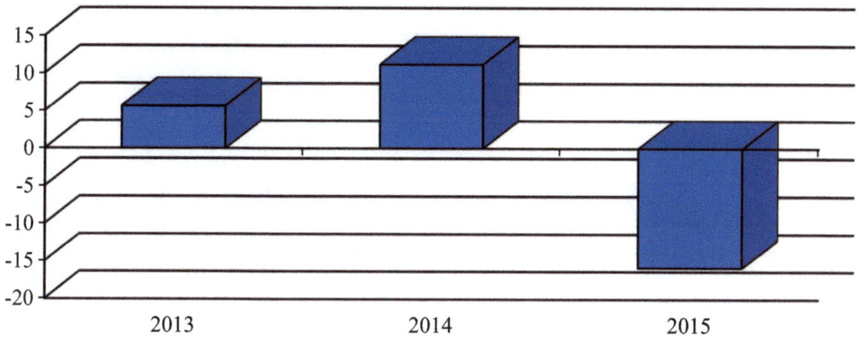

Fig. 5.5 Total return Romgaz

S.N.G.N. Romgaz S.A.

$$\text{Total return SNG}_{2013-2015} = \frac{7,3698 + (27,,2 - 34,,40)}{34,40} = +0,49\%$$

Romgaz entered the stock exchange around the end of 2013, having a positive return in 2014 and negative return in 2015. The investors still keep their focus on this company, as it is a significant gas manufacturer and has important cash reserves, which may be invested in the future for the discovery of new gas deposits. For the analyzed period, the positive return of dividends was practically cancelled by the negative return given by the decrease in the share price (Table 5.6, Fig. 5.6).

Table 5.6 Determining total return in Societatea Energetică Electrica S.A

Name of the company	Years	Total net profit (thousand RON)	Net divi dends (thousand RON)	Distri bution rate (3:2) (%)	Closing price – prev. year (RON)	Closing price – curr. year (RON)	Increase in added value (6–5) (RON)	Gross divi dends (RON)	Net divi dends 8×(1−T) (RON)	Total output $(\frac{7+9}{5})$ (%)
0	**1**	**2**	**3**	**4**	**5**	**6**	**7**	**8**	**9**	**10**
EL	June 2014	269,489.52	249,664.85	92.64	11.99	11.37	−0.62	0.7217	0.606	−0.11
	2015	300,864.49	297,508.34	98.88	11.37	12.20	0.83	0.86	0.7224	13.65

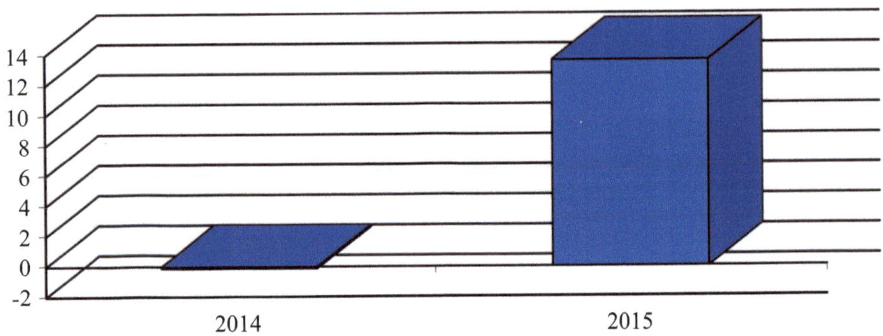

Fig. 5.6 Total return Electrica

Societatea Energetică Electrica S.A.

$$\text{Total return EL}_{2014-2015} = \frac{1,3284+(12,,2-11,,99)}{11,99} = +12,83\%$$

Electrica is the only public company where the majority package of 51% was listed on the BVB, on June 27, 2014 (its trading began on July 4, 2014). It has significant cash and is looking for investments in development. Unfortunately, since it was listed, it has not yet managed to invest the money; all the discussions it has had with various entities in order to purchase assets have failed. Therefore, without significant investments, the quotation went slightly up from the listing, bringing a modest output to shareholders from the capital increase. Corroborated with the return of dividends, the company had a total return of more than 12% (Table 5.7, Fig. 5.7)

Table 5.7 Determining total return in Conpet S.A

Name of the company	Years	Total net profit (thousand RON)	Net divi dends (thousand RON)	Distri bution rate (3:2) (%)	Closing price – prev. year (RON)	Closing price – curr. year (RON)	Increase in added value (6–5) (RON)	Gross divi dends (RON)	Net divi dends 8× (1−T) (RON)	Total output $(\frac{7+9}{5})$ (%)
0	**1**	**2**	**3**	**4**	**5**	**6**	**7**	**8**	**9**	**10**
COTE	Sept 2013	31,297.56	29,522.17	94.33	44.00	45.00	+1.00	3.41	2.8644	+8.78
	2014	51,434.19	51,425.72	99.98	45.00	55.05	+10.05	5.94	4.9896	+33.42
	2015	63,198.99	63,191.30	99.99	55.05	77.00	21.95	7.299	6.934	+52.47

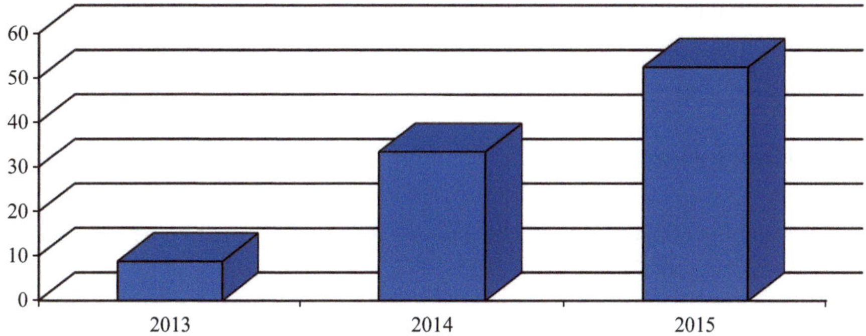

Fig. 5.7 Total return Conpet

Conpet S.A.

$$\text{Total return COTE}_{2013-2015} = \frac{14,788 + (77 - 44)}{44} = +108,60\%$$

Starting September 5, 2013, the shares issued by Conpet S.A. are being traded on the regulated market administered by BSE, under COTE symbol.

Conpet Ploiesti witnessed a major increase in its quotation in the last years, after having sold its shares in Fondul Proprietatea to the latter. The company deals with the transportation of oil through pipes and has had several large customers that ensure the proper development of its activity: Petrom, Rompetrol, and Lukoil. The company has major cash reserves, which makes it attractive for additional dividends from the profits of past years.

The total return of more than 108% during 2013–2015 is due both to the return given by the increase in added value (75%) and the return from dividends (about 33%). The return of COTE is one of the best on the capital market in the latest years.

For a pertinent analysis, for comparability reasons, we considered we had to determine total return for the period 2013–2015, for the quotes shares as well, much before this analyzed period.

Thus:

$$\text{Total return TGN}_{2013-2015} = \frac{59,31+(277-218)}{218} = 54,27\%$$

$$\text{Total return TEL}_{2013-2015} = \frac{6,47+(29,,15-12,,69)}{12,69} = +182,82\%$$

$$\text{Total return SNP}_{2013-2015} = \frac{0,035+(0,,29-0,,4281)}{0,4281} = -24,08\%$$

5.3 Conclusions

Considering the obtained results, the analysis may be split into two periods: 2008–2012 (the crisis period) and 2013–2015.

Table 5.8 The monetary policy interest rate, the credit facility interest rate, and the deposit facility interest rate

Date	The monetary policy interest rate	The credit facility interest rate (Lombard)	The deposit facility interest rate
March 5, 2013	5.25	8.25	2.25
February 7, 2013	5.00	8.00	2.00
June 8, 2013	4.50	7.50	1.50
January 10, 2013	4.25	7.25	1.25
June 11, 2013	4.00	7.00	1.00
September 1, 2014	3.75	6.75	0.75
May 2, 2014	3.50	6.50	0.50
May 8, 2014	3.25	6.25	0.25
January 10, 2014	3.00	5.75	0.25
May 11, 2014	2.75	5.25	0.25
August 1, 2015	2.50	4.75	0.25
May 2, 2015	2.25	4.25	0.25
January 4, 2015	2.00	3.75	0.25
July 5, 2015	1.75	3.25	0.25

In the first period, three of the seven companies were listed (TGN, TEL, SNP). The evolution of the three companies was completely different in terms of returns. Thus, TGN and SNP had a return of around 0, which was due to the fact that the decrease in quotations was not so strong. Instead, TEL had a negative return, of more than 180%, due to the aggressive decrease in the rate, up to 12.69 RON at the end of 2012 (from 40 RON).

The conclusions resulting from the analysis of the second period 2013–2015 are very interesting. Thus, two shares (TEL, COTE) have a total return of 182.82% and 108.60%, respectively. A very good return in this period was also seen in Transgaz, more than 54%.

Interestingly, the three companies operate in the field of energy and gas transmission. The sector of energy, oil, and gas production had a modest return (0.49% – SNP), even negative (more than 30% in SNN and more than 24% in SNP).

Electrica S.A., the energy provider, had a total return of more than 12%. In order to launch the challenge to invest on the capital market, we consider that a minimum comparison should be made with the monetary policy interest rate, the credit facility interest rate, and the deposit facility interest rate, for the last 3 years (Table 5.8).

We may see that the returns of TEL, COTE, and TGN are clearly higher than the interest rates in the table. Equally true, we also have three companies with a lower performance: SNG, SNN, and SNP. Moreover, SNP was also affected by the severe increase in the oil barrel price.

The fact that some companies, even from the same field, had a positive evolution, while others had a negative evolution in terms of returns, reinforces our belief that a portfolio should be diversified.

Thus, the state's need for money is expected to result in the award of dividends from the reserves and unallocated profits of energy companies. This may result in an increase in the stock exchange rate of the shares of the concerned companies, as well as an excellent total return for shareholders.

Chapter 6
Financial Intermediation in Modern Europe Time: Evidence from Romania

Renate Bratu

Abstract In a world governed by complex financial and economic systems, knowing the process of financial intermediation becomes a must. We face times when the process of financial intermediation seems to change nearly as a natural phenomenon. Financial intermediation stakeholders find constantly new ways to interact on behalf of obtaining funds they need and returns they expect and manage risks they try to avoid. The article's aim is to take a snapshot of a financial intermediation process that manifests in Europe Modern Era, specifically in one EU member like Romania, in contrast with other two EU member – Bulgaria and Croatia. In the same time, we also outline the relation between financial development and economic development, mostly after EU accession. In terms of Romania's financial intermediation, we confirm that the banking sector represents the main component of financial system and that bank credit represents the most important financing channel for nonfinancial sector, denominated, mostly in national currency. Despite all that, Romania's EU accession has led to a constant changing in financial structure, with more active nonbanking financial intermediaries.

Keywords Financial intermediation • Financial education • Growth • European Union

6.1 Introduction

Financial research literature includes many papers that analyze the relation between financial development and positive economic development. Many of them suggest that both financial intermediaries and markets influence growth, but the same theoretical and empirical evidence make it difficult to conclude that the financial system merely – and automatically – determines growth (Levine 2005). There are finings

R. Bratu (✉)
Lucian Blaga University of Sibiu, Sibiu, Romania
e-mail: renate.bratu@ulbsibiu.ro

S.C. Mărginean et al. (eds.), *Emerging Issues in the Global Economy*, Springer Proceedings in Business and Economics,
https://doi.org/10.1007/978-3-319-71876-7_6

(Thiel 2001) that sustain finance as an important stone for growth at early stages of economic developments. Trew (2008) demonstrates that the best model of finance and growth is one that departs from the standard depth-growth link.

Our paper outlines another important issue, and that is financial access, based on how, when, were, and why people can demand and receive proper financial services in order to accomplish the role of financial intermediation and to help individuals to realize their financial goals. That is financial inclusion based on acquiring financial knowledge, skills, behavior, and so on that we called financial literacy or financial education. There are evidence that financial inclusion of individuals can help reduce poverty and inequality by helping people invest in the future, smooth their consumption, and manage financial risks (Demirguc-Kunt et al. 2017).

A study that investigated the role of financial intermediation on the growth of members of the SADC (the Southern African Development Community), for the time 1965–1995, reveals some positive correlation between financial development and growth of real GDP per capita (measured by liquid liabilities of financial institutions). Not the same level of relevance between financial development and growth resulted when they had taken into account financial indicators like credit by banks and credit to the private sector (Allen 1998).

One specific article related to our paper is that of Oks (2001) which presents empirical evidence between financial sector development and economic growth among Central and Eastern European countries (CEE), for the period 1992–1998. The results showed that for Bulgaria, Czech Republic, Estonia, and Poland, a test indicates the casual relationship to run from financial sector development and growth. For countries like Lithuania, Latvia, Slovenia, and also Slovak Republic, results reveal that economic growth seems to cause financial sector. In this context, based on those differences in findings, Oks (2001) does not sustain the proposed hypothesis that financial development causes economic growth.

In this context our findings based on empirical analysis reflect a positive correlation between financial development and growth, for the post-accession period of Romania, Bulgaria and Croatia, in this Modern Europe Era.

6.2 Theoretical Correlations

As we already know from theoretical and empirical studies, the development of financial system determines in the same sense the development of economy, considering the main variables that determine the change in stock of financial assets and implicit, economic development.

$$\mathrm{FA}(\uparrow) \rightarrow \mathrm{GDP}(\uparrow) \tag{6.1}$$

Furthermore, financial development should influence, at least indirectly, positive changing of real GDP per capita. There are models and empirical evidence in which financial intermediaries affect the rate of per capita growth (Levine 1992).

$$FA(\uparrow) \rightarrow GDP(\uparrow) \rightarrow R\_GDPp(\uparrow) \tag{6.2}$$

Thus, we mention the main variables that constitute or could affect those key factors (FA, GDP, R_GDPp) in developing process.

We consider that (i) FA = financial assets, (ii) GDP = gross domestic products, (iii) R_GDPp = real GDP per capita, and (iv) FI = financial inclusion.

After the financial crisis of 2007–2010, there is a constant attention on financial inclusion degree. For that, in 2011, at G20 initiative, a framework about financial inclusion (WB 2011) was created, which becomes the base for various specific indicators in these aspects (World Bank 2017). In 2014, the following were pointed out again:

(i) There is a different financial inclusion degree among countries.
(ii) Financial inclusion is a key factor that influences the development and degree of poverty among individuals.
(iii) Financial inclusion could be more extended by using new technologies and well-designed and targeted interventions.
(iv) In some cases, the use of financial services is constrained by regulatory impediments or dysfunctions of markets.
(v) There is a need for addressing market failures (World Bank 2014).

Thus, we consider that financial inclusion is an important variable in the real GDP per capita indicator in every economy.

In our opinion, real GDP per capita is determined in the same way by the performance of financial allocation in real economy that could produce a higher GDP and by the degree of financial education of every household. And that is because before an individual becomes an investor or entrepreneur or freelancer, that man is a natural person who needs to have financial education skills in order to be able to allocate efficiently financial resources (incomes, wealth, business, financial market dividends, and so on). Moreover, if an individual is aware about the importance of financial education, then he will study financial system, he will seek to take the best financial opportunities, and he will design sorts of financial strategies in order to improve or develop personal wealth. We consider that whatever is financial development in some countries, if there is a low financial education of individuals, we cannot exploit properly that financial intermediation development. We consider more appropriately the following expression:

$$FA(\uparrow) + FI(\uparrow) \rightarrow GDP(\uparrow) \rightarrow R\_GDPp(\uparrow) \tag{6.3}$$

In terms of concepts, instruments, strategies, and date, it seems that after the financial crisis of 2007–2010, international authorities, central banks, universities, nongovernmental organizations, companies, etc. notice that this feature of financial development has developed educational programs that seek to improve the financial education of individuals.

6.3 Methodology

In order to articulate correctly characteristics of financial system, international institutions constantly improve the framework through which we can benchmark the financial world. This is also because more and more findings reveal a strong connection between financial development – financial institutions, financial markets, and financial infrastructures – and economic development, poverty alleviation, and economic stability (Čihák et al. 2012). In August 2012, Čihák, Demirgüç-Kunt, Feyen, and Levine published a matrix of financial indicators distributed in four main categories that reflect principal aspects of a financial development benchmarking across different countries. Those are financial depth, financial access, financial efficiency, and financial stability. Thus, our paper is based on this framework and the available data about those features of financial systems.

This article presents the characteristics of Romanian financial system compared with other two financial systems, of Bulgaria and Croatia, in the European Union context and Euro Area benchmark. The selection of those economies is based on few criteria as the following: they are members of EU (since 2007 for Bulgaria and Romania and 2013 for Croatia) (European Union 2017), they belong to the Central and Eastern European Countries (CEECs) (OECD 2017), and also they are classified in the same group by income in the World Bank methodology acceptation, as upper middle income (World Bank 2017).

The comparative analysis is based on specific data of financial sector published by World Bank, ECB, national central banks, and other relevant institutions.

Furthermore, to a more complete comparative analysis, close to those three countries, we present facts specific for upper middle-income group (at median/general level, of currently 56 countries) and world levels.

For every country, we use the international symbols as Bulgaria (BGR), Croatia (HRY), Romania (ROU), European Union (EUU), Euro Area (EMU), upper middle-income countries (UMC), and world (WLD).

Our paper is based on panel cross-sectional data of the main financial and economic activity indicators. Starting from that, we assume the fact that, like in other research on the link between financial intermediation and economic growth, there are some unresolved issues (Badjun 2009). Here we mention the short period of analysis, 2007–2015, and that is because we wanted to capture some intuitive causality between EU accession, financial development, economic growths, and real GDP per capita. In the same time, we propose for future research to test econometrically the robustness of intuitive results and also to investigate more accurately the main characteristics of financial development that could influence positively economic activity, and implicitly, real GDP per capita.

6.4 Data and Facts

6.4.1 Time in Romanian Banking Sector

Before the Great Depression, Romania had a quite well-developed financial system, mainly banks. Shortly before 1934, there were 1204 banks, and under the reforming law from 1934, only 246 banks remained (at 31 December 1944). Among those, the first eight biggest banks concentrated 39% of banking capital, 60% of savings, 77.6% of cash in current banking accounts of all Romania's banks of that time and also more than 50% of total rediscount loans from the central bank (Kirițescu 1997). In the centralized system period, Romanian banking system adopted a mono-bank soviet model. The National Bank of Romania (NBR) executed central bank function and also commercial bank function alongside with other four specialized state-owned banks (BRCE, Banca Agricolă, Banca de Investiții, CEC) and another foreign bank with limited exchange currency function (like Manufacturers Hanover Trust, Société Générale, Banque Franco-Roumanie, and Frankfurt Bucharest Bank) (Chirleşan 2008). In December 1990, the reform of the Romanian banking sector based on two levels started, specific to market economy. In 1997, Romania had a developed and diversified banking system, characterized by a high level of concentration and segmentation of banking activity. In that time there were active 47 banks (6 state-owned banks, 30 banks with domestic and foreign private capital, and 11 branches of some foreign banks) (Isărescu 2007).

In 2007, Romania became an EU member, with all rights from this status, along with Bulgaria. At that time, the banking sector faced a new challenge: that was raising the competition of Romanian banks with other EU banks that required structural measures. The structure of the banking sector was formed by 42 credit institutions and 143 notifications from other credit institutions from other EU member states and also 221 nonbanking financial institutions submitted at the financial authority (National Bank of Romania 2007).

Nowadays, the financial system in Romania is more developed, especially on the structural level of nonbanking sector. In 2016, the Romanian banking sector continued to consolidate the structural stability of aggregate balance sheet (by attracting more domestic savings even though the interests are historically low, by managing efficiently the volume of nonperforming loans, and by stimulating lending in national currency – RON). As a business model, Romanian banks are more oriented to retail lending (mostly in RON) and for sovereign exposure. The dimension of banking sector includes 29 credit institutions, Romanian legal entities (2 state-owned banks, 3 with majority domestic private capital, and 24 banks with majority foreign private capital), and 8 branches of credit institutions from other EU state members. For June 2017 statistical data shows that there were (i) a number of 36 credit institutions, (ii) total assets of 97,908.94 million USD (with 4.0714 ROL per USD, June 2017), (iii) solvability ratio of 19.83% (>8%), (iv) ROA of 1.36% and ROE of 12.91%, (v) credit/deposit ratio of 79.99%, and (vi) no-performance loan rate (EBA definition) of 8.32% (National Bank of Romania 2017a,).

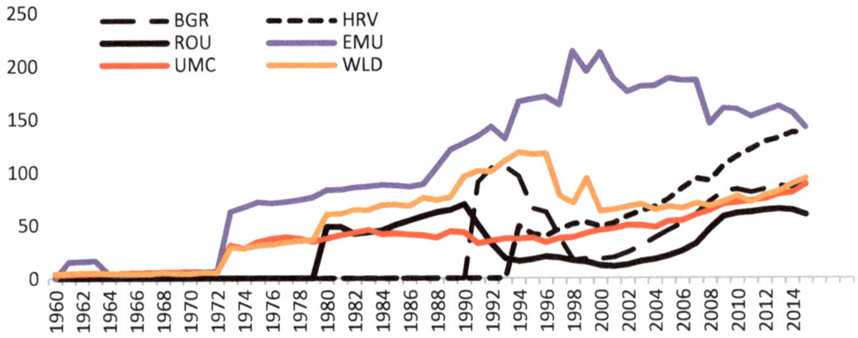

Fig. 6.1 Financial institutions' assets to GDP (%) (World Bank 2017) (For the general level of indicator "financial assets to GDP (%)," we add available data about deposit money bank's assets to GDP (%), insurance company assets to GDP (%), mutual fund assets to GDP (%), nonbank financial institutions' assets to GDP (%), and pension fund assets to GDP (%) (World Bank 2017))

6.4.2 Romanian Financial System in Global Context

We mentioned earlier that Romania is classified by the international institutions as an upper-middle-income country (UMC) considering the level of GDP per capita, along with Bulgaria and Croatia. Thus, in order to observe the development of the financial sector in Romania, we need to present the evolution of the main specific indicators: financial depth, financial efficiency, financial stability, and financial access.

Financial depth As we can notice from Fig. 6.1, in Romania there is the lowest degree of financial depth compared with the general level of UMC, BGR, HRV, and WLD, with the mention that after 2007, this level is increasing, that being a confirmation of a continuing process of development in this sector. The main feature of all financial systems presented is that the majority of financial assets are those of credit institutions considered like "deposit money banks." In 2015, those credit institutions attracted assets about 42.03% of GDP in ROU, 67.98% of GDP in BGH, 97.01% of GDP in HRY, 58.19% of GDP in UMC, and nearly 55% of GDP at WLD level. It is also worth mentioning that the banking intermediation level assessed with the "private credit by deposit money banks to GDP (%)" indicator which, for the same year, reflects the same hierarchy with 29.68% of GDP in ROU, 57.23% of GDP in BGR, 67.09% of GDP in HRY, 47.176% of GDP in UMC, and 44.54% of GDP at WLD level. Again, this is a confirmation that financial systems in those regions are still conducted by baking sectors and in a short level of nonbank financial sector.

Financial depth can be sustained also through capital markets. Analyzing the evolution of stock market capitalization to GDP, we notice the lower use of capital market (different from banking market) as a source of opportunity to invest or to attract investors, especially in Romania (Fig. 6.2). Latest data reveal that stock market

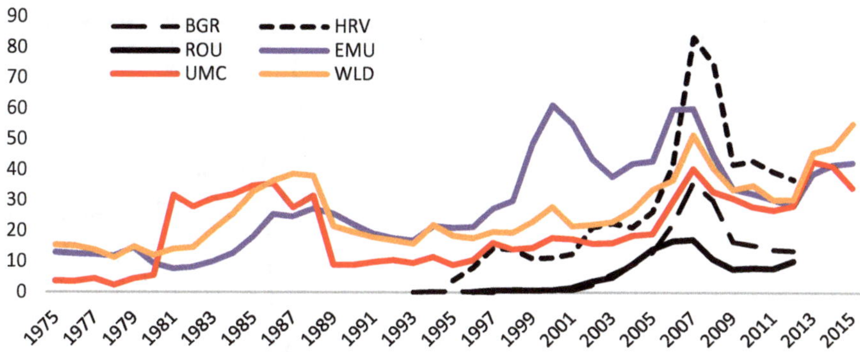

Fig. 6.2 Stock market capitalization to GDP (%) (World Bank 2017)

capitalization in Romania developed from 0.75% of GDP in 1998[1] to 17.29% of GDP in EU accession year (the highest level in the entire period) (World Bank 2017) and nearly 10% in 2012 and almost 12% of GDP in May 2017 (Bucharest Stock Exchange 2017). In the studied context, again, in Romania financial markets are less intense compared with others – BGR, HRY, UMC, EMU, and WLD.

Financial efficiency Commercial banks' ROA and ROE (after taxes) had an appropriate behavior, visible being influenced by the latest international financial crisis and also by national specifics. In Romania case, after 1996 we notice a constant reduction of bank lending-deposit spread from 17.87 pp. to 4.88 pp. (2015) being more appropriate by the average EMU level (3.98 pp. – 2015). And this has a positive effect on growth (Cojocaru et al. 2015). In the same time, the bank net interest margin oscillated from 5.03% in 1996 to a maximum of 9.9% in 2004 and 3.62% in 2015; this is also in alignment with business model that Romanian banks practice (more oriented on business margin). The same evolution of bank net interest margin is also for BGR which reported a 3.54% as well as HRY with 3.13% and EMU with 1.795%, in 2015 (Figs. 6.3 and 6.4).

For the correlation of profits and costs, in the financial sector, the Boone indicator[2] data reflects a slice deterioration in the competitive conduction of financial intermediation starting from 2009 (−0.9) to 2014 (0.01) and 2015 (−0.04).

In terms of capital market efficiency, in ROU the level of stock market turnover ratio was relatively stable after financial crisis with levels near to 12% (2009–2012), except for the year 2011 when the indicator was 20.17% (Fig. 6.5), thus making ROU an interesting capital market for investors among emerging markets. For instance, in BGR, in the same period, stock market efficiency oscillated near to 4–5.7% and in HRY in the range 2.7–5.6%.

---

[1] After 3 years from the date when the Bucharest Stock Exchange was reopened in 1995.

[2] A measure of degree of competition based on profit efficiency in the banking market and is indirectly proportional to the competitive conduct of financial intermediaries (World Bank 2017).

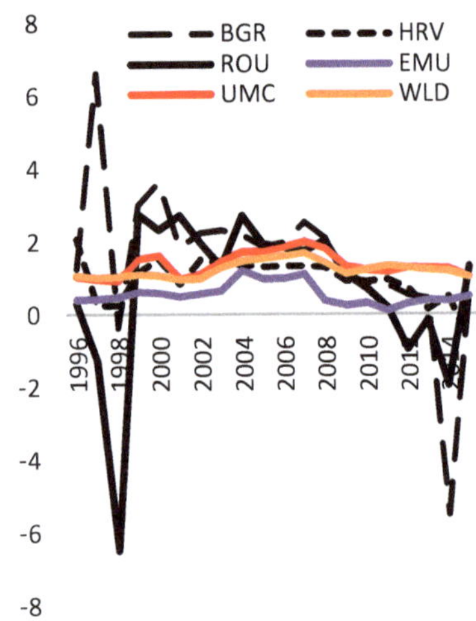

Fig. 6.3 Commercial banks' ROA (World Bank 2017)

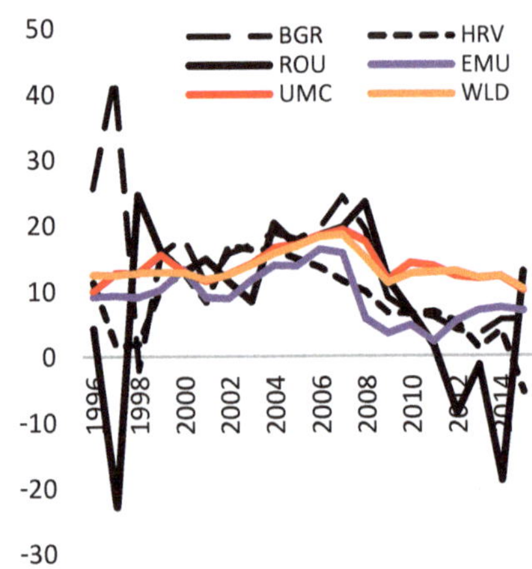

Fig. 6.4 Commercial banks' ROE (World Bank 2017)

Financial stability Concerning Romania, the banking sector is characterized by good stability, with great scores at the stress test applied by the National Central Bank. Bank regulatory capital to risk-weighted asset indicator raised from 13.8% (2007) to 19.16% (2015) (Fig. 6.6). This reflects, besides a good stability, also an opportunity for banks to be more active in intermediation activity for companies from different industries. We notice a degree of stability on capital market too. The stock market volatility indicator seems to converge in the same way for all the country/region analyzed (Fig. 6.7), close to 20 points.

As we mentioned before, in Romania, banks are oriented mostly to household lending. That is why the banking sector is facing high levels of nonperforming loans (NPLs) (Fig. 6.8). In the last years, one of the challenges for the commercial banks was to clean the balance sheets from bad loans (Fig. 6.9).

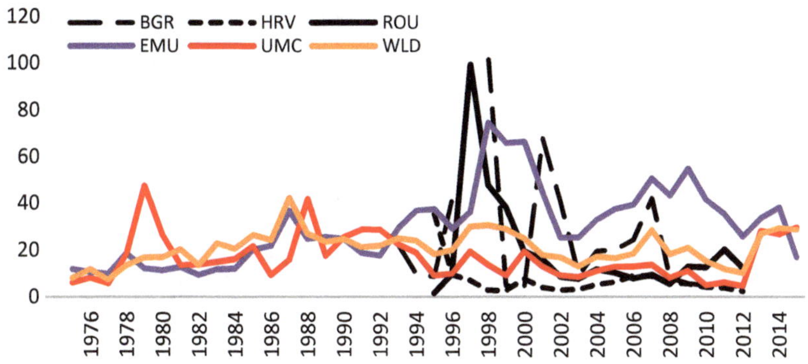

Fig. 6.5 Stock market turnover ratio (%) (World Bank 2017)

Fig. 6.6 Bank regulatory capital to risk-weighted assets (%)

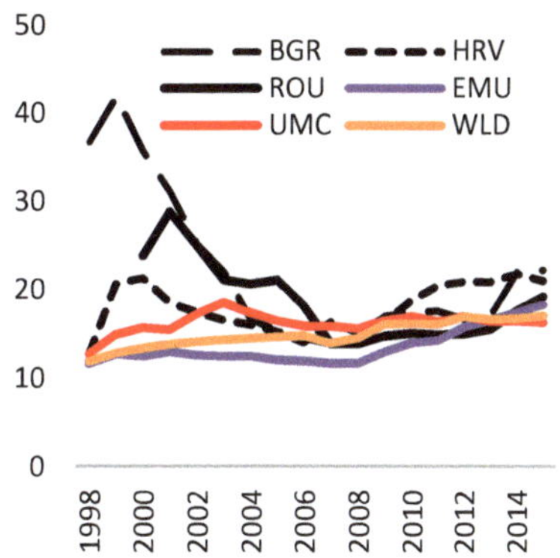

Fig. 6.7 Stock price volatility (World Bank 2017)

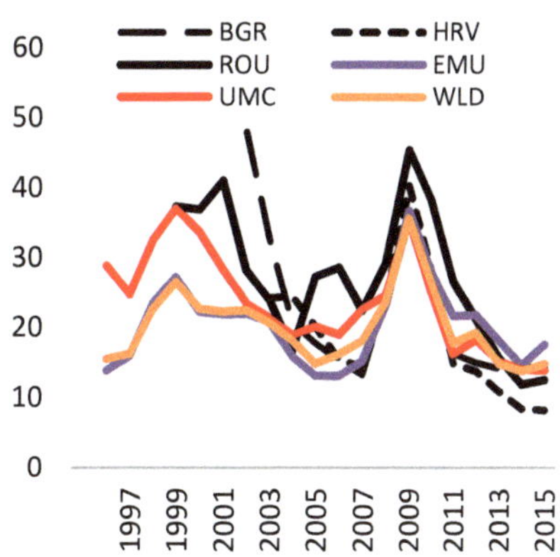

On behalf of stability, Romanian commercial banks constituted proper provision in order to cover potential risks from bad loans (Fig. 6.7). As we can notice from the reported data, the levels of provision to NPLs have slice deteriorated in 2014–2015, but there is a conformable level, 57.72% in 2015 (48.77% in BGR, 61.91% in HRY, and 47.64% in EMU, in the same year).

Fig. 6.8 Bank nonperforming loans to gross loans

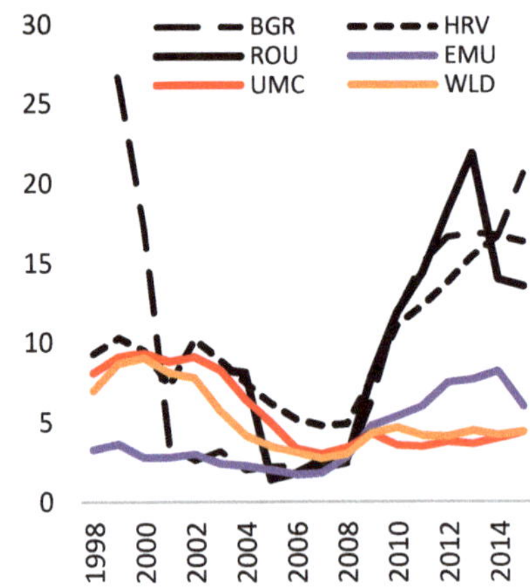

Fig. 6.9 Provisions to nonperforming loans (%) (World Bank 2017)

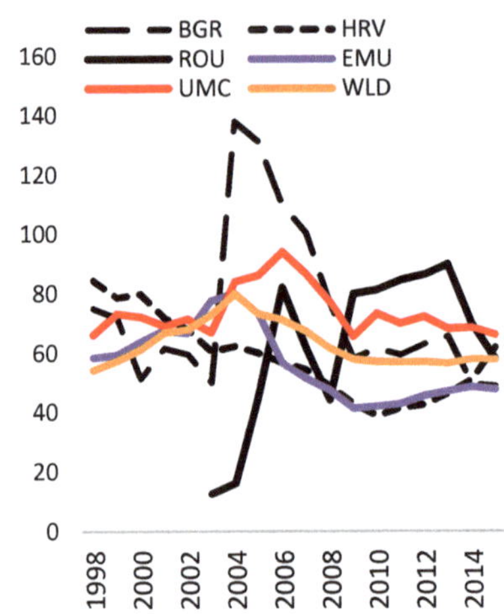

In a way, high nonperforming loans ratio could be a real threat for national banking sectors in terms of efficiency and stability, even though there is a high provision ratio for those loans. But, in other way, this feature could be an excellent investment opportunity for other financial institutions (investment banks or other financial holdings). For that Romania was declared in 2016 the most active market, with 3.5 billion euros (approx. $3.87 billion) in 2015 and 2016 for selling NPLs (Delloite 2016). And the forecasts reveal that there will be more underwritings in these fields for the years to come because Romanian commercial banks seek to reduce NPL ratio near to EUU and EMU averages.

Financial access In 2015, Romania was characterized as an EU member with the lowest financial literacy rate by 22% among individuals, after Bulgaria and Cyprus with 35% of the same indicator (Klapper et al. 2015). Studying the available data (Appendix 6.3: Figs. 6.10, 6.11, 6.12, 6.13, and 6.14), we notice an improvement in financial access levels, in terms of spreading of financial institution local units.

Even if there is a tendency to reduce the geographical presence of bank local unit in order to make more efficient financial intermediations and to educate consumers to access financial services by e-finance technologies, we notice also that there are increasing individuals (age + 15) that use saving and loan financial services, mostly from commercial banks, but still at low level. 13.27% for savings and 11.85% for loans (Figs. 6.12 and 6.13). In the same time, it seems that near half of companies have a checking or savings account and a bank loan or line of credit (49.4%, checking/savings accounts; 47.4%, bank loan or line of credit, 2013) (Figs. 6.15, 6.16, and 6.17).

Moreover, in 2013 it was reported that only 43.9% of small firms have had a bank loan or a line of credit. In our opinion this is correlated with the level of financial education (literacy). If an individual has limited financial literacy, the same individual which becomes an entrepreneur has limited financial literacy. There are evidence that educational programs for improving financial education among students do not have a great impact on financial knowledge, skills, attitude, behavior, and so on for those individuals. Better impact could have those "teachable moments," when individuals start a job or purchase a major financial product (World Bank 2014).

Thus, we consider that it is difficult to evaluate the degree of financial literacy on short term, and this is what the available data show us. We have to assess as a unit all aspects of financial data (financial depth, financial efficiency, financial stability and financial access, and others) in order to consider if financial intermediation represents the milestone for macroeconomic growth and also for individual well-being.

6.4.3 Financial Systems in CEE and Growth

Central and Eastern Europe is a special region, on the one hand, because of the geographical position and the similarities in political history and economic development in the European Union context on the other hand. Many studies are focused on this part of the world, to express the gap of economic development between CEE and EU (or Euro Area). Cojocaru et al. (2015) studied the relation between financial development and growth in CEE and the CIS countries during 1990–2008. They found that analyzed economies are broadly consistent with the overall positive findings in the financial development–economic growth literature.

In the 2017 Q1, growth in the Central and Eastern European (CEE) economy had a 4.0% expansion of GDP, driven mainly by investments sustained also by EU development funds and solid demand for exports from the Euro Area. Some forecasts suggest that CEE will have a GDP growth of 3.6% by 2017 and 3.3% by 2018. For Romania a continuing robust growth of 4.6% in 2017 and 3.7% in 2018 is predicted, in the context of overheating risks fueled by strong consumer spending due to matrix of tax cuts and wage hikes (Focus Economics 2017). As we can see from cross-sectional data presented in Appendix 6.1, Romania is the largest country with 19,705.30 thousand of people (BGR 7127.82 and HRY just 4171) and with GDP per capita of $9474.1 (after HRY with $12,090.7 and before BGR with $7350.8, before average of UMC of $7937.28 and slightly lower than WLD average of $10,150.78, in 2016). Considering the stock of population, Romania is the seventh EU member, after other well-developed Euro Area countries like Germany, the UK, France, Italy, Spain, and Poland (Worldometers 2017). In social-economic terms, intuitively, we can sustain that Romania can represent the seventh market for goods and services, labor force, financial intermediaries, and capital. But, if we look just at the GDP per capita indicator, we notice that this supposed "seventh place" in EU for now represents only a potential opportunity. In fact, the latest data reveal that Romania and Croatia have a GDP per capita of around 40% below the EU-28 average (placing ROU on the 27th place, HRY on the 26th place) and Bulgaria around 52% below that average (being the 28th member at this indicator) (Eurostat 2017). Also, in December 2016, Romania reported one of the lowest financial intermediation degrees among EU member states, about 75.2% of GDP (with 75.5% of GDP at the end of 2015) (National Bank of Romania 2017a, b). Studding the evolution of financial assets, of 2007–2015 (Appendix 6.2), we notice that Romania has increased this value with 27.56%, in nominal terms compared with Croatia that faced an increase of 20.69% and Bulgaria of 15.77%.

Thus, starting from relation (1) and (2), we can make some empirical and methodological observations:

- Empirical data reveal that (Table 6.1):

- Logical assumption:
  - Based on empirical results (with some reserves of data relevance, mostly because of short period of analysis, only 9 years), we confirmed that, possibly, an increase of financial assets determines an increase of GDP (smaller) and an increase of real GDP per capita (in some cases).
  - Also, we notice that in Romania and Bulgaria, financial assets had the higher positive impact on GDP and on real GDP per capita. Can we assume that EU accession of those countries has that major impact on higher development of financial intermediation? Could the EU financial funds for EU members with a real GDP per capita equal and below than EU average influence a develop-

Table 6.1 Average annual percent change rate of financial assets, GDP, and real GDP per capita indicators, in 2007–2015

Region/countries	Level of indicators and their relationship (%)	Type of effects
EMU19	FA (↑) 3.3591 → GDP (↑) 1.3919 → R_GDPp (↓) 0.0639	+ / + / −
EUU28	FA (↑) 3.3107 → GDP (↑) 1.6486 → R_GDPp (↑) 0.1628	+ / + / +
BGR	FA (↑) 5.4410 → GDP (↑) 4.3552 → R_GDPp (↑) 1.9323	+ / + / +
HRY	FA (↑) 2.4086 → GDP (↑) 0.1279 → R_GDPp (↑) −0.7532	+ / + / −
HRY (2013–2015)	FA (↑) 3.7806 → GDP (↑) 0.1163 → R_GDPp (↑) 0.6568	+ / + / +
ROU	FA (↑) 3.1289 → GDP (↑) 3.4211 → R_GDPp (↑) 1.9323	+ / + / +

ment of financial intermediation? Could the EU financial regulation influence financial intermediation increase? For all these questions, the intuitive answers could be yes. But we outline another question. Why a positive change in financial assets stock determines a smaller positive change of GPD and much smaller positive change of real GDP per capita? In our opinion this effects should be opposite.

– A higher degree of financial inclusion (financial access and financial education) could be an important factor that driven both, in parallel, financial development (by demanding more financial services tailored on the specific consumers) and economic growth (by learning and doing better investments based on financial interaction experiences).

6.5 Conclusions

The purpose of this paper was to take a snapshot of Romania's financial development after almost 10 years from EU accession benchmarking with other two countries – Bulgaria and Croatia – Euro Area data, and upper-middle income and world group.

The research work was focused on the four main indicators for assessing financial development (depth, efficiency, stability, and access). Our results reveal that Romania's financial system is more developed before 2007 (the moment of EU accession), but not so fast in terms of depth. In that concern efficiency part, this is difficult to evaluate comparing with regions taken into account, and this is because, we think there are still financial crisis recovering time. The main issue for Romania's banking sector seems to be the NPL problem, but we consider that as an opportunity for future development of national capital market. Stability is featured by soundness of the financial system, especially the banking sector, being well capitalized (in some cases over capitalized), and having high grades in the stress test of the central bank. This could be another opportunity for Romanian banks to extend lending activities. The financial access in Romania is low, at least this is revealed by the little data that we have, but in developing process.

Another part of the research was to analyze if there is a confirmation of a direct relation between financial development, economic growth, and real GDP per capita. Thus, we notice a positive correlation between those variables, and we add that it would be constructive if in financial and economic strategies, the financial inclusion data are included. This is because we think that represent a milestone for future financial development as well as for future economic development.

Moreover, we also think that the relationship between financial development, economic growth, and real GDP per capita is more complex, and it could be analyzed also in the context of social and political issues, not just from the macroeconomic point of view, especially when we consider financial inclusion a key feature of financial development (Table 6.2).

Appendix 6.1

Table 6.2 Social and economic development indicators – selection, 2016

	Indicator	BGR	HRV	ROU	EU	EA	UMC	WLD
1	Access to electricity (% of population) (2014)	100 (rank 1)	100 (rank 1)	100 (rank 1)	100	100	99.31 (2014)	85.33 (2014)
2	Ease of doing business index (1 = most business-firmly regulations)	39 (rank 2)	43 (rank 1)	36 (rank 3)	30	33	NA	NA
3	Exports of goods and services (% of GDP)	63.6 (rank 1)	51.4 (rank 2)	41.4 (rank 3)	43	44	24.2	29.36 (2015)
4	Imports of goods and services (% of GDP)	60.5 (rank 1)	48.2 (rank 2)	42.3 (rank 3)	39.7	40	22.9	23.6 (2015)
5	GDP per capita	7350.80 (rank 3)	12,090.70 (rank 1)	9474.10 (rank 2)	32,058.80	34,866.10	7937.28	10,150.78
6	Government expenditure on education, total (% of GDP)	4.062 (2013) (rank 2)	4.582 (2013) (rank 1)	3.129 (2014) (rank 3)	5.285 (2014)	5.383 (2014)	4.74 (2013)	4.70 (2013)
7	Gross savings (% of GDP)	26 (rank 1)	23.794 (2015) (rank 2)	23 (rank 3)	22	23	32.79 (2015)	25.05 (2015)
8	Labor force, total (% of total population)	0.46 (rank 2)	0.44 (rank 3)	0.47 (rank 1)	247,824.30	163,160.83	1,346,046.29	3,426,614.45
9	Literacy rate, adult total (% of people ages 15 and above)	98 (rank 2)	99 (rank 1)	99 (rank 1)	N/A	N/A	94.2 (2010)	85.3 (2010)
10	Personal remittances, received (% of GDP)	3.17 (rank 2)	4.46 (rank 1)	1.86 (rank 3)	0.65	0.65	0.66	0.72

11	Population, total (thousand)	7127.82 (rank 2)	4171 (rank 3)	19,705.30 (rank 1)	511,497.41	340,894.61	2,579,909.67	7,442,135.58
12	Researchers in R&D (per million people) (2014)	1833.13 (rank 1)	1437.31 (rank 2)	921.505 (rank 3)	3480.54	3573.83	1266.31 (2014)	1281.67 (2010)
13	Total reserves (includes gold, current US$) (million)	25,176.06 (rank 2)	14,244.34 (rank 3)	39,953.48 (rank 1)	N/A	N/A	N/A	N/A
14	Unemployment, total (% of total labor force) (modeled ILO estimate)	8 (rank 2)	13.5 (rank 3)	6.4 (rank 1)	8.6	10	6.2	5.74
15	Urban population (% of total)	74 (rank 1)	59 (rank 2)	55 (rank 3)	75	76	65.05	54.2
	Total rank 1	**6/15**	**6/15**	**6/15**	–	–	–	–

Source: World Bank – Data Bank Indicators, https://data.worldbank.org/indicator, 2016

Appendix 6.2

Financial assets (million euro)	2007	2008	2009	2010	2011	2012	2013	2014	2015	Average of annual change rate (%)	Period change (2007–2015) (%)
European Union (28 countries)	58,811,607.0	59,774,830.7	59,034,389.7	63,560,605.3	66,728,558.3	69,413,742.3	68,772,991.9	75,880,006.6	79,753,959.3		
Annual change rate (%)		1.6378	−1.2387	7.6671	4.9841	4.0240	−0.9231	10.3340	5.1054	3.3107	35.6092
Euro area (19 countries)	44,579,202.2	44,510,494.7	45,498,048.2	47,698,418.2	49,315,014.5	52,088,909.8	52,481,689.8	57,836,811.8	61,364,785.9		
Annual change rate (%)		−0.1541	2.2187	4.8362	3.3892	5.6248	0.7541	10.2038	6.0999	3.3591	37.6534
Bulgaria	112,867.9	118,385.3	125,159.0	124,177.3	135,270.5	142,587.2	156,722.6	163,326.0	171,872.9		
Annual change rate (%)		4.8884	5.7217	−0.7844	8.9334	5.4089	9.9135	4.2134	5.2330	5.4410	15.7785
Croatia	153,709.4	150,056.1	156,803.2	164,391.2	165,070.2	165,986.5	171,445.8	177,612.6	185,526.7		
Annual change rate 2007–2015 (%)		−2.3768	4.4964	4.8392	0.4130	0.5551	3.2890	3.5969	4.4558	2.4086	20.6996
Annual change rate 2013–2015 (%)							3.2890	3.5969	4.4558	3.7806	8.2130
Romania	278,511.3	280,698.3	274,020.4	278,934.0	292,647.6	307,863.3	330,043.1	344,518.1	355,286.5		
Annual change rate (%)		0.7852	−2.3790	1.7932	4.9164	5.1993	7.2044	4.3858	3.1256	3.1289	27.5663

Source: Authors' calculations based on EUROSTAT: Financial Balance Sheets, 2017 http://appsso.eurostat.ec.europa.eu/nui/show.do?dataset=nasa_10_f_bs&lang=en

Gross domestic product at market prices (million euro)	2007	2008	2009	2010	2011	2012	2013	2014	2015	Average of annual change rate (%)	Period change (2007–2015) (%)
European Union (28 countries)	12,966,403.5	13,040,309.4	12,292,959.4	12,818,381.8	13,192,373.8	13,445,756.5	13,554,117.0	14,007,869.8	14,720,020.2		
Annual change rate (%)		0.5700	−5.7311	4.2742	2.9176	1.9207	0.8059	3.3477	5.0839	1.6486	13.5243
Euro area (19 countries)	9,383,907.2	9,619,070.2	9,284,155.4	9,546,292.9	9,798,991.1	9,832,819.8	9,927,596.1	10,140,441.0	10,463,656.6		
Annual change rate		2.5060	−3.4818	2.8235	2.6471	0.3452	0.9639	2.1440	3.1874	1.3919	11.5064
Bulgaria	32,449.1	37,200.1	37,317.7	38,230.5	41,292.0	41,947.2	42,011.5	42,762.2	45,286.5		
Annual change rate (%)		14.6414	0.3161	2.4460	8.0080	1.5867	0.1533	1.7869	5.9031	4.3552	39.5617
Croatia	43,925.8	48,129.8	45,090.7	45,004.3	44,708.6	43,933.7	43,487.1	42,977.8	44,068.0		
Annual change rate 2007–2015 (%)		9.5707	−6.3144	−0.1916	−0.6570	−1.7332	−1.0165	−1.1712	2.5367	0.1279	0.3237
Annual change rate 2013–2015 (%)							−1.0165	−1.1712	2.5367	0.1163	1.3358
Romania	125,403.4	142,396.3	120,409.2	126,746.4	133,305.9	133,511.4	144,253.5	150,357.5	159,963.7		
Annual change rate (%)		13.5506	−15.4408	5.2631	5.1753	0.1542	8.0458	4.2314	6.3889	3.4211	27.5593

Source: Authors' calculations based on EUROSTAT: GDP and main components (output, expenditure, and income), 2017 http://appsso.eurostat.ec.europa.eu/nui/show.do?dataset=nama_10_gdp&lang=en

Real GDP per capita, EUR per inhabitant	2007	2008	2009	2010	2011	2012	2013	2014	2015	Average of annual change rate (%)	Period change (2007–2015) (%)
EU (28 countries)	26,200	26,200	25,000	25,500	25,800	25,600	25,700	26,000	26,500		
Annual change rate		0.0000	−4.5802	2.0000	1.1765	−0.7752	0.3906	1.1673	1.9231	0.1628	1.1450
Euro area (19 countries)	29,400	29,400	28,000	28,500	28,900	28,600	28,400	28,700	29,200		
Annual change rate		0.0000	−4.7619	1.7857	1.4035	−1.0381	−0.6993	1.0563	1.7422	−0.0639	−0.6803
Bulgaria	4900	5200	5100	5200	5300	5300	5400	5500	5700		
Annual change rate (%)		6.1224	−1.9231	1.9608	1.9231	0.0000	1.8868	1.8519	3.6364	1.9323	16.3265
Croatia	11,200	11,500	10,600	10,500	10,500	10,300	10,200	10,200	10,500		
Annual change rate 2007–2015 (%)		2.6786	−7.8261	−0.9434	0.0000	−1.9048	−0.9709	0.0000	2.9412	−0.7532	−6.2500
Annual change rate 2013–2015 (%)							−0.9709	0.0000	2.9412	0.6568	2.9412
Romania	6100	6700	6300	6300	6400	6400	6700	6900	7200		
Annual change rate		9.836066	−5.97015	0	1.587302	0	4.6875	2.985075	4.347826	2.1842	18.0328

Source: Authors' calculations based on EUROSTAT: real GDP per capita, growth rate and totals, 2017 http://ec.europa.eu/eurostat/tgm/table.do?tab=table&init=1&plugin=1&pcode=tsdec100&language=en

Appendix 6.3: Financial Access Indicators

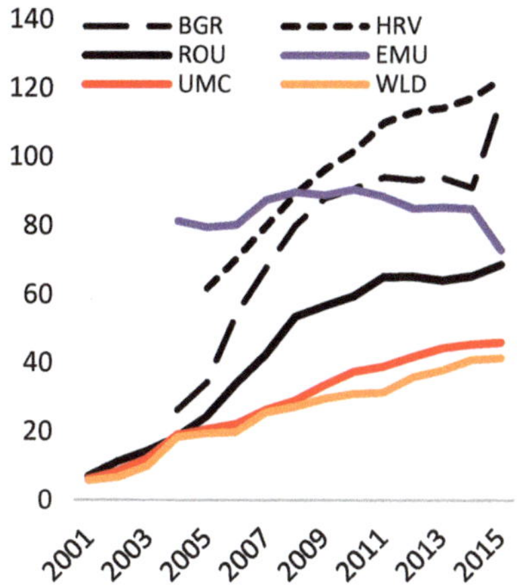

Fig. 6.10 ATMs per 100,000 adults (World Bank 2017)

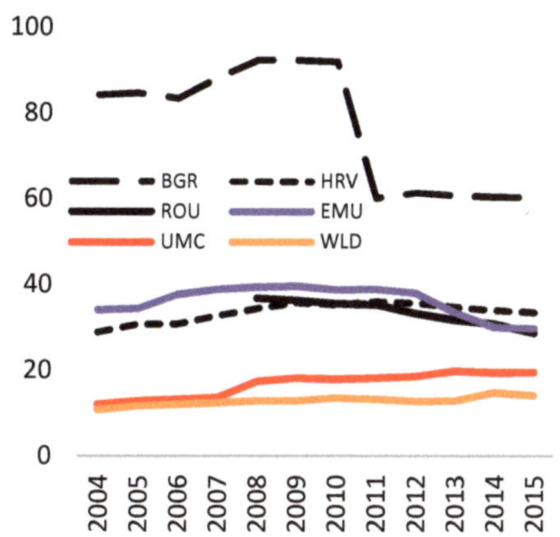

Fig. 6.11 Bank branches per 100,000 adults (World Bank 2017)

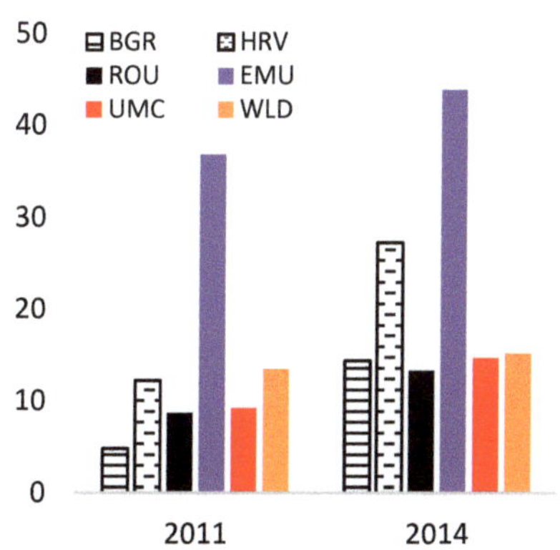

Fig. 6.12 Saved at a financial institution in the past year (% age 15+) (World Bank 2017)

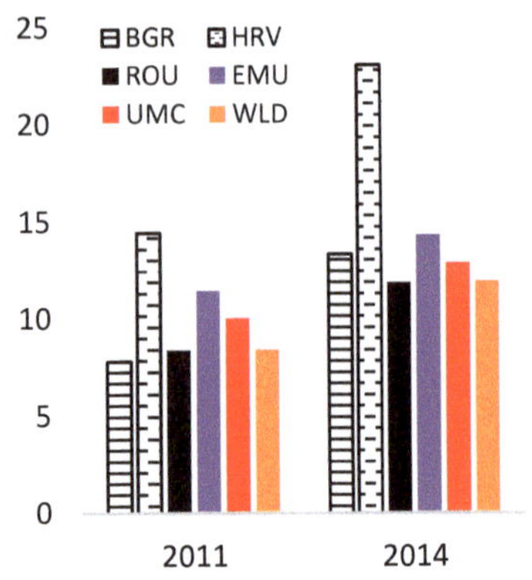

Fig. 6.13 Loan from a financial institution in the past year (% age 15+) (World Bank 2017)

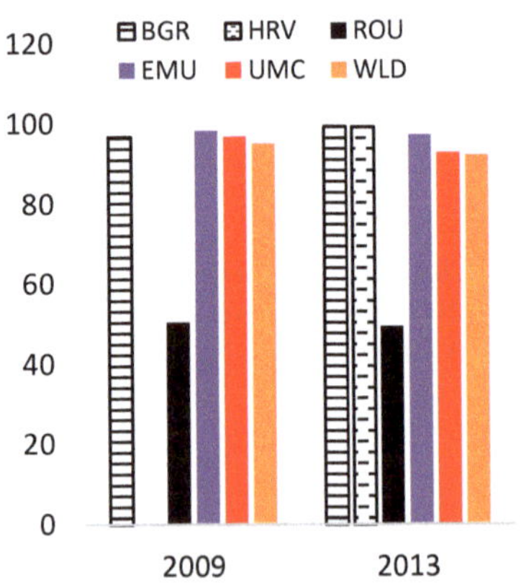

Fig. 6.14 Firms with a checking or saving account (%) (World Bank 2017)

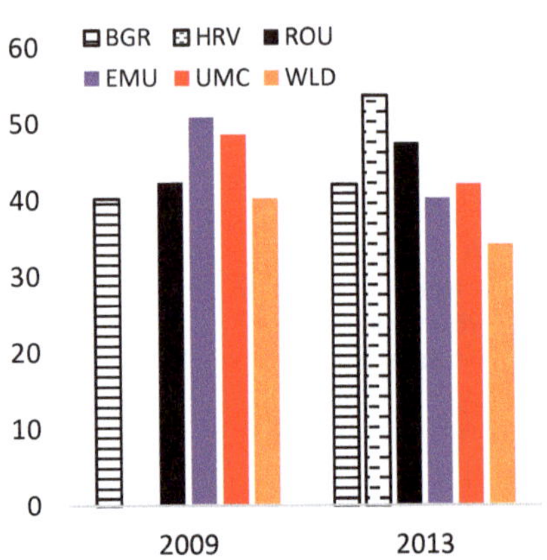

Fig. 6.15 Firms with a bank loan or line of credit (%) (World Bank 2017)

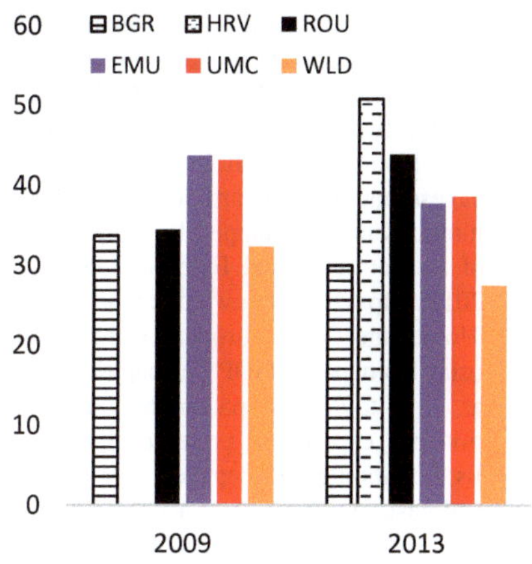

Fig. 6.16 Small firms with a bank loan or a line of credit (%) (World Bank 2017)

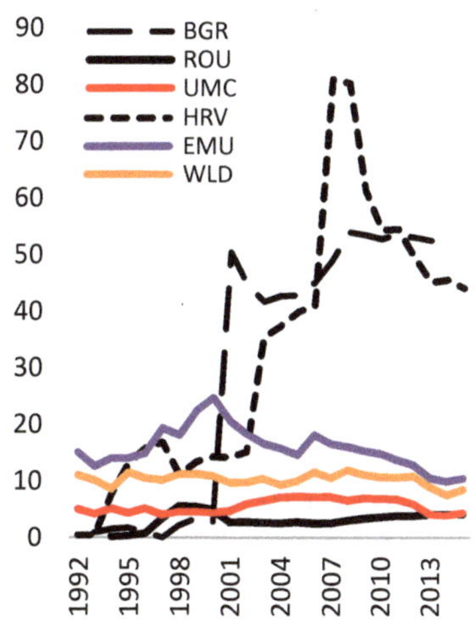

Fig. 6.17 Number of listed companies per 1,000,000 people (World Bank 2017)

References

Allen, D., Ndikumana, L.: Financial Intermediation and Economic Growth in Southern Africa. Working Paper, St. Louis: Federal Reserve Bank of St. Louis. (1998). Accessed 2017. https://research.stlouisfed.org/wp/1998/98-004.pdf

Badjun, M.: Financial intermediation by banks and economic growth: a review of empirical evidence. Inst. Pub. Financ. 1–32 (2009.) Accessed 2017. http://www.ijf.hr/eng/FTP/2009/2/badjun.pdf

Bucharest Stock Exchange Homepage: Romanian Companies see Capitalization over euro 20 billion for the first time in 9 years. (2017).Available at: https://www.bvb.ro/press/2017/Press_Release_BVB_Capitalization.pdf

Chirleşan, D.: Metodele acţiunii bancare & gestiunea finanţelor publice (Methods of Bank Action & Public Finance Management), vol. II, pp. 364–365. Alexandru Ioan Cuza University Publishing House, Iaşi (2008)

Čihák, M., Demirgüç-Kunt, A., Feyen, E., Levine, R.: Benchmarking Financial Systems Around the World Policy Research Working Paper 6175, pp. 2–3. World Bank, Washington, DC (2012)

Cojocaru, L. Falaris, E.V., Hoffman, S.D., Miller, J.B.: Financial System Development and Economic Growth in Transition Economies: New Empirical Evidence from CEE and CIS Countries (2015). Accessed 2017. http://www.lerner.udel.edu/sites/default/files/ECON/PDFs/RePEc/dlw/WorkingPapers/2015/UDWP2015-04.pdf

Delloite Homepage, Delloite. (2016.) [Online] Available at: https://www2.deloitte.com/ro/en/pages/about-deloitte/articles/2016-a-record-year-for-NPLs.html

Demirguc-Kunt, A. Klapper, L., Singer, D.: Financial Inclusion and Inclusive Growth: A Review of Recent Empirical Evidence. Policy Research Working Paper, pp. 2–4 (2017). Accessed 2017. https://openknowledge.worldbank.org/handle/10986/26479

EU Homepage, 2017. European Union. Last accessed (2017)

Eurostat Homepage: GDP per capita, consumption per capita and price level indices. Available at: http://ec.europa.eu/eurostat/statistics-explained/index.php/GDP_per_capita,_consumption_per_capita_and_price_level_indices. Last accessed (2017)

Focus Economics Homepage.: Available at: http://www.focus-economics.com/regions/central-and-eastern-europe. Last accessed (2017)

Isărescu, M.C.: Reflecţii economice (Economic Reflections), 2nd edn, pp. 193–200. Romanian Academy. The Romanian Center of Comparative and Consensus Economy, Bucharest (2007)

Kiriţescu, C.: Sistemul bănesc al leului si precursorii lui (The Money System of Lion Currency and It's Precursors), pp. 88–90. Enciclopedică Publishing House, Bucharest (1997)

Klapper, L., Lusardi, A., Oudheusden, P.: Financial literacy around the world. Insights from S&Ps Rating Services Global Financial Literacy Survey. The Globa Center For Financial Literacy, The George Washington University School of Business, 8. http://gflec.org/wp-content/uploads/2015/11/Finlit_paper_16_F2_singles.pdf (2015)

Levine, R.: Financial intermediary services and growth. J. Jpn. Int Econ. **6**, 383–405 (1992). https://doi.org/10.1016/0889-1583(92)90005-O

Levine, R.: Finance and growth: theory and evidence. In: Handbook of Economic Growth, pp. 866–910. Elsevier B.V. (2005). https://doi.org/10.1016/S1574-0684(05)01012-9

National Bank of Romania Homepage: Annual Report. 21–22 (2007). Available at: http://www.bnro.ro/Publicatii-periodice-204.aspx. Last accessed (2017)

National Bank of Romania Homepage: Financial Stability Report. 65–66 (2017a), Available at: http://www.bnro.ro/Publicatii-periodice-204.aspx, last accessed (2017)

National Bank of Romania Homepage.: Available at: http://www.bnro.ro/Baza-de-date-interactiva-604.aspx#. Last accessed (2017b)

OECD Homepage. Available at: https://stats.oecd.org/glossary/detail.asp?ID=303. Last accessed (2017)

Oks, A.: Efficiency of the Financial Intermediaries and Economic Growth in CEEC. Tartu University Press, Tartu (2001). http://www.mtk.ut.ee/sites/default/files/mtk/toimetised/febawb8.pdf

Thiel, M.: Finance and economic growth – a review of theory and the available evidence, s.l.: European Communities. http://ec.europa.eu/economy_finance/publications/pages/publication884_en.pdf (2001)

Trew, A.: Efficiency, depth and growth: quatitative implications of finance and growth theory. J. Macroecon. **30**, (2008). https://doi.org/10.1016/j.jmacro.2007.12.005. 1550-1568

World Bank Homepage: Financial inclusion data – Assessing the landscape and country level target approaches. Global Partnership for Financial Inclusion. International Financial Corporation. Available at: https://openknowledge.worldbank.org/bitstream/handle/10986/21741/947340WP0Box3800GPFI0Data0SG0Report.pdf?sequence=1&isAllowed=y (2011)

World Bank Homepage: Database. Available at: https://data.worldbank.org/indicator. Last accessed (2017)

World Bank: Global Financial Development Report 2014: Financial Inclusion, pp. 3–4. World Bank, Washington, DC (2014). https://doi.org/10.1596/978–0–8213-9985-9

Worldometers Homepage. Available at: http://www.worldometers.info/population/countries-in-europe-by-population/. Last accessed (2017)

Chapter 7
Linking Online Marketing Practices in Romania to Global Trends

Camelia Budac

Abstract The very fast online transformations cause rapid changes in consumers' behavior and, implicitly, the need for businesses' adaptation to market trends and wants. We are now at that moment when a business's survival and development essentially depend on understanding the importance of marketing and on adjustment to online marketing trends like ultimate elements in bringing its success. Thus, online marketing is a business culture, an entrepreneurial mindset in all over the world, for each type of business. This paper aims to give an overview on Romanian online advertising market by presenting data, trends, and main players. Many recent studies showed that the online is in a growing process, and this will keep going at least till 2021. Therefore, Romanian audience is still enjoying smart advertising content. One of the most attractive this year is the mobile sector, because consumers will use, even more, smartphones in their buying process. Thus, advertising should go through creative campaigns, imagined for these kinds of devices. Romania is a great potential for online advertising, but there is still some space for quality content. In order to gain a great image, a brand should use in its creative campaigns last innovations and databases offered by Facebook, Google, YouTube, and so on. Thus, for Romanian audience, the way of displaying an ad is still very annoying.

Keywords Online Romanian Marketing • Creative Advertising • Global Online Advertising Trends

7.1 Introduction

Due to the fact that innovation is everywhere, it is constantly raised the question about what is next and how new practices can be used. Moreover, marketers are thinking about what they can do differently while retaining brand identity but

---

C. Budac (✉)
Lucian Blaga University of Sibiu, Sibiu, Romania
e-mail: camelia.budac@ulbsibiu.ro

S.C. Mărginean et al. (eds.), *Emerging Issues in the Global Economy*, Springer Proceedings in Business and Economics,
https://doi.org/10.1007/978-3-319-71876-7_7

integrating components such as video, VR, email, and mobile marketing, how much more impact Facebook will have, and how many other platforms will develop.

Market evolution forces companies to constantly adapt marketing tools, so that the budget allocated does not prove to be too high compared to the proposed objectives – profit, public reaction, etc. (Prasad and Sethi 2009; Aaker and Carman 1982). Users are adapting faster and faster to new technologies, which requires rapid application of technological novelties to make this development a competitive advantage.

Whether we talk about trends such as big data, influencers, content marketing, native advertising, or personalization, the common thing that they have is to increase brand relevance and brand experience online. Through new technologies, brands one can and must bring more value to the consumer (Tiago and Tiago 2012; Strauss et al. 2003; Rodriguez and Peterson 2012; Kondopoulos 2011). The mere intrinsic value of products and services is no longer sufficient. To survive, each brand must take technological progress so as to be able to provide specific digital relevance to meet the needs of the consumer in a superior way.

7.2 Online Romanian Advertising Market

According to the latest edition of the ROADS, the total reported value of the online advertising market in Romania for the whole year 2016 was about 41 million euros (190,541,366 lei), recording a 22% increase over the previous year (like for like).

As a result of a robust countrywide consumer-driven growth, the online advertising market in Romania has registered strong growth last year, confirming the long-standing potential of this segment, which had not yet materialized in previous years. However, in order to capitalize on this favorable trend, publishers must come up with quality content that meets the need for companies to target different niche markets.

According to survey results, the top five industries account for 45% of total online advertising investment. Even if the order has changed, the top industries of digital advertising investments remain the same. The unquestionable leader of 7 years is the telecom industry (6 million euros), followed by finance (3.5 million euros – fourth in 2015), cosmetics (3.4 million euros – fifth rise), beverages (3 million euros – dropped a position compared to last year), and online retail (2.9 million euros – which last year ranked second).

As the evolution of the European market is concerned, Romania has the most visible growth rate (36.9% – calculated as like-for-like percentage and gross value), being in line with the dynamics at European level (+ 12.3% calculated as like-for-like percentage to gross value) (see Fig. 7.1)

Although Romania is still below the European average, the growth rate underlines the high potential of the market which needs to be sustained both through education and good practice of the local industry.

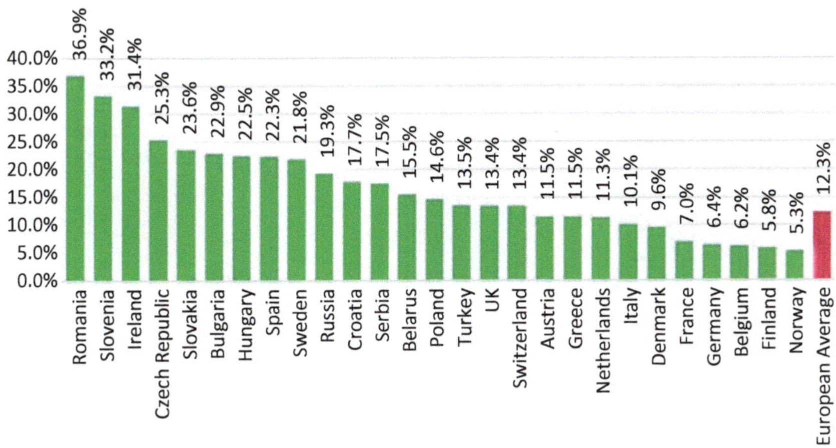

Fig. 7.1 Online advertising YoY growth in 2016 (%) (Adex Benchmark 2016)

Also in the first semester of 2017, communications market players are the largest investors in digital advertising, with over 9 million euro card rates, followed by media and entertainment/free time (8.69 million euro card rates), automobile, business, industry and technological equipment, and retail stores.

The digital platforms that attracted the largest advertising budgets in the first half of 2017 are the following: adevarul.ro, stirileprotv.ro, and mediafax.ro (MIPO 2017).

According to the ADEX Benchmark 2016 study on online advertising consumption at the European level, digital has strengthened its position as the main advertising environment and surpassing TV over 8 billion euros, which confirms the importance of innovation in this ever-changing industry.

Mobile and video advertisings are according to the study the main reasons for this growth in the industry that allows advertisers to meet the changing habits of their audience. Both the mobile display and the mobile search increased by more than 52% in 2016.

The video advertising has also grown considerably, accounting for 18.5% out of the total European display market, the market that thus gained 14.1% in 2016 (see Fig. 7.2). These mobile and video advertising moves are expected to continue in the years to come; the brands that will choose them in an attempt to train their audience will be able to reach their business goals.

The total European online advertising market reached 41.9 billion euros in 2016, that is, 37.3% of the European media advertising market (due to increases registered in each individual markets) which is close to almost 6.5 times more than in 2006, successive growth in each of these years, but the growth rate has stabilized in recent years (see Fig. 7.3) The largest increases came from the markets of Romania (36.9%), Slovenia (33.2%), and Ireland (31.4%).

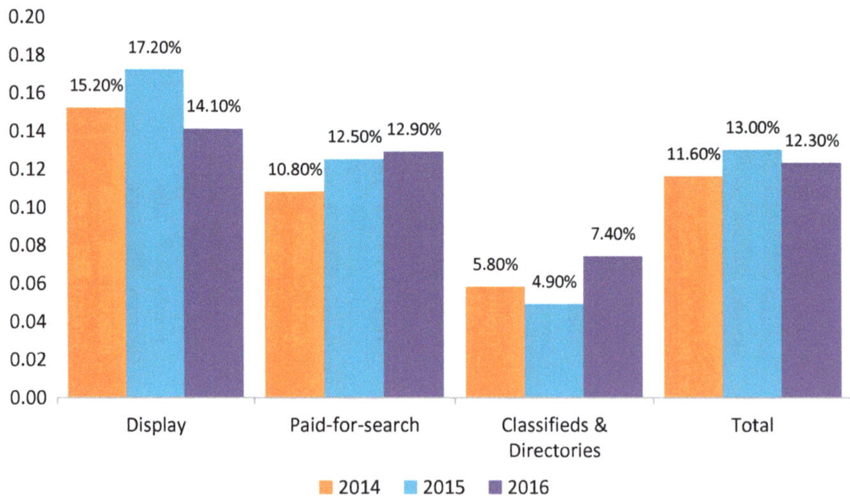

Fig. 7.2 Online advertising formats YoY growth (%) (Adex Benchmark 2016)

Fig. 7.3 Online advertising YoY growth (%) (Adex Benchmark 2016)

7.3 Trends in Consumer Behavior

Analyzing and putting up together the main online marketing trends, globally, we come to the conclusion that customers are the ones who will set trends. Customer satisfaction is the performance indicator that marketers adopt; this is a clue related to the fact that the boundaries between marketing, services, and sales are fading. Today, consumers interact with the brand and even build it, in collaboration with other consumers, but also with the marketing team. And all these are possible because the technology allows it.

The consumer's journey incorporates any technology that transforms a simple shopping experience into a personalized and unique one. The trend is to bring online facilities directly into store shelves, making retail and technology inseparable.

Artificial intelligence, enhanced and virtual reality, and Internet of things will greatly contribute to personalized shopping experience by perfectly blending online and offline for the benefit of the consumer. Today's consumers make their purchases whenever they want, using any device they want. For them, it is no longer so important to be present in the online or offline store. It is important that the brand should be present anytime and anywhere they shop. The digital domain must now be a part of everything that happens, so the two must be fully integrated. Companies do not necessarily need a digital strategy; the thing they really need is knowing the way to connect the digital component to the complex process that shows them how consumers are making purchasing decisions.

The main source of online information for both online and offline consumers is searching for desired products through search engines: about 68% of them use Internet searches for information when they want to make a purchase (Consumer Barometer 2017). It has become normal for information to be a click away, and buyers can become frustrated if they do not have immediate access to details about the products they are looking for. In recent years, there have emerged companies which have developed a policy focused on transparency and sustainability.

Consumers use virtual space to make purchasing decisions – from YouTube to Facebook – and it is getting harder, even harder than it used to be, putting buyers of certain products into one category or another. The categories of consumers such as "mainstream" – the vast majority or "high-end" and "low-end" – buyers of expensive products and cheap products start to disappear.

Consumer segmentation is becoming more and more complex. It can happen that the same customer is buying at the same time a luxury and an inexpensive product. These days you can easily find a person who might take a plane of a cheap airline to fly to Milan to buy a luxury handbag. When choosing the products, consumers apply an unequal combination of emotions and reasoning. They may have no emotional connection to aviation, and thus the cheapest product will be good enough for them. But when it comes to buying a luxury handbag, they might appreciate the tradition and craftsmanship invested in that product.

7.4 Trends in Online Marketing

By comprehensive processing of the information contained in the large databases, companies find out a bunch of new things about customers and their preferences, becoming better and better to identify the target audience and to communicate most effectively with their consumers (Oancea 2015), taking into account their buying and Internet search habits.

Due to large and complex customer databases and processes that can be processed and exploited, as well as social networking and flexible manufacturing processes, more and more companies are learning how to deliver products and designs tailored to the needs and preferences of each customer (Reto et al. 2017).

7.4.1 Social Media Marketing

Social networks have greatly changed the way that consumers across the world access information; communication has undergone a major change in accessibility, and content has changed in relation to user needs, becoming real centered customer experiences (Von Lieven 2016).

According to statistics provided by Statista (2017), the penetration rate of social networks is globally increasing. Thus, 71% of Internet users use social networks in their daily online activities, and they do so mostly on the smartphone. At both instrument and support level, this is a revolution; environments have to adapt to a wide variety of virtual and real-life systems (Yadav et al. 2015), formats, and devices that allow a dynamic stage and excellent opportunities. Mobile devices have brought new opportunities for mobile social networks including location features (Foursquare, Google Now) or social games.

Due to the abundance of information that the user is subjected to in the online environment, marketers are forced to propose solutions through social media marketing as a vital tool of online marketing strategy (Ahmad et al. 2016; Constantinides 2014).

As for social media, the number of social media channels with interest potential for the Romanian consumer is increasing by entering the area of relevance and reach of the Instagram and Pinterest platforms. As part of social media strategies, these platforms will become part of the mix, alongside Facebook, YouTube, and, in some cases, LinkedIn.

7.4.2 Video Marketing

Video content is increasingly present (the audience is showing increasing interest in this area; see Fig. 7.4.), and, with only a few exceptions, it is the only one that generates positive engagement in an organic way in social media. We can no longer talk about video as content but the experience it offers. The user begins to discover it gradually; from a subjective perspective, he feels he lives that moment. Whether we are talking about 360 videos, augmented reality or virtual reality videos definitely represent one of the areas with the greatest potential for exploitation.

Lately, the video has proven to be one of the most effective marketing strategies, especially for branding and engagement. The video helps to increase the e-mail opening rate, to make it easier to find the brand on search engines and to differentiate it from competition.

Creating video content is the main challenge that prevents more businesses from using this type of content and to be able to overcome its competition.

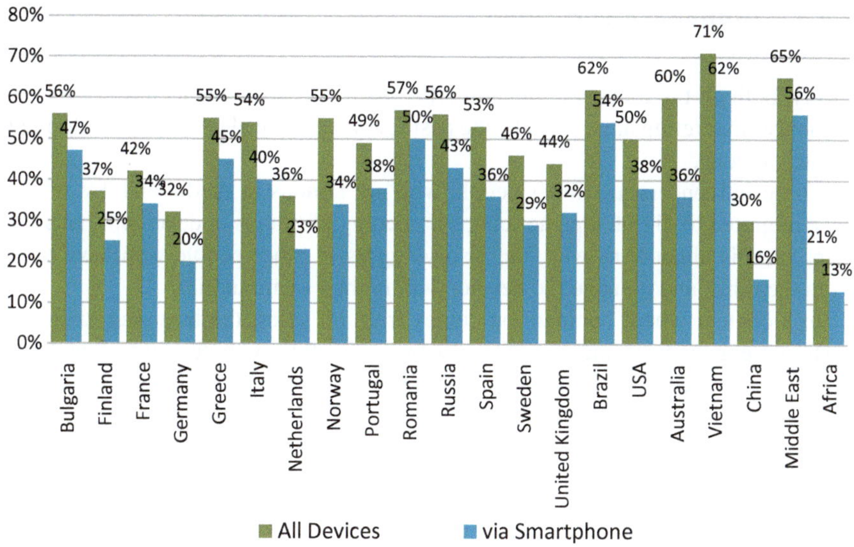

Fig. 7.4. Daily watching online videos (Data provided by Consumer Barometer (2017))

7.4.3 Content Marketing

Content marketing has been a trend in recent years, along with the assumption of the first mobile paradigm by more and more marketers.

2016 was the year when mobile Internet consumption exceeded the desktop worldwide, and this is also visible in Romania, where there are already big brands whose campaigns have generated mobile traffic and majority engagement. To adapt to this new reality, it is necessary to rethink not only the interfaces and engagement modes but also the content strategy.

Mobile content differs greatly from desktop usage: mobile has a much higher affinity than multimedia content (video and photo), different engagement modes, and more personalization capabilities (taking advantage of the fact that much of the time spent on social networks comes from mobile).

The fact that the product says a story is more relevant to consumers who are increasingly mindful of how they interact with a brand (Thomas 2011).

Digital relevance can take many forms: from a better understanding of the consumer, his needs, and his values (profiling, prototyping) to the anticipation and addressing to these needs (big data, personalization), their satisfaction under conditions of increased accessibility (UX), or even creating new needs (big data, content marketing).

7.4.4 *Influencer Marketing*

Lately, both on the local and global market, there has been a tendency to go to the influencer marketing area. Locally, the past few years have allowed the development of such a niche.

These influencers are either people who are famous in media and TV or who have migrated to digital area noticing the opening of brands in developing relationships on this channel as well, but also vloggers or other people who have raised from the ranks and managed to develop within their communities.

In a context where competition comes from all sides, the best way to shorten customer engagement and confidence is by associating with people or brands that have already succeeded in doing so. Partnerships with those who already have the support of their community can result in highly creative and effective campaigns.

7.5 Conclusions

Developing video content and the desire to personalize communication as much as possible will create strong relationships between brands, influential people, and their communities. Content remains the most relevant for marketing, but the context in which it is delivered has become more important than ever. Good content is organically delivered with an influence.

The future sounds promising, with a lot of news that it would be appropriate to take into account an online marketing strategy. As long as the public's need is the one that counts and the information that is of utmost interest to it is delivered, one will surely get the desired results from an online marketing campaign.

References

Aaker, A., Carman, J.M.: Are you overadvertising? J. Advert. Res. **22**(4), 57–70 (1982)

Ahmad, N.S., Musa, R., Harun, M.H.: The impact of social media content marketing (SMCM) towards brand health. Procedia. Econ. Financ. **37**, 331–336 (2016). https://doi.org/10.1016/S2212-5671(16)30133-2

Constantinides, E.: Foundations of social media marketing. Procedia. Soc. Behav. Sci. **148**, 40–57 (2014). https://doi.org/10.1016/j.sbspro.2014.07.016

Consumer Barometer with Google. https://www.consumerbarometer.com (2017)

IAB Europe and IHS Markit: Adex Benchmark 2016. European Online Advertising Spend. https://www.iabeurope.eu/wp-content/uploads/2017/06/IABEurope-AdExBenchmark-2016-full-report.pdf (2017). Accessed 28 July 2017

Kondopoulos, D.: Internet marketing advanced techniques for increased market share. Chim. Oggi. **29**(3), 9–12 (2011)

MIPO – Monitorizarea Investițiilor în Publicitatea Online Study, Biroul Român de Audit Transmedia – BRAT, http://www.forbes.ro/publicitatea-pe-internet-debutat-forta-2017-81147 (2017). Accessed 5 Aug 2017

economy. However, they regarded interests in themselves as suprahistorical, as the product of an unchanging "human nature."

A scientific analysis of economic interests was given by Marxism, which proceeded from the concept that social phenomena are based on relations of production among people, relations that reflect the interests of particular classes.

Relations of production are manifested through the motivations of human behavior as interests that belong to the objective conditions for the existence of society; economic interests are reflected in consciousness of people in the form of desired goals and motives for their achievement.

Interest, in the broad sense of the term, is a person's participation in or concern for a cause, advantage, and responsibility. In a narrow sense, interest means benefit of an individual or a certain group of people, opposed to benefit of others.

The following are the forms of self-interest orientation:

1. Obedience is an example of a weak self-interest orientation. A. Low formulates it as follows: "One can imagine the limiting case of a monolithic collectivism in which the prescriptions of the central plan are carried out by functionaries who fully identify with the imposed macrogoals." This type is unlikely to exist in its pure form in economy, so it is applied to study the evolution of human socialization than explaining the decision-making motives.
2. Following one's interests is a kind of egoism that is accepted in neoclassical economic theory. Agents start a process of exchange, knowing in advance the initial positions of an opposite side. All their actions are stipulated; all information about the surrounding they will have to face is known. There are no obstacles in the form of nonstandard or irrational behavior, as well as deviations from the rules.
3. Opportunism involves distortion of information, concealment of truth, and entanglement of counterparty and generates certain side effect of opportunistic behavior that also involves agents.

In addition to the effects of opportunistic behavior, agency costs include:

1. Control cost is a type of costs that a principal bears in order to ensure the appropriate fulfillment of the terms of a contract by an agent.
2. Indication costs incurred by an agent trying to gain trust of a principal and convince him of his abilities or good intentions.

For a particular employee, indication costs include getting a diploma or academic degree, a certificate of advanced training; for an enterprise, these costs mean the production and distribution of free product samples for potential customers, printing materials, and other methods of advertising and promotion. Managers assume the indication costs when they submit accounting reports openly, invite independent auditors for regular inspections, or attract financial resources, not through additional share issue, but issuing bonds or resorting to bank loans. (Unlike dividend payments, debt repayment does not depend on current business situation of a company, so this decision limits managers' freedom, including the opportunity to use such a valuable asset as a "quiet life." That's why issuing bonds usually

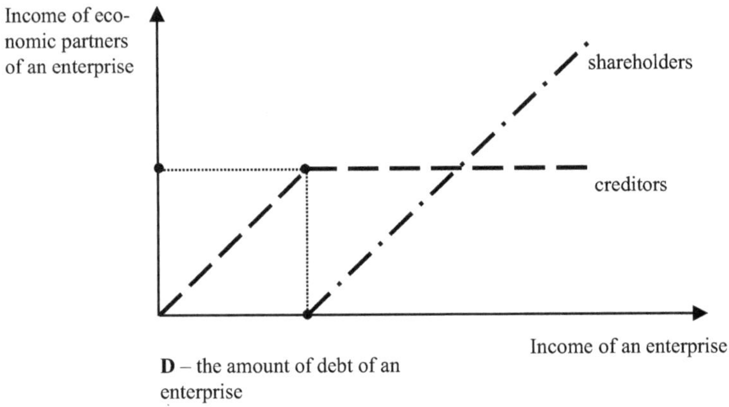

Fig. 8.1 Difference in the ways of obtaining income by owners and creditors of an enterprise as the basis of the distributive conflict between them (Minakova 2012)

increases shares rate.) Such decisions are a kind of guarantee of manager integrity for shareholders.

Within bankruptcy institute, agency relationship appears between shareholders and a principal of an enterprise, creditors and a principal, shareholders, and creditors. The relationship between these parties is characterized by numerous conflicts of interest.

- *Conflict of Interests Between Men of Property (Shareholders) and Creditors* (Fig. 8.1)

Such a conflict of interests between creditors and shareholders leads to a danger of a suboptimal investment *policy*: *underinvestment or reinvestment* (De Meza and Webb 1987).

Reinvestment Risk

This risk exists since the head of an enterprise usually acts in the interests of shareholders. At the same time, creditors are not in a position to control the use of loans granted to the enterprise. As a result, the head gets the opportunity to raise funds from creditors to finance one project, but actually brings these recourses to another project with a higher level of risk without making creditors known.

To illustrate this risk, we will present an enterprise with one shareholder in arrears to the creditor equal to 10. This enterprise can invest in two projects: the first project guarantees the income equal to 10. The second one is a kind of a lottery ticket with a 10% probability you can get 100 or nothing in 90% of cases. In case of choosing the first project, all income received will go to pay off the debt to the creditor; the shareholder's income will be zero. If a preference is given to the second project, in one case out of ten, a shareholder has an opportunity to get 90. Thus, if a principal acts in the interests of a shareholder, he will choose the second project to the detriment of the interests of creditors.

Underinvestment Risk

An increase of the enterprise debt can become an obstacle for implementation of economically viable investment projects, since the funds received from these projects will primarily be sent to creditors whose maturity dates are approaching (Myers 1984). Thus, the probability of receiving income by new creditors that provided funds for the project is reducing.

Suppose that an enterprise has a debt equal to 100. This enterprise has the opportunity to implement an investment project that will bring income equal to 120, but requiring for its implementation costs of 50. If the debt to creditors is paid in chronological order (starting with the very first creditors), then this project will not be realized, in spite of the fact this project is profitable. This is due to the fact that the new lender financing this project will receive only 20 (with incurred costs equal to 50).

This example justifies the existence in the legislation of a number of the countries of provisions in accordance with which the indebtedness to creditors who have provided funds to an enterprise that is in bankruptcy procedures is repaid in priority order (Article 40 in France) (Blazy 2000).

On the other hand, this problem can be solved if the investment project is financed by the original creditors, without involving new creditors.

Differences in the way of receiving income by shareholders and creditors create a conflict between them in determining the way to resolve the current crisis situation: shareholders are more likely to find it more profitable for the enterprise to continue functioning (i.e., to preserve an insolvent business entity), and creditors would prefer enterprise liquidation. At the same time, for receiving the fastest payout, creditors will prefer to liquidate even an enterprise that could survive and eventually regain its solvency under the condition of competent management. Because of the long process that bankruptcy procedures take, production capacities can be lost, which does not correspond to the objective conditions of the Russian economy interested in preserving its production potential.

On the contrary, if a decision is made in shareholders' interests, then there is a risk of preserving nonviable enterprises that create a significant burden on the budget and restrain structural changes in the economy. In this situation, the interests of shareholders and a principle of an enterprise coincide with the interests of employees, as well as municipal and regional authorities. Authorities often oppose a liquidation of large and politically significant enterprises that are major employers in regions. As a result, governors and managers of such enterprises act in collusion in order to use procedures of external management and financial recovery for avoiding payment of federal taxes and non-return of credits to external investors (Ermolaev and Minakova 2012).

As a result, obsolete enterprises often continue to function because they are the largest employers in cities. Municipal and regional authorities do everything to save them: provide them with hidden subsidies that come from additional taxes and fees payed by financially sustainable firms.

The conflict of interests between creditors and shareholders in the absence of effective mechanisms for resolving it leads to a decision that contradicts the principles of optimal choice, efficient use of resources, and social justice.

- *Conflict of Interest Between Shareholders and a General Manager of an Enterprise*

Relationship between a general manager of an enterprise and shareholders can be considered as a "principal-agent" relationship, in which a principal (shareholder) delegates the authority to manage the enterprise to a general manager (agent). The activities of a general manager have a direct impact on the value of the enterprise and on the well-being of shareholders. But shareholders (principals) have only a superficial understanding of the nature of the efforts spent by a general manager, his true intentions and conscientiousness. This is despite the fact that a general manager and shareholders have opposite interests (Jensen 1986). So, shareholders are interested in the growth of the share price and the dividends received, while a general manager himself does not participate in their distribution receiving a fixed reward, and his main function is to ensure the sustainable development of an enterprise in achieving its mission and goals. This conflict of interest can be reduced if (1) a general manager owns a part of the shares of an enterprise headed by him or his remuneration will be proportional to shares price (Leland and Pyle 1977) and (2) probable bankruptcy of an enterprise is accompanied by costs for a general manager himself (loss of business reputation, loss of job, penalties).

At the same time, despite the differences in interests of shareholders and managers of an enterprise, in the situation of insolvency in determining the outcome of the crisis, their common choice will be keeping an economic entity going.

- *Conflict of Interest Between Creditors and a General Manager of an Enterprise*

Creditors, on the one hand, and a general manager of a debtor enterprise, on the other hand, are guided by the opposite motives in the situation of insolvency. Creditors are interested in prompt return of their funds, which is most likely to be achieved in the process of liquidation of an economic entity, and a general manager is interested in preserving an enterprise, because with company liquidation he loses not only control over it but also his reward.

In accordance with the certain targets, economic agents form their behavioral strategies. In particular:

- Shareholders and a general manager under any conditions will be interested in preserving an enterprise that is related to the nature of remuneration they receive. In addition, shareholders' demands are satisfied at last, and in the situation of company liquidation, there is a strong possibility that they will get nothing.
- Satisfaction of creditors' claims is not in the first instance, so they may also prefer to run a company, even if its liquidation is economically viable. Such a decision is made by them in the situation if the liquidation value is clearly not sufficient to satisfy all requirements.

Table 8.1 Arbitration between the preservation of an insolvent enterprise and its liquidation

	Date 1	Date 2	Date 3
Enterprise income	5	5	5
Debts for the period t[a]	10	10	10
If an enterprise continues its business			
Amount of funds transferred to creditors for the period t + 1[b]	–	3	3
Amount of funds transferred to creditors for the period t	5	2	2
If an enterprise goes through liquidation ($V_l = 0$)			
Amount of funds transferred to creditors for the period t	5	0	0

[a]A period before *debt announcement*
[b]A period after starting insolvency proceedings

- Creditors of the first priority, on the contrary, are more likely to give preference to liquidation of a viable enterprise facing temporary financial difficulties.

Uncovered conflicts of interest have a significant impact on the effectiveness of the entire bankruptcy institute because they determine which method of resolving the crisis will be given preference: rehabilitation or liquidation procedures.

If a final decision in perspectives of a debtor enterprise is made by a separate category of interested parties (having certain rights with respect to a debtor enterprise), as a rule, this decision is not appropriate. In other words, this decision is made exclusively in the interests of this group and at the expense of the national economic system.

At the same time, a rational solution to this dilemma between the preservation of an insolvent enterprise and its liquidation should be based on the following provisions:

1. An enterprise that does not need new borrowings to ensure its further functioning should be retained for the economic system, if its value during the continuation of its activity (Vc) exceeds the liquidation value (Vl) and vice versa.
2. If the enterprise is unable to continue its activities without resorting to new loans, its preservation is advisable only if Vc-Vl exceeds the value of a new loan (Table 8.1, De Meza and Webb 1987).

The decision to continue business activity is taken after the first period, when an enterprise is unable to pay its debts in time. In order to continue its business, such an enterprise has to get a new loan. This loan repayment will be paid in the order of *preference* to creditors' claims of period t (assume that creditors of period t + 1 receive three in the second period and three in the third period). At the same time, amounts sent to pay off debts to creditors of period t will be two in the second and third periods; when an enterprise is in liquidation, income of these creditors is zero (liquidation value of an enterprise is considered zero). Therefore, enterprise preservation for creditors is more preferable. Thus, the chosen solution of the current crisis situation should ensure the maximization of the value of the economic entity and public welfare.

8.4 Conclusion

Thus, the focus of the neo-institutional theory is contractual relationships, which can be classified as agency relationships. Agency relationships arise whenever one of the parties, called an agent, takes decisions on behalf of or represents the interests of the other party, called a principal (Jensen and Meckling 1976).

In the frame of bankruptcy, institute agency relationships are established between creditors and shareholders, as well as in the situation of delegating powers of shareholders or creditors to a general manager of an enterprise. All these economic agents are characterized by opposite interests. That is why, if the enterprise becomes insolvent, and a decision in its perspectives (liquidation or preservation) is taken by a separate group of interested parties, this decision is often not appropriate from a point of maximizing social welfare.

Ideally, the main function of bankruptcy institute is to reconcile interests of all interested parties, first of all, creditors and debtors. It should be done by resolving the emerging distributive conflicts when the conditions for maximizing the objective function of one group of economic agents coincide with the conditions under which the increase in the welfare of this group is impossible without reducing the welfare of another (pareto-optimal state).

References

Blazy, R.: La faillite: éléments d'analyse économique. Economica, Paris (2000)
De Meza, D., Webb, D.C.: Too much investment: a problem of asymmetric information. Q. J. Econ. **102**, 281–289 (1987). https://doi.org/10.2307/1885064
Eggertsson, T.: Economic Behavior and Institutions. Cambridge University Press, Cambridge (1990). https://doi.org/10.1017/CBO9780511609404
Ermolaev, D., Minakova, I.: Management of Socio-Economic Development of the Region: Theoretical and Methodological Concept and Institutional Constrains. Southwest State University, Kursk (2012.) (in Russian)
Jensen, M.C.: Agency costs of free cash flow, corporate finance and takeovers. Am. Econ. Rev. **76**, 323–339 (1986). https://doi.org/10.2139/ssrn.99580
Jensen, M., Meckling, W.: Theory of the firm: managerial behavior, agency costs and ownership structure. J. Financ. Econ. **3**, 305–360 (1976). https://doi.org/10.1016/0304-405X(76)90026-X
Leland, H., Pyle, D.: Information asymmetries, financial structure, and financial intermediation. J. Financ. **2**, 371–387 (1977). https://doi.org/10.2307/2326770
Minakova, I.: Behavioral patterns of economic agents in different types of contractual relationships: neo-institutional approach. Izvestia Southwest State University. **2-2**(41), 29–34 (2012.) (in Russian)
Myers, S.: Determinants of corporate borrowing. J. Financ. Econ. **5**, 147–175 (1977). https://doi.org/10.1016/0304-405X(77)90015-0
Myers, S.: The capital structure puzzle. J. Financ. **3**, 575–592 (1984). https://doi.org/10.3386/w1393
Ross, S.A.: The determination of financial structure: the incentive Signaling approach. Bell J. Econ. **1**, 23–40 (1977). https://doi.org/10.2307/3003485
Shleifer, A., Vishny, R.W.: Management entrenchment – the case of manager-specific investment. J. Financ. Econ. **25**, 123–139 (1989). https://doi.org/10.1016/0304-405X(89)90099-8

Chapter 9
The Influence of Business Ecosystems on Innovation-Based Industries: A Research on the Mechanical Sector in Italy

Anatolie Caraganciu, Fabio Musso, and Barbara Francioni

Abstract The business ecosystem perspective can be considered as a more advanced point of view for interpreting the development of local economic systems, if compared to more traditional concepts such as clusters, industrial districts, local or regional systems, and local networks. The business ecosystem perspective allows to better highlight the adaptive and evolutionary nature of local systems in front of the changing external environment and dynamics on national and international markets. The aim of the research was to analyze the key characteristics of firms belonging to a local business ecosystem specialized on an innovation-driven industry – the mechanical sector – in order to verify which kind of influence the local context still exerts on firms' management, competitiveness, and relationships. A quantitative survey has been conducted on a sample of 104 firms located in Italy, focusing on organization, strategies, and relationships with both the internal (at the local system level) and external networks, and to relationships with the local environment and market. Results highlight the ability of firms belonging to a business ecosystem to take advantage of innovation diffusion processes and also to better develop the quality of products. An important issue that emerges is related to the cohesion of ties within the local context. When relationships are based on knowledge exchange, the evolution of smaller and weaker firms can be fostered, bringing to a general strengthening of the local system.

Keywords Business ecosystems • Local economic systems • Clusters • Industrial districts • Mechanical industry

A. Caraganciu
Lucian Blaga University of Sibiu, Sibiu, Romania
e-mail: an.caraganciu@gmail.com

F. Musso (✉) • B. Francioni
Carlo Bo University of Urbino, Urbino, Italy
e-mail: fabio.musso@uniurb.it; barbara.francioni@uniurb.it

S.C. Mărginean et al. (eds.), *Emerging Issues in the Global Economy*, Springer Proceedings in Business and Economics,
https://doi.org/10.1007/978-3-319-71876-7_9

9.1 Introduction

The local concentration of manufacturing activities has been widely analyzed in literature. On this respect, several concepts have been proposed in order to interpret the dynamics within local economic systems, such as industrial districts (Becattini 1990), clusters (Porter 1990), innovative milieu (Camagni 1991), local systems (Becattini and Rullani 1996), and local networks (Grandori and Soda 1995). More recently, the concept of business ecosystems (Iansiti and Levien 2004a; Pierce 2009; Peltoniemi 2006; Koenig 2012; Adner 2006) has been introduced, which better highlights the adaptive and evolutionary nature of the local system facing the changes in the external environment and in markets. According to this perspective, the dynamic character of the local system whose components interact, adapt, and evolve has been highlighted (Eisenhardt and Galunic 2000; van der Borgh et al. 2012).

All the perspectives described above point out the advantages of local systems in terms of firms' competitiveness, bringing to a general economic growth of the region they belong to. However, the emergence of global supply chains and ICT-based extended business networks is calling into question the role and future of local systems (Whitford 2001), since knowledge can be transmitted and exchanged much more easily than in the past. As a consequence, it has been argued if the development of global value chains may affect local manufacturing systems (Humphrey and Schmitz 2002).

This research analyzes the key characteristics of firms belonging to a local system, according to the business ecosystem perspective, with the objective of verifying which kind of influence the local context still exerts on firms' management, competitiveness, and relationships. To achieve this goal, a survey was carried out on a sample of 104 mechanical firms located inside an Italian local system.

The chapter is organized as follows. After the literature review, the methodology is described, and results are presented and discussed. Finally, conclusions, limitations, and future research directions are indicated.

9.2 Literature Review: Local Systems and the Business Ecosystem Approach

Porter (1990) introduced the concept of cluster for defining local economic systems and described them in terms of (i) geographic concentration, (ii) interconnection of firms and institutions, (iii) presence of both competition and cooperation, and (iv) specialization.

In this context, the relational dynamics have been considered in terms of inter-firm relationships and relationships with the local context. The focus has also been predominantly on economic factors, especially those influencing internal (to the local system) relationships and also external relationships, with supplying and selling markets (Brown et al. 2007).

Within the cluster literature, a focus on the regional development has been also addressed by the "innovative milieu" approach (Camagni 1991), which analyzed the causes of different regional capabilities to innovate. According to this perspective, the innovative milieu was defined as "... the set or the complex network of mainly in-formal relationships on a limited geographical area, often determining a specific external 'image' and a specific internal 'representation' and sense of belonging, which enhance the local innovative capability through synergetic and collective learning processes" (Camagni 1991: 3).

Another relevant concept that has been adopted for interpreting local systems is that of industrial districts. Unlike clusters, in case of industrial districts, two more elements are highlighted: a homogeneous system of values and a strong influence of the social dimension (Zucchella 2006).

Becattini and Rullani (1996) identified different success factors related to industrial districts. A key feature is the presence of information flows occurring not only through formalized channels but also through informal and social-based channels. Such information flows foster learning and innovation processes, which cannot then be easily transferred to other systems (Maskell 2005). Other key concepts related to industrial districts seem to be those of embeddedness (Boschma et al. 2002; Nordhaug 2003; Uzzi 1997), by which "economic and social cohesion are intertwined so that economic and social actions and structures blend together" (Zucchella 2006: 22), and trust. Trust, however, did not receive adequate attention and has not been analyzed in its determinants and dimensions.

More recently, the business ecosystem perspective has been adopted. The concept of business ecosystem emerged in the 1990s as an extension of works based on ecological systems, being defined as "a system of interactions between people of different species in the same site, and between people and the physical environment" (Hannan and Freeman 1989).

On the economic domain, the concept stems from the organizational ecology literature, which analyzes the financial condition of firms' agglomerations, which collectively form ecosystems (Carroll and Hannan 2000). Doing so, the ecological metaphor has been transposed to relations between firms.

Different authors (Moore 2006; Lewin et al. 1999; Hannan and Freeman 1989) attempted to apply this concept to the business environment and corporate behavior.

Participants in a business ecosystem "are not all created equal and do not necessarily pursue the same strategies" (Iansiti and Levien 2004a). Divisions of labor can develop and stabilize over time, but the ways in which roles are distributed among interacting firms are not determined by the technology itself, since they can vary, based on institutional, historical, and national differences (Tee and Gawer 2009).

According to the strategy literature, business ecosystems arise around core firms that define a technological architecture (Teece 2007). However, they can also be based on brand, geography, or product characteristics. Unlike organizational ecology literature, the strategy perspective highlights organizational adaptation as a key issue. Individual actors are mainly driven by seeking personal advantages, and the competitive environment exerts a selection on those firms that could be an obstacle to the community's economic health (Pierce 2009). Adaptation for these firms is constrained by structural inertia, and their survival depends on how well their features match the changing competitive environment.

Iansiti and Levien (2004b) suggested productivity, robustness, and niche creation as the three main factors for evaluating the health of a business ecosystem. They proposed four different roles that firms can have within business ecosystems: keystones (acting as enablers, with a great influence on the whole system), niche players (the largest base of the population), dominators, and hub landlords (attracting resources from the system but not reciprocally).

Most studies on business ecosystems use the perspective of a keystone firm to ad-dress relationships with other members of the ecosystem (Iansiti and Levien 2004b; Cusumano 2010). Therefore, the business ecosystem perspective, with its focus on common platforms and relationships among actors (members or stakeholders), is a good setting in which to examine the dynamic adaptation process of a local system to the external environment (included markets) changes and the mechanisms of knowledge transmission and generation of innovation.

9.3 Methodology: Sampling and Data Collection

To achieve our objectives, a survey was conducted in Italy, involving small-medium-sized firms belonging to the mechanical sector and manufacturing machinery, components, and equipment.

The mechanical sector was chosen because its competitive dynamics are strictly dependent on innovation, and the aim of this research was to analyze the role of the local system in affecting innovation generation/transmission processes. Moreover, the choice of a specific sector is due to the need to reduce heterogeneity among firms depending on structures and processes that are sector-related (Francioni et al. 2015).

The survey has been conducted between July and October 2016 in the province of Pesaro-Urbino, in the center of Italy, where an important local system specialized in mechanics exists. The sample was obtained from a list provided by the Pesaro-Urbino Chamber of Commerce, including all the companies of the mechanical industry in the province.

The questionnaire was addressed to the entrepreneur (if operating in the firm) or the general manager. A total of 104 valid responses have been collected. The analysis of responses was carried out through descriptive statistics and a cluster analysis.

Finally, results have been discussed within a focus group composed by representatives of manufacturers associations, local chamber of commerce, banking system, and entrepreneurs.

9.4 Findings

9.4.1 Descriptive Statistics

Almost half of the companies (49%) produce components (metal carpentry, turning, foundry, and precision mechanics), and 16.3% performs third-party processing (sheet metal processing, assembling, etc.). Machinery, manufacturing plants, and tools are produced by 26% of firms. Finally, 8.7% produces industrial equipment.

The average number of customers per firm shows a weakness and risky condition in market relationships for microenterprises (below 10 employees) and those with up to 20 employees: respectively, 65% and 70% of these firms counts 80% of turnover with less than 10 customers and 85% of them with less than 20 customers. Increasing the size of firms, the number of customers increases. Dependence on a few customers is more pronounced for components manufacturers, turners, and third-party manufacturers.

Looking at the strength points and distinctive elements of firms, according to what the respondents stated, a clear focus on technological innovation and efficiency in the supply chain emerged from larger firms. In fact, innovation and efficiency in the supply chain are key issues to achieve levels of excellence compared to competitors, and they require investment capacity and adequate organizational dimension.

Research and development (R&D) is carried out by 68.3% of firms. The relationship between firm size and investments on R&D is clear: 41.9% of smaller firms report no R&D, and, as the firm size increases, the percentage of no R&D decreases.

Relationship with suppliers is based on trust in 83.7% of cases, and two-thirds of those relying on trust also indicate two essential requirements: reliability and quality. In 12.5% of cases, the relationship is based on price and only in 3.8% of cases on R&D and innovation-based collaboration.

The tight dependence of smaller firms on the local system is confirmed by the analysis of the international suppliers, which shows a clear relationship between firm size and the presence of international suppliers. Larger companies have in almost all cases (91.7%) international suppliers. Smaller firms have much lower percentages, respectively, 52.4% for firms from 21 to 50 employees and 25.9% for firms with less than 21 employees.

Alliances with other firms are not widely adopted. Only 23.5% of respondents stated that they had alliances with other firms. Machinery and tools manufacturers are those who have made the most use of agreements and alliances (45% of cases). On the contrary, firms producing components and third-party processing are those who have made less use of agreements.

9.4.2 Cluster Analysis

In order to outline different typologies of firms, a cluster analysis has been performed. The cluster analysis permits to group into subsets (clusters) elements belonging to a larger set, in order to determine groups that are internally more homogeneous and, at the same time, more heterogeneous to the other groups. For this purpose, a nonhierarchical cluster analysis, usually applicable to quantitative data sets (Malhotra and Birks 2007), has been performed.

A K-Mean methodology has been followed, which allows minimized inertia within single groups and between clusters. Clusters have been identified on the basis of the main characteristics of firms. After a series of test, the number of the singled-out cluster that emerged is 4. Cluster 4 resulted as the most numerous one with 44 units, followed by cluster 2 (28 units), cluster 1 (27 units), and finally cluster 3 (5 units).

Through the ANOVA, we found that product/process specialization, the percentage of export sales on turnover, and the type of R&D conducted are the variables that can better define the clusters within the sample.

The four clusters that emerged have been named as Following the Partners, Innovation Leaders, Independents, and Service- and Quality-Based Followers (Table 9.1).

By comparing the characteristics of clusters and their profiles, it is possible to highlight the distinctive elements for successful or unsuccessful results in terms of managing the clubs and attracting practitioners.

Cluster 1 ("Following the Partners") consists of 27 firms that mainly produce components, although several of them are specialized on third-party manufacturing. The entrepreneur and his family predominantly manage firms. On average, the number of employees is between 11 and 20, but several firms also have a number of employees less than 10. The turnover does not exceed two million euros per year, and the export percentage is less than 20%, with many cases where no exports were reported.

Although most companies stated that strategic planning is clear to the management, the indicators considered show that planning is almost nonexistent.

These firms are poorly structured/organized and do not pursue product innovation of their own initiative. However, they respond to customers' requests about collaboration in the development of innovative products and components.

Competitiveness is mainly based on price, but there are also several firms competing on quality, service, speed, and flexibility. However, their condition is dependent on relationships with the local system.

Firms in this group are those who have made less use of formal agreements with other companies. Even the relationship with local stakeholders is loose and in some cases not constructive (e.g., with the banking system). Among these groups of firms, several ones are those concerned for their survival, especially among smaller firms.

Cluster 2 ("Innovation Leaders") consists of 28 firms and is mainly composed of machinery and industrial plants manufacturers. However, also other types of product

Table 9.1 Firms' profiles based on cluster centers

	Cluster			
	1. Following the partners (27 firms)	2. Innovation leaders (28 firms)	3. Independents (5 firms)	4. Service- and quality-based followers (44 firms)
Main production type	Components	Machinery and manufacturing plants	Industrial equipment	Turners, third-party manufacturers
Management	Entrepreneur and his/her family members	General manager (mainly with a career internal to the firm)	Entrepreneur and his/her family members	Entrepreneur and his/her family members
Local/national/ international customers	Local/national	International/ national	Mainly national and international and also local	Local/national
Total number of employees	11–20	51–250	11–20	11–20
Percentage of export sales on turnover	Less than 20%	41–60%	41–60%	Less than 20%
Type of R&D	None	Relevant and structured	Existing and informal	None
Main competitors	Local, national, and international (from emerging markets)	International (from developed countries)	National and international (from developed countries)	Local
Type of strategic planning	Almost nonexisting	Clear to the management and communicated inside the company	Clear to the management and area responsible	Almost nonexisting
No. of customers	Low	High	Medium-high	Medium-low

specialization are present in this group, such as those that produce industrial tools. Firms within this group have a managerial character, although the entrepreneur presence is always active and has central role on decisions. These companies have a higher number of employees than the other clusters, between 50 and 250.

What is most commonly associated with this type of firms is their high level of internationalization, which is typically between 41% and 60% of turnover, with several companies exporting between 61% and 80% and five of them with export rate between 81% and 100%.

Strategic planning is always carried out in the case of larger companies within this group. Moreover, precise R&D programs are also conducted in a structured manner, both in cooperation with customers and suppliers.

In addition to the agreements for R&D, about half of the firms developed agreements at the distribution level for foreign market development and for organizing pre- and post-sale services to international customers.

The key factors of success for these companies are innovation, quality, and service. Relationships with local stakeholders are mildly established and mainly involve institutional stakeholders and trade associations. Several firms have collaborative relationships with universities for studying and developing innovation in products, materials, and processes. Despite this group of firms resulted as better positioned in the market with satisfactory economic results, some companies reported critical conditions, perceiving a real risk of exiting the market.

Cluster 3 ("Independents") is the smaller one (5 firms) and consists of companies that mainly produce industrial equipment and heating/cooling plants. Businesses are mainly managed by the entrepreneur and members of his family. They have long experience in the market, being founded between 31 and 40 years ago, and have a staff of between 11 and 20 employees, although in one case the size is between 50 and 250. The percentage of export on total turnover is between 41% and 60%.

These companies are well structured and have sufficient resources and skills for developing foreign markets. Moreover, continue R&D is conducted, but predominantly out from systematic processes, by looking at the opportunities coming from innovation in the components and materials markets.

Collaboration with other firms within the local system is limited and focused on components production. Marketing activities and new markets development are conducted autonomously, without any relationship with other firms of the local system. This group is the least affected by the threats deriving from the market. However, in this case, the explanation can be mainly found on the product specialization.

Cluster 4 ("Service- and Quality-Based Followers") is composed of 44 firms, most of which are specialized on precision turnstiles and precision mechanics. In addition, some firms produce metal carpentry. The average age of these firms is between 21 and 30 years, and, similarly to clusters 1 and 3, management is in the hands of the entrepreneur and his family. The average number of employees is between 11 and 20, although nearly half of the cluster has fewer than 10 employees. The export percentage on turnover is, as for cluster number 1, less than 20%, and in more than half the cases, there is no export.

What makes this group different from cluster 1 mainly concerns the type of production and turnover, which in cluster 4 is higher.

The main distinctive feature of these companies is that they base their competitiveness on the quality of product and workmanship, together with a highly qualified services offered in terms of flexibility and willingness to participate in joint projects for the development of new products or processes. Relationships for quality improvement and innovation are mainly developed with customers belonging to the same local system, where the main competitors are also located. The dependence on local customers is not the same as for cluster 1, since in cluster 4 several firms have a significant share of customers in the national market. This is due to the ability to compete on price with bigger firms and those better organized, having enough levels of efficiency economies of scale.

In this group of companies, agreements and partnerships are more informal, with the possibility of relying on a significant trusteeship base for relationships with the local system firms. Among these companies, there are a number of criticalities with a frequent perception of market exiting risk.

9.5 Conclusions

This research had the objective of analyzing the key characters of firms belonging to a local system in order to verify which kind of influence the local context still exerts on firms' management, competitiveness, and relationships. A survey conducted on a sample of 104 companies located within an Italian local system, specialized in the mechanical industry, allowed to examine a number of variables concerning structural, organizational and strategic aspects of firms. In addition, supplying relationships, relationships with the markets and with the local context have been analyzed.

Through the cluster analysis, it has been possible to identify different firms' profiles, with characteristics partially corresponding to the different roles of firms to a business ecosystem as identified by previous literature on business ecosystem (Iansiti and Levien 2004b). More in depth, a correspondence between the group defined as "Innovation Leaders" and the role of "keystones" proposed by Iansiti and Levien (2004b) has emerged clearly. Similarly, cluster 1 ("Following the Partners") seems to be more corresponding to the role of "niche players," although with a less autonomous and more adaptive character. On the other hand, the other profiles which emerged did not match the roles of "niche players-dominators" and "hub landlords." The only partial exception is cluster 3 (Independents) which can be partially associated with the latter, since it benefits from belonging to the local system more than it contributes.

The most prominent profile for the local system is that of the "Innovation Leaders," which have developed power-based not formalized relationships (El Ansary and Stern 1972) with their local supply chain partners. Thanks to these relationships, the "Innovation Leaders" are able to involve suppliers in R&D processes, also encouraging the exchange and dissemination of knowledge and addressing suppliers in increasing quality levels of production and reliability on relationships. On this point, it is interesting to note that smaller firms, which would have difficulties in developing autonomously new products, processes, and service improvements, and even less innovation, are able to effectively respond to major firm's stimuli, contributing to a widespread strengthening process within the local system, even if often limited to the relationships among firms.

The implications of this study are numerous.

Firstly, there are many indications on which areas public policies could be addressed to. It is possible to identify the key recipients of public actions, that is, the leading companies, focusing on their ability to involve the followers, on one side, and the weaker firms to help them to overcome their limits, and addressing them to correct evolutionary paths, on the other side. However, the focus of intervention tools should be projects, more than subjects. Secondly, implications from this study come also for the strategic choices of individual businesses, since it was possible to identify for each profile which weaknesses must be overcome and which directions of change/evolution can be identified.

There are several limits in this research. The first one refers to the lack of trustworthiness of the information provided by firms on issues related to their strategic consciousness and their commitment on R&D and innovation policies. On this issue, future investigations should enforce the use of more objective indicators to complement the information directly provided by respondents. Another limit to this research is that it did not sufficiently deepen the processes of change, in order to better highlight the dynamics of evolution, coevolution, and selection of the local system. In this regard, a longitudinal analysis on indicators capable of describing such change processes would be advisable.

References

Adner, R.: Match your innovation strategy to your innovation ecosystem. Harv. Bus. Rev. **84**(4), 98–107 (2006)

Becattini, G.: The Marshallian industrial district as a socio-economic notion. In: Pyke, F., Becattini, G., Sengenberger, W. (eds.) Industrial Districts and Inter-Firm Cooperation in Italy, pp. 37–51. International Institute for Labour Studies, Geneva (1990)

Becattini, G., Rullani, E.: Local systems and global connections: the role of knowledge. In: Cossentino, F., Pyke, F., Sengenberger, W. (eds.) Local and Regional Response to Global Pressure: The Case of Italy and its Industrial Districts. International Institute for Labour Studies, Geneva (1996)

Boschma, R.A., Lambooy, J.G., Schutjens, V.: Embeddedness and innovation. In: Taylor, M., Leonard, S. (eds.) Embedded Enterprise and Social Capital: International Perspectives, pp. 19–35. Ashgate, Aldershot (2002)

Brown, K.A., Burgess, J.D., Festing, M., Royer, S., Steffen, C., Waterhouse, J.M.: Towards a new conceptualisation of clusters. In: Chapman, R. (ed.) Proceedings Managing Our Intellectual and Social Capital: 21st ANZAM 2007 Conference, pp. 1–13, Sydney (2007)

Camagni, R.P. (ed.): Innovation Networks: Spatial Perspective. Belhaven, London (1991)

Carroll, G.R., Hannan, M.T.: The demography of corporations and industries. Princeton University Press, Princeton (2000)

Eisenhardt, K.M., Galunic, D.C.: Coevolving: at last, a way to make synergies. Harv. Bus. Rev. **78**, 91–101 (2000)

El-Ansary, A.I., Stern, L.W.: Power measurement in the distribution channel. J. Mark. Res. **9**(1), 47–52 (1972)

Francioni, B., Musso, F., Cioppi, M.: Decision-maker characteristics and international decisions for SMEs. Manag. Decis. **53**(10), 2226–2249 (2015)

Grandori, A., Soda, G.: Inter-firm networks: antecedents, mechanisms and forms. Organ. Stud. **16**(2), 183–214 (1995)

Hannan, M.T., Freeman, J.: Organizational Ecology. Harvard University Press, Cambridge, MA (1989)

Humphrey, J., Schmitz, H.: How does insertion in global value chains affect upgrading in industrial clusters? Reg. Stud. **36**(9), 1017–1027 (2002)

Iansiti, M., Levien, R.: Strategy as ecology. Harv. Bus. Rev. **82**(3), 68–78 (2004a)

Iansiti, M., Levien, R.: Keystone Advantage: What the New Dynamics of Business Ecosystems Mean for Strategy. Innovation, and Sustainability. Harvard Business School Press Books, Boston (2004b)

Koenig, G.: Business ecosystems revisited. Management (France). **15**(2), 208–224 (2012)

Lewin, A.Y., Long, C.P., Carroll, T.N.: The coevolution of new organizational forms. Organ. Sci. **10**(5), 535–550 (1999)

Malhotra, N., Birks D.: Marketing research: An integrated approach. Prentice Hall, Harlow (2007)

Maskell, P.: Towards a knowledge-based theory of the geographical cluster. In: Breschi, S. (ed.) Clusters, Networks, and Innovation, pp. 411–432. Oxford University Press, Oxford (2005)

Moore, J.F.: Business ecosystems and the view from the firm. The Antitrust Bulletin. **51**(1), 31–75 (2006)

Nordhaug, K.: Globalisation, Embeddedness and Disembeddedness Working Paper No. 1. Centre for Technology, Innovation and Culture, University of Oslo, Oslo (2003)

Peltoniemi, M.: Preliminary theoretical framework for the study of business ecosystems. Emerg. Comp. Org. **8**(1), 10–19 (2006)

Pierce, L.: Big losses in ecosystem niches: how core firm decisions drive complementary product shakeouts. Strateg. Manag. J. **30**, 323–347 (2009)

Porter, M. E.: The competitive advantage of nations. Harvard business review. **68**(2), 73–93 (1990)

Tee, R., Gawer, A.: Industry architecture as a determinant of successful platform strategies: a case study of the i-mode mobile internet service. Eur. Manag. Rev. **6**(4), 217–232 (2009)

Teece, D.J.: Explicating dynamic capabilities: the nature and microfoundations of (sustainable) enterprise performance. Strateg. Manag. J. **28**, 1319–1350 (2007)

Uzzi, B.: Social structure and competition in interfirm networks : the paradox of embeddedness. Adm. Sci. Q. **42**(1), 35–67 (1997)

Van der Borgh, M., Cloodt, M., Romme, A.G.L.: Value creation by knowledge-based ecosystems: evidence from a field study. R&D Manag. **42**(2), 150–169 (2012)

Whitford, J.: The decline of a model? Challenge and response in the Italian industrial districts. Econ. Soc. **30**(1), 38–65 (2001)

Zucchella, A.: Local cluster dynamics: trajectories of mature industrial districts between decline and multiple embeddedness. J. Inst. Econ. **2**(2006), 21–44 (2006)

Chapter 10
Energy Perspective 2030 for Ukraine in the Context of the EU Integration

Oleksandr Chernyak, Ganna Kharlamova, and Andriy Stavytskyy

Abstract Today there is no state that can be sure in its energy security. States and its citizens are constantly faced with new threats. The layout of the article is as follows: Section 10.1 describes the introduction to the problem, highlighting the scope and agenda of the energy security study. Section 10.2 describes the concept of the energy security for Ukraine, current trends, and calculative assessments available in the world and considers the position of Ukraine in the World Energy Council (WEC) index in details. Section 10.3 provides expert scenario forecasting of the balance of electricity in Ukraine up to 2030 with regard to world megatrends and EU integration of the state. Comparison assessment of the international risk index for energy security of EU states and Ukraine is presented. Section 10.4 provides the VAR modeling and impulse analysis of Ukraine's energy security to resource shocks. Those are followed by short conclusion and discussion. Results of this paper have a few policy implications for the energy strategies of Ukraine and the EU. First of all, it is a high time to review the energy policy in the aspect of the energy security adequate assessment and forecasting. It is also necessary to improve the Ukrainian legislation in the field of energy efficiency, in particular regarding the use of renewable energy sources (RES) in Ukraine, according to optimistic scenario of the development.

Keywords Energy security • Ukraine • Assessment • EU

10.1 Introduction

The high competitiveness of the national economy is one of the most important tasks to ensure sustainable economic development nowadays.

However, in terms of the spread of globalization and the relentless growth of interdependence and interconnectedness of national economies, revitalization

O. Chernyak • G. Kharlamova (✉) • A. Stavytskyy
Taras Shevchenko National University of Kyiv, Kyiv, Ukraine
e-mail: akharlamova@ukr.net

S.C. Mărginean et al. (eds.), *Emerging Issues in the Global Economy*, Springer Proceedings in Business and Economics,
https://doi.org/10.1007/978-3-319-71876-7_10

efforts of the state to ensure their independence and national security are much needed. This includes the energy and economic security along with the sovereignty. In this context, the considerable attention of countries and regions should be focused on energy as one of the most important components of sustainable development and national security and, in this way, the competitiveness of the national economy.

Projections show that in the next decade, the energy consumption will tend to decrease. Uneven providing of countries and regions by energy resources would rise the threats to the energy security and, consequently, economic risks and can cause the fragility of the national security.

Background Energy is the basis of the Ukrainian economy, providing functioning of all branches, forming a significant proportion of budget revenues and currency inflows. Therefore, the efficient use of the energy potential acts as a basis for further economic development. That is the key to independence, social (Stavytskyy and Sadovenko 2013) and political stability, and ability to facilitate the integration of Ukraine into the European and world community. Energy security of Ukraine and the EU has attracted considerable attention in recent literature: Sovacool (2012), Dziadykevych (2014) and Dziadykevych (2015), Kulyk et al. (2017), Kiss (2008), Showstack (2014), Łucka (2010), Kharlamova (2013), and others. The aim of this article is to contribute to the ongoing academic discussion related to the energy security of Ukraine in the perspective of EU integration.

The objective of the paper To evaluate and predict the development of efficient consumption of electricity in terms of energy security for Ukraine in the context of European integration. *The methodological basis of the study* is based on the use of descriptive statistics, expert scenario analyses, and econometric methods. *Information base of the research* contains the Energy Strategy of Ukraine until 2035, textbooks and monographs devoted to this subject, publications of authors in the field of energy security, and national and international regulations, legislations, and official Ukrainian and European statistical data.

10.2 Literature Review

10.2.1 The Concept of Energy Security: General Description of the Problem – National Level

The World Energy Outlook 2012 newsletter answered some of the issues such as "How will global energy markets evolve in 2035?":

1. Despite innovative developments in the field of the ES, and the intentions of politicians, the world is still unable to put the global energy system on a more sustainable path.
2. Developing economies are a good piece for countries that are dominating on the global energy markets.

3. Energy subsidies are very important for the growth of renewable energy sources, since renewables are still more expensive than conventional sources (Kharlamova 2015).

The term "energy security" is used almost everywhere in the economic and political discussions related to energy supply. But various authors input different meanings in the concept of energy security.

Attempts to determine the essence of concept "power safety/energy security" were not systemized and marked by the varieties of approaches, and some even have insufficient ground. Existent definitions are based on a few basic approaches that energy security is examined as:

- The state of security of citizens, society, and economy from the threats of unsatisfactory energy supply (Wallace 1997)
- The state of safety interests (national, state, public) in the energy field (Burstein et al. 1990)
- The state of the systems of energy supply (in particular, fuel-power complex) in different terms (Ibrahim et al. 2008)

For clearance, first we need to determine the object of the energy security. If we consider the energy security in the scale of the country, we can distinguish two approaches. The first approach considers the energy complex or the national system of energy supply as the energy security object (Cherp and Jewell 2014). In the second approach, the economy, society, and state are considered as objects of energy security (Ciută 2010). Energy security threats come primarily from unattractive energy sector (or energy system supply at all). The rest of the approaches are just variations of the abovementioned.

A necessity to assess the energy strength of Ukrainian security, both separately and in composition of estimations for the economic strength of European security, is in the urgent necessity. All mentioned above need the universal understanding of the concept of energy security and determination of its object. The development of methodical base to assess energy strength, criteria, and indexes of energy security and the management of the informative data supply of such estimations are in the high demand.

Besides, it is quite crucial to come to joint understanding of threats. Threat to the energy security is the event of short- or long-duration character that can destabilize the activity of power complex, limit or violate energy supply, and lead to accidents and other negative consequences for energy, economy, and the society (Yergin 2006); (Winzer 2012).

Enforcement of the energy security is impossible without identifying factors that may negatively affect the development of the fuel and energy complex. One of the main goals of the state energy policy in the energy strategy by 2030 is the satisfaction of Ukraine in fuel and energy recourses by increasing the amount of own production and reducing external energy sources by reducing the import duties (Yermilov 2006) (Energy Strategy of Ukraine toward 2030 2006). But the strategy is not a panacea, since Ukraine in the year 2030 will achieve the level which Poland has already achieved in the past year. So, it turns out that the strategy cast offs Ukraine for almost 20 years in the concurrence with the EU countries. It is necessary to find an efficient mechanism for new energy sources but not to increase "steam boilers." A positive shift is the initiatives on the exploration of the accession of the Ukrainian energy system to the ENTSO-E. In the case of an amalgamation of the United Energy Systems of Ukraine and the energy system of Europe, the electricity markets of Ukraine will be integrated into the energy market of the European Union, which includes 41 system operators and 34 participating countries. Establishing the corresponding work with a powerful energy system in Europe will significantly increase the efficiency and reliability of Ukrainian energy system and will reduce Ukraine's dependence on the Russian Federation. It will also allow adjusting the export of electricity to Europe through the development of cheaper energy on Ukrainian NPPs (nuclear power plants).

10.2.2 WEC Index: Case of Ukraine

Currently, the methods of monitoring and indicative analysis are mainly used to assess the level of energy security in the country. The objective is to compare individual indicators and energy security indicators that characterize certain properties of energy (economic) objects or processes and reflect the degree of impact of a certain security threat on the system, with their threshold values. However, this method of assessing the level of energy security does not allow to quickly take into account the impact of the risks of energy market actors on the level of energy security. Thus, most of the indicators used to assess the level of energy security are based on the statistical data of the country's energy industry, which can be freely accessible with considerable delay (Khomenko 2016). All these methods, in particular, are based on the methods of data analysis, which are based on energy safety indicators. The methods for the final diagnosis of energy safety are scalarization, discriminative analysis, and the theory of fuzzy sets.

Since 2011, the World Energy Council (WEC) meets and develops national energy rating tables based on the Energy Trilemma Index:

- Energy security
- Energy consumption to generate energy (level of electrification)
- The ecology of the energy sector

Determining the value of this index is based on a series of data sets that display the energy productiveness in the context of energy efficiency.

Indicators of the energy efficiency take into account the supply and demand, the level of attention to energy sources, and the environmental impact of production and usage of energy. Contextual indicators take into account the broader scope of energy efficiency; thus, they can provide a coherent, predictable, and accountable energy policy and regulatory framework.

Table 10.1 The value of the Energy Trilemma Index for Ukraine in 2014–2016

Parameter	2014	2015	2016	2016 Trend	2016 Score
Index rank	65	65	63	▶	ABD
Energy security	26	28	28	▶	A
Energy equity	59	60	61	▶	B
Environmental sustainability	112	111	108	▶	D

Source: World Energy Council official web site (2016)

For a more in-depth analysis of the index, countries are divided into four economic groups:

Group I: GDP per capita of more than $ 33,500
Group II: GDP per capita of $ 14,300–$ 33,500
Group III: GDP per capita of $ 6000–$ 14,300
Group IV: GDP per capita less than $ 6000 (World Energy Trilemma Index Report 2016)

According to the results of the 2016 ranking, the top five most energy-efficient countries are:

1. Denmark
2. Switzerland
3. Sweden
4. The Netherlands
5. Germany

Over the past years, the key goal of these countries was to reduce their dependence on traditional energy sources and prioritize alternative sources. For example, in Denmark, the government developed an energy strategy to ensure energy efficiency by 2050, according to which the country should switch to a 100% utilization of renewable energy sources. For this transition to the RES, the budget of the country planned significant investments in the development of energy efficiency, RES, and the overall energy system of the whole country (Khomenko 2016).

Ukraine in 2016 improved its position in line with the Energy Trilemma Index by 2 points and occupied the 63rd place. Competitive advantage, according to the ranking, is the energy security – 28th place (Table 10.1).

According to the World Energy Council, in terms of energy generation, the largest part is thermal power engineering and nuclear energy, which is the same as for the smelting of minerals that is coal. The general primary energy reserves are more or less diversified, but there are rather large amounts of coal, natural gas, and nuclear power (Fig. 10.1).

First of all, the energy efficiency of Ukraine holds out such a factor as a rather significant part of import of fuels; in particular it concerns natural gas and oil. On the part of the environmental criterion, this factor is the high carbon dioxide emissions due to the old technologies of purification at the enterprises of industrial

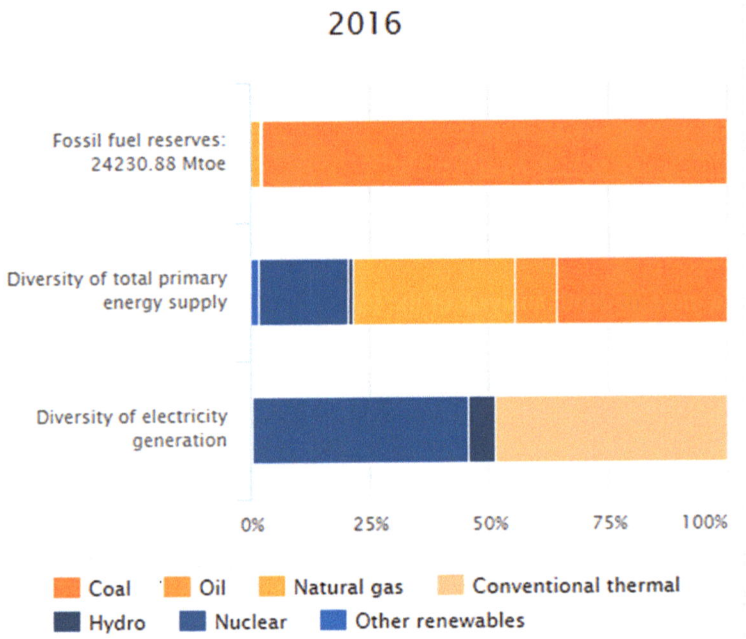

Fig. 10.1 Energy profile of Ukraine according to the Energy Trilemma Index in 2016 (World Energy Council official web site (2016))

branches, in particular, in the field of heavy industrial applications. In addition, a significant deterrent factor is the energy infrastructure, which requires serious investments for its modernization.

But there are also positive trends regarding the diversification of energy sources associated with the abandonment of natural gas from Russia, through increased domestic oil and gas production, as well as the development of Ukrainian nuclear energy (World Energy Trilemma Index Report 2016).

According to the results of the Ukrainian Energy Index, the energy efficiency indicator for the domestic economy counts 54.2% of the EU level (Ukrainian Energy Index 2013). Energy-efficient industrial production amounts to 51.1% of the EU level; the number of state contracts, 37.1%; the sector of enterprises, 46.1%; construction, 11.3%; and housing sector 61.9%. The ranking of energy efficiency in the regions is headed by Zakarpattya, Chernihiv, and Vinnytsia regions, with energy efficiency indicators of 64.3%, 63.8%, and 62.9% of the EU level, respectively. The energy saving potential for Ukraine is estimated at 26.5 mln. in oil equivalent, about 29.3 billion cubic meters of natural gas. In monetary terms, potential savings will be 11.4 billion euros (2010 price level). The industrial and residential sectors have the highest potential for energy saving, as they are the largest consumers of energy resources. The share of industrial and residential sectors in energy saving in Ukraine is 48.0% and 34.9%, respectively.

It should be noted that owing to the energy efficiency, industrialized countries provide about 60–65% of economic upswing. Each 1% of GDP growth is regarded to only 0.4% of energy consumption increasing. Therefore, for energy efficiency, Ukraine needs:

1. To develop a short circuit strategy for the import substitution of fuel reclamations by 2025, taking into account the necessary annual investments
2. To create a long-term energy strategy by 2050, the priority of which will be reorientation to the RES
3. To completely modernize the energy infrastructure of the country and its energy networks

10.3 Scenario Perspective of Ukrainian Energy Security up to 2030

Review of literature shows that various indicators and methods have been applied to measure the relationship in question; therefore, the authors have selected the regression analysis as the most appropriate method to suit the objectives of this research. The purpose of this unit is to find the key factors influencing the state of energy security of the group of countries from each cluster (Table 10.2).

Electricity is one of the most important energy resources, since its technological usage is more efficient. But the consumption of other energy resources should be reduced to ensure the efficient energy consumption. That is why the next step in the study is to forecast the balance of electricity for Ukraine by 2030 under the perspective of the EU integration. The forecasts were created by expert assessment, which was based on the following information:

- Analysis of statistical reporting, for the period from 2007 to 2015, provided by the State Statistics Service of Ukraine
- Consideration of perspective directions of development of the branches of the economy and its separate sectors, including branches of fuel and energy complex
- Assessment of the impact of the latest technologies on the energy sector and its future applications
- Evaluation of the structure and volumes of energy savings
- Estimation of the indicators that force the volumes of energy consumption, such as technical level of production, environmental costs, etc.

The data for forming the energy balance for the projected periods (2020, 2025, 2030 years) are based on the results of the analysis of the trends toward changes in the macroeconomic indicators of the Ukrainian economy, reflecting the projected trends in the development of the economy and resource base, taking into account the possibilities for its expansion.

Table 10.2 Comparison assessment of the international risk index for energy security for each of the three clusters

Cluster	Countries	The most significant influence factors	Econometric model
I	Denmark, Germany, Norway, United Kingdom	Total volume of energy imports per GDP Intensity of energy consumption Volatility of energy consumption	Index1kl = 572.06 + 0.11 Fossil_Fuel_Import_Expenditure_per_GDP + 0.29 Energy_Expenditure_Intensity + 0.12Energy_Expenditure_Volatility
II	France, Italy, the Netherlands, Spain, Poland	Intensity of energy consumption Volatility of oil prices CO2 emissions	Index1k2 = 6.198e + 02 + 2.063e-01 Energy_Expenditure_Intensity +1.066e- Crude_ Oil_Price_Volatility +1.553e-01·CO_2_Emissions_Trend
III	Ukraine	Total volume of import of energy resources GDP per capita	log(index_ukraine) = 7.294+ 1.685e-04 Total_Energy_Import_Exposure +7.051e-05 GDP_per_Capita

Source: Authors' calculations in RStudio tools based on Large Energy User Group Index Scores and Rankings (1980–2014) (2016)

Table 10.3 The basic scenario of the balance of electricity in Ukraine up to 2030, million kWh

Article of balance	2015 (fact)	Forecast 2020	2025	2030
I. Resources, total	**215**	**236**	**259**	**282**
1. Production, total	216	236	259	282
1.1 Power generation at NPPs	91	96	115	133
1.2 Power generation at the hydroelectric power station	12	13	14	14
1.3 Power generation at the PSP	3	7	7	7
1.4 Electricity production at TPP – coal	85	86	87	91
1.5 Electricity production at TPP – gas	2	2	2	2
1.6 Electricity production at PHES and block stations	19	20	21	21
1.7 Electricity production at RES	3	12	13	14
2. Import	0	0	0	0
II Allocation of resources	**214.9**	**236**	**259**	**282**
1. Electricity consumption net, including:	186.5	208.5	231.4	253.5
1.1 Industry and agriculture	111	120.4	131	139
1.2 Commercial (service sector and transport)	35.4	41.4	48.5	57.8
1.3 Population	40.1	46.7	51.9	56.8
2. Transportation and distribution costs	22.9	22	22.1	23
3. Electricity consumption gross – total	209.4	230.5	253.5	276.5
4. Export	5.5	5.5	5.5	5.5

Source: Created by authors based on State Statistical Agency of Ukraine. Energy (2017), Energy Strategy of Ukraine Towards 2035 (2016)

It is also necessary to take into account some uncertainty about changes in external conditions of socioeconomic development of the country in the future, the impact of certain subjective, and hardly predicted factors that may unexpectedly affect positively or negatively the consumption of electricity. Therefore, along with the basic state electric balance forecasting, pessimistic and optimistic electric balances are also considered. These electric balances outline the upper and lower limits of possible deviations of production and electricity consumption ratios from the baseline forecast for the period up to 2030, respectively (Table 10.3).

In 2015, the electricity consumed amounted to 209.4 billion kWh. In the future, there is the gradual growth of electricity consumption with the achievement of 230.0 billion kWh, 2020; 253.5 billion kWh, 2025; and 276.5 billion kWh, 2030 (Table 10.3). The average annual growth of electricity consumption by 2030 is expected at 8.84%. Thus, the growth is planned but a slow one (Tables 10.4 and 10.5). The main negative factors that may affect the energy consumption are:

- The slow integration of the gas and electricity markets of Ukraine into the EU energy space or its fail
- Increase in the energy intensity of GDP
- Focusing on fossil energy sources – natural gas, oil, etc.
- Slow or non-implementation of the high technologies in the energy sector
- Unstable political situation in the country
- Force majeure circumstances that are difficult to be predicted

Table 10.4 The pessimistic scenario of the balance of electricity in Ukraine up to 2030, million kWh

Article of balance	2015 (fact)	Forecast		
		2020	2025	2030
I. Resources, total	215	220	234	244
1. Production, total	216	220	234	244
1.1 Power generation at NPPs	91	96	107	115
1.2 Power generation at the hydroelectric power station	12	13	14	14
1.3 Power generation at the PSP	3	7	7	7
1.4 Electricity production at TPP – coal	85	80	81	76
1.5 Electricity production at TPP – gas	2	2	2	2
1.6 Electricity production at PHES and block stations	19	19	19	20
1.7 Electricity production at RES	3	3	4	10
2. Import	0	0	0	0
II. Allocation of resources	214.9	220	234	244
3. Electricity consumption gross – total	209.4	214.5	228.5	238.5
4. Export	111	5.5	5.5	5.5

Source: Created by authors based on State Statistical Agency of Ukraine. Energy (2017), Energy Strategy of Ukraine Towards 2035 (2016)

Table 10.5 The optimistic scenario of the balance of electricity in Ukraine up to 2030, million kWh

Article of balance	2015 (fact)	Forecast		
		2020	2025	2030
I. Resources, total	215	243	278	315
1. Production, total	216	243	278	315
1.1 Power generation at NPPs	91	96	115	138
1.2 Power generation at the hydroelectric power station	12	13	14	14
1.3 Power generation at the PSP	3	7	7	7
1.4 Electricity production at TPP – coal	85	88	102	114
1.5 Electricity production at TPP – gas	2	2	2	2
1.6 Electricity production at PHES and block stations	19	21	21	22
1.7 Electricity production at RES	3	16	17	18
2. Import	0	0	0	0
II. Allocation of resources	214.9	243	278	315
3. Electricity consumption gross – total	209.4	237.5	272.5	309.5
4. Export	111	5.5	5.5	5.5

Source: Created by authors based on State Statistical Agency of Ukraine. Energy (2017), Energy Strategy of Ukraine Towards 2035 (2016)

Taking into account the analyzed data, based on the basic, pessimistic, and optimistic scenarios, we will construct a graph illustrating all three forecasted situations of Ukrainian electricity consumption by 2030 (Fig. 10.2). As can be seen, the difference between the received scenarios of 2030 is quite significant: from the baseline to the pessimistic level, it makes 38 million kWh and from the baseline to the optimistic level, 33 million kWh.

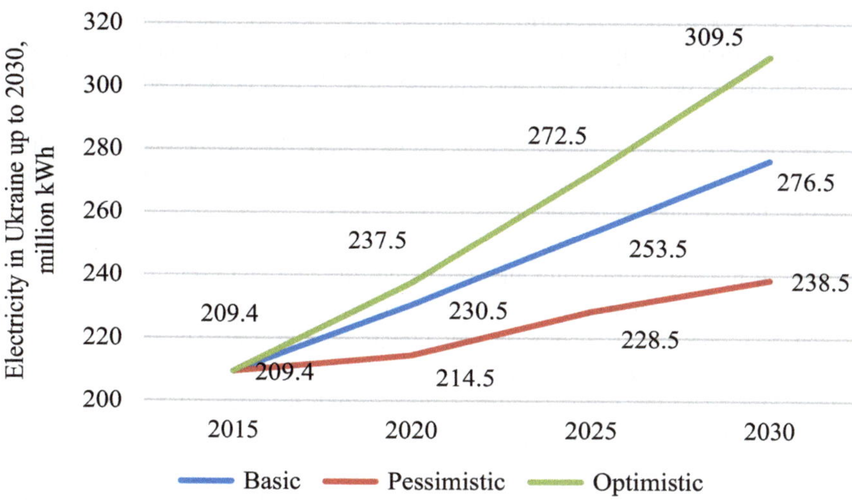

Fig. 10.2 The basic, pessimistic, and optimistic scenarios of electricity consumption by 2030 (Source: Created by authors based on State Statistical Agency of Ukraine. Energy (2017), Energy Strategy of Ukraine Towards 2035 (2016))

Table 10.6 The structure of electricity production in Ukraine by three scenarios in 2030, %

Production mode	2015	Basic scenario	Pessimistic scenario	Optimistic scenario
NPP	42.13	47.16	47.13	43.81
HPP	5.56	4.96	5.74	4.44
PSP	1.39	2.48	2.87	2.22
TPP with coal	39.35	32.27	31.15	36.19
TPP with gas	0.93	0.71	0.82	0.63
PHES and block stations	8.8	7.45	8.2	6.98
READ	1.39	4.96	4.1	5.71

Source: Created by authors based on State Statistical Agency of Ukraine. Energy (2017), Energy Strategy of Ukraine Towards 2035 (2016)

The next stage is to consider the structure of electricity production in Ukraine in three of the received scenarios separately (Table 10.6). As we see, the use of renewable energy sources (RES) is almost at the last place that is not a positive indicator, given the fact that European countries are gradually moving precisely to alternative energy sources to ensure efficient energy production and consumption. Comparing current data with projections in the basic scenario, it is easy to see that the share of energy produced by the NPP increased from 42.13% to 47.16%, but at the same time, the share of RES has increased to almost 5%, which means that Ukraine will move slowly toward efficient energy production. The coal TPP (thermal power plant) still remains in the second place and in the third place – again – the PHES (pumped hydroelectric energy storage) and the block station, although with a lower value of 7.45%. In general, the overall picture is more or less typical, not counting the concentration of power generation at the NPP.

As to the pessimistic scenario, its indicators are not very altered from the basic one. It is difficult to say clearly whether it is productive for the energy security or not, although, even in this scenario, the use of RES will grow steadily, compared with 2015.

Of course, the optimistic scenario is the most appealing to the predicted values. Here, the share of RES in the structure of production is the largest of all scenarios, and the share of nuclear power plants is the smallest.

However, to ensure Ukraine's energy independence, one must rely on the development of nuclear energy, although this is not the best and safest option. So, the reform of the energy market is needed – the conception of a new market model. That is, the basic electricity generation will remain atomic way. The construction of nuclear fuel fabrication plants with the involvement of foreign companies from the United States and the EU is important for ensuring the fuel independence of the Ukrainian nuclear power industry. In the new model of the electricity market, it is necessary to ensure timely and full payment of the NPP-produced energy.

During the transition to a new model of the electricity market, the following mechanisms need to be developed and formulated: market, its capacity, new regulatory environment, and dedicated funds, which will ensure guaranteed accumulation of necessary funds for the reliable operation of the NPP under the new conditions of work on the liberalized market. Creating a transparent, liberalized fuel market will support the modernization of thermal generation with the gradual transfer of its work to state-of-the-art technologies (Energy Strategy of Ukraine Towards 2035 (2016)).

So, to summarize, for the future perspective by 2030, there are three variants of the development of the Ukrainian electricity sector: basic, optimistic, and pessimistic. The difference between each one is quite significant, which means that at the moment, the state still has the opportunity to choose the one that will be the best. In fact, from one point of view, even the pessimistic scenario is relatively fine, since it gives a chance to the energy independence of the country, due to the increased use of nuclear power plants. As for the optimistic scenario, it pre-sees a decrease in the share of nuclear power plants and an increase in RES, which is prospective in terms of safety. And the basic scenario is almost a middle option, if to rely on a change in the share of alternative energy sources.

10.4 Impulse Analysis of Ukraine's Energy Security to Resource Shocks

The purpose of this chapter is to study the changes in the response of the international energy security risk index of Ukraine to the variation in prices of basic energy resources: oil, natural gas, and coal.

In order to construct the VAR model, the time series of the international energy security risk index and the price of oil (Brent), natural gas, and coal were initially

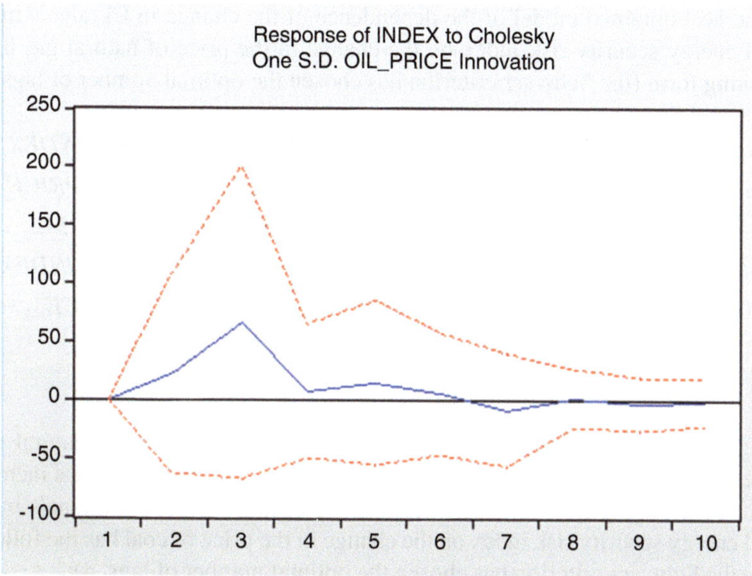

Fig. 10.3 Impulse response of the international risk index for Ukraine's energy security to change oil prices (2005–2014) (Source: Authors' calculations in EViews based on Large Energy User Group Index Scores and Rankings (1980–2014) (2016) and BP Statistical Review of World Energy 2016 (2016))

adapted as stationary series by the subtraction method with a reliability level of 90%, since its stationarity according to the Dickey-Fuller test was unsteady. EViews application was used to build VAR models that allow analyzing the impact of fuel price shocks on the international energy security risk index (case of Ukraine). With the help of the Schwarz criterion, the optimal number of lags was chosen, 2. The best obtained model has the following form:

$$\begin{aligned} \Delta INDEX_t &= 116.2742 + 0.4123^* \Delta INDEX_{t-1} - 0.1487^* \Delta INDEX_{t-2} \\ &\quad + 2.2529^* \Delta OIL\_PRICE_{t-1} + 6.1656^* \Delta OIL\_PRICE_{t-2}, \\ \Delta OIL\_PRICE_t &= -6.6681 + 0.04528^* \Delta IINDEX_{t-1} - 0.0337^* \Delta INDEX_{t-2} \\ &\quad 0.3664^* \Delta OIL\_PRICE_{t-1} + 0.0708^* \Delta OIL\_PRICE_{t-2}. \end{aligned} \tag{10.1}$$

On the model (10.1), the impulse reaction graph for 10 years – from 2005 to 2014 – was constructed (Fig. 10.3).

Figure 10.3 demonstrates that along with the growth of oil prices in 2007, the value of Ukraine's international energy security risk index has also increased, indicating a deterioration in the state of energy security of the country. The result is true, since Ukraine is a net importer of oil, so the rise in fuel prices has a negative impact on its energy security. In 2008, there was a decrease in the price of oil; therefore, the state of Ukraine's energy security improved fairly.

The best obtained model of the dependence of the change in Ukraine's international energy security risk index on the change in the price of natural gas has the following form (the Schwarz criterion has chosen the optimal number of lags, 4):

$$\begin{gathered}\Delta INDEX_t = 0.4194^* \Delta INDEX_{t-1} + 0.36224^* \Delta INDEX_{t-2} - 0.43956^* \Delta INDEX_{t-3} - \\ 0.0686^* \Delta INDEX_{t-4} + 52.4070^* \Delta GAS\_PRICE_{t-1} + 29.9378^* \Delta GAS\_PRICE_{t-2} - \\ 64.5206^* \Delta GAS\_PRICE_{t-3} - 21.6943^* \Delta GAS\_PRICE_{t-4} + 54.7542 \\ \Delta GAS\_PRICE_t = -0.0066^* \Delta INDEX_{t-1} + 0.0031^* INDEX_{t-2} + 0.0022^* INDEX_{t-3} - \\ 0.0004^* INDEX_{t-4} - 0.6133^* GAS\_PRICE_{t-1} - 0.3479^* GAS\_PRICE_{t-2} - \\ 0.1930^* GAS\_PRICE_{t-3} - 0.6257^* GAS\_PRICE_{t-4} + 1.7124.\end{gathered} \tag{10.2}$$

Figure 10.4 demonstrates that with the increase in the price of natural gas in 2006, the value of Ukraine's international energy security risk index has increased.

The best obtained model of the dependence of the change in Ukraine's international energy security risk index on the change in the price of coal has the following form (the Schwarz criterion has chosen the optimal number of lags, 4):

$$\begin{gathered}\Delta INDEX_t = 0.3140^* 4INDEX_{t-1} + 0.3791^* \Delta INDEX_{t-2} - 0.4628^* \Delta INDEX_{t\,3} - \\ 0.0385^* \Delta INDEX_{t-4} - 0.0332^* \Delta COAL\_PRICE_{t-1} + 0.1600^* \Delta COAL\_PRICE_{t-2} - \\ 5.0758^* \Delta COAL\_PRICE_{t-3} - 4.3093^* \Delta COAL\_PRICE_{t-4} + 116.8348, \\ \Delta COAL\_PRICE_t = -0.0102^* \Delta INDEX_{t-1} + 0.0097^* \Delta INDEX_{t-2} + 0.0250^* \Delta INDEX_{t-3} \\ +0.0373^* \Delta INDEX_{t-4} - 0.7742^* \Delta COAL\_PRICE_{t-1} - 0.6825^* \Delta COAL\_PRICE_{t-2} - \\ 0.1435^* \Delta COAL\_PRICE_{t-3} + 0.1696^* \Delta COAL\_PRICE_{t-4} + 4.0582.\end{gathered} \tag{10.3}$$

Figure 10.5 demonstrates that with the decrease in the price of coal in 2008, the value of Ukraine's international energy security risk index has decreased, that means improving the level of energy security. Similarly, one can see the slight decline in coal prices in 2012 and the index reaction on this shock.

Conclusions and Discussion Ukraine in 2016 improved its position in line with the Energy Trilemma Index by 2 points and occupied the 63rd place. Competitive advantage, according to the ranking, is the energy security – 28th place. Energy-efficient basket of Ukraine holds a significant part of importing fuels, in particular natural gas and oil. Although there are positive trends in diversification of energy sources, which is related to the abandonment of natural gas, there is as well the development of nuclear energy. The results of the Ukrainian Energy Index rating show that the energy efficiency indicator for the domestic economy will be 54.2% of the level of the EU countries up to 2030. The energy intensity of Ukraine's GDP depends on the total consumption of natural gas and energy generated by renewable energy sources. As for natural gas, it is not surprising, because it is used most of all from the fuel and energy complex. The impact of energy consumption indicators of RES can be explained by the fact that in recent years, alternative energy sources

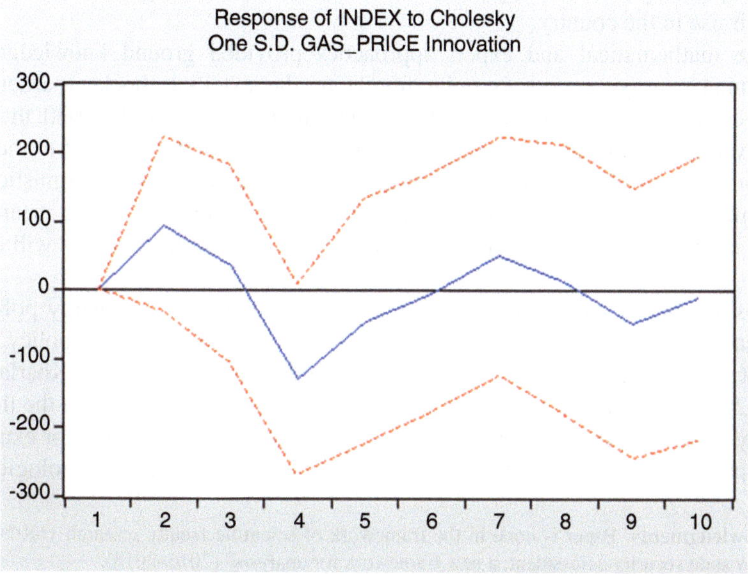

Fig. 10.4 Impulse response of the international risk index for Ukraine's energy security to change the price of natural gas (2005–2014) (Source: Authors' calculations in EViews based on Large Energy User Group Index Scores and Rankings (1980–2014) (2016) and BP Statistical Review of World Energy 2016 (2016))

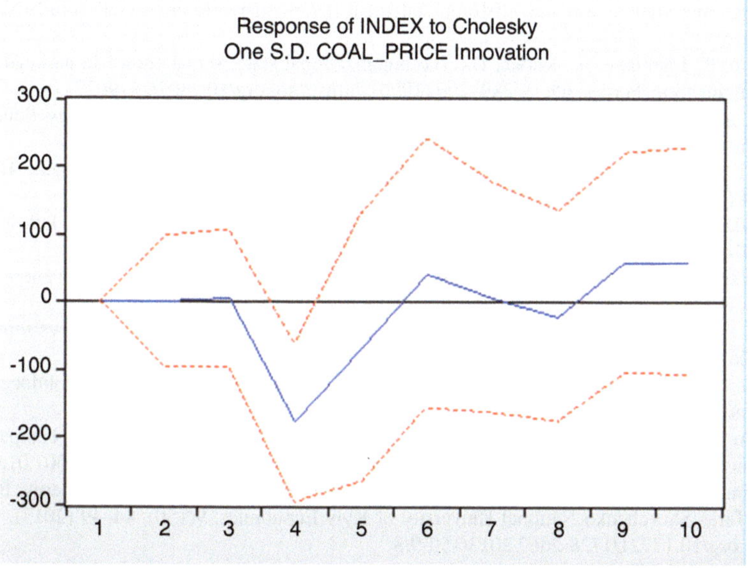

Fig. 10.5 Impulse response of the international risk index for Ukraine's energy security to change the price of coal (2005–2014) (Source: Authors' calculations in EViews based on Large Energy User Group Index Scores and Rankings (1980–2014) (2016) and BP Statistical Review of World Energy 2016 (2016))

have begun to gain popularity in Ukraine, which has led to expansion of the limits of their use in the country.

The mathematical and expert approaches provided ground knowledge that Ukrainian energy security is quite fragile to the external shocks (particularly, changes in prices of energy resources). For the future perspective by 2030, there are three variants of the development of the Ukrainian electricity sector up to the integration to the EU and supporting strong energy security: basic, optimistic, and pessimistic. The difference between each one is quite significant, which means that at the moment, the state still has the opportunity to choose the one that will be the best.

Results of this paper have a few policy implications for the energy policy of Ukraine and the EU. First of all, it is a high time to review the energy policy in the aspect of the energy security adequate assessment and forecasting (Kharlamova et al. 2016). It is also necessary to improve the Ukrainian legislation in the field of energy efficiency, in particular regarding the use of RES in Ukraine, for example, wind power engineering or the development of biogas production technologies.

Acknowledgments Paper is done in the framework of scientific faculty research 16КФ040-04 "Steady state security assessment: a new framework for analysis" (2016–2018).

References

BP Statistical Review of World Energy 2016.: https://www.bp.com/content/dam/bp/pdf/energy-economics/statistical-review-2016/bp-statistical-review-of-world-energy-2016-full-report.pdf (2016)

Burstein, P., Laumann, E., Knoke, D.: The organizational state: social choice in national policy domains. Soc. Forces. **69**(1), 289–290 (1990). https://doi.org/10.2307/2579627

Cherp, A., Jewell, J.: The concept of energy security: beyond the four As. Energy Policy. **75**, 415–421 (2014). https://doi.org/10.1016/j.enpol.2014.09.005

Ciută, F.: Conceptual notes on energy security: total or banal security? Secur. Dialogue. **41**, 123–144 (2010). https://doi.org/10.1177/0967010610361596

Dziadykevych, I.: The directions in increasing energy security of Ukraine. Adv. Sci. J. **9**, 123–127 (2014). https://doi.org/10.15550/asj.2014.09.123

Dziadykevych, I.: The Cooperation of Ukraine with the European Union – the key to energy security. Adv. Sci. J. **1**, 106–110 (2015). https://doi.org/10.15550/asj.2015.01.106

Energy Strategy of Ukraine towards 2030.: http://zakon1.rada.gov.ua/laws/show/145-2006-%D1%80 (2006)

Energy Strategy of Ukraine towards 2035.: http://mpe.kmu.gov.ua/minugol/doccatalog/document?id=245032412 (2016)

Ibrahim, H., Ilinca, A., Perron, J.: Energy storage systems – characteristics and comparisons. Renew. Sust. Energ. Rev. **12**, 1221–1250 (2008). https://doi.org/10.1016/j.rser.2007.01.023

Kharlamova, G.: An ecological-economic convergence: transition to sustainable energy. Bulletin of Taras Shevchenko National University of Kyiv Economics. **9**(150), 44–49 (2013). https://doi.org/10.17721/1728-2667.2013/150-9/8

Kharlamova, G.: The energy component of the environmental security: Ukraine in the mirror. Bulletin of Taras Shevchenko National University of Kyiv Economics. **1**(166), 72–79 (2015). https://doi.org/10.17721/1728-2667.2015/166-1/11

Kharlamova, G., Nate, S., Chernyak, O.: Renewable energy and security for Ukraine: challenge or smart way? J. Int. Stud. **9**(1), 88–115 (2016). https://doi.org/10.14254/2071-8330.2016/9-1/7

Khomenko, O.: Energy trilateral index: is Ukraine energy efficient? https://uifuture.org/uk/comment/indeks-energeticnoi-trilemi-ci-energoefektivna-ukraina_15 (2016)

Kiss, P.: Hungary-Ukraine Energy Cooperation and its contribution to the security of supply in the European Union. Energy Environ. **19**, 1155–1160 (2008). https://doi.org/10.1260/095830508786939901

Kulyk, M., Malyarenko, O., Maystrenko, N., et al.: Application of the method of complex forecasting for the determination of long-term demand for energy resources. Probl. Gen. Energy. **1**(48), 5–15 (2017). https://doi.org/10.15407/pge2017.01.005

Large Energy User Group Index Scores and Rankings (1980–2014): Edition final (2016)

Łucka, I.: Economic and environmental aspects of renewable energy. Econ. Soc. **3**, 119–140 (2010). https://doi.org/10.14254/2071-789x.2010/3-1a/9

Showstack, R.: Experts examine Ukraine energy security needs. EOS Trans. Am. Geophys. Union. **95**, 254–255 (2014). https://doi.org/10.1002/2014eo280002

Sovacool, B.: Energy security: challenges and needs. Wiley Interdiscip. Rev. Energy Environ. **1**, 51–59 (2012). https://doi.org/10.1002/wene.13

State Statistical Agency of Ukraine. Energy.: http://www.ukrstat.gov.ua/ (2017)

Stavytskyy, A., Sadovenko, O.: Analysis and modeling of social security index in Ukraine, Lithuania and Scandinavian countries. Economika. **92**(4), 37–53 (2013)

Ukrainian Energy Index.: http://energyindex.scm.com.ua/media/report/pdf/UEI_13_3.pdf (2013)

Wallace, W.: The retreat of the state: the diffusion of power in the world economy. Int. Aff. **73**, 573–573 (1997). https://doi.org/10.2307/2624300

Winzer, C.: Conceptualizing energy security. Energy Policy. **46**, 36–48 (2012). https://doi.org/10.1016/j.enpol.2012.02.067

World Energy Council official web site.: https://trilemma.worldenergy.org/#!/countryprofile?country=Ukraine&year=2016. Energy profile 2016 of Ukraine (2016)

World Energy Trilemma Index Report 2016.: https://trilemma.worldenergy.org/reports/main/2016/2016%20Energy%20Trilemma%20Index.pdf (2016)

Yergin, D.: Ensuring energy security. Foreign Aff. **85**(2), 69–82 (2006). https://doi.org/10.2307/20031912

Yermilov, S.: Energy strategy of Ukraine to 2030: problematic issues of content and implementation. Zerkalo nedeli 20 (2006)

Chapter 11
Quality Management Determinants of Hospital Services Case Study: Pneumophthisiology Hospitals in Romania

Emilia Ciobanu, Maria Viorica Bedrule Grigoruta, and Elisabeta Jaba

Abstract The present paper aims to study the influence of the determinants: category, size, and residence environment of the public hospitals of pneumophthisiology in Romania, on the quality management components through the opinion of their manager/director. The degree of satisfaction of human resources in the above-mentioned hospitals depends on the importance given to the quality management components by the manager/director, influencing their commitment. Data were gathered using the questionnaire method (CHMQ) of hospital leadership, regarding quality management on its components and employees' satisfaction in terms of working conditions, vocational training, and safety policy (health and safety) of the workplace. Each of the seven components of quality management, policy, objectives, planning, implementation, control, improvement, and commitment of human resources, is influenced by the size, category, and environment of the hospital. The importance given to quality management on its components influences all the processes of hospital management.

Keywords Hospital management • Quality management • Hospital leadership

11.1 Introduction

The main objective of the Romanian health system is "to improve the health status of the Romanian population" (Vladescu 2000). Romania's public hospitals are experiencing severe attempts either externally, from inadequate funding from the health system and from patient's dissatisfaction, or internally, from hospital

E. Ciobanu • M.V. Bedrule Grigoruţă (✉) • E. JABA
Romania Faculty of Economics and Business Administration,
Alexandru Ioan Cuza University of Iaşi, Romania
e-mail: pislariu61@gmail.com; maria.bedrulegrigoruta@uaic.ro; ejaba@uaic.ro

S.C. Mărginean et al. (eds.), *Emerging Issues in the Global Economy*, Springer Proceedings in Business and Economics,
https://doi.org/10.1007/978-3-319-71876-7_11

management to its various components. In this paper we will focus on the leadership and human resources of the hospital. The approach of quality management of hospital medical services is difficult, especially through the complexity of the interpersonal relationships that arise in the course of these medical services. Health services are, in fact, services to restore, maintain, and improve the health of the population from a psychological, physical, and spiritual point of view, for a higher quality of life, for the prolongation of man's work capacity (Borgonovi et al. 2009).

Quality is the degree of excellence, compliance to requirements (Crosby 1979), and a dynamic state associated with the products, services, people, processes, and the environment in which their expectations meet, which help create plus value (Knowles 2011), the "exercise for use" (Juran 1951). In its broadest sense, quality is an attribute of a product or service. The perspective of the person evaluating the product or service influences its attributes with its judgment. According to Deming (Deming 1986), quality should be the expression of "customer needs, present and future." Quality management defines quality by ensuring patient's satisfaction with the efficient use of resources (Chiru 2006). Quality in most services, but especially the quality of healthcare, is difficult to measure due to its characteristics: intangibility, heterogeneity, and inseparability (Naidu 2009). Healthcare services are dynamic and important worldwide, mainly due to changes in customer psychology and growing competition (Naidu 2009). Specifically, patient satisfaction is defined as an assessment of distinct health dimensions (Linder-Pelz 1982). This could be considered as one of the desired outcomes from care services, and so patient satisfaction information should be indispensable for assessing the quality of hospital care services for their management (Turner and Pol 1995). Patient's satisfaction leads to an improvement of the hospital's image, which translates into an increase use of services and market share of the hospital (Andaleeb 1988). Important factors in patient satisfaction are those related to care, empathy, trust, and reaction (Tucker and Adams 2001). Ware and his associates (Ware 1978) identify the factors that guide patient assessments: physician behavior, availability of services, continuity, trust, efficiency, and outcomes. Patients' perceptions, especially on the physician's communication skills, are also significant determinants. In other studies (Butler et al. 1996), it was explained that 66% of the variation in the perception of quality of service to patients is due to "facilities made available to the patient" and "staff performance."

Also important are the working and safety conditions of both the employees and the patients. The paradox of today's hospital management is that the manager of the Romanian public hospital has a much lower decisional power, the legislative restrictions leading to a lack of authority in the management and human resources management and the impossibility to motivate them on performance principles (Vladescu 2000). Many other studies have also emerged, focusing on the quality of medical services in Romania and approaches such as the three-dimensional approach to quality, with the three main actors: patients, specialists, and quality management (Chiru 2006), in which the two aspects of the quality of sanitary services appear, the technical side and the interpersonal side, the second one being significantly influenced by the satisfaction of human resources (Chiru 2006). There are also numerous other quality-related studies covering this subject. The components of total quality management are quality policy, quality objectives, quality planning, quality implementation, quality control, and quality improvement, plus the commitment of the human resources (Stanciu et al. 2015). In order for the human resources to be involved, a significant role is their satisfaction with the working conditions, the safety and health of the workplace, and their personal development, through the vocational training policies.

The aim of the research is to find some determinants that influence the quality of the hospital medical services in order to take measures to improve the quality management of the pneumophthisiology hospitals in Romania. The assumption on which the present research (Hypothesis 1) is based is "quality management of hospitals is different depending on the following criteria: category, size, and hospital's residence."

11.2 Methodology

In this research both quantitative (questionnaire survey, quantitative analysis) and qualitative (interpretation, qualitative analysis) methods have been used. It has been conducted for 33 public pneumophthisiology hospitals in Romania (the data collected is only from 32) dispersed throughout the country. From the hospitals' sites, contact data was collected, telephones, e-mail, county, etc., later used for the introduction of the research methodology, the submission of questionnaires, and data reception. These methods have taken into account principles such as anonymity of the respondent, confidentiality of data, agreement of the respondent, and agreements with collaborating institutions.

11.2.1 Data Collection

Data was collected using the CHMQ of hospital leadership on "quality management on its components" and "satisfaction degree of hospital's employees, regarding working conditions, vocational training policy, and safety (health and safety) of the workplace."

The questionnaire survey of hospital leadership was conducted through "questionnaire on quality management in the Romanian public hospital," which contains 14 closed questions (three regarding the satisfaction of hospital employees), five questions regarding the profile of the manager/director, and an open question on proposals to improve the quality of hospital services. The administration of the questionnaire was done in a computerized system by e-mailing to each hospital (eventually the manager or director), before having a telephone conversation with at least one representative of the hospital management (manager or medical director, financial accountant, or caretaker). The responses representing the data of this investigation were also obtained through e-mail.

The questions for the CHMQ questionnaire, for the present study, are as follows:

In order to find out the opinion of hospital managers/directors about the need to improve quality management, CHMQ has broken down the hospital quality management into seven components (Q6 question), namely, "quality policy," "quality objective," "quality planning," "quality implementation," "quality control," "quality improvement," and "human resources involvement." Questions Q7, Q8, and Q9 from CHMQ will be conducted to discover the satisfaction degree of hospital employees, related to the work conditions/vocational training, health, and security of the workplace. All these closed questions have five answer options, namely, 1, "very satisfied"; 2, "content"; 3, "neither satisfied nor dissatisfied"; 4, "upset"; and 5, "very upset." In the CHMQ questionnaire, included are the following four questions, referring to data that classifies the hospitals, in function of the differentiating criteria:

- Q11 – number of employees, with five criteria: less than 500, between 500 and 100 employees, between 101 and 250 employees, between 251 and 500 employees, and the last category with more than 500 employees, pneumophthisiology hospitals having single specialty, with employees of up to 670 employees (National Institute of Pneumophthisiology)
- Q12 – hospital category; in Romania there are five hospital categories, from I, the most complex hospital, to V, single-specialty hospitals
- Q13 – belonging region; there are eight regions in Romania: North-East, South-East, South-Muntenia, South-West Oltenia, West, North-West, Center, and Bucharest-Ilfov; pneumophthisiology hospitals exist in each of them
- Q14 – urban or rural residential area of the hospital

Questions about the profile of managers/directors lead to findings about gender, age, graduated schools, residence environment, and managerial experience. The last one is an open question asking the manager/director to make personal proposals to improve hospital's quality management.

11.2.2 Data Used in the Research

The population observed during CHMQ survey is 33 public hospitals of pneumophthisiology in Romania, through their representatives, managers, or directors (medical, financial accounting, caretakers). The data gathered with CHMQ survey is from 32 pneumophthisiology hospitals, and the answers were provided by hospital managers or directors. CHMQ questionnaires were sent by e-mail and fax, where no electronic transmission could be possible. Responses arrived by e-mail; only one was received by fax. In the hospitals included in the research, there are, apart from the departments/compartments with the specialty of pneumology/phthisiology (multiple drug-resistant tuberculosis (MDR-TB)), in the hospitals included in the research, there are also adults and children, palliative care departments, oncology (usually pulmonary), medical recovery (usually respiratory), thoracic surgery and Anesthesia and Intensive Care (AIC), infectious diseases.

11.2.3 Data Processing

The methods used in the research are questionnaire survey. The questionnaires used (CHMQ) were described above. Responses gathered on the basis of questionnaires from hospital managers/directors were introduced in Excel format first, and the processing was done using SPSS software. Each hospital on both databases was encoded with SP1. The questions were encoded with Q1A, Q1B, Q2A–Q2E, Q3A–Q3E, Q4A–Q4D, Q5A–Q5F, Q6A–Q6G, Q7, Q8, Q9, Q10A–Q10D, Q11, Q12, and Q13 for the CHMQ survey, and questions Q14–Q20, about the hospital managers/directors profile, were added. The answers to questions were in the form of scores from 1 to 5, at different levels, with the following meanings: very satisfied, 1; content, 2; neither satisfied nor dissatisfied, 3; upset, 4; very dissatisfied, 5; very little, 1; a bit, 2; no more, no less than, 3; more, 4; and very much, 5 for the CHMQ questionnaire. In the case of the CHMQ questionnaire, the processing was done in relation to the average score on each quality management component (Q6) and the overall score on Q6, in order to obtain an order of importance for these components, in the opinion of the manager/director. Managers'/directors' responses regarding employees' satisfaction are also being processed on the three components: working conditions (Q7), vocational training policy (Q8), and occupational health and safety at work (Q9). It will be considered that the sum of the scores obtained by managers'/directors' answers to questions Q7, Q8, and Q9 will be the satisfaction score of the employees of the pneumophthisiology hospitals, according to their opinion. We will follow the correlations that exist, if any, between the importance given to quality management components and employee satisfaction.

$$y = f\left(\sum SQ_{6A},, SQ_{6B},, \ldots SQ_{6G}\right)$$

where y is the satisfaction of the employees and SQ_{6A},........ SQ_{6G} the scores obtained on each component of the quality management.

11.3 Analysis and Results

The analysis of the data obtained and processed is based on the proposed assumptions.

The analysis of quality management on the seven components – (a) quality policy, (b) quality objectives, (c) quality planning, (d) quality implementation, (e) quality control, (f) quality improvement, and (g) human resources involvement – in accord with Hypothesis 1 starts with the descriptive analysis presented in Table 11.1.

The highest average value, 3.03, is obtained from Q6E (quality control improvement), followed by Q6D (improving quality implementation), with an average of 2.91. These values correspond to the level of opinion "neither much nor little" and signify that most hospital managers/directors feel that they are somewhere in the

Table 11.1 Quality management description on six components Q6A–Q6G (statistics)

		Q6A	Q6B	Q6C	Q6D	Q6E	Q6F	Q6G
N	Valid	32	32	32	32	32	32	32
	Missing	1	1	1	1	1	1	1
Mean		2.53	2.38	2.47	2.91	3.03	2.66	2.84
Std. deviation		1.344	1.314	1.319	1.353	1.470	1.260	1.417
Sum		81	76	79	93	97	85	91

middle with the improvements that should be made to quality management. The smallest average, 2.38, is obtained from Q6B component (improving the quality objectives), meaning a value close to "little."

First the analysis of the quality management components according to the criterion related to the hospital category (Q12) is presented. Only two single cases are a single pneumophthisiology hospital in category I and one in category IV, the rest being in category IIM or V. There is a maximum value of 5, in the category II of pneumophthisiology hospitals; a single hospital manager (SP13) considers that there is still "much to do" to improve the policy; the median is 3, "neither much nor little"; the minimum is 2; the lower quartile is 2; and the upper one is 4. The group of questions Q1-5-Q6A has a minimum value of 1 and a maximum value of 5; only one hospital manager, of category V (SP), considers that there is still "much to do" to improve the quality policy; and the median is 2. There are several fifth-grade hospitals whose managers have "very little" or "little" to do to improve the quality policy; the lower quartile is 1 and the upper quartile is 4, analogous to the other Q6B–Q6G quality management components.

In the case of analysis of the quality management components based on the criteria related to the urban or rural environment of the hospital (Q14), the results (Q14-1-Q6A) indicate that in the category of pneumophthisiology hospitals from the urban region, the median is 3, "no more or less," to improve the quality policy, the minimum being 1 and maximum 5, the lower quartile is 2, and the upper one is 4.

In the case of analysis of the answers of Q14-2-Q6A questions, the minimum value is 1 and maximum value is 4, two hospital managers/directors from the rural region consider that they still have "a lot" to do in order to improve the quality policy, and the median is 1.5. There are many rural hospitals whose managers have "very little" or "little" to do in order to improve the quality policy; the lower quartile is 1 and the upper quartile is 2, analogous to the other Q6B–Q6G quality management components.

11.4 Discussions

The research on the importance of quality management, under all its components, could lead to further results such as:

- Improving the quality of medical services by continuously improving each hospital's process.

- High visibility of hospitals that grant importance to quality management.
- Hospital performance and, implicitly, top managements will be increased by improving specific indicators, especially the quality indicators: in-hospital mortality rate, nosocomial infections rate, re-infected sickness rate within the 30 days of discharge, concordance indices of diagnosis at admission and discharge, percentage of patients transferred to other hospitals out of the total hospitalized patients, and number of complaints/complaints of patients registered.
- Hospital accreditation.
- Sustainable development of the hospital.

11.5 Research Limitations

The limits of the analysis, in the survey based on the CHMQ questionnaire, are related to the degree of subjectivity with which the answers were filled by the managers/directors.

11.6 Conclusions

In this research, we managed to present some of the determinants of hospital quality management, for the case of pneumophthisiology hospitals in Romania.

Thus, the importance given to the quality management of these hospitals, through all its seven components, quality policy, quality objectives, quality planning, quality implementation, quality control, quality improvement, and commitment to human resources, influences the satisfaction of employees, being a single hospital of pneumophthisiology in category I and one in category IV, the rest being in category IIM or V, two cases of pneumophthisiology hospitals with more than 500 employees (clinical hospital), three hospitals with a number of employees between 251 and 500, 12 hospitals with a number of employees ranging from 51 to 100, and 15 hospitals with a number of employees ranging from 101 to 250. No hospital has less than 50 employees.

Each component of quality management is influenced by the size, category, and environment of the hospital. The analysis of quality management components based on the urban or rural environment criterion of the hospital (Q14) reveals that only one rural hospital manager believes he still has “much to do” to improve the quality policy. There are several rural hospitals whose managers have “very little” or “little” to do to improve quality policy. By analogy these results have been extended to the other components of quality management.

Learning these determinants is an important managerial process, a team process in which both staff and hospital leadership need to be involved, as well as patients, insurers, financiers, and policymakers on the other hand, because the benefits, resulting from the continuous improvement of the quality of these services, will affect all of the above.

References

Andaleeb, S.: Determinants of customer satisfaction with hospitals: a managerial model. Int. J. Health Care Qual. Assur. **11**(6), 181–187 (1988). https://doi.org/10.1108/09526869810231541
Borgonovi, E., Fattore, G., Longo, F.: Management delle institutioni pubbliche, 2nd edn. Egea, Milano (2009)
Butler, D., Oswald, S.L., Turner, D.E.: The effects of demographics on determinants of perceived health-care service quality – the case of users and observers. J. Manag. Med. **10**(5), 8–20 (1996)
Chiru, L.: Evolutions in health services quality approach. The amphitheatre. Econ. J. **8**(20), 169–176 (2006)
Crosby, P.B.: Quality Is Free: the Art of Making Quality Certain. McGraw-Hill, New York (1979)
Deming, W.E.: Out of the Crisis. MIT Press, Cambridge, MA (1986)
Juran, J.M.: Quality-Control Handbook. McGraw-Hill, New York (1951)
Knowles, G.: Managing Quality in the 21st Century. Bookboon (2011), http://bookboon.com/en/managing-quality-in-the-21st-century-ebook
Linder-Pelz, S.: Toward a theory of patient satisfaction. Soc. Sci. Med. **16**(5), 577–582 (1982)
Naidu, A.: Factors affecting patient satisfaction and healthcare quality. Int. J. Health Care Qual. Assur. **22**(4), 366–381 (2009). https://doi.org/10.1108/09526860910964834
Stanciu, I., Petrescu, I., Pascu, E., Ţîţu, M.A.: Contribuţii româneşti la dezvoltarea managementului calităţii totale. In: Petrescu, I. (ed.) Contribuţii la conturarea unui model românesc de management, Vol. 1. Expert Edition, Bucharest (2015)
Tucker, J., Adams, S.R.: Incorporating patients' assessments of satisfaction and quality: an integrative model of patients' evaluations of their care. Manag. Serv. Qual. **11**(4), 272–286 (2001). https://doi.org/10.1108/EUM0000000005611
Turner, P., Pol, L.: Beyond patient satisfaction. J. Health Care Mark. **15**(3), 45–53 (1995)
Vladescu, C.: Managementul serviciilor de sănătate [Health Services Management]. Expert Edition, Bucharest (2000)
Ware Jr., J.E.: Effects of acquiescent response set on patient satisfaction ratings. Med. Care. **16**, 327–336 (1978)

Chapter 12
Taxation in Emerging Market and Middle-Income Economies: Similarities and Differences Between Countries from Europe and Central Asia

Carmen Comaniciu

Abstract The studies and the research from specialty literature demonstrate that a free-open policy and an efficient governance of the economy are the basic pillars for economic and social growth, taxation having an essential role in the life of any nation. A fiscal system based on horizontal and vertical equity, stability, predictability, and efficiency contributes significantly to the sustainability of public finances. Based on these considerations, through this article, we will highlight the main similarities and differences in the field of taxation at the level of countries that are included in the emerging market and middle-income economies category from Europe and Central Asia, to identify best practices and to highlight the impact of taxation on economic and social development. Without claiming an exhaustive approach, by analyzing some indicators of the fiscal field, we will try to achieve a ranking of these countries, to identify the most attractive country from the perspective of taxation.

Keywords Taxation • Emerging market • Similarities and differences

12.1 Introduction

Taking into account, on the one hand, the action of each tax as economic and financial leverage (Cope 1988) as well as the functions it performs (Leroy 2008) and, on the other hand, the impact that taxation has on the level of development (Burgess and Stem 1993), each state pursues the construction of a fiscal system based on horizontal and vertical equity, in full accord with the economic, social, and political

C. Comaniciu (✉)
Lucian Blaga University of Sibiu, Sibiu, Romania
e-mail: carmen.comaniciu@ulbsibiu.ro

S.C. Mărginean et al. (eds.), *Emerging Issues in the Global Economy*, Springer Proceedings in Business and Economics,
https://doi.org/10.1007/978-3-319-71876-7_12

changes at the national and international level. In this regard, countries pay particular attention to tax rates, from the perspective of maintaining the sustainability of public finances (Kondo 2016), increasing voluntary compliance, and reducing tax evasion (Janský and Prats 2015).

According to IMF Fiscal Monitor, the 40 countries included in the emerging market and middle-income economies category are divided into five subcategories, namely, Asia, Europe, Latin America, East and North Africa and Pakistan, and Africa (IMF 2017). The present paper refers to countries' fiscal field of the second subcategory, Europe and Central Asia (ECA), namely, Azerbaijan (AZE), Belarus (BLR), Croatia (HRV), Hungary (HUN), Kazakhstan (KAZ), Poland (POL), Romania (ROU), Russia (RUS), Turkey (TUR), and Ukraine (UKR).

In order to identify the similarities and differences in the fiscal field at the level of the ten ECA states, in the first part of this article, we will analyze the evolution of the following indicators: the fiscal deficit, the corporate tax rate, the marginal tax rate for individuals, the standard and the reduced VAT rate, and the level and structure of social security rate. The second part of this article includes analyses on ease of tax payment and the impact of taxation on the economic freedom index. Based on all indicators analyzed, using a scale of 1–10, we will be granted scores to each country, so that, at the end of the article, we will be able to make a ranking on attractiveness from the perspective of the fiscal field.

12.2 Evolution of the Main Fiscal Indicators

According to IMF Fiscal Monitor (IMF 2017), in 2012–2016, on total emerging market and middle-income economies, the fiscal deficit depreciated significantly, from an average of 0.9% of GDP to an average of 4.8% of GDP. If, in 2012, the ECA states had a negative impact on this deficit, with an average of 1.06% of GDP, in 2016, the fiscal deficit in the ECA states increased by an average of 1.61 percentage points. The evolution of general government revenue (percent of GDP) and general government expenditure (percent of GDP) in the ECA states, as well as the recent changes in fiscal and budgetary policies, determines an optimistic forecast for the period 2018–2022, with a fiscal deficit in 2022 on average of 1.62% of GDP, as can be seen in Fig. 12.1. For the projected period, higher values on fiscal deficit are found in Belarus, Romania, Poland, and Ukraine, at the opposite pole being Russia and Azerbaijan.

In the last period, a particular importance is attached to corporate taxation, given its impact on intellectual property (Griffith et al. 2014), quality of research and development (Ernst et al. 2014), FDI attractiveness (Kersan-Skabic 2015), and corporate social responsibility (Avi-Yonah 2014).

From the analysis of how the companies are taxed worldwide is remarkable the tendency to differentiate the tax rates according to the activities carried out, the place of activity, the promotion of investments, the size of the entities, and the regime of the deductibility of the expenses, in order to maximize the profit and to reduce the tax evasion.

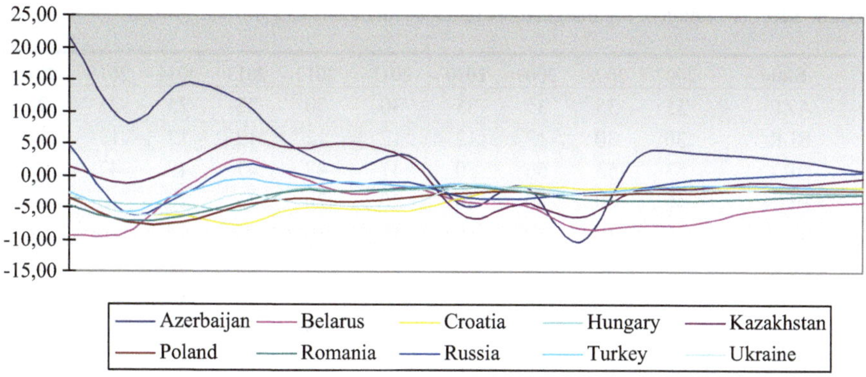

Fig. 12.1 Evolution of general government overall balance (% of GDP) (Source: IMF Fiscal Monitor April 2017)

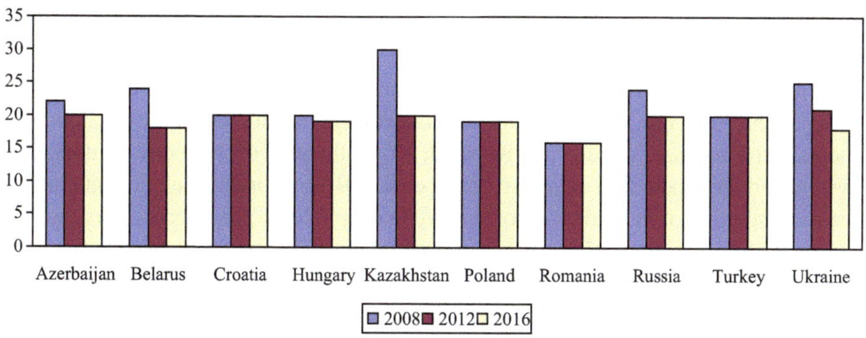

Fig. 12.2 Evolution of corporate tax rate (%) (Source: Trading Economics)

According to the data presented by the Trading Economics (Trading Economics 2017), in 2016, the corporate tax rate in ECA states from emerging market and middle-income economies recorded values between 16% (Romania) and 20% (Azerbaijan, Croatia, Kazakhstan, Russia, Turkey). As can also be seen in Fig. 12.2, compared to the situation from 2008, in 2016, with the exception of Croatia, Poland, Romania, and Turkey where the corporate tax rate was retained, in the other emerging countries, there was a reduction of the tax rate, the largest being in Kazakhstan (−10 percentage points). Changes in the corporate tax rate in 2017 compared to 2016 are in Croatia (18% versus 20%) and Hungary (9% versus progressive quotas 10% and 19%). Therefore, according to KPMG (KPMG 2017a), in 2017, all states register the corporate tax rate below the global average (24.26%); Azerbaijan, Kazakhstan, Russia, and Turkey are the only countries that exceed Europe average (by +0.29 percentage points); Hungary practices a tax rate well below Europe average (by −10.71 percentage points) and global average (by −15.26 percentage points).

The specialized literature offers a series of studies and research designed to give personal income taxation a special importance, whereas the share of individuals which

Table 12.1 Evolution of top marginal tax rate for individuals (%)

State	2007	2008	2009	2010	2011	2012	2013	2014	2015	2016
AZE	35	35	35	35	30	30	25	25	25	25
BLR	30	30	12	12	12	12	12	12	13	13
HRV	53	53	56	50	47	47	47	47	47	47
HUN	40	40	40	40	20	20	16	16	16	15
KAZ	10	10	10	10	10	10	10	10	10	10
POL	40	40	32	32	32	32	32	32	32	32
ROU	16	16	16	16	16	16	16	16	16	16
RUS	13	13	13	13	13	13	13	13	13	13
TUR	35	35	35	35	35	35	35	35	35	35
UKR	15	15	15	15	17	17	17	17	20	18

Progressive rate	Flat rate

Source: KPMG, Individual income tax rates table

contributes to the constitution of public revenues is significantly higher than the share of legal entities. Thus, the following are noteworthy: the studies on the essential elements of the tax base (Gordon and Kopczuk 2014); the relationship between the taxing system and the production volatility (Rieth et al. 2016); the influence of the tax rate on the redistribution of individual income (Bird and Zolt 2014);the effects of tax rates on the level of tax evasion and economic and social development (Ameyaw et al. 2015).

In 2007–2016, the top marginal tax rate for individuals in most ECA states from emerging markets and middle-income economies has undergone significant changes, according to the data presented in Table 12.1.

During the analyzed period, Kazakhstan, Romania, Russia, and Turkey have kept the tax rate unchanged; Azerbaijan, Belarus, Croatia, Hungary, and Poland have made a reduction in this rate, the largest reduction being in Hungary (from 40% in 2007 to 15% in 2016) and in Belarus (from 30% in 2007 to 13% in 2016); the tax rate was increased in Ukraine by 5 percentage points in 2015 compared to 2007 and then reducing it from 20% in 2015 to 18% in 2016 (KPMG 2017a).

Equality of taxpayers with respect to taxes, the existence of a constant ratio between the income earned and the tax due, compliance with the principles of fiscal equity, and simplicity in administration are just some of the benefits which causes states to apply the single tax rate. So, in ECA states from emerging market and middle-income economies, 60% of countries (Belarus, Hungary, Kazakhstan, Romania, Russia, and Ukraine) practice the single tax rate for personal income tax, with values between 10% (in Kazakhstan) and 18% (in Ukraine).

At present, value-added tax is the main consumer tax, being found in more than 130 countries (Keen and Lockwood 2010), with a significant contribution to the formation of public financial resources. At EU level, aspects of the common VAT system are reflected in the content of Council Directive 2006/112/ EC, with effect from January 1, 2007 (EUR-Lex 2006), with issues related to taxable persons, taxable

Table 12.2 Evolution of standard VAT rate

State	2007	2008	2009	2010	2011	2012	2013	2014	2015	2016
AZE	NA	NA	NA	NA	NA	NA	NA	18	18	18
BLR	18	18	18	20	20	20	20	20	20	20
HRV	22	22	22	23	23	25	25	23	25	25
HUN	20	20	25	25	25	27	27	27	27	27
KAZ	14	13	12	12	12	12	12	12	12	12
POL	22	22	22	22	23	23	23	23	23	23
ROU	19	19	19	24	24	24	24	24	24	20
RUS	18	18	18	18	18	18	18	18	18	18
TUR	18	18	18	18	18	18	18	18	18	18
UKR	20	20	20	20	20	20	20	20	20	20

Source: Trading Economics

transactions, the place of the operation, chargeability of VAT, tax base, standard VAT rate, VAT exemptions, right of deduction, and special VAT arrangements being specified.

The importance of VAT is also visible in emerging markets and middle-income economies, taking into account the existence of VAT in the tax system of all emerging countries and significant changes in tax rates and goods/services subject to VAT, the evolution of the standard VAT rate being presented in Table 12.2.

In the period 2007–2012, the most spectacular evolution of the standard VAT rate is observed in Romania (a significant increase in 2010 compared to 2009 by 5 percentage points, followed by a decrease in 2006 from 24% to 20%) and in Hungary (an increase of 5 percentage points in 2009 compared to 2008, followed by an increase of 2 percentage points in 2012).

According to the European Directive, EU member states can apply one or two reduced VAT rates not less than 5% for the products and services specified in Annex III to the VAT Directive, except those provided electronically (EUR-Lex 2010). The common system of value-added tax in the European Union also refers to special VAT rates, respectively, to the exceptions to standard rate rules, allowing member states to apply super-reduced VAT rates (rates below 5%, including zero and reduced rates for goods and services other than those specified in Articles 102–128 of the Directive). These aspects can be observed from Table 12.3, for the year 2017 (Avalara VATlive 2017).

In any democratic state, social protection occupies a particularly important place in government policies to cover all or part of the risks of illness, disability, old age, death, unemployment, maternity or work-related accidents. So, there is a need for public financial resources for the financing of the national pension system, and the health system, the social assistance system. In this context, providing financial resources is mainly done on the basis of social security contributions supported by employees, employers and insured persons, who are representing mandatory payments which confers the taxpayer the right to receive social benefits in the future (old-age pension, survivor's pension, temporary or permanent incapacity benefit, family allowances, provision of medical and hospital services).

Table 12.3 Standard and reduced VAT rate in 2017

Country	Standard VAT rate	Reduced VAT rate	Examples of products/services with a reduced VAT rate
Azerbaijan	18	0	Exports and international transportation
Belarus	20	–	–
Croatia	25	13	Some foodstuffs, newspapers, periodicals, hotel accommodation, restaurants
		5	Some foodstuffs, pharmaceutical products, some medical equipment, books, admission to cinema
		0	Intra-community and international transport
Hungary	27	18	Certain foodstuffs, hotel accommodation, restaurant services
		5	Certain foodstuffs, pharmaceutical products, newspapers and periodicals, social housing
		0	Intra-community and international transport
Kazakhstan	12	0	Exports, international transport services
Poland	23	5	Some foodstuffs, certain books and periodicals, some agricultural supplies
		8	Certain foodstuffs, pharmaceutical products, domestic passenger transport, social housing, hotel accommodation, restaurants, admission to sports events, some building supplies
		0	Intra-community and international passenger transport
Romania	19	9	Foodstuffs, pharmaceutical products, books, newspapers, restaurants, and catering services
		5	Social housing, books, newspapers and periodicals, admission to cultural and sporting events
		0	Intra-community and international passenger transport
Russia	18	10	Foodstuffs, certain children's supplies, medicine, books
		0	Exports and associated services
Turkey	18	8	Certain basic foodstuffs, pharmaceutical products, medical products, books
		1	Some basic foodstuffs, newspapers, and magazines
		0	Exports of goods and related services
Ukraine	20	7	Pharmaceutical supplies
		0	Exports, international transportation

Source: Avalara VATlive, International VAT and GST rates 2017

From the analysis of social security data for the period 2012–2016 (Trading Economics 2017), the following are observed:

Azerbaijan, Belarus, Croatia, Russia, and Ukraine have maintained social security rate for companies and employees, the highest values being in Ukraine (total social security rate of 53.3%) and the lowest in Azerbaijan (total social security rate of 25%).

Hungary has increased social security rate for employees since 2013 by 10 percentage points, compared to the situation in 2012, thus registering a total tax rate of 47%.

Fig. 12.3 Structure of social security rate (Source: Trading Economics)

Since 2014, a social security rate for companies of 31% is practiced in Kazakhstan, an increase of 5 percentage points compared to the situation in 2013.

If in 2015 Poland reduced the social security rate for both companies and employees (a total reduction of 8.63 percentage points), in 2016 the social security rate for employees is maintained (13.71%), but it increases social security rate for companies, from 20.12% to 22.41%.

Romania maintains unchanged social security rate for employees (16%) and makes a reduction in the social security rate for companies in 2015, from 28.45% to 23.45%.

Turkey's social security rate for employees is maintained at 15%, but social security rates for companies are rising from 16.5% in 2012 to 17.5% in 2014 and 22.5% in 2015.

As can be seen from Fig. 12.3, the ratio between social security rate for companies and social security rates for employees is very different at ECA states level.

Thus, the EU member states practice a social security rate for employees with values between 13.71% (Poland) and 20% (Croatia); Turkey, as an EU candidate country, has a 15% social security rate for employees, and the rest of the states practice a social security rate for employees with values between 0% (Kazakhstan and Russia) and 3.6% (Ukraine).

12.3 Ease of Paying Taxes and Fiscal Freedom

Every year, PricewaterhouseCoopers International Limited, the World Bank, and International Finance Corporation make a world ranking based on the indicators that measure ease of tax payment, considering taxing costs and the administrative burden of tax compliance. The 11th edition – Paying Taxes 2017 – shows the world ranking of 190 economies based on four indexes, namel: total tax rates (% of commercial profit), time to comply (number of hours), number of payments, and postfiling index, respectively (PwC 2017).

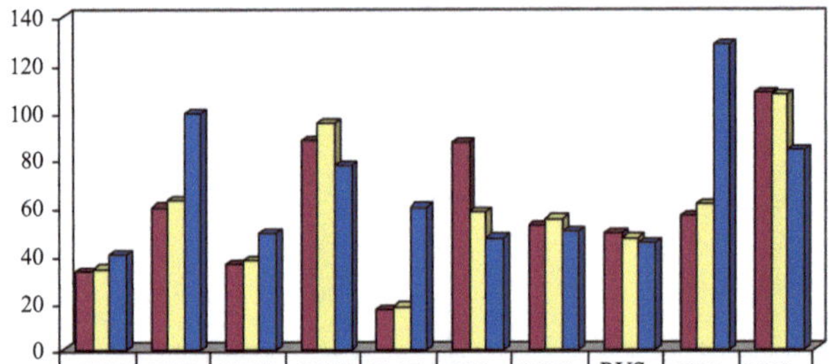

	AZE	BLR	HRV	HUN	KAZ	POL	ROU	RUS	TUR	UKR
Overall ranking 2015	33	60	36	88	17	87	52	49	56	108
Overall ranking 2016	34	63	38	95	18	58	55	47	61	107
Overall ranking 2017	40	99	49	77	60	47	50	45	128	84

Fig. 12.4 Ease of tax payment (Source: PwC, Paying Taxes 2017)

Table 12.4 Impact on ease of paying taxes

Indicators	AZE	BLR	HRV	HUN	KAZ	POL	ROU	RUS	TUR	UKR
Total tax rate		–	–	+		–	+	–	–	+
Time to comply		+	+		+	+	–		+	–
Number of payments	+		–		–	+				
Post-filing index	+	+	+	+	–	+	+	+	–	+

Source: PwC, Paying Taxes 2017

The fiscal and budgetary policy measures taken by the ECA states in the post-crisis period (effective or less effective) are also visible in the place occupied by these states in the ease-of-payment ranking. As shown in Fig. 12.4, significant changes in the position occupied by the ECA states in Paying Taxes 2017 against Paying Taxes 2016 are recorded in Belarus (from rank 63 to rank 99), Kazakhstan (from rank 18 to rank 60), Turkey (from rank 61 to rank 128), Poland (from rank 58 to rank 47), and Ukraine (from rank 107 to rank 84).

The causes that generate the change of position (positive or negative) in the ranking on ease of tax payment for each ECA state under analysis are shown in Table 12.4, the biggest negative impact being found in Turkey, due to increased total tax rate and the very low value of the post-filing index (a score of 3.9 points out of 100 points, obtained from a non-refundable VAT and the number of hours for correcting a corporate income tax return and dealing with any corresponding tax audits).

Annually The Heritage Foundation, in partnership with *The Wall Street Journal*, carries out a world ranking of economic freedom, taking into account 12 quantitative and qualitative indicators, grouped into four categories (rule of law, property rights, government integrity, judicial effectiveness; government size, government

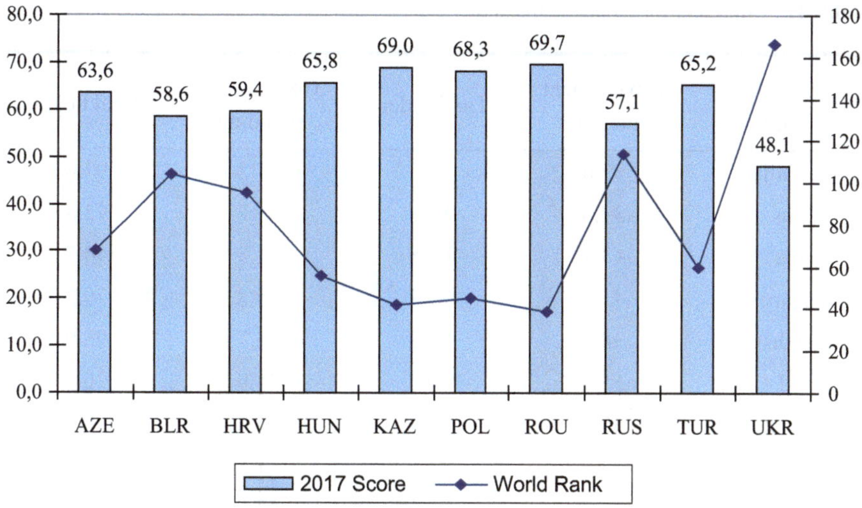

Fig. 12.5 The 2017 Index of Economic Freedom (Source: The Heritage Foundation 2017)

spending, tax burden, fiscal health; regulatory efficiency, business freedom, labor freedom, monetary freedom; and open markets, trade freedom, investment freedom, financial freedom), each of which is classified on a scale from 0 to 100 (Heritage Foundation 2017).

Based on some formulas established for each indicator, the index of economic freedom is built, and the values obtained specify the economic freedom of each state (free, 80–100 points; mostly free, 70–79.99 points; moderately free, 60–69.99 points; mostly unfree, 50–59. 99 points; repressed, 0–49.99 points).

For the year 2017, the index of economic freedom, for the ten states under analysis, has values between 48.1 points and 166th place (Ukraine) and 69.7 points and 39th place (Romania), as shown in Fig. 12.5.

Although, according to the general score, the vast majority of states are included in the moderately free category, fiscal and budgetary indicators have values between 20.2 (Ukraine, government integrity) and 98.9 (Kazakhstan, fiscal health), the highest being found for fiscal health and tax burden and the lowest for government integrity, as seen in Table 12.5.

Compared to the world average, in year 2017, the following are found (PwC 2017):

Azerbaijan, Croatia, Kazakhstan, Poland, and Romania record values for total tax rates below the world average (40.6%).

Hungary, Poland, and Ukraine record values for time to comply above the world average (251).

Only Croatia records a value higher than the global average for total tax payments (31 tax payments versus 25 tax payments).

The highest values for post-filing index are found in Croatia (97.88) and Poland (92.18).

Table 12.5 Indicator for economic freedom

Country name	Government integrity	Tax burden	Government spending	Fiscal health
Azerbaijan	37.6	87.7	57.5	97.4
Belarus	37.6	89.8	48.7	92.8
Croatia	43.4	66.8	31.3	44.7
Hungary	41.5	79.3	25.3	79.3
Kazakhstan	38.0	93.3	85.7	98.9
Poland	55.5	76.0	46.9	76.1
Romania	45.9	87.4	65.3	90.9
Russia	38.2	81.8	61.5	93.4
Turkey	40.7	75.5	57.7	95.7
Ukraine	29.2	78.6	38.2	67.9

Free	Mostly free	Moderately free	Repressed

12.4 The Attractiveness of the Fiscal Field in ECA States

In order to achieve a ranking of the ten ECA countries from the tax perspective, we proceeded to assign scores from 1 to 10 for the following indicators analyzed: general government balance (% of GDP), corporate tax rate, top marginal tax rate for individuals, standard VAT rate, paying taxes (overall ranking), and fiscal health.

The centralization of these scores allowed us to achieve the ranking as shown in Table 12.6, the first position being occupied by Azerbaijan and the last position by Croatia.

The first position occupied by Azerbaijan is confirmed by the values recorded for GDP growth rate for 2016 −3.8%, 5-year GDP growth rate −4.4%, and FDI Inflow −16,508 million (Heritage Foundation 2017).

With a fairly low level for general government balance, top marginal tax rate for individuals, and fiscal health, Croatia is facing with a high unemployment rate (16.1% in 2016) and a low level of foreign direct investment (173.9 million in 2016), which justifies the last position occupied in the ranking of attractiveness of the tax area (Heritage Foundation 2017).

Table 12.6 Ranking on attractiveness of the fiscal field

Rank	Country	Indicators with the best values
1	Azerbaijan	General government overall balance; social security rate; paying taxes, overall ranking; standard VAT rate; fiscal health
2	Kazakhstan	Top marginal tax rate for individuals, standard VAT rate, fiscal health, general government overall balance
3	Russia	Top marginal tax rate for individuals; standard VAT rate; paying taxes, overall ranking; general government overall balance; social security rate
4	Belarus	Top marginal tax rate for individuals, social security rate, corporate tax rate
5	Romania	Corporate tax rate, standard VAT rate
6	Hungary	Corporate tax rate, top marginal tax rate for individuals
7	Poland	Paying taxes, overall ranking
8	Turkey	Standard VAT rate, fiscal health
9	Ukraine	Corporate tax rate
10	Croatia	Corporate tax rate

12.5 Conclusions

Without claiming an exhaustive approach, the data presented in this article emphasizes once again the impact of taxation on economic and social development. We believe that a sustainable fiscal policy, alongside reforms to increase productivity, stimulates investment and creates new jobs, and institutional reforms to reduce inefficiency are key pillars for economic growth.

References

Ameyaw, B., Addai, B., Ashalley, E., Quaye, I.: The effects of personal income tax evasion on socio-economic development in Ghana: a case study of the informal sector. British Journal of Economics, Management & Trade. **10**, 1–14 (2015)

Avalara VATlive Homepage, International VAT and GST rates 2017: https://www.vatlive.com (2017). Last accessed 12 July 2017

Avi-Yonah, R.S.: Corporate taxation and corporate social responsibility. NYUJL & Bus. **11**, 1 (2014)

Bird, R.M., Zolt, E.M.: Redistribution via taxation: the limited role of the personal income tax in developing countries. Annals of economics and. Finance. **15**(2), 625–683 (2014)

Burgess, R., Stern, N.: Taxation and development. J. Econ. Lit. **31**(2), 762–830 (1993)

Cope, J.M.: Business Taxation: Policy and Practice. Van Nostrand Reinhold Co. Ltd, London (1988)

Ernst, C., Richter, K., Riedel, N.: Corporate taxation and the quality of research and development. Int. Tax Public Financ. **21**(4), 694–719 (2014)

EUR-Lex Homepage: Council Directive 2006/112/EC – the EU's common system of value added tax (VAT). http://eur-lex.europa.eu (2006). Last accessed 12 July 2017

EUR-Lex Homepage: Council Directive 2010/88/EU of 7 December 2010 amending Directive 2006/112/EC on the common system of value added tax, with regard to the duration of the obligation to respect a minimum standard rate. http://eur-lex.europa.eu (2010). Last accessed 20 Apr 2017

Gordon, R.H., Kopczuk, W.: The choice of the personal income tax base. J. Public Econ. **118**, 97–110 (2014)

Griffith, R., Miller, H., O'Connell, M.: Ownership of intellectual property and corporate taxation. J. Public Econ. **112**, 12–23 (2014)

Heritage Foundation Homepage: The 2017 Index of Economic Freedom. http://www.heritage.org (2017). Last accessed 19 June 2017

IMF Fiscal Monitor Homepage: Achieving More with Less. http://www.imf.org (2017). Last accessed 19 June 2017

Janský, P., Prats, A.: International profit-shifting out of developing countries and the role of tax havens. Development policy review. **33**(3), 271–292 (2015)

Keen, M., Lockwood, B.: The value added tax: its causes and consequences. J. Dev. Econ. **92**(2), 138–151 (2010)

Kersan-Skabic, I.: The importance of corporate taxation for FDI attractiveness of southeast european countries. Panoeconomicus. **62**(1), 105 (2015)

Kondo, A.: Sustainability of Public Debt in an AK Model with Complex Tax System. Shiga University, Faculty of Economics, Center for Risk Research. No. 20 (2016)

KPMG Homepage: Corporate tax rates table. https://home.kpmg.com (2017a). Last accessed 30 July 2017

Leroy, M.: Tax sociology. Sociopolitical issues for a dialogue with economists. Revues Sociologos 3 http://socio-logos.revues.org/2073#tocfrom1n1 (2008)

PwC Homepage: Paying taxes 2017. https://www.pwc.com (2017). Last accessed 05 Aug 2016

Rieth, M., Checherita-Westphal, C., Attinasi, M.G.: Personal income tax progressivity and output volatility: evidence from OECD countries. Canadian Journal of Economics/Revue canadienne d'économique. **49**(3), 968–996 (2016)

Trading Economics Homepage.: https://tradingeconomics.com (2017). Last accessed 30 July 2017

Chapter 13
The Audit of SME's Informatics Systems

Marian Pompiliu Cristescu

Abstract Basically, ERP implies a policy that reflects what it means to think and act for the purpose of economic processes and is therefore considered a strategic management solution. The new business model with process-focused operations increases productivity and meets the economic performance standards. The economic operational stages must be integrated in order to trigger workflows, to control the flow of information, and to create connections between the organization, suppliers, and customers. All this requires organizational changes, technological updates, and, eventually, a new identity for the organization itself. The present paper proposes a specific approach to the procedures needed to perform the audit of integrated informatics systems of the SMEs. Concrete methods of undertaking audit operations for the financial accounting modules of integrated informatics systems of the SMEs are presented in the present work.

Keywords Integrated informatics systems • Internal audit • Risk management • System implementation • Procedures

13.1 Introduction

The ERP applications form the backbone or basis of an organization and are "responsible" for data and information operations and with the internal organizational knowledge. The core of this application package has to administer internal data. They are organized in data warehouses, from where they are extracted and analyzed through decision support systems using OLAP- or OLTP-type tools (Fotache and Munteanu, 2005/2006). Overall, "data warehouses provide architecture and useful tools for the entity's top management by means of systematic organization, the understanding and usage of data for strategic decisions" (Popa and Ionescu 2005); in particular, they support information processing procedures by providing a solid platform for strengthening historical data for analysis.

M.P. Cristescu (✉)
Lucian Blaga University of Sibiu, Sibiu, Romania
e-mail: marian.cristescu@ulbsibiu.ro

S.C. Mărginean et al. (eds.), *Emerging Issues in the Global Economy*, Springer Proceedings in Business and Economics,
https://doi.org/10.1007/978-3-319-71876-7_13

According to Popa and Ionescu (2005), "the integration can be achieved at any business level using any type of technology. The key to success lies in choosing the best performing technologies that comply with the following criteria: the support provided to users, technological longevity, adaptability, scalability and the fast feedback of a solution":

- The application of the system, the data, the accessibility to the data, and the graphical user interface are harmonized and standardized for users.
- The rationality of data corresponding to the enterprise – the data has the same status in different systems and modules and are coherently defined at the organizational level.
- All management applications and computerized media are scalable, portable, and cover multiple functions.

From a technological point of view, the applications can be quickly reconfigured according to the amended business processes and must show flexibility. The code and the structure of the data support changes and replicates.

13.2 Performing Fundamental Procedures

During an audit, the audit team must choose and apply those procedures that comply with audit standards and at the same time meet the objectives of that audit. Fundamental procedures represent tests conducted by auditors in order to obtain proof or evidence needed to detect major inaccuracies in the financial statements. There are two types of substantive procedures: analytical procedures and substantive tests.

To understand the quality and the fairness of the financial accounting systems' operation carried out within an entity and to rule over the truthfulness and accuracy with which financial statements were prepared for the financial term, auditors have to make a series of investigations:

(a) Describing the procedures

In a system that collects and processes data it is needed to determine, for each significant field (purchase of goods and services, storage, production, sales), which are the procedures used by the company for collecting information, drafting registers, data processing, and recording of synthetic and analytical accounting in a chronological and systematic way. The legal provisions of the national accounting standards state as follows: "The supporting documents that help base the underlying accounting records make liable the individuals who have drafted, authorized, approved or made the registration in the accounting"; this claim is also found in the Financial and Regularity Audit Manual, Romanian Court Of Accounts (2003), European Court Of Accounts: European Auditing Standards of the International Organization of Supreme Audit Institutions (INTOSAI) (2002), European Court of Accounts: European Auditing Standards of the International Organization of

Supreme Audit Institutions (INTOSAI) (2002), and European Court Of Accounts, Romanian Court Of Accounts: European Implementing Guidelines for the INTOSAI Auditing Standards (2002).

(b) The compliance tests

The compliance tests are designed to determine whether the procedures described above are real, regardless if they are applied or not. At this stage, the main focus is not on discovering the errors in the functioning of financial accounting information system but on determining whether the system described above is, of course, the real one.

(c) Preliminary assessment of the risk of errors

Once a description of the accounting data collection and processing is established in the financial system, a preliminary assessment of the reliability of the organization will be undertaken in order to highlight the strengths and weaknesses of the system procedures.

At this stage, the system is analyzed in order to assess the design and to highlight the design errors, making sure that the stage that follows will verify the functionality of the system.

The strengths consist of controls, placed in the data processing flow, which guarantee a correct accounting procedure.

The weaknesses are represented by the deficiencies of the system that may give rise to risks of errors or fraud.

(d) Test of continuity

The aim is to monitor if the procedures are implemented in a permanent manner without fault. These tests must be broad enough to provide certainties for the functioning of the system.

To detect the risks that occurred in the functioning of the system, an analysis of the preventive and detection controls provided by the company must be enforced. The affiliated institutions are to be listed directly below the names of the authors. Multiple affiliations should be marked with superscript Arabic numbers, and they should each start on a new line as shown in this document. In addition to the name of your affiliation, we would ask you to give the town and the country in which it is situated. If you prefer to include the entire postal address, then please feel free to do so. E-mail addresses should start on a new line and should be grouped per affiliation.

13.3 Performing Analytical Procedures and Documentation

The auditors design and perform substantive procedures to account for the assessment regarding significant audit risk at the level of assertion. The substantive procedures applied by the auditors at the assertion level may be derived from tests of details, from substantive analytical procedures, or from a combination of both of the above.

In accordance with the International Standards on Auditing, the analytical procedures are used for the following purposes:

(a) As risk assessment procedures to gain an understanding of the entity and its environment
(b) As substantive procedures, when their usage can be more effective or efficient compared to the tests of details, in reducing audit risk at the level of assertion at an acceptable low level
(c) As an overall review of computer systems and of the financial statements at the end of the year

The first stage of an analytical procedure is to determine the acceptable difference between the forecast made by the auditor and the numbers stated in the financial statements. Furthermore, the auditor will take into account the relationship between the total value of the category of operations and the basis of materiality, calculating the acceptable difference according to the following formula (Financial and Regularity Audit Manual, Romanian Court of Accounts (2003)):

$$\text{The acceptable difference} = \text{The level of materiality} \times \text{V} \tag{13.1}$$

(The value of the transaction category/the square root of the basis of materiality)

Example:
An auditor determines the materiality level at 450,000 euros for entity X. The total expenditure of 50 million euros forms the basis of materiality. The auditor wants to perform an analytical review of the transaction category for staff salary of 40 million euros.

The method of calculation:
The sum of 40 million euros (the value of the transaction category) divided by 50 million euros (the basic materiality) is equal to 0.8, from which the auditor extracts the square root (0.8944). Then, he multiplies this result with the materiality level (450,000 euros) obtaining the acceptable difference of 402,292 euros.

The second stage of an analytical procedure is to make an estimate. The auditor should perform this procedure before knowing the value noted in the financial statements. Therefore, the forecast that the auditor makes must result from independent data than those foreseen by the accounting records. In this case, it results that the information obtained from outside sources of the entity are more valuable than those obtained from the inside.

Example:
If the auditor inspects a school with 150 employed teachers who earn 2000 euros per year, then the total value of expenses encountered for paying wages is expected to be of 300,000 (150 × 2000).

Table 13.1 Data adherent to the process of estimation

	Number	Value	Total income
Apartments	20,000	100 euros	2000,000 euros
Houses	5000	150 euros	750,000 euros
			2,750,000 euros

If an audited entity collects local taxes from the population, the auditor will be able to estimate what would be the total income. Thus, if the entity collects 100 euros per apartment in the area and 150 euros per house, and there are 20,000 apartments and 5000 houses, then the expected income will be (Table 13.1):

The third stage of the analytical procedures is to compare the forecast with the value of the account. This is a simple procedure that the auditor must register within the work papers, and then he must assess whether the actual numbers correspond within the acceptable ranges, meaning that the difference between forecast and account numbers is lower than the accepted difference. In case the value ranges within these limits, the auditor is certain that the verified transactions are in accordance with the existing regulations. Only a small difference between the actual and the estimated number (maximum tolerance of 1%) is accepted where those differences cannot be adequately explained.

If the numbers surpass the limits, the auditor should request punctual explanations. He will use open questions as "what factors have influenced those incomes?" and he will not ask "why the resulted income is bigger or smaller this year."

Example:
If the recorded incomes in the financial accounting information system related to concessions and corporate rents are about 4,000,000 euros and the forecast situations had been about 2,750,000 euros, then the audit team will request explanations for the variation of the 1,250,000 euros sum. The informatics system should be equipped with a warning system in case of increased variation (45%). If the credit accountant will explain to the audit team that this increase is due to the new spaces used during the year, then the team will have to determine how many such spaces were built and which was the surface given for rent, as well as the commencement date of collecting the rents.

Considerations regarding the evaluation of the analytical procedures and tests of control regarding the informatics systems:

Evaluation of the analytical procedures	If the analytical procedures allow the formulation of a forecast in the limits of an acceptable difference, then the auditor can rely on the planned insurance. In the case where the analytical procedures do not indicate a forecast within the limits of the acceptable difference, then the planned insurance cannot be taken into consideration, and the audit must adopt alternative procedures aimed to obtain the planned insurance.
Evaluation of the control tests	If the auditors find that certain controls have not given the proper result, they will analyze the possibility of conducting other controls (alternatives). In case there are no alternative controls or they prove to be ineffective, the auditor should revise the audit plan. For example, if a monthly variation analyzed is not undertaken for individual wages, this does not necessarily mean that the payroll for that month is incorrect.

13.4 The Audit Report

The audit report should contain a clear opinion based on the evaluation of the conclusions drawn in accordance with the evidence obtained during the audit. According to the Audit Standard No. 700, "The audit report must contain, in writing, a clear opinion on the financial statements considered as a whole." Before drafting the audit report, it is recommended to verify the decision tree that might look like this (Fig. 13.1):

To select the most appropriate audit procedures to be used for checking the financial accounting information system, it is considered that the auditors should use the decision tree (Whittington et al. 2008; Champlain 2003).

According to Boulescu et al. (2005), Eden and Stanciu (2004), Munteanu (2001), and Popa and Ionescu (2005), it all starts with the risk assessment for the information system as a whole and for each separate module. If major error risks were identified, the auditors must verify the internal controls of the entity carried out for preventing and reducing risks.

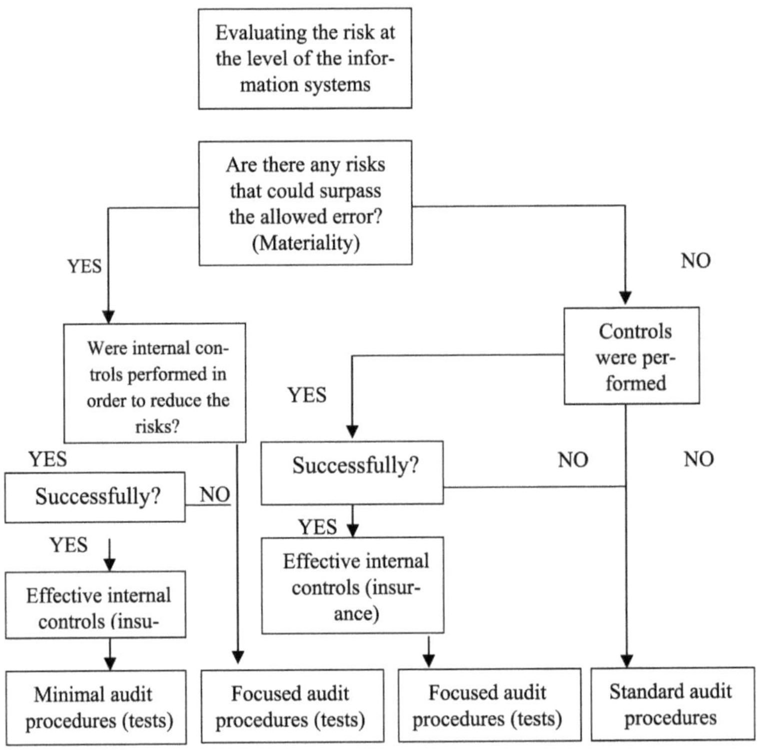

Fig. 13.1 The decision tree

13.5 Conclusions

Following the analysis and the comparison of the European Standards (European Court of Accounts: European Auditing Standards of the International Organization of Supreme Audit Institutions (INTOSAI) (2002), European Court of Accounts: European Auditing Standards of the International Organization of Supreme Audit Institutions (INTOSAI) (2002), and European Court Of Accounts, Romanian Court Of Accounts: European Implementing Guidelines for the INTOSAI Auditing Standards (2002)) used in the auditing of the financial and accounting information systems, a number of common elements that need to be introduced and used in Romanian standards were identified.

As such, the financial and accounting information systems' audit should be:

(a) *Easy to understand* – a clear, simple language must be used, to the extent permitted by the objectives of the audit.
(b) *Unambiguous/clear* – the auditor will ensure that all the findings are expressed accurately and leave no room for interpretation; the easiest way to be fully understood is to use standard formulas that are generally accepted.
(c) *Complete* – an audit must contain all the information necessary to firstly fulfill the objectives of the audit and then the requirements of the audited entity.
(d) *Accurate* – an accurate description implies, with accuracy, the scope of the audit and the methods used. Any inaccuracy that occurred within the audit report may create doubts on the validity of the report as a whole and can distract the attention from the purpose of the report.
(e) *Objective* – an audit report has a considerably greater credibility if the evidence is presented in an impartial manner.
(f) *Persuasive/convincing* – the user must be convinced by the reality of the findings, by the reasonableness of conclusions, and by the benefit of applying the formulated recommendations.
(g) *Concise* – the audit should be concise and contain conclusions and recommendations to support the evidence presented.

An audit report must specify the type and extension of the paper regarding the works that were carried out, according to IFAC International Standards on Auditing and the Guidelines for Internal or International Audit (ISA 520 n.d.; ISA 700 n.d.)

References

Boulescu, M., Fusaru, D., Gherasim, Z.: Auditul sistemelor informatice financiar-contabile. Tribuna Economică, Bucureşti (2005)
Champlain, J.: Auditing Information Systems. John Wiley & Sons, Inc., USA (2003)
Eden, A., Stanciu, V.: Auditul sistemelor informatice. DuAl Tech, Bucureşti (2004)

European Court Of Accounts: European Auditing Standards of the International Organization of Supreme Audit Institutions (INTOSAI) (2002)

European Court of Accounts, Romanian Court of Accounts: European Implementing Guidelines for the INTOSAI Auditing Standards (2002)

Financial and Regularity Audit Manual. Romanian Court Of Accounts: Bucharest (2003)

Fotache, D., Munteanu, A.: Auditarea sistemelor integrate de aplicaţii. Analele ştiinţifice ale Universităţii, Alexandru Ioan Cuza" din Iaşi, Ştiinţe Economice. LII/LIII, 283–287 (2005/2006)

International Standards on Auditing no. 520, paragraph 7 (n.d.)

International Standards on Auditing, no. 700, "Auditor's Report" (n.d.)

Munteanu, A.: Auditul sistemelor informaţionale contabile. Polirom, Iaşi (2001)

Popa, S., Ionescu, C.: Audit în medii informatizate. Expert, Bucureşti (2005)

Whittington, O.R., Pany, K., Meigs, W., Meigs, R.: Principles of Auditing, p. 150. IRWIN, Boston (2008)

Chapter 14
Empirical Analysis of the Relationship Between CSR and Company's Market Capitalization: Evidence from Bucharest Stock Exchange

Adina Dornean and Dumitru-Cristian Oanea

Abstract The practice of corporate social responsibility (CSR) is much debated and criticized. There is a continuous debate regarding the link between CSR and corporate financial performance (CFP) because the narrative reviews of the literature and the empirical evidence are too varied and mixed in different country context to allow for definitive conclusions. This paper aims at empirically analyzing the relationship between CSR and company's market capitalization, the indicator which measures the investors' evaluation of a firm value. Starting from the existing literature, our paper investigates this relationship for the Romanian companies listed on Bucharest Stock Exchange (BSE). From a total of 85 listed companies, we selected only 70 of them which were listed on the BSE during the period 2010–2015, without being excluded from trading. Using panel least squares methodology, our results suggest a positive relationship between CSR activities and market capitalization of firms, which are also impacted by the dividend paid and return on equity. This is a clear clue that besides the financial performance of a firm, the investors take into account also the attitude of a firm regarding its CSR activities. Moreover, this paper highlights the benefits for both managers and investors, since CSR exerts a significant positive impact on the firm value.

Keywords Corporate social responsibility • Bucharest stock exchange • Panel least squares

---

A. Dornean (✉)
Alexandru Ioan Cuza University of Iaşi, Faculty of Economics and Business Administration, Iaşi, Romania
e-mail: amartin@uaic.ro

D.-C. Oanea
Bucharest University of Economic Studies, Faculty of Finance and Banking, Bucharest, Romania

S.C. Mărginean et al. (eds.), *Emerging Issues in the Global Economy*, Springer Proceedings in Business and Economics,
https://doi.org/10.1007/978-3-319-71876-7_14

14.1 Introduction

The growth of corporate social responsibility (CSR) on public financial markets has drawn considerable academic attention beginning with the late twentieth century.

Perhaps the most popular and one of the most used definitions of CSR belongs to Archie Carroll (1979, 1999) that in his articles, considered also oft-cited foundations of current CSR research, attempt to separate business's social obligations into four responsibility categories: economic, legal, ethical, and discretionary (philanthropic). Carroll (1979) recognizes that "These four categories are not mutually exclusive, nor are they intended to portray a continuum of economic concerns on one end and social concerns on the other. That is, they are neither cumulative nor additive." In distinguishing between ethical and discretionary responsibilities, Carroll also recognizes, however, that ethical responsibilities, like economic and legal responsibilities, are not voluntary.

The economic responsibility is to produce goods and services desired by individuals and to be profitable. Secondly, the legal responsibility of firms consist into abide by law. The last two dimensions, the ethical and the discretionary/voluntary/philanthropic, specify a set of expectations that exceeds any formal legal system (Baleanu et al. 2011): the ethical responsibility to do what is right and fair beyond that required by law and a philanthropic responsibility to contribute to various kinds of social, educational, recreational, or cultural purposes.

By placing these four dimensions of CSR in a pyramid, starting off with economic obligations and topping up with philanthropic responsibilities, Carroll (1991) defines the responsible firm as the organization which "strives to make a profit, obey the law, be ethical, and be a good corporate citizen."

Sacconi (2004) proposed the following definition of CSR: "a model of extended corporate governance whereby who runs a firm (entrepreneurs, directors, managers) have responsibilities that range from fulfilment of their fiduciary duties towards the owners to fulfilment of analogous fiduciary duties towards all the firm's stakeholders."

According to Benabou and Tirole (2010), there are three views on CSR: the adoption of a more long-term perspective, the delegated exercise of philanthropy on behalf of stakeholders, and insider-initiated corporate philanthropy. The first vision supposes "win–win" principle ("doing well by doing good"): according to some advocates of CSR, being a good corporate citizen can also make a firm more profitable on long term. The second vision refers to delegated philanthropy (the firm as a channel for the expression of citizen values): some stakeholders (investors, customers, employees) are often willing to sacrifice money for social goals. And the third vision, insider-initiated corporate philanthropy, considers that corporate prosocial behavior is (at least, partially) not motivated by stakeholders' demands or willingness to sacrifice money for a good cause but rather reflects the management's or the board members' own desires to engage in philanthropy. In the authors' opinion, these three motives are mutually interdependent, and both policy-makers and social activists must have a good understanding of these interactions in order to properly harness people's desire to behave prosocially.

In another approach, CSR is a form of corporate self-regulation integrated into a business model (Baker and Nofsinger 2012). That is, CSR is the decision-making and implementation process that guides all company activities in protecting and promoting international human rights, labor and environmental standards, and compliance with legal requirements within its operations and in its relations to the societies and communities where it operates. CSR involves a commitment to contribute to the economic, environmental, and social sustainability of communities through the ongoing engagement of stakeholders, the active participation of communities affected by company activities, and the public reporting of company policies and performance in the economic, environmental, and social arenas.

Thus, the definition of CSR is complex (Sheehy 2015) not only because of the multifaceted nature of the problem and the number of actors, locations, and institutions, but it is also complicated by four distinct agendas which are engaged in the definitional enterprise. He defined it as a form of international private self-regulation focused on the reduction and mitigation of industrial harms and provision of public good.

Despite the long history of the term CSR, no consensus has been developed among the industry participants, academics, or other interested parties. In our research we will focus on the relationship between CSR and company's market capitalization. Thus, the structure of the paper is as follows: Section 14.2 reviews the literature and the most important papers which have analyzed the relationship between CSR and capital market, including market capitalization and corporate financial performance of listed companies. Section 14.3 focuses on the methodology, describing the model, the data, and the descriptive statistics, and Sect. 14.4 presents the results obtained from the regression model. Finally, Sect. 14.5 concludes and presents policy recommendations.

14.2 Literature Review

The CSR, considered as "a combination of good corporate governance, sound environmental standards, and care of stakeholder relations" (Renneboog et al. 2008), can be rationalized as a signaling device of firms' trustworthiness in providing quality products or a means of softening competition in product markets. One of the main arguments in favor of CSR is that CSR is consistent with shareholder value maximization (Renneboog et al. 2008), which is similar also to the findings of Besley and Ghatak (2007) that CSR is in line with profit maximization in competitive markets. Furthermore, they mentioned that, while the literature documents a generally positive relation between CSR and firms' financial performance, especially in terms of accounting measures, there is no convincing evidence on the direction of the causality and on whether or not CSR is priced in capital markets.

On the Greek capital market, Maggina and Tsaklanganos (2012) investigated differences in the market variables of companies listed on the Athens Stock Exchange that show CSR compared with those that do not. They used discriminant analysis and logistic regression, and their results indicated that very few of the analyzed market variables—stock price, stock returns, earnings per share, and dividends—play a role in discriminating between these two categories of companies (companies with or without CSR), while firm size plays almost no role at all.

In his study, Sudha (2014) empirically analyzed the value relevance of CSR on the share prices of the companies controlling for major variables that impact firm value. The research considered a purposive sample from the Indian S&P 500 companies, listed on the National Stock Exchange of India (NSE), who have obtained a CSR rating for the year 2010. Applying the cross-sectional multivariate ordinary least squares regression, the author showed that CSR had a significant positive relationship on the share price of the firm implying that companies who have exhibited a superior CSR performance have been valued higher than those who have an inferior CSR performance.

On the Italian capital market, we have found a research conducted by Nigro et al. (2015), on a sample of Italian listed firms, composed both by the 64 companies listed on the STAR Market and by a sample of control, composed by the 20 listed companies with the higher capitalization, for a total of 84 corporations. The authors investigated the relationship between CSR, measured by an index, and corporate financial performance (CFP), measured by ROA (return on assets), ROS (return on sales), and ROE (return on equity), for the 2012–2013 financial year. Using the Tobit regression model, they cannot state that there is a positive relationship between CSR and CFP.

Similar result was obtained by Waworuntu et al. (2014). They conducted a study regarding the correlation between the CSP and CFP of the top 40 companies (the constituents of the FTSE/ASEAN 40 index) in the ASEAN (Association of Southeast Asian Nations) region (Singapore, Malaysia, the Philippines, Indonesia, and Thailand) by analyzing the economic, environmental, and social disclosure against the profitability ratios of the firms. They found a moderate positive correlation between all corporate social performance (CSP) and CFP variables.

Mishra and Modi (2016) conducted a research on a sample of 1725 firms over the period 2000–2009. Their results indicate that the effects of overall CSR efforts on stock returns and idiosyncratic risk are not significant on their own but only become so in the presence of marketing capability. Furthermore, they obtained that although marketing capability has positive interaction effects with verifiable CSR efforts—environment (e.g., using clean energy), products (e.g., providing to economically disadvantaged), diversity (e.g., pursuing diversity in top management), corporate governance (e.g., limiting board compensation), and employees (e.g., supporting unions)—on stock returns (and negative interaction effects with these CSR efforts on idiosyncratic risk), it has no significant interaction effect with community-based efforts (e.g., charitable giving).

An extensive review was made by Raza et al. (2012) in order to conclude about the relationship between CSR and CFP using content analysis of 45 studies covering the period from 1972 to 2012. They concluded, based on empirical literature evidences, that CSR is highly linked with CFP. Firstly, 35 studies out of 45 found that

CSR is positively correlated with CFP, 1 study found mixed correlation between CSR and CFP, no study found negative correlation between CSR and CFP, and 9 studies out of 45 found no relationship between CSR and CFP using ROA, ROE, and ROS. Secondly, six studies out of six found positive relationship between CSR and CFP using market-to-book ratio/Tobin's Q. Lastly, 7 studies out of 25 studies found positive relation between CSR and CFP, 3 studies out of 25 studies found mixed relation between CSR and CFP, 8 studies out of 25 studies found negative relation between CSR and CFP, and 7 studies out of 25 studies found no relation between CSR and CFP using stock market returns.

It is very interesting also to see how the CSR reporting is affecting the companies. Lungu et al. (2011) studied the sustainability reports of the largest 50 companies classified by Global Fortune in 2009. Using the websites and the CSR reports as regularly published document to comply with voluntarily requirements, they found that size characteristics measured by assets and revenues cannot be correlated to the extent of CSR reports published by companies, but there is a significant negative correlation between change in revenues and return on equity and social and environmental disclosure for the sampled companies.

In the case of the Romanian companies listed on Bucharest Stock Exchange, Dumitru et al. (2011) found that there is a correlation between the degree of transparency (dependent variable) of CSR disclosure on the websites and the type of shareholders of the companies has not been scientifically validated (the corresponding null hypothesis was accepted).

Baleanu et al. (2011) investigated the extent to which the top 100 Romanian companies practice CSR. In order to highlight this, they analyzed the corporate website of each company, and they found that almost half of the firms analyzed (49%) affirmed in one way or the other their engagement to CSR, which is relatively low compared to Western companies. Also, they outlined that companies prefer inexpensive intervention instruments and prove weak coordination with other social and political actors.

There are two studies (Simionescu and Dumitrescu 2014; Simionescu and Gherghina 2014) analyzing the Romanian companies listed on Bucharest Stock Exchange (BSE) in order to determine whether the CSR practices can be linked to companies' financial performance during an economic downturn. The first paper analyzed 81 companies listed on BSE and considered only 19 companies that are active in CSR. The period analyzed is between 2006 and 2012. Results suggest a positive relation between CSR practices and companies' financial performance. The second paper empirically investigated the relationship between CSR and corporate performance by using both accounting-based performance measures (e.g., ROA, ROE, and ROS) and market-based firm performance measures (e.g., PER, EPS, and PBV), for a sample of companies listed on the BSE during the period 2008–2011. The authors (Simionescu and Gherghina 2014) used panel data regression models without cross-sectional effects, and they found a negative relationship between CSR and ROS, as well as a positive association between CSR and EPS.

According to Simionescu and Dumitrescu (2014) and Servaes and Tamayo (2013), CSR activities have a significant positive impact on market capitalization of the firms, which is a logic finding from the economic perspective, because these companies are more valuable in the investors' eyes.

In our previous research (Dornean and Oanea 2016), we have analyzed the impact of CSR on stock price and other market variables (dividends and stock return) for the companies listed on Bucharest Stock Exchange (BSE) in 2014. Using three statistical techniques, discriminant analysis, probit analysis model, and logistic regression, we showed that the stock price is the main driver for CSR activities of a company, while the others—dividend and stock return—do not have a significant impact. In this context, in order to add more clarity to our results, we conducted an analysis on listed companies on Romanian capital market over the period 2010–2015.

14.3 Methodology

14.3.1 The Model

The question we raise in our study is the following: which is the impact of CSR practices on companies' market capitalization? The present study attempts to fill in this gap by analyzing the companies listed on the Bucharest Stock Exchange (BSE) in Romania between 2010 and 2015, highlighting the postcrisis period.

Our research has as main objective to identify the impact of CSR activities on market capitalization of a firm, based on the methodology used by previous research on this topic (Simionescu and Dumitrescu 2014; Servaes and Tamayo 2013). In order to analyze this, we formulate the following hypothesis:

H_0: CSR has a positive impact on market capitalization.
H_1: CSR has a negative impact on market capitalization.

Using multiple regression model based on panel data for the period 2010–2015, we try to highlight the main factors affecting market capitalization pointing out the impact of CSR activities. The equation can be described by relation (14.1):

$$MCAP_{t,i} = \alpha_0 + \alpha_1 \cdot CSR_{t,i} + \alpha_2 \cdot DIV_{t,i} + \alpha_3 \cdot ROE_{t,i} + \varepsilon_{t,i} \tag{14.1}$$

where $MCAP_{t,i}$ is the dependent variable, showing the market capitalization of company i for year t; $CSR_{t,i}$ is the proxy variable for corporate social responsibility actions, equal to 1 if the company has CSR activities and 0 otherwise; $DIV_{t,i}$ is the dividend paid by company i for year t; $ROE_{t,i}$ is the return on equity for company i and year t; $\alpha_0, \alpha_1, \alpha_2, \alpha_3$ are the discriminant coefficients; and ε is the error term.

Table 14.1 Descriptive statistics for analyzed variables

Variable	Mean	Median	Std. Dev.	Skewness	Kurtosis
CSR companies					
ln_MCAP	19.7380	19.4931	1.7742	0.3958	2.5286
ln_DIV	10.1388	14.7005	8.5580	−0.2794	1.2124
ROE	0.21%	6.81%	0.5102	−9.3209	9.9949
NON-CSR companies					
ln_MCAP	16.4661	17.0376	3.6926	−3.6073	16.7001
ln_DIV	4.6184	0.0000	6.9832	0.8879	1.8792
ROE	−9.20%	1.79%	1.3241	−5.1678	9.7883
All companies					
ln_MCAP	17.5260	17.5442	3.5458	−3.1793	17.2691
ln_DIV	6.4066	0	7.9517	0.4944	1.3703
ROE	−6.2%	2.6%	1.1269	−6.0013	9.6317

14.3.2 Data and Descriptive Statistics

Our sample is formed by the companies listed at BSE, by excluding 15 companies which were excluded from the trading in the period 2010–2015. The analyzed sample is formed by 70 companies, from which only 23 of them have CSR activities, which are clearly stated in the annual reports or websites.

For each company we computed the following variables as follows:

- Market capitalization—the product between the final price for each year and the number of shares. Average stock price for year 2015. These values will be linearized by applying logarithmic function.
- Dividend paid—dividend value paid in each year by each companies. In case one company did not pay dividends, we equal the value for this variable with 0; these values will be linearized by applying logarithmic function.
- ROE (return on equity)—ratio between the profit and equity value for each company for each year.

In Table 14.1 we present the descriptive statistics for the selected variables, from where we can observe that there are notable differences between CSR companies and NON-CSR companies.

In CSR companies, all variables recorded higher values, namely, higher market capitalization, higher dividend paid, and higher return on equity, because all these CSR activities offer a better position of these companies in investors' eyes.

At a first glance, we can see that CSR companies are paying higher dividends versus the NON-CSR companies. At the same time, when we analyze the ROE for these two categories, CSR companies recorded positive ROE, while the NON-CSR companies recorded a negative ROE for the period 2010–2015.

Based on correlation coefficients presented in Table 14.2, we are able to see that the correlations between independent variable are small, so the multicollinearity in the regression model is avoided.

Table 14.2 Correlation coefficients

Variable	ln_MCAP	CSR	ln_DIV
ln_MCAP	1.0000		
CSR	0.4323	1.0000	
ln_DIV	0.3091	0.3252	1.0000
ROE	0.1949	0.0391	0.1582

Table 14.3 Unit root test for panel data (Levin et al. (2002))

Variables	t-test	p-value
ln_MCAP	−130.49***	0.0000
ln_DIV	−125.53***	0.0000
ROE	−9.55***	0.0000

*, **, ***indicate significant at the 0.1 level, 0.05 level, and 0.01 level

Through the regression model, we want to capture the influence of CSR activities to market capitalization taking into consideration also the influence of dividend paid by each company and ROE. In order to do this, we have to test the stationarity of these series of data. This is the reason why we applied unit root (Levin et al. 2002) test for panel data. According to the results from Table 14.3, all series are stationary.

14.4 Results

The estimated coefficients for the regression model described in the relation (14.1) are given in Table 14.4.

Based on the results presented in Table 14.4, we noticed that all three independent variables are affecting positively the market capitalization, which is the expected result. At the same time, we conclude that CSR activities have a significant positive impact on market capitalization of the firms listed on BSE during the period 2010–2015.

We obtained similar results with the previous literature (Simionescu and Dumitrescu 2014; Servaes and Tamayo 2013), which also highlighted the positive impact of CSR activity on firm financial performance.

14.5 Conclusion

The aim of this paper was to analyze the relationship between companies' CSR activities and market capitalization, for listed companies on Bucharest Stock Exchange over the period 2010–2015. Thus, our contribution consists in improvement of the existing literature.

Table 14.4 Regression model estimation

Depended variable: ln_MCAP	
Constant	16.1744*** (0.2063)[a]
CSR	2.8261*** (0.3392)
ln_DIV	0.0728*** (0.0202)
ROE	0.4860*** (0.1350)
R-squared	*0.2419*
R-squared (adjusted)	*0.2365*

[a]—standard errors in parentheses
*, **, ***indicate significant at the 0.1 level, 0.05 level, and 0.01 level

BSE introduced a mandatory code that all companies must adhere to the corporate social responsiblity, but only 23 of 85 listed companies have clear activities regarding CSR, for the period 2010–2015. Also this aspect was pointed out in our previous research (Dornean and Oanea 2016).

Analyzing the descriptive data for the two groups of companies (CSR and NON-CSR companies), we were able to conclude that the average market capitalization, the average dividend paid, and also the average ROE are higher for CSR companies compared with NON-CSR companies for the analyzed period (2010–2015).

Based on the regression model estimation, we obtained similar results with the results obtained by other researchers (Simionescu and Dumitrescu 2014; Servaes and Tamayo 2013), and we highlighted that CSR activities have a significant positive impact on market capitalization of the firms, which is logical from the economic approach, because these companies are more valuable in the investors' eyes.

Despite the positive implications of CSR on society, there remains an extensive debate regarding its consequences for companies' shareholders.

This study, which is limited to companies listed on the Bucharest Stock Exchange, has significant practical implications because it can motivate potential investors and/or the large public to decide to invest in companies that demonstrate a higher degree of CSR and improve policymaking through appropriate policies or incentives for CSR programs.

Further research can extend the analyzed period, to include also the years before 2010, for example, for the period between 2007 and present in order to capture also the crisis effect.

References

Baker, K., Nofsinger, J.: Socially Responsible Finance and Investing: Financial Institutions, Corporations, Investors, and Activists. Wiley, Hoboken (2012)

Baleanu, T.E., Chelcea, L., Stancu, A.: The social responsibility of the top 100 Romanian companies. An analysis of corporate websites. Amfiteatru Econ. **13**(29), 235–248 (2011)

Benabou, R., Tirole, J.: Individual and corporate social responsibility. Economica. **77**, 1–19 (2010). https://doi.org/10.1111/j.1468-0335.2009.00843.x

Besley, T., Ghatak, M.: Retailing public goods: the economics of corporate social responsibility. J. Public Econ. **91**(9), 1645–1663 (2007). https://doi.org/10.1016/j.jpubeco.2007.07.006

Carroll, A.B.: A three-dimensional conceptual model of corporate social performance. Acad. Manag. Rev. **4**(4), 497–505 (1979). https://doi.org/10.2307/257850

Carroll, A.B.: The pyramid of corporate social responsibility: toward the moral management of organizational stakeholders. Bus. Horiz. **34**(4), 39–48 (1991). https://doi.org/10.1016/0007-6813(91)90005-G

Carroll, A.B.: Corporate social responsibility: evolution of a definitional construct. Bus. Soc. **38**(3), 268–295 (1999). https://doi.org/10.1177/0007650315575488

Dornean, A., Oanea, D.C.: The impact of CSR on Company's stock price: evidence from Bucharest stock exchange. In: 27th IBIMA Proceedings, I – VI, pp. 1200–1210 (2016)

Dumitru, V., Ionescu, I., Calu, A., Oancea, M.: An investigation regarding the disclosure of corporate social responsibility information for listed companies from Romania. Amfiteatru Econ. **13**(29), 146–161 (2011)

Levin, A., Lin, C.F., Chu, C.S.J.: Unit root tests in panel data: asymptotic and finite-sample properties. J. Econom. **108**(1), 1–24 (2002). https://doi.org/10.1016/S0304-4076(01)00098-7

Lungu, C.I., Caraiani, C., Dascălu, C.: Research on corporate social responsibility reporting. Amfiteatru Econ. **13**(29), 117–131 (2011)

Maggina, A., Tsaklanganos, A.A.: Predicting the corporate social responsibility of listed companies in Greece using market variables. J. Appl. Bus. Res. **28**(4), 661–672 (2012). https://doi.org/10.19030/jabr.v28i4.8398

Mishra, S., Modi, S.B.: Corporate social responsibility and shareholder wealth: the role of marketing capability. J. Mark. **80**(1), 26–46 (2016). https://doi.org/10.1509/jm.15.0013

Nigro, C., Iannuzzi, E., Cortese, F., Petracca, M.: The relationship between corporate social responsibility and financial performance. An empirical analysis on a sample of Italian listed firms. In: Vrontis, D., Weber, Y., Tsoukatos, E. (eds.) Innovation, Entrepreneurship and Sustainable Value Chain in a Dynamic Environment (8th Annual Conference of the EuroMed-Academy-of-Business), pp. 1626–1639. Verona, Italy (2015)

Raza, A., Ilyas, M.I., Rauf, R., Qamar, R.: Relationship between Corporate Social Responsibility (CSR) and Corporate Financial Performance (CFP): literature review approach. Elixir Fin. Mgmt. **46**, 8404–8409 (2012)

Renneboog, L., Horst, J.T., Zhang, C.: Socially responsible investments: institutional aspects, performance, and investor behavior. J. Bank. Finance. **32**(9), 1723–1742 (2008). https://doi.org/10.1016/j.jbankfin.2007.12.039

Sacconi, L.: Corporate Social Responsibility (CSR) as a Model of 'Extended' Corporate Governance: An Explanation Based on the Economic Theories of Social Contract, Reputation and Reciprocal Conformism. LIUC, Ethics, Law and Economics. Paper No. 142. (2004). doi: https://doi.org/10.2139/ssrn.514522

Servaes, H., Tamayo, A.: The impact of corporate social responsibility on firm value: the role of customer awareness. Manag. Sci. **59**(5), 1045–1061 (2013)

Sheehy, B.: Defining CSR: problems and solutions. J. Bus. Ethics. **131**, 625–648 (2015). https://doi.org/10.1287/mnsc.1120.1630

Simionescu, L., Dumitrescu, D.: Corporate social responsibility and financial crisis. In: Roman, A., Anton, S.G. (eds.) Monetary, Banking and Financial Issues in Central Eastern EU Members Countries: How Can Central and Eastern EU Members Overcome the Current Economic Crisis, vol. 2, pp. 281–289. Alexandru Ioan Cuza University, Iasi (2014)

Simionescu, L., Gherghina, Ş.C.: Corporate social responsibility and corporate performance: empirical evidence from a panel of the Bucharest Stock Exchange listed companies. Management. Mark. Theory. **9**(4), 439–458 (2014)

Sudha, S.: Impact of corporate social responsibility on firm value – evidence from the Indian stock market. SS Int. J. Bus. Manag. Res. **4**(5), 58–75 (2014)

Waworuntu, S.R., Wantah, M.D., Rusmanto, T.: CSR and financial performance analysis: evidence from top ASEAN listed companies. Procedia. Soc. Behav. Sci. **164**, 493–500 (2014). https://doi.org/10.1016/j.sbspro.2014.11.107

Chapter 15
Study of Behavior Dimensions of the European Consumer of Financial Products and Services

Oana Alexandrina Duralia

Abstract While marketing can be considered an activity mainly focused outside the organization, particularly on consumers, in order to meet their needs and gain profit, we cannot talk about a uniform implementation of marketing strategies, policies, and tactics for all areas, since the field of services and specifically of financial services entails customizing the marketing approach based on a provider-consumer relationship.

In this context, the present paper aims to highlight the characteristics of the purchasing behavior of the consumer of financial services, having as a starting point the emphasis placed on the characteristics of activities specific to financial services, which leads to a different perception of the consumers in what regards the quality of services that are inherently intangible and highly diversified in terms of the criteria of time, the degree of complexity of operations, or the manifestation of market demand.

Keywords Financial products and services • Service marketing • Consumer behavior

15.1 Introduction

In specialized literature, most expert approaches on marketing services are aimed at highlighting the characteristics that distinguish the sector of services from the goods sector, and hence the need to substantiate marketing strategies operationalized through a marketing mix tailored on the general characteristics of services, namely, intangibility, inseparability, variation (heterogeneity), and perishability.

Outstanding contributions can be found in the work of authors such as Shostack (1977), Zeithaml et al. (1985), Lovelock (1983), Bowen and Schneider (1988), Berry and Parasuraman (1991), Kotler (1994), and McKechnie (1992). In one of the

---

O.A. Duralia (✉)
Lucian Blaga University of Sibiu, Sibiu, Romania
e-mail: oanaalexa@yahoo.com

S.C. Mărginean et al. (eds.), *Emerging Issues in the Global Economy*, Springer Proceedings in Business and Economics,
https://doi.org/10.1007/978-3-319-71876-7_15

most popular approaches to services marketing, Philip Kotler (1994) highlights the so-called triangle of marketing services underlying that, in the sector of services, an organization providing services should focus on all three aspects of marketing, namely, (1) the organization-consumer relationship, in terms of external or conventional marketing; (2) the organization-staff relationship, in terms of internal marketing; and (3) the staff-consumer relationship, in terms of interactive marketing.

A very interesting classification of services is provided by Lovelock and Yip (1996), according to which services can be grouped as follows: (1) people processing services, including services that address consumers directly, openly contributing to the achievement and consumption of services (healthcare, passenger transport, travel, etc.); (2) possession processing services, highlighting the services adding value to the possession of various goods, such as warranty and maintenance services, cleaning services, household maintenance services, etc.; and (3) information processing services, focused on telecommunications, financial services, services provided by various media, etc. The great advantage of this type of services is that their inseparability can be partially overcome by providing remote services, since the physical presence of the consumer in delivering the service is not mandatory.

We may notice that a differentiated operationalization of marketing in the banking field results from a number of features of the provider-consumer relationship, namely, the existence of mutual obligations, the responsibility for privacy, and the presence of a two-way information flow between the financial organization and the client.

Thus, specialized literature highlights three characteristics of financial services that customize the marketing approach in this area, namely (Ennew and Waite 2007):

1. Responsibility for money circulation (fiduciary responsibility) – focused on fund management and implicitly on the financial advisory services aimed at the client.
2. The duration of consumption or the contractual relationship – in most cases, the contractual relationship in the financial sector requires a long-term horizon and a wide range of services, which requires special attention to clients in order to exploit cross-selling opportunities, without assaulting the consumer with offers that do not correspond to their real needs.
3. Contingent consumption – reveals that, in some situations, the money invested in purchasing financial products and services may result in future consumer opportunities while in some cases may not result in a tangible consumption for the buyer.

Although the differentiated approach to services marketing mix (the 7 Ps: product, price, placement, promotion, personnel, process performance, and physical aspects) is better known than the traditional marketing (the 4 Ps), we should not overlook the fact that marketing mix, as a tool to operationalize the marketing strategy of the organization, must lead, on the one hand, to strengthening the competitive position on the market and, on the other hand, to increasing the satisfaction of the targeted customer segments. The synergic effect of marketing mix elements will be higher if the organization succeeds in objectively defining its market position compared to the competition while identifying and selecting the best target customer segments.

15.2 Characteristics of the Purchasing Behavior of the Financial Services and Products Consumer

Regarding the issue of studying the behavior of the financial products and services consumer, the major objectives aim to identify factors that influence financial services consumer behavior and to understand the decision-making process when buying financial products and services, from the moment when a problem is identified until the moment after the purchase, when the satisfaction or the cognitive dissonance (dissatisfaction) regarding the financial products and services purchased and consumed is expressed.

Unlike conventional products, studying the behavior of financial services consumer is somewhat restrictive, since for many consumers, financial products and services are, on the one hand, associated with a higher risk and, on the other hand, are seen as "unattractive," since they do not necessarily generate a consumption benefit or because this benefit is only relevant as a future opportunity.

The first step in understanding the decision-making process of acquiring financial services is the identification of the problem or the consumer's need awareness, a process that can be extremely difficult for two reasons (Ennew and Waite 2007): (1) for many consumers accessing financial services is directly subject to the occurrence of unforeseen events of force majeure, causing consumers to identify possible sources of financing or insurance to cover illness or even death events, and (2) the lack of transparency of the bidders regarding marketing activities, which does not allow consumers to fulfill their needs in terms of the financial products and services offered.

Creating selective demand, which means encouraging the consumer to use the financial products and services offered by one financial institution instead of another, can be achieved only if the primary application is already in place. As a result, marketing professionals must convince consumers that choosing the financial services of an organization compared to a similar one will eliminate the difference between their current state and the desired one.

Because of the intangibility and inseparability of financial services, during the information searching stage, an important role in influencing the purchasing decision of the consumer is taken by the personal information sources, along with the previous experience of the consumer (Dumitrescu 1998). Therefore, the recommendations of other consumers, as well as the credibility of the organization, are considered sources that facilitate the perceptual process of the quality of the service to be provided, which is intangible, par excellence (Zeithaml 1981).

The influence of these sources of information varies according to the category of the financial products and services targeted by the particular buyer, while the extent of the information search process differs depending on the importance of the acquisition, on the need to learn more about the targeted financial product/service and on the ease of obtaining relevant information.

Even if the consumer succeeds to overcome the barrier raised by the "availability" of information regarding financial services found on the market at a specific time, issues regarding the accuracy of the information are still a concern, more specifically in what regards the extent to which they fail to truthfully reflect reality. Hence, since the consumer obtains a lot of information from the external search process, the recommendations of the others are a personal source influencing the decision, and it is possible that the experience of the others regarding the financial services purchased might not identify with the current need of the potential consumer in terms of various socioeconomic and demographic variables (e.g., age, income, marital status, etc.). In addition, even if the potential buyer has access to information on financial products and services, the lack of expertise in the field hinders their perception and interpretation, and, in this context, the quality of the advisory service offered in the stage before the purchase is a determining factor in deciding upon the acquisition.

Regarding the alternative evaluation phase, the consumer reaction to the information acquired during the information searching stage may be different, because they can be integrated by the consumer as such or may be distorted or simply ignored.

The degree of coverage and the extent of the alternative evaluation stage are influenced by a number of factors (Cătoiu and Teodorescu 2004): (1) the experience of the consumer, which makes the evaluation process be quicker and less extended; (2) the reasons requiring a more urgent need force the buyer to make a more rapid evaluation; (3) the demo-economic and cultural characteristics offer the consumers a greater capacity of operational evaluation and determine a broader assessment, while the cost of taking an incorrect decision becomes higher; (4) the increasing complexity of the alternatives requires a more extensive assessment; and (5) the importance of the product or service enhances the evaluation of the alternatives.

A particularly important problem is to identify the criteria the consumer uses in the evaluation and comparison of the identified alternatives and then the ranking of the criteria based on the importance attributed by the consumer. Since the structure of values and beliefs of the consumer may differ, it is likely that different consumers be positioned differently, although they use the same criteria with the same degree of importance. Furthermore, if the consumer has been somewhat inactive during the problem identification stage, the criteria for evaluating alternatives will also be very briefly defined, and the barriers to evaluation are most often determined by the intangibility of the financial products and services and implicitly by the lack of expertise of most of the consumers.

Buying the financial product/service as result of the evaluation of alternatives is most often the result of the marketing approach initiated by the provider. Whereas, because of inseparability of the services, the consumer has an active role in the production and consumption of financial services, the interaction between the staff of the providing institution and the potential buyers is significant.

Given, on the one hand, the high degree of risk associated to the purchase of financial products and services and, on the other, the complexity and lack of the standardization and warrantees, we can say that, generally, the consumer is vulnerable to the "overselling" offers of the bidder.

During the last stage of the decision-making process, the post-purchase stage, the consumer will evaluate the extent to which the decision was optimal or not. If the performances of the product/service live up to their expectations, the consumer will be satisfied, and the information acquired will be stored in memory for further use in decision-making; otherwise the consumers will be facing a state of dissatisfaction, known as cognitive dissonance.

The difficulties in assessing the financial products and services are determined by the fact that, in general, the functional aspects of the financial services provided are evaluated in comparison with the technical ones, which leads to the conclusion that the risk of cognitive dissonance is extremely high in the case of financial products and services, which results in a reduction of brand loyalty in this field (Zeithaml et al. 1985).

15.3 Research from Secondary Data Sources of the European Consumer of Financial Products and Services

One of the objectives of the European Commission has been the concern to facilitate access to individual, retail, and organizational consumers to the market of financial products and services. In this respect, the recent years have recorded major advances aimed at more measures to protect consumers and investors on the market of financial products and services, but the big challenge remains cross-border access to financial products and services (http://www.europa.eu).

In this context, in April 2016, the European Commission carried out and published a Eurobarometer research aimed at studying the purchasing behavior of the consumer of financial products and services offered both internally and at the level of the other UE member states.

Thus, at the EU28 level, we can observe that 88% of the respondents said they had purchased at least one financial product or service, of which 16% have purchased two financial products/services, while 57% of the European consumers bought three financial products/services, while only 15% of them have purchased a single product or financial service (Fig.15.1).

With regard to the financial products/services purchased, the aforementioned study reveals that 76% of the Europeans admitted they have a current bank account, while 54% of the respondents have car insurance, and only 44% of the respondents said they own a savings account. In the first quarter of 2016, approximately 43% of the Europeans were holders of a credit card, 17% had a mortgage, and a rate of only 11% had a personal credit (Fig. 15.2).

In what concerns the Romanian consumers, the analysis of the information published reveals that Romania holds one of the last places in the EU28 in terms of the number of those who have a current bank account (29%), of those who completed a car insurance (23%), or have a savings account (8%). Also, a rate of only 2% of the Romanian respondents declared they had a mortgage, 10% a personal loan, and 38% (the highest figure for the EU28) said they did not purchase any financial product.

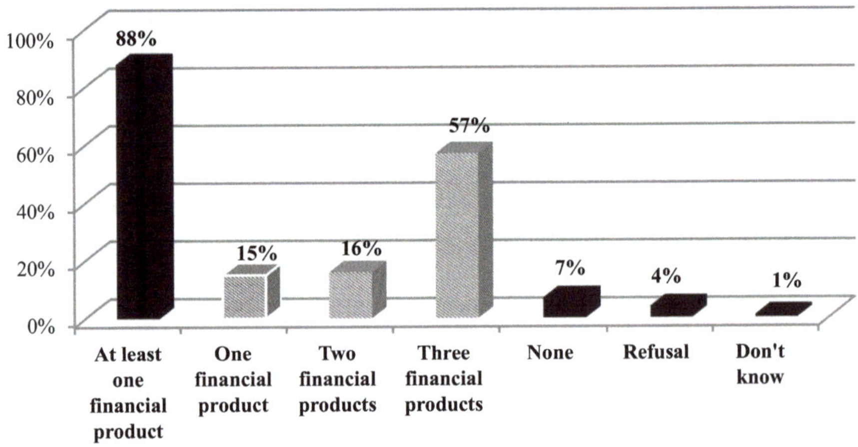

Fig. 15.1 Share of financial products/services purchased in the EU28 (Source: European Commission, Special Eurobarometer no.446, April 2016, p.6, http://www.europa.eu)

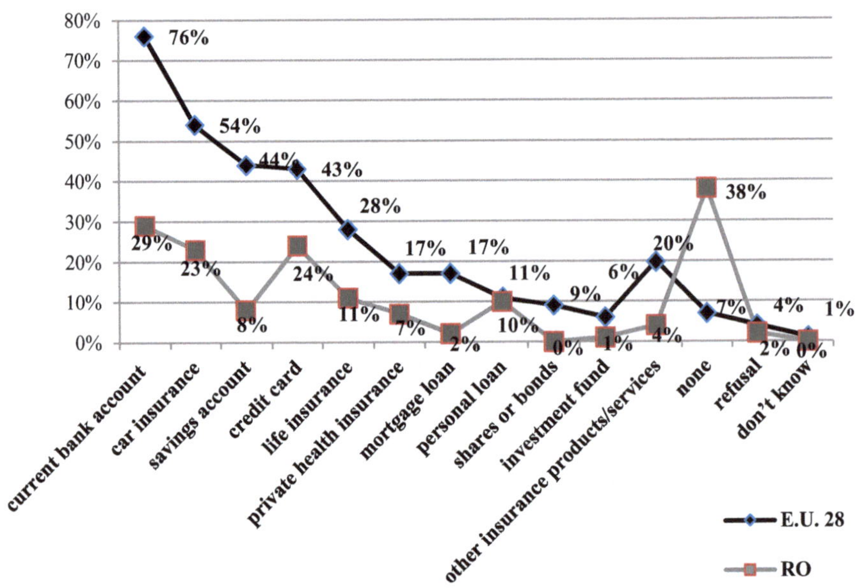

Fig. 15.2 Main categories of financial products/services held by European consumers' multiple possible answers (Source: European Commission, Special Eurobarometer no.446, April 2016, p.9/10, http://www.europa.eu)

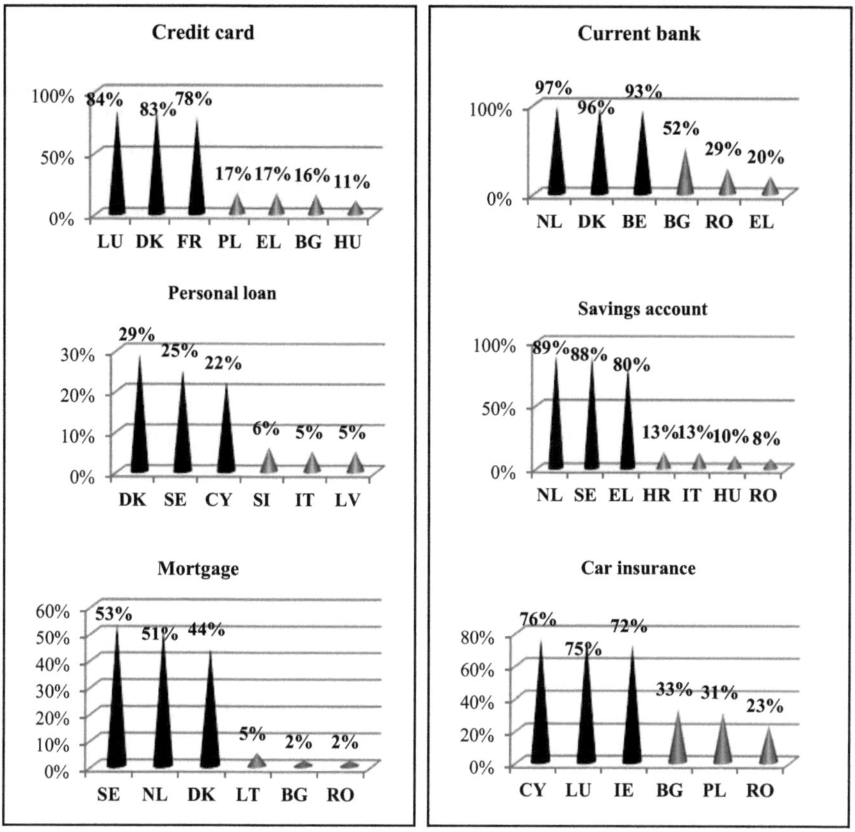

Fig. 15.3 EU member states holding leading/laggard positions regarding the degree of acquisition of financial products/services on the internal market multiple possible answers (Source: European Commission, Special Eurobarometer no.446, April 2016, p.9/10, http://www.europa.eu)

In contrast, the leading positions are occupied by the Netherlands, Luxembourg, Denmark, Sweden, and Belgium, as the consumers in these countries are most willing to purchase financial products/services on the internal market (Fig. 15.3).

Another objective of the study conducted by the European Commission was to identify the attitude of the European consumers regarding the purchase of financial products/services on the markets of other EU member states.

Thus, in April 2016, most interviewed consumers (i.e., 92%) of the 28 EU member states (sample made up of 27,969 respondents) declared they did not acquire any financial product or service from another EU country, the share of those who bought such products/services being of only 7% (Fig.15.4).

The decisions of the European consumers who have purchased financial products/services from another EU member country were directed toward the establishment of current accounts (3%) and savings accounts (1%) and obtaining credit cards (1%) and closure of life or car auto insurance policies (both by 1%).

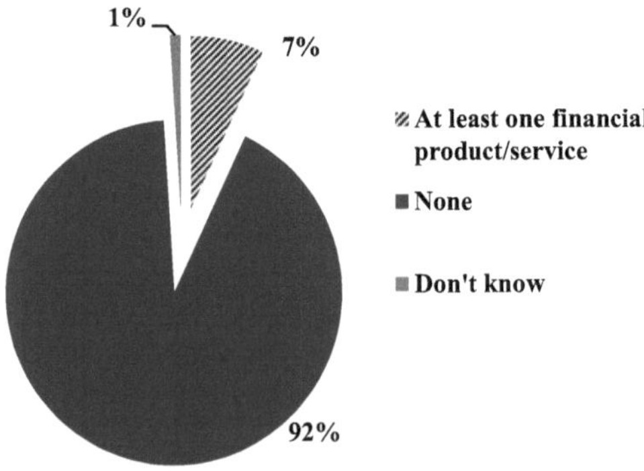

Fig. 15.4 Share of European consumers who purchased financial products/services from another EU country (Source: European Commission, Special Eurobarometer no.446, April 2016, p.15 http://www.europa.eu)

In what regards the reasons for not purchasing financial products and services on another market in the EU, the European consumers mentioned (within a maximum of three possible reasons):

- They can purchase any necessary financial product/service on the domestic market (33%).
- They prefer to purchase financial products/services from the local market (21%).
- They lack clear information on financial products/services (17%).
- They are concerned about fraud (16%).
- They prefer direct purchase (14%).
- They are not familiar with legislation if problems occur (13%).
- The existence of language barriers (12%).
- They lack information about the possibilities of purchasing financial products/services from another EU market (6%).
- The existence of higher prices or additional costs (4%).
- The lack of the existence of legislation of consumer protection on another EU market (4%).

Another very interesting result after analyzing the data of the study mentioned above is related to the reliability of the European consumers for the suppliers of financial products/services purchased during the last 5 years. 71% of the Europeans admitted they did not change the supplier of products and financial services, while a rate of only 25% of the respondents said they had switched suppliers for at least one financial product/service (Fig. 15.5).

15.4 Conclusions

The peculiarities of studying the behavior of the financial products and services consumer stem from the materialization of the characteristics of financial services such as intangibility, inseparability, variability, and perishability, which hamper their favorable perception by the consumers who lack a tangible representation.

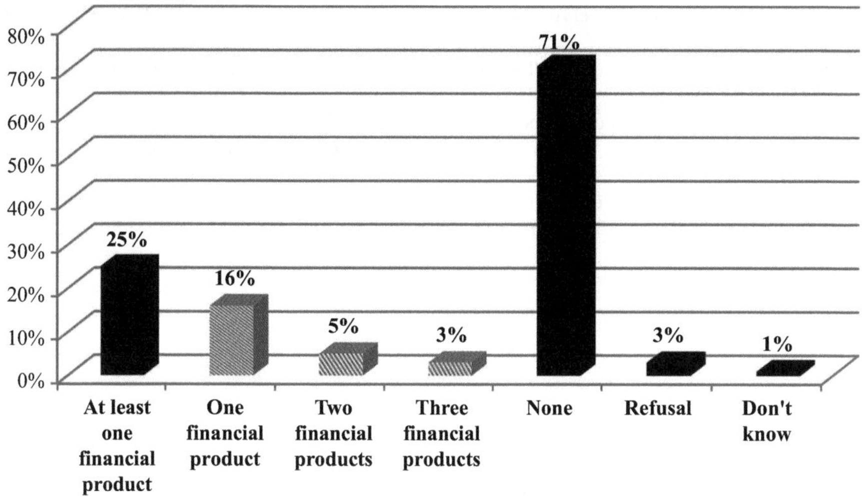

Fig. 15.5 The extent to which European consumers have switched suppliers of financial products and services purchased during the last 5 years (Source: European Commission, Special Eurobarometer no.446, April 2016, p.33, http://www.europa.eu)

Moreover, the growing number of intermediaries on the financial market and the drop in the differences between the providers of financial products and services on all components of marketing mix determine the increase of the marketing efforts on the part of the providers of financial products and services, aimed at studying the real needs of the consumers and consequently at tailoring products and financial services according to their requirements.

References

Berry, L., Parasuraman, A.: Marketing Services: Competing Through Quality. The Free Press, New York (1991)

Bowen, D.E., Schneider, B.: Services marketing and management: implications for organizational behavior. In: Cummings, L.L., Staw, B.M. (eds.) Research in Organizational Behavior, vol. vol. 10, pp. 43–80. CT: JAI Press, Greenwich (1988)

Cătoiu, I., Teodorescu, N.: Comportamentul Consumatorului. Uranus Publishing House, Bucharest (2004)

Dumitrescu, L.: Marketingul Serviciilor, pp. 115–126. Imago Publishing House, Sibiu (1998)

Ennew, T.C., Waite, N.: Financial Services Marketing. An International Guide to Principles and Practice. Butterworth-Heinemann/Elsevier, Oxford (2007)

European Union: Special Eurobarometer no.446, http://www.europa.eu (2016). Accessed 21 Feb 2017

Kotler, P.: Marketing Management: Analysis, Planning, Implementation and Control, 8th edn. Prentice-Hall, Englewood Cliffs (1994)

Lovelock, C.H., Yip, G.S.: Developing global strategies for service businesses. Calif. Manag. Rev. **38**(2), 64–86 (1996)

Lovelock, C.H.: Classifying services to gain strategic marketing insights. J. Mark. **47**(3), 9–20 (1983)
McKechnie, S.: Consumer buying behavior in financial services: an overview. Int. J. Bank Market. **10**(5), 4–12 (1992)
Shostack, G.L.: Breaking free from product marketing. J. Mark. **41**, 73–80 (1977)
Zeithaml, A.V., Parasuraman, A., Berry, L.: Problems and strategies in service marketing. J. Mark. **49**(2), 33–46 (1985)
Zeithaml, V.: How consumer evaluation processes differ between goods and services. In: Donnelly, J.H., George, W.R. (eds.) The Marketing of Services, pp. 186–190. AMA Proceedings, Chicago (1981)

Chapter 16
The Investment on Capital Market: From Target Price Valuation Models to Investor Final Decision

Mihaela Herciu

Abstract The investments on capital market are more attractive nowadays considering the short-term potential earnings that this particular market can offer but also the opportunities generated by the new entry companies. The aim of the paper is to present different valuation models of share in order to identify/calculate a target price, on one hand, and to emphasize the impact of both internal and external information on price per share, on the other hand. The target price is an important instrument that drives, alongside with industry, financial, and risk analysis, the investment decision to buy, to hold, and to sell. The key issues in determining target price are equity analysis, cash flow forecasts, dividend forecast, peer valuation, and so on. But even if a fair/true target price of a given share according to valuation models was established, the external information (from the macroeconomic environment or related to the government policies) could have a huge impact on price per share and on investor decision to buy, to hold, or to sell.

Keywords Share • Target price • Valuation models • Investment decision

16.1 Introduction

The investment on capital market is not a randomized process and is based on fundamental and technical analysis. In a market in which everyone is trying to make money, if some strategies were to achieve this, everybody would be searching for it because "a dollar lost is twice as bad as a dollar gained is good" (Sharpe and Litterman 2014).

Equity valuation relates the practice and theory of corporate finance. In order to evaluate equity, analysts must evaluate first the firm's financial standing and consider

M. Herciu (✉)
Lucian Blaga University of Sibiu, Sibiu, Romania
e-mail: mihaela.herciu@ulbsibiu.ro

S.C. Mărginean et al. (eds.), *Emerging Issues in the Global Economy*, Springer Proceedings in Business and Economics,
https://doi.org/10.1007/978-3-319-71876-7_16

the implications of up-to-date research on valuation consequences of corporate financial decision (Billingsley 1995).

16.2 Literature Review: Presenting Valuation Models

The equity valuation is a very difficult and complex job for financial analysts. In many cases the investment decision on capital market is based on the chartered financial analyst recommendation. Chartered financial analysts or sell-side analysts issue in their equity research report the target price (Demirakos et al. 2010) using one or more of the most suitable valuation model by considering the business specific.

But what is valuation? According to Stowe et al. (2007), "valuation is the estimation of an asset's value based either on variables perceived to be related to future investment returns or on comparisons with similar assets." The same authors have identified five steps for each individual valuation, as follows: (1) understanding the business, (2) forecasting company performance, (3) selecting the appropriate valuation model, (4) converting forecasts to a valuation, and (5) making the investment decision (recommendation). So, in order to be able to make a recommendation or to invest, it is very important to understand the business and to forecast the company financial performance. More, choosing the right or appropriate valuation model for calculating the target price is very challenging because according to many specialists (Demirakos et al. 2010; Gleason et al. 2013; Imam et al. 2013; Bradshaw et al. 2013), the valuation models affect target price accuracy.

Financial analysts provide investment recommendations – to buy, to hold, or to sell – based on the single-point target price forecast (Joos et al. 2013) that is very valuable for investors (Bilinski et al. 2012) when comparing with the current/real stock price on the capital market. In equity valuation model earnings, book value, dividends, and forecasted cash flow are vital variables (Ohlson 1995) and drive to target price forecast (Da et al. 2016).

Parrino (2005) has argued that even if there are many valuation models, most of them can be grouped into three categories: *assets/cost approaches*, *market approaches*, and *income approaches*. But as regarding stock evaluation and target price determination, the last two categories are more appropriate.

16.2.1 Market Approaches

In the market approach, the most important is P/E (price/earnings).

$$P_0 = \frac{DIV_1}{k_E - g} = \frac{EPS_1 b}{k_E - g} \Rightarrow \frac{P_0}{EPS_1} = \frac{b}{k_E - g}$$

Table 16.1 Calculating FCFF and FCFE

FCFF: WACC method	FCFE
Net revenue – Operating expenses	Net revenue – Operating expenses
EBITDA (earnings before interest, taxes, depreciation, and amortization – Depreciation and amortization	EBITDA (earnings before interest, taxes, depreciation, and amortization – Depreciation and amortization
EBIT (operating profit) X (1 – Average tax rate)	EBIT (operating profit) – Interest expense X (1 – Average tax rate)
Operating profit after tax + Depreciation and amortization – Capital expenditure – Addition to working capital	Net income + Depreciation and amortization – Capital expenditure – Addition to working capital + Proceeds from new debt issues – Principal repayments
Free cash flow to the firm (FCFF)	*Free cash flow to equity (FCFE)*
$V_f = \sum_{t=0}^{\infty} \frac{FCFF_t}{(1+WACC)^t}$	$V_f = \sum_{t=0}^{\infty} \frac{FCEF_t}{(1+k_E)^t}$
Where: WACC – Weighted average cost of capital used to discount FCFF K_E – Cost of equity to discount FCFE t – The period when cash flow is received	

Source: Parrino (2005)

where:

DIV_1 – dividends in period 1
EPS_1 – earnings per share in period 1
b – payout ratio
k_E – cost of equity
g – dividends/earnings growth rate

When comparing companies price per earning is more appropriate (Cheng and McNamara 2000).

16.2.2 *Income Approaches*

FCFF and FCFE

In the income approach, the models are based on free cash flow to the firm (FCFF) or free cash flow to equity (FCFE) (Table 16.1).

According to Mukherjee et al. (2004), the discounted cash flow method is more popular for valuating publicly held companies compared with closely held ones.

Discounted Dividend Model

The DDM is the simplest and oldest present value approach to valuing stock (Stowe et al. 2007).

$$V_0 = \sum_{t=1}^{n} \frac{DIV_t}{(1+k_E)^t} + \frac{TV_n}{(1+k_E)^n}$$

Where:

V_0 – value per share
TV – terminal value

16.3 Data and Results

In order to show how target price can be determinate, Electrica SA was selected, as a group. Electrica SA is a key player in the field of distribution, supply, and other electricity-connected services in Romania, both in terms of areas covered and number of users served. 120 years of experience on the market and good economic results strengthen the company's position on the market, putting Electrica into a leading position.

Over the years, Electrica SA obtained financial results that led to the possibility of admission to trading on the stock exchange. In 2014, Electrica's shares were admitted to trade on both the BSE and LSE following a successful IPO with a deal size above 400 million euros. The structure of the transaction and the clear equity story of Electrica attracted great demand from both local and international institutional investors.

According to our estimations, Electrica has a great growth potential in terms of revenue, covering all operating costs, but also in terms of net income, dividends, quantity distributed, and customers.

16.3.1 Discounted Dividend Model

We calculate beta by regressing both daily returns of Electrica and BET. The result is 0.6482. Also, we compare our beta with 0.54 the value of world beta industry (as it is calculated by Damodaran). Given the higher volatility of the Romanian market, a beta of 0.64 is a reasonable one.

For equity risk premium, we used 7.08%, result obtained by Aswath Damodaran (2017) for Romania at the beginning of 2017. The ERP (equity risk premium) is based on Moody's rating for Romania (Baa3) and country risk premium (3.13%).

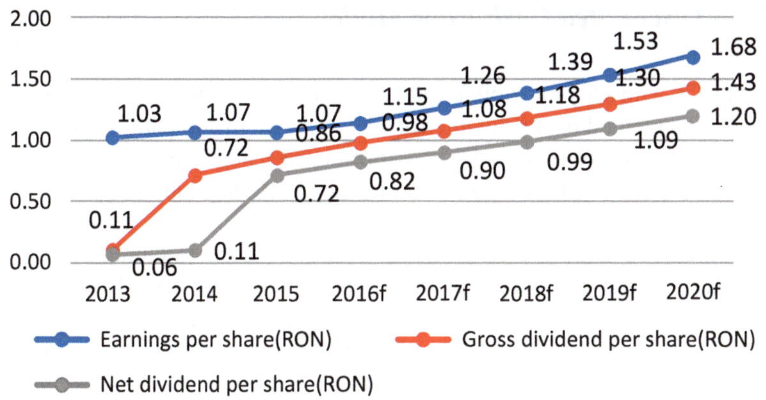

Fig. 16.1 Forecasting EPS for Electrica (based on own calculation and assumptions)

Table 16.2 Valuation assumptions for DDM

Beta		0.6482
Risk-free rate		3.30%
Equity risk premium		7.08%
Cost of equity		*7.89%*
Year	*Dividend value*	*NPV of dividend*
D1–2016	0.8200	0.7600
D2–2017	0.9000	0.7732
D3–2018	0.9900	0.7883
D4–2019	1.0900	0.8045
D5–2020	1.2000	0.8209
Terminal value	18.0089	12.3192
Estimative price		*16.27 RON*

Given the fact that the risk-free rate on primary market operations is 3.30% (according to NBR) for 70-month government bond yield, the cost of equity will be 7.89%.

At the end of 2015, Electrica announced a 0.722 net dividend/share (0.86 gross dividend per share). We estimated net income for 2016–2020 based on forecasted revenues, operating costs, and taxes. Historical analysis shows that a 75% from net income returns to shareholders. Moreover, according to the annual report, as regarding dividend policy, Electrica intended to retain 85% from net income of shareholders for dividends. Considering that, we forecasted every dividend for every year (around 10% growth rate) for the next 5 years, and we used 1.15% for terminal value based on ROE and retained earnings. After dividends and terminal value estimation, we valuate a target price for Electrica of 16.27 RON with an upside potential of 12.51% (Fig. 16.1 and Table 16.2).

Comparing with the price at September 05, 2017 of 14.46 RON, Electrica shares have an upside potential of 12.51%.

16.3.2 Discounted Cash Flow Model

We used DCF with a 5-year explicit forecast, using a benchmark formula for allowed revenues, this method being suitable for Electrica due to company's specific activities. The base case for this model was formulated using guidance form historical performance (2011–2015), industry outlook, ANRE regulations, and Electrica's competitive position.

We estimate revenues by considering operational costs (including costs of network losses), working capital, depreciation, regulated asset base (RAB), and regulated rate of return (RRR). We considered that operating costs will increase only with 2% y-o-y, given the important level of the investment for the forthcoming years and the probability of reducing costs of network losses.

We estimate the level of WC based on operational costs per month and RRR. Even if at the end of 2015 Electrica has a huge NWC (2548 mil. RON), in order to estimate the change in net working capital, we subtracted from balance sheet short-term investment (government bonds).

The depreciation level is around 60% from CAPEX. The level of CAPEX is already approved by ANRE till 2018 and is growing with an average level of 12% y-o-y. We consider that after 2018, the CAPEX will increase with 10% y-o-y. The regulated asset base level for 2015 was 4423 mil. RON representing 97% forms the total fixed assets. We estimate that the value of fixed assets per year will increase with the value of CAPEX from previous year. Regulated return rate level is 7.7% based on ANRE regulations.

Considering 5-year forecasts, we used for estimating cost of debt the following: the risk-free rate for 70-month government bond yield (3.30%), the interest rate of margin 3.51% (according to NBR), and a tax rate of 16%. The cost of debt will be 5.72%. Based on capital structure (77% equity and 23% debt) and both cost of equity, as it was estimated for DDM (7.89%), and cost of debt, the WACC will be 7.39%.

After estimation of free cash flows, we discounted them with 7.39% WACC. Due to energy market balance after 2020 (after 2 years of total liberalization), we assume that the terminal value will grow with 1%. Enterprise value represents the sum of both discounted cash flows and discounted terminal value. The market value of net debt was calculated by considering short- and long-term liabilities minus cash and cash equivalents. The fair value of equity (5511.81 million RON) divided at total number of shares conducted to an estimative price of 15.93 RON for Electrica (Tables 16.3 and 16.4).

Comparing with the price at September 05, 2017 of 14.46 RON, Electrica shares have an upside potential of 10.16%.

As it can be oserved, the estimative prices were identified by using DDM and DCF models. To calculate the target price, the two prices were weighted by 50/50. According to calculated target price of 16,09 RON, a buy recommendation can be issued (Fig. 16.2).

Table 16.3 Calculating WACC

Cost of equity	7.89%
Cost of debt	5.72%
Equity as % of assets	77%
Debt as % of assets	23%
WACC	*7.39%*

Table 16.4 Calculating the fair value of equity and the estimative price

Terminal value (mil. RON)	6.989,14
PV of terminal value (mil. RON)	4.893,10
PV of FCF (mil. RON)	1.673,91
Enterprise value (mil. RON)	6.567,01
– Market value of net debt (mil. RON)	1.055,20
Fair value of equity (mil. RON)	*5.511,81*
Number of shares	345.939,929
Estimative price RON	*15,93*

Fig. 16.2 Investment recommendation

16.3.3 Sensitivity Analysis

In Electrica case the models (DDM and DCF) are sensitive to risk-free rate (considering the macroeconomic instability) and perpetual growth rate for terminal value which can provide three sensitivity analyses (scenarios) with different results for target price. In the first scenario, both cost of equity and cost of debt are changing, while in the other two, only the terminal value is affected by the assumptions.

As it can be observed from Table 16.5 according to the first scenario, the recommendation is to hold because the target price is almost equal with the price at September 05, 2017. In the other two scenarios, the recommendation remained to buy, but in those cases the terminal value is growing. If the terminal value will decrease, the buy recommendation has to be changed into to hold.

Table 16.5 Scenario development and target prices

First scenario	Second scenario	Third scenario
The risk-free rate is 3.96% (126 months GBY)	The terminal value in DDM will grow with 2%	The terminal value in DCF will grow with 2%
Risk-free rate 3.93%	TV growth rate 2%	TV growth rate 2%
Estimative price DDM 14.75	Estimative price DDM 18.16	Estimative price DDM 16.27
Estimative price DCF 14.20	Estimative price DCF 15.93	Estimative price DCF 18.72
Target price 14.48	*Target price 17.05*	*Target price 17.50*

16.3.4 News Impact on Price per Share

Most of the analysts will make the recommendation for the investment decision based on estimation, forecasts and financial standing, and evolution of the company. Beyond earning per share, dividend yield, or dividend policy, in many cases there are also external factors that can affect price per share, such as macroeconomic environment (Nikkinen and Sahlstrom 2015; Cutler et al. 1989) and news about the company (Li et al. 2014; Boudoukh et al. 2013).

In Electrica case the price of electricity on the electricity market or electricity market regulations can affect price per share. More, the strategic decision made by Electrica has influenced the price per share. For instance, the revocation of sales manager has conducted to the growth of price per share with 3.18% at London Stock Exchange.

Electrica has to comply with regulatory requirements given by the Romanian Energy Regulatory Authority (ANRE) and has to keep in place regulated approvals, being exposed to significant liabilities in case of non-compliance. The regulation risk generated by the frequent changes of the methodology during the regulatory period and the lack of predictability and stability of the regulatory environment may have a negative impact on the electricity prices. Also, the changing tariffs on the regulated market can negatively influence the group's financial performance (for instance, the average regulated tariff for low voltage in 2015 was 191.04 RON/Mwh, decreasing in 2016 to 110.25 RON/Mwh and then to 103.27 ROM/Mwh in 2017).

16.4 Conclusions

The investor decision to invest on capital market is an act of trust. Equity or chartered financial analysts have to convince the investor that the decision recommendations – to buy, to sell, or to hold – are valuable and that they issue a fair target price. But even if they have used the most suitable valuation models for estimating the target price, the reality can be different precisely because the target price is calculated based on estimation, forecasts, and assumptions.

According to calculated target price for Electrica, there is an upside potential of 11.27% against the price per share from May 09, 2017 if these are considered DDM and DCF valuation models. But in terms of sensitivity, it is very important to find out if the recommendation remains the same. Equity analysts have to offer also a worst scenario to the investor in order to take the final decision because they are playing with their money.

References

Bilinski, P., Lyssimachou, D., Walker, M.: Target price accuracy: international evidence. Account. Rev. **88**(3), 825–851 (2012)

Billingsley, R.S.: Corporate financial decision making and equity analysis: an overview. In: AIMR Conference Proceedings. Association for Investment Management and Research, Vol. 1995, No. 4, pp. 1–4 (1995)

Boudoukh, J., Feldman, R., Kogan, S., Richardson, M.: Which news moves stock prices? A textual analysis (No. w18725). National Bureau of Economic Research (2013)

Bradshaw, M.T., Brown, L.D., Huang, K.: Do sell-side analysts exhibit differential target price forecasting ability? Rev. Acc. Stud. **18**(4), 930–955 (2013)

Cheng, C.A., McNamara, R.: The valuation accuracy of the price-earnings and price-book benchmark valuation methods. Rev. Quant. Finan. Acc. **15**(4), 349–370 (2000)

Cutler, D.M., Poterba, J.M., Summers, L.H.: What moves stock prices? J. Portf. Manag. **15**(3), 4–12 (1989)

Da, Z., Hong, K.P., Lee, S.: What drives target price forecasts and their investment value? J. Bus. Finan. Acc. **43**(3–4), 487–510 (2016)

Damodaran, A.: http://pages.stern.nyu.edu/~adamodar/New_Home_Page/datafile/Betas.html (2017). Accessed 25 Mar 2017

Demirakos, E.G., Strong, N.C., Walker, M.: Does valuation model choice affect target price accuracy? Eur. Account. Rev. **19**(1), 35–72 (2010)

Gleason, C.A., Bruce Johnson, W., Li, H.: Valuation model use and the price target performance of sell-side equity analysts. Contemp. Account. Res. **30**(1), 80–115 (2013)

Imam, S., Chan, J., Shah, S.Z.A.: Equity valuation models and target price accuracy in Europe: evidence from equity reports. Int. Rev. Financ. Anal. **28**, 9–19 (2013)

Joos, P., Piotroski, J.D., Srinivasan, S.: Can analysts assess fundamental risk and valuation uncertainty? An empirical analysis of scenario-based value estimates. J. Financ. Econ. **121**(3), 645–663 (2013)

Li, X., Xie, H., Chen, L., Wang, J., Deng, X.: News impact on stock price return via sentiment analysis. Knowl.-Based Syst. **69**, 14–23 (2014)

Mukherjee, T.K., Kiymaz, H., Baker, H.K.: Merger motives and target valuation: a survey of evidence from CFOs. J. Appl. Finan. **14**, 7–24 (2004)

Nikkinen, J., Sahlström, P.: Impact of scheduled US macroeconomic news on stock market uncertainty: a multinational. Perspective. (2015)

Ohlson, J.A.: Earnings, book values, and dividends in equity valuation. Contemp. Account. Res. **11**(2), 661–687 (1995)

Parrino, R.: Choosing the right valuation approach. In: CFA Institute Conference Proceedings, Vol. 2005, No. 4, pp. 15–28. CFA Institute (2005)

Sharpe, W.F., Litterman, R.: Past, present, and future financial thinking. Financ. Anal. J. **70**(6), 16–22 (2014)

Stowe, J., Robinson, Th., Pinto, J., McLeavey, D.: Equity Asset Valuation, CFA Institute, John Wiley & Sons, Inc., New Jersey, (2007)

Chapter 17
Evaluation of Female Entrepreneurs' Emotional Feedback

Esra Kahya Ozyirmidokuz and Eduard Alexandru Stoica

Abstract Female unemployment rates are very high in Turkey. Women's participation in the work force will not only increase the national income but also increase the number of female entrepreneurs in business life to join what is traditionally considered a man's world. Although there are few (only about 8.5%) women in management, there are women in top and decision-making positions. To encourage Turkish women into entrepreneurship, there are third-party online organizations which share and publicize online success stories of Turkish female entrepreneurs. This research aims to discover the factors related to female entrepreneurs' success in business life. The aim of the research is to evaluate female entrepreneurs' emotional feedback in order to provide a general conceptual overview of the current situation in Turkey on the subject. To achieve this, 69 successful female entrepreneurs' online feedback which was collected from third-party organizations was analyzed in order to extract the factors contributing to the success of female entrepreneurs in Turkey.

Keywords Female entrepreneurship • Happiness • Online feedback analysis

17.1 Introduction

Unemployment is the biggest obstacle to the economic development of a country. The most practical solution to remove unemployment is entrepreneurship (Ciftci 2010). Female unemployment rates are very high in Turkey. Women's participation in the work force will not only increase the national income but also increase the

E.K. Ozyirmidokuz (✉)
Erciyes University, Kayseri, Turkey
e-mail: esrakahya@erciyes.edu.tr

E.A. Stoica
Lucian Blaga University of Sibiu, Sibiu, Romania
e-mail: eduard.stoica@ulbsibiu.ro

S.C. Mărginean et al. (eds.), *Emerging Issues in the Global Economy*, Springer Proceedings in Business and Economics,
https://doi.org/10.1007/978-3-319-71876-7_17

number of female entrepreneurs in business life to what is traditionally considered a man's world. In Turkey, labor force participation overall by women is low, less than 22% compared to an average of 62% in OECD countries and compared to an average of 33% in a group of selected countries with similar levels of economic development. In fact, women's share in the labor force has fallen from 34.3% in 1988 to 21.6% in 2008; Turkey now has the distinction among OECD countries or any country in the European and Central Asian regions of having the fewest women participating in its economic development (Welsh et al. 2016). Turkey is a country where men have a leading role in economic development and women have significant importance to participate in economic development.

According to recent data (Aycan 2004), Turkish women make up 32% of professionals in scientific and technical jobs, 35% of managerial personnel, and 11% of entrepreneurs, directors, and top management positions. Turkish women also represent a substantial proportion in professions such as pharmacists (60%), physicians (19%), dentists (30%), lawyers (34%), and professors (23%) (Aycan and Eskin 2005). Another problem for Turkey is its inability to make the best use of female and young entrepreneurs, an important entrepreneurial potential within the Turkish population (Gurol and Atsan 2006). The percentage of female employers among all employers in Turkey is as low as 3.3% (TUSIAD Report 2002). The proportion of female entrepreneurs as a share of the total number of entrepreneurs in Turkey is around 10%, compared with 16–40% in European countries (Cetindamar et al. 2012).

Turkey is a developing country where women seek self-employment as a means to overcome occupational segregation and participate in economic development. The small size of this country, its predominantly strong family orientation, and overall education level of women reflect social structures which differ from many developed countries. Moreover, little is known about the performance of female-owned businesses in Turkey or any entrepreneurship in the country, for that matter (Hisrich and Ozturk 1999).

Understanding women's involvement in economic life is the key to developing effective policy (Zhu and Chu 2010). Numerous researchers have investigated female entrepreneur studies to understand female entrepreneurs and their enterprises (Hisrich and Ozturk 1999; Welsh et al., 2016; Maden 2015; Boz and Ergeneli 2014; De Vita et al. 2014; Ince 2012; Cetindamar et al. 2012; Landig 2011; Gurol and Atsan 2006; Aycan 2004; Levent et al. 2003; Ufuk and Ozgen 2001; Hisrich and Ozturk 1999; Esim 1997). Gurol and Atsan (2006) explored the entrepreneurship profile of Turkish university students and made an evaluation of their entrepreneurial orientation by comparing them with non-entrepreneurially inclined students. They explained one of their findings to be due to Turkey's unique characteristics such as the significantly low rate of women entrepreneurs and the fact that women participate in working life mostly as salaried workers.

As the recognition of the importance of entrepreneurial activity for the economy and the gender gap in entrepreneurship in Turkey have increased, the profile of entrepreneurs becomes an interesting research topic (Boz and Ergeneli 2014). Increasingly, female entrepreneurs are considered as important for economic development. Not only do they contribute to employment creation and economic growth through their increasing numbers, but they also make a contribution to the diversity of entrepreneurship in the economic process (Ince 2012).

Female entrepreneurship has been recognized as an important source of economic growth. To encourage Turkish women into entrepreneurship, there are third-party online organizations which share and publicize the online success stories of Turkish female entrepreneurs. These data must be analyzed in order to understand successful female entrepreneurs.

Although researchers have analyzed emotional online customer feedback, reviews, etc., there has been very little research reported on analyzing entrepreneurial feedback. In spite of the fact that happiness has long been studied in many fields of research, there are only a few studies about happiness and entrepreneurship (Bista 2016; Moodley 2016; Lackéus 2017, Murnieks et al. 2017). Kahya Ozyirmidokuz and Stoica (2016) analyzed the world's best 100 websites for entrepreneurs according to Forbes 2015 to discover the ideal average happiness value of the entrepreneur website. There is no research which measures online happiness from successful Turkish female entrepreneurs' feedback. This study employed a mining research methodology to understand female entrepreneurs' feedback in Turkey by examining the impacts of prior experiences of successful female entrepreneurs on an online third-party organization. The aim of the research is to evaluate female entrepreneurs' emotional feedback in order to provide a general conceptual overview of the current situation in Turkey on the subject.

17.2 Application

The study comprised 69 online feedback data with successful Turkish female entrepreneurs which were collected from a third-party online organization. The organization carefully selected successful entrepreneurs to inspire and encourage Turkish female investors. Sixty nine successful female entrepreneurs expressed their feelings and ideas about being entrepreneurial women in Turkey. In addition, we also evaluated 29 online videos of these female entrepreneurs.

In order to analyze online feedback, it is converted to documents by applying natural language processing (NLP) techniques. The word vector, which is a numeric matrix (Stoica and Kahya Ozyirmidokuz 2015), is extracted after applying NLP techniques. TF-IDF (term frequency-inverse document frequency), which is a numeric statistic, is applied to online feedback to measure the importance of the tokens (Kahya Ozyirmidokuz 2014). In this phase, tokenization is applied to break up the streams of documents into tokens, which are meaningful elements. Then transform cases are used to convert words into lowercases. The unnecessary words, Turkish conjunctions, and the html codes are deleted from the word lists. We also filter tokens by length, removing all the words composed of less than two characters and more than ten characters from the documents. The Turkish Snowball stemming algorithm is used to obtain the root of the words. Consequently, the word lists are

Table 17.1 Document occurrences of the words in the word list

Translation in English	Word in Turkish	Total frequency	Document frequency
Woman	Kadın	875	69
Entrepreneur	Girişimci	303.0	69.0
Life	Hayat	243.0	69.0
Child	Çocuk	221.0	69.0
Year	Yıl	212.0	55.0
Time	Zaman	191.0	50.0
Big	Büyük	163.0	43.0
Herself	Kendi	161.0	53.0
Business	İş	160.0	41.0
Subject	Konu	156.0	45.0
Work	Çalışma	156.0	47.0
World	Dünya	134.0	41.0
Education	Eğitim	126.0	35.0
Important	Önemli	117.0	43.0
Project	Proje	115.0	32.0
Different	Farklı	114.0	43.0
Art	Sanat	108.0	24.0
Successful	Başarı	107.0	69.0
Decision	Karar	100.0	38.0
Road	Yol	96.0	40.0

extracted for each document. Thus, 3086 regular attributes (entries) were applied in 69 documents, and, in total, 250 words were extracted. Table 17.1 presents the most commonly used words and their frequencies in the final word list. Woman, life, child, year, and time are the most frequently used words in the documents. "Woman," "entrepreneur," "life," and "child" are used by all women. Also, when we also read the feedback and watch the videos, the successful women talk about their life and having a child while introducing their entrepreneurial experiences. The most interesting finding is that the word "doubt (şüphe in Turkish)" occurred in just two documents. Only two women used the word "doubt."

We translated ANEW (Bradley and Lang 1999) into Turkish to use the average emotional valences which are in the ANEW dictionary (Kahya Ozyirmidokuz and Stoica 2016). We calculated the average happiness scores per documents to measure the happiness of successful female entrepreneurs. There are two fundamental dimensions rather than a range of differing kinds of emotions (Fox 2008). First, the valence of an experienced emotion is the degree to which it is strongly positive or negative. Second, the level of arousal felt is the amount of energy perceived (e.g., from lethargic to hyperactive). Identifying valence and arousal is likely to be far easier and more reliable than identifying other types of emotion detection (Thelwall et al. 2009). Affective Norms for English Words (ANEW) was developed to provide a set of normative emotional ratings for a large number of words in the English language, in order to provide standardized materials that are available to researchers

Table 17.2 Some average valence values of words

Translation in English	Word in Turkish	Average valence
1	2	1.394
1	24	1.410
15	35	1.337
23	27	1.411
33	35	1.356

Table 17.3 The average emotional valence values of some feedback

Women's feedback number	Average valence
1	6.0023
7	6.8471
8	5.1742
12	3.3162
27	5.7228

in the study of emotion and attention (Bradley and Lang 1999). There are studies which measure online happiness from big data (Kamvar and Harris 2010; Dodds and Danforth 2010; Dodds et al. 2015) by using ANEW.

To estimate the overall valence score for a text, which we denote by ν_{text}, we determine the frequency f_i that the ith word from the ANEW study word list has in the text; we then compute a weighted average of the valence of the ANEW study words as in Eq. (17.1). The ν_i is the ANEW study's recorded average valence for word i (Dodds and Danforth 2010). The distribution of psychological valence will show us the customer's happy words. The average valence of a text is given in Eq. (17.1) (Bradley and Lang 1999).

$$\gamma_{\text{text}} = \frac{\sum_k \gamma_k - f_k}{\sum_k f_k} \tag{17.1}$$

To measure the average emotional valences of the documents, the Turkish translation of ANEW emotional valence values is used (Kahya Ozyirmidokuz and Stoica 2016). If a word which is in the word vector is in the ANEW translation dictionary, then we use that word and its frequency in the document/documents to calculate the average valence values. Some of the words in the dictionary and their average valence values are shown in Table 17.2.

Table 17.3 presents the average emotional valences of some successful women's feedback. We also order the feedback according to their average valence scores. The average valence score of 69 documents is 5.7631. According to the results, one entrepreneur's valence score is very low (3.3162). When we read the document, she describes the difficulties of her life before becoming an entrepreneur. She says "Life does not always offer people good things. Difficulties, illness, failures, losses... Negative experiences and fears have become a part of our lives. Pain is sometimes embodied, it becomes like a hand. Then I have my daughter. And suddenly I find an idea…." Some documents which have lower average valence scores point out the difficulties of being a woman in a man's world and also advise women. Documents which describe very happy female entrepreneurs generally express their happiness and dreams.

What are the factors that affect the happiness of successful female entrepreneurs? To answer this question, we selected seven very happy entrepreneurial feedback documents which have average valence scores of more than 6.7. We applied a qualitative approach. Thematic analysis, which is a widely used method of analysis in qualitative research (Braun and Clarke 2006), was applied to these seven documents to extract the common factors contributing to the success of happy female entrepreneurs. After reading the data while looking for patterns in them, we generated codes which were then used to identify themes. We applied the thematic coding qualitative research technique (Gibbs 2007; Guest et al. 2012) to the feedback data. After coding, we achieved Table 17.4, which presents some data set examples after coding. According to the study results, happy female entrepreneurs have five common categories which are also presented in Table 17.4.

Table 17.4 Categories and some samples after coding

Categories	Some coded phrases of feedback
Thinking you are doing the job you really want to do	"My life is my work, my work is my life. I am very happy and I am loving it" "You should do a job which you love, I have a job which is as good as making a cake"
Thinking that doing the job is very useful to others and/or others give very positive feedback about the job	"Making a product for kids and designing something new for kids are the most motivating points for me." All this functional creation and sharing with people makes me feel that I have a very important place in the world. What I have accomplished up to now is my self-confidence and my desire to live. I live with joy, happiness, and peace. "The fact that outgoing guests choose us again on their next trip shows that I really do my job well." "I was excited to have achieved a lot of praise from the place I designed." "I am happy if we can help others and help them to discover new things and make them healthier…" "It makes me very excited to see the individual responses of the customers when they receive my products."
Thinking successfully (has no negative thoughts about the job and thinking she will become a successful entrepreneur)	"I am proud of my work." "In the 6 years following the success of my job…" "It makes us so happy that we are in this business." "To achieve your dream of doing the job makes you a successful entrepreneur. The best ideas and the greatest sensations lie there. Moreover, the subject you love is constantly inspiring."

(continued)

Table 17.4 (continued)

Categories	Some coded phrases of feedback
Thinking her dream has come true	"I think the greatest happiness in the world is to realize your desires." "It has been my dream for 25 years…" "In life there are dreamers and those who realize their dreams. I think I've completed this task."
Having different new dreams about the future	"Now I have different dreams. To create and sell products globally in the style and level that will shape the new interpretations of the products…" My future objectives are to ensure the protection of the town, to prevent the contamination of concrete and noise pollution that destroy our coasts, and to contribute to the development of the town's social welfare (especially when we have done a lot of good work with children)
Working for happiness	"Whatever I do, I am ready to pay. As long as I'm happy." "…because this makes me happy and the meaning of life is the desire for happiness..." "It is such a joy that this belief is not over yet…"

17.3 Conclusions

Entrepreneurship is one of the most important factors that play a role in economic growth and development. In addition, it is a source of innovation and creativity. In recent years there has been an increase in the number of female entrepreneurs in Turkey, despite many problems. In order to explore the emotional feedback of female entrepreneurs, this study analyzes the impacts felt by successful Turkish female entrepreneurs of prior experiences. According to the results, we discovered five categories which happy entrepreneurial women have in common.

This research presents an introduction to the literature on the subject. Future research could be done in order to understand the relation between these five codes and the happiness of female entrepreneurs. A mixed approach could be used to implement the research to explore the relationship between happiness and successful entrepreneurs.

The limitation of the research is that it uses a translated dictionary which is not designed for Turkish. In addition, we plan to design a Turkish happiness dictionary for online research to develop a set of normative emotional ratings for the Turkish language in order to standardize materials for researchers in the field of emotion.

Acknowledgment This research was supported by Erciyes University Research Fund under the title "Formalizing and Analysing Users' Feedback to Evolve the STSs" project (Project id: FBA-2014-5364).

References

Aycan, Z., Eskin, M.: Relative contributions of childcare, spousal support, and organizational support in reducing work–family conflict for men and women: The case of Turkey. Sex Roles. **53**(7/8.), Springer), 453–471 (2005). https://doi.org/10.1007/s11199-005-7134-8
Aycan, Z.: Key success factors for women in management in Turkey. Appl. Psychol. Int. Rev. **53**, 453–477 (2004)
Bista, R.B.: Enterprises: necessity or opportunity to women empowerment and happiness: a case of western Nepal. In: Radovic-Markovic, M., et al. (eds.) Entrepreneurship: Types, Current Trends and Future Perspectives, Serbia, USA, UK: Valjevo Print, ISBN: 978-1-5323-2194-8, pp. 83–93 (2016)
Boz, A., Ergeneli, A.: Women entrepreneurs' personality characteristics and parents' parenting style profile in Turkey. Procedia Soc. Behav. Sci. **109**, 92–97 (2014)
Bradley, M.M., Lang, P.J.: Affective Norms for English Words (ANEW): Instruction Manual and Affective Ratings, Technical Report C-1, The Center for Research in Psychophysiology, University of Florida. http://www.uvm.edu/~pdodds/teaching/courses/2009-08UVM-300/docs/others/everything/bradley1999a.pdf (1999). Accessed 07 June 2017
Braun, V., Clarke, V.: Using thematic analysis in psychology. Qual. Res. Psychol. **3**(2), 77–101 (2006)
Cetindamar, D., et al.: What the numbers tell: the impact of human, family and financial capital on women and men's entry into entrepreneurship in Turkey. Entrep. Reg. Dev. **24**(1–2), 29–51 (2012)
Ciftci, M.: Türkiye'de işsizliğe çözüm önerisi olarak kadın girişimciliğin geliştirilmesi: Mikro kredi uygulamaları, (2010). 42–54, http://www.ceis.org.tr/dergiDocs/makale315.pdf. Accessed 7 June 2017
De Vita, L., et al.: Women entrepreneurs in and from developing countries: evidences from the literature. Eur. Manag. J. **32**, 451–460 (2014)
Dodds, P.S., et al.: Human language reveals a universal positivity bias, PNAS. Proc. Natl. Acad. Sci. USA. **112**, 2389–2394 (2015)
Dodds, P.S., Danforth, C.M.: Measuring the happiness of large-scale written expression: songs, blogs, and presidents. J. Happiness Stud. **11**, 441–456 (2010)
Esim, S.: Can feminist methodology reduce power hierarchies in research settings? Fem. Econ. **3**(2), 137–139 (1997)
Fox, E.: Emotion Science. Macmillan, England (2008)
Gibbs, G.R.: Thematic Coding and Categorizing. Analyzing Qualitative Data. Sage Publications, Ltd., London (2007)
Guest, G., et al.: Applied Thematic Analysis. SAGE Publications, Inc, Los Angeles (2012)
Gurol, Y., Atsan, N.: Entrepreneurial characteristics amongst university students: some insights for entrepreneurship education and training in Turkey. Educ. Train. **48**(1), 25–38 (2006)
Hisrich, R.D., Ozturk, S.A.: Women entrepreneurs in a developing economy. J. Manag. Dev. **18**(2), 114–125 (1999)
Ince, M.: Obstacles and future prospects of women entrepreneurs: the Turkish context. Economia Marche J. Appl. Econ. **31**(2) 61–72 (2012)
Kahya Ozyirmidokuz E., Stoica E.A.: Girişimci firmaların web sitelerinden duygusal bilgi çıkarımı. In: 3rd International Information Management Systems Conference (IMSC'16), İzmir, Turkey, 6–8 October 2016, pp. 25–31 (2016)
Kahya Ozyirmidokuz, E.: Analyzing unstructured Facebook social network data through web text mining: a study of online shopping firms in Turkey. Inf. Dev. **32**, 70–80 (2014)
Kamvar, S.D., Harris, J.: We feel fine and searching the emotional web. In: Proceedings of the WSDM'11, ACM 978-1-4503-0493-1/11/02, Hong Kong, China, , 9–12 February 2011, pp. 1–11 (2010)
Lackéus, M.: Does entrepreneurial education trigger more or less neoliberalism in education? Educ. Train. **59**(6), 635–650 (2017)

Landig, J.M.: Bringing women to the table: European Union funding for women's empowerment projects in Turkey. Women's Stud. Int. Forum. **34**, 206–219 (2011)

Levent, T.B., et al.: Diversity in entrepreneurship: ethnic and female roles in urban economic life. Int. J. Soc. Econ. **30**(11), 1131–1161 (2003)

Maden, C.: A gendered lens on entrepreneurship: women entrepreneurship in Turkey. Gend. Manag. Int. J. **30**(4), 312–331 (2015)

Moodley, N.: Exploring the experience of flow by portfolio entrepreneurs, Master thesis, Mini Dissertation (MBA), University of Pretoria, http://repository.up.ac.za/handle/2263/52263 (2016). Accessed 7 June 2017

Murnieks, C.Y., et al.: Does congruence with an entrepreneur social identity encourage positive emotion under environmental dynamism? J. Small Bus. Manag. 1–19 (2017). https://doi.org/10.1111/jsbm.12335

Stoica, E.A., Kahya Ozyirmidokuz, E.: Mining customer feedback documents. Int. J. Knowl. Eng. **1**(1), 68–71 (2015)

Thelwall, M., et al.: Data mining emotion in social network communication: gender differences in MySpace. J. Assoc. Form. Sci. Technol. **61**(1), Wiley Online Library, 190–199 (2009)

TUSIAD Report: Türkiye'de Girisimcilik (Entrepreneurship in Turkey) (2002). http://tusiad.org/tr/yayinlar/raporlar/item/1880-turkiyede-girisimcilik. Accessed 29 June 2017

Ufuk, H., Ozgen, O.: Interaction between the business and family lives of women entrepreneurs in Turkey. J. Bus. Ethics. Kluwer Academic Publishers. **31**, 95–106 (2001)

Welsh, D.H.B., et al.: An empirical analysis of the impact of family moral support on Turkish women entrepreneurs. J. Innov. Knowledg. **1**, 3–12 (2016)

Zhu, L., Chu, H.M.: Motivations, success factors and problems encountered by Chinese women entrepreneurs: A Factor Analysis, International Review of Business Research Papers, **6**(5), 164–180 (2010)

Chapter 18
Creative Economy and Competitiveness: Case of Ukraine

Ganna Kharlamova and Oleksandra Gumenna

Abstract The Europe 2020 strategy bases the future development of the EU on smart, sustainable growth fostering social inclusion. One of its dimensions concerns the creative economy concept. Creativity comes from the combination of ability and environment. It relates to the capacity of people to think with imagination and challenge the existing. Creativity and science become twins in the aspect of impacting the future economy development. The cultural and creative industries are important drivers of economic and social innovation in other sectors according to the European Commission agenda "An Integrated Industrial Policy for the Globalization Era – Putting Competitiveness and Sustainability at Centre Stage" (2011). The article deals with the essence of creative industries and their state of formation and development in Ukraine with exact examples. This research examines the role of the creative approach to business activity and economic development in general. First, the difference between creativity and innovation has been described. Second, foundations of creative thinking have been discussed in details. The authors attempted to analyze the connection between global competitiveness, levels of development, and the creativity index. The coefficient of rank correlation may be considered as a reliable one. In this manner, there is a connection between Countries' Creativity Index and the Global Competitive Index.

Keywords Creativity index • Creative industry • Ukraine

G. Kharlamova (✉)
Taras Shevchenko National University of Kyiv, Kyiv, Ukraine
e-mail: akharlamova@ukr.net

O. Gumenna
National University "Kyiv-Mohyla Academy", Kyiv, Ukraine

S.C. Mărginean et al. (eds.), *Emerging Issues in the Global Economy*, Springer Proceedings in Business and Economics,
https://doi.org/10.1007/978-3-319-71876-7_18

18.1 Introduction

As for today, there are a lot of opinions that countries' economies are discovering six stages (eras) during their development. The stages are determined by the main directions, resources, and products, which characterize the growth of the economy. Those stages are:

- Preindustrial (the main role depends on agriculture)
- Industrial (the main role depends on the industry)
- Postindustrial (service industries matter)
- Information economy (growth of the economy depends on information systems and technologies)
- The economy of knowledge (intangible assets and intellectual property play the main role)
- Creative or innovation society (new ideas and innovations play the main role in the process of society development) (Bozhedarnik and Vasylyk 2015)

In this way, the new approach should be based on the creative nature of economy – on the ability to conduct the combination of technologies, engineering, science, education, culture, identity, heritage, and social problems. The creative approach is based on the capitalization of human talent and intellectual potential. Accelerated progress of creative economy is based on ICT. Together they are able to accelerate the creation of strategic capacity of the national economy and become a catalyst of its modernization for creating a new high-tech economy.

The traditional thinking is connected to analysis, opinions, and disputes. And if it were the sustainable world around us, it would be enough. Therefore, accordingly, to the uncertain reality where standard decisions may appear inadequate, there is a serious need in new approaches and decisions. There is a lack of creative thinking and constructive thinking, which allow creating and finding out new ways for developing.

18.2 Literature Review

The creativity and creative thinking have been started to be actively discussed in the middle of the twentieth century. In particular, one of the first was H. Anderson (1959) who actively had studied the creativity and its development. Famous researcher of the creativity phenomenon Edward de Bono proposed the term "lateral thinking" in 1967 (Bono 2005). The theoretical analyses say that de Bono determines thinking in general meaning as the working process with the information and as the operational skill (Bono 2005). "Lateral thinking" means the process of information processing, which has been directed to change the existing stereotypical model of reality perception, making new alternative approaches to resolve some problem. Lateral thinking, including parts of divergent and convergent thinking, is a basis of the **creative process**.

Since the late 1990s of the last century, and especially in the early 2000s, the rapid growth of a number of studies on creativity and creative economy has begun. Many researchers such as Caves (2002), Howkins (2013), Bradford (2004), Hanburry (2005), Gloor (2006), Bilton (2007), Throsby (2007), Towse and Handke (2014), Edwards (2008), and many others have written about the importance of a creative approach to economics and management.

Particularly worthy to be noted are the works of Richard Florida (2002), who studies the creative class and its role in economic development. Today, the research base is concentrated on creative focus in management and in education of creative skills and creative confidence (Kelly and Kelly 2015).

Currently, the creative economy is becoming a foundation for the world economy. Present fast-paced changes in global creation processes and the introduction of inventions indicate that all of the future economies will be creative. The creativity of economy is the definition of its quality as well as efficiency. The economic measurement for creativity is its impact on business and the ability to generate and promote innovation, productivity, and economic growth.

Creativity means finding new ways of development, producing new things, new processes, and new ways. The most important is the connection between creativity and innovations, whereas creativity provides productive solutions to innovation – that is realization (commercialization) of the most viable and competitive ideas. As usual, there is always the question how to provide some creative idea in practice. In the case if the ideas of new products and services are not transformed into practice, they will not reach the market and will not capitalize, and there is no actualization for the different audience. There are hundreds of creative thoughts, but innovation means practical creativity.

According to the UN, the share of the creative economy is 3.4% of the world GDP, which is almost 1.6 trillion USD and twice the volume of annual revenues from international tourism. Annual growth rates in different countries range from 4.3% to 17.6%, exceeding twice the rate of growth of service economy and four times the growth rate of industrial production (Global Creativity Index 2017).

The volume of world exports of creative goods and services achieved an average annual growth of 8.7%. Revenue from creative industries in the EU, which employ 5.6 million people, has a growth rate 12.3% higher than the rate of revenue growth of overall economic activity. Concerning the matter of development of creative economy, the best example is Estonia, which at present has 5.7% of national product and 12% of all companies related to the creative economy (Creative Economy Report 2016).

According to the economic era changes, the role of working class as for today significantly decreased in the world. It has been dismissed by service class people. Nowadays that is the most numerous class, but it is decreasing in the economic competition because of the creative class. The number of the creative class is already about 25% of the population: as programmers, architects, coaches, scientists, engineers, designers, journalists, and advertisers. Also, managers, financiers, "close to business" persons, advocates, and doctors are in the pull. Those persons who do not use elements of creative thinking in their professional life appeared to have much fewer possibilities, especially financial.

18.3 Methodology and Empirical Results

As to the countries' problems in case of economic growth today, we should make stress on the fact that creativity and innovations are making a serious difference in the global countries' competitiveness.

According to the rating of global competitiveness created by the World Economic Forum in 2015, Ukraine lost 3 positions and changed 76 locations (2014) on 79 between 140 countries. And also Ukraine's competitive index has been decreased: 0.11 (from 4.14 to 4.03). In the same time, based on the 2015 results, Ukraine has some competitive advantages in innovations. Ukraine occupies the 29th place in the rating on availability of scientific and engineering sources, 43rd on research centers quality, and 50th on new patents. Obviously, innovations create the potential for economic growth. Both governmental and business efforts are required to grow up governmental high-tech products procurement (for today Ukraine occupies the 98th place) and to improve universities and business cooperation in the science and innovations development (74 place) (Chukhai et al. 2016).

Martin Prosperity Institute (University of Toronto, Canada) has published annual rating, which analyzes data about creativity and creativity class in different regions and countries all over the world. Global Creativity Index estimates countries taking into account three main key economic growth indicators – technologies, talents, and tolerance. In this way, during the process of plan production, it is important to define investments in the scientific research and development, researchers' quantity and patents per capita, educational level, and sociological surveys by Gallup in the case of citizens from different countries attitude to immigrants, race, and ethnic minorities and also to sexual minorities.

In 2015, Australia became the most creative country, after that the USA and New Zeeland. On top of the most creative countries, we may also discover Canada, Denmark, Finland, Sweden, Iceland, Singapore, and Netherlands. Ukraine occupies the 45th position in this list of 139 states, what is enough high result. By the way, the level of technologies and talents available in Ukraine has a good value in comparison with other countries. It should be useful to lift Ukraine up in this list. But Ukraine seriously loses in the case of Society Tolerance Index. Moreover, the double difference between Talents Index and Technology Index (24 and 43) shows that level of new developments in Ukraine is considerably lower than people quantity who possibly can provide those developments.

In the table below, there are some details about Global Competitive Index and Countries' Creativity Index; sample by GDP per capita has been provided. Ease of Doing Business Index has been determined.

Table 18.1 Global Creativity Index correlation with other global indices

Country	Technologies	Talent	Tolerance	Global Creativity Index (2015)	Country rank	Global Competitive Index (2015–2016)		GDP per capita, USD	Ease of Doing Business Index
	(1 – highest score)					Place in Rating	Rank		
Australia	7	1	4	0.970	1	21	17	43,374	14
USA	4	3	11	0.950	2	3	3	53,813	8
New Zealand	7	8	3	0.949	3	16	14	35,185	2
Canada	13	14	1	0.920	4	13	13	43,418	14
Denmark	10	6	13	0.917	5	12	12	44,169	3
Finland	5	3	20	0.917	6	8	8	39,501	10
Sweden	11	8	10	0.915	7	9	9	44,926	8
Iceland	26	2	2	0.913	8	29	23	41,976	19
Singapore	7	5	23	0.896	9	2	2	80,003	1
Netherlands	20	11	6	0.889	10	5	5	46,399	28
Norway	18	12	9	0.883	11	11	11	64,877	9
Great Britain	15	20	5	0.881	12	10	10	39,092	6
Ireland	23	21	7	0.845	13	24	20	47,739	17
Germany	7	28	18	0.837	14	4	4	44,342	15
Switzerland	19	22	17	0.822	16	1	1	57,713	26
France	16	26	16	0.822	16	22	18	37,822	27
Slovenia	17	8	35	0.822	16	59	37	29,594	29
Belgium	28	18	14	0.817	18	19	15	41,922	43
Spain	31	19	12	0.811	19	33	26	33,630	33
Austria	4	3	11	0.950	20	23	19	44,911	21
Hong Kong	32	32	30	0.715	21	7	7	54,030	5
Italy	25	31	38	0.715	22	48	33	34,816	45
Portugal	35	36	22	0.710	23	38	28	28,141	23
Japan	2	58	39	0.708	24	6	6	36,314	34
Luxembourg	20	48	32	0.696	25	20	16	92,697	61
Uruguay	48	45	7	0.688	26	73	40	…	92
Argentina	48	35	19	0.681	27	106	45	18,046	121
Hungary	34	33	41	0.673	28	63	38	24,216	42
Brazil	27	68	15	0.667	29	75	41	14,874	116
Israel	3	28	93	0.665	30	27	22	32,444	53
South Korea	1	50	70	0.660	31	26	21	34,021	4
Nicaragua	56	–	27	0.631	32	108	46	…	125
Estonia	33	16	87	0.625	33	30	24	26,406	16
Chile	56	39	31	0.611	34	35	27	22,583	48
Czech Republic	29	30	80	0.609	35	31	25	29,530	36
Costa Rica	47	61	20	0.607	36	52	35	…	58

(continued)

Table 18.1 (continued)

Country	Technologies	Talent	Tolerance	Global Creativity Index (2015)	Country rank	Global Competitive Index (2015–2016)		GDP per capita, USD	Ease of Doing Business Index
	(1 – highest score)					Place in Rating	Rank		
Belarus	41	8	97	0.598	37	…	–	…	44
Russia	22	15	123	0.579	38	45	31	25,364	51
South Africa	30	62	57	0.564	39	49	34	12,859	73
Latvia	54	22	77	0.563	40	44	30	23,397	22
Cuba	94	17	37	0.556	41	…	–	…	…
Laos	–	97	23	0.555	42	…	–	…	134
Malta	73	49	25	0.550	43	48	32	…	80
Ecuador	43	90	25	0.532	44	76	42	…	117
Ukraine	**43**	**24**	**105**	**0.518**	**45**	**79**	**43**	**8709**	**83**
Poland	46	25	101	0.516	46	41	29	24,462	25
Montenegro	51	34	83	0.516	46	70	39	…	46
Bulgaria	78	38	47	0.505	48	54	36	16,139	38
Belize	–	88	48	0.504	49	…	–	…	120
Jamaica	42	79	49	0.502	50	86	44	…	64

Source: http://martinprosperity.org/media/Global-Creativity-Index-2015.pdf; http://worldcompetitiveness.imd.org/countryprofile

At first sight, it may seem that there is no obvious connection between those indicators, but we are going to check our hypothesis (Table 18.1).

Now we will try to determine whether there is a relationship between the Creativity Index and Global Competitive Index using rank correlation and Spearman correlation coefficient (ρ):

$$\rho = 1 - \frac{6\sum a^2}{n\left(n^2 - 1\right)} \tag{18.1}$$

To calculate this coefficient, we should know quantitative (or qualitative) features for studied series of values, defining conditional rejection (the rank difference by line) and summarizing conditional deviations to square and defining sum of squares conditional deviations and calculating correlation coefficient (taking into consideration only 46 countries in case of absence of more details for those 4 countries in the list):

$$\rho = 1 - \left[\left(6^{*}5361\right) / \left(97336 - 46\right)\right] = 0.67 \tag{18.2}$$

Then we are checking the result credibility for the discovered coefficient using t-criteria Students. Having ten and more observations, evaluation of the significance can be provided by the formula below:

$$t = \rho\sqrt{\frac{n-2}{1-\rho^2}} \tag{18.3}$$

In our case the discovered meaning is t = 5993.

In this way, using t-Students' table (n′ = 44), compare the calculated value to the Student table meaning. In this case, table value with the level of significance determined as 0.95 is equal to 0.31. Therefore, the coefficient of rank correlation may be considered as a reliable one. In this manner, there is a connection between Countries' Creativity Index and Global Competitive Index.

Despite the growing role of creativity in an economy, we should declare (and that is not a pleasure) that for today, more people are thinking with templates. The theme of future education was risen during the World Forum 2016 in Davos. One of the Wikipedia creators, entrepreneur Jimmy Wales, has noted that formal education is so traditional that in most cases we do not react on children creativity and do not use new technologies in this way. Humanity needs to change the global approach to the study processes, needs to understand how to involve students, and needs to help in developing individual creativity. To support this thesis, Professor of the Public Understanding of Philosophy at the University of Sheffield, Angela Hobbs, notes: there is strong need to go away from the opinion that education is the process of knowledge transfer and consider the education as a skill to ask; as a critical thinking – discussions and debates; as a learning of other cultures and cooperation with people all over the world; and as an active creative dialogue. The creative economy not only requires new and rapidly changing skills, but it requires a completely new approach to education in which collaborative learning and mutual respect between the traditional disciplines of arts, science, and technology will be crucial.

A cluster of creative industries begins to form in Ukraine – it is the industry originating from individual creativity, skill, and talent and has the potential to create wealth and jobs through the generation and economic implementation of intellectual property.

Today, in the EU, types of economic activity are being categorized according to statistical classification (adopted by the European Parliament and by the Council), relating to the creative industries, into:

- Publishing production of films
- Videos and television programs, soundtracks, and music publishing
- Development and broadcasting of events
- Computer programming, consultation, and related activities
- Media services
- Architectural and engineering activities
- Scientific research and development
- Advertising and market research

Table 18.2 Creative economy concept and its components

The concept and components of the creative economy	Characteristic
Creative economy	Creative people are present in all sectors of the economy
Creative industry	Business that creates added value/value in the sector
Creative and cultural sectors	Organizations and people who create the cultural and creative products
Creative/cultural clusters	Geographical networks, which concentrate creative and cultural activities
Cultural hub	Multi-consumer centers or areas – local points for the development of creative entrepreneurship and incubation of ideas and products

Source: Creative Economy Report

- Other professional, scientific, and technical activities
- Art and entertainment events
- Sport events

These sectors of economic activity are defined as knowledge-intensive service sectors and services with high added value (Table 18.2).

The current state of the formation of creative industries in Ukraine reflects their urban orientation (centers of development are major Ukrainian cities – Kiev, Lviv, Dnipro, Odessa, Kharkiv, Zaporizhzhya, etc.) and their cluster model of organization (IT, art, education, design). At the same time, Ukraine has not yet created a complete infrastructure of creative industries; however various organizational creative hubs are being actively developed: co-working spaces, workshops, incubators, laboratories, and clusters. These new spaces allow a greater number of people to efficiently realize and develop their talents and creativity.

Today the regions of Ukraine have already seen successful attempts to create clusters of creative industries (Foresight of Economy of Ukraine 2016). Here are some of them.

In Lviv, the work is going on the implementation of an art cluster "Jam Factory." Now it is a free place for lectures, open-air film screenings, and cinema workshop, where a professional team of artists from Sweden, Belarus, and Ukraine teaches young people to make films.

In Ivano-Frankivsk, a concept of revitalization is being worked out for plant "Prompribor" with its transformation into a hub of creativity and knowledge. The idea is to fill it with new features: modern informal education, contemporary art, new economy, and urban studies.

A network is being developed for ICT co-working under the brand iHUB (business incubator). Currently, it has workshops open in Kiev, Lviv, Vinnytsia, Chernihiv, and Ivano-Frankivsk. iHUB is a network of centers of innovation and entrepreneurship, which gives access to education, communities, investors, and space for work for tech companies in Eastern Europe.

Another center of attraction for the creative class in Kiev last year was Art-Works "Platforma," also a co-working space. Its description from the official website: "A creative cluster in Kiev, a space of opportunities that connects people, ideas and work. A promising center for IT development, education, music, design, fashion and art. The concept of 'city within a city', designed for work and leisure."

Worth attention is a Ukrainian business school "SELab," which is an intensive modular course on the basis of social entrepreneurship for those who are starting their own business or developing and improving their social enterprise. The school is designed for those seeking to build a social enterprise in Ukraine to become a "pioneer" in the field and create new jobs and opportunities.

A large number of cultural projects are being developed, more specifically private educational organizations, based on the principle of social entrepreneurship. But beyond the formal definition, those are also an open space for people with similar interests and open communication.

A library of creative economy was opened, where a translation of the book from David Parish *T-Shirts and Suits: A Guide to the Business of Creativity* was presented. It is a progressive work relevant enough for the given state of maturity of the current creative business in Ukraine.

Different educational programs are being actively developed, which help prepare teenagers for maturity and finding their own way in the innovative economy of the future. Next Generation Business School is an educational platform of innovation economy and creative entrepreneurship for young people founded by the Agency for Cultural Strategies in partnership with Smart Education Agency.

Another one is Creative Management Camp, which is a course for managers of cultural projects and urban entrepreneurs which was first held in 2015. The target audience is event managers; marketers; PR people; managers of cultural departments; organizers of festivals, concerts, and educational initiatives; project managers; and art directors.

Overall, Ukraine has people emotionally charged, talented people, and people with different cultural backgrounds. This is a great strong point. However, there is an important weakness, which is the inability to present themselves, sell, and build large ecosystems. We usually can do something in a small group. Hence the boom in places, like co-working, already exists almost in every regional town.

Therefore, Ukraine should display the creative orientation of economy and culture in its economic and political documents.

Specifically, in the foresight for Ukraine, there are proposed sectors and clusters of the future economy, where the share of the creative economy by 2020 should be 26%, and by 2030, this share could rise up to 42% (see Fig. 18.1).

The first attempt of systematic display preconditions to build and develop creative industry is the development of the strategic document "Doctrine of sustainable development: Ukraine 2030" (Gumenna and Kharlamova 2017). This is important because today, the adopted plan in Ukraine for cultural redistribution and survival may lead to extinction, while only a culture of creativity and collaboration (creative) can lead the nation to prosperity.

Overall, the support for the creative sector is the simultaneous development of five core components:

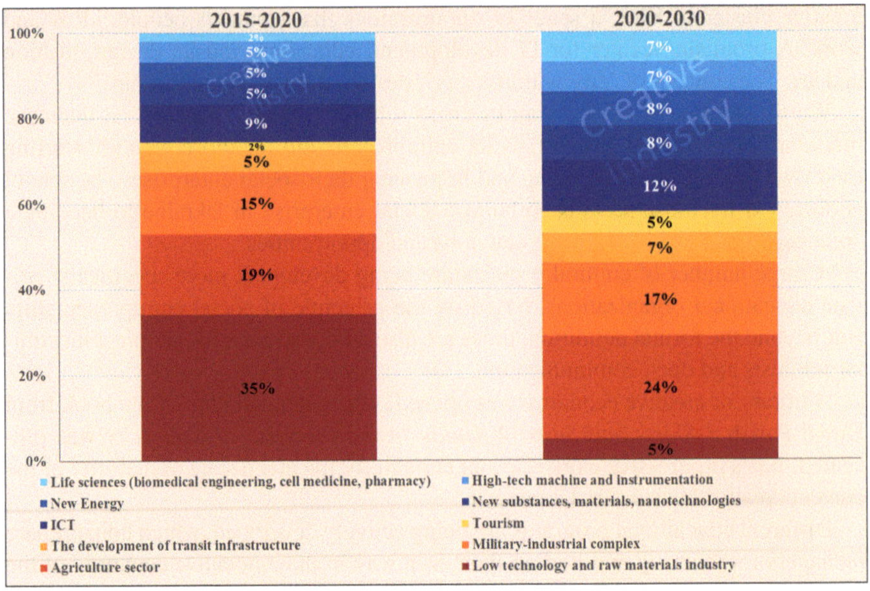

Fig. 18.1 Forecast of sectors/clusters of economy of Ukraine 2030 (Source: Foresight of Economy of Ukraine 2016)

1. Policy making and advocacy and activity of professional networks and associations
2. Strengthening institutional capacity, especially through special education and lifelong learning
3. Work of incubators and accelerators
4. Creation of clusters and hubs
5. Internationalization (focus on global markets and global creative scene)

Effective economic realization of the creative potential of Ukraine requires development and implementation of systematic measures, as shown in Fig. 18.2.

18.4 Conclusion

Thus, the development of the creative industry in Ukraine involves forming spaces and institutions that bring together technology, engineering, science, education, culture, identity, and heritage in order to create a new meaningfulness and solving social problems.

Jamie Anderson, a member of the top 25 management thinkers in the version of Business Strategy Review, highlights the "three pillars of creativity" – inspiration, intuition, and imagination (Skiba 2017). At his training of creativity, he said that the secret of most successful people is that they no longer trust their feelings, not logic.

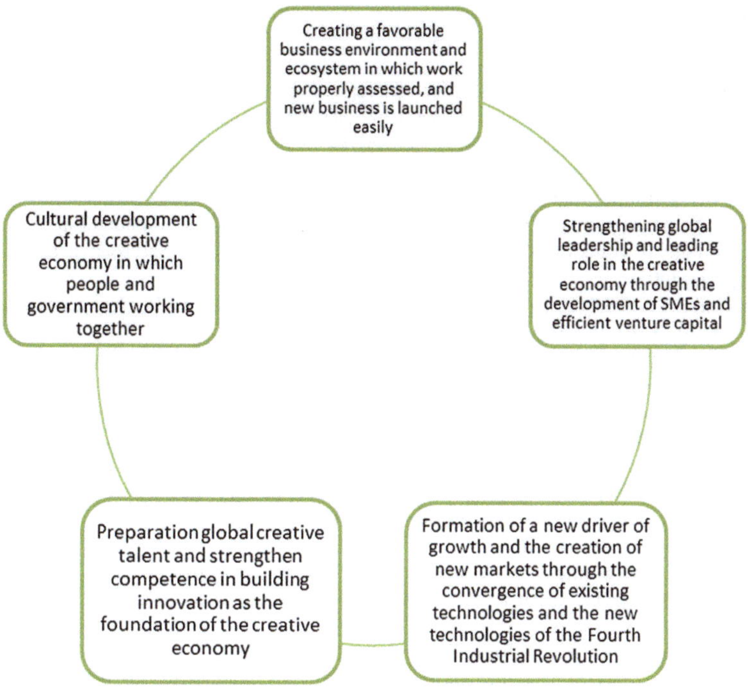

Fig. 18.2 Systematic measures to stimulate development of creative industry in Ukraine (Source: Gumenna and Kharlamova 2017)

Intuition is the emotional aspect of the process of personal creativity. Imagination is the final step in active thinking. What has come to us in the form of a spark and became realistic because of the feeling then creates a picture. In the process of creativity, we let the picture grow, and give it a clear outline and real form, so you can imagine the idea. Imagination is the ability to think and visualize ideas' endpoint, making it visible. Move forward – that is currently the main task for Ukrainian business. Anderson emphasizes that today, creativity is a key skill for leaders and organizations, which helps not only to adapt to changes but also to create new industries and markets. And the country needs to form a team that would be engaged in practical drafting strategic "road map" of innovation.

To reach creativity people should challenge their established rules and statements (Asian Development Bank 2014; Creative Vitality Index 2017). After moving through the lowed path, our mind often produces the sight of hidden opportunities that are out of it. Today, the creative energy is one of the most valuable resources of mankind. It can help us find fresh solutions to the most difficult tasks. People with high creative confidence have a valid impact on the environment.

References

Anderson, H.: Creativity and Its Cultivation. Addresses Presented at the Interdisciplinary Symposia on Creativity (1957/58), 1st edn. Harper, Row, New York (1959)

Asian Development Bank 2014. Creative Productivity Index: Analysing Creativity and Innovation in Asia. Manila: ADB. http://www.adb.org/publications/creative-productivity-index-analysing-creativity-and-innovation-asia (2014). Accessed 10 Aug 2017

Bilton, C.: Management and Creativity, 1st edn. Blackwell Publishing, Malden (2007)

Bono, E.: Lateral Thinking: Creative Thinking Textbook (trans. by Samsonova P.A.). Minsk. Poppuri. (2005)

Bozhedarnik, T., Vasylyk, N.: Formation and development company's creative management. Economist. **3**(March), 37–39 (2015)

Bradford, N.: Creative Cities, 1st edn. Canadian Policy Research Networks, Ottawa (2004)

Caves, R.: Creative Industries, 1st edn. Harvard University Press, Cambridge, MA (2002)

Chukhai, A., Strakhova, V., Ivanov, P: Ukraine in global competitive rate 2015. http://reforms.in.ua/ua/news/ukrayina-u-reytyngu-globalnoyi-konkurentospromozhnosti-2015 (2016). Accessed 11 Aug 2017

Creative Economy Report: Widening local development pathways 2013. Special edition. UNDP. http://ssc.undp.org/content/ ssc/news/events/widening_local_ development_ pathways.html (2016). Accessed 9 Aug 2017

Creative Vitality Index. https://cvi.westaf.org/ (2017). Accessed 15 Aug 2017

Edwards, D.: Artscience: Creativity in the Post- Google Generation. Harvard University Press, Cambridge, MA (2008)

Florida, R.: The Creative Class. Basic Books, New York (2002)

Foresight of Economy of Ukraine: Term (2015–2020) and long term (2020–2030) time horizons, "KPI named Igor Sikorsky" World Data Center for Geoinformatics and Sustainable Development. http://ied.kpi.ua/wp-content/uploads/2015/10/Foresight-2015.pdf (2016). Accessed 15 Jun 2017

Global Creativity Index: Ukraine became 45th among 139 countries. http://www.5.ua/suspilstvo/Hlobalnyi-indeks-kreatyvnosti-Ukraina-stala-45iu-zi-139-krain-95726.html (2017). Accessed 15 Jul 2017

Gloor, P.: Swarm Creativity, 1st edn. Oxford University Press, New York (2006)

Gumenna O., Kharlamova G., etc.: Ukraine 2030: the doctrine of sustainable development. Lviv. Calvary (2017)

Hanburry, B.: The creative revolution and rise of the democratic media. BSc (Hons) Medialab Arts. (2005)

Howkins, J.: The Creative Economy, 1st edn. Penguin, London (2013)

Kelly, T., Kelly, D.: Creative Confidence. How to Release and Implement Personal Creative Forces. Azbuka Business, Moscow (2015)

Skiba, M.: Creative industry in Ukraine: to stand, to educate. http://tyzhden.ua/Society/158758 (2017). Accessed 12 Jul 2017

Throsby, D.: Preferred work patterns of creative artists. J. Econ. Financ. **31**, 395–402 (2007). https://doi.org/10.1007/bf02885729

Towse, R., Handke, C.: Handbook on the Digital Creative Economy, 1st edn. Edward Elgar, Cheltenham (2014)

Chapter 19
Dynamics of the Transaction Sector in the Countries of the Eurasian Economic Union

Galina Litvintseva and Nadezhda Gakhova

Abstract The paper deals with the gross output and GDP dynamics along with the trends in the development of the base (transformation) and transaction sectors of the economy including changes of their industry leaders in the countries of the Eurasian Economic Union (EAEU). Gross value added growth rates in both sectors of the economies of these countries are studied and analyzed. Transaction costs of the economy are measured as a share of the transaction sector gross output in the gross output of the economy using North-Wallis's method and the approach proposed by the author. The impact of transaction costs on the GDP dynamics in Russia and some EAEU countries is also shown. Some conclusions about the trends in the transaction sector change and its effect on the GDP dynamics are made based on calculations. These trends indicate the heterogeneity of these countries' economies and their gradual modernization under the influence of market reforms and integration processes.

Keywords Gross output • GDP • Productivity of economy • Transaction sector • Members of the Eurasian Economic Union

19.1 Introduction

The development of the transaction sector in the countries of the Eurasian Economic Union is of particular interest due to the activation of integration processes in the Eurasian space. These countries include Armenia, Belarus, Kazakhstan, Kyrgyzstan, and the Russian Federation.

G. Litvintseva (✉) • N. Gakhova
Novosibirsk State Technical University, Novosibirsk, Russia
e-mail: litvintseva-g@mail.ru

S.C. Mărginean et al. (eds.), *Emerging Issues in the Global Economy*, Springer Proceedings in Business and Economics,
https://doi.org/10.1007/978-3-319-71876-7_19

Studies of the transaction structure of the EAEU countries' economy are few and uncoordinated and are carried out based mainly on current prices of the major macroindicators. Note that the transaction sector includes wholesale and retail trade, real estate transactions, finance, insurance, public management, and military security.

At the macroeconomic level, transaction costs (TAC) measured as a share of the transaction sector in the main macroeconomic indicators are an important parameter characterizing the rates, proportions, and peculiarities of modern economy.

19.2 Literature Review

D. North and G. Wallis were the first to measure directly transaction costs at the macroeconomic level based on the transaction sector share in the US GNP over the period of 1870–1970. They took into account the total volume of transaction services consisting of two parts: (1) services of the transaction sector including wholesale and retail trade, insurance, banking, etc. and (2) transaction services rendered within the transformation sector, i.e., administrative expenses along with supply and sales costs in various industries of this sector. Besides, the authors singled out private and public transaction sectors. According to calculations based on national accounts, the share of transaction services rendered by the private sector in the US GNP increased from 23% in 1870 to 41% in 1970, while in the public sector, it increased from 3.6% in 1870 to 13.9% in 1970, which on the whole shows the growth from 26.1% to 54.7% (North and Wallis 1986).

The paper published by V. Kokorev in 1996 was one of the first publications in post-Soviet Russia devoted to the subject. Transaction costs were measured by the share of overhead production costs in the structure of costs, and the author noted their growth in 1991–1993 (Kokorev 1996). In 2001, multiplicative transaction costs were measured based on the data of the interindustry balance of the Russian national account system over 1990–1997. Multiplicative TACs increased in the period under study in various industries from 10–20% to 30–50% and more (Blokhin 2001).

As for the EAEU countries, the first data on the GDP dynamics of the transaction sector were published in Armenia (Erznkyan and Kazbakova 2002). The share of the transaction sector in the GDP of Armenia grew by 1.72 times in the period of 1990–2000. This indicator is much lower than in Russia and other post-Soviet countries in view of a higher value of this sector share in 1990, which was approximately two times higher in Armenia.

An analysis of the GDP production structure of Kyrgyzstan over the period of 1990–2000 showed that in 1990 the share of the base sector amounted to 91%, while the share of the transaction sector was 9% in 2000 and 79% and 21%, respectively. An increase in the share of the transaction sector was caused by the development of trade and public catering as well as management. The transaction sector in Kyrgyzstan like in Russia was developing apart from the base sector suppressing it (Bazarbaeva 2013).

As concerns Belarus, overhead costs act as transaction costs, and the cost structure in the transformation sector of the economy in 1990–1998 is considered in the study. A considerable growth (by more than four times) is caused by such factors as an adaptation of enterprises to market conditions, underdevelopment of the market infrastructure, privatization processes, creation of new companies, etc. (Lemeshchenko 2015). It is interesting to note that in our opinion, the transaction sector boom occurred in 1995 when the structure of the post-Soviet countries' economies including Russia changed radically and in the 1998 crisis year.

19.3 Research Methods

Along with using the well-known North-Wallis's method, TACs can be measured at the macrolevel as a share of the gross output (and its components) of the transaction sector in the gross output (and its components) of the economy as a whole, which was proposed in the paper published in 2003 (Litvintseva 2003) and used further in the analysis of the economy of modern Russia (Litvintseva and Gakhova 2016).

Both approaches will be used in the present study to estimate changes in the transaction sector in modern economies of the EAEU countries. Indicators of national account systems of the five countries given in the EAEU statistics over 5 years make up the information base. The data were taken in monetary units of corresponding countries (National accounts 2015).

To analyze the influence of transaction costs on GDP, such indicators were calculated as gross output unit costs in comparable prices of 2010, gross output and its components growth rates in 2010–2014 (comparable prices of 2010, % to 2010), correlation coefficients between time series of costs per unit (in prices of 2010), and growth rates of real gross output and its components of both the economy as a whole and its sectors in 2010–2014. Some essential positive and negative correlations were revealed. To determine essential correlations, approximation functions with high coefficients of determination R2 were chosen, and appropriate diagrams were built.

19.4 Gross Output Structure and Transaction and Base Sectors of EAEU Countries

An analysis of the gross output (GO) dynamics of the EAEU countries' economies in terms of GDP and intermediate consumption (IC) has shown that an evident decrease in relative productivity of the economy (a share of gross value added (GVA) or GDP in gross output) is observed only in the Russian Federation. The rest EAEU countries do not show such a trend. Besides, a decrease in real GDP as compared to 2010 is observed only in the Russian Federation (Table 19.1).

Table 19.1 Dynamics of real GDP production (2010 = 100) and its share in the gross output in the economies of EAEU countries (in current prices, in percentage to total)

Indicator	2010	2011	2012	2013	2014
Armenia					
GDP and GO share	63.0	61.0	61.0	63.0	63.0
GDP growth rates	100.0	104.7	112.2	115.9	120.0
Belarus					
GDP and GO share	41.0	39.0	40.0	43.0	45.0
GDP growth rates	100.0	105.5	107.3	108.4	110.2
Kazakhstan					
GDP and GO share	57.0	57.0	57.0	59.0	59.0
GDP growth rates	100.0	107.2	112.1	118.6	123.5
Kyrgyzstan					
GDP and GO share	42.0	42.0	42.0	43.0	43.0
GDP growth rates	100.0	106.0	105.9	117.4	121.7
Russia					
GDP and GO share	49.0	49.0	49.0	49.0	48.0
GDP growth rates	100.0	99.6	100.4	100.3	98.0

Industry leaders in GDP production vary greatly in the EAEU member states. In Armenia they are agriculture, forestry, and fishery (20.3% of GDP); in Belarus it is the manufacturing industry (24.5%); and in Kazakhstan and Kyrgyzstan, they are wholesale and retail trade along with transport vehicle and motorcycle repair (17.3, 19.5, and 17.3%, respectively).

The indicators of gross output, intermediate consumption, and gross value added of the base and transaction sectors of the EAEU member states reveal essential differences in their productivity (Table 19.2).

The highest relative productivity of the base sector is seen in Armenia, and the lowest one is observed in Belarus and Kyrgyzstan. A relative productivity of the transaction sector is higher in Armenia and Belarus and lower in Russia. Note that a relative productivity of the base sector grew by 1 pp., while a relative productivity of the transaction sector decreased by the same value. Real estate business in Armenia, research and engineering activities in Kazakhstan, and education in Belarus, Kyrgyzstan, and Russia were industry leaders in relative productivity in 2014.

The following aspects (Fig. 19.1) characterize the GVA dynamics of the base sector (BAS) and the transaction sector (TAS).

In Armenia average annual growth rates of the base sector and the economy as a whole are approximately equal and lower than in the transaction sector (GVA growth of the economy by 19.9%). The GVA of the transaction sector of Armenia increased by a factor of 1.22 over the period under study. The GVA of the transaction sector of Belarus increased by a factor of 1.21, while the GVA dynamics of the base sector is characterized by lower average annual growth rates than the rates of the economy and the transaction sector (the GVA growth of the economy by 9.3%). In 2014, the transaction sector of Kazakhstan produced GVA by a factor of 1.37 greater than in 2010. The GVA of the base sector increased only by a factor of 1.18

Table 19.2 Relative productivity of two sectors in the EAEU member states (GVA of GO %)

Indicator	2010	2011	2012	2013	2014
Armenia					
Base sector	62	61	60	60	59
Transaction sector	69	69	70	77	76
Belarus					
Base sector	36	34	35	38	40
Transaction sector	71	70	70	69	71
Kazakhstan					
Base sector	55	52	52	52	54
Transaction sector	65	67	71	73	69
Kyrgyzstan					
Base sector	38	39	39	38	38
Transaction sector	62	62	60	65	66
Russia					
Base sector	42	43	43	43	43
Transaction sector	61	61	61	60	60

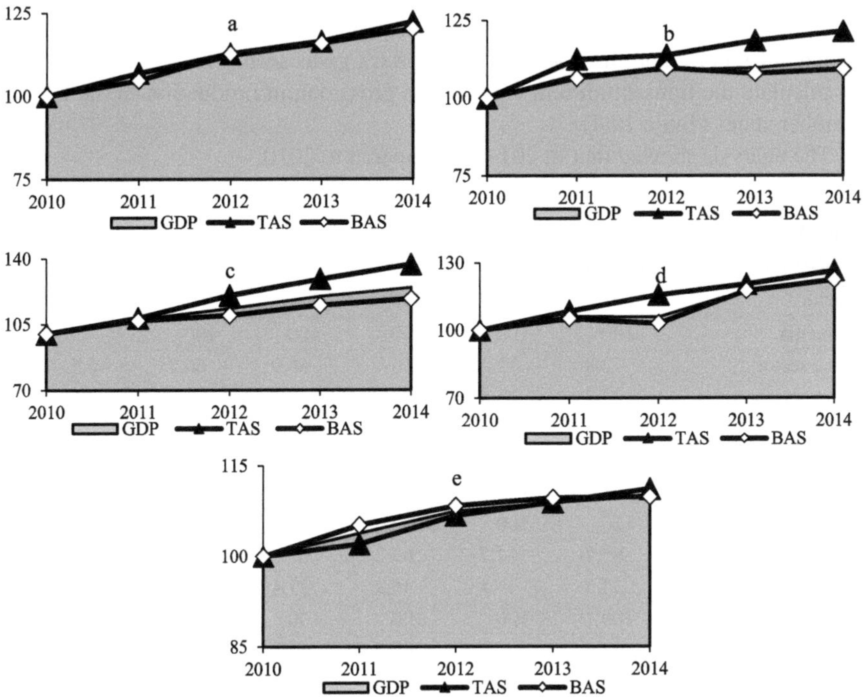

Fig. 19.1 Dynamics of GVA production in the two sectors of the economy (%, 2010 = 100): (**a**) Armenia; (**b**) Belarus; (**c**) Kazakhstan; (**d**) Kyrgyzstan; (**e**) Russia

over the period studied, which is lower than the GVA growth of the economy as a whole. The dynamics of the base sector in Kyrgyzstan is characterized by high growth rates (by a factor of 1.22 over the period), while the GVA growth rates in the transaction sector were higher and amounted to a factor of 1.26. The GVA growth of the base sector in Russia was 9.8% (similar to the economy as a whole). The transaction sector of GVA increased by a factor of 1.11.

19.5 Changes in Transaction Costs at the Macrolevel and their Influence on GDP in some EAEU Member States

Transaction costs in the EAEU member states' economies calculated by the North-Wallis's method decreased by 1.4 pp. only in Russia over the period studied and amounted to 41.4% in 2014 (Table 19.3).

In spite of this, the highest transaction costs are observed in Russia. In Armenia, Belarus, Kazakhstan, and Kyrgyzstan, shares of the transaction sector increased. In Kyrgyzstan the minimum value was registered in 2011 (30.5) and in the rest member states in 2010. The greatest growth of the transaction sector was observed in Armenia (6.5 pp), and the lowest growth (58.6%) was seen in Russia in 2014. Let us calculate the transaction unit costs of the gross output production in the EAEU member states (Table 19.4).

The analysis showed that in 2014 as compared to 2010:

Table 19.3 GDP production structure in terms of the base and transaction sectors of the economy in 2010–2014 (current prices in percentage to the total)

Sector	2010	2011	2012	2013	2014	Growth
Armenia	100	100	100	100	100	
Base sector	72.8	72.4	716	66.9	66.2	−6.5
Transaction sector	27.2	27.6	28.4	33.1	33.8	6.5
Belarus	100	100	100	100	100	
Base sector	70.5	67.9	70.2	69.1	68.7	−1.8
Transaction sector	29.5	32.1	29.8	30.9	31.3	1.8
Kazakhstan	100	100	100	100	100	
Base sector	65.7	64.7	63.2	62.6	61.7	−4.0
Transaction sector	34.3	35.3	36.8	37.4	38.3	4.0
Kyrgyzstan	100	100	100	100	100	
Base sector	67.6	69.5	67.7	66.8	65.0	−2.6
Transaction sector	32.4	30.5	32.3	33.2	35.0	2.6
Russia	100	100	100	100	100	
Base sector	57.2	59.7	59.1	58.9	58.6	1.4
Transaction sector	42.8	40.3	40.9	41.1	41.4	−1.4

Table 19.4 Structure of unit costs of gross output production in terms of the transaction sectors in 2010–2014 (current prices in percentage to gross output)

Indicator	2010	2011	2012	2013	2014	Growth
Transaction sector in Armenia:						
IC	7.7	7.6	7.7	6.5	6.7	−1.0
GVA	17.4	17.4	17.8	21.5	21.6	4.2
GO (TAC)	25.1	25.0	25.5	28.0	28.4	3.2
Transaction sector in Belarus:						
IC	5.0	5.5	5.2	6.0	6.1	1.1
GVA	12.5	12.9	12.1	13.6	14.5	2.1
GO (TAC)	17.5	18.4	17.3	19.6	20.7	3.2
Transaction sector in Kazakhstan:						
IC	10.6	9.6	8.5	8.1	10.0	−0.7
GVA	19.9	20.0	21.1	21.9	22.7	2.8
GO (TAC)	30.5	29.6	29.6	30.0	32.6	2.1
Transaction sector in Kyrgyzstan:						
IC	8.5	8.2	9.4	7.9	8.0	−0.5
GVA	14.1	13.3	14.2	14.6	15.6	1.5
GO (TAC)	22.6	21.5	23.6	22.5	23.6	1.0
Transaction sector in Russia:						
IC	13.2	12.5	13.0	13.3	13.5	0.24
GVA	20.9	19.7	20.0	20.0	20.0	−0.85
GO (TAC)	34.1	32.2	32.9	33.3	33.5	−0.61

- Unit transaction costs in Armenia grew by 3.2 pp. and amounted to 28.4 lumas per 1 Armenian dram of GO (the unit GO of the base sector decreased by the same value).
- Unit transaction costs in Belarus grew by 3.2 pp. and amounted to 20.7 kopeks per 1 Belarusian ruble of GO (the unit GO of the base sector decreased by the same value).
- Unit transaction costs in Kazakhstan grew by 2.1 pp. and amounted to 32.6 tyiyn per 1 tenge of GO (the unit GO of the base sector decreased by the same value).
- Unit transaction costs in Kyrgyzstan grew by 1.0 pp. and amounted to 23.6 tyiyn per 1 som of GO (the unit GO of the base sector decreased by the same value).
- Unit transaction costs in Russia decreased by 0.61 pp. and amounted to 33.5 kopeks per 1 ruble of GO (the unit GO of the base sector increased by the same value).

Thus, using both the method proposed by the author and the North and Wallis method, it was shown that transaction costs in the economies of the EAEU member states increased with the exception of Russia where they decreased at the highest absolute level.

The calculation of the GO production unit costs of the countries in comparable prices showed that transaction costs in 2014 as compared to 2010 increased after some fluctuation in Belarus, Kazakhstan, and Russia, while they decreased in

Table 19.5 Correlation coefficients of unit costs (prices of 2010) and volumes of production of real GO in terms of its components in Armenia

	Unit costs per one monetary unit of GO							
	Base sector Transaction sector Economy as a whole							
Sector	IC	GVA	GO	IC	GVA	GO	IC	GVA
Base								
IC	0.997	−0.786	0.924	−0.868	−0.705	−0.924	0.821	−0.821
GVA	0.986	−0.718	0.951	−0.895	−0.723	−0.951	0.769	−0.769
GO	0.994	−0.755	0.938	−0.882	−0.714	−0.938	0.798	−0.798
Transaction								
IC	−0.346	−0.228	−0.638	0.748	−0.250	0.638	0.249	−0.249
GVA	0.999	−0.775	0.933	−0.885	−0.674	−0.933	0.805	−0.805
GO	0.935	−0.920	0.751	−0.656	−0.819	−0.751	0.959	−0.959
Economy as a whole								
IC	0.986	−0.843	0.873	−0.800	−0.762	−0.873	0.882	−0.882
GVA	0.990	−0.721	0.955	−0.904	−0.697	−0.955	0.765	−0.765
GO	0.972	−0.826	0.863	−0.779	−0.816	−0.863	0.881	−0.881

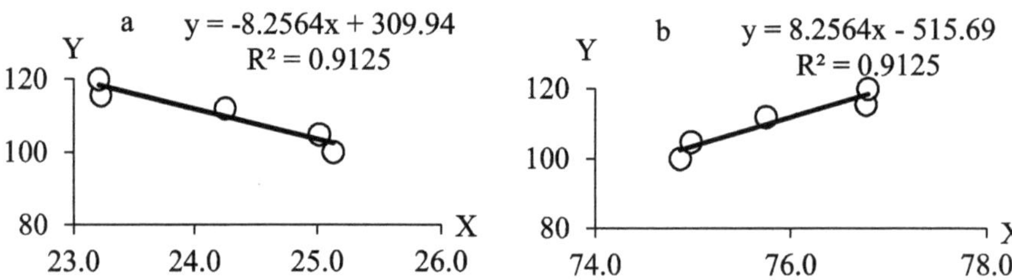

Fig. 19.2 Dependence of GDP (y, % to GDP, 2010) on gross output per unit in Armenia (x, luma per 1 Armenian dram in prices of 2010): (**a**) transaction sector; (**b**) base sector

Armenia and Kyrgyzstan. To analyze the impact of unit costs on the GO dynamics, volumes of production are calculated in terms of its components in comparable prices (2010) and are expressed in percentage to 2010.

The correlation analysis of the time series of unit costs in comparable prices and growth rates of IC, GVA, and GO made it possible to determine a sufficient dependence only for Armenia because of a different structure of costs, their multidirectionality, and insufficiently long time series. The correlation coefficients have shown that unit GO and GVA of the transaction sector of Armenia have a high negative correlation with volumes of GO and GDP, while unit IC and GVA of the base sector have a high negative (GVA per unit) and positive (GO per unit) correlation (Table 19.5).

A linear function approximating the correlation between real volumes of GDP production and TACs per unit in Armenia demonstrates that the higher the transaction costs in the economy, the lower the GDP growth rates (Fig.19.2a). The GO per unit in the base sector depends directly on GDP production volumes (Fig. 19.2b).

A similar dependence was observed in Russia in 1990–2001 when the growth of GO and GVA per unit in the transaction sector led to the decline in volumes of GO and GDP production in the Russian economy (Litvintseva 2003). In 2002–2014, the

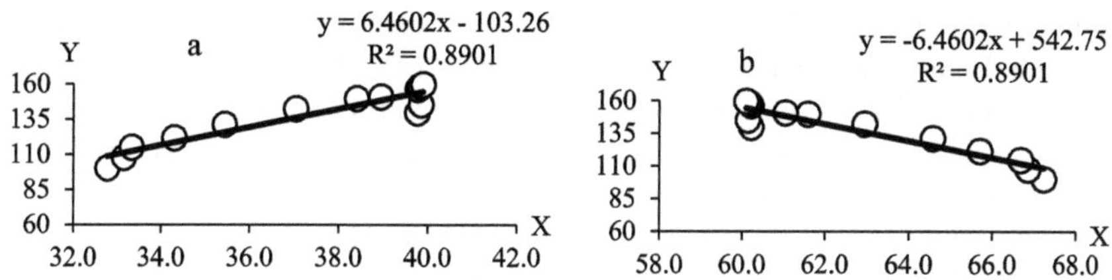

Fig. 19.3 Dependence of GDP (y, % to GDP, 2002) on gross output per unit in Russia (x, kopeks per 1 ruble in prices of 2002): (**a**) transaction sector; (**b**) base sector

situation reversed, i.e., based on calculations (National accounts of Russia 2015), the growth of TAC and GVA per unit in the transaction sector leads to the growth of GO and GDP production volumes and vice versa (National accounts of Russia 2010). A linear function approximating the correlation between real volumes of GDP production and TACs per unit is shown in Fig. 19.3 (Litvintseva and Gakhova 2016).

Costs per unit in the base sector and all their components are in inverse relationship with GDP production volumes (Fig. 19.3b). The GVA per unit in the base sector has the greatest negative impact on the GDP growth (the correlation coefficient is −0.968).

Thus, the transaction and base sectors of the economy of modern Russia have an opposite effect on the development of the economy by increasing gross output volumes by 1 ruble of GO in the economy. Growth of transaction services by 1 ruble of GO results in the growth of gross output volumes and its components, namely, intermediate consumption and GDP. An increase in gross output volumes by 1 ruble of GO in the base sector leads to a GDP decline. In the long-term period, any significant dependence between an absolute productivity of the economy (GDP production volumes) and its relative productivity (DP and GO shares) is not observed. This change of the TAC influence on GDP is caused by a radical change in the structure of the Russian economy as a result of reforms and, in recent years, of economic sanctions. In implementing a national economic policy (Gil'Mundinov et al. 2016) and harmonizing policies of the EAEU member states, it is necessary to take into account the heterogeneity of their economic development and multi-directionality of the effect of the base sectors of the economy on the main macroindicators.

19.6 Conclusions

In 2010–2014, the volume of real GDP production and relative productivity of the economy decreased only in Russia among other EAEU countries. Only Russia demonstrates some growth of the base sector share in creating the GDP of the country. The rest countries show an increase in the transaction sector share.

In 2014, industries of the transaction sector dominated in Armenia, Belarus, Kazakhstan, and Kyrgyzstan, while in Russia, industries of the base sector prevailed as leaders in relative efficiency of production. The GVA dynamics of the EAEU countries' economies can be characterized by the following aspects: (a) average annual growth rates of the base sector were lower than in the transaction sector in Armenia, Belarus, and Kazakhstan; (b) the highest growth of the transaction sector as compared to the initial period was observed in Kyrgyzstan and Kazakhstan.

Transaction costs in the EAEU countries' economies except Russia increased, which is proved by calculations using the above two methods. The retention of the economy's productivity in Armenia and its growth in Kazakhstan and Kyrgyzstan was the result of the growth of the unit GVA in the transaction sectors of these countries. An increase in the Belarus economy efficiency is caused by the growth of the unit GVA in both the base and transaction sectors. A decrease in the efficiency of the Russian economy (−0.39) was caused by the growth of the unit GVA of the base sector and a greater decrease in the unit GVA of the transaction sector.

A significant correlation found for Armenia shows that the higher the transaction costs, the lower the GDP growth rates. A similar dependence was seen in Russia in 1990–2001 when the growth of the unit GO and GVA of the transaction sector caused a decrease in the GO and GDP production in the economy of Russia. In 2001–2014, the situation reversed, i.e., the TAC growth is followed by the GO and GDP growth in the economy of Russia. These differences in the structures of the economies should be taken into account when pursuing national economic policies and harmonizing the EAEU countries' policies.

References

Bazarbaeva, R.S. (ed.): Institutional Changes in Transformational Economies of CIS Countries: Contradictions and Ways of Solution. NII IE in KEU, Bishkek (2013)

Blokhin, A.A.: Institutional aspect of the Russian reforms price analysis. Forecast. Probl. **1**, 116–136 (2001)

Erznkyan, B.A., Kazbakova, E.L.: Dynamic transaction sector and steady development strategy of Russia. In: Theory and Practice of Institutional Transformations in Russian Economy **3**, pp. 126–134. TSEMI-RAN, Moscow (2002)

Gil'Mundinov, V.M., Melnikov, V.V., Petrov, S.P.: Optimization of the Russian macroeconomic policy in 2016–2020. World Econ. Manag. **16**(4), 5–19 (2016)

Kokorev, V.: Institutional transformations in modern Russia: analysis of transactional costs dynamics. Econ. Quest. **12**, 61–72 (1996)

Lemeshchenko, P.S.: Institutional Economics: Theory, Policy, Practice: Teaching Aid. Misanta, Minsk (2015)

Litvintseva, G.P.: The Productivity of Economy and the Institutions at the Present Stage of Development of Russia. Science, Novosibirsk (2003)

Litvintseva, G.P., Gakhova, N.A.: Dynamics of the transaction sector of the Russian economy: as taught by D. North. J. Inst. Stud. **8**(2), 38–50 (2016)

National accounts of Russia in 2002–2009: Stat. Collection. Rosstat, Moscow (2010)

National accounts of Russia in 2007–2014: Stat. Collection. Rosstat, Moscow (2015)

National accounts. Statistics of the Eurasian Economic Union: Statistical collection, pp. 98–127 (2015)

North, D.C., Wallis, J.J.: Measuring the transaction sector in the American economy, 1870–1970. In: Engerman, S.L., Gallman, R.E. (eds.) Long-Term Factors in American Economic Growth, pp. 95–161. University of Chicago Press, Chicago (1986)

Chapter 20
Globalization Is Dead: Long Live the Globalization!?

Silvia Mărginean

Abstract Globalization was the mainstream paradigm in the last 70 years, long enough to create and explain prosperity and welfare in a connected world. Recently, there are many signs that we are reaching a turning point. From jobs, wages, and unemployment to immigrants and Brexit, all the key debates emphasize that the world is preparing for a new kind of globalization which will be less about countries and multinationals and more about people. There is no doubt that old globalization had winners and losers, but more than ever, the voice of the people who reject globalization was heard in 2016, specifically in the UK and USA. The world will have to deal with new institutions, and technologies and will have to find new indicators to measure these trends. European Integration itself, the most powerful success story of the post-War World II, is under question. The aim of this paper is to examine how, in the last year, mainstream economists and organizations reacted and contributed to the idea that the old globalization will be replaced by a new kind of globalization or if there are signs that a completely different paradigm will emerge. The methodology was to systematize the contributions as they were reflected in journals, scientific articles, conference papers, and different reliable online sources. As we emphasize in the title, the results of the review show that there are visible signs for the end of globalization as we know it and the seeds of a new form of globalization are already visible.

Keywords Globalization • Brexit • New globalization

S. Mărginean (✉)
Lucian Blaga University of Sibiu, Sibiu, Romania
e-mail: silvia.marginean@ulbsibiu.ro

S.C. Mărginean et al. (eds.), *Emerging Issues in the Global Economy*, Springer Proceedings in Business and Economics,
https://doi.org/10.1007/978-3-319-71876-7_20

20.1 Introduction

Globalization was the mainstream paradigm in the last 70 years, long enough to create and explain prosperity and welfare in a connected world. Recently, there are many signs that we are reaching a turning point. The globalization, as we learn about it in the 1990s, is based on three pillars: international trade, foreign direct investments, and ICT (information and communication technologies). The 2008–2009 crisis was a turning point for many things, including ideas and theories. During the crisis and also during the recovery, globalization was a central debate, for two reasons: some voices claim that the cause of the crisis is globalization and its rules and others say that anti-crisis measures and recovery are limiting the free trade, and foreign direct investments slow down because there is not enough capital available and the risks are too high, so the globalization looks to be in retreat.

Last year's headlines look to be connected to globalization and its rejection by people in many developed countries: Brexit, Trump victory in the USA, and refugee crisis in European Union – all are related to anti-globalist discourses.

The world is changing, and the economy needs something new to go back on the track of high growth and positive results. The questions about the future are very complicated: will we replace globalization with protectionism? Can we go back where we were in the nineteenth century, before the first wave of globalization, and do we want this? Will it be a new world with new rules? Some of the analysts call it new globalization, and they try to anticipate how it will look.

The rest of the paper is organized in five parts, each focused on one idea: globalization is good, globalization is bad, globalization is irreversible, globalization is dead, and new globalization emerged; these are followed by some concluding remarks.

20.2 Globalization Is Good: The Beginning

The world experienced a long period of growth, with a significant improvement in the quality of life and strengthen the middle class in many countries. The explanation was all these years linked to globalization and the positive effect on the world economies were unquestionable.

There are hundreds or thousands of books, articles, and blogs about globalization and its consequences, most of them published by authors from developed countries, which experienced globalization simultaneously with economic growth and amazing life-changing technologies. There are of course pros and cons; there are some globalization critiques but they are not the mainstream, and they are referring to the North-South divide, to developing world, which didn't have its fair share right from the beginning.

Explaining the impact and the mechanisms of globalization was challenging, and there are many different ways to approach these problems. One of the newest books on globalization, *The Great Convergence: Information Technology and the New Globalization*, written by Richard Baldwin has a good explanation regarding the stages and changes of globalization. One of the book's central premises is that understanding globalization requires a sharp distinction between the three types of "separation costs": trade costs, communication costs, and face-to-face costs (Baldwin 2016).

The economic development in the past 150 years was always about the distance and about the difficulty of moving three types of things: goods, ideas, and people. This "three – cascading – constrains – perspective" (Baldwin 2016) starts with the period before 1820, when all three constraints were present, and continues with the second period, between 1820 and 1990, when only two remain (the cost of moving goods dropped dramatically) and the third stage when only one is still important (the cost of moving ideas almost disappeared). In Baldwin's vision, the old globalization was at the beginning about the first unbundling, the physical separation of production and consumption. As markets expanded globally, production clustered locally, and the costs of moving goods decreased. The root cause of *The Great Divergence* was, according to Baldwin, the fact that the costs of moving ideas remained high in the first stage of globalization. The ICT revolution relaxed this second constraint and has led globalization in a new acceleration phase. The next step will be *The Great Convergence*, "a radical new transformation which will only happen if the cost of moving people falls in the future as the cost of moving ideas has in the recent past" (Baldwin 2016).

20.3 Globalization Is Bad

Baldwin's book talks about *The Great Divergence*. Before him, we read about North-South gap, about globalization as a "winner takes all society" and about a world where rich countries will became richer and poor countries will became poorer. The dark side of globalization was always related to the inequality. The long period of economic growth registered by developed countries was related to globalization, but the rise of Western Europe and North America drove up the global inequality, since Industrial Revolution to the 1990s.

Recently, there are changes regarding the global inequality (Milanovic 2016): even if the inequalities inside rich countries decreased and people are living a better life than their parents and grandparents, the problem seems to be lower gap between rich and poor. People in developed countries see themselves less rich only because the middle class in developing countries has a similar revenue; they could buy the same things and the visit same places. The inequality challenge and the Milanovic book itself seem to be of great interest (Keech 2017; Lawson 2017) at global level, but there are studies that focused on specific area – East Europe, for example (Pichanic, Stankova 2016), or on a specific measure of inequality like GDP distribution (Wen et al. 2016; Fioramonti 2016).

Anti-globalist movements in developed countries are also connected to labor market. Unemployment (in developed or developing countries) (Buchtova 2016), migration (Kubicova 2016; Portes 2016), and labor organization (Antentas 2016) are all tight together because of the direct impact on the quality of life.

20.4 Good or Bad: Globalization Is Irreversible

The idea of irreversible globalization stands up in many ways. This was a mainstream opinion since 1990s and it could be found everywhere: in scientific journals and Nobel prize winners contributions, in books ("globalization is like sunrise, like it or not, still happen every day") (Friedman 2001), and in mass-media ("the world has already changed and the egg can't be unscrambled"). It was the argument for more trade liberalization and for governmental policies which support globalization and open economies.

20.5 Globalization Is Dead

The pushback against globalization has some explanations: inequality, immigration, and labor market issues. The signs that the world is reaching a turning point are visible in many ways, but most important is the people's vote for anti-globalist opinions (Brexit and Trump are the typical examples).

There are many arguments to say that the Great Britain vote for leaving the European Union was more a vote against globalization than a vote against EU. The roots are related to the deindustrialization, a process which took place in the UK after the 1970s and had negative impact on the labor market. The World Economic Forum (Was Brexit a vote against globalization? 2016) or Bloomberg (Schuman 2016) had published opinions in this direction. There are already many articles in scientific journals about Brexit, and specialists in economics, politics, or social studies are looking for answers. Often, these answers are related to the impact of globalization on the Great Britain's economy and to the perception of the people regarding negative effects on the home markets (Kostadinova 2017; Obstfeld 2016).

Soon after the big crisis of 2008–2009 in the economic and political journals emerge the idea that globalization seems to be in retreat.

There are not many positions for more globalization, but we can still find some position arguing that we have to move in the same direction, to create an open and borderless world economy. Why? Because the slowdown of globalization could have a negative impact on the developed economies. Globalization is not only about trade and low-cost wages, but it is about labor market and immigration. But, in this area, developed countries are confronted with a paradox: even if in terms of short-term gains and losses, immigration could be perceived as bad for the receiving country, and there are some positive effects. For example, the positive impact of the immigration on the pension system in receiving country shows that the slowdown of immigration (as a consequence of a less globalized world) has a negative impact on the public finances (Armstrong, Van de Ven 2016).

Globalization and trade are not the same, but for a long time, the growth of trade (and foreign direct investments) was the core indicator for a more globalized world. The volume and the growth rate of trade decrease dramatically after the 2008 crisis, and many specialists argue that globalization slowed down as a result of changes in international trade, and this influenced the nature and structure of globalization (Neumann 2016). International trade could be seen as a downsize of globalization because of contagion (Zhou, Coleman 2016).

Another approach puts together all the bad things which happened in the past 10 years and tries to find if these are the signs of the ending globalization (Rolenc 2016): the 9/11 terrorist attacks in the USA; the post-2008 economic crisis; the unsuccessful Arab Spring; the conflicts in Syria, Libya, or Yemen; the conflict in Ukraine and colder relations between Russia and the West; the emergence of the Islamic State; the terrorist attacks in Paris, Brussels, and elsewhere; the migration crisis in Europe; or recently the "Brexit."

20.6 New Globalization

The globalization is not dead. The world is changing, and we are confronting a new kind of globalization. First, this new globalization is still related to trade, but there are new and different patterns of trade: we are registering huge digital flows (old globalization was more about moving goods); the growth and competitive advantage for today's companies are about complex value chains and about production processes sliced up in different stages and countries; and also, the flow of goods is changing – it is wider, and a higher number of countries are involved in the global processes.

New globalization is more about developing countries, in terms of trade, institutions, and migration. Fifty two percent of the developing countries' exports go to other developing countries, and new countries are included; new institutions are built, for and with developing countries; 38% of immigrants go from one developing country to another (Schuman 2016).

New globalization is the subject of the Richard Baldwin's last book *The Great Convergence: Information Technology and the New Globalization* (Baldwin 2016). The most important change is related to the organization of production. The fact that intra-factory flows became international flows had an amazing impact on the globalization as we know it. The most important implications are comparative advantage is denationalized; value is shifted to services; new winners and losers are created within nations; and globalization gets wilder (Baldwin 2016).

New globalization is about new countries. At the beginning, globalization was "a movement from the West to the rest" (Schuman 2016), but now it is a development paradigm for countries from all over the world, from China, Thailand, and Indonesia to Africa, Latin America, or Islamic countries (Otsubo 2016).

New globalization is more about microeconomic decisions and behavior, different from the first wave of globalization which was more about nations, trade, foreign direct investments, and macroeconomic rules (Marginean 2015).

20.7 Conclusions

The change of the world as we know it is real. In our attempt to anticipate how our future will look, it is rational to look at globalization, as the main development paradigm of the past 30 years. A literature is emerging that seeks to identify new features of globalization, which could be the answer to our questions, and in the same time the starting point for a completely new world economic order.

References

Antentas, J.M.: Internationalist challenges: antiglobalisation, occupy, and indignados. Globalizations. **13**(4), 469–483 (2016). https://doi.org/10.1080/14747731.2015.1041270

Armstrong, A., Van de Ven, J.: The impact of possible migration scenarios after 'Brexit' on the state pension system. Economies. **4**(4), (2016). https://doi.org/10.3390/economies4040023

Baldwin, R.: The Great Convergence. Information Technology and the New Globalization. The Belknap Press of Harvard University, Cambridge, MA (2016)

Buchtova, B.: Unemployment – a Phenomenon of Globalization? Globalization and its Socio-Economic Consequences, 16th International Scientific Conference Proceedings, Pts I-V (2016)

Fioramonti, L.: A post-GDP world? Rethinking international politics in the 21(st) century. Global Pol. **7**(1), 15–24 (2016). https://doi.org/10.1111/1758-5899.12269

Friedman, T.L.: Lexus şi măslinul. Editura Fundaţiei Pro, Bucureşti (2001)

Keech, W.R.: Global inequality: a new approach for the age of globalization. Indep. Rev. **21**(4), 632–635 (2017)

Kostadinova, V.: Brexit is unlikely to provide answers to governance problems under globalisation. Econ. Aff. **37**(1), 135–140 (2017). https://doi.org/10.1111/ecaf.12219

Kubicova, J.: Exit Tax in the World of International Migration of Companies and Individuals. Globalization and its Socio-Economic Consequences, 16th International Scientific Conference Proceedings, Pts I-V (2016)

Lawson, R.A.: Global inequality: a new approach for the age of globalization. Public Choice. **170**(1–2), 175–176 (2017). https://doi.org/10.1007/s11127-016-0390-z

Marginean, S.: Economic globalization: from microeconomic foundation to National Determinants. Procedia Econ. Financ. **27**, 731–735 (2015)

Milanovic, B.: Global Inequality: A New Approach for the Age of Globalization. Harvard University Press, Cambridge, MA (2016)

Neumann, P.: Is Trade Decline a Start of a New Globalization Trend? Globalization and its Socio-Economic Consequences, 16th International Scientific Conference Proceedings, Pts I-V (2016)

Obstfeld, M.: The initial economic impact of Brexit: an update to early December 2016. Brook. Pap. Econ. Act. **2016**, 359–366 (2016)

Otsubo, S.T. (ed.): Globalization and Development, Vol III: In Search of a New Development Paradigm (2016)

Pichanic, M., Stankova, A.: "Can The Globalization Reduce Inequality Among The Central European Countries?" (The Case Of Czech Republic). Globalization and Its Socio-Economic Consequences, 16th International Scientific Conference Proceedings, Pts I-V (2016)
Portes, J.: Immigration after Brexit. Natl. Inst. Econ. Rev. **238**(1), R13–R21 (2016). https://doi.org/10.1177/002795011623800111
Rolenc, J.M.: Do Recent International Crises Represent the "End of Globalization"? Globalization and its Socio-Economic Consequences, 16th International Scientific Conference Proceedings, Pts I-V (2016)
Schuman, M.: Brexit Won't Stop Globalization. https://www.bloomberg.com/news/articles/2016-07-14/brexit-won-t-stop-globalization. Bloomberg Businessweek (2016). Accessed 15 April 2017
Was Brexit a vote against globalization?. https://www.weforum.org/agenda/2016/08/was-brexit-a-vote-against-globalization (2016). Accessed 15 April 2017
Wen, J., Chang, C.P., Weng, J.H., Liu, J.L.: Globalization and real GDP: new evidence using panel vector autoregression. Singap. Econ. Rev. **61**(5), 1550065 (2016). https://doi.org/10.1142/s0217590815500654
Zhou, Y.R., Coleman, W.D.: Accelerated contagion and response: understanding the relationships among globalization, time, and disease. Globalizations. **13**(3), 285–299 (2016). https://doi.org/10.1080/14747731.2015.1056498

Chapter 21
Role of Corporate Governance in the Context of Globalization

Bogdan Mârza, Alina Mărcuţă, and Liviu Mărcuţă

Abstract The globalization process, although criticized, is constantly growing, contributing to the internationalization of activities performed by companies and to the internationalization of markets. This also resulted in the occurrence of important changes regarding the operation and functioning of organizations, as well as regarding the operating mode of governments that have to adopt their policies to a changing market. In addition, the corporate governance, besides the ethical principles it observes, and the social responsibility also use rules and procedures aimed to increase the value of the company. Moreover, the emergence of the economic crisis showed that accounting frauds are a result of the lack of control or of control deficiencies, and that is why the corporate governance is even more important. This paper intends to analyze the different systems of corporate governance and to highlight the difficulties the companies are facing as a result of their adapting to the globalization system.

Keywords Accounting • Globalization • Corporate governance • Investors • Shareholders

21.1 Introduction

Corporate governance is a concept that is increasingly concerned with the profession account, being defined by various economists, and there is still no unanimously accepted definition. It is considered either a system by which companies are run and

B. Mârza (✉)
Lucian Blaga University of Sibiu, Sibiu, Romania
e-mail: bogdan.marza@ulbsibiu.ro

A. Mărcuţă • L. Mărcuţă
University of Agronomic Science and Veterinary Medicine Bucharest, Bucharest, Romania

S.C. Mărginean et al. (eds.), *Emerging Issues in the Global Economy*, Springer Proceedings in Business and Economics,
https://doi.org/10.1007/978-3-319-71876-7_21

controlled or a combination of processes and structures implemented by the board of directors to inform, direct, and monitor the organization's activities. In order to achieve the predetermined goals (the US Institute of Internal Auditors), a set of practices of the board of directors and executive management are exercised to ensure strategic direction of action, achievement of objectives, risk management, and responsible use of resources (International Federation of Accountants).

The generally accepted aspect of corporate governance is that effective corporate governance is one that can ensure both the setting of long-term strategic objectives and plans and the provision of leadership so that the set goals can be reached. Moreover, because there was a separation between shareholders and management, there was a need to increase investors' confidence in the security of investments they make, which requires transparency on all transactions and the adoption by companies of standards of transparency in their relationship with investors or creditors.

In this context, corporate governance is also an attempt to implement risk analysis, verification, evaluation, and control systems that can help deliver effective corporate management.

Corporate governance therefore needs to be tackled with risk management, financial management, internal control, and internal audit, as corporate governance requires transaction transparency and monitoring of control systems to ensure a fair assessment of the risks that may threaten society's activity.

21.2 The Role of Corporate Governance

Given the particularly important role of corporate governance, this is a topic of global interest at the level of large organizations operating at macroeconomic level. One of the results of the economic globalization has been to reach consensus on the international development of core corporate governance principles that are centered on equity, transparency, and accountability (Fulop and Pintea 2015), five of which are fundamental.

These principles relate to providing the foundations for a framework for effective corporate governance; ensuring shareholders' rights; fair treatment for all shareholders; recognizing the role of all parties involved in corporate governance; nonacceptance of directors to occupy positions of conflict of interest; the need for managers themselves to be content with the risk identification, monitoring, and management system; the existence of an internal audit effectively supervised by the audit committee; developing and implementing transparent processes and procedures; the existence of clear policies setting out the responsibilities and duties of the board; the need for the board to set performance indicators for senior management to create an effective performance monitoring system; and the need for an adequate control system to ensure that the board complies with all applicable regulatory requirements.

The success of good corporate governance is due to the fact that it provides appropriate incentives for board and company management to achieve its goals, facilitates effective monitoring, and encourages the most efficient use of resources.

On the other hand, inefficient corporate governance is one that implies insufficient oversight of board management, inappropriate risk management, and the use of structures and nontransparent and unjustified complex activities.

21.3 Corporate Governance Systems

Over time, there have been several corporate governance systems that have tried to improve the relationship between managers, investors, employees, and governments by providing complete and accurate information.

Thus, starting from the fact that in the 1970s and 1980s, the role of large business managers diminished as a result of the decline in the importance of these companies, and it changed the vision of the manager-oriented model that the technocratic managers acted in the investors' interest, as they actually pursued their own interests, however well-intentioned they were.

Another model was the employee-oriented model, according to which employees as members of the boards of directors had to be directly involved in governance. This model was tried in Germany and then taken over by other European countries. Subsequently, significant participation in the vote of workers was considered to lead to inefficient management boards generating costs that outweigh the potential benefits of applying this model.

In France and Japan, the state-oriented model was adopted and started from the performance of state-run Asian economies. But the collapse of communism contributed to the decline of the model, considering that free state intervention in corporate affairs does not have beneficial results for them.

The shareholder-driven model safeguards the interests of all shareholders, minority or majority shareholders, thereby helping corporations manage their funding by capital. At the same time, it is intended to protect other corporate actors, employees, creditors, the state, etc. (Feleagă et al. 2011).

Although each of the presented methods has its advantages, whatever the agreed model, it must be taken into account that an efficient corporate governance method is one that can ensure overall social welfare and where corporate managers are responsible for meeting the interests of shareholders.

In order to avoid inappropriate governance, top management must have particular preoccupations for strategy development, policy-making, and the organization of the internal control system to master and assess the organization's risks.

Moreover, the role of corporate governance has also been influenced by the importance of internal auditing of organizations in the context of the economic crises generated by financial scandals that have taken place both in Europe and in America and has highlighted the fact that accounting fraud is due to the absence of formal control foreseen in the company's internal regulations, resulting in the relationship between fraud, corporate governance, and internal audit. There were doubts about the ability of investors to make informed decisions based on information provided by companies and the capital market.

These failures were either due to the lack of integrity of leeways or due to legislative evasion, events that led to doubt and uncertainty in the capital market.

In Europe, for example, there was a resounding financial collapse of British Barings, which, although survived financial turbulence in the nineteenth century and world wars, collapsed in 1995 following unauthorized trading of Singapore-derived contracts by an inexperienced employee, which led to losses of £ 827 million, mainly from speculation on futures contracts. Although the bank had losses, profit was reported in the financial statements as a result of the use of an unauthorized account to hide trade losses. Another cause was his undetectment by external and internal auditors, which led to the collapse of the oldest London bank. If the financial engineering used were discovered, the collapse could have been avoided.

Another failure is that of the audit and accounting firm Arthur Andersen, a reputable company with the five largest international audit firms and accountants, whose bankruptcy is linked to another financial failure, that of the American company Enron.

The collapse of this company has had implications for the international market, as it has been demonstrated that large corporations need more than an accounting firm for audit services.

Andersen has processed Enron's accounting records and has received audit fees and financial consulting fees of $25 million per year. However, Enron went bankrupt, and the audit firm was convicted of obstructing justice and deliberately destroying documents related to Enron's audit.

Another European firm involved in financial scandals was Parmalat, a global dairy maker who has issued bonds worth 300 million euros but who due to the lack of transparency has not benefited from the expected success due to related suspicions to the financial stability of the company. To hide this fact, in 2003, the company turned to an engineering firm to guarantee its loans, which consisted of a 4 billion-euro deposit, a Cayman-owned company, money that did not exist and which led to the bankruptcy of the company in 2003 which resulted in the overthrow of over 100,000 investors.

The apparent financial solidity of the company was built on the basis of nonexistent amounts in the accounts of some Caribbean and South American banks, which were presented in the financial statements and hiding huge losses. Pretending to have funds that he did not have, Parmalat was fooling investors with new loans. The main cause of bankruptcy was the fact that the only one who controlled the management of the Italian company was its founder who had total control over the company, while the other managers were devoted to him and not the investors.

And in America, there were bankruptcy cases, the most well-known being the Enron case, which went bankrupt in 2001 amid billions of dollars of debt. Bankruptcy has led to the unemployment of 20,000 employees and the loss of billions of dollars to investors. At the company level, it was suggested that the company would not have needed "assets," valuing them at market value, which led to anticipating future profits from transactions, which are treated as current revenues that have led to the recording of some valuable gains, as they lost losses over a period of time. These speculations led to the writable increase in the value of shares that at the end of the 1990s were traded at prices of $80–90 per share. Moreover, in the summer of 2001, triple gains were reported over the same period in 2000, owing to the overestimation of profit and the underestimation of debt. The Enron scandal was not as big as the human and financial costs involved.

Therefore, beyond the benefits and opportunities of development, globalization and the market economy also offer countless solutions whereby large companies, led by executives with various financial interests, can lead to financial collapses that often have serious consequences for people row. That is why solutions are sought to avoid these problems by implementing effective corporate governance systems that differ from one country to another and directly affect both the development of global strategies and the types of strategies that can be adopted. The vast majority of developed and developing countries have a Corporate Governance Code issued by different regulatory bodies.

At European level, corporate governance is achieved through the application of three methods: the Community method, the intergovernmental method, and the open coordination method.

The Community method was based on several factors, namely, the unification of sovereignty, which gave the possibility of more efficient and shared management of the resources belonging to the member states, and the efficient functioning of the markets. Another aspect related to the way in which the economic integration of economic integration, Community law, etc., was introduced, which were advantages of the Community method.

Among these advantages is the renunciation by member states of a part of national sovereignty in favor of the European Union, thereby communicating that they want cooperation and decision-making at Community level. This also means making common decisions for all member states, taking into account the interest of each state, so that the final decision is a common agreement. Another important aspect is related to Community law which, through the set of rights and obligations granted, transforms the status of citizen of a national state into a citizen of a supranational state. On the other hand, the Community method also has its disadvantages, for example, joint decision-making can be hampered by divergent interests of states. There may also be situations in which the general interest of the European Union does not correspond to the national interest of the member states, which leads to delays in making decisions.

As the Community method has not always been able to apply the principles of the organization and functioning of the European Union, other methods have been sought, such as the intergovernmental method, which refers to governmental cooperation, finding solutions to decision-making through diplomatic negotiations between member states, and advantage that allows cooperation in some areas where integration has become more difficult. This method allows states to maintain their sovereignty and act in accordance with their own national interest.

The disadvantage of the method is that it has no general applicability and can be applied to areas such as fiscal policy, environmental policy, foreign policy, defense, justice, and common security.

The open method of coordination has a nonbinding and decentralized nature, has a high degree of openness and flexibility, but involves a large number of actors involved in decision-making. This method aims to create a European social model that is complementary to other instruments such as legislation, social dialogue, structural funds, analysis, and research. The guidelines are transposed into national and regional policies by setting specific targets that take into account national and regional differences.

By this method, deadlines are set for reaching short-, medium-, or long-term goals, deadlines member states have to meet, and certain performance indicators through which growth and economic growth are pursued.

This policy promotes diversity and diminishes the influence of political factors. However, the interdependencies of policies and the need for their coordination lead to polarization and conflicts related to development and promotion of competitiveness, which can be a disadvantage of the method.

At the level of Romania, the changes in the landscape of corporate governance have occurred not as a result of a reform in this field but as a secondary element of wider reforms applied to the economic and social system that have made corporate governance a particular aspect of economic policy. The emergence of the market economy, the privatization of companies, their listing, and the reform of the capital markets that allowed for stock transactions, for the first time after several decades, contributed to the emergence and development of the concept of corporate governance (Vasile 2009).

The first Corporate Governance Code was adopted in 2001, when it was created for Categorization Plus listing, to which listed companies could have access only after fully incorporating the provisions of the Corporate Governance Code into their articles of incorporation. Because one company applied for promotion in the plus category, the Corporate Governance Institute was set up in the years to educate listed issuers on the application of corporate governance standards and to contribute to the adoption of the White Paper on Corporate Governance in the countries in Southeastern Europe. The Corporate Governance Code was adopted in 2008 and has been applied voluntarily since 2009, similar to those adopted by the other EU member states. The Code provides for new compliance recommendations, but the application of corporate governance rules has encountered numerous difficulties, such as lack of detail analysis of owner-manager relationships; lack of a conceptual framework for an efficient market; poor involvement of auditors in promoting corporate governance, as well as participants in decision-making; the failure of reforms to implement an accounting system in line with international developments; and the deficiencies of control mechanisms for relevant, reliable, intelligible, comparable, and meaningful financial information.

Important steps were taken in 2011 with the emergence of Government Emergency Ordinance 109/2011 on Corporate Governance of Public Undertakings approved with amendments to Law no. 11/20/2016 and by the advent of Government Decision 722/2016 on the approval of the Methodological Norms for Application of Certain Provisions of EGO no. 109/2011 on corporate governance of public enterprises and by the advent of Law 111/2016 approving the Government Emergency Ordinance no. 109/2011 on corporate governance of public enterprises.

Nevertheless, the results of the corporate governance application made investors, on the one hand, to give it more importance and credit to it, due to good results, and on the other hand, they made companies deposit much more effort and time to reach corporate governance standards because they allow for a more accurate evaluation and monitoring of performance and maximize the value of the company from the shareholders' perspective.

The advantages of applying corporate governance are that applying governance measures and principles will increase the transparency of entities and attract investors who are willing to pay in addition to achieve good results in this area, which is considered an added value domain to a companies.

It has been found that those entities that apply corporate governance systems are able to maximize their value, meet the requirements of their customers, employees, suppliers, etc., and allow managers to evaluate and monitor their performance.

Thus, corporations that comply with corporate governance standards will gain customer trust and shareholder confidence, which will result in better performance on the market.

An important aspect to be given is the correct, complete, and scientifically substantiated risk assessment, so that the entity focuses on maximizing its potential by formulating strategic objectives or by optimizing the level of risk associated with its operations.

Ensuring effective corporate governance must be based on fairness, credibility, and transparency in relation to shareholders, investors, creditors, etc., on assuming management responsibilities and optimizing risk management in a company.

Therefore, corporate governance is a priority for the management of those companies that want success, as transparency and the correct application of corporate governance principles will lead to increased performance (Răileanu et al. 2011).

21.4 Conclusions

Corporate governance gains new dimensions because their phenomena and effects are expanding globally, and globalization is a phenomenon that has contributed both to the liberalization of capital flows and a more efficient allocation of resources, this being determined by opportunities to attract investment.

Although the globalization of financial markets has helped to reduce the differences between the various economies, the existence of cultural, economic, and social factors prevents an exhaustive approach to this concept.

Corporate governance not only involves supervising financial activity and boosting performance but also defending investor interests, ensuring social stability, and increasing the quality of human capital and orderly development of production processes, all this respecting the cultural values of each country.

The economic crisis has been a triggering factor in the analysis of the role and efficiency of corporate governance systems (Bulata 2014). The models applied to date are constantly changing, their application revealing over time the main corporate governance problems of modern companies. Thus, the source is represented by the complexity of the organizational structures, each institution being obliged to develop structures, processes, and practices appropriate to its needs. Evolution of society, globalization will contribute to changing the perception of corporate governance that corporate will need to be integrated into the business strategy of companies and not just as a mere obligation of compliance. We will not be able to talk about efficient corporate governance without the support of the company's management, whose role is to ensure the sustainable growth of the company. At the same time, shareholders will have to be accountable for decision-making, engaging in a reasonable and responsible manner in the company's business.

Applying a good corporate governance framework encourages business development with a positive impact on growth, while a poor-quality corporate governance framework leads to incidents related to political or fiscal events that contribute to destabilizing economic activity.

In the future, corporate governance will take on the place it deserves, as the premises of a better-organized and stronger financial market will be created, less sensitive to economic gaps and more accessible and transparent to all actors involved.

References

Bulata, D.: Corporate governance and economic crisis. Economia Online. http://economiaonline.ro/guvernanta-corporativa-si-criza-financiara/ (2014). Accessed 30 Sept 2016

Feleagă, N., Feleagă, L., Dragomir, V., Bigioi, A.: Corporate governance in emerging economies: the case of Romania. Theor. Appl. Econ. **9**(562), 3–15 (2011)

Fulop, M.T., Pintea, M.O.: The link between corporate governance and performance. Evidence from Romania. Manag. Intercult. **33**, 81–90 (2015)

Răileanu, A., Dobroțeanu, C., Dobroțeanu, L.: Current issues regarding the measurement of corporate governance level in Romania. Financ. Audit. **1**, 11–15 (2011)

Vasile, C.M.: Managerial Authority and a New Model of Corporate Governance Applicable to Romanian Enterprises, Ph.D. Thesis, the Bucharest University of Economic Studies (2009)

Chapter 22
Financial Synergies of Mergers and Acquisitions: Between Intentions and Achievements

Diana Marieta Mihaiu

Abstract Mergers and acquisitions (M&A) market is a barometer of the attractiveness of the national economy for the foreign capital but also for the local capital to develop its businesses. In recent years, worldwide, foreign investments have resulted mainly in M&A transactions than in green field investment. The objective of this article is to analyze the financial performance of companies in Romania which went through a M&A transaction, before and after this transaction. The purpose of this research is to determine if the financial performance of these companies has improved after a M&A transaction. The financial performance of M&A transactions in Romania will be analyzed, during the 2010–2013 period, taking into consideration a sample of ten transactions from several industries. The objective of the study is to analyze the impact of M&A transaction on the financial performance of the companies involved. We consider that a M&A transaction is efficient in financial terms if it generates growth in profit and if it generates an increase in value for shareholders, compared to previous values before the transaction. Financial performance measurement method used in this study is accounting-based measure, using financial indicators analysis. Through this method, it will be established: the impact of M&A transaction on the profitability of companies and the impact of M&A transaction on the value created for shareholders.

Keywords Merger • Acquisition • Financial performance

D.M. Mihaiu (✉)
Lucian Blaga University of Sibiu, Sibiu, Romania
e-mail: diana.mihaiu@ulbsibiu.ro

S.C. Mărginean et al. (eds.), *Emerging Issues in the Global Economy*, Springer Proceedings in Business and Economics,
https://doi.org/10.1007/978-3-319-71876-7_22

22.1 Introduction

The merger and acquisition (M&A) market, characterized by the number of transactions and value of transactions, is also a barometer of the attractiveness of the national economy for foreign capital but also for the domestic market to develop its business. Over the last few years, on a worldwide level, foreign investments have become predominantly M&A transactions, rather than green field investment.

The objective of this article is to analyze the financial performance of Romanian companies that have gone through an M&A transaction before and after this type of transaction. The purpose of the research is to see if the financial performance of the companies under review has improved as a result of this M&A transaction.

Although the value of M&A transactions is estimated at $5 trillion in 2015, representing 12% of GDP, according to J.P. Morgan statistics (J.P. Morgan, 2016), however, studies show high rates of failure of these transactions. Favorable impact has been identified in the case of hostile takeovers and unrelated takeovers; gains were recorded in the case of the shareholders of the target company who benefited from the cash payment (Wang and Moini 2012).

First of all, we should determine what is meant by the financial performance of a company. When can we consider a company to be financially competitive? The performance definition varies depending on the stakeholders' interests (Gruian 2010), the aspects of performance being multiple. In the present situation, we will consider that a company is financially competitive if it generates profits and generates value for shareholders. The profit ensures the future performance of the company's business and indicates a low risk of insolvency. The value generated for shareholders keeps the company attractive for current shareholders, but also for potential investors, thus giving them access to their own funding sources.

The paper is structured in a logical and gradual way, as follows: the introductory part in which the subject of this paper is mentioned; part II, literature review, containing a presentation of the recent debates on the success and failure rates in M&A transactions; and part III, the analysis of financial performance of mergers and acquisitions in Romania with the methodology used, results, and conclusions.

22.2 Literature Review

M&A transactions are based on diverse motivations but always optimistic from the perspective of the transaction's initiator.

G. Hurduzeu identified the following business motivations: commercial and industrial motivations (obtaining operational synergies, company development, survival, penetration of new markets, increasing market power, and diversification), financial motivations, and special motivations (high-performance management teams, highly qualified specialists, operating licenses) (Hurduzeu 2002).

M. Sehleanu shared the M&A determinants into two categories:

- *Macroeconomic determinants*: economic boom, technological innovations, globalization, and national laws and regulations. An increase in M&A operations in growth periods, with low interest rates, with a rise in the capital market, in sectors that have suffered a deregulation, has been found.
- *Microeconomic determinants*: strategic motivation, economic motivations, and hubris syndrome (Sehleanu 2013, pp. 62, 71).

But, while they are based on positive incentives, obtaining positive synergies, some studies show that most M&A transactions do not reach their targets. According to Thomas Straub's study, two-thirds of M&A transactions are doomed to failure (Straub 2007). The analysis by Daojuan Wang and Hamid Moini identified that the failure rate of M&A is between 40% and 80% of cases, without significant variations over time (Wang and Moini 2012). Other studies have shown that 83% of transactions do not generate long-term competitive advantage, 60% of transactions destroy the firm's value, and 66% of transactions have not generated shareholder value (Pacquisitions Blog 2014); operating performance decreased over the next 3 years after the M&A operation (Rao-Nicholson et al. 2016). The same idea is supported by a study on M&A transactions on the banking market, which concludes that M&As do not create value for the firm and the analysis of operational performance based on 20 financial ratios has shown that it has not improved (Liargovas and Repousis 2011). Some more concrete results from a study on a sample of 80 transactions show that EBITDA/sales ratio fell 3.3% on average on M&A and profit fell as a result of M&A by about $ 4 million, so the impact of M&A transactions was an unfavorable one over the value of the companies involved (Grigorieva and Petrunina 2015).

The results of research in the field are not unitary. Some research has shown that M&A transactions generate greater returns for investors in the post-merger period but do not contribute significantly to improving the company's liquidity or profit before tax/total income (Sinha et al. 2010, p. 194). Sidjabat and Prijadi study shows that most companies increased their profitability and liquidity as a result of such a transaction, but operating efficiency has not improved (Sidjabat and Prijadi 2013). The performance analysis of M&A transactions undertaken by Joash and Njangiru in the banking sector concludes that these transactions lead to the rise of shareholder value, earnings per share, and the profitability of companies that have undergone such an operation (Joash and Njangiru 2015, p. 1111). In the long run, M&A transactions generate favorable synergies such as cost reductions, business diversification, and net cash flow growth in Kumar S. and Bansal L. opinion (Kumar and Bansal 2008).

It can be seen that most studies demonstrate that M&A transactions do not reach all of their targets, registering some degree of failure, not being fully performing. But the problem is:

1. *How is the performance of M&A transactions defined?*
2. *How is the performance of M&A transactions measured?*

The results of M&A transaction performance studies depend on the way performance is defined, the measurement methodology, the time horizon analyzed, the sample used, and the benchmarks of stability (Wang and Moini 2012, p. 1).

Defining the performance of M&A transactions is not unitary, but it is considered that a transaction is competitive if the resulting company creates a value superior to the pre-transaction situation. But the problem now arises in defining the value. The company has an accounting value, a market value, an economic value, and a shareholder value (Radici n.d.). I consider that a transaction is performing if it generates profit, generates a growing market value of the firm, and offers competitive returns to shareholders. Also, in analyzing the performance of a transaction, the reasons behind the transaction have to be analyzed and whether they have been reached.

Wang and Moini in the *Performance Assessment of mergers and acquisitions: evidence from Denmark* made a presentation of the methods used to measure the performance of M&A transactions, namely (Wang and Moini 2012, pp. 2–9):

- Event studies
- Accounting-based measures
- Managers perceived performance
- Experts informants' assessment
- Divestment measure

Numerous studies use the accounting-based measure as the method to analyze the pre- and post-merger financial performance of transactions, although it is not a method without imperfections (Huian 2012). It is relatively simple to use this method because it offers the possibility of calculating many financial indicators, but the information is influenced by the accounting policies used, by the legal regulations that may differ from one company to another located in different countries, and by the accounting information users.

In Romania, the M&A market began to recover starting in 2014 when 181 transactions were made in the amount of 2.24 billion euros, and in 2016, there were 136 transactions worth 3.54 billion euros, almost reaching the level of 2008 when the transaction value was 3.62 billion euros. The evolution of Romania's merger and acquisitions market is closely linked to the overall economic situation of the country as well as to the evolution of the global economy. Most investors in Romania are strategic; in the year 2016, they were 81%, and the rest of 19% were financial investors; between 50% and 60% of transactions are local purchases of foreigners, domestic purchases being fewer (M&A Barometer Romania n.d.and Emerging Europe, 2016).

22.3 Data and Methodology

In this section, we will analyze the financial performance of MA transactions in Romania, from 2010 to 2013, taking a sample of ten transactions from several fields of activity.

The objective of the study is to analyze the impact of the M&A transaction on the financial performance of the companies involved. We will consider that an M&A transaction is financially feasible if it generates rising profit and generates value for shareholders rising from the previous transaction.

The method of measuring the financial performance used in this study is the accounting-based measure, using the analysis of financial indicators. Through this method, there will be analyzed:

- The impact of the M&A transaction on companies' profitability
- The impact of the M&A transaction on the value created for shareholders

To perform the *financial performance analysis in terms of profitability*, we will calculate and compare the following indicators:

- Evolution of turnover
- Evolution of the asset
- Evolution of gross profit
- ROA (return on assets)
- Money availability rate (cash ratio)
- Debt ratio
- ROE (return on equity)

In order to perform *the financial performance analysis from the point of view of the value created for the shareholders*, we will calculate and compare *the return on social capital = net profit/share capital.*

It has been decided to choose this indicator because the earnings per share (EPS) cannot be determined, since not all companies are listed on the stock exchange and thus they do not publish the number of shares in the share capital (Fig. 22.1).

These indicators will be calculated for the pre-M&A, 2010–2012, and post-M&A, 2013–2015, respectively.

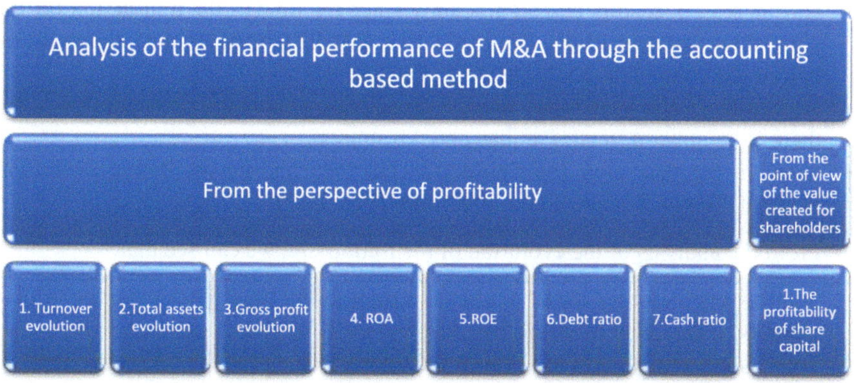

Fig. 22.1 Analysis of the financial performance of M&A through the accounting-based method

Table 22.1 M&A transactions analyzed

	Year of transaction	Type of transaction	Target company	Acquirer	Resulting entity
1	2012	Merger	Real hypermarket	Auchan	Auchan
2	2012	Acquisition	Pambac	Comfert, Popasul Trebes	Pambac
3	2012	Acquisition	Azomures	Ameropa holding	Azomures
4	2012	Acquisition	Rombat	Metair group	Rombat
5	2012	Acquisition	Zaharul Ludus	Tereos	Tereos Romania
6	2012	Acquisition	eJobs	Ringier	eJobs
7	2011	Acquisition	Dialmed clinic	Diaverum	Dialmed clinic
8	2011	Acquisition	Spumotim	Johnson controls	Spumotim
9	2011	Acquisition	Eva clinic	MedLife	MedLife Eva
10	2011	Acquisition	Bramac	Monier group	Bramac

The companies analyzed are presented in the following table as well as the type of transaction. It can be noticed that most of the transactions in this period on the Romanian market were acquisitions (Table 22.1).

22.4 Results

The results of the calculation of the financial indicators in Fig. 22.2 are shown in the table in Appendix 22.1.

The chart below shows the CA evolution of the companies analyzed in pre- and post-M&A period.

It can be noticed that *turnover*:

- Has increased steadily and significantly since the time of the transaction for the companies: Auchan, eJobs, Dialmed Clinic, MedLife Eva, Bramac, representing half of the companies analyzed
- Decreased in the year following the transaction versus the pre-trade level, but there is an upward trend: Pambac and Azomures
- Grew in the year after the transaction but then had an oscillating evolution: Rombat, Tereos Romania, and Spumotim (Fig. 22.3)

From the analysis of the evolution of *the total asset*, we can see that:

- Total assets increased steadily after the transaction time for companies: eJobs, Dialmed Clinic, and MedLife Eva.
- Total assets increased in the year of the transaction, but in the following years, it also recorded declines: Auchan, Pambac, Azomures, Rombat, Tereos Romania, Spumotim, and Bramac (Fig. 22.4).

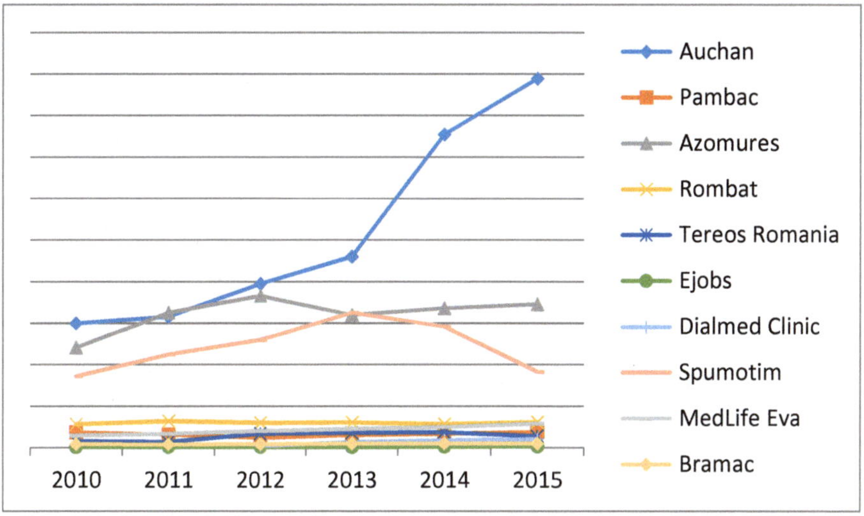

Fig. 22.2 Turnover evolution of analyzed companies, pre- and post-merger (Author's own elaboration based on data from Appendix 22.1)

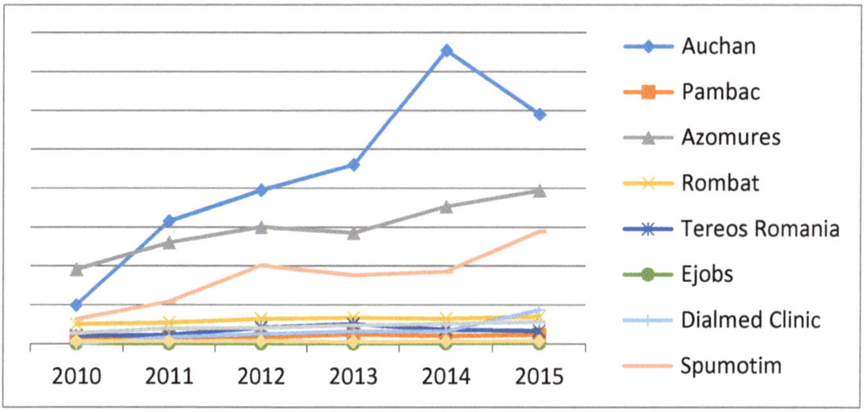

Fig. 22.3 Total assets evolution of analyzed companies, pre- and post-merger (Author's own elaboration based on data from Appendix 22.1)

From the analysis of the evolution of *gross profit*, it can be noticed that:

- It increased in the year of the transaction, but then losses were recorded: Auchan and Tereos Romania
- It increased in the year of the transaction but then dropped below pre-transaction level: Rombat.
- It decreased in the year of the transaction, but in the years to come, it grew and exceeded the pre-transaction level: Pambac, eJobs, and Bramac.
- It decreased in the year of the transaction as well as in subsequent years, standing below pre-transaction level: Azomures.

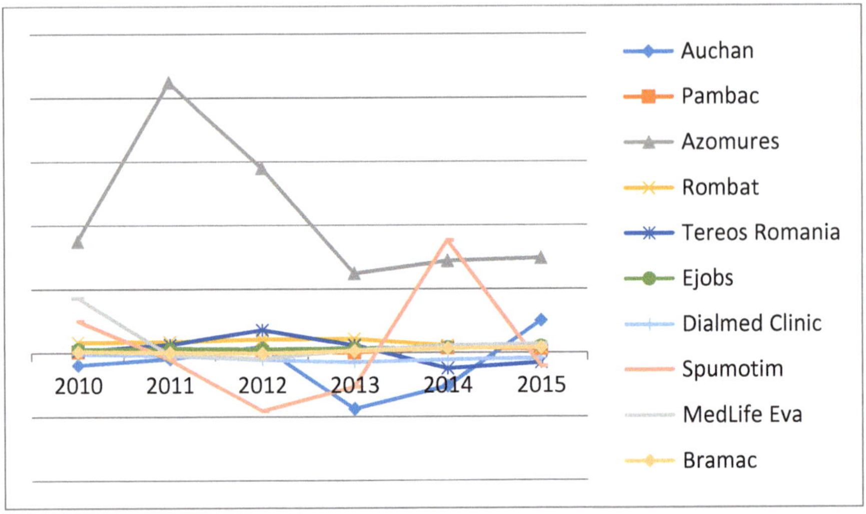

Fig. 22.4 Evolution of *gross profit* of the analyzed companies, pre- and post-merger (Author's own elaboration based on data from Appendix 22.1)

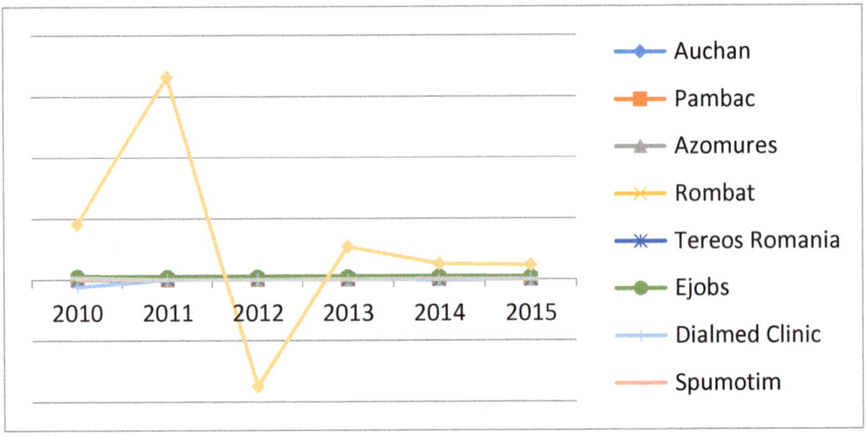

Fig. 22.5 ROA evolution of the analyzed companies, pre- and post-merger (Author's own elaboration based on data from Appendix 22.1)

- It has recorded losses that have accentuated after the transaction: Dialmed Clinic.
- It has incurred losses in the year of the transaction, and then the loss and profit periods alternated: Spumotim.
- It has incurred losses in the year of the transaction and then increased in profit but at a lower level than that from the pre-transaction period: MedLife Eva.

Therefore, in only 40% of cases, it is possible to see a gross profit increase above the level recorded in the pre-transaction period (Fig. 22.5).

Analyzing the ROA indicator of the year before the transaction with the last year analyzed after the transaction, it is noted that this indicator has improved only in

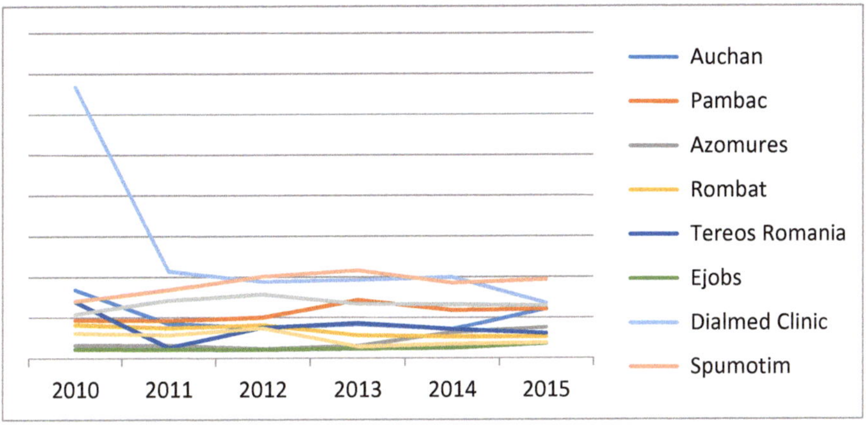

Fig. 22.6 Evolution of the debt ratio of the analyzed companies, pre- and post-merger (Author's own elaboration based on data from Appendix 22.1)

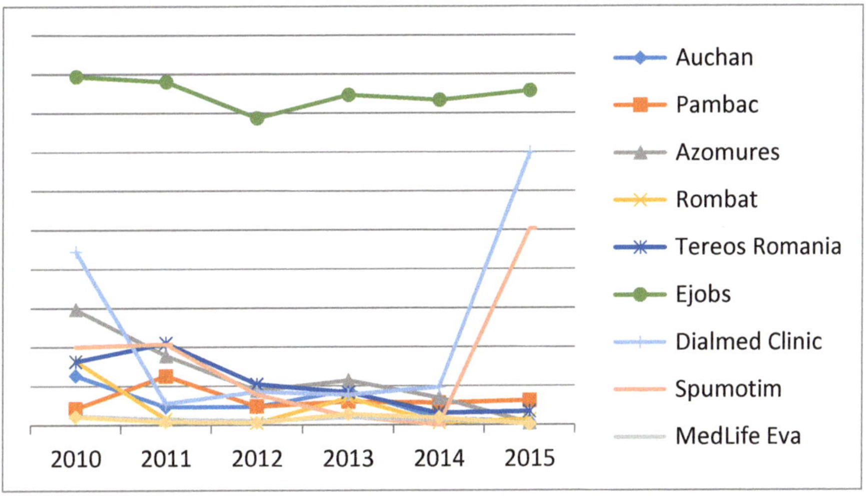

Fig. 22.7 Cash/total assets ratio evolution of analyzed companies, pre- and post-merger (Aauthor's own elaboration based on data from Appendix 22.1)

20% of the analyzed cases, i.e., for the companies Auchan and Pambac. In the rest of the cases, the evolution is unfavorable (Fig. 22.6).

Analyzing the debt ratio, it is found that in most cases, it recorded an increase in the after-transaction period compared to the pre-transaction level (in five out of the ten cases analyzed); in three cases, there was a decrease and in two cases, comparable levels.

Azomures presents a specific situation in which the debt ratio increases, but ROA records depreciation that denotes a decline in return on assets funded in part by debt (Fig. 22.7).

Cash/total assets ratio declined in the post-transaction period compared to the pre-transaction period in four cases, i.e., in 40% of the analyzed cases. A relatively

Fig. 22.8 ROE evolution of analyzed companies, pre- and post-merger (Author's own elaboration based on data from Appendix 22.1)

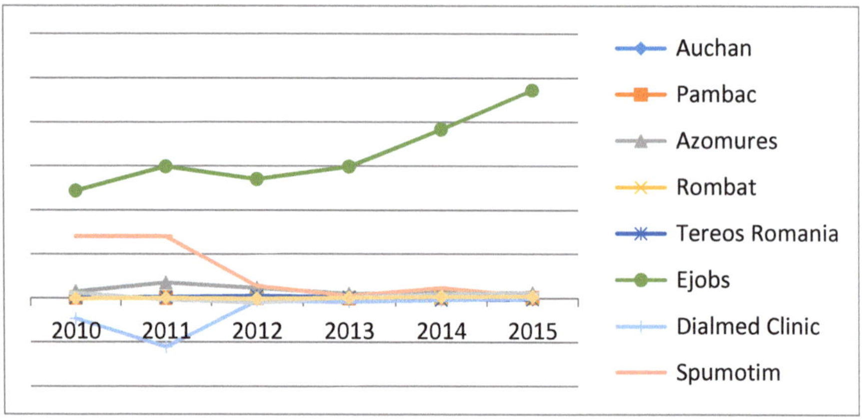

Fig. 22.9 Evolution of profitability of the social capital of the analyzed companies, pre- and post-merger (Author's own elaboration based on data from Appendix 22.1)

constant evolution, with no major fluctuations, was recorded in three cases (eJobs, MedLife, Bramac) and in the other cases' oscillatory evolutions (Rombat, Dialmed Clinic, Spumotim) (Fig. 22.8).

ROE recorded an improvement only in two of the analyzed cases: Pambac and Bramac. In the rest of the situations, the evolution of ROE is unfavorable or uncertain (Fig. 22.9).

The profitability of the share capital increased in the case of the companies Auchan, Pambac, eJobs, and Bramac, i.e., in 40% of the cases. In the rest of the analyzed situations, the profitability of the registered capital has decreased compared to the pre-M&A situation or is not positive.

22.5 Conclusions

The main reasons leading to merger or acquisition decisions are mainly synergies and acquisition of strategic assets. The success of a merger or acquisition is closely related to the correct forecast of the opportunity, taking into account several factors, such as corporate resources, legal and regulatory restrictions, and macroeconomic environment. It is essential to analyze the competitive position of the buyer and the target company, making an objective evaluation of the operation (Ulijin et al. 2010, p. 32). Once the merger or acquisition operation has been carried out, its success could be jeopardized by neglecting the integration and subsequent planning process if the company is too focused on reducing costs and neglecting core activities, staff, and stakeholders (Straub 2007, p. 64).

Following the analysis carried out, on a sample of ten companies, it can be noticed that:

- The financial performance analyzed in terms of profitability through the seven financial indicators reflects the following situation: in 70% of the cases, sales clearly increased as a result of the transaction, which means that in general M&A transactions increase market share and gain of commercial synergies; in 100% of the cases, the total assets of the companies surveyed have increased today compared to the pre-transaction period due to the pooling of the assets of the companies involved in the transaction and due to the investments made to maintain the market competitiveness; only in 40% of the cases an increase of the gross profit over the level recorded in the pre-transaction period can be seen, and, consequently, the ROA indicator registered a favorable trend only for 20% of the analyzed companies; in 50% of cases, the debt ratio of companies that have undergone an M&A transaction has increased as a result of real investments; in 30% of the cases, cash/total assets ratio improved, while in the rest of the cases, there were decreases or relatively constant evolutions; ROE has experienced an improvement in only 20% of the analyzed cases. These results cannot be generalized as M&A transactions increase business profitability.
- Financial performance in terms of value created for shareholders increased in 40% of the cases due to the favorable evolution of the profit registered by the companies as a result of the M&A transaction; in the rest of the cases, it registered decreases or failed to record positive values due to the losses. It cannot be concluded that M&A transactions produce value increases for shareholders.

The limits of this study are the low number of firms analyzed due to the lack of comparable information and the analysis of financial performance based on strictly financial indicators using only the accounting-based method, most of the transactions under consideration being acquisition and fewer mergers.

Appendix 22.1

The results of the indicators of the analyzed companies

Company	2010	2011	2012	2013	2014	2015
1. *Real-Auchan*						
Turnover	1,498,002,996	1,578,059,613	1,973,757,257	2,300,730,369	3,770,686,684	4,444,160,904
Gross profit	−19,302,726	−9,679,764	9,591,917	−88,003,347	−52,346,933	50,654,365
Total assets	498,000,000	1,578,000,000	1,973,760,000	2,300,730,000	3,770,000,000	2,950,464,738
ROA %	−4	−1	0	−4	−1	2
Cash ratio %	13	5	5	9	2	1
Roe %		−5	2	−12	−7	5
Debt ratio %	84	42	37	42	35	61
Profitability of the share capital %		−3	1	−10	−5	4
2. *Pambac*						
Turnover	181,933,815	156,688,866	119,977,880	152,149,704	171,316,469	191,099,466
Gross profit	2,370,644	4,015,409	659,092	361,535	7,459,141	5,981,725
Total assets	80,350,000	81,630,000	81,960,000	123,580,000	103,200,000	120,824,774
ROA %	3	5	1	0	7	5
Cash ratio %	4	12	5	6	6	6
Roe %	5	8	1	0	15	12
Debt ratio %	47	46	50	71	59	60
Profitability of the share capital %	9	15	2	0	28	25
3. *Azomures*						
Turnover	1,202,016,666	1,625,577,204	1,829,333,521	1,599,340,920	1,681,092,188	1,728,273,019
Gross profit	955,260,000	1,305,130,000	1,503,250,000	1,430,800,000	1,763,800,000	1,971,282,603
Total assets	175,102,672	424,060,846	289,676,859	124,246,007	143,940,842	148,365,307
ROA %	18	32	19	9	8	8
Cash ratio %	30	18	9	11	7	1
Roe %	21	33	18	8	10	10
Debt ratio %	16	16	11	15	31	38

Profitability of the share capital %	293	694	464	199	234	234
4. *Rombat*						
Turnover	280,515,928	319,058,489	299,046,836	305,193,974	285,774,995	309,568,697
Gross profit	254,350,000	273,650,000	322,160,000	335,710,000	327,500,000	351,521,984
Total assets	16,928,957	17,619,904	21,853,420	21,926,044	11,054,740	8,122,586
ROA %	7	6	7	7	3	2
Cash ratio %	16	2	1	7	1	1
Roe %	10	9	10	9	5	3
Debt ratio %	41	37	41	28	26	26
Profitability of the share capital %	45	46	56	57	28	21
5. *Zaharul Ludus*						
Turnover	77,417,982	72,534,749	171,634,181	180,831,715	184,987,939	140,058,177
Gross profit	105,530,000	117,360,000	211,760,000	255,580,000	183,630,000	169,693,028
Total assets	3,368,463	13,126,603	36,017,098	11,608,142	−24,896,568	−15,623,748
ROA %	3	11	17	5	−14	−9
Cash ratio %	16	21	10	8	3	3
Roe %	9	11	23	7	−21	−15
Debt ratio %	70	13	37	43	35	30
Profitability of the share capital %	9	36	98	30	−80	−49
6. *eJobs*						
Turnover	8,344,911	10,172,223	10,194,929	10,293,780	12,983,551	16,758,477
Gross profit	4,863,239	6,060,000	5,510,000	6,200,000	7,980,000	10,453,409
Total assets	5,939,800	6,367,838	5,793,768	6,371,252	8,191,939	10,081,609
ROA %	122	105	105	103	103	96
Cash ratio %	89	88	79	85	83	86
Roe %	100	98	98	98	98	99

(continued)

(contiued)

Company	2010	2011	2012	2013	2014	2015
Debt ratio %	11	11	10	12	12	18
Profitability of the share capital %	4866	5969	5399	5972	7657	9436
7. *Takeover of Dialmed clinic by Diaverum*						
Turnover			19,474,039	68,975,842	90,235,250	104,017,564
Gross profit	756,061	87,504,615	128,599,396	160,755,340	163,751,215	435,323,342
Total assets	−1,858,360	−4,425,209	−11,421,017	−15,218,822	−11,082,011	−8,520,694
ROA %	−246	−5	−9	−9	−7	−2
Cash ratio %	44	5	8	8	10	70
Roe %	105	71	−144	−222	−648	−6
Debt ratio %	334	107	94	96	99	68
Profitability of the share capital %	−930	−2213	−124	−165	−93	−5
8. *Takeover of Spumotim*						
Turnover	857,879,057	1,119,868,177	1,295,437,947	1,627,526,538	1,460,796,608	912,612,963
Gross profit	321,159,768	539,979,539	1,005,716,044	883,291,548	928,837,705	1,449,492,233
Total assets	50,410,739	−10,661,767	−91,185,056	−53,301,928	176,381,410	−20,894,850
ROA %	16	−2	−9	−6	19	−1
Cash ratio %	20	21	8	2	0	50
Roe %		46	12	2	9	4
Debt ratio %	70	84	101	108	93	97
Profitability of the share capital %	#div/0!	2813	550	110	465	103
9. *Takeover of Clinica Eva by MedLife*						
Turnover	144,779,891	166,457,784	201,636,884	228,588,566	251,092,044	291,014,966
Gross profit	140,833,628	200,630,612	207,557,054	241,037,040	259,119,712	285,298,826
Total assets	86,939,108	−3,227,339	−9,695,387	3,752,415	11,200,926	13,627,270

ROA %	62	−2	−5	2	4	5
Cash ratio %	2	1	1	2	1	0
Roe %	175	−6	−22	3	10	11
Debt ratio %	54	71	79	67	66	65
Profitability of the share capital %	231	−74	−206	46	187	220
10. *Takeover of Bramac by Monier*						
Turnover	42,910,703	41,804,287	42,362,496	49,687,419	51,101,284	51,358,008
Gross profit	1,870,192	513,433	−1,053,581	2,612,791	6,531,539	7,866,840
Total assets	34,113,215	34,088,577	36,771,593	28,324,725	33,762,921	37,686,142
ROA %	1824	6639	−3490	1084	517	479
Cash ratio %	2	1	1	3	2	0
Roe %	−13	2	−6	8	22	25
Debt ratio %	31	28	37	14	17	19
Profitability of the share capital %	−33	4	−15	20	61	75

Source: Author's own calculation based on data reported by http://doingbusiness.ro/financiar/?financiar=financiar and by http://www.risco.ro, https://www.listafirme.ro/

References

Emerging Europe: M&A Report 2016, available online at https://cms.law/en/INT/Publication/Emerging-Europe-M-A-Report-2016-17 (2016). Accessed on 10 Feb 2017

Grigorieva, S., Petrunina, T.: The performance of mergers and acquisitions in emerging capital markets: new angle. J. Manag. Control. **26**, 377 (2015). https://doi.org/10.1007/s00187-015-0219-9

Gruian, C.M.: What do we mean by Company Performance, Analele Universităţii "Constantin Brâncuşi" Târgu Jiu, Seria Economie, Nr. 4/2010 (2010)

Huian, C.M.: Post M&A accounting performance of Romanian banks. J. East. Eur. Res. Bus. Econ. article ID 184557, IBIMA Publishing (2012), https://doi.org/10.5171/2012.184557

Hurduzeu, G.: Achiziţiile de firme pe piaţa de capital, Ed. Economică, Bucureşti (2002)

Joash, G.O., Njangiru, M.J.: The Effect of mergers and acquisitions on financial performance of Banks (A survey of commercial banks in Kenya). Int. J. Innov. Res. Dev. **4**(8) (2015)

Kumar, S., Bansal, L.K.: The impact of mergers and acquisitions on corporate performance in India. Manag. Decis. **46**(10), 1531–1543 (2008)

Liargovas, P., Repousis, S.: The impact of mergers and acquisitions on the performance of the Greek banking sector: an event study approach. Int. J. Econ. Finance. **3**(2) (2011)

Morgan, J.P.: 2016 M&A Global Outlook, higher deal count drives continued strength, available online at https://www.jpmorgan.com/global/insights/maglobaloutlook (2016). Accessed on 10 Feb 2017

M&A Barometer Romania 2016, available online at http://www.ey.com/Publication/vwLUAssets/2017-MA-BarometrCSE/$FILE/M&A2016_CSEl.pdf (n.d.). Accessed on 13 Feb 2017

Pacquisitions Blog: What Happens When I Change My Mind (and don't complete the transaction)?, available online at https://pacquisitions.wordpress.com/2014/08/14/what-happens-when-i-change-my-mind-and-dont-complete-the-transaction/ (2014). Accessed on 02 Feb 2017

Radici, C.: Modalităţi de creare de valoare într-o societate comercială, available online at http://mastermrufeaa.ucoz.com/Cristina_Radici-Modalitati_de_creare_de_valoare_in.pdf (n.d.). Accessed on 06 Feb 2017

Rao-Nicholson, R., Salaber, J., Cao, T.H.: Long-term performance of mergers and acquisitions in ASEAN countries. Res. Int. Bus. Finance. **36** (2016)

Sehleanu, M.: Fuziuni şi achizitii de intreprinderi. Particularităţi europene şi naţionale, Ed. Economică, Bucureşti (2013)

Sidjabat, M.R., Prijadi, R.: Firms Performance after Mergers and Acquisition in Indonesia, Universitas Indonesia, Graduate School of Management Research Paper No. 13–72. Available at https://ssrn.com/abstract=2330695 or https://doi.org/10.2139/ssrn.2330695 (2013)

Sinha, N., Kaushik, K.P., Chaudhary, T.: Measuring post-merger and acquisition performance: an investigation of selected financial sector of organizations in India. Int. J. Econ. Finance. **2**(4) (2010)

Straub, T.: Reasons for Frequent Failure in Mergers and Acquisitions, A Comprehensive Analysis. Deutscher Universitäts-Verlag/GWV Fachverlage GmbH, Wiesbaden (2007)

Ulijin, J., Duysters, G., Meijer, E.: Strategic Alliances, Mergers and Acquisitions – The Influence of Culture on Successful Cooperation. Edward Elgar Publishing Limited, Cheltenham (2010)

Wang, D., Moini H.: Performance Assessment of Mergers and acquisition: Evidence from Denmark , Available online at http://www.g-casa.com/PaperDatabase.htm (2012). Accessed on 08 Feb 2017

Chapter 23
Rural and Gastronomical Tourism in Baltic Countries

Virgil Nicula and Simona Spânu

Abstract The Baltic countries are apparently similar but actually very different not only concerning their language and culture but also their lifestyle. Regarding rural tourism, Latvia, Estonia, and Lithuania have many common points: given the care for the remarkable natural environment and for preserving traditions and rural tourism practiced in each of the Baltic countries, filled with recreation and active desire for knowledge, traditional life, and beauty of nature in protected areas. Rural tourism also contributes to preserving the cultural heritage, and youth people are encouraged to know and keep the traditions alive. The rural tourist offer is complemented by the variety of gastronomy, which benefits from the rich offer of products from the natural environment of the Baltic countries.

Keywords Rural tourism • Gastronomy • Heritage

23.1 Introduction Countries

Rural tourism in the Baltic is relatively recent, but the professionalism it provides is a guarantee for its sustainable development. Even if they are very different to landscape, lifestyle, language, and traditions, these countries have some common characteristics: remarkable environmental care, capitalizing on natural and cultural potential, a gastronomy that combines tradition with modernity, and the desire to preserve all values that individualize this part of Europe. Rural tourism benefits

V. Nicula (✉)
Lucian Blaga University of Sibiu, Sibiu, Romania
e-mail: niculavirgil@yahoo.com

S. Spânu
Lucian Blaga University of Sibiu, Sibiu, Romania
e-mail: simona_spanu@yahoo.com

S.C. Mărginean et al. (eds.), *Emerging Issues in the Global Economy*, Springer Proceedings in Business and Economics,
https://doi.org/10.1007/978-3-319-71876-7_23

from government support, European programs, and the safest promotion, directly through tourists who communicate to those who know their special experience in the Baltic rural area.

Residents in the Baltic Sea area have a close relationship with their nature and annual cycle. Traditional and seasonal holidays make use of natural products in the area such as mushrooms, berries, herbs and spontaneous aromatic herbs, or fish.

The rural area is a haven for nature-loving travelers, who respect the traditions and want to experience rural tourism and in-depth knowledge of the traditional Baltic culture. Circuits for tourists and information on specialized sites are based on the accommodation in small units, farms, and local producers, where visitors can come into contact with traditions, life, and people in rural areas. Associations regularly inventory local farms and growers, encouraging them to develop new tourism products, so those organizations involved in rural tourism activities are real experts.

The gastronomy of rural communities on the shores of the Baltic Sea uses natural forest gifts, meadows, rivers, lakes, and the sea. During the short northern summer, vegetables are carefully grown in small gardens and farms. People think about future generations and use organic farming methods so that the ingredients are fresh, clean, healthy, and nutritious.

Throughout the year, Baltic cuisine offers rye bread, cereals, fresh and fermented dairy products, as well as various cheeses. During spring and summer, lighter dishes of fresh vegetables, herbs, berries, mushrooms, and fish predominate. In winter and autumn, the kitchen gets its substance with meat, vegetables, and legumes and spicy, pickled, and marinated dishes, which are supplemented with aromatic spices. It is a matter of honor to prepare food from high-quality ingredients that are bought from local producers and local suppliers.

A brief review of the natural environment, the Latvian, Lithuanian and Estonian gastronomic traditions show enough arguments for choosing a holiday in Baltic rural areas (Cimdina and Hanovs 2011).

23.2 Rural Tourism and Gastronomy in Baltic Countries

23.2.1 Particularities of Rural Tourism and Gastronomy in Latvia

A mosaic of frequent forests, crystalline lakes, and sinuous ribs, Latvia is a true giant park unspoiled around a single metropolis, the capital of Riga. Latvia is the perfect destination for those who want to spend a quiet holiday by hiking, cycling, or dreaming about a white sandy beach bordered by pine forests. This small country is one of the most popular Baltic countries that attract visitors with spectacular landscapes, a fascinating culture, and vibrant and modern capital (Dreifelds, 1996).

Table 23.1 Statistical data on foreign tourists arriving in Latvia (1996–2015)

Year	*1996*	*1997*	*1998*	*1999*	*2000*	*2001*	*2002*	*2003*	*2004*	*2005*
Number of tourist arrivals (thousands of tourists)	1713	1824	1801	1718	1914	2039	2273	2470	3033	3774
Number of overnights (thousands of tourists)	–	–	3721	3457	3397	3670	4821	4641	5208	5790
Minimum amount spent by a tourist (Euro)	155	169	140	94	106	101	137	177	202	270
Year	*2006*	*2007*	*2008*	*2009*	*2010*	*2011*	*2012*	*2013*	*2014*	*2015*
Number of tourist arrivals (thousands of tourists)	4645	5236	5496	4727	5042	5538	5569	5822	6246	6842
Number of overnights (thousands of tourists)	6758	7140	7841	6137	3224	7121	6823	8027	9085	9516
Minimum amount spent by a tourist (Euro)	379	481	574	490	475	540	546	608	559	742

Source: www.csb.gov.lv, 2016

Latvia is among the greenest countries in the world. Concerning the share of the forest area, Latvia ranks fifth place in the European Union, after Sweden, Finland, Estonia, and Slovenia.

Forests cover 56% of the country's total land area. To say that Latvia boasts a clean nature is no exaggeration, because it benefits from a natural setting suitable for green tourism, from simple walks in the forest to special tracks for birds, insects, friends, and nature connoisseurs.

Latvia includes 706 protected (Latvia, 2014) natural areas: 4 national parks (Vidžeme Gauja National Park, Kemeri National Park in Zemgale, the Slītere National Park in Kurzeme, and the Rāzna National Park in Latgale), a Biosphere Reserve at North Vidžeme, 42 natural parks, 9 protected areas, 260 nature reserves, 4 strict natural reserves, 355 nature monuments, 7 protected marine areas, and 24 micro reserves. The welcoming attitude of the Latvians derives from the fact that they are less pragmatic and have a higher artistic sense than the other Baltic countries (Plakans, A, 2010).

Latvia has become a tourist attraction, which results from the steady increase in the number of visitors. According to the statistical data downloaded from the website www.csb.gov.lv, the number of overnight stays of foreign tourists increased, as well as the minimum amount spent by them during their stay in Latvia (Table 23.1).

Even though during the economic and financial crisis, the Latvian tourism recorded decreases in the number of tourist arrivals and overnights, the occupancy rate of the accommodation establishments, and the minimum daily/tourist expenses; the situation gradually improved, the 2015 figures indicating increases by more than 25% compared to 2008, for all tourism indicators analyzed. Thus, in 2015, the employment rate is slightly above 26% only in January and December, but in the summer, this indicator reaches values above 60%.

The beauty of the landscape brings an increasing number of tourists to the rural area, which is why the number of visitors and overnight stays in the reception structures with the function of agritourist hostels, campsites, or caravan parks increased.

Table 23.2 Number of tourist arrivals and overnights in accommodation facilities per quarter, in 2015

	Quarter I	Quarter II	Quarter III	Quarter IV
Number of arrivals				
Total number of tourist arrivals	360,421	577,565	782,013	419,364
Number of tourist arrivals in hotels	332,502	508,477	637,786	386,524
Number of tourist arrivals in hostels, pensions, cottages	26,858	53,512	93,183	31,890
Number of tourist arrivals in campsites, caravan parks	1091	15,576	51,044	950
Number of overnights				
Total number of tourist arrivals	693,680	1,081,895	1,503,406	830,929
Number of tourist arrivals in hotels	592,769	913,266	1,164,237	703,796
Number of tourist arrivals in hostels, pensions, cottages	98,996	142,445	241,996	125,835
Number of tourist arrivals in campsites, caravan parks	1915	26,184	97,173	1298

Source: www.csb.gov.lv, 2016

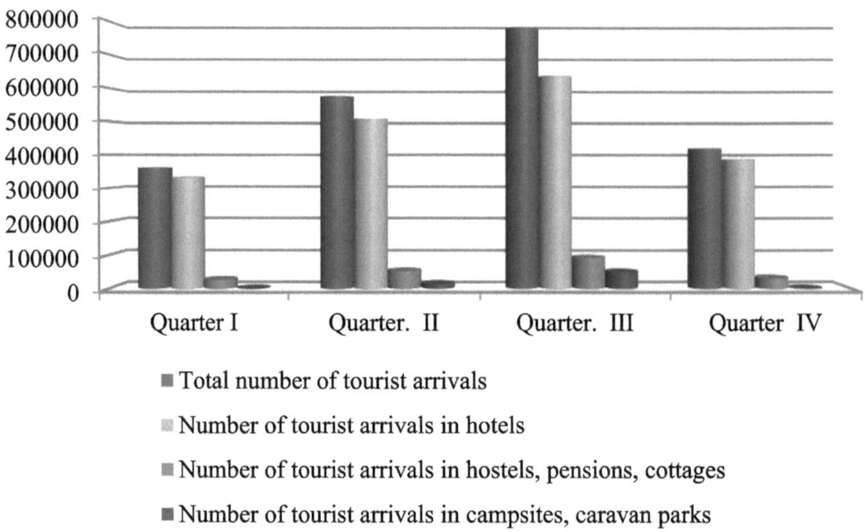

Fig. 23.1 Number of tourist arrivals in accommodation establishments per quarter, in 2015

According to Latvian statistical data, the quarterly situation in 2015 for these indicators is as follows (Table 23.2):

In agritourist boarding houses, cottages, and hostels, the number of overnight stays increased by 43% in the second quarter versus the first quarter and 2.4 times in the third quarter. Those who chose this type of accommodation are 3.46 times more in the third quarter compared to the first quarter (Fig. 23.1).

In 2015, the EDEN (European Destinations of Excellence) project awarded the best rural tourism emerging destinations in the world. *Kuldiga* occupies the ninth place, being considered the Latvian Venice. The village is located in the valley of the *Venta* River. The main tourist attraction of the area consists of cultural, historical, and architectural riches. The Venta River, known as the country's most beautiful river, ends in the widest waterfall in Europe (240 m from one shore to the other). The cultural and historical heritage of Kurzeme (Courland) is as colorful as the *Suiti* women's long skirt and as diverse as the natural environment on the Baltic Sea Livonian coast. Kurzeme is the paradise of fishermen and fish consumers. Sold in the villages on the shore or even along the roads, fish is a good pretext to interact with the local community. In the villages, locals invite tourists to participate in the process of preparing smoked fish, a local delicacy. Each Latvian region has its own traditional food, and Kurzeme is no exception. Sklandrausis (carrot mash with potatoes made from rye flour), *biguzis* (rye bread dessert), and *bukstiņputra* (potato barley stew) are just a few recommendations. These dishes are complemented by wines from the *Vina kalns* vineyard, introduced in the Record of Records as being at the northernmost latitude in the world. With wonderful scenery around, tourists can visit wine cellars where wine producers explain the whole process, subject to wine tasting – depending on time and energy.

For centuries, the Kurzeme northern coast has been "home" for the lion-dwellers, today's Latin predecessors. This small community stubbornly resists and forms a unique entity in the Kurzeme Region, represented by the population of Suiti of Catholic faith, whose territory inhabited in a modest number has been recognized and registered in the UNESCO patrimony. The Suiti community, from a cultural point of view, is made up of Lions, Poles, and Germans and is remarkable in their colorful folk costumes. Some unique trails enhance tourist attractions:

- "The barefoot way" is a popular road of 2.6 km, being regarded as a great opportunity in the summer months for tourists who want to walk barefoot on this route, covered by the feeling of freedom of the body.
- The "scenic path" is 4.5 km long and is an invitation to tourists to explore the natural environment, because in the woods, there are colored "frozen" frames full of natural beauty. This path is exciting for tourists regardless of age, as it includes over 20 varied difficult games.
- "Labyrinth of meditation" is an opportunity for tourists to spend a few moments alone. There are several options; the Gothic designed in 2010 is similar to the thirteenth-century labyrinth of the Chartres Cathedral in France.
- Cycling trails near lake Valguma: There are three routes of choice (16 km, 17 km, and 22 km), plus a series of nature trails. Besides, these trails are also practiced by schoolchildren to explore nature alive, not just on the pages of textbooks or science books. It can be seen from the decomposing forests of termites, forest areas with pine trees, conservation biotopes, rock outcrops, and the bears that have their habitat here, and, with some luck, they can see foxes and deer.
- Bird-watching: Wild duck, wren, yellowhammer, thrush, blackheads, or black stork, an optimal way of relaxing for those who love nature.
- Sportfishing: Lake waters are populated with perch, pike, wicker, cod, and dace.

Also in the Kurzeme Region lies the *Pape Nature Park*. Being a protected area, any excursion and hiking around pastures are always done with a specialized guide. Among the interesting trails of this natural park, there are:

- The "Orchid Way" offers visitors the opportunity to see rare species of orchids.
- "Pape, bird-watching paradise"(bird-watching): Since 1966, an observation, call, and recording station for migratory birds has been operating in Pape. In the fall and spring, thousands of birds use the strip of land between Lake Pape and the sea as part of their migratory routes. More than 200 species of birds migrate each autumn along the Pape shore.
- Fishermen's villages: The Park includes the villages of Pape and Koņu, with fishing farms, which keep alive the interest for the rich cultural and historical heritage as well as for the old buildings.

Laumu Nature Park is a private park developed in Talsi District with special trails to explore nature. Active leisure, cycling, and sportfishing are practiced in the park. Those who choose the *Bee Path*, led by a knowledge guide in the field, can understand the role of bees, and old beekeepers can come to know the secrets of the bee kingdom. *The Bird's Way* provides insight into the fascinating world of birds, the history and origin of the birds present in the park, as well as the possibility of looking closely at bird feathers, the construction of wings, the diversity of nesting sites, and the diversity of bird eggs, beaks, and legs, in thematic collections. Plant lovers can choose the "Plant Way" and observe about 40 species of fruit yew, juniper of various forms, and other perennials.

The Baltic Sea sandy beaches are excellent for walking and cycling, plus the possibility of sailing to the Kolka lighthouse. The national park is on the path of the migratory birds, which come in large numbers in the spring, crossing the sand dunes and the grassy marshes among them and which, as a whole, form a unique landscape in Europe. Fishermen's villages located on the territory of the National Park give visitors the chance to know the cultural heritage of the Livonian, which is also an important part of the cultural and historical heritage of Northern Europe (Jarvis and Kallas 2008).

The southern part of Latvia is occupied by the Zemgale region, a flat area with one of the most fertile fields in Northern Europe, suitable for grain cultivation, which has ensured the prosperity of the local population for centuries. Rural tourism benefits from the possibility of accommodation in the castles of Zemgale and manor houses, proof of the luxury and prosperity of the old times. The landscapes in Zemgale are characterized by extensive cultivated fields, grain and rape, windmills, and modern wind generators. Part of the Ķemeri National Park, which is known for curative sludge, sulfur waters, and mineral waters, is located in the northern area of Zemgale. Women in Zemgale are known to be very hardworking, welcoming, and good housewives, ready to welcome with a good meal for their guests at any time. Local foods in Zemgale are karaša or barley milk and sour milk porridge, along with fish.

Tervete Nature Park with its wooden sculptures with winding paths and bridges stretching along the valley of the River Tervete transposes visitors into the world of fairytale populated by the characters of the books of Latvian writer Anna Brigadere. Nature lovers can admire the pine forests of nearly 300 years or the observation tower that prides itself proudly on the top of the trees and is one of the most impressive structures of its kind in Latvia. Tourists can also visit the scenic Swan Lake, combining hiking with a fishing party with a renting boat. The tourist products include *Mammadaba Deka* (a mother nature adventure) – a chance for tourists who come to the area to combine active leisure time with the exploration of the forest – but also *Zala klase* (green class), an excellent opportunity to learn about friends and the pests of the forest and the diversity of animals and to sensitize participants to this program against one of the greatest treasures of Latvia, the forest. Tourists eager to experience Gauja with waterfalls and thresholds and cyclists who can choose one of Gauja National Park trails or the bay beaches between *Salacgrīva* and *Tuja* can also fly to *Aerodium* – the vertical wind tunnel. In Sigulda, the interest for tourists is the *Tarzāns* amusement park, obstacle races, or bungee jumping from the *Sigulda* cable car above the Gauja Valley.

Gauja National Park has a vast network of natural hiking trails, many of which are adapted to the needs of wheelchair users and families with children in trolleys. Cycling routes in the Gauja National Park are mostly for experienced cyclists, who can approach narrow paths or sandy paths. The best time to go for a bike ride is from May to September. The most popular cycling routes are nearby Sigulda, Ramkalni, Ezu, Cesis, and Valmiera or Apalkalna in the Pargauja region. In winter, Sigulda becomes the ski center of Latvia.

The characteristics of local culture are visible in architectural monuments (cathedrals, churches, public buildings), as well as in households, mansions, and parks that were built in the eighteenth and nineteenth centuries, in Krāslava, Preili, and Kameņeca mural paintings, mansion houses with annexes of servants, barns, and stables. The old Daugavpils fortress is now a multifunctional art center. Rēzekne hosts one of the largest concert halls in the Baltic countries – *Latgale Gors*, considered to be a courageous combination of old and modern architecture. Traditional foods of the Latgale region include *kļocka* (guinea pigs), guļbišņīki (potato balls), *buļbu blini* (potato pancakes), *asuškas* (small white-bread rolls) served with milk and cream sauce, and *slokatnis* (pie with rye flour).

Latgale is a destination especially recommended for gourmets, thanks to both its local delicacies and its specialized farms. The various farms offer visitors the chance to taste cheeses, different types of honey, and herbal teas as well as the chance to take part in the baking process and to taste local wines.

The Rāzna National Park is a "Natura 2000" site and occupies an area of 59,615 ha. It was created to protect the natural values of Rāzna Lake and the surrounding areas, as well as the cultural environment and the landscape that characterize the entire Latgale territory. The sinuous valley of the Daugava River, considered to be the oldest water course in Latvia and where the river has retained its natural character, is part of the area protecting the Augsdaugava landscape, which was declared a "Natura 2000" site in 2004 and included in UNESCO list in 2011.

In 1993, the Latvian Rural Tourism Professional Association with over 330 members, generally owners of rural accommodation establishments, was established. The association is a member of Eurogîtes. Representatives of the association are passionate about outdoor activities and nature. All proposed routes and offers are being tested by specialized guides. The association focuses on small businesses that provide a personal touch and local experience in detail. The association boasts collaboration with some of Latvia's best bird-watching and environmental experts.

Specialists offer advice on planning holidays in the Latvian countryside, setting routes for individual trips and small groups – cycling, boat or bus trips, hiking, bird-watching, visits to craftsmen and local artists, etc (Tourism in Latvia, 2016). The services offered by the association are realized in creation of personalized packages for groups and individuals; reservation accommodation and related services to hotels, guesthouses, mansions, self-catering, and farms; providing specialist guides, publications, professional maps, route descriptions, and specialized tour guides; rental of boats, cars, and bicycles; and transfer services (Rutkis 1997).

Latvia's professional tourism association offers tourists a number of circuits, including *the road of cheese*, *the Baltic country holidays*, and *the Seniors Go Rural*.

Following the *Cheese Road*, tourists learn about the types and assortments of cheese that are produced in small processing units located in rural areas and can enjoy the variety of products they can taste and buy on the farms included in the trail. At the same time, tourists can see the way of production that proves craftsmanship in cheese making, can socialize with small producers about the manufacturing process, and can receive samples for tasting or purchasing, with the Master Cheese rural product label.

Animal husbandry and milk processing are traditional occupations in Latvia, dating back over 2000 years, and cheese is one of the preferred Latvian foods. Jan Siers cheese has the longest tradition and, along with beer, is part of the traditional menu at the Midsummer Day feast; this type of cheese has received the Protected Geographical Indication Certificate as Traditional Specialty Guaranteed – TSG – as it highlights the traditional character in both composition and processing.

The Latvian National Tourism Association, *Lauku ceļotājs*, has edited the "Tasty *Cheese Road*" brochure – *Gardā siera ceļš* – where the Sierzinis holdings are presented to farms and production facilities that prove their craftsmanship in cheese making. The title is also awarded to rural pensions and catering establishments offering in their meals cheeses produced by local recipes.

Baltic country holidays are a tourist product developed by the National Tourism Association of Latvia together with the Estonian Rural Tourism Association and the Regional Tourism Association in Southern Finland. Together, the three associations have produced promotional materials for Japanese target audience about rural touristic circuits and the beauty of nature of the Baltic states and Southern Finland.

The pure nature of Latvia, the countryside of traditions and customs, and the welcoming people and tourists are the certainty of a sustainable rural tourism.

23.2.2 Lithuanian Specificity of Rural and Gastronomical Tourism

The largest of the three Baltic countries, *Lithuania*, has over 700 rivers and nearly 3000 lakes, its territory being covered by 28% of forests. The scenic landscape of Lithuania with low hills, forests, numerous rivers, and more than 3000 lakes, with a stretch of 100 km from lakes, lagoons, and white sandy beaches, attracts tourists not only as a natural paradise but also a modern country with beautiful cities, unique museums, and shops with style. Lithuania is a country where jazz lovers can enjoy good music and gourmets of a select gastronomy and for those who want relaxation of well-rated SPAs. The largest of the three Baltic countries is known for its exceptional basketball performances, jazz festivals, or the beauty of amber objects and less as a tourist destination. Tourists choose for their trips to the capital Vilnius, the Baltic Sea coast, or UNESCO World Heritage Sites – the Nerja Isthmus (Courland), the Kernavė Archaeological Site, or the three observation points of the Struve Geodetic Arc – but Lithuania is also known as a destination for medical tourism, with balneotherapeutic treatment facilities for tourists who choose Northern Europe or Baltic Sea cruises.

According to the annual tourism report in Lithuania, the total number of tourist accommodation facilities increased by more than 100 units in 2015 compared to 2014, as did the number of detailer tour operators and tour operators (Table 23.3).

The analysis of the number of tourists, compared to 2014 and 2015, shows that it is growing. Even if most tourists choose hotels, the second place in accommodation preferences is tourist and agritourism lodges, villas, and holiday homes (Table 23.4).

According to data provided by the World Travel and Tourism Council, tourism's contribution to Lithuania's GDP has steadily increased (Table 23.5).

Table 23.3 Analysis of tourism indicators (2014–2015)

On subsectors of activity (no.)	2014	2015
Tourist structures with accommodation function	1032	1217
Retail travel agencies	214	231
Tour operator travel agencies	108	119
Number of accommodation places by types of tourist structures (thousands of places)		
Hotels	26,6	26,9
Hostels	1,5	1,7
Camping and caravan parks	2,5	2,7
Tourist and agritourist guesthouses, villas, and holiday homes	25,1	26,0
Employees in tourism subsectors (thousands of people)		
In tourist structures with accommodation function	11	11,3
Public alimentation	30,5	30,6
Retail travel agencies	1,3	1,2
Tour operators travel agencies	0,8	0,9

Source: www.csb.gov.lv, 2016

Table 23.4 Analysis of tourist traffic (2014–2015)

Number of tourist arrivals (thousands)	2014	2015
Number of tourist arrivals of residents and foreigners in tourist accommodation structures	1977.5	2184.5
Number of tourist overnights of residents and foreigners in tourist accommodation structures	5265.6	5563.3
Number of residents traveling abroad	1707.5	1764.2
Number of overnights of the residents traveling abroad	6885.7	6993.2
Occupancy in tourist structures with accommodation function (%)		
Hotels	58.7	59.7
Tourist and agritourist guesthouses, villas, and holiday homes	36.7	35.3
Travels lasting 4 days or longer		
Number of trips of foreign tourists (thousands of trips)	630.3	647.3
Percentage of total foreigners' travels (%)	33.2	35.8
Percentage of total residents' travels (%)	17.2	20.1

Source: www.csb.gov.lv, 2016

Table 23.5 Evolution of tourism's contribution to Lithuania's GDP (2010–2015)

	2010	2011	2012	2013	2014	2015
Direct tourism contribution (million euro)	1665.1	1896,7	2036,0	2181,4	2340,9	2316,6
Total tourism contribution (million euro)	4379.2	4862,2	5212,1	5523,4	5912,2	5836,3

Source: www.csb.gov.lv, 2016

The annual budget allocated for tourism promotion has grown from 2973.3 thousand euros in 2014 to 3829.6 thousand euros in 2015, as it is obvious the role that this industry has in the country's economic development. The projects from European funds in the field were also growing, so the structural and cohesion funds were allocated 1707.3 thousand euro in 2014 and 2942.3 thousand euro in 2015.

Rural tourism emerged in Lithuania in 1997, when there were only 17 pensions. The activity has grown continuously so that nowadays tourists can accommodate over 600 boarding houses in the countryside. Rural tourism is considered as an alternative to the usual activities in the villages. The Lithuanian Rural Tourism Association is an independent, nonprofit organization that gathers together members from all over the country involved in rural tourism activities: consultancy actions, training farmers to manage their rural tourism business, promoting rural tourism through Specific marketing activities, and cooperation with central and local authorities.

The region of *Žemaitija* is the home of craftsmen: carpenters, coopers, tailors, blacksmiths, and potters have their workshops in the rural areas and small towns of this region, *Kursenai*, being declared the capital of pottery in Lithuania. Outdoor museums allow visitors to know how people lived a hundred or two hundred years ago: the Stone Processing Museum, the Ethnographic and Folk Civilization Museum, and the Alka History Museum. The historic site Deal of the Cruces was visited in 1993 by Pope John Paul II, an event that gathered hundreds of thousands of people at the liturgy of the sovereign Pontiff, during which His Excellency blessed Lithuania and all of the Christian Europe. The moment was marked by the tide raised on the Hill of the Cross a year later after the pope's visit. The flag and flag of the region are decorated with a dark brown bear symbolizing the temper of the locals and their heroic deeds throughout history.

The Aukstaitija region is located in the northeast and east of the country and is the area where the core of the Grand Duchy of Lithuania was formed around the eleventh century. Aukštaitija is the largest Lithuanian region that differentiates itself from the rest of the country through households and villages systematized on the basis of rigorous plans, but also through the production of beer and amazing folklore. It's hard to tell if the people in Aukštaitija started singing or drinking beer first. Aukštaitija's songs are distinguished by the uniqueness of the sounds (the famous *sutartinės*, the old songs of Aukštaitija, preserved the typical musical and poetic form). The region is also renowned for traditional colorful textiles and national costumes. In addition, culinary art and beer factories are also characteristics of Aukštaitija, a member of European culinary heritage. In Aukštaitija there are many tourist attractions:

- The longest lake in Lithuania, *Sartai*, is not only a spectacular oasis but also a favorite place for tourists coming from all over the country as well as from neighboring countries including winter to enjoy the lively nature spectacle.
- A giant rock, *Puntukas*, which weighs about 265 tones and which, according to archaeologists, was brought there by Scandinavian glaciers; mythology says that the stone was carried by the waters of a river that turned into a drop and disappeared when the first rays of sun appeared.
- Stelmužė oak, the oldest tree in Lithuania and one of the oldest in Europe, about 1500 years old, has a diameter of 3.5 m.
- A unique museum dedicated to horses: On the first Saturday of June, the museum invites tourists to participate in a traditional sport and a cheerful ethnographic celebration, called "Run, horse, run!"

The Southwest Lithuanian region, located between two of the country's main rivers, Nemunas and Neris, is the area with the oldest weavers in the country, as well as the most talented singers. Currently, there are several villages designed as true outdoor museums, where visitors can spend a few days in the midst of local communities. Particular for their diversity are the Druskininkai and Trakai resorts, where tourists come for vacation and romantic weekends or benefit from wellness treatments where clean, unpolluted, salty air brings curative benefits.

The Suvalkija region is located in southern and southwest Lithuania, on the left bank of the Nemunas River, which also explains the name *Uznemunė* (the other side of the Nemunas River). The Suvalkija region covers the lands of the historical tribe of Sūduviai, a clay-lined land with herbaceous vegetation. Suvalkija boasts its folk festivals, such as *Gegužinė* (Feast of May). The capital of the region is *Marijampolė*, the seventh largest city, famous for the oldest fabric in Lithuania. Suvalkija people are renowned for their ingenuity but also for stinginess.

There is also a series of anecdotes about the lifestyle of Suvalkians. One of them might translate as follows: "What does a Suvalkian do when it is very cold in winter?

He stands in front of a candle. But what does he do when it is really very cold in the winter? Light the candle."

The ethnographic region of Lower Lithuania is located in the west of the country. In fact, the region is also included the Kaliningrad area, which now belongs to Russia. Lower Lithuania includes the most beautiful natural heritage in Lithuania, the small Curonian promontory of sand, which is included in the UNESCO World Heritage, because the nature and archaic folk architecture made of wood are united in one particular ensemble. The largest city in Lower Lithuania is Klaipėda, a city that belonged to Prussia and in 1923 only returned to Lithuania, explaining the cultural variety, including architecture and good knowledge of the German language.

In 2001, when UNESCO declared the list of the first 19 intangible patrimonies, the Lithuanian crafts (*kryždirbystė*) and their symbolism were also included. Traditional crosses in Lithuania are unique artisanal objects, a combination of architectural elements, blacksmithing, sculpture, and painting. Crosses with iron countertops, ornaments, and wooden sculptures with various themes are important elements of Lithuanian folk heritage. The craftsmanship is closely related to some Lithuanian traditions and customs: they are crosses made for the dead or as a mystical spiritual preservation, placed in special places as gifts. Crafts have become symbols of Lithuanian nationalism, and the works of the craftsman Vincas Svirskis (1835–1916) are preserved in national museums. After the Lithuanian handcrafted cross was included in UNESCO's List of Intangible Cultural Heritage objects, public organizations became more active in preserving and fostering the preservation of this craft.

Lithuania is also called the country of the storks, the stork being also the high-ranking bird of distinctive character of this country. On its entire surface, there are approximately 13,000 pairs of storks. This is why the households included in the Lithuanian Rural Tourism Association are classified into five categories on storks rather than flowers, as in other European countries (Table 23.6).

Statistical data indicates that most rural households are classified as three berms (42%) and two berms (35%). In the category "a barge," 10% of the rural tourism

Table 23.6 Classification criteria for rural tourism pensions

Classification	Requests
	Basic conditions for accommodation and facilities but very few leisure opportunities
	Rural household with minimum facilities. Tourists live in the same house with homeowners. Minimum offer for facilities and recreation
	Rural environment of average comfort. There is a wide variety of leisure facilities, quality accommodation. Most of the menu is self-catering
	Comfortable rural house for rest and various events. Quality accommodation and food, a wide range of leisure facilities
	Exclusive rural household. Well-managed facilities, excellent accommodation services, dining, and a wide range of leisure facilities are provided

Source: www.csb.gov.lv, 2016

pensions are included, and those providing a high comfort of four and five storks represent only 12% and 1%, respectively (Official Statistics Portal, Tourism. Vilnius, Statistics Lithuania 2014).

Regarding the number of accommodation places in rural tourist pensions, the region Utena in the Molėtai District attracts the most visitors due to the beauty of nature and rich cultural heritage. The 220 lakes in this area are distinguished by their clearness and cleanliness. Visitors can get acquainted with the history of the district in the local and fishery museums (with a rich collection of fishing gear and trophies). The clean waters of the local lakes create favorable conditions for the existence of many species of fish and crustaceans. An interesting museum is *Ethnocosmology*, with the astronomical observer. In the Molėtai District, there is Asveja, the largest lake in Lithuania. In the village of Balninkai, there is a museum of glass where you can make an insight into the history of the way of making Lithuanian glass and you can admire glass exhibits, real works of art. The Molėtai District is one of the cleanest areas in Lithuania, with the largest number of households practicing rural tourism. For tourists, all the conditions for an active holiday are created:

- "Duonos sodyba" (Bread House of Peasants), where visitors follow the bread baking process from the ingredients to the finished product
- "Gojaus smuklė," entertainment evenings for visitors who can enjoy local gastronomy while listening to traditional folk music
- "Įlankos sodyba," where boat tours on Lake Bebrusai, fishing trips, or ceramic courses are organized for tourists (Table 23.7)

A total of 392 farms and agritourism boardhouses in the year 2015 are distributed in the 4 ethnographic regions: 197 pensions in Aukštaitija, 91 in Žemaitija, 85 in Dzukija, and 19 in Suvalkija (Table 23.8).

Table 23.7 Farms, tourist boarding houses, and agritourism by counties (2014–2015)

County	Number of accommodation structures		Number of rooms		Number of beds	
	2014	2015	2014	2015	2014	2015
Total	590	615	3878	4231	12421	13332
Alytus	95	94	593	591	2010	2018
Kaunas	65	70	549	587	1871	1943
Klaipėda	37	46	279	310	874	973
Marijampolė	20	22	128	139	570	613
Panevėžys	22	29	194	208	618	630
Šiauliai	13	16	126	132	381	425
Tauragė	19	17	151	192	332	306
Telšiai	41	41	302	312	878	885
Utena	193	184	901	866	2835	2688
Vilnius	85	102	655	954	2052	2851

Source: www.csb.gov.lv, 2016c

Table 23.8 Number of tourist arrivals and overnights in farms, tourist and agritourist boarding houses (2014–2015)

County	No. of arrivals (thousands)		Number of overnights (thousands)		Average duration of stay (no. of days)	
	2014	2015	2014	2015	2014	2015
Total	227,5	252,8	379,8	453,4	1,67	1,79
Alytus	37,8	40,8	58,5	62,0	1,55	1,52
Kaunas	41,8	44,1	70,3	73,8	1,68	1,67
Klaipėda	15,4	17,1	23,4	31,6	1,52	1,85
Marijampolė	11,1	8,8	17,7	19,1	1,59	2,16
Panevėžys	12,3	12,4	23,0	24,5	1,87	1,97
Šiauliai	5,7	8,2	8,5	12,8	1,49	1,56
Tauragė	4,3	4,3	12,4	12,5	2,90	2,90
Telšiai	15,0	15,0	21,4	21,1	1,40	1,40
Utena	38,6	39,6	71,4	85,1	1,85	2,15
Vilnius	45,7	62,3	73,3	110,8	1,61	1,78

Source: www.csb.gov.lv, 2016

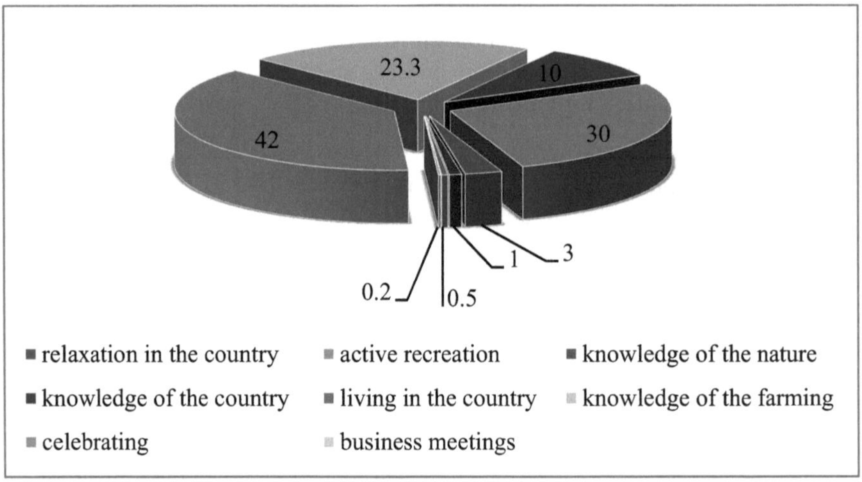

Fig. 23.2 Tourist motivations in the choice of rural tourism and agritourism destinations (%) (Source: www.atostogoskaime.lt)

Rural tourism in Lithuania is complemented by active recreation, with the desire to know the traditional life and beauty of nature in protected areas, as well as business tourism, events, and celebration of traditional religious holidays (Fig. 23.2).

1. Each Lithuanian region has something to offer to rural tourism consumers: different traditions, ethnographic elements, and folk architecture. Rural tourism in Aukštaitija is better developed. In addition to the attractions of the lakes, tourists

can also be familiar with the pottery. Žemaitija attracts tourists with the seaside area and the national park, plus the Virgis and Plateliai areas, which propose to familiarize tourists with culinary heritage items through the products of rural bakeries. Dzukija successfully uses the richness of its forests and traditions in buckwheat culture. Tourists can take part in mill activities that squeeze buckwheat and prepare culinary products (Bučienė and Merkienė 2014).

Within the Rural Development Program measure "Encourage rural tourism activities," the villages received financial support from both the EU and the government.

The Lithuanian Rural Tourism Association is a member of Eurogîtes and takes on the French experience in the sustainable development of rural tourism but adapting it to local realities and the requirements of the target audience.

Regarding the specific features of the activities of rural tourism, based on direct communication with hosts in rural guesthouses, tourists return to the same hostels, through a system that has grown, called "personal communication for accommodation services." Such communication is highly appreciated, and this is a distinct feature of rural tourism in Lithuania (Rupnik et al. 2003).

Individuals involved in Lithuanian rural tourism have understood that rural tourism is not a regular business, but much more is needed. The visitor can be offered not only a night stay but also a certain program of activities. Guests see or feel something new, something they did not experience before. Such a way of spending a holiday allows the tourist to get familiar with their everyday life in the guesthouse that hosts them and can experience the usual household activities as a family member. He does not only consume healthier products but also has the opportunity to participate in the whole process of obtaining those products; how these products find their way from the farm to consumption; the way the grain is grown on the farmland or on the neighboring farms, such as cows; and how the dishes are prepared. There is a wide range of activities of choice, so some tourists find pleasure in the tranquility of the landscape, admire the mist rising above the lake early in the morning, and listen to song of birds, while others can spend their most active time through trips and hiking, bathing, fishing.

In 2011, a number of priorities have been established to ensure the harmonious and sustainable development of rural tourism. The first nominee was sanitation in rural tourism pensions, in order to be responsible and support for nature and environmental protection activities, so that the tourist product does not affect nature.

Funds allocated through the measure on "Encouraging rural tourism, including development trades in rural households," have been used to develop nature knowledge trails and a workshop to build traditional craft. With such initiatives, rural tourism is constantly being developed, the beneficiaries being not only domestic tourists but also those in neighboring Poland, Latvia, Russia, Germany, Sweden, Denmark, and Finland or from more remote countries like the United Kingdom; Russians and Germans prefer rural tourism in the localities situated in the coastal area, although it was not the Russians who first appreciated the rural tourism products. They have begun to discover their advantages in their immediate vicinity: nature is similar to Russia, conditions are even better, and prices are lower. In addition, in Lithuania many Russian tourists can communicate in their mother tongue.

Through the "Encouragement of Tourist Activities" measure under the Rural Development Program, areas of activity are supported, such as developing crafts in rural households, improving the quality of rural tourism services and increasing their diversity, and implementing innovations in rural tourism businesses. The attempt to diversify rural tourism services is encouraged to complement traditional agricultural activities with the provision of quality services to tourists (supply of fresh farmed products, recreational services such as sports, horseback riding, agricultural training courses, or traditional crafts). There are touristic boarding houses offering boating or on canoeing, cycling, and hiking trails. In this way, rural residents are stabilized by creating long-term jobs and complementary rural tourism revenues.

Rural tourism also contributes to the valorization of cultural heritage, and young people are encouraged to know and maintain the Lithuanian traditions.

Initially, rural tourism represented the desire to be closer to nature; those who started business in the field had a holiday home where they came with friends, relatives, and acquaintances. Gradually they found that everyone liked to relax in nature, and because most of them had large areas of land, they set up ponds, playgrounds, parking lots, alleys, and themed trails in the attractive landscape. As the business has grown, the owners of rural pensions have organized a wide variety of leisure activities at the request of their clients. Traditionally, live music festivals with campfire events are organized. Regardless of the season, tourists can find attractions such as swimming in the pond or sink in winter, sauna, and archery – recalling the weapons used by medieval archers.

Those who choose rural tourism products do it for the natural landscape and the traditional spirit of the household. This is why tourists most often choose rural pensions for family celebrations, for generations of birthdays. It is also the reason why the owners of the hostels make every effort to preserve their authenticity and tradition by collecting ethnographic exhibits, old household utensils, old pieces of furniture, etc. In recent years, it has been found that young people are increasingly interested in the ancestors' lifestyle. The touristic packages offered by the tour operators are adapted to the new requirements and include courses in ethnography and folk culture, taught by recognized specialists. Such courses also include students who are fascinated by the authenticity of country life and the abundance of traditional exhibits. Most young people prefer to sleep in the rooms set in the old barns, where in winter it is heated by old stoves on wood.

Lithuanian rural tourism, encouraged by the increased demand for products launched and the large number of visitors, is on the rise. This is done in a sustainable way, with care for the authentic immaterial patrimony but also for the generous natural environment. With climate change, the challenge is immense, as Lithuania will be one of the first countries to disappear from the map if mankind fails to find a solution to global warming. Over a few hundred years, the city of Vilnius and the medieval castles, villages, and traditions kept for centuries may only exist in the history books.

23.2.3 Rural Tourism and Gastronomy in Estonia

Estonia is a small country on the southern shore of the Baltic Sea, with an area almost as large as Denmark and the Netherlands. However, Estonia has three times fewer inhabitants than Denmark and ten times less than in the Netherlands. The low population density allowed a better preservation of the natural environment than in densely populated Western European regions. Estonia has a long and curved shoreline, measuring approximately 3800 km. More than 2500 km are the shores of approx. 1500 islands. Approximately half of Estonia's territory is covered with forests. The natural river system can be considered one of the most important values of Estonian nature, with a wealth of natural habitats. There are about 1500 lakes of considerable size, with countless ponds and marshes. The lakeside area occupies over 2000 km2, of which two thirds belong to Lake Peipsi, the fifth largest lake in Europe. Estonians are one of the oldest nations in Europe, traces of the presence of ancestors of today's population dating back to about 5000 years. Just a hundred years ago, the Estonians were largely peasants, depending on their ability to coexist with nature. This is reflected in rural settlements but also in Estonian folklore. The dramatic political transformations of the past century have had a severe impact on the landscapes in Estonia, one fifth of the villages being destroyed. Estonian landscapes can be divided into three major types: the first category is the estuary areas situated to the west by the mountain regions, which rarely exceed 30 m; the second category consists of the vast plains and plateaus that occupy the north of the country, the central part and the surroundings of Tartu; the third type of landscape is formed by the mountain areas Pandivere, Sakala, Vooremaa, Otepää, Karula and Haanja.

Starting with 2006, the tourist villas, the pensions, the houses, and the holiday villages were registered in the National Economic Registry and ranked in quality classes, depending on endowments. The introduction of the classification of accommodation units in rural areas allowed:

- Establishing the classification category for each structure with accommodation function
- Increasing the credibility of accommodation providers
- Entrepreneurial planning
- Determining the needs and expectations of the target customer group
- Increasing the credibility of the tourist destination and increasing the competitiveness of the entrepreneurs

As a symbol of the quality of the accommodation units in the countryside, the cornflower was chosen as the national symbol plant, with the flowers that have been embellished in the fields of Estonia over the centuries. MTÜ Eesti Maaturism (Estonian Rural Tourism Association) has the right to classify accommodation facilities in rural areas that maintain their classification for 3 years (Table 23.9).

At the level of 2016, agritourist hostels were approved  and . The number of agritourist pensions does not show spectacular increases, but the

Table 23.9 Capacity of accommodation establishments

Year	Territory	Number of establishments	Number of rooms	Number of beds
2014	Whole country	1419	23,971	58,095
	Northern Estonia	237	8796	19,410
	Central Estonia	130	1644	4276
	Northeastern Estonia	75	1584	3986
	Western Estonia	548	6871	17,458
	Southern Estonia	429	5076	12,965
2015	Whole country	1417	23,754	58,072
	Northern Estonia	240	8670	19,267
	Central Estonia	133	1655	4258
	Northeastern Estonia	79	1567	3917
	Western Estonia	541	7053	17,937
	Southern Estonia	424	4809	12,693
2016	Whole country	1454	24,503	59,471
	Northern Estonia	254	8983	19,957
	Central Estonia	146	1776	4425
	Northeastern Estonia	78	1625	4221
	Western Estonia	549	7068	17,745
	Southern Estonia	427	5051	13,123

Source: www.csb.gov.lv, 2016

Table 23.10 Accommodated tourists by year

Year	Categories of tourists	Number of tourists
2014	Accommodated tourists total	3,087,070
	Accommodated residents of Estonia	1,103,755
	Accommodated foreign visitors	1,983,315
2015	Accommodated tourists total	3,112,143
	Accommodated residents of Estonia	1,182,979
	Accommodated foreign visitors	1,929,164
2016	Accommodated tourists total	3,324,914
	Accommodated residents of Estonia	1,268,388
	Accommodated foreign visitors	2,056,526

Source: www.csb.gov.lv, 2016

number of tourists and overnight stays in these accommodation structures has increased (Table 23.10).

The most numerous tourists come from neighboring countries and especially from Russia. The fact that Estonia, as well as the other Baltic countries, was part of the Soviet Union was materialized, among other things, in the obligation to know and use Russian. This is now an advantage, as Russian tourists know that in the Baltic countries they can understand the hosts in Russian. More and more Europeans discover the beauty of the Baltic landscape, so the presence of foreign tourists is growing. At country level, the situation between 2013 and 2015 is as follows (Table 23.11):

Table 23.11 Accommodated tourists by country of residence

Country	2013	2014	2015
Albania, Bulgaria, Romania	900	1093	1629
Austria	3487	5757	9368
Belgium	2828	4043	4940
Czech Republic	2111	4433	5046
Denmark	14,894	13,915	15,407
Estonia	448,755	547,712	619,168
Finland	706,473	843,871	799,139
France	8326	15,086	16,921
Germany	68,151	85,643	109,346
Greece	1240	1564	1696
Hungary	1489	2267	3464
Iceland	..	916	2209
Ireland	2073	3058	4841
Italy	13,127	25,642	26,712
Cyprus	..	..	223
Latvia	29,230	40,956	51,558
Lithuania	14,320	20,555	24,703
Luxembourg	350	454	561
Malta	..	..	169
Netherlands	7826	10,490	12,714
Norway	29,842	35,798	41,273
Poland	13,018	11,301	14,194
Portugal	1131	2781	3488
Russia	37,320	42,348	53,427
Slovakia	513	564	1255
Slovenia	478	740	1298
Spain	7921	12,177	15,533
Sweden	66,751	89,042	108,234
Switzerland	3791	4694	5258
Ukraine	..	..	1861
United Kingdom	30,151	38,903	62,926
Other European countries	13,236	15,888	11,669
United States of America	12,761	19,411	19,506
Canada	1567	2981	3254
Japan	6901	7362	8066
Other countries	10,540	10,681	11,530

Source: www.csb.gov.lv, 2016

The number of foreign tourists visiting Estonia is increasing significantly. For example, in only 3 years (2013–2015), the number of English and Spanish tourists has doubled, and the Russians reach approx. 10,000 more each year.

Table 23.12 Accommodated tourists by year and purpose of trip

2014	Total	3,087,070
	Holiday trip	2,106,909
	Business trip	676,983
	Participation in conference, training	95,735
	Other trips	303,178
2015	Total	3,112,143
	Holiday trip	2,113,176
	Business trip	698,261
	Participation in conference, training	117,308
	Other trips	300,706
2016	Total	3,324,914
	Holiday trip	2,289,237
	Business trip	730,290
	Participation in conference, training	109,956
	Other trips	305,387

Source: www.csb.gov.lv, 2016

The reasons why tourists visit Estonia are numerous: spending holidays, business trips, and attending trainings and conferences. It is remarkable that a small country like Estonia attracts twice as many tourists (Table 23.12).

The EHE symbol is a quality label for labeling tourism products in accordance with the principles of ecotourism. The objective of the EHE brand is to promote the principles of ecotourism among tourist units, tourism consumers, and the general public. By applying the EHE mark to its products, the entrepreneur commits itself to the principles of ecotourism and meets the requirements set for such products. The Estonian Ecological Tourism Society, in cooperation with MTÜ Eesti Maaturism and other relevant organizations in the field, launched the eco-labeling scheme for EHE – Ehtne ja huvitav Eesti (Interesting Estonia) – in 2001. The tourist units have joined voluntarily, and their adherence to the system gives the tourism company a competitive advantage and a growing market share. The keywords of the organization are ecological awareness and authentic natural and cultural experiences.

Other meanings have been promoted, including the swallowtail bird, always present near the human settlements, which cheered farmers during their daily work with their optimistic chirp. Limestone, the rock chosen as a national symbol, is found in Northern and Western Estonia. While many farmers have encountered difficulties due to limestone, the Estonian architecture has gained much from this remarkable building material. The oak was unofficially recognized as the Estonian national symbol tree, on the plateaus of this country reaching the northern limit of its natural area of spreading. The Estonians appreciated the tree for both practical utility and the holy symbol. Throughout history, Estonian cuisine has depended much on the season and has focused on simple peasant food, being influenced by many countries. Today, it includes many international dishes. Estonian foods are black bread, pork, potatoes, and dairy products. Traditionally, in the summer and spring, Estonians eat fresh food: fruits, vegetables, and whatever is collected directly from the garden. Hunting and fishing are also common, though they have become just hobbies. The outdoor grill in the summer has become popular. In winter, jams, preserved foods, and pickles are consumed. Estonia has gone through difficult years in the past and that's why gathering and preserving fruit, mushrooms, and vegetables for the winter have always been essential activities. Today, gathering and preserving are not so frequent, but the preparation of winter food remains popular in the country and still has a somewhat ritual significance. In Estonian national cuisine, most dishes are known and recognized throughout the country, but there are also regional differences and peculiarities. Traditional food choices are the result of holidays and seasons, and dishes made from national cuisine are found in the menus of many agritouristic boarding houses and restaurants. The "house specialty" symbol is sometimes completed with "host specialty."

The rye reef has always been a part of the Estonian mass. To this, add graham bread, sauce with barley flour, pies and pudding. Of the meat types, Estonians prefer pork, which is usually consumed with potatoes, vegetables and herbs. Typical dishes in Estonian national cuisine are boiled cabbage with pork or veal and spicy flavored spices. Estonians have always preferred fish. Delicious culinary experiences are provided by boarding houses that prepare barbecue or smoked fish. As beverages, Estonians prefer quartz and birch and maple syrup. Homemade beer is prepared, and juniper flavor is added to it. The national project in Estonia, based on a national partnership for rural tourism, has shown that this form of tourism offers the best prospects for a new economic activity in rural Estonia. Project experts have suggested that a central, unified, professional, and autonomous organization can establish and coordinate the promotion and marketing of rural tourism products in the country as well as abroad. In January 2000, 19 tourism entrepreneurs set up the Estonian Rural Tourism Organization (ERTO) as a nonprofit body. ERTO has started from the belief that life in rural areas can be best preserved and exploited through rural tourism. The purpose of the organization is to bring Estonian entrepreneurs together with stakeholders involved in rural tourism-related activities so that a common database is accessible to all those interested in the lives of Estonian people and their history.

ERTO's efforts have focused on organizing, developing, and building confidence in its activities, as well as reuniting rural tourism entrepreneurs in order to commercialize their activities and provide new opportunities to support and strengthen their operations. On the training line, counseling and marketing services are offered to members of ERTO. The Ministry of Agriculture, the Ministry of Business and Environment, the Estonian Tourism Agency, the Estonian Ecotourism Association, and local NGOs are the most important ERTO partners at the national level. There is also a close partnership with foreign institutions such as the Rural Tourism Organization in Latvia and Finland but also with the Scottish Farm College.

By the end of 2000, ERTO had attracted 195 members, the top 100 joining the ERTO's marketing scheme, which includes the advertising website and the publication.

The travel guide for the countryside is accessible in five languages, of which three of international circulation, and also contains information on the telephone support service. The ERTO marketing strategy has focused on a number of distinct tourist products that target traditional Estonian markets for tourism as well as new ones. These products include holidays in rural production farms, nature and cultural tourism, children and family in rural tourism, health tourism, active holidays, seminars, and anniversary parties. ERTO has worked closely with its members to ensure quality.

Circuits and other tourist products are being offered, and this quality has been constantly monitored. In 2001, ERTO focused on diversifying and improving the travel packages offered by members of the organization, as well as their more efficient marketing through tourism fairs and neighboring countries, with 130 tourism entrepreneurs being involved in the marketing program. By the end of 2002, ERTO had completed the criteria, ensuring the quality of tourist accommodation services in rural areas, similar to the "stars" system used in hotels. Over the next few years, more and more rural tourism entrepreneurs have participated in training programs, including three specialties in the field of active tourism, nature and culture, and tourism and holidays on agricultural farms.

At present, ERTO has 266 members from all rural Estonia, of which 210 are tourist accommodation providers, accounting for around 30% of such Estonian suppliers.

23.3 Conclusions

From their experience so far in rural tourism, Latvia, Lithuania, and Estonia have learned to professionally promote nature, the most valuable asset of these Baltic countries. Several measures on rural tourism have been taken to improve the situation in rural areas. The establishment of rural tourism organizations provides access to information and good practice materials on European rural tourism and the organization of courses for rural residents in order to improve the quality of services provided by potential tourists. For the development of rural tourism, the governments of the Baltic countries have been allocated funds as a direct support for the development of tourism products. At the same time, the state provides economic support and guarantees for loans for investment in rural tourism.

Rural tourism activity has been increasing in recent years and is an important form of sustainable development. Baltic rural communities have identified a number of regional problems with relatively poor peripheral infrastructure compared to urban areas, depopulation and migration to the urban area, increased unemployment among local communities, and sea and fishing dependency. All this can be solved by developing rural tourism and agritourism.

The central objective of Baltic tourism policy is to ensure the rational use of natural resources, tourism contributing to the development of a diverse and profitable economy capable of providing modern services but also a means of slowing migration from rural areas to urban areas. An important way to achieve these goals is to diversify the hospitality industry through rural tourism.

References

Bučienė, R., Merkienė, J.: Sustainable development and rural tourism in Lithuania, Rotur. Revista de Ocio y Turismo. **7**, 10–19 (2014)

Cimdiņa, A., Hanovs, D.: Latvia and Latvians: A People and a State in Ideas, Images and Symbols. Zinātne Publishers, Rīga (2011)

Dreifelds, J.: Latvia in Transition. Cambridge University Press, Cambridge (1996)

http://osp.stat.gov.lt (2016). Last accessed 2017/05/21

Jarvis, J., Kallas, P.: Estonian Tourism and the Accession Effect: The Impact of European Union Membership on the Contemporary Development Patterns of the Estonian Tourism Industry, Tourism Geographies – An International Journal of Tourism Space, Place and Environment , Volume 10, Issue 4: Tourism in transition economies, National Centre for Estonian Tourist Board, Enterprise Estonia, Tallinn, Estonia, 474–494 (2008)

Official Statistics Portal, Tourism. Vilnius, Statistics Lithuania (2014)

Plakans, A.: The A to Z of Latvia. The Scarecrow Press, Lanham (2010)

Rupnik, J., Pettai, V., Zielonka, J.: The Road to the European Union: Estonia, Latvia, and Lithuania. Manchester University Press/Palgrave, Manchester/New York (2003)

Rutkis, J.: Latvia: Country & People. Stockholm, Latvian National Foundation (1997)

www.atostogoskaime.lt (2016b). Last accessed 2017/05/21

www.countryside.lt (2016c). Last accessed 2017/05/21

www.wttc.org (2016d). Last accessed 2017/05/21

*** Latvia, OECD Tourism Trends and Policies, OECD Publishing (2014)

*** Tourism in Latvia, Collection of Statistics, Riga (2016)

Chapter 24
The Dynamics of the Global Multinationals: Determinants of New Global Configurations and New Management Challenges

Claudia Ogrean

Abstract During the last few decades, the complex interplay between (the process of) globalization and (the evolution of global) multinationals has radically changed both the architecture of the global economy and the characteristics of their main players – the global multinationals; new configurations have emerged, while new complexities have replaced them, in unprecedented (in terms of speed, breadth, and depth) manners, adding new valences to the challenges firms and their strategists are confronting nowadays. The aim of the paper is to identify (some of) the most significant shifts that have marked the dynamics of the global multinationals during the last two decades, in order to sketch the new realities and trends that define the global economy as is it today, on one hand, and to determine the challenges these new (diverse and dynamic) conditions raise in front of firms and their strategic management, on the other hand. Against the background offered by the literature review – on the mutually reinforcing and ever-emerging relationships between globalization and (the global) multinationals, the paper will develop a (historical) comparative analysis of the world's largest companies – based on Fortune Global 500 rankings (which represent a widely recognized benchmark); the combination of the two methods (literature review and analysis of real data) will ensure significant insights on the subject while setting the premises for reliable findings and conclusions, as well as for future research directions.

Keywords Globalization • Global shifts • Global multinationals • Management challenges

---

C. Ogrean (✉)
Lucian Blaga University of Sibiu, Sibiu, Romania
e-mail: claudia.ogrean@ulbsibiu.ro

S.C. Mărginean et al. (eds.), *Emerging Issues in the Global Economy*, Springer Proceedings in Business and Economics,
https://doi.org/10.1007/978-3-319-71876-7_24

24.1 Introduction and Literature Review

Globalization and multinationals are two constructs that undeniably dominate the business environment nowadays, following quite parallel paths of symbiotic dynamics. Despite the controversies on the emergence and evolution of both globalization (Hirst et al. 2015) and multinationals (Wilkins 2009), the histories of the two phenomenon are strongly correlated – as academia have consistently and substantially argued. Thus, "multinational enterprises (MNEs) are the key drivers of globalization" (Rugman and Verbeke 2004), while "the emergence and activities of multinational enterprises (MNEs) stand in the center of the theoretical explanation of the globalization process" (Kleinert 2004). But, just as it is true that "globalization depends on multinationals" (McCann 2008), it is also true that "globalization has changed the nature of the MNE" (Narula and Dunning 2010).

Within this ever-evolving framework, with multinationals fueling the globalization process and benefiting from its spillovers, a new "species" has occurred and gained momentum on the global arena – the global multinationals. This tendency of firms toward going global has been quite intensely analyzed and theorized by academia: (a). the organization theory perspective considers that multinationals become global by following a four-stage evolution process and argues that "although few companies are genuinely fully global, (…) truly global companies no longer think of themselves as having a single home country and, indeed, have been called stateless corporations" (Daft et al. 2010); (b). in a similar line of thinking, the international business perspective identifies – when classifying firms by multinationality on a matrix basis taking into account the extent of geographic spread on one hand and the depth of market engagement on the other hand – seven types of global firms, which "conduct business in all six regions (…) based on the inhabited continents" (Aggarwal et al. 2010).

During the last few decades, the complex interplay between (the process of) globalization and (the evolution of global) multinationals has radically changed both the architecture of the global economy and the characteristics of their main players (the global multinationals).

As regards the global landscape, its dynamics and characteristics, (a). some are talking about "global shift: the changing global economic map" (Dicken 2007) – driven by and resulted into a series of "processes of global shift" (referring to technological change, transnational corporations, transnational production networks, variation in state economic policies, and uneasy relationship between transnational corporations and states), which have redesigned different sectors (clothing, automobile, semiconductor, agro-food, financial services, logistics, and distribution), while leading to "winning and losing in the global economy" (Dicken 2007); (b). others are introducing the concept of globality (Sirkin et al. 2008) – in order to define the "new era emerging "– "a different kind of environment, in which business flows in every direction. Companies have no centers. The idea of foreignness is foreign. Commerce swirls and market dominance shifts. Western business orthodoxy entwines with eastern business philosophy and creates a whole new mind-set that embraces profit and competition as well as sustainability and collaboration" (Sirkin et al. 2008).

As concerns the global multinationals, academia has brought into attention new forms/varieties, developing new patterns of evolution, new (global) strategies and business models – that all reflect the new global shifts, being, in the same time, significant contributors to them:

(a) The born-global firms – also called "international new ventures" or "global start-ups" (Knight and Cavusgil 2005) – which "are companies that, from or near founding, obtain a substantial portion of total revenue from sales in international market" (Knight and Cavusgil 2005).
(b) The globally integrated enterprise – which is "a new corporate entity based on collaborative innovation, integrated production, and outsourcing to specialists, (…) a company that fashions its strategy, its management, and its operations in pursuit of a new goal: the integration of production and value delivery worldwide" (Palmisano 2006).
(c) The meta-national firm – which is born in the "wrong" place but successfully survive "by searching out and mobilizing untapped pockets of technology and market intelligence that are scattered across the globe" (Doz et al. 2001).
(d) The Dragon multinationals – which "are firms from the Asia-Pacific region – historically a peripheral region in the world economy (…) firms that start from behind, and overcome their deficiencies to emerge as industry leaders, in sometimes astonishingly short periods of time, without any of the advantages of the incumbent industry leaders" (Mathews 2006).
(e) Global Latinas – which are "Latin American companies that have come on to the world stage and have succeeded in the United States, European Union or Asia" (Casanova 2009). A series of other studies has emphasized on the "Russian multinationals: from regional supremacy to global lead" (Panibratov 2012), "the global impact of China's emerging multinationals (Williamson and Zeng 2008), or on the "India's global powerhouses: how they are taking on the world" (Kumar 2009).

Regardless of this apparent "liberalization" and global spread of global multinationals, some well-grounded empirical studies have led to quite different findings: (a). following the examination of Fortune Global 500 companies during the period 1981–2001, the conclusion was that "very few are 'global' firms (…) instead, nearly all the top 500 firms are regionally based" (Rugman 2005); moreover, the retake of the study referring to the period 1999–2008 has confirmed that "most of the large firms remained in their home region in regard to both sales and assets" (Hoon and Rugman 2014); (b). after leading "the first investigation of the architecture of the international ownership network, along with the computation of the control held by each global player," the findings were "that transnational corporations form a giant bow-tie structure and that a large portion of control flows to a small tightly knit core of financial institutions. This core can be seen as an economic "superentity" that raises new important issues both for researchers and policy makers" (Vitali et al. 2011).

Given the abovementioned, it became obvious that new configurations have emerged, while new complexities have replaced them, in unprecedented (in terms of speed, breadth, and depth) manners: on one hand, globalization as it is today is a process of rapid international integration toward a geo-economy of complexity (Mayrhofer and Urban 2011), and therefore it "should be conceptualized as a series of adapting and coevolving global systems each characterized by unpredictability, irreversibility, and co-evolution" (Urry 2005); on the other hand, the (global) multinationals experience shifts of their own – the traditional modes of internationalization (foreign direct investments and trade) are increasingly complemented by the non-equity modes: "exporting, licensing, franchising, contractual agreements such as outsourcing, and service management" (Mikler 2013), while the "emerging giants use potent strategies to transform themselves into global contenders" (Khanna and Palepu 2006), as they turn "initial disabilities into sources of advantage – by leapfrogging to advanced technological levels, for example, or by leveraging their way into new markets through partnerships and joint ventures" (Mathews 2006).

The new realities and trends characterizing the global economic system and its main actors – the (global) multinationals – are adding new valences to the challenges firms (no matter if they are multinationals or not) and their strategists are confronting nowadays. In their search for strategic competitiveness – which "is achieved when a firm successfully formulates and implements a value-creating strategy" (Hitt et al. 2013) – strategist should pay attention to "improving decision making in complexity environment" (Gorzeń-Mitka and Okręglicka 2014); a sine qua non condition in doing that is by "creating the environmentally aware organization" (Dess et al. 2014) – one that, through environmental scanning and monitoring, combined with competitive intelligence, is able to develop reliable environmental forecasting – a prerequisite for a well-designed and executed strategy.

The following two sections of the paper will comparatively analyze, based on Fortune Global 500 data (Fortune Global 500 n.d; Fortune Magazine 1996a, 1996b), the overall dynamics of companies, as well as the country-based dynamics of the Fortune Global 500 companies, in order to identify the main shifts that characterize the world of global multinationals during the last two decades; the final section of the paper is dedicated to conclusions – emphasizing on the managerial challenges the new global configurations raise in front of strategists and their (global) search for competitiveness – and future research directions.

24.2 Overall Dynamics in Fortune Global 500: 2016 Comparative to 1996

The overall dynamics registered by the Fortune Global 500 companies – 2016 comparative to 1996 – show (Fig. 24.1) significant but quite different changes as concerns: profits (which have more than quadrupled during the reporting period) and assets (which have more than tripled in the same period), on one hand, and

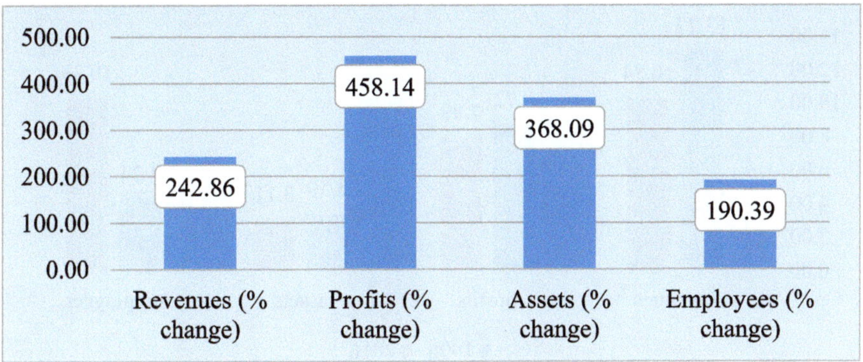

Fig. 24.1 Overall dynamics of FG 500 companies – 2016 comparative to 1996

Table 24.1 Top 10 companies in FG 500: 2016 comparative to 1996

2016 Top 10 companies		Country	Years in list	1996 Top 10 companies		Country
1	Walmart	USA	**22**	1	Mitsubishi	Japan
2	State Grid	China	16	2	Mitsui	Japan
3	China National Petroleum	China	16	3	Itochu	Japan
4	Sinopec Group	China	18	4	General Motors	USA
5	Royal Dutch Shell	Netherlands	**22**	5	Sumitomo	Japan
6	Exxon Mobil	USA	**22**	6	Marubeni	Japan
7	Volkswagen	Germany	**22**	7	Ford Motor	USA
8	Toyota Motor	Japan	**22**	8	Toyota Motor	Japan
9	Apple	USA	14	9	Exxon	USA
10	BP	Britain	**22**	10	Royal Dutch/Shell Group	Netherlands

revenues (which have more than doubled) and employees (which have less than doubled), on the other hand.

The analysis of the Top 10 companies in Fortune Global 500–2016 comparative to 1996 – reveals some interesting insights (Table 24.1 and Fig. 24.2):

- In terms of represented countries: if in 1996 Japan was leading – with six companies in Top 10 FG 500, followed by the USA with three companies, and Netherlands with one company; in 2016 the USA and China are both represented by three companies, followed by Netherlands, Germany, Japan, and Britain – each one with one company in Top 10 FG 500.
- Only three companies – a Japanese one (Toyota Motor), a Netherlander one (Royal Dutch Shell), and a US one (Exxon Mobil) – are present in both the Top 10 companies of FG 500.
- Five out of the 2016 Top 10 MNEs in FG 500 have a "full" 22 years of history in FG 500 (Walmart, Royal Dutch Shell, Exxon Mobil, Volkswagen, and Toyota

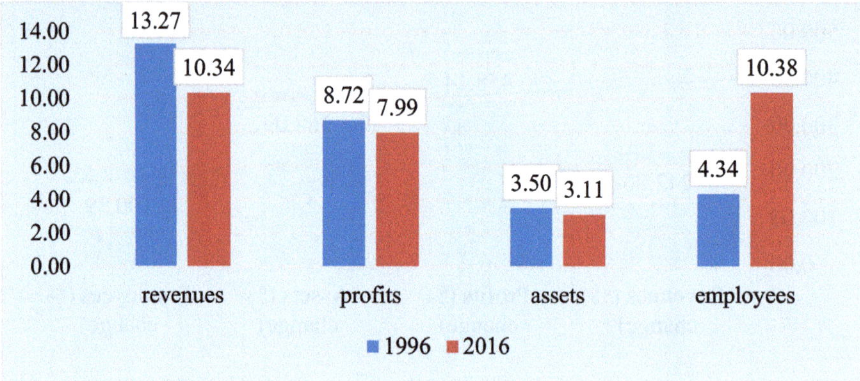

Fig. 24.2 Top 10 companies' contribution to total FG 500 (%)

Motor), while five of them are either more recently comers (the Chinese companies: Sinopec Group, 18 years; and State Grid and China National Petroleum, 16 years) or companies with a fluctuating performance during the two decades (the US-based Apple, 14 years).

- In terms of represented industries: the 2016 Top 10 FG 500 gathers six energy companies – five of them operating into petroleum refining (China National Petroleum, Sinopec Group, Royal Dutch Shell, Exxon Mobil, and BP) and one into utilities (State Grid), two motor vehicles and parts companies (Volkswagen and Toyota Motor), one retailing/general merchandisers company (Walmart), and one technology/computers, office equipment company (Apple), respectively; the 1996 Top 10 has gathered five (Japanese) trading companies (Mitsubishi, Mitsui, Itochu, Sumitomo, and Marubeni), three motor vehicles and parts companies (General Motors, Ford Motor, and Toyota Motor), and two petroleum refining companies (Exxon, and Royal Dutch/Shell Group).
- Top 10 companies' contribution to total FG 500 has decreased in terms of revenues (from 13.27% in 1996 to 10.34% in 2016), profits (from 8.27% to 7.99%), and assets (from 3.5% to 3.11%), and it has quite significantly increased in terms of employees (from 4.34% in 1996 to 10.38% in 2016).

24.3 Country-Based Dynamics in Fortune Global 500: 2016 Comparative to 1996

The country-based survey of the FG 500 companies (2016 comparative to 1996) has led to the following findings:

- The number of countries/entrances represented by their companies in FG 500 (Table 24.2) has increased from 27 in 1996 to 34 in 2016 ("entrances" are Britain/Netherlands, both in 2016 and 1996; Belgium/Netherlands, Netherlands Antilles, and Hong Kong, in 1996).

Table 24.2 No of companies in FG 500 by countries/entrances

Countries/entrances		2016	Countries/entrances		1996
1.	USA	134	1.	USA	153
2.	China	103	2.	Japan	141
3.	Japan	52	3.	France	42
4.	France	29	4.	Germany	40
5.	Germany	28	5.	Britain	32
6.	Britain	25	6.	Switzerland	16
7.	Switzerland	15	7.	South Korea	12
8.	South Korea	15	8.	Italy	12
9.	Netherlands	12	9.	Netherlands	8
10.	Canada	11	10–11.	Canada; Spain	6
11–12.	Italy; Spain	9	12.	Belgium	5
13.	Australia	8	13–14.	Australia; Brazil	4
14–16.	Brazil; India; Taiwan	7	15.	Sweden	3
17.	Russia	5	**16–19.**	China; Britain/Netherlands; Norway; Finland;	2
18–19.	Sweden; Singapore	3	**20–27.**	India; Taiwan; Mexico; Turkey; Belgium/ Netherlands; Hong Kong; Netherlands Antilles; Venezuela	1
20–22.	Belgium; Mexico; Ireland	2			
23–34.	Britain/Netherlands; Norway; Turkey; Austria; Denmark; Indonesia; Luxembourg; Malaysia; Poland; Saudi Arabia; Thailand; UAE	1			

- Twelve countries were represented with more than 5 companies in FG 500 in 1996 – making a total of 473 companies out if 500 (94.6%), while in 2016 their number has increased to 17 (countries with more than 5 companies in FG 500) – making a total of 476 companies (95.2%).
- The Top 10 countries/entries – by number of companies in FG 500 has reunited: 462 companies out of 500 (92.4%) in 1996 and 424 companies (84.8%) in 2016, respectively.
- Except from Italy and Spain, all the other 1996 Top 10 countries/entries – by number of companies in FG 500 have kept a spot in the 2016 Top 10 (but not necessarily their position and/or their number of companies); the spectacular "new entry" is China (which has reached the second place in 2016 – with 103 companies in FG 500, starting from just 2 companies in 1996), while Japan has suffered the most dramatic loss in terms of number of companies in FG 500 (from 141 in 1996 to 52 in 2016) – although, in terms of ranking, the drop was only from the second place (in 1996) to the third one (in 2016).

Table 24.3 Top 10 countries/entrances in FG 500: by revenues

2016				1996			
Countries/entrances and no of companies			Revenues ($M)	Countries/entrances and no of companies			Revenues ($M)
1.	USA	134	8,467,058	1.	Japan	141	3,984,793.5
2.	China	103	5,885,016	2.	USA	153	3,221,391.2
3.	Japan	52	2,577,664	3.	Germany	40	1,017,207.5
4.	Germany	28	1,872,883	4.	France	42	880,112.4
5.	France	29	1,650,219	5.	Britain	32	515,871.5
6.	Britain	25	1,146,393	6.	Switzerland	16	345,140.2
7.	South Korea	15	725,225	7.	South Korea	12	262,991.2
8.	Switzerland	15	719,065	8.	Italy	12	254,937.7
9.	Netherlands	12	702,762	9.	Netherlands	8	170,609.9
10.	Italy	9	591,029	10.	Britain/Netherlands	2	159,571.7

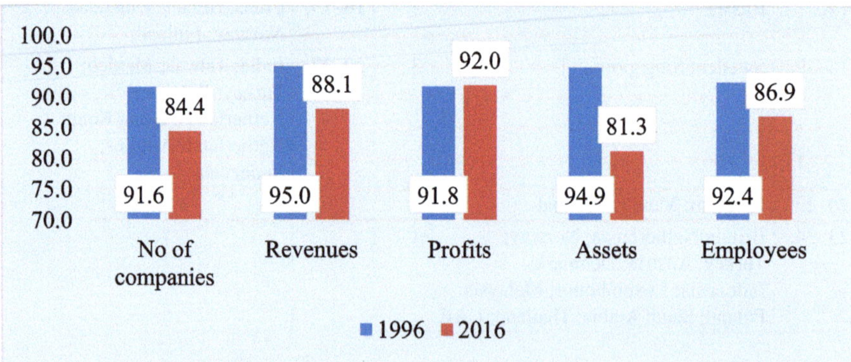

Fig. 24.3 Contribution of Top 10 countries/entrances – by revenues – to total FG 500 (%)

- The two Top 10 countries/entrances – by revenues – in FG 500 (Table 24.3) have reunited: 458 companies out of 500 in 1996 (91.6%) and 422 companies (84.4%) in 2016, while, for both 1996 and 2016, the first nine of the Top 10 countries, by number of companies and by revenues, are the same (although if occupying different positions); only the last positions are totally different: in 1996, the revenues of the two Britain/Netherlands companies have allowed this entrance to reach Top 10 countries, by revenues; in 2016, the revenues of the nine Italian companies have allowed Italy to reach Top 10 countries, by revenues (instead of Canada that has had 11 companies in FG 500).

- The contribution of Top 10 countries/entrances – by revenues to FG 500, 1996 comparative to 2016 (Fig. 24.3) has slightly increased in terms of profits (from 91.8% to 92%), and it has decreased in terms of revenues (from 95% to 81%), assets (from 94.9% to 81.3%), number of companies (from 91.6% to 84.4%), and employees (from 92.4% to 86.9%).

24.4 Conclusions and Future Research Directions

The most significant conclusions that could be drawn based on the comparative examination of the two FG 500 rankings (2016 and 1996), together with some short comments – which will actually represent starting points for future research endeavors that will be developed in order to (a). forecast possible patterns of new developments (based on the analysis of both the causes and the consequences of the explored dynamics); (b). identify benchmarks of best practices (based on the analysis and comparison of the strategic decisions, corporate strategies, and business models that FG 500 companies have developed in their search for global leadership) – refer to:

Overall dynamics: the huge discrepancy between profits increasing and employees increasing – which is accompanied by the "moderate" increasing of revenues and assets. Besides technological progress and work productivity increasing, other possible causes of the abovementioned evolutions – that need further investigation – could refer to strategic decisions (such as relocation of companies' headquarters) and/or corporate strategies (such as offshore outsourcing) FG 500 companies have made and/or pursued in their search for both efficiency and effectiveness.

Top 10 companies' dynamics: the massive reconfiguration of the "picture" encompassing the main actors of the global economy – in terms of both overall and structural dynamics regarding the companies that are present in both rankings (only three out of ten), the represented industries (five in 2016 comparative to three in 1996), and the represented countries (six in 2016, comparative to three in 1996) – accompanied by an interesting evolution as regards the Top 10 companies' contribution to total (revenues, profits, assets, and employees) FG 500. All these shifts deserve a closer look, in order to identify the general, industry- and firm-related effects contributing to the performance of the Top 10 winners.

Country-based dynamics: (a). the combination of "democratization" with "concentration" – reflected into the increasing number of countries represented, through their companies, in FG 500 (34 in 2016, comparative to 27 in 1996); the increasing number of countries with more than five companies in FG 500 (17 in 2016, comparative to 12 in 1996); and the decreasing number of companies Top 10 countries, by number of companies in FG 500, have reunited (424 in 2016, comparative to 462 in 1996) and (b). the "Asian battle": the extraordinary evolution of the Chinese-based companies (from two companies in 1996 to 103 in 2016) that have brought China on the second place in terms of number of companies in FG 500 in 2016, on one hand and the severe decreasing of Japan in terms of number of companies in FG 500 (from 141 in 1996 to 52 in 2016), on the other hand (although it has meant for Japan "only" changing the second place to the third one in terms of number of companies in FG 500). What is interesting to know in respect to the country-based dynamics are the broader (macro-environmental) contexts that have shaped the evolution of the FG 500 companies, as well as the corporate strategies and the specific business models that have determined the performance of FG 500 companies.

Top 10 countries/entrances by revenues' dynamics: at a first glance, concentration – reflected into the decreasing number of gathered companies (422 in 2016 comparative to 458 in 1996) – and consolidation, as the countries represented in the two series of data are almost the same (except from China, placed the second in 2016), seem to be the main characteristics here. Further analysis will be needed here not only on identifying the inner dynamics that took place (together with their possible determinants and consequences) but also on explaining the interesting evolution registered by the contribution of Top 10 countries/entrances – by revenues to total (revenues, assets, profits, and employees) FG 500 (considering that only the contribution of profits has slightly increased, while the contribution of assets, for instance, has decreased the most).

To sum up, the interdependencies between the process of globalization and the evolution of the global multinationals have led to significant shifts affecting both the global (economic) architecture and the characteristics of the (global) multinationals: (a). the emergence of some apparent paradoxes (combining, in different forms, the increasing of "democracy" with the consolidating of "oligopoly", or globalization with regionalization and localization); (b). the impetuous rise of "global challengers", global multinationals from emerging markets that "are here to stay." Under these new and ever-changing circumstances, new challenges for strategic management occur, asking for more alertness and flexibility when dealing with (the new global) opportunities and threats – in (the global) search for competitiveness.

References

Aggarwal, R., Berrill, J., Hutson, E., Kearney, C.: What is a multinational corporation? Classifying the degree of firm-level multinationality. Int. Bus. Rev. **20**(5), 557–577 (2010)

Casanova, L.: Global Latinas: Latin America's Emerging Multinationals. Palgrave Macmillan, London (2009)

Daft, R.L., Murphy, J., Willmott, H.: Organization Theory and Design. Cengage Learning EMEA, Andover (2010)

Dess, G.G., Lumpkin, G.T., Eisner, A., McNamara, G.: Strategic Management. McGraw Hill Education, New York (2014)

Dicken, P.: Global Shift: Mapping the Changing Contours of the World Economy. SAGE Publications, London\Thousand Oaks\New Delhi (2007)

Doz, Y.L., Santos, J., Williamson, P.: From Global to Metanational: How Companies win in the Knowledge Economy. Harvard Business Press, Boston (2001)

Fortune Global 500., http://fortune.com/global500/ (n.d.). Accessed 11 June 2017

Fortune Magazine, Fortune's Global 500 ranked within countries, http://archive.fortune.com/magazines/fortune/fortune_archive/1996/08/05/215441/index.htm (1996a). Accessed 11 June 2017

Fortune Magazine., http://www.fortunechina.com/fortune500/c/1996-11/01/content_9659.htm (1996b). Accessed 11 June 2017

Gorzeń-Mitka, I., Okręglicka, M.: Improving decision making in complexity environment. In: Mihaescu, L., et al. (eds.) Procedia Economics and Finance, 21st International Economic Conference of Sibiu 2014, IECS 2014 Prospects of Economic Recovery in a Volatile International Context: Major Obstacles, Initiatives and Projects, vol. 16, pp. 402–409. Elsevier, Amsterdam (2014)

Hirst, P., Thompson, G., Bromley, S.: Globalization in Question. Polity. Cambridge, Malden (2015)
Hitt, M.A., Ireland, D.R., Hoskisson, R.E.: Strategic Management: Concepts and Cases: Competitiveness and Globalization. Cengage Learning, Mason (2013)
Hoon, O.C., Rugman, A.M.: The dynamics of regional and global multinationals, 1999–2008. The. Multinatl. Bus. Rev. **22**(2), 108–117 (2014)
Khanna, T., Palepu, K.G.: Emerging giants. Building World-Class Companies in Developing Countries. Harv. Bus. Rev. 1–11 (2006)
Kleinert, J.: The Role of Multinational Enterprises in Globalization, vol. 326. Springer-Verlag, Berlin Heidelberg (2004)
Knight, G.A., Cavusgil, S.T.: A taxonomy of born-global firms. MIR: Manag. Int. Rev. **45**(3), 15–35 (2005)
Kumar, N.: India's Global Powerhouses: How they Are Taking on the Wworld. Harvard Business Press, Boston (2009)
Mathews, J.A.: Dragon multinationals: new players in 21st century globalization. Asia Pac. J. Manag. **23**(1), 5–27 (2006)
Mayrhofer, U., Urban, S.: Management International. Des pratiques en mutation. Pearson Education France, Paris (2011)
McCann, P.: The economic geography of globalization: technology, institutions and multinationals. Keynote speech at the Congress of the European Regional Science Association (ERSA). Liver. 27–31 (2008)
Mikler, J. (ed.): The Handbook of Global Companies. John Wiley and Sons Ltd., Chichester (2013)
Narula, R., Dunning, J.H.: Multinational enterprises, development and globalization: some clarifications and a research agenda. Oxf. Dev. Stud. **38**(3), 263–287 (2010)
Palmisano, S.J.: The globally integrated enterprise. Foreign Aff. **85**(3), 127–136 (2006)
Panibratov, A.: Russian Multinationals: From Regional Supremacy to Global Lead. Routledge, London\New York (2012)
Rugman, A.M.: The Regional Multinationals: MNEs and 'Global' Strategic Management. Cambridge University Press, Cambridge (2005)
Rugman, A.M., Verbeke, A.: A perspective on regional and global strategies of multinational enterprises. J. Int. Bus. Stud. **35**(1), 3–18 (2004)
Sirkin, H.L., Hemerling, J.W., Bhattachrya, A.K.: Globality. Competing with Everyone from Everywhere for Everything. The Boston Consulting Group, Inc. Headline Publishing Group, London (2008)
Urry, J.: The complexity turn. Theory Cult. Soc. **22**(5), 1–14 (2005)
Vitali, S., Glattfelder, J.B., Battiston, S.: The network of global corporate control. PLoS One. **6**(10), 1–6 (2011)
Wilkins, M.: The history of multinational enterprise. In: Rugman, A.M., Brewer, T.L. (eds.) The Oxford Handbook of International Business, pp. 3–35. Oxford University Press, New York (2009)
Williamson, P.J., Zeng, M.: The global impact of China's emerging multinationals. In: McNally, C.A. (ed.) China's Emergent Political Economy: Capitalism in the Dragon's Lair, pp. 83–101. Routledge, London\New York (2008)

Chapter 25
International Exchanges in a Globalized World

Oana Oprişan and Cosmin Tileagă

Abstract A reality today is that the economy, characterized by the expansion and development of financial mechanisms, cannot be conceived without the stock exchange: the real economy is reflected in the trend of stock, and, in turn, the stock can influence – good or bad – the economic life. Thus, by the rise of globalization, as instruments of capital accumulation, stock exchange has become the most effective way of targeting the capital available in the economy to the most profitable use. The market will determine which companies will be funded and what is the cost of their capital. The decisive factor is the efficiency with which companies use this capital. In this way, international stock markets have taken a central role in macroeconomic development of various countries of the world.

Keywords Stock exchange • Financial market • Globalization • Capital

25.1 Introduction

The modern economy characterized by expansion and increasing complexity of financial mechanisms cannot be conceived without the stock exchange: the economy is reflected in the stock market trend, and, in turn, the stock market may influence, positively or negatively, the economic life.

World stock exchanges are under the pressure of consolidation trends, amid the requirements of customers who are interested in global services and lower rates (Pratt 2002).

O. Oprişan (✉)
Ovidius University, Constanța, Romania
e-mail: oana.oprisan@yahoo.com

C. Tileagă
Lucian Blaga University of Sibiu, Sibiu, Romania
e-mail: cosmin.tileaga@ulbsibiu.ro

S.C. Mărginean et al. (eds.), *Emerging Issues in the Global Economy*, Springer Proceedings in Business and Economics,
https://doi.org/10.1007/978-3-319-71876-7_25

The interpretation of stock exchange as a landmark of the business world should take into account its imperfections as economic indicator; in some cases, the exchange may reflect an unfounded optimism, a false promise of gain, leading to detachment of the stock trend from the real economic situation or even to opposition between the financial economy and the real one – reflected by the stock crash (Lease et al. 2000). This is because the stock trend is determined not only by rational expectations, grounded in economic terms, but also by subjective factors and reactions. However, in assessing the role of stock exchange in the economic and financial life, we cannot consider the magnitude of the consequences which can have a very intense exchange activity, the risks of some uncontrollable speculations that may cause stock panic and even crashes (Grigore 2011).

However, beyond the above adverse circumstances, market proved to be an essential institution to the functioning of the market economy.

25.2 New Dimensions of Stock Market

The trend of financial markets globalization printed new dimensions to world stock market.

Although all over the world there is a large number of stock exchange, the world market is based on the United States–Japan–United Kingdom triangle. If the major stock markets have a significant share in the world, each of them is represented by an internationally recognized financial center: New York, Tokyo, and London; the position of these centers nationally and internationally is determined by the number of securities listed on the representative exchanges (NYSE, TSE, LSE) and by the potential and the workload of the three major ("The Big Three").

Triangle influence is exercised on other stock centers and, especially, on those financial centers in the regions found under the economic impact of the three stock titans. In other words, each of the three exchange centers is, in itself, a financial center of a subordinate region: New York, Canada and Latin America; London, the European financial market; Tokyo, the financial markets of SE Asia (Brigham and Ehrhardt 2002).

TSE has regional offices in each of the three major financial areas: North America, Europe, and Asia. Tokyo Stock Exchange shows that Japan, as the largest financial market, holds one of the major securities markets in the world. This component has several features: financial institutions have a significant power and share (Nomura securities house occupies one of the top 15 places in the top of Japanese companies); the abundance of liquidity makes the weight of shares that are likely to be negotiated in the short term to be reduced.

On the markets that became global, the various financial centers and major banks launched a competitive unprecedented process. Centers such as London, Paris, and Frankfurt are rapidly modernizing to cope the great offensive center, Tokyo (Lupan 2005).

Interdependence relation of the major exchanges manifests itself both in the fields of cooperation and of the high competition to attract capital. In recent years, there have been two kinds of actions taken in this regard (Ross et al. 2001):

- Regulators (i.e., reduction of the exchange control forms)
- Modernization (introduction of electronic equipment on the stock exchange)

The result of these measures was the differentiated dynamics of the three major stock markets.

25.3 Dynamics of Three Large Stock Markets

For "The Big Three" the situation is favorable. The links between the three major stock centers, in terms of their being in different time zones, create prerequisites for the establishment of unified global transactions with continuous operation during the 24 h. Experts say that in America, conjuncture momentum is predictable, but equity markets are more expensive than in Europe and Asia. In Asia, the conjuncture momentum is now. Europe does everything now to return to precrisis 2008 level – favorable quotation is shown to have significant growth potential (Dincă and Dincă 2007).

So if 11 years ago, companies wishing to raise funds from abroad at affordable prices turned their attention to the United States, the situation is now quite different.

The competition, which until recent years was not a problem for US markets, began to be strengthened as the development of financial markets from outside the United States resulted in a more active participation of US companies in these markets. There is talk even of a competition between Wall Street and London, because European markets, although fragmented, have attracted the attention of institutional investors, as the European Union has strengthened its position in the world.

When they are rivals, the three stock exchanges work with rules of oligopoly and cooperate with those of monopoly. It is unknown the alternation between oligopoly and monopoly.

The speed with which the exchange rates volatility can be transmitted between different financial markets is demonstrated by the survey indices of the three major exchanges, caught in their development of economic crisis in.

25.4 Conclusions

2008 will remain written in financial history, because of the events that have collapsed ideologies and economic doctrines and reformulated the top of the world giants. The decline in financial and banking system of the United States, which has spread around the world, has also affected international stock exchange, causing the decline and even the collapse of the stock systems. International trades al exchanges have been influenced by some notorious events that have happened in isolation. But a chain of events, some important, others less important, had an effect on the evolution of the global economy.

In this study, the situation of the studies indices recorded lows below average performance during the economic crisis. The crisis brought the record of the low values, valid for all three indices analyzed, by the domino effect caused global, that included the exchange system.

Also, the year 2010 is a common benchmark for this indicator, because this year records an improvement of the situation in the average over the period the evolution of these indicators was followed.

Globally, it is observed that the developments of these stock exchanges, through performed transactions, are closely dependent on each other.

In 2008, the Tokyo Stock Exchange ended the worst year in its history, during which it lost 42% in value because of the financial crisis. It is, statistically, the largest decrease since the creation of the Tokyo Stock Exchange in 1949.

Tokyo Stock Exchange is looking for partnerships to remain the first financial market in Asia, coveted by the stock exchanges in China, especially the one in Hong Kong. TSE tried to conclude an alliance with the New York Stock Exchange. The first two capital markets in the world could thus create an extensive exchange network stretched across three continents, because the NYSE is preparing a merger with pan-European stock exchange Euronext, grouping capital markets in Paris, Amsterdam, Brussels, and Lisbon.

International exchanges preferred lately alliances and mergers to share the costs related to investments in new generation systems and to keep pace with the competitive environment and the global spread of information and transactions.

It is important to note that multibillion dollar mergers are not the only way exchanges can work together. Many stock exchanges establish links between them through sales of small holdings or partnerships.

Prices, in the case of transactions, are extremely low, but the hope is that these alliances will be a first step toward broader agreements in the future. For large stock exchanges, with important capitalization, these alliances may be a way of gaining a position, no matter how small, on emerging markets, and perhaps to convince the biggest companies here to list abroad. For smaller stock, purely local, a major partner with international experience can bring benefits in terms of promotion, technology, and attracting a large number of foreign investors. Over several years, these alliances may lead to mergers (Pascu-Nedelcu 2011).

The activity of major stock centers is dominated by deregulation, i.e., attenuation of the exchange control forms, as well as its modernization, which involves introducing electronic computing technology in the mechanism of exchange transactions.

Combined, the three markets accounted for over three quarters of the global market capitalization in 1990 and had reached 77% at the end of August 1992.

Currently, “The Big Three” holds together about 70% of global market share, but sharp differences of the three stock market developments affected their size.

The best example is the decrease of the Tokyo Stock Exchange, which in the 1980s recorded a trend in market capitalization three times higher than the London Stock Exchange and about the same with New York Stock Exchange. Nowadays this momentum has been significantly reduced since the capitalization share of the exchanges has reached a similar performance with the London Stock Exchange and only a fifth of the New York Stock Exchange capitalization.

Through information above, it has been shown that the global market is dominated by the potential and the workload of "The Big Three," respectively, the New York Stock Exchange, Tokyo Stock Exchange, and London Stock Exchange.

According to statistical data, those financial centers detach in terms of their potential and the number of companies listed, as well as continued growth in the share of institutional investors.

References

Brigham, E.F., Ehrhardt, M.C.: Financial Management: Theory and Practice, 10th edn, pp. 420–422. Canada and Latin America\European financial market\Financial markets in SE Asia, New York\London\Tokyo (2002)

Dincă, M., Dincă, G.: Models of analysis of the company expenses using indexes, ICBE, Review of Management and Economical Engineering (2007)

Grigore A.: Capital Markets – Courses Notes. Bucharest (2011)

Lease, R.C., Kose, J., Avner, K., Uri, L., Oded, H.S.: Dividend Policy: Its Impact on Firm Value. Harvard Business School Press, Boston, MA (2000)

Lupan, M.: Globalization – Visions, Contexts, Trends. Economic Publishing House, Bucharest (2005)

Pascu-Nedelcu, M.: Merton valuation model of the cost of capital, mathematical sum but not economic, CAPM and APT models. J. Doctoral Res. Econ. **III**, 1 (2011)

Pratt, S.: Cost of capital. Estimation and Apllication (2002)

Ross, S., Westerfield, R., Jordan, B.: Corporate Finance. McGraw-Hill Irwin Inc (2001)

Chapter 26
Global Powers and the International Currencies: What Does the Last Years Suggest for the Future?

Ramona Orăştean

Abstract Starting from the literature that identifies different factors which determine whether a currency plays a global role, we propose an analysis of international status of major currencies using the following criteria: the demographic, economic, commercial, and financial size and importance of the currency issuer, the currency issuer's financial market, and the history of using currency. We consider that the international use of a currency is mainly defined by the issuer's place in the global economy, including its share of world trade and the size of its economy and financial market. The US dollar's reference position was less influenced by the introduction of the euro, but nowadays it may be affected by the growing importance of China, the decline of the US political and economic power, and the crisis of the European Union.

Keywords Global powers • International currencies • Criteria

26.1 Introduction

There are a number of criteria by which a currency qualifies for international status. The share of different currencies and their importance depend on their relative position on the criteria and the relative importance of the criteria.

Bergsten (1996) lists five factors that determine whether a currency plays a global role:

- The size of its economy and global trade
- The economy's independence from external constraints
- Avoidance of exchange controls

R. Orăştean (✉)
Lucian Blaga University of Sibiu, Sibiu, Romania
e-mail: ramona.orastean@ulbsibiu.ro

S.C. Mărginean et al. (eds.), *Emerging Issues in the Global Economy*, Springer Proceedings in Business and Economics,
https://doi.org/10.1007/978-3-319-71876-7_26

- The breadth, depth, and liquidity of its capital markets
- The resilience and stability of the economy and its external position

Tavlas (1998) finds several elements underlying international currency use: confidence in the currency value and in the issuing country's inflation performance, confidence in the political stability of the issuing government, free of controls and large and deep financial markets of the issuing country, and the issuing country's economic characteristics, including its share of world trade and the size of its economy.

Analyzing the literature, Chinn and Frankel (2008) identify a number of variables of international currency status:

- Output and trade
- The country's financial markets
- Confidence in the currency
- Network externalities

To become a dominant currency is a question of time, that currency having to satisfy a number of conditions, including to play a significant role in commercial, noncommercial, and financial international transactions, to be important as an investment currency, to be attractive for central banks as a reserve currency, and to hold a major position in exchange regimes.

We further propose an analysis of international status of major currencies using the following *criteria:*

A. *The demographic, economic, commercial, and financial size and importance of the currency issuer*
B. *The currency issuer's financial market*
C. *History of using currency*

26.2 Characteristics of the Main International Currencies

Characteristics of the main international currencies (US dollar, euro, Japanese yen, Chinese yuan/renminbi) and issuing economies overtake the implications of global macroeconomic imbalances on the international monetary system components.

26.2.1 Demographic, Economic, Commercial, and Financial Size and Importance of the Currency Issuer

We analyzed a set of macroeconomic indicators in the main currency issuers (the United States, Euro area, China, and Japan) such as population, GDP, exports and imports, inflation, and interest rate.

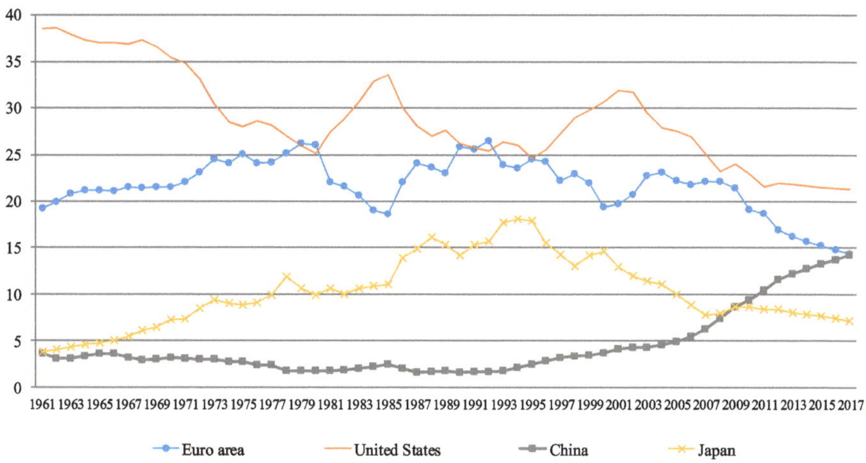

Fig. 26.1 GDP of the main currency issuers, 1960–2017 (% of global GDP)

With a *population* of over 1.37 billion people in 2016, China is the largest economic entity in the world (18.5% of total population), far exceeding the Euro area's population (340.9 million people, 4.5%), the United States (323.1 million people, 4.3%), and Japan (127 million people, 1.7%).

GDP share of each area in global GDP was in 2016 of 24.6% for the United States, 15.7% for the Euro area, 14.8% for China, and 6.5% in Japan. Since 1973, the EU has become the economy with the largest share in terms of global GDP (with a maximum of 34.5% in 1980 and decreasing trends in the next period, reaching 21.7% in 2016). The United States registered a contraction in the share of global GDP (from 33.3% in 1973 to 26% in 1980 and 24.6% in 2016). Japan ranked third until 2010 (with shares rising in the period 1973–1994 from 9.4% in 1973 to a peak of 18% in 1994, followed by significant reductions between 1995 and 2016, reaching 6.5% in 2016). Since 2010, China moved to third place as share of global GDP, accounting 9.4% in 2010 and 14.8% in 2016 (Fig. 26.1).

The global crisis has strengthened the changes of the balance in the global economy and determined mutations of the exports distribution, where there is an increase of trade between developing countries.

According to the World Trade Organization (2016), the value of merchandise trade and trade in commercial services declined in 2015 following modest growth in 2012 to 2014. The share of developing economies in merchandise *exports* increased from 33% in 2005 to 42% in 2015. China's share in world merchandise exports reached 14.2% in 2015, consolidating its top position it occupies since 2009, followed by the United States (9.4%) and Japan (3.9%). As regarding world merchandise *imports*, 2015 placed the United States (19.3%) in the first position, followed by China (10.3%) and Japan (4.0%) (Fig. 26.2).

As it is, the international trade has strong intracontinental network and is arranged in three clusters: American (the United States, Canada, Mexico), Asian (China,

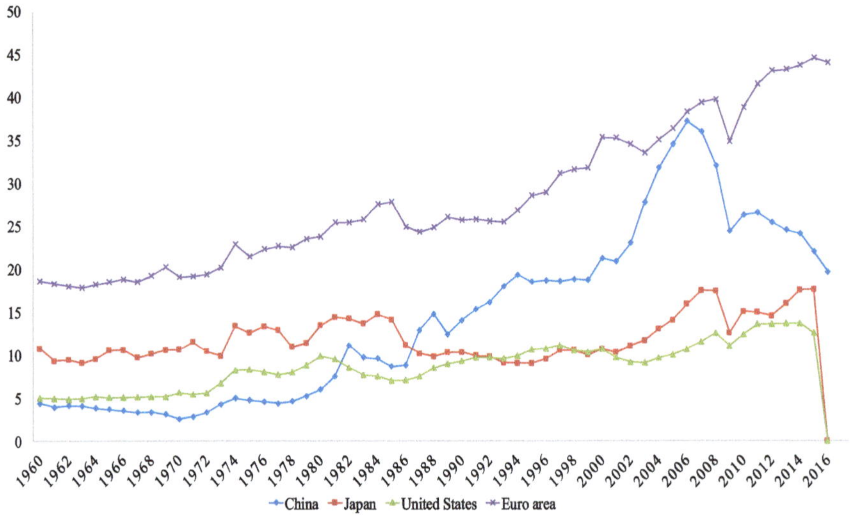

Fig. 26.2 Exports of goods and services, 1960–2016 (% of GDP)

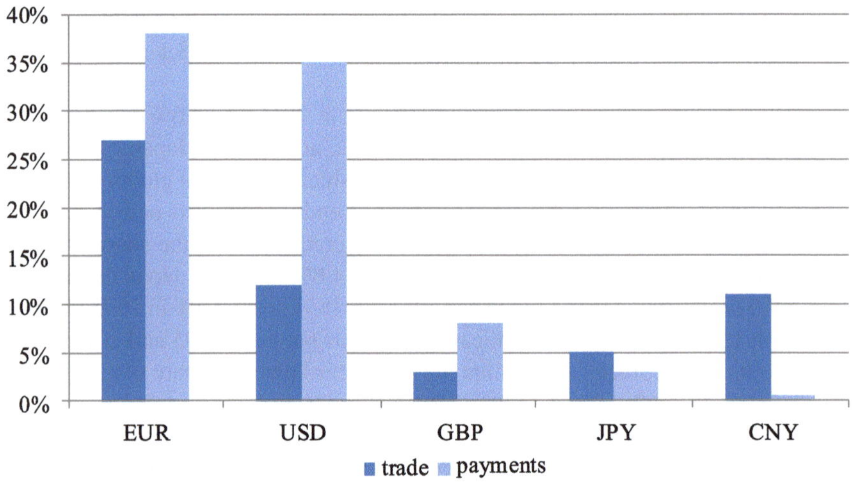

Fig. 26.3 International trade and payment currencies in 2010 (%) (Auboin 2012, p. 10)

Singapore, Hong Kong, Korea, Japan), and European (Germany, the United Kingdom, Spain, Italy). As a result, the main *payment currencies* were in 2010 as follows: euro, US dollar, pound sterling, and Japanese yen (Fig. 26.3). Although China had 11.4% of global trade, the renminbi's share of international payments was 0.24%.

Starting with 2012, the United States, China, and Germany are the countries where links to other points of the network are established, which mean that their currencies are mainly used as means of payment, as can be seen in Fig. 26.4.

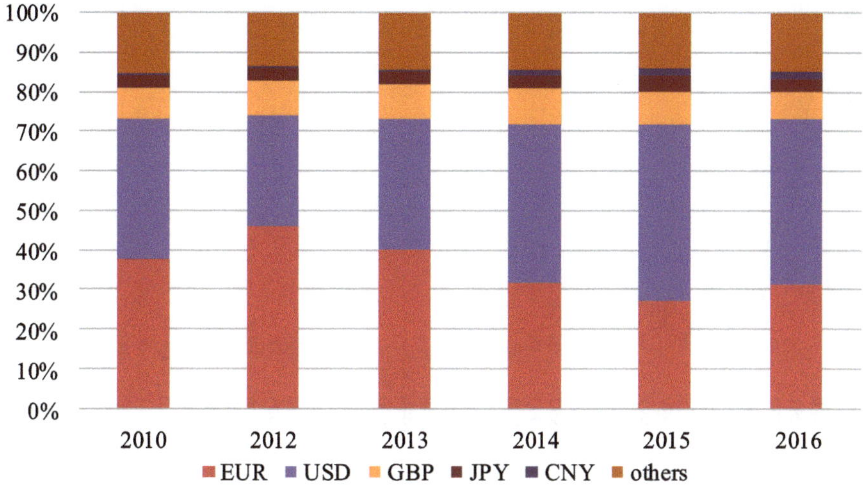

Fig. 26.4 Share of payment currencies in 2010–2016 (%)

According to the European Central Bank (2015), the share of the renminbi in global payments has risen from 0.8% in October 2013 to about 2% in January 2015, moving from 12th to 5th rank and surpassing the Australian dollar, Hong Kong dollar, Swiss franc, and Canadian dollar, among others. The euro lost its first place starting with 2014 in the favor of the US dollar, reaching 31.2% of international payments in 2016 compared with 41.8% in the case of US dollar.

A SWIFT report (2017) states that in 2016, the value of renminbi payments was on a negative trajectory and fell by 16% compared to 2015, dropping from 2.03% in March 2015 to 1.78% in March 2017. This decline can be assigned to the slowdown of the Chinese economy and volatility of the renminbi exchange rate. There is no doubt that the renminbi will become an important currency in international trade on the medium and long term.

In terms of *inflation*, in the 1970s the monetary authorities in Japan and Germany set a record low inflation rates better than the United States. In the 1980s, inflation rate in the United States was higher than those of Japan and Germany but lower than those of the United Kingdom and France. On a declining trend, in the 1990s, the highest levels were recorded in the United States and the United Kingdom, followed by China, Euro area, and Japan. During the global crisis, the downward trend continued reaching minimum values in 2009. Starting with 2010, the inflation rate gradually increased but inflationary pressures remained relatively limited in developed countries and accentuated in emerging countries, as seen in Fig. 26.5. In 2016, consumer prices in the United States increased by 1.2% while in the Euro area from 0 to 0.2% and in China rose 2.0%.

In the period of crisis, the *monetary policy* of major central banks was one of the cheap moneys through reducing policy interest rates at historical levels between 0 and 1% (Fig. 26.6). Low levels were recorded by the Federal Reserve System (0–0.25% in December 2008), the European Central Bank (0.75% in July 2012),

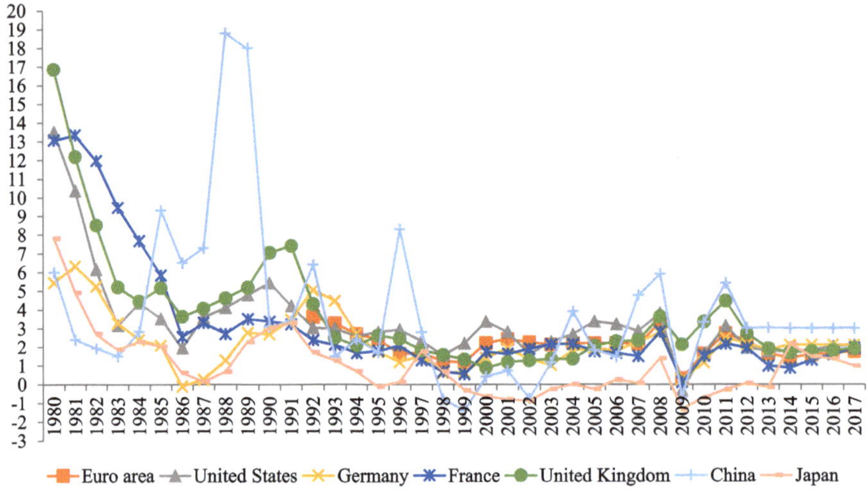

Fig. 26.5 Inflation, average consumer prices, 1980–2017 (%)

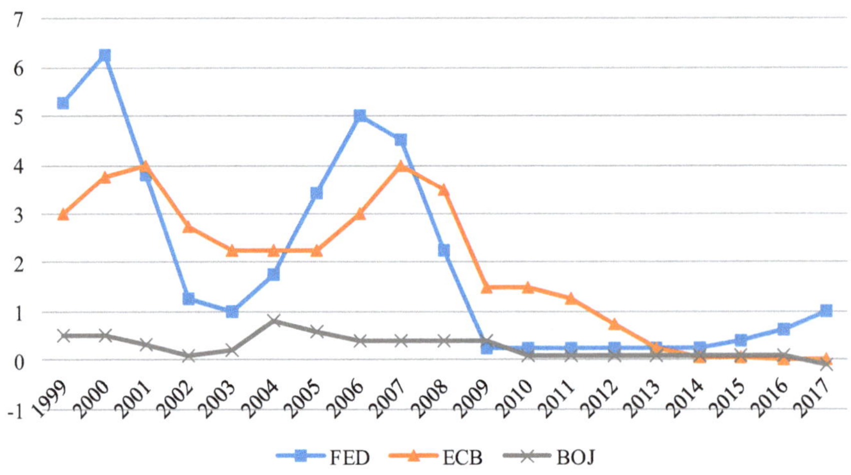

Fig. 26.6 Monetary policy rate of FED, ECB, and BOJ, 1980–2017 (%)

and the Bank of Japan (0–0.1% in October 2010), which were maintained for a period thereafter. Likewise, for the first time in their modern history, some central banks have used unconventional monetary policy measures.

Since 2016, the monetary policy decisions of the major banks are very different. The Federal Open Market Committee has been gradually increasing its target range for the federal funds rate, bringing it to 1–1.25% in June 2017, taking into account the monetary policy objectives of maximum employment and price stability. From February 2016, the Bank of Japan decided to apply a negative interest rate of minus 0.1% to excess reserves that financial institutional place at the bank, as not to further

Table 26.1 Global economic role of the United States, Euro area, China, and Japan (2016)

Indicators	Euro area	United States	China	Japan
Population (millions)	340.9	323.1	1378.7	127.0
GDP (% of global GDP)	15.7	24.6	14.8	6.5
Inflation (annual, %)	0.2	1.3	2.0	–0.1
General government fiscal balance (% of GDP)	−1.7	−4.4	−3.8	−4.2
Central government debt (% of GDP)	91.5	99.8	84.0	198.1
Exports of goods and services (% of world exports)	26.2	10.9	10.6	3.7
Exports of goods and services (% of GDP)	44.0	12.6*	19.6	17.6*
Imports of goods and services (% of GDP)	40.0	15.4*	17.4	17.9*
Trade balance goods and services (billions USD)	553.7	−500.6	249.6	40.3
Current account balance (% of GDP)	3.4	−2.6	1.8	3.9
Deposit interest rate (% per annum)	0.78	0,34	1.5	0.3
Lending rate (% per annum)	–	3.5	4.4	1.0
Government bond yield (% per annum)	0.93	1.8	–	−0.07

*2015

affect the inflation trend. Starting with March 2016, the Governing Council of the ECB decreased the interest rate on the main refinancing operations by 5 basis points to 0.0%. As regarding China, monetary policy is on a modernization phase bringing closer to the characteristics of developed markets.

Periods of low interest rates since 2008 put some pressure on global financial markets, adding to the risks arising from sovereign debt crisis in Europe and geopolitical risks in the Middle East.

In a synthesis, the main features of the international use of a currency derive from the place held by the currency issuer in the global economy as shown in the Table 26.1 (based on data from IMF - World Economic Outlook Database, 2017; IMF - International Financial Statistics; UNCTADstat; World Bank - World Development Indicators Database, 2017).

As the data for 2016 show, the United States is the first country as share of global GDP, followed by the Euro area, China, and Japan. In terms of population size, China ranks first. Euro area occupies the first place regarding the share in GDP of exports and imports of goods and services.

26.2.2 *The Currency Issuer's Financial Market*

The financial market can be analyzed based on the following features: breadth, liquidity, depth, and liberalization.

An investigation of the major regions highlights that the size of the European banking sector is much larger than that of the United States, Japan, or China. Moreover, there are significant differences in size and structure of the national banking sectors in Europe, such as different economic structures and different types of

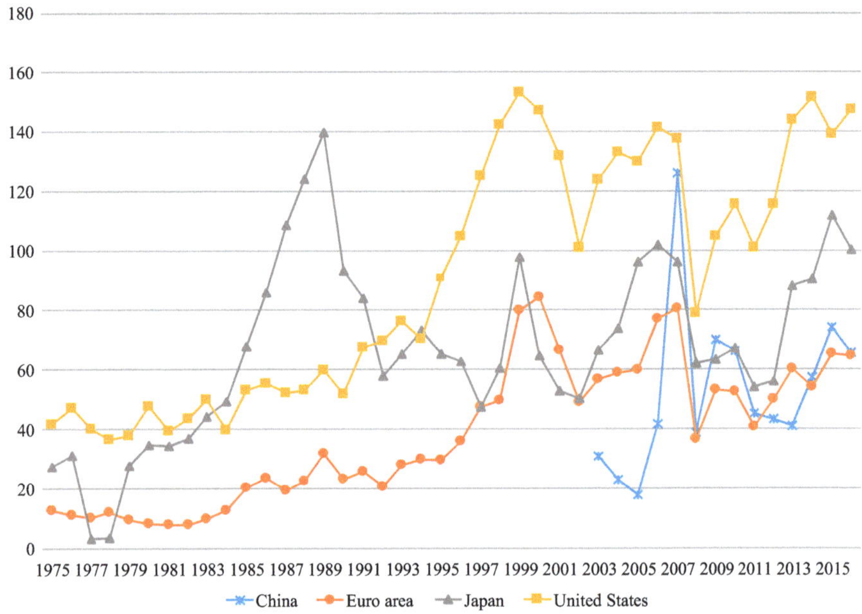

Fig. 26.7 Market capitalization, 1975–2016 (% of GDP)

clients. These systems are often seen as overbanked, and many banks are currently focusing on rebuilding their capital base (ECB 2017, p. 60).

On the other hand, the American economy can be described as a strongly capitalized economy, with 78.5% of GDP in 2008 and 147.3% of GDP in 2016 as market capitalization (two times more than in the Euro area that recorded 36.4% of GDP in 2008 and 64.4% of GDP in 2016) and which is financing on the capital market and more less through banks (Fig. 26.7, based on data from World Federation of Exchange 2017).

In Japan, the market capitalization of listed domestic companies was 61.8% of GDP in 2008 and 100.3% of GDP in 2016.

Although the real economy of the Euro area is almost as large as the United States, European capital markets are less comparable to their American correspondents, which are huge and very liquid and higher than in the Euro area. The New York and London Stock Exchange favor the US dollar and pound sterling against euro and Japanese yen, while Tokyo remains far behind, but Hong Kong and Shanghai are gaining important positions.

Not only the size of financial market matters but also its degree of liberalization. Thus, American market presents both greater depth and liquidity and a wider range of sophisticated financial instruments. As regarding China's financial market, there are still significant gaps, especially in terms of stability, liquidity, capital controls, and regulations that limit access.

Brexit has forced the European Union to find an alternative financial market to London and to speed up its capital markets union (CMU) project – the creation of a single market for capital in the EU by 2019 – to make the financial system more resilient and robust. According to the European Commission (2016), the goal is to complement Europe's strong tradition of bank financing by providing alternatives to credit-based financing.

26.2.3 *History of Using Currency*

It has proven that there is a preference for a currency that was strong in the past.

The seventeenth and eighteenth centuries were commercially and financially dominated by the Netherlands, where paper money became important for international operations. In the nineteenth century, Great Britain has held the largest share in international trade reviving strength of pound sterling role. During 1860–1914, about 60% of world trade was denominated and settled in pounds (Eichengreen 2005, p. 4). Pound domination before 1914 is often cited as proof that there can be only one international currency for a specific period of time. This was the case in the nineteenth century with pound sterling and then with the US dollar in the twentieth century. In the late nineteenth century, the American economy has exceeded the largest British economy. The United Kingdom lost its economic, colonial, and military supremacy, but pound sterling remained an important international currency.

After the Second World War, the international monetary system created at Bretton Woods was designed having as a reference currency the US dollar. The US dollar became the main currency in the global market, a position which is maintained today.

Year 1999 marks the creation of the euro and European Central Bank in the context of new dimensions and characteristics of the international monetary system but without a significant change in terms of international use of the US dollar.

Recently, on November 2015, the International Monetary Fund awarded the yuan/renminbi status as a reserve currency and added it to the special drawing rights basket on October 2016.

26.3 Conclusions

In conclusion, two of the features of an international currency – the development of the financial market and historical continuity – support the US dollar against the euro or other currencies. From the point of view of the other criterion – the issuer's demographic, economic, commercial, and financial dimension and importance – it can be said that the US dollar and the euro are in the same position, but the role of China and hence of the renminbi should not be neglected.

As the data for 2016 show, the United States is the first country as share of global GDP, followed by the Euro area, China, and Japan. In terms of population size, China ranks first. Euro area occupies the first place regarding the share in GDP of exports and imports of goods and services.

Solans (2003) perceived the introduction of the euro as the start of competition between different currencies on international financial markets. Actually, international monetary system did not seek to get the euro gains that would lead to losses for the US dollar. Both currencies have had their place in the global economy, and from the introduction of the euro, it has benefited both the Euro area and the rest of the world.

Over time, despite the increase in the volume of foreign exchange transactions and exchange rate volatility, the market remained one centered on the US dollar. The US dollar continues to dominate its use on the capital market, the money market, the banking market, the foreign exchange market, and in foreign exchange reserves of the central banks.

The US dollar's reference position was less influenced by the introduction of the euro, but nowadays it may be affected by the growing importance of China, the decline of the US political and economic power, and the crisis of the European Union. It can be said that the US dollar has so far benefited from the lack of alternatives but now has real international rivals, the euro and the Chinese renminbi, though the voices are very different. For example, Eichengreen (2016, p. 48) believes that China's currency remains far behind the US dollar and the euro on every relevant dimension in spite of the publicity regarding renminbi internationalization. On the other side, Cohen (2017) considers that mercantilist agenda of the Trump administration will determine over time the US dollar to lose ground to the renminbi.

Changing the US dollar's stand may have consequences on seignorage revenues and the US financing costs and global influence. Global crisis, changes in the US dollar's value, Euro area crisis, and more recently US elections and Brexit are challenges to the current US dollar's position in the global markets. Although if we cite Bergsten (2015), domestic economy must be able to avoid undue direct repercussions from foreign events.

References

Auboin, M.: Use of currencies in international trade: any changes in the picture? WTO Staff Working Paper, ERSD-2012-10 (2012)

Bergsten, C.F.: The Dilemmas of the Dollar: The Economics and Politics of United States International Monetary Policy. A Council on Foreign Relations Book. M.E. Sharpe, New York (1996)

Bergsten, C.F.: The Dilemmas of the Dollar: The Economics and Politics of United States International Monetary Policy. A Council on Foreign Relations Book, 2nd edn. Routledge, London/New York (2015)

Chinn, M., Frankel, J.: The euro may over the next 15 years surpass the dollar as leading international currency. NBER Working Paper, 13909 (2008)

Cohen, B.: Renminbi Internationalization: a Conflict of Statecrafts. Prepared for presentation at the ISA International Conference 2017, Hong Kong 15–18 June 2017, http://web.isanet.org/Web/Conferences/HKU2017-s/Archive/ab9b21df-37a2-403a-8492-d964e3d5d01d.pdf (2017). Accessed 8 Aug 2017

ECB: International Role of the Euro, July (2015)

ECB: Financial Integration in Europe, May (2017)
Eichengreen, B.: Sterling's Past, Dollar's Future: Historical Perspectives on Reserve Currency Competition. NBER Working Paper, 11336 (2005)
Eichengreen, B.: Global Monetary Order, in Conference proceedings The future of the international monetary and financial architecture, 27–29 June 2016, Sintra, Portugal, pp. 21–63. https://www.ecb.europa.eu/pub/pdf/other/ecbforumcentralbanking201606.en.pdf (2016). Accessed 09 July 2017
European Commission: Conference report European financial market integration – Opportunities and challenges from a transatlantic perspective (6.6.2016). https://ec.europa.eu/germany/sites/germany/files/cmu_event_report.pdf. Accessed 25 August 2017
IMF: World Economic Outlook Database, April (2017). Accessed July 2017
IMF: International Financial Statistics database
SWIFT: RMB Tracker, April (2017)
Solans, D.: The international role of the euro in a globalised economy. Pareto Securities Economic Conference, Oslo, March (2003)
Tavlas, G.: The international use of currencies: the U.S. dollar and the euro finance and development, June 1998, **35**(2). http://www.imf.org/external/pubs/ft/fandd/1998/06/tavlas.htm
UNCTADstat database
World Bank: World Development Indicators Database, April (2017). Accessed June 2017
World Federation of Exchange: WFE Database (2017). Accessed June 2017
World Trade Organization: World Trade Statistical Review (2016)

Chapter 27
The E-Government Role in the Future of Jobs in Accounting and in Auditing: A Theoretical Proposal Applied to the Italian Public Sector

Massimo Pollifroni, Gheorghe Militaru, Adrian Ioana, and Augustin Semenescu

Abstract The article attempts to outline possible future developments in the field of the public accounting and auditing professions resulting from the present e-government processes, which dates back to the early 2000s. This change has an untapped potential that could have a profound effect in many areas, such as the rationalization of public spending, business ethics, and university education to new professions required by the future labor market. It should be noted also that the future change of labor is a generalist issue proposed in many prestigious international researches: the paper seeks to make a contribution specifically oriented to the field of accounting and auditing professions applied to the public sector. After a methodological premise of systematization of the related topics of reference – whose origins can be traced back to the New Public Management Theory – the theoretical approach of the contribution will try to develop some Italian real implications regarding the change under study.

Keywords Public management • E-government • Business ethics

27.1 Introduction

The future change of labor is a generalist issue proposed in different international researches (Berra 2017; World Economic Forum 2016). The present proposal seeks to make a contribution specifically oriented to the field of accounting and auditing

M. Pollifroni (✉)
University of Turin, Turin, Italy
e-mail: massimo.pollifroni@unito.it

G. Militaru • A. Ioana • A. Semenescu
University Politehnica of Bucharest, Bucharest, Romania
e-mail: militaru@upb.ro; adyioana@gmail.com; augustin.semenescu@upb.ro

S.C. Mărginean et al. (eds.), *Emerging Issues in the Global Economy*, Springer Proceedings in Business and Economics,
https://doi.org/10.1007/978-3-319-71876-7_27

professions applied to the public sector, a sector – this latter – deeply reformed by the "New Public Management Theory" (in acronym NPMT) in the 1990s.

At the present time, the NPMT finds empirical evidences in e-government processes that "(…) are referred to the use of modern Information and Communication Technologies (ICT) linked to the development of electronics and the Internet in the modernization process of the Public Administration (…)" (Pollifroni 2003: p. 3).

E-government processes will play an important role in managing change of the work in the Public Administration: in the future as in the present.

The central part of the paper presents a case study applied to the audit activities applied to the Italian public sector: this case already represents an important e-government application oriented to change the work in auditing and concerns the automatized random choice of the audit boards in the Italian municipalities, an electronic procedure of choice introduced in accordance with Article 16, Paragraph 25, of the Decree Law 13 August 2011, n. 138.

The final part of the contribution will try to propose some changes in the Italian Case for improving the biphasic action of e-government processes (Pollifroni 2010), in which it is possible to observe the following dynamics: on the one hand, these processes represent a right way to introduce efficiency and effectiveness in the public management (short-period analysis); on the other hand, e-government applications can have a useful effect on the ethical shared behaviors (long-period analysis).

27.2 Analysis of the NPMT Evolution in the Present E-Government Processes

The research methodology applied to the present study is oriented to the "aprioristic theory" (Ayres 1961; Freadman and Miller 1992; Haspelmath 2012), where its potential is to provide a theoretical framework for improving the biphasic action of e-government processes carried out in order to increase efficiency and ethics in the public sector.

These e-government processes represent the modern representation of theorization started in the 1990s under the diction of "New Public Management" or also "New Public Management Theory" (in acronym NPMT) (Barzelay 2000; Christensen 2002; Navarra and Cornford 2006; Osborne and Gaebler 1992), through which many new features were introduced in the management of Public Administration (or in the public management), such as:

- Rigid, hierarchical, bureaucratic form changing to flexible
- Change role of government in society
- Change in relationship between government and citizenship
- "Entrepreneurial governments" promoting competition between service providers
- Measuring performance by outcomes
- Pushing control into the community

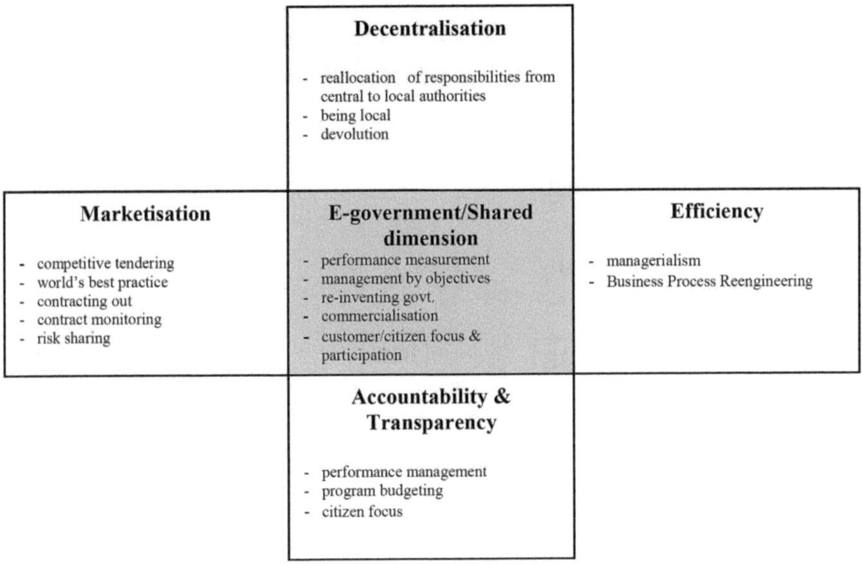

Fig. 27.1 The four drivers of NPMT: reforms in government and the location of e-government (Source: Navarra and Cornford 2006: p. 3).

In other words, the following figure (see Fig. 27.1) attempts to highlight and summarize the main NPMT drivers characterizing the present e-government processes which are – following Navarra and Cornford's approach – decentralization, efficiency, accountability/transparency, and marketization.

NPMT finds current evidence in different processes of e-government that may be analyzed with reference to the various models applied to the public institutions during their modernization and since the 2000s, and the academic debate and the international literature have tried to systemize the e-government models through the following schema:

- G2C model (government-to-citizen model) that concerns the activities carried out by the public institution toward citizens (e.g., building Institutional Portal Web to provide Internet online services to the citizens, such as the presentation of the individual tax return in electronic format or the application of electronic document delivery to the public offices, etc.).
- G2B model (government-to-business model) regarding the activities carried out by the public institution toward business companies (e.g., to provide Internet online services such as the presentation – in electronic format – of the following documents: income tax return, annual report, etc.).
- G2E model (government-to-employees model): this model concerns the activities carried out by the public institution toward employees (e.g., to provide Internet online services such as e-learning activities, teleworking activities, etc.).
- G2G model (government-to-government model) includes the activities carried out by the public institution toward other domestic public institution (electronic

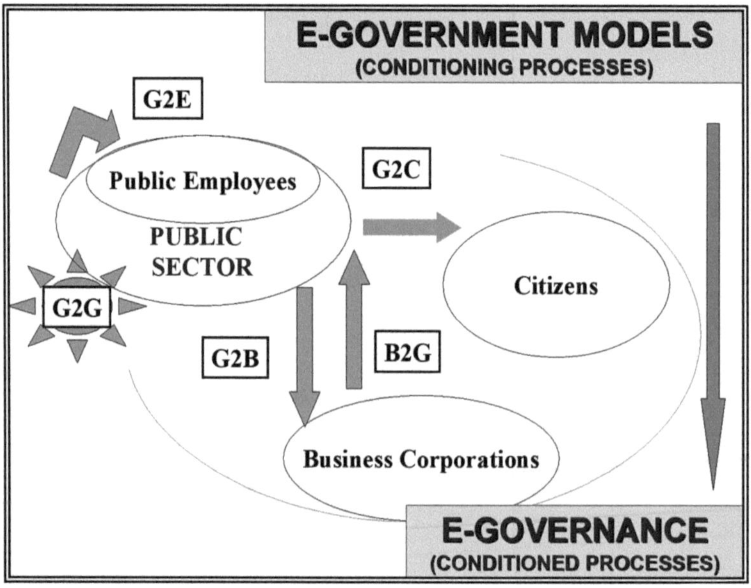

Fig. 27.2 The relationships between e-governance processes and e-government (processes and models) (Source: Pollifroni 2003: p. 5)

integration between several departments or between central and local public institution) or toward other international or foreign public institutions (e.g., activities in intelligence cooperation to contrast organized crime or international terrorism).

- B2G model (business-to-government model) that includes the activities carried out by the public institution toward external supplier (e.g., e-procurement activities, e-auctions online, etc.; in Italy, these activities are centralized by Consip S.p.A., a company owned by the Italian Treasury Department).

The development of the e-government processes (conditioning processes or causes) determines an improvement in the governance processes of the public institution that – using highly technological solutions – are named e-governance processes (conditioned processes or effects). Consequently, e-government and e-governance processes are the two clusters of the aspects of technological innovation applied to public administration processes: the following figure (see Fig. 27.2) tries to show the main relationships between e-governance processes and e-government (processes and models).

The e-governance processes include, for example, direct participation of the employees to the internal decision of the public institution: these processes influence the internal governance with activities, e.g., of internal electronic poll (e-decision), and may support the assessment of external consensus in different activities (e.g., of e-voting activities, so-called digital democracy or e-democracy).

The case that will be presented and discussed in the next paragraph represents an application oriented to the B2G model and concerns the automatized random choice of the audit boards in the Italian municipalities and provinces, an electronic procedure of choice introduced in accordance with Article 16, Paragraph 25, of the Decree Law 13 August 2011, n. 138.

27.3 The New Automatized Random Choice Model Applied to the Elections of the Audit Boards in the Italian Municipalities and Provinces: Presentation and Discussion

This paragraph is dedicated to present and discuss a new Italian application oriented to the B2G model and full adhering to the four NPMT drivers shown in the previous Fig. 27.1.

The application concerns the automatized random choice of the audit boards in the Italian municipalities and provinces, an electronic procedure of choice introduced in accordance with Article 16, Paragraph 25, of the Decree Law 13 August 2011, n. 138.

The automatized random choice is operated on a list of auditors (public accounts) managed by the Ministry of Interior and divided into 20 regional sub-lists, in relation to the public account residence.

Every regional list is electronically managed by the regional unit of the Ministry of Interior (called "prefecture") and is divided in three sections identified in relation to the population of the municipality or of the province:

- The first section regards the municipalities until 4.999 inhabitants.
- The second section regards the municipalities from 5.000 to 14.999 inhabitants.
- The third section regards the municipalities from 15.000 inhabitants and all the provinces.

Professionals (auditors and public accountants) must meet the following requirements for enrollment on the sections:

- The first section regards for the municipalities until 4.999 inhabitants: 2 years of enrollment in the Register of the Chartered Accountants and Accounting Experts (or in the Register of Auditors), ten professional training credits per year, and no prior assignments are required.
- The second section regards for the municipalities from 5.000 to 14.999 inhabitants: 5 years of enrollment in the Register of the Chartered Accountants and Accounting Experts (or in the Register of Auditors), ten professional training credits per year, and one prior triennial assignment are required.
- The third section regards for the municipalities from 15.000 inhabitants and the provinces: 10 years of enrollment in the Register of the Chartered Accountants

and Accounting Experts (or in the Register of Auditors), ten professional training credits per year, and two prior triennial assignments are required.

Inclusion in the list is done in the regional section of the applicant's residence and in one of the bands of local authorities in relation to the requirements for enrollment in each section.

Upon registration, applicants can ask to be placed in one or more groups of municipalities, if they meet the requirements, and can exclude one or more provincial territories for which are not intended to express willingness to hold the assignment.

The professionals sign on the website at least ten professional training credits per year in the period from 1 January to 30 November of the previous year: the credit training in public accounting and financial and economic management of local authorities for participation in events that have been previously agreed upon by the Ministry of the Interior; for these events, a final test is required.

The professionals should be proven annually the meeting of the requirements for the maintenance in the list: otherwise their positions will be delisted in the case of absence of requirements.

The request for registration and maintenance in the list must be performed through electronic procedure, in the manner and within the time specified in the appropriate public notices branched from the Ministry of Interior.

The random sorting from the lists for the subsequent appointment of auditors by the Local Government Council is carried out by the regional unit of the Ministry of Interior (called "prefecture" or – in Italian language – "Prefettura Ufficio Territoriale del Governo") through the informatics system.

The technical features of the extraction procedure of names from the lists of auditors of municipalities are disclosed through the algorithm description of the IT procedure management software used, based on the principles of randomness.

The process begins by creating a list of random selected candidates, by choosing, from the list's subscribers, all candidates who, at the time of the draw:

- Are resident in the region of the requesting entity
- Have not excluded, under demand, the county of the same entity belonging
- Are enrolled in the local authorities of the belonging institution

Since extraction of the list of random selected candidates, a standard function is used to create another random list. On this list, you proceed following the Java programming language standards to get a number that represents the position in the list of the first single extract name.

The generator of random values uses the system timestamp in nanoseconds (value that changes continuously), in order to avoid two different launches from getting the same sequences of random numbers.

This operation is repeated a number of times equal to three times of auditors required for the entity, in order to extract the names for possible replacements in case of renunciation or impediment, as required by law.

Therefore, at the end of the process, you get two lists:

- The drawn names (in order of extraction, including the names for possible replacements)
- The names who took part in the draw

Both lists are attached to the extract of the verbal automatically generated by the procedure: the names that are extracted for the renewal of the body of a local authority, those designated for appointment, and those subsequently extracted for replacement continue to contribute to the formation of lists of random selected candidates valid for subsequent extractions.

The related local authority will verify any cases of incompatibility for reaching the limit of assignments at the time of the appointment, as required by Article 5 of the Decree of the Minister 15 February 2012, n. 23.

After presenting the model, it is possible to proceed to the critical analysis of the same in terms of strengths and weaknesses.

On the strengths, it is possible to observe that the automatized random choice of the audit boards in the Italian municipalities and provinces reduces to zero the interference of politics in this choice, but the model could still be greatly improved.

Primarily, it has been said that every regional list is electronically managed by the regional unit of the Ministry of Interior (called "prefecture") and is divided in three sections identified in relation to the population of the municipality or of the province.

It is important to observe that the access to the second and third sections is subordinated to previous assignments they had in the past and before the reform the choice was of political emanation: this creates a discrimination among those who had assignments in the past and who did not have them; this discrimination could be eliminated by creating a single list.

Secondly, the remuneration for the audit activities is still very discretionary: it should be defined by the same website procedure.

Thirdly, today auditors' activities are more than 100 per year: it might think of a reduction obtainable through e-government processes that can be implemented on the same Web platform dedicated to the random choice of the audit boards.

Fourthly, the automatized random choice of the audit boards – introduced in accordance with Article 16, Paragraph 25, of the Decree Law 13 August 2011, n. 138 – only regards the Italian municipalities and provinces: could it not be extended to all sectors of the Italian public administration? This last solution would offer greater transparency to the entire Italian public administration sector.

Fifthly, could the model be adapted to the stock market, given the importance of listed companies in terms of corporate social responsibility (in acronym CSR)?

Last but not least, could the model be implemented also for the business consultancy that public administration requires from professionals?

This final proposal – concerning the consultancy solutions – would be of enormous contribution for reducing the public spending, in addition to the issues of transparency and ethics, previously discussed.

As announced the following paragraph is dedicated to draw the conclusion of the paper.

27.4 Conclusion

The paper has tried to show the biphasic action of e-government processes, as described in the previous pages: on the one hand, these processes represent a right way to introduce efficiency and effectiveness in the public sector management (short-period analysis); on the other hand, e-government applications can have a useful effect on the ethical shared behaviors, such as tax evasion control, observance of the law, reengineering a public merit rating system, etc. (long-period analysis).

The biphasic action of e-government processes has had an empirical evidence in the Italian Case represented and discussed in the previous paragraph, concerning the new automatized random choice model applied to the elections of the audit boards in the Italian municipalities and provinces.

It is evident that the model should have important reflections on the future profile of audit professionals, such as:

- A greater independence from politics
- A continuous professional upgrade on public management issues
- A greater domesticity with the ICT tools
- A sure and preventive definition of the professional remuneration

Finally, the paper also wanted to introduce the debate on the potential adoption of the model in the stock market: a proposal that could surely generate a profound discussion on the subject.

Perhaps the proposed discussion and conclusion are a little utopian, but as it is said in these cases: who will live will see!

References

Ayres, C.E.: Review of epistemological problems of economics. South. Econ. J. **28**(2), 199–202 (1961)

Barzelay, M.: The New Public Management: Improving Research and Policy Dialogue. University of California Press, Berkeley (2000)

Berra, Y.: The future ain't what it used to be, University of Kent (2017). Available at: https://www.kent.ac.uk/careers/Choosing/future-jobs.htm. Accessed 14 June 2017

Christensen, T.P.L.: New Public Management: The Transformation of Ideas and Practice. Ashgate, Aldershot (2002)

Freadman, R., Miller, S.: Re-Thinking Theory: A Critique of Contemporary Literary Theory and an Alternative Account. Cambridge University Press, Cambridge (UK) (1992)

Haspelmath, M.: Deductive vs. aprioristic theories: continuing the debate on word-class universality (2012). Available at http://dlc.hypotheses.org/250. Accessed 14 June 2017

Navarra, D.D., Cornford, T.: The state, democracy and the limits of new public management: exploring alternative models of E-government. In: Proceedings of eGovernment Workshop '06 (eGOV06), pp. 1–14. Brunel University, London (2006)

Osborne, D., Gaebler, T.: Reinventing Government: How the Entrepreneurial Spirit Is Transforming the Public Sector. Penguin Books, London (1992)

Pollifroni, M.: Processi e modelli di e-government ed e-governance applicati all'azienda pubblica. Giuffrè, Milan (2003)
Pollifroni, M.: Some empirical evidences about the biphasic action of e-government processes. In: Proceedings of the Challenges for Analysis of the Economy, the Businesses, and Social Progress International Scientific Conference, pp. 332–350. Unidocument Kft, Szeged (Hungary) (2010)
World Economic Forum: The Future of Jobs Employment, Skills and Workforce Strategy for the Fourth Industrial Revolution (2016). Available at: http://www3.weforum.org/docs/WEF_Future_of_Jobs.pdf. Accessed 14 June 2017

Chapter 28
The Fascination of History Ignored: Explosive Economic Paths for Which We Pay a Huge Price

Dan Popescu

Abstract The paper is presenting a series of examples of ignored history – facts which were overlooked and the humankind who didn't seem to learn anything. The examples are many: from the eighteenth-century revolutions to the First and Second World Wars and from the economic crisis of 2008–2009 to recent developments in East European countries, particularly in Romania, the people ignore the lessons, and the price paid for this ignorance is huge.

Keywords Economic history • Crisis • Wars

28.1 Introduction

Globalization has been and still is ineluctable. Many factors have contributed and are still contributing to this effect. Here is a brief overview. Man, as an individual, has "moved" toward family, even though, originally, people gathered in packs. A tough way of life and common interests, primarily of mutual help, and a relatively primitive, difficult life have led to families joining into communities. In this way, families were better protected by the very solidarity of their members, communities, originally villages, then along other directions, especially important economic functions, mainly market towns, but also defense citadels, harbors, etc., have become cities. Hundreds of thousands of years have thus gone by (Toynbee 1998). The picture is, of course, incomplete, but I am referring here to the main directions of evolution and not only in Europe.

In time, nations came into being and subsequently or simultaneously countries, with the resulting alliances, treaties, state communities, etc. With economic development, modernization of communication systems, and huge advances in

D. Popescu (✉)
Lucian Blaga University of Sibiu, Sibiu, Romania
e-mail: dan.popescu@ulbsibiu.ro

S.C. Mărginean et al. (eds.), *Emerging Issues in the Global Economy*, Springer Proceedings in Business and Economics,
https://doi.org/10.1007/978-3-319-71876-7_28

transportation – from the cart to modern, high-speed, large-capacity airplanes – alongside widespread and generalized literacy and the disappearance of harmful, crude ignorance and the spread of information technologies and many others, we are becoming people, citizens of the Earth. We have not only our own worries and hopes but also those of our fellow human beings from other places, with whom we are interconnected, regarding development, health, culture, society, etc. As concerns clime, unfortunately, NASA's recent and dramatic warning about the Earth's clime is something I was discussing in the 1980s (Popescu 1981, 1984, 1987). But as I was living and working in Romania, nobody paid any attention to me. But let us come back. Nations and nationalities are not disappearing, and interconnectedness is starting to prevail, even though timidly at first.

From the United States to the states of Russia, in their extended form, to Europe's communities, and to those of South America and from the Asian alliances increasingly replacing Pan-Asianism (Toynbee 1998), more and more differences are reduced and thus we are heading for the United States of the World. And then it seems highly probable that we are going to have a global state of the world, with global institutions, with global interests, both specific and general, a state taking over more and more responsibilities "upriver" (Popescu 2007, 2011). However, I don't think that this will be a serious inconvenience, provided that national states are preserved. They have so much more to say. However, as far as Europe is concerned, in addition to the nation, from the perspective of the European production system, the individual has been and still is the core, the main element. Even the states of Asia, more or less now with their group-based production system, are oriented toward the individual. See China and India, the emergent economies of Southeast Asia (Toynbee 1998).

This is, of course, only a simple outline of our evolution toward globalization. There are objective laws and complex developments which make such an evolution objective, too. The process is difficult, long, and highly complex. But people and what unites them, wisdom, hopes, and beliefs, will prevail; history will prevail in a complicated future. And it is a good thing that we are heading in this direction, as resistance would cost us dearly now or later. We can identify well-defined stages in this framework, which significantly illustrate the directions shown. Very briefly, in my opinion, a first stage of globalization was constituted by the Roman Empire, stretching out on three continents: Europe, Asia, and Africa. The empire fell apart, but the civilization promoted by the Romans endured, even developed, being incorporated in traditions, generating evolutive principles, behaviors, etc., including the "Pax Romana" (Popescu 2007). And doesn't Israel contribute in this direction, too, as a civilized formation of the ancient world which has spread then all over the world through its people for hundreds and thousands of years (Attali 2011)?

Then came a second stage, that of geographical discoveries, large and small, which, especially starting with the fifteenth century, have "aligned" to Europe the two Americas, including Canada, then Australia, and then more recently the two "cold" continents (the Arctic and the Antarctic). They were "aligned" to Europe as regards religions, science, economic methods and technologies, expenditures and benefits, even language in general, activities and lifestyle, etc. (Popescu 2007). Next came a third stage, with substages that are still continuing today and will continue for a long time, the industrial revolutions, the stage of transition from wood to coal and metal, the mechanical revolution, the electricity revolution, of oil and its derivatives, the cybernetic and informatics revolution, nanotechnologies, the post-industrial revolutions, etc. (Popescu 2007). Those who have understood this and have acted accordingly have been successful and still are. Those who have not understood have largely, sooner or later, failed and will continue to do so (Popescu 2014). But evil; terrorism, in particular diseases; and poverty are also globalized, which hugely increases the complexity and costs of globalization. Unfortunately, I don't think anyone has calculated these costs (Popescu 2014). We are, however, with rights and responsibilities, individuals, citizens of a country and of a community, but also "global people." We have common interests, hopes, sorrows, achievements, aspirations, and illusions. I do not believe in any other variant.

28.2 What Have We Learned from History?

This is, of course, a hypothesis, a hypothesis regarding a certain evolution we have been following. It seems highly probable that it is the most natural one. It is, of course, not a linear evolution. There have always been divisions, serious backlashes, enormous conflicts, wars, most of them awful, coup d'etat, genocides, death, horrible epidemics, catastrophic cataclysms, confrontations of all sorts, divergent interests and discrepancies. But despite all these, we are heading in this direction.

One way or another, we reset ourselves based on the principles of biblical genesis or on those of other important religions, principles regarding humanism, tolerance, understanding, and even peace (Popescu 2014). It is true that starting with a certain moment, when we became increasingly aware of our actions, mainly from the modern period, many of the divisions we have mentioned, originally conflicts, wars, but also others, often "in the name of development," have related to a certain fascination which ignored history that seems to have been exerting over us. What have we learned from history to help us pay a lower price for the good things we have obtained and are obtaining? Almost nothing. We are repeating our mistakes. There have been – and still are – explosive developments for which a huge price has been paid and still is, the disregard for history appearing to be contagious and dramatic. We are going to refer here to several such explosive economic developments generated by the disregard for history, developments for which costs have been and are huge. Of course, we are talking about the past 100 years since the First World War. And we will often highlight, as it is natural, certain developments and regresses in Romania. And from such a complex perspective, what future and destinies can be foreseen?

Here are some questions in this respect. How important is the nation as a form of meditation and mediation (Pomeranz 2016) between the isolated individual and the human race? And for how long? Should we close frontiers, for fear of terrorism and of a somehow prejudicial integration for some, or should we keep them open but beware of the "evil," and develop their capacity to "breathe" toward the world? Are nations dynamic categories, with openings toward the world, increasingly interconnected, or are they mere citadels under siege within which any difference must be reduced, even exterminated (Veverca 1941)?

Are wars inevitable for the simple reason that we cannot imagine – we cannot adhere to – a perpetual peace, even if this does not exclude keen competition, tough fight for resources, and fight for a better life in which often some win noisily, while the others lose tragically (Toynbee 1998)? Can't we possibly amend the second term of this relation, by finding those contexts and situations in which exchanges and competition will end, one way or another, with advantages for all participants, of course without excluding hierarchies? Why are the great powers less global and more national, while smaller countries are called upon to open up their economic borders and embrace globalization at any cost (Popescu 2014)? Is it so difficult for us to formulate the theory of labor value according to the views of the Vienna and later American marginalists, who believe that utility confers value to products and through the exchange of products everybody can – and must – gain the maximum advantage (Popescu 1999)? And so much more. But let us refer concretely to the more or less recognized experiences together with the things they have revealed, good and bad, to our disregard for these experiences and the huge price paid for this disregard.

28.3 Revolutions

We are at the middle of the eighteenth century and later. It is the "century of lights," but "lights" come in with difficulty. In France, for example, despite the advances made by the Mercantilist School and especially by the Physiocracy School, which launched the famous words "laissez-faire, laissez-passer, and le monde va de lui même," an unaltered and unalterable invitation to trade, development, and progress, despite the advances made by the Enlighteners, the disdain of the nobility, in its largest part, for the "commoners," for both the rural population and the urban marginal one, was as huge as it was consistent (Popescu 1999). Nothing had been learned from the experience of the unfortunate king across the Channel, Carol I of Stuart, who, 130 years before, had been beheaded not over family or religious intrigues, but mainly for social reasons. Cromwell meant something totally different than the Stuarts' steady belief in a world of advantages and privileges which, according to them, should not and could not change. If someone powerful and influential had read these pages in the history of England, then royalty in its entirety might not have been so strongly shaken by a huge earthquake which sometimes continues to be felt even today.

The institution of monarchy might have become wiser and come down from the ivory tower of wealth and power to which they had been living, paying more attention to the demands of the people and of the time – with great economic gains for everybody. In another context, how sad but how suggestive wrote Vlahuta, the

Romanian: "Lie sits at the table with the king." We must say, however, that, to her honor, Romania's monarchy cannot be described in this way. For example, three great kings – Carol I, the founder (of course we do not forget Alexandru Ioan Cuza, with a much shorter reign, the founder as well); Ferdinand, the unifier; and King Michael – risked their lives and throne to serve the interests of the country.

Even nowadays – especially in less developed countries and not only in Europe, where there are monarchies or pretenders supported in various ways – too little has been learned from these times and events. More and more people understand that real life is real life and there is less and less room in it for anachronistic characters, some of them cardboard characters but noisily claimed. Dictatorships, very close to the royal absolutism found several centuries ago, and even in some decades of the twentieth century, have revealed the same logic of force and abuse and of disdain for and severe punishment of those who do not accept them (Bainville 1935), going as far as murder, extermination, and genocide. Which explains why, no matter how they started, most dictatorships ended – and still end – badly for dictators and their supporters (Bainville 1935; Popescu 2011). Have societies learned anything from such developments, nipping dictatorships in the bud, preventing their harmful effects? Very little, not few dictatorships still exist today.

But let us continue. According to many opinions – which we credit – large-scale, mass poverty, "popular" poverty in fact, has generated and is still generating revolutions, just like wise reforms with well-defined social objectives leading to the most genuine material and spiritual emulation, equality of opportunity for everybody, etc. which have generated progress. I believe, however, that not all revolutions are "bad" (Lăcusteanu 2015), on the contrary. And we have, among others, the examples of some Romanian revolutions – "Tudor Vladimirescu," the revolution of 1848, etc. According to most calculations ante and post factum, evolution represents a smoother and less costly way toward progress, even if some people overrate revolutions and wars.

I have to say that I have no doubts regarding, for example, the great significance of the French Revolution of 1789, a revolution conceived, animated, and carried out, victorious under the umbrella of the "Enlightenment," of the slogan "Liberté, Egalité, Fraternité!" It meant so much for civilization, although it also incorporated some bloody components. But I am not convinced of the genuine system change – what a revolution aims to do and does – of some "revolutions," too frequent and thus almost commonplace, from states in South America (Bainville 1935) and Africa. I have doubts regarding partly or wholly stolen revolutions (Portocală 1991), etc. – a lot of noise, tirades, and declamations, a lot of blood, but too little for society. And we also have the example of the two most disastrous world catastrophes of the last century but also of some small, internal wars of unimaginable cruelty. What have the rulers, the privileged thus learnt, what have those learnt who could – and can – make decisions? Almost nothing, as being rather worthless and highly ignorant, they hope for immutability, for the eternity of the world in which they have prospered and still do.

What huge differences exist between the lowest incomes in the world (of course, for the countries capable of calculating them) – of only several cents – and the highest ones, of billions and billions of dollars? And what has come out of such opaqueness, of the fights thus conducted? Huge loss and a true hemorrhage of social substance, dead people, grieving families, shattered hopes, and destitution still continue to exist. And it is mostly for these reasons, including those of morbid social contrasts, that the Earth is sitting on a powder keg (Popescu 2014). Anyway, things have been and still are complex. Many times, in the name of "justice" and "good" (in whose name really?) and of religions, lately mainly fundamentalist, wars, genocides, abominable crimes, spectacular poisonings, horrible beheadings, numerous and hasty shootings, and merciless fights for fortunes have been conducted; flagrant lies have been and are still being told. And the consequences have been and still are terrible. This is why decision-making requires marked sensibility and balance, positive restraint, and control now more than ever. But let us continue.

28.4 Migration

Of course, the examples we are referring to can be – and are – numerous. For greater accuracy of the enquiry, let us limit ourselves to the nineteenth century and some of its industrial revolutions and developments. Let us limit our enquiry to the area of mutations taking place in productivity and production, of social structures, and of families and individuals and to the area of capital constitution and loss, especially for Europe, the Two Americas, Asia, and Africa. Of course, a special situation is represented by emigration and immigration. As we were saying, the long-distance motivations for emigration and immigration (processes that have always existed) have been starvation, destitution, and the hope for a better life in another place, even if this place was far away (of course, originally closer) – a certain desire of those involved generally determined by economic reasons (Popescu 2010). We should add refugees, "forced" emigrations, representing an important part – according to some calculations the most important one, actually forced by the "others" and by other factors. To these we should add military colonization and then exiles to distant places, the serving of punishment by prisoners from England in Australia, and similar deportations, not only from England, to Asia, Africa, and the archipelagoes (also see Henri Charrière, "Papillon," etc.).

Last but not least, there were emigrations generated by fear of death, by fear of crime. Political persecutions are not unimportant either, on the contrary, etc., for example, political deportations not only from Russia, from the Tsarist Empire, to Siberia, mainly after the nineteenth century (see, e.g., C. Stere "In preajma revoluției"). Then deportations of prisoners, etc. What about racism, racist policies, and the huge curse of genocide that we have mentioned, which, besides death, have moved and are still moving around tens and tens of millions of people? Many times history has preferred to record these events as merely spectacular and dramatic rather than as economically motivated movements – unfairly considered to be "commonplace," indistinct. But this is the direction in which we are going to conduct our research.

As shown by the American professor Kenneth Pommeranz of Chicago University, starting with the nineteenth century, population migration was overwhelmingly determined by concrete and fast structural changes in production and productivity. It was not forced migration, but mostly "free migration," willingly generated by certain freedoms and great advances in certain parts of the world and not by typical constraints. In other words, it was migration well-designed and freely conducted by its very subjects (Pomeranz 2016). What triggered such a change, how have the dimensions of migration been amplified like this, and the question remains: can we resist it?

In the first decades of the nineteenth century – in England even earlier, as they started here – industrial revolutions take place, generally defined as the transition from manual labor to machines. In addition to England, machines will prevail in France, Belgium, the Netherlands, Italy, the United States, Germany, and a little bit later Russia. They will spread then to countries of Asia and Africa and Australia (Popescu 1981). It is true, in many colonial territories, industrial revolutions will involve mainly the construction of railways, as there is too little industry in the colonies where the new technologies expand. They will be used eventually in the extractive industry. Industrial revolutions will also concern the great maritime lines increasingly endowed with steamers, mechanized harbors, etc., so as to facilitate and reduce the cost of carrying raw materials from colonies to metropolises, and of finished goods from metropolises to colonies (Pomeranz 2016).

Products one country or another did not have and needed were in this way exchanged largely over long distances. As we were saying, these products usually included raw materials and primary food products (mainly exotic products) from the colonies, and finished products from industrialized countries. We are not going to address the advantages and disadvantages of this exchange pattern; it is clear how they were distributed. The Argentinian economist Raul Prebisch was one of the first to explain this in his theory "the price scissors" (Popescu 1981).

Slowly, a change is becoming more and more apparent. It originated in the United States – which, from a colony, turned into an industrialized country – through the integration of West territories into the American economic circuit. Such an integration also occurs in Canada, Australia, and other countries of Asia which develop beyond the boundaries of colonization. Transport is faster and cheaper, and machines make their way into agriculture – an agriculture largely dominated by great land properties – of course, excluding the American North with a much more mobile agriculture organized around farms. This, on the one hand. At the same time, we must take into account the advanced globalization of capital markets, of goods markets, of labor markets, etc. In these conditions, when product "a" is exchanged for product "b," the prices of agricultural products, for example, are no longer producers' prices but those found in the international market. Thus, many households in South Italy, France, Germany, England, Ireland, the Netherlands, etc. become inefficient as they are obsolete and cannot cope with the inflow of cheaper products coming to the market from the United States, for example, wheat. The same applies to wool from Australia and New Zealand; meat, already carried in fridge trains and containers from Argentina; hide, from the same place; etc. The traditional local markets of advanced European countries will be faced with big difficulties, low productivity, higher costs, and households will go bankrupt (Pomeranz 2016).

What did these Europeans choose to do? To emigrate massively to America, to other countries. Tens and hundreds of millions of people. Of course, the picture rendered by Kenneth Pomeranz is slightly more complex, but things are essentially like this. You can resist the market using autarchic economies only in strictly limited areas, which for several hundred years, in our times of integrated economies and of an increasingly globalized economy, has proven to be disastrous. Who was able to fight – and why – the huge inflow of immigrants after the eighteenth century coming to America from the Netherlands, France, Germany, Ireland, Russia, and even Romania? Nobody, and they couldn't have. Economic and social criteria of development were actively at work. And here is today's United States, where according to some statistics about 15% of the population has German origins, 5–6% Italian, then Spanish, Irish, etc. Who could fight – and why – the huge wave of emigrants from the poorly developed Italy to Argentina, a cradle of hope, in the years at the end of the nineteenth century and the beginning of the twentieth century? Nobody, and the Italians fit in. Who opposed those coming in search of a job to Germany – ruined by the Second World War – but capable of reaching a genuine construction boom, first from Italy and then from Turkey? Nobody, the process being highly successful, and the German economy flourishing with this kind of support, too (Popescu 2016).

The present-day waves of emigrants from Asia and Africa to Europe are generated; beyond the flight from death, persecution, and war, beyond torn countries, they are generated by economic causes of a similar type. As international trade is no longer represented by the classical exchange between metropolises and colonies, mainly finished goods for raw materials or unfinished goods, but now also involves wheat for wheat, wool for wool, cotton for cotton, fruit for fruit, etc., small farmers from developing countries can no longer produce their own food for consumption. They lose on price. They will first emigrate to the slumps, reservations on the outskirts of big cities, where they will be poorer, not needed by anyone, and then to the "bright horizons" of developed countries – with or without papers, with or without the consent of those countries (Pomeranz 2016; Popescu 2016).

28.5 Cultural Differences

It is very difficult to oppose such advances of regresses. Border "walls" are becoming permeable; they are broken into, jumped over, and even pulled down with the sacrifices of those hoping for a better life. It becomes so much harder to deny the process as European developed economies – economies with a population whole life expectancy is difficult to imagine by the "aspiring poor" – acutely need labor force of a certain type, generally primary, who would accept much lower salaries than those of the local people (Popescu 2016). Whether we admit it or not is an entirely different matter. The wave of immigrants with everything it brings with it and after it, especially in the political context of relaxing restrictions on family reunion, reunion which is one of the fundamental rights of man, this wave can be somehow reduced, I believe, only by stimulating development and progress in the economically retarded areas of the world. However, this has a price, too. A price which, if paid, does not necessarily offer us the desired efficiency. And if we do not pay it, it is even worse (Popescu 2015a, b).

As regards the last waves of Asian and African immigrants looking for a future in Europe, especially in Germany, but also in other countries, including Romania, some of them actually refugees, the protests of political people in some European countries – but not at the level of the European Union – have often been vehement. Borders have been reinforced and consolidated, new walls have been erected, and small ships and boats carrying immigrants have been "hunted down." In this situation, besides the tens and hundreds of thousands of immigrants who have been admitted to the EU, Germany, Italy, France, Romania, then Turkey, etc., there have been thousands and thousands of deaths among those "hunted down," including, and especially, women and children. "Fortresses" of one kind or another and restrictions have had an enormous cost, but things have calmed down eventually, although the integration process of the newcomers has been slow and very difficult: different cultures, different customs, and a different horizon of expectations. Despite a well-organized bureaucratic activity of integration, especially in Germany, which gave priority to those immigrants considered useful for its labor market.

Things were also complicated from the perspective of the fact that very many Muslims among the newly arrived Asian and African immigrants were potential terrorists, actually consolidating that segment in different countries. Finally, things have calmed down, and it has become obvious that not few of the terrorists caught or wanted – in France, in Germany, in Belgium, in Spain, in the United States, in Russia, in Turkey, etc. – were citizens of those countries, many of them born there but preserving intact the jihad, revenge, terror in their intimate faith, although these are not allowed by the Islamic religion or by any other recognized religions of Asia, Europe, etc. Without such criminal acts, generated by a certain marginalization and isolation of the poor population in Western Europe and the United States, by a non-existent or extremely difficult process of social insertion (Popescu 2015b, 2014), these integration processes would have been much easier and the positive results more consistent. But this would have meant not to ignore the economic history of the world, because, regardless of punitive measures and actions, you cannot really oppose emigration which is determined by the hope for a better life and good integration of the newcomers (see among others "les emeutes des banlieues" in France in the early 2000s). The limited, not unlimited, number of newcomers. We are not talking here about a reconquest of Europe by Asia, the return of the Islamic occupation to the old European borders – sometimes up to the walls of Vienna – but much more simply, I believe we are talking about economic criteria and laws being applied in an ever-changing world.

28.6 World Wars

The First World War, to which we have referred before and since when 100 years have passed, broke out mainly for conquest reasons (mainly on Germany's and Austria-Hungary's part) and ended in a peace which left Germany in nominal incapacity for development, while Austria-Hungary fell apart. It was only natural – France, Great Britain, Italy, Belgium, Romania, etc. were victorious, and Bolshevism was setting in Russia. However, the largest war compensations were cashed in only by some. Let us remember some of the effects: several tens and tens of millions of people dead, injured, missing; other tens of millions of people prey to disease and poverty, also deceased; hundreds of thousands of people maimed by war; the destruction of huge economic potential, especially in the countries where battles were fought; wasted money; shattered hopes; dreadful poverty; and destitution. In addition to these, there was a demographic disequilibrium in many of the belligerent states, a scarcity of men – a situation from which these states have recovered with great difficulty. Some have still not recovered. Disastrous economic consequences. One would have thought that, with such a bloody and dreadful result, war of these dimensions would be forever removed from the political and "post-political" arsenal of the world's great powers. Treaties, declarations, the setting up of the League of Nations and its activity seemed to be favourable signs for a period of time.

But a little more than two decades had passed (21 years), and, in 1939, the Hitlerian Germany and Stalin's Russia would start another confrontation which, through the natural reactions of Poland, the United Kingdom, France, then the United States, etc., would rapidly become the Second World War. So the wisdom of those who had started the war lasted only for two decades. And this time the aftermath was even more terrible. Almost the whole of Europe was conquered by Hitler's Germany, a Reich – the third one – which, however, did not last for 1000 years as Hitler had promised, but only a few years ...Russia was operationally "disabled" by Germany, with huge losses, but then expanded its Bolshevism and dictatorial influence all over Eastern and Central Europe. At the same time, during the war and as a result of Hitlerism, genocides, and exterminating racial policies, there were tens and tens of millions of deaths and shattered people and families. Then, possibly as a result of some erroneous calculations, came the nuclear bomb dropped by the Americans at Hiroshima and Nagasaki in Japan, a country with imperial dreams for the entire Asia. Here, in addition to mass deaths, the result was horrible pain to several generations: disease and the perpetuation in time of radiation diseases ...The redrawing of the world map, the collapse of the colonial system to an equal extent, in fact a world largely destroyed for many years and which recovered with great difficulty, paying with starvation, disease, poverty, persecution, and a huge shortage of active and professional population. It is true, however, and we must mention this aspect too, this period also saw several fundamental technological advancements.

But this type of conflict – the war – continues to occupy an important place, despite the efforts made to remove it from the "communication" arsenal of states. For various reasons, we have reduced their world dimension, as agreement, peace, and negotiation between states have been promoted. But wars have become localized and, in addition to this, have slowly turned into a world war against terrorism. Anyway, this has meant and means something, and I feel that progress has been made. Even if shyly, slightly, with small steps, in a changing world where the very configuration of interest and power poles is changing. But let us still hope.

28.7 Crises

How about the world crises, the two great economic world crises, the one of 1929–1933 and the one of 2007–2008, which is actually still continuing in the present, and what have we learned from them? Very little. The speculative economy, at the expense of the productive one, and excessive financial involvement, the two main causes of the two crises, continue to occupy an important part today, too (Colson 1918; Landes 1998; Gendarme 1963; Popescu 2002a, 2015a, b). We will never be able to eat papers, only products. Then, sometimes leaving healthy practices aside, such as those put in place by the great American entrepreneur Henry Ford, which helped the recovery of the American economy after 1929–1933 by increasing the number of jobs and wages, thus stepping up production and spending, I have written repeatedly about these aspects (Popescu 1999, 2011) – other "specialists," mainly of the present time, have recommended the exit from the crisis through unemployment, poverty, the destruction of the public sector, and the reduction in wages and pensions. They have thus created resources but mainly for their own enrichment, the compensation of bank CEOs, etc.

The efforts to recover from the crisis were made at the expense of common people, of the population (Popescu 2012). And we are and have been in a "drifting boat": we do not know whether it will float or sink. Have we learned anything from the IMF's tarnished reputation at the end of the 1990s in Southeast Asian countries? These economies have recovered from the crisis, but without the IMF and through economic policies of investment, formulated with difficulty but still formulated, through policies of production growth and correlation with competition, through policies of income increases.

28.8 Romania

As regards Romania and Romania's economy, apart from several accomplishments – in particular the NATO entry and the European Union entry, the attainment of membership with full rights but also with full obligations (negotiations were led timidly and from a position of subordination, which did not happen in the case of the Visegrad countries), the winning of freedoms, which is huge – we have proven and are still proving that, unfortunately, we have a "calling" for ignoring the sacred lessons of history, with not at all negligible effects (Popescu 1990, 2002a, b). To a large extent, the ruin of a large part of the economy proves this. The reduced efficiency of privatizations, in the context of the extremely disadvantageous privatization of important industries which manufactured and sold products at competitive prices, is another important aspect. Most of these enterprises have been plundered by various and "skilled" technologies – some of them finally becoming showrooms and clubs, equipment and machinery being scrapped – thus bringing huge losses to the national wealth and huge fortunes to the accounts of various conmen, who become in this way the country's "upper class." Have the culprits answered and has the stolen money been restored to the natural economic flow? Not at all or to a very small extent. Another aspect is research has been destroyed, technical, social, and cultural research in particular. And we have lost and are losing a lot in this way, too.

And another aspect is the culpable and prejudicial sale of natural resources, of the economy's resources, from ore to oil and forests, and land too, at a time when their value was huge. Several foreign companies in cahoots with crooks and politicians – crooks themselves, too – have got rich and nothing else. The culprits are "missing" again, only "scolded." Justice, in some of its key departments, has proven to be selective, slow in many cases, with endless retractions and postponements, while highly negative characters, often ignorant or poorly educated, are free and disdainful, seemingly mocking the Romanian people. Unfortunately, they are becoming models. Jean Valjean from Victor Hugo's "Les Misérables" is back but only in his first facet – that of convict (Popescu 2014).

The situation in our agriculture is equally compromising. We largely have a broken agriculture, hardly a subsistence one, which has replaced the relatively productive agriculture we have inherited. Rash measures, which haven't been able to either prevent or eliminate theft and corruption, have amplified and are still amplifying our agricultural impairments, making us strictly dependent on the external market and its prices, although we do not have many real reasons to be so. And this is in the context of the proliferation of a very severe world food crisis, with further disastrous effects for the country. We haven't learned anything from Cuza's Agrarian Reform of 1863, from the Agrarian Reform of 1918–1921, or from the "Conversion Law" between the two wars or the Communists' "Agrarian Reform" of 1946. We haven't learned anything from the Soviet-Communist "collectivization" drama, carried out with the bat, etc. (Popescu 2002b). Anyway, let us hope.

Those politicians who have promoted not the best interests of the country and of Europe, but their own self-interest, turning out to be fools, liars, and crooks to an equal extent – something between the "hardworking fool" and the "smart villain" – are further plunging the Romanian economy and even society into depression. The press, of one type or another, is proving this. It has been published: everyday (October 2016) about 300 small- and medium-sized enterprises are closing down, most of them forced into bankruptcy. Of course, official figures may be different, but the stark reality is visible in the wallets of citizens of every type, Romania alongside Bulgaria sometimes having the lowest incomes of the countries in the European Union. Unclear situations brought about by poverty and destitution, in addition to this, the effects of German occupation, mostly, but also Turkish and Bulgarian occupation during and immediately after the First World War, when the country went through its hardest times (Cancicov 2016), seem not to have taught us anything. The Second World War and subsequent period, when a handful of leaders offered Romania, with its arms and belongings, to the "great Eastern neighbor," also taught us nothing (Popescu 2002b). And so we continue to pay the price.

As a matter of fact, for the Romanian economy to maintain its substance even in the context of its natural integration and involvement in the EU and the global economy, two aspects are essential: (a) jobs at the necessary level of competitiveness, an essential condition for the existence of an economy, even if this economy is exporting 2–3 million workers by emigration, by "free emigration," and (b) the incomes of those in work have to repay their labor but also attract future workers. In our country, these incomes are often about ten times lower than those in developed European countries with whose economies we want to and not only that we want to but we actually have to compete. And we do compete. Tough competition. And both within and outside the European Union, no gifts are made.

What have we learned from the depression of 1929–1933 when the United States came out of the crisis through Roosevelt's New Deal and by increasing salaries? Nothing (Popescu 1999, 2010). Education through teachers; health through doctors; culture through its people, museographers, experts, writers, and artists; and then research through researchers are at the forefront of this unfortunate situation. In technological competition, we are completely outpaced, mainly for lack of resources. How are we stimulating the business environment, which is the main employer in an economy? We are not stimulating it properly. We are talking, of course, about a real business environment and not about those conmen who, for example, without having any property before 1944, have bought in recent years the "litigious rights" of the rightful owners – the latter's claims being indeterminately postponed – and were then "compensated" with huge amounts of public money, much more than the real price of that property. These too, as well as others, are the beneficiaries of a corrupt, venal system. A system that is more speculative than productive, hardly productive at all. A system in which fortunes have been and are still made, some say most of the times, not through production and competition, but through speculation in land and houses, through the corrupt benefits of corrupt politicians (Popescu 2016). Its successful subjects have perfectly "learned" – even without reading him as most of them are ignorant or uneducated – the great French playwright Marcel Pagnol, whose "hero" Topaze from the play with the same name says: "If you want to have money, you have to get it from where it is." And where is the money in a little productive economy? Mostly in the public area, as much as there is (taxes are high and many as compared to what we get in return from a social point of view).

Not all politicians are the same, of course. There are people of good faith in Romania's service, too, who give the country more than they take from it. Some of them "voice" their reactions to such bad, fateful situations, but it is not enough. We thus risk, but risk is not the right word as the process is already underway, experiencing a demographic and economic hemorrhage that will empty the country of its people, especially young, intelligent, educated, hardworking people who lack the necessary "connections" and often have their way blocked not only toward the management of a shrinking economy but also toward politics, so much more in a country where – as it has very often been stated at all levels – corruption has become endemic, plunders succeed each other, and the often theatrical attitudes of politicians have little effect. "Theatrical" because there is no thorough analysis of the current situation, of jobs and incomes, of the present and future demographic situation. And of the fact that a large part of the population cannot even make a living from the wages they are paid. "Vocalization" cannot replace either reality or social aspects.

It seems that in our country the political position is much more profitable – practice has proven this and continues to do so – than almost any honest management position in the economy. And much easier. One says words and has money, influence, power, and nominal prestige, although not real. And then how could corrupt politicians step aside, when they do not do anything and are socially useless – people who have stood out very little or not at all in their previous jobs? They do not step aside; they cling to their positions (Popescu 2016). As a matter of fact, their evaluation system is unconvincing: so many times have they given their address in Parliament or anywhere else but have done nothing concrete for the recovery of the country; they have pointed fingers at culprits but have not proceeded to their punishment. But how could they have done so when they themselves are guilty, too? Let the worthy ones wait. At the same time, I do not understand why our present-day politicians at the highest levels, ministers, secretaries of state, senators, deputies, etc. have voted increased salaries and benefits for themselves, close to those in the West. Not to mention the increase in their own pensions. One more reason why many of these politicians should not occupy the positions they are occupying. But who can change this situation? With whom to replace them? And we keep hoping that things are going to look up. But they aren't.

28.9 Conclusions

It turns out again that we have learned nothing from history. What is coming next? Difficult to say, in a country where pseudo-politics has largely replaced politics, and the same all over the world. Of course, beyond the underground, fundamental, serious, efficient maneuvers of the very important figures who are setting the main trends to their own advantage. A world in which, unfortunately, we occupy peripheral positions. A world of huge social discrepancies. If the spread between the average income per capita in the poorest and richest countries was 1 to 6 in the nineteenth century, today it is 1 to 50 – significant and serious. There are countries where national economies are stalling. Even more serious is that in these circumstances, a large, maybe the largest, part of the world's population is living at or below the poverty line – a line calculated at the lowest level (Popescu 2014; Gendarme 1963; Landes 1998). Poverty and destitution do not help the progress and strengthening of nations, neither of communities nor of the global world.

And how many lives, disasters, and genocides have the two world wars cost the world, which started from and in the context of similar circumstances, as well as other wars and conflicts? It is true we have highlighted only some aspects. There are, obviously, good things, too, and not few. But the negative ones are enough to allow us to give a clear warning signal for many of the present developments which can lead to nothing good.

Let us almost end with a famous parable from the late eighteenth century, from Claude Henri de Rouvroy, comte de Saint-Simon, and his book "L'Organisateur." The parable showed, as far as I remember, that if France would lose the king, the king's brother, all the members of the royal family, its court members, its ministers with or without their ministries, the politicians and high officials, the ministry clerks, etc. and, in addition to this, the ten thousand owners, the wealthiest ones, and the aristocrats, the French people will experience a feeling of pity, as they are a compassionate people – it will be a sentimental loss, but the country, the economy will go on. But if France were to lose its first 50 physicists, first 50 chemists, first 50 philosophers, first 50 bankers, first 200 merchants, first 600 farmers, first 50 blacksmiths, and other industrial professions, if it were to lose the most productive Frenchmen, the nation would become a soulless body, would immediately fall into a state of inferiority toward other nations with which it is competing today, and would continue to remain in a position of inferiority until it recovered this loss. In fact, France will be destroyed.

Let us remember from these words, which also apply to Romania. Do we have any reason not to believe Saint-Simon? I believe not. Let us also refer to "Les trentes glorieuses," Europe's and the world's "30 glorious years," years of real, actual economic growth (1946–1975), brilliantly discussed by the French sociologist Jean Fourastié (Fourastié 1979), followed by over "30 sad years" (about 40 years), broadly examined by myself among others. Let us ask ourselves: What is next for Romania and the world – more years of growth or more disastrous years? The answer is closely linked to the lessons we have learned and are learning from history.

References

Attali, J.: Evreii, lumea şi banii (Istoria economică a poporului evreu). Univers, Bucureşti (2011)
Bainville, J.: Les dictateurs. Denoële et Steele, Paris (1935)
Cancicov, V.: Jurnalul din vremea ocupaţiei. Impresiuni şi păreri personale din timpul războiului României. Jurnal zilnic, august 1916-decembrie 1918, vol. I – II. Humanitas, Bucureşti (2016)
Colson, C.: Organisme économique et désordre social. Flammarion, Paris (1918)
Fourastié, J.: Les trentes glorieuses. Fayard, Paris (1979)
Gendarme, R.: La pauvreté des nations. Cujas (1963)
Landes, D.S.: The Wealth and Poverty of Nations. W.W.Norton and Company, New York/London (1998)
Lăcusteanu, G.: Amintirile colonelului Lăcusteanu. Polirom (2015)
Pomeranz, K.: La mondialisation du XIX siècle. Naissance du monde. L'Histoire. 425–426 (2016)
Popescu, D.: Civilizaţie şi industrie. Albatros, Bucureşti (1981)
Popescu, D.: Cornul abundenţei, un miracol? Albatros, Bucureşti (1984)
Popescu, D.: Universul în alb-negru. Albatros, Bucureşti (1987)
Popescu, D.: Domnul Interes şi Doamna Iniţiativă. In: Liberalul, vol. 1. Bucureşti (1990)

Popescu, D.: Istoria gândirii economice de la începuturi până la sfârşitul secolului XX. Continent, Sibiu-Bucureşti (1999)
Popescu, D.: De la protection du developpement national à la protection de l'interet du capitalism international? Étude de cas: l'économie roumaine. In: Popescu, D. (ed.) Les pays de l'Europe Centrale et de l'Europe de l'Est: allez, retour, allez vers l'économie de marché, pp. 1850–2000 (2002a)
Popescu, D.: Istorie economică–Istoria economiei naţionale. Continent, Sibiu-Bucureşti (2002b)
Popescu, D.: Jurnal economic. Continent, Sibiu-Bucureşti (2007)
Popescu, D.: Cataclismele economice care zguduie lumea. Continent, Sibiu-Bucureşti (2010)
Popescu, D.: Amurgul lumilor paralele. Continent, Sibiu-Bucureşti (2011)
Popescu, D.: Criza indecentă. Continent, Sibiu-Bucureşti (2012)
Popescu, D.: Ameninţări pentru secolul XXI. Continent, Sibiu-Bucureşti (2014)
Popescu, D.: Alungarea hughenoţilor... Toleranţă şi intoleranţă. In: Vacarel, I. (ed.) Studii de istorie economică şi istoria gândirii economice, vol. 17. Editura Academiei, Bucuresti (2015a)
Popescu, D.: Confruntările muncitorilor cu patronatul. Succintă privire în timp şi spaţiu. Transilvania(8), 76–82 (2015b)
Popescu, D.: Amplificarea emigrării şi imigrării generată de integrare şi globalizare. Capacitatea reală de ocupare a economiei. In: Penser l'Europe. Editura Academiei, Bucuresti (2016)
Portocală, R.: Autopsia unei lovituri de stat. În ţara în care a triumfat minciuna. Continent, Agora Timişoreană (1991)
Toynbee, A.J.: Studiu asupra istoriei. Humanitas, Bucureşti (1998)
Veverca, I.: Naţionalismul Economic. Analele economice şi statistice, Bucureşti (1941)

Chapter 29
Sales Management Mechanism and Methodologies for Solving the Problems of Special-Purpose Product Management and Sales

Elvira A. Pyanikova, Anna E. Kovaleva, and Mariya A. Zaikina

Abstract This article discusses the mechanisms of sales management and offers some methodologies that allow us to solve the problems of special-purpose product management and marketing. Our study considers special-purpose products as functional nutrition products with a balanced composition that are enriched in specific components, the main role of which is body process regulation to maintain its effective life. The article has undertaken the analysis of existing techniques for managing the production process, output, and delivery of goods and managing sales directly in trade. There have been singled out positive and negative aspects of these techniques and on the basis of that we have proposed some methodologies that help to identify potential customers for a specific product with the use of integrated events to promote products. Methodologies allow us to evaluate the efficiency of special-purpose product production, through the example of bread products, depending on demand for them, taking into account a combination of integrated events to promote this category of goods. This technique makes it possible to obtain the ratio of anticipated sales with due account for growth output indices and to determine the necessary quantity of shipped product from manufacturers to trade outlets. Methodologies include targeting mathematical methods of processing statistical data obtained in real-life conditions. Practical approval of mathematical apparatus was carried out on the example of citizens living in Kursk.

Keywords Management • Methodologies • Efficiency

E.A. Pyanikova (✉) • A.E. Kovaleva • M.A. Zaikina
Southwest State University, Kursk, Russia
e-mail: pyanikovaelvira@yandex.ru

S.C. Mărginean et al. (eds.), *Emerging Issues in the Global Economy*, Springer Proceedings in Business and Economics,
https://doi.org/10.1007/978-3-319-71876-7_29

29.1 Introduction

"Sales management" is a multidimensional concept for which there is no unambiguous definition. While considering the notion of "sales management," one relies upon the fact that it includes both people management and process management in the field of sales. From our point of view, sales management is a field of practice emerging at the intersection of management, marketing, and sales art itself (Pikalova 2013).

Manufacturing, output, and supply of products are inextricably connected with planning and sales management. In this regard, there is such a component as "production" in the concept of "sales management." The existing modern mathematical models and methods for planning production process management, the constituent elements of which are raw materials, material and technical resources, labor forces, finished products, and waste product, have wide possibilities of adaptation to different types of businesses (Lutsiak 2015).

While optimizing the structure of product portfolio, companies must consider their own capabilities during the period of production planning. They must also consider markets, where their products will be sold, and the possibility of large capital investments in the case of production expansion (Shirokov and Rassadina 2013).

A large number of questions concerning relationships between commodity producers and retail chains on the regional food market remain open. Understanding their depth, complexity, and ambiguity must contribute to more successful solution of existing accumulated problems in the management of the regional food market as well as in the activities of business entities (Neganov and Neganov 2012).

29.2 Data and Methodology

There are two methods to identify factors influencing the level of sales. The first method is the collection and processing of expert estimates and is based on interpreting the opinions of various experts. The second method is econometric modeling that serves as an alternative to the first one (Kuznetsova 2012). According to the latter one, information from the accumulated data systems are used as factors of evidence about the sales process. All obtained results are analyzed to determine whether the verification of all factors is possible in a practical way.

In the given paper, we propose to use the methodologies of modeling and solving of special-purpose product range optimization in the form of a dynamic problem of optimal management being adapted to the market conditions. The developed methodologies provide an opportunity to assess the likelihood of purchases made by a certain group of population and to obtain a numerical value for the potential buyer for a specific product and to calculate the required amount of release of special-purpose goods according to a particular list.

As a certain group of population, we mean a target audience being interested in purchasing a particular product (Armando et al. 2014). In this regard, we can use a new tool of targeting.

Targeting (from the English word "target") is an advertising mechanism that makes it possible to select from all available audience only that part that meets the criteria (target audience) and to present advertising to it (Vijay et al. 2015).

One of the most consumed food products by the population is bakery products. Priority direction of the modern society development is a healthy lifestyle and eating healthy (special-purpose) food products.

The analysis of bakery product range by branch enterprises shows that each of them produces special-purpose products being consumed for preventive causes.

Currently, the market of bakery products for preventive and therapeutic nutrition is various. Prophylactic and therapeutic properties of breads are reached with the help of extra ingredients, rich in nutrients (amino acids, vitamins, micro- and macronutrients), as well as changes in the technology of product preparation (Beznosov 2012).

Bakery products are one of the main foodstuffs for people, through which we receive the necessary body nutrients: proteins, carbohydrates, minerals, vitamins, and dietary fibers (Pyanikova 2014a).

Baked goods from grain are the main supplier of major energy food components – carbohydrates. After the consumption of 500 g of wheat bread made from white flour, the human body gets 21–64% of the 24-h requirements in essential amino acids (except lysine that is contained in bread in small quantities) (Zhuravleva and Moiseenkov 2015).

An important index of our country's well-being is, first of all, providing the population with products from grain crops (wheat, rye) and a stable level of prices for them. However, the factors influencing the growth and development of bakery businesses do not always depend on them. There are also external factors. Companies must find their consumers and markets for their products to remain competitive and not lose their position. In this situation, the marketing approach to the problems of management and sales is of great importance.

Sales of products for enterprises is the final stage of all production and business activities (Umut et al. 2014).The question of improving the mechanism of products sale is of particular significance in bakery industry. A large part of grain products (bakery and confectionery products) has a short shelf life. In this regard, even with large production capacity, bakery companies are trying to produce products in such volume that could be sold afterward. Due to the fact that now a lot of enterprises, joint stock companies, as well as private ones are engaged in the production of bakery products, their sales services departments need to convince a potential buyer that their products are tastier, healthier, etc. through the development of effective marketing mechanisms.

The probability of increasing the volume of bakery product market is low. Most likely, there will be a change in its structure by broadening the range of bakery products, appearing and growing the popularity of different bread and flour products having a functional orientation.

29.3 Models and Results

The proposed methodologies include a range of activities, for example, sales promotion and presentation of products to the final consumer (Jens et al. 2014). The principal purpose of these events is to appeal to the target audience through some local view representations (Theodore et al. 2014).

A special program was developed to obtain the appropriate value of potential buyer ratio, including oral presentation, store demonstration, sampling, and interviewing.

The information on four types of bread for oral presentation was used.

To calculate potential buyer ratio, all the proposed promotional activities were used.

Together with the manufacturers of the selected samples of bread, the days of the week and time of carrying out a group of activities were set. Thursday, Friday, and Saturday were chosen as optimal days of store demonstration. The period of time from 16 h 30 min to 19 h 30 min hours on weekdays and from 11 h up to 14 h on Saturday.

During the store demonstration, a questionnaire survey based on a specially made questionnaire was conducted.

During the store demonstration, an anonymous survey of buyers of five shops located in the city of Kursk was conducted. In all trade outlets, about 700 respondents were chosen. The selection of respondents was carried out using a quota sample, and quota settings were gender and age (Ivanova 2005).

In most respondents' view (94%), the best means of advertising bakery products is store demonstration as it allows a person to evaluate the product by directly tasting it. Six percent of respondents said that the best advertisement is a gift for purchase (Pyanikova 2014b).

The simplest method of determining the economic efficiency of integrated activities to promote sales is to compare the supply of products before and after the event. According to this method, the economic efficiency of a promotional event is determined either by matching the supply of products for a certain period of time when goods were exposed to advertising with data for the same period of time when the goods were not advertised or by matching shipments from an enterprise for days before and after the promotional event.

The first way requires information about the volume of sales from each trade outlet for each item of advertised bread when we analyze data obtained at different periods of time. When we use the second way, we usually focus on data for the period of a promotional event taking into account the shipments of the product (in kg, it is also possible to calculate in pieces). That is why it is possible to directly compare the figures in the period before advertising and after-advertising period. The analysis of the obtained results makes it possible to predict the required output of products to provide consumers with the necessary amount of special-purpose bakery products.

The economic efficiency of an integrated promotional event can be judged by comparing changes in the volume of output in the period before the advertisement and after it.

While analyzing the economic efficiency of promotional events to stimulate sales of bakery products, statistics on shipments from an enterprise serve as essential information. On the basis of these events, it is possible to study not only the economic efficiency of one or several events but also the entire performance of a company.

The economic effect from the stimulating events can be seen immediately after them, but soon afterward, this effect may decline. If one aims at obtaining more accurate results from promotional activities, they should not be carried out together with other similar activities in a given period of time, when the influence of other (unrelated to the promotional events being conducted) factors affecting the level of shipments is weak or predictable enough to be taken into account in the following calculations.

After conducting the survey procedure, there were modeled methodologies to identify a potential buyer for special-purpose products. We have obtained the following formula:

$$K_{\text{пп}} = \frac{(m \cdot n - S)}{0{,}5 \cdot m \cdot n \cdot (m-1)} \tag{29.1}$$

where m is the number of potential respondents, n is the number of indicators (in this case n = 3), and

$$S = \Sigma x_{1j} + \Sigma x_{2j} + \Sigma x_{3j} \tag{29.2}$$

Given the obtained data, Formula (29.1) changes:

$$K_{\text{пп}} = \frac{(3m - S)}{1{,}5 \cdot m \cdot (m-1)} \tag{29.3}$$

Using this formula, we calculated the ratios of potential buyer for the products under study. The ratio of potential buyer who purchased products before the promotional event amounted to 0.268; the ratio of potential buyer who purchased products during the event is 0.553, and the ratio of occasional potential buyer is equal to 0.179.

The total value of potential buyer ratios for all the indicators should not exceed 1. The value of potential buyer ratio during the promotional event tends to increase. What is clearly confirmed by our study results: the value of potential buyer ratio during the promotional event as compared to the period prior to the event increases 2,06 times.

The proposed methodologies allow us to evaluate the effectiveness of growth index (I) of bread production depending on demand. We take into account here such factors as the supply of bread to the studied outlets and demand for it.

The index of output growth depending on the supply of bakery products is calculated according to formula

$$I_1 = \frac{V_{prior\ to\ the\ event}}{V_{during\ the\ event}} \tag{29.4}$$

where $V_{prior\ to\ the\ event}$ is the volume of bread production before the promotional event and $V_{during\ the\ event}$ is the volume of bread production during the event.

The index of output growth depending on the demand of customers is calculated according to formula

$$I_2 = \frac{S_{prior\ to\ the\ event}}{S_{during\ the\ event}} \tag{29.5}$$

where $S_{prior\ to\ the\ event}$ is demand for bread before the promotional event and $S_{during\ the\ event}$ is demand for bread during the promotional event.

The studies were conducted in five stages the data for which were obtained from enterprises. The first stage (I) is the relation of the first period of holding a promotional event to the advertising period. The index of output growth for trade outlet No. 1 was equal to 7,38; for trade outlet No. 2, 3,86; for trade outlet No. 3, 8,75; for trade outlet No. 4, 2,62; and for trade outlet No. 5, 3,3.

The second stage (II) is the relation of the first advertising period to the following after-advertising period. The index of output growth for trade outlet No. 1 for 3 days amounted to 0,51; for trade outlet No. 2, 1,05; for trade outlet No. 3, 0,83; for trade outlet No. 4, 1,02; and for trade outlet No. 5, 1,15.

The third stage (III) is the relation of the second advertising period to the first after-advertising period. The index of output growth for trade outlet No. 1 for 3 days was equal to 2,55; for trade outlet No. 2, 1.39; for trade outlet No. 3, 1,79; for trade outlet No. 4, 2,51; and for trade outlet No. 5, 2,51.

The fourth stage (IV) is the relation of the second advertising period to the following after-advertising promotional period. The index of output growth for trade outlet No. 1 for 3 days was equal to 2,8; for trade outlet No. 2, 1,8; for trade outlet No. 3, 2,59; for trade outlet No. 4, 2,51; and for trade outlet No. 5, 2,51.

The fifth stage (V) is the relation of the period after holding two advertising promotional events to the period prior to advertising that would show the effectiveness of the events and will give an idea whether there was increase in demand for these products. The index of output growth for trade outlet No. 1 for 3 days amounted to 3,28; for trade outlet No. 2, 3,07; for trade outlet No. 3, 4,25; for trade outlet No. 4, 2,69; and for trade outlet No. 5, 2,8.

The ratio of anticipated sales is calculated by the formula

$$\text{КР}_{\text{ПР}} = \text{К}_{\text{ПП1}} \cdot I_I + \text{К}_{\text{ПП2}} \cdot (I_{II} + I_{IV}) + \text{К}_{\text{ПП3}} \cdot ((I_V - I_I) + I_V) \quad (29.6)$$

Taking into account all the studied periods, the ratio of anticipated sales was equal to 4,43. Thus, in order to calculate the quantity of shipped bread in five trade outlets, the formula was developed:

$$\text{ПР}_{\text{В}} = \frac{\text{КР}_{\text{ПР}} \cdot B_V}{\sum I_{Vj}} \quad (29.7)$$

where B_V is the volume of shipped bread in the fifth period for five trade outlets, kg. $\text{ПР}_{\text{В}} = 179,33\ kg$.

29.4 Conclusion

As a result of implementing the developed program of promotional events, a formula for calculating the ratio of potential buyer of special-purpose products on the example of bread with additives was deduced. Taking into account the factor of potential buyer ratio of sold products, we have also developed the formula for determining the prediction number of shipped bread. The information for the created methodology and its testing was obtained on the basis of experimental studies conducted in real-life conditions that include an oral presentation of products, store demonstration, sampling, and interviewing.

The proposed methodologies will allow both manufacturers and trading companies to organize their commercial activities in such a way that manufacturers will produce as much product as trading outlets will subsequently be able to sell. Hence, risks will decrease for both businesses.

References

Armando, L.V., Heidi, W., Christine, E.: The effects of relationship marketing on share of business: a synthesis and comparison of models. J. Business-to-Business Market. **21**(2), 85–110 (2014)

Beznosov, Y. V.: Development of innovative technologies in modern trade – key to achievement of high competitiveness. Modern trade: theory, practice, development prospects. Y.V. Beznosov, E. O. Ermolaeva. Materials of the First International Innovation Scientific-Practical Conference. Moscow. pp. 1422–1425 (2012)

Ivanova, T. N.: The analysis of consumer preferences on the food market of the Orel region. Marketing in Russia and abroad. №2 (2005)

Jens, L.-H., Frida, L., Andrea, P.: Customer involvement in product development. An industrial network perspective. J. Business-to-Business Market. **21**(4), 257–276 (2014)

Kuznetsova, O.A.: Econometric modeling: Tutorial. O.A. Kuznetsova, M. S. Tatarnikova. Samara: Samara Aerospace State University Press, pp.44 (2012)

Lutsiak, V.: Methodology of small production enterprises' marketing on the example of the food industry enterprise: product quality aspect. Економічний часопис-XXI, №7–8 (2) pp. 27–31 (2015)

Neganov, S.A., Neganov, I. S.: Relationship of producers and retailers at the regional food market. Economy of regions, №4. pp. 100–108 (2012)

Pikalova, M. B.: Technology management of assortment using product categories. News of Southwest State University. № 2 (47). pp. 37–41 (2013)

Pyanikova, E. A.: Functional bakery products JSC Kurskkhleb. E.A. Pyanikova, A. E. Kovaleva, M. S. Larionova. Commodity of food products. №3. pp. 27–32 (2014a)

Pyanikova, E.A.: Marketing research of consumer preferences of the city Kursk inhabitants in the bakery products segment with a special purpose, manufactured by JSC Kurskkhleb. Pyanikova E.A., Kovaleva A.E. Commodity of food products. №5. pp. 15–22 (2014b)

Shirokov, A.F., Rassadina, E.S.: Dynamic optimization of complex adaptive control structure of the company product range. Economy of regions, №2. pp. 176–184 (2013)

Theodore, J.-N., Fabrizio Di, M., Kyle, B.-M.: The role of arousal in congruity-based product evaluation. J. Consum. Res. **41**(4), 1108–1126 (2014)

Umut, K., Scott, A.N., Petr, C.V.: The effect of search channel elimination on purchase incidence, order size and channel choice. Int. J. Res. Mark. **31**(1), 49–64 (2014)

Vijay, G.H., Debabrata, T., Changhvun, K.: Optimal targeting of advertisement for new products with multiple consumer segments. Int. J. Res. Market. Market. Innov. **32**(3), 263–271 (2015)

Zhuravleva, Ya. Yu, Moiseenkov, E.G.: Improvement of assortment and nutritional increasing value of bread and bakery products. XXXIV International Student Scientific-Practical Conference «Scientific community of students XXI century». [Electronic resource]. sibac.info/14258 (2015)

Chapter 30
Short-Termism: A Step Forward Toward Long-Term Performance or a Dead End

Radu-Alexandru Şerban

Abstract The debate around short-termism and its effects on the economic life, rather negative than positive, is far from ending, having academics, practitioners, and pundits arguing on this topic. The purpose of this paper is to determine if short-termism is part of the process of creating long-term performance (value) in an organization or it is harmful for harnessing performance, by presenting the definitions of the concept, who are the main promoters of short-termism, opinions of both academics and practitioners, and studies and examples that sustain on the one side the fact that short-termism encourages the manipulation of numbers in order to meet quarterly earnings, by cutting investments from R&D and innovations, and on the other side the fact that short-term approach is the cornerstone of the future and, without short-term performance, there is no long-term future for an organization.

Keywords Short-termism • Value • Long-term performance • Investors • Strategy

30.1 Introduction

If we look at the main difference between East and West, the thing that strikes is how they make important decisions, related to the time frame, long-term vs short-term. Comparing the USA and Europe with Asia, we can see that short-term became the norm in the first two; meanwhile, Asians think on long-term, typically 10–15 years (Barton 2011).

The debate on how huge is the impact of short-termism on value (destruction) continues among analysts, economists, and executives due to the fact that the business environment became highly complex and is not a matter of one measure that indicates the result. Academic research tried to explain the influence of short-termism by linking the impact of "short-termism to lower investment rates for

R.-A. Şerban (✉)
Lucian Blaga University of Sibiu, Sibiu, Romania
e-mail: radu.serban@ulbsibiu.ro

S.C. Mărginean et al. (eds.), *Emerging Issues in the Global Economy*, Springer Proceedings in Business and Economics,
https://doi.org/10.1007/978-3-319-71876-7_30

publicly traded companies" and the "decline of returns over a multi-year time frame" (Barton et al. 2017), and others tried to quantify economic growth as a result of cuts in research and development driven by short-termism.

A recent survey of executives and board members concluded that short-termism approach is still predominant in the business environment due to fact that publicly traded companies are pressured by the financial markets, from where the large investors came – "pension funds, mutual funds, insurance firms and sovereign wealth funds" – and they put pressure for short-term results (Barton and Wiseman 2013).

The paper is organized as follows. In the next part, I will review the literature in order to identify the relevant definitions and factors that will show different approaches to the impact/influence of short-termism on long-term performance.

Other distinct parts of the paper are focused on presenting a model that proves the fact that adopting a long-term approach will benefit the organization, improving performance. The different opinions on this topic, the limitations of the study, and its conclusions are presented in the last part of the paper.

30.2 Literature Review

The Financial Times Lexicon claims that short-termism "refers to an excessive focus on short-term results at the expense of long-term interests."

Haldane and Davies (2011) on the other hand claims that short-termism refers "to the tendency of agents in the financial intermediation chain to weight too heavily near-term outcomes at the expense of longer-term opportunities. This has opportunity costs, for example in forgone investment projects and hence future output."

Based on broad definitions of Marginson and McAulay (2008), Aspara et al. (2014) define corporate short-termism as the "inclination of corporate management to orient corporate strategies towards maximization of STEs at the cost of long-term objective." Same authors suggest that corporate short-termism can be replaced by "managerial myopia," a similar term defined by Samuel (2000) as "managerial behavior focused on improving earnings in the short-term at the expense of long-term growth." STEs "represent the company's realized accounting earnings during the current year and forecast earnings for the following two years" (Tonello 2006; Jackson and Petraki 2011). Literature that approaches short-termism suggests several determinants of this phenomenon:

- "The increased number of short-term trades by stock market investors" (Johnson and Kaplan 1987; Jacobs 1991; Porter 1992; Bushee 2004).
- Others see that "investors have the tendency to pursue short-term gains" (Jensen 1986; Hansen and Hill 1991; Laverty 1996; Marginson and McAulay 2008).
- Some authors emphasize the fact that "short-termism is when companies focus on maximizing the value for shareholders, and long-term approach means

maximizing value for both shareholders and stakeholders without making any trade-offs" (Stout 2012; Freeman et al. 2007; Mackey and Sisodia 2014).

- On the one hand, there are empirical studies that suggest "a negative association between short-term investors and their long-term investments in R&D" (Graves 1988; Samuel 2000; Cohen et al. 2013; Ferreira et al. 2012) and on the other hand studies that "report a positive association between them" (Baysinger et al. 1991; Hansen and Hill 1991; David et al. 2001; Aghion et al. 2013).

The research in strategy underlines the idea that in order to achieve competitive advantage, unique resources, and distinctive organizational competencies, sustained investments over long periods of time are the essential element (Dierickx and Cool 1989).

One of the reasons why companies face problems when it comes to discontinuous technological changes, based on the work in the innovation tradition, suggests that companies invest in the status quo rather than in "next-generation" technologies (Christensen 2013). Likewise, short-term measurable performance can determine managers to pass by those tasks for which clear performance indicators are not available (Holmstrom and Milgrom 1991).

Opposite, the studies and literature in accounting indicate that "managing earnings" and "meeting analysts' expectations" are linked with high performance (Rahmandad et al. 2015). Bhojraj et al. (2009) claims that companies who manage to exceed earnings forecast by manipulation will improve their stock price in short-term and will lower ROA in long-term. Likewise, "companies that meet or exceed analysts expectations frequently report superior operating profits" Bartov et al. (2002) claim, while Gunny (2010) finds that "real" actions such as "reducing investments in R&D" and reducing SG&A to increase income have a positive impact on future ROA.

The results above suggest according to some agency theories and information problems. Bowen et al. (1995) and Burgstahler and Dichev (1997) claim that managers who "manage numbers" increase their "reputation" with top management and as a result, they obtain better trade terms. On the other hand, Farrell and Whidbee (2003) claim that "making the numbers" is a career preoccupation of those senior managers who otherwise will lose their jobs.

30.2.1 What Drives Short-Termism?

A report from the "Business Roundtable Institute for Corporate Ethics" and the "CFA Institute: Breaking the Short-term Cycle" (2006) says that "an excessive short-term focus by some corporate leaders, investors, and analysts combined with insufficient regard for long-term strategy can tip the balance in value-destructive ways for market participants, undermine the market's credibility, and discourage long-term value creation and investment." Certain research of the global economic downturn found that financial institutions and lenders are the root cause of short-termism. As we will point out in the following part, several reasons are considered to be the causes of short-termism. As the report above suggests, the investors and the pressure of financial markets are considered the causes by most of the researchers.

Short-term strategies fail to consider the future opportunities, are associated with high risk, are based on accounting metrics and profit maximization, and do not reflect the complexities and importance of corporate management and investment. The most common metric used is EPS (earnings per share). Also, researchers claim that managers take major decisions to hit their quarterly targets, for example, cutting resources from R&D, hiring, or maintaining important employees (Graham et al. 2005).

Corporate governance is a concept that has its roots in the 1930s, at the seminal work of Adolf and Means (1932), but as a field emerged only in the 1970s and today is an important topic (Subramanian 2015), considered to be a decisive factor in the performance of a company, especially after the financial crisis in 2007, which revealed the importance of corporate governance in the pay-for-performance scheme, incentives, and compensations for executives particularly in the financial and banking industry. The fact that companies pay particular attention to short-term performance and managers spend both time and money in order to achieve quarterly earnings and increase shareholders' return putting in danger the future of the company is considered to be the biggest failure of corporate governance.

Jones and Burchman (2016) claim that another big factor that is not so obvious influenced short-termism and the way incentives are related to performance. They claim that executives adopted short-termism like never before, for two reasons:

1. Earnings are used to buy back share, even when those shares cost more than they even worth.
2. Increased dividends that redirect the resources from long-term investments.

In the study of Graham et al. (2005), in which they interviewed 401 CFOs of large US public companies, the results were that almost 80% admitted that they would sacrifice economic value, so they can meet quarterly earnings targets. In his research, Bill Lazonick (2014) reveals that corporate buybacks are an increasing practice in the USA and companies "are using large amounts of their earnings to repurchase their own stock, rather than investing for the future."

Also, Benner (2007, 2010) suggests that companies who are involved in an important technological transition are dealing in addition to the pressure from analysts, determining them to reduce investments in research and development and investment capital.

According to a Darr and Koller (2017), in the USA, 25% of public companies are owned by short-term investors and 75% by long-term investors. Even though the number of short-term investors is low compared to long-term ones, the most active participants, the volume, and the pace of the daily transactions are dominated by short-term investors. For this reason, Darr and Koller (2017) suggest "they have the power to pressure for short-term performance (quarterly earnings) at the expense of long-term value." In 2015, 471 companies from S&P 500 bought back stock, and

372 increased their dividends, although they had to invest heavily to keep up with global market changes (Darr and Koller 2017).

When researchers, analysts, etc. ask why executives are putting in danger the long-term perspective of their company, would sacrifice sustainable value creation, and focus on methods to improve short-term indicators and why those gains are not invested in the development of the business for the long-term, ironically, one answer comes from the reform that was meant to be for the benefit of long-term investments.

Jones and Burchman (2016) opine that since the Dodd-Frank reform was adopted almost 7 years ago, the corporate governance groups with their policy that requires half of long-term incentives to be performance-based determined the companies' options with multi-years with performance plans. Those performance plans require performance targets. For most of the companies, planning work was in 3-year cycles. Based on that, the "performance period" for long-term incentives is similar to those cycles. Starting then, those 3 years become the standard performance horizon and the norm after which companies invested billions to achieve "long-term" value. The proof that these 3-year windows became a standard to pay for performance widely adopted among analysts, investors, etc. is that four out of five S&P 500 companies use it in their long-term incentives (Jones and Burchman 2016). Not only that, 3 years is now considered long-term view, but when companies link EPS and other financial metrics, to compensate executive performance for long-term, it is not wondering why this approach becomes "shareholder friendly." If the earning targets are hard to achieve, from internal growth, the company uses the money to buy back share in order to achieve 3-year EPS targets (Jones and Burchman 2016).

In order to improve and support the 3-year view, researchers propose that companies should use strategic milestones, considered to be a key element. These strategic milestones must be specific, objective strategic achievements, having zero room for interpretation, and should provide the path to strategic success. Companies could tie the strategic goals with restricted-stock or next-generation options. These actions combined should determine the executives to extend their 3-year view to a 10-year horizon (Jones and Burchman 2016). The financial institutions are pointed out to be those who promoted this type of approach, and it was spread through the whole system. "Pension funds, insurance companies, mutual funds, and sovereign wealth funds hold $65 trillion," Barton (2011) claims. If those who provide the capital promote short-termism, then the whole system will adapt also, in theory. Not all Western companies took the short-term approach; Intel, Apple, Google, Unilever, Coca-Cola, and Ford are examples of companies that are not aligned with the trend (Barton, 2011).

The pressure created by the regulators, increasing the frequency of reporting, was identified by Gigler and Hemmer (2001), who argued that moral hazard problems could arise if reporting frequency is increased. The debate on mandating quarterly financial reporting in Europe, Singapore, and Australia received a lot of critics. Bhojraj and Libby (2005) reported from the excerpts of popular press (Financial Times) that the investor's side claimed that quarterly financial reporting did not prevent corporate scandals in the USA and encourage short-termism. Rahman et al.

(2007) summarized the European debate, on the one side those who were in favor of quarterly financial reporting, arguing that "more frequent reporting of earnings increases analyst following of firms, improves the timeliness of earnings, and improves stock trading." On the other side, those who opposed argued that "it encourages short-termism, which can lead to earnings management and stock price volatility."

30.2.2 The Corporate Horizon Index

A very recent research (2017), made by "McKinsey Global Institute" in cooperation with "FCLT Global" and MGI, shows that organizations with long-term approach deliver superior results despite the pressure that came from analysts and investors to achieve quarterly earnings.

In their research, they prove with data that companies with a long-term view, like Unilever, AT&T, and Amazon, outperformed their peers (period 2001–2014), in relevant and important financial measures such as company revenue, company earnings, economic profit, and market capitalization (Barton et al. 2017). The study reveals that besides the growth and increased revenues for the companies who adopted the long-term view, the returns to society are another important aspect, focusing not only on the shareholders needs but also satisfying the needs of the stakeholder's. The companies with a long-term perspective "added nearly 12,000 jobs" on average than their peers, between 2001 and 2015 (Barton et al. 2017).

In their research, MGI, McKinsey, and FCLT Global "tried to measure short and long-termism at the company level," by developing the "Corporate Horizon Index." The data is from 615 non-finance companies, with reported results between 2001 and 2015, and a market capitalization higher than 5 billion dollars, in at least 1 year. The last condition was so they could focus on large companies where there is the possibility of short-term pressure from stakeholders. The Corporate Horizon Index consists of five financial indicators, each with his hypothesis, to show in which ways companies with short-termism differ from those with long-termism (Barton et al. 2017):

- "Investment – The ratio of CapEx to depreciation. We assume long-term companies will invest more and more consistently than other companies."
- "Earnings quality – Accruals as a share of revenue. Our belief is that the earnings of long-term companies will rely less on accounting decisions and more on underlying cash flow than other companies."
- "Margin growth – Difference between earnings growth and revenue growth. We assume that long-term companies are less likely to grow their margins unsustainably in order to hit near-term targets."
- "Earnings growth – Difference between earnings-per-share (EPS) growth and true earnings growth. We hypothesize that long-term companies will focus less on things like Wall Street's obsession with earnings per share, which can be

influenced by actions such as share repurchases, and more on the absolute rise or fall of reported earnings."

- "Quarterly targeting – Incidence of beating or missing EPS targets by less than two cents. We assume long-term companies are more likely to miss earnings targets by small amounts (when they easily could have taken action to hit them) and less likely to hit earnings targets by small amounts (where doing so would divert resources from other business needs)."

30.2.3 Managerial Relevance: Who Is Right?

According to Goedhart et al. (2015), "the guiding principle of business value creation is that companies that grow and earn a return on capital that exceeds their cost of capital create value." They suggest that creating value for shareholders is different from maximizing short-term profits. And focusing on building value for shareholders from business is not the problem, but short-termism is.

A long-term approach is considered to be a better alternative for short-termism, because long-term promotes value creation, takes into consideration the stakeholders not only shareholders, and is not paying leaders for short-term earnings and in this situation, shareholders will act like owners and will be more involved in their business. But according to researchers, this debate on short-termism is not settled yet. Both academics and pundits are blaming short-termism and the "tyranny of quarterly earnings" for the decline of western economies, as the main factor (Laverty 1996; The Aspen Institute 2009; Haldane and Davies 2011; Dallas 2011).

A former head of the SEC said when he was asked to comment about the meltdown of the US financial system: "The excessive focus by too many corporations on achieving short-term results...certainly is one of the root causes for some of the problems we face today (Rummel 2008)."

Larry Summers (2015), on the other hand, economist and hedge fund adviser cautions about the possible side effect of reforming "quarterly earnings," claiming that this will lead to "Japan's keiretsu system, which insulated corporate management from share price pressure by tying large companies together."

Ken Favaro considers that companies cannot sacrifice short-term and expect to build something in the future. He claims that managers don't see the link between short-term results and investing for the future and in their attempt to find the balance they will neglect one in favor of the other (Favaro 2014).

Peter Drucker (1986) said that there is no excuse for the management team to not manage both short- and long-term no matter if there are stakeholders with different needs and time frames. He also said that all companies are facing the situation where they have to invest for the future in order to have one, but they also need to produce earnings in present to pay the investment for the future.

30.3 Conclusion

In the study, I have approached short-termism, what drives it, the consequences, and points of view of academics and practitioners and presented a model that supports the idea of long-term as beneficial for performance. The findings support both the idea of short-termism as beneficial for long-term performance and the idea that short-termism is damaging long-term performance, but even if it is not settled, the majority are blaming short-termism pointing out investors, the financial markets, and managers as main causes of promoting this type of behavior.

Based on the results provided by the Corporate Horizon Index, the fact that investors and large asset holders are starting to look after companies with the long-term view should question more seriously the role of short-term approach in building a sustainable future. Therefore, it is very important that things are changing and investors and financial markets and big companies are realizing the consequences of the short-term approach.

References

Adolf, B., Means, G.: The Modern Corporation and Private Property. Commerce Clearing House, New York (1932)

Aghion, P., Van Reenen, J., Zingales, L.: Innovation and institutional ownership. Am. Econ. Rev. **103**, 277–304 (2013)

Aspara, J., Pajunen, K., Tikkanen, H., Tainio, R.: Explaining corporate short-termism: self-reinforcing processes and biases among investors, the media and corporate managers. Soc. Econ. Rev. **12**, 667–693 (2014)

Barton, D.: Capitalism for the long term. Harv. Bus. Rev. https://hbr.org/2011/03/capitalism-for-the-long-term (2011). Accessed 15 Mar 2017

Barton, D., Wiseman, M.: Focusing capital on the long term. McKinsey&Company. http://www.mckinsey.com/global-themes/leadership/focusing-capital-on-the-long-term (2013). Accessed 13 Mar 2017

Barton, D., Manyika, J., Williamson, S.K.: Finally, evidence that managing for the long term pays off. Harv. Bus. Rev. https://hbr.org/2017/02/finally-proof-that-managing-for-the-long-term-pays-off (2017). Accessed 15 March 2017

Bartov, E., Givoly, D., Hayn, C.: The rewards to meeting or beating earnings expectations. J. Account. Econ. **33**, 173–204 (2002)

Baysinger, B., Kosnik, R., Turk, T.: Effects of board and ownership structure on corporate R&D strategy. Acad. Manag. J. **34**, 205–214 (1991)

Benner, M.: The incumbent discount: stock market categories and response to radical technological change. Acad. Manag. Rev. **32**, 703–720 (2007)

Benner, M.: Securities analysts and incumbent response to radical technological change: evidence from digital photography and internet telephony. Organ. Sci. **21**, 42–62 (2010)

Bhojraj, S., Libby, R.: Capital market pressure, disclosure frequency-induced earnings/cash flow conflict, and managerial myopia (retracted). Account. Rev. **80**, 1–20 (2005)

Bhojraj, S., Hribar, P., Picconi, M., McInnis, J.: Making sense of cents: an examination of firms that marginally miss or beat analyst forecasts. J. Financ. **64**, 2361–2388 (2009)

Bowen, R., DuCharme, L., Shores, D.: Stakeholders' implicit claims and accounting method choice. J. Account. Econ. **20**, 255–295 (1995)

Burgstahler, D., Dichev, I.: Earnings management to avoid earnings decreases and losses. J. Account. Econ. **24**, 99–126 (1997)
Bushee, B.: Identifying and attracting the "right" investors: evidence on the behavior of institutional investors. J. Appl. Corp. Financ. **16**, 28–35 (2004)
Christensen, C.: The innovator's Dilemma: when New Technologies Cause Great Firms to Fail. Harvard Business Review Press, Boston (2013)
Cohen, L., Diether, K., Malloy, C.: Misvaluing innovation. Rev. Financ. Stud. **26**, 635–666 (2013)
Dallas, L.: Short-termism, the financial crisis, and corporate governance. Journal of Corporation Law. **37**, 265–364 (2011)
Darr, R., Koller, T.: How to build an alliance against corporate short-termism. McKinsey&Company. http://www.mckinsey.com/business-functions/strategy-and-corporate-finance/our-insights/how-to-build-an-alliance-against-corporate-short-termism (2017). Accessed 17 Mar 2014
David, P., Hitt, M., Gimeno, J.: The influence of activism by institutional investors on R&D. Acad. Manag. J. **44**, 144–157 (2001)
Dierickx, I., Cool, K.: Asset stock accumulation and sustainability of competitive advantage. Manag. Sci. **35**, 1504–1511 (1989)
Drucker, P.: A crisis of capitalism. The Wall Street Journal. **30**, 30–31 (1986)
Farrell, K., Whidbee, D.: Impact of firm performance expectations on CEO turnover and replacement decisions. J. Account. Econ. **36**, 165–196 (2003)
Favaro, K.: Long-termism is just as bad as short-termism. Harv. Bus. Rev. https://hbr.org/2014/09/long-termism-is-just-as-bad-as-short-termism (2014), Accessed 15 Mar 2017
Ferreira, D., Manso, G., Silva, A.: Incentives to innovate and the decision to go public or private. Rev. Financ. Stud. **27**, 256–300 (2012)
Freeman, R.E., Harrison, J.S., Wicks, A.C.: Managing for Stakeholders: Survival, Reputation, and Success. Yale University Press, New Haven/London (2007)
Gigler, F., Hemmer, T.: Conservatism, optimal disclosure policy, and the timeliness of financial reports. Account. Rev. **76**, 471–493 (2001)
Goedhart, M., Koller, T., Wessels, D.: The real business of business, McKinsey&Company. http://www.mckinsey.com/business-functions/strategy-and-corporate-finance/our-insights/the-real-business-of-business. **2**, 101–109 (2015.) Accessed 10 Mar 2017
Graham, J.R., Harvey, C.R., Rajgopal, S.: The economic implications of corporate financial reporting. J. Account. Econ. **40**, 3–73 (2005)
Graves, S.: Institutional ownership and corporate R&D in the computer industry. Acad. Manag. J. **31**, 417–428 (1988)
Gunny, K.: The relation between earnings management using real activities manipulation and future performance: evidence from meeting earnings benchmarks*. Contemp. Account. Res. **27**, 855–888 (2010)
Haldane, A.G., Davies, R.: The short long. Paper presented at the 29th SUERF (Société Universitaire Européene de Recherches Financières) Colloquium in Brussels on 11th May 2011
Hansen, G., Hill, C.: Are institutional investors myopic? A time-series study of four technology-driven industries. Strateg. Manag. J. **12**, 1–16 (1991)
Holmstrom, B., Milgrom, P.: Multitask principal-agent analyses: incentive contracts, asset ownership, and job design. J. Law Econ. Org. **7**, 24–52 (1991)
Jackson, G., Petraki, A.: The Sustainable Company: a New Approach to Corporate Governance, pp. 199–225. ETUI, Brussels (2011)
Jacobs, M.T.: Short-Term America: the Causes and Cures of our Business Myopia. Harvard Business School Press, Boston (1991)
Jensen, M.C.: The takeover controversy: analysis and evidence. Midland Corp. Financ. J. **4**, 6–32 (1986)
Johnson, H., Kaplan, R.: The rise and fall of management accounting. IEEE Eng. Manag. Rev. **15**, 36–44 (1987)

Jones, B., Burchman, S.: How incentives for long-term management backfire. Harv. Bus. Rev. https://hbr.org/2016/05/how-incentives-for-long-term-management-backfire (2016). Accessed 19 Mar 2017

Laverty, K.: Economic "short-termism": the debate, the unresolved issues, and the implications for management practice and research. Acad. Manag. Rev. **21**, 825–860 (1996)

Lazonick, W.: Profits without prosperity. Harv. Bus. Rev. https://hbr.org/2014/09/profits-without-prosperity (2014). Accessed 20 Mar 2017

Mackey, J., Sisodia, R.: Conscious Capitalism, with a New Preface by the Authors: Liberating the Heroic Spirit of Business. Harvard Business Review Press, Boston (2014)

Marginson, D., McAulay, L.: Exploring the debate on short-termism: a theoretical and empirical analysis. Strateg. Manag. J. **29**, 273–292 (2008)

Porter, M.E.: Capital disadvantage: America's failing capital investment system. Harv. Bus. Rev. **70**(5), 65–82 (1992)

Rahman, A., Tay, T., Ong, B., Cai, S.: Quarterly reporting in a voluntary disclosure environment: its benefits, drawbacks and determinants. Int. J. Account. **42**, 416–442 (2007)

Rahmandad, H., Henderson, R., Repenning, N.: Making the numbers? "Short termism" and the puzzle of only occasional disaster. Acad. Manag. Proc. 17632–17632 (2015)

Rummel, N.: Short-term earnings focus led to wall street woes, former SEC chief Donaldson says. *Financial Week* (2008)

Samuel, C.: Does shareholder myopia lead to managerial myopia? A first look. Appl. Financ. Econ. **10**, 493–505 (2000)

Stout, L.A.: The Shareholder Value Myth: how Putting Shareholders First Harms Investors, Corporations, and the Public. Berrett-Koehler Publishers, San Francisco (2012)

Subramanian, G.: Corporate governance 2.0. Harv. Bus. Rev. **93**(3), 17 (2015)

Summers, L.: Taking a long view on corporate reform, The Washington Post. https://www.washingtonpost.com/opinions/taking-a-long-view-on-corporate-reform/2015/08/09/c786cdb8-3d0c-11e5-9c2d-ed991d848c48_story.html (2015). Accessed 17 Mar 2017

The Aspen Institute: Overcoming Short-Termism: a Call for a more Responsible Approach to Investment and Business Management. The Aspen Institute, New York. https://assets.aspeninstitute.org/content/uploads/files/content/docs/pubs/overcome_short_state0909_0.pdf (2009). Accessed 21 Mar 2017

Tonello, M.: Revisiting stock market short-termism. Research report, Corporate/Investor Summit Series, The Conference Board (2006)

Chapter 31
Cultural and Creative Economy: Challenges and Opportunities for Romania

Marta-Christina Suciu, Laura Istudor, Diana Florentina Spînu, and Christian Năsulea

Abstract The main aim of our paper is to highlight the importance of creative and cultural economy (CCE) for Romania on its road towards a knowledge and innovation-based society. In order to express the accelerated importance of CCE for ranking countries performance based on the new competitiveness framework specific to this new type of economy and society, we apply some of the most relevant new benchmarking methodologies such as the *Global Creativity Index*, *European Innovation Scoreboard*, *Cultural Employment Index* and *Beyond GDP*. The authors identify some of the key drivers of competitiveness specific to these new benchmarking methods. We also include a comparative analysis between these methods. We also compare the different ranking positions of Romania according to these methods, on one hand, and the performance of the top five countries corresponding to each of the benchmarking tool. Special attention had been given to Romania both from a static and dynamic point of view considering its expected evolution and trends based on different dimensions of development (economic, social, cultural, environment) under the broader umbrella of CCE. For further research we intend to enlarge our perspective including an alternative mix of socio-economic-cultural and environmental policies that would contribute and make the difference for a long-run smart, sustainable and inclusive development at all the levels of activities (micro-, mezzo- and macroeconomics). We will also take into account the specific ways in which these interconnected policies are affected by the emergence of CCE.

Keywords Creative and cultural economy • Cultural-creative industries • Creative class • Creative and innovative communities • Smart cities

---

M.-C. Suciu (✉) • L. Istudor • D.F. Spînu
Bucharest University of Economic Studies, Bucharest, Romania
e-mail: christina.suciu@economie.ase.ro

C. Năsulea
University of Bucharest, Bucharest, Romania

S.C. Mărginean et al. (eds.), *Emerging Issues in the Global Economy*, Springer Proceedings in Business and Economics,
https://doi.org/10.1007/978-3-319-71876-7_31

31.1 Introduction

Human civilization is evolving more and more towards an economy and society based on creativity, innovation, knowledge and talent. Even it is considered to be a modern evolution, it seems that it started to be addressed since the late eighteenth century. Adam Smith had illustrated the key role of human capital considering it as the "fourth factor of production" (Smith 1990). Nevertheless, the new economic rules specific to the digital era, also known as the *network society* or *knowledge and innovation-based economy*, are more and more present within the recent research developments.

31.1.1 The Importance of Creativity and Innovation in the Context of the Creative and Cultural Economics (CCE)

The cultural and creative economy (CCE), with its three main elements – *creative class*, *creative-innovative communities* and *cultural-creative industries* – represents a new research field with an increasing importance in order to better understand today's economic, social and cultural challenges (Howkins 2001).

Creativity is defined by the Oxford Dictionary (2017) as the use of imagination in order to generate new contents, ideas, services and products, namely, by using both tangible and intangible assets. Creativity and innovation are considered to be key engines of development and important sources for obtaining and keeping a long-term competitive advantage (Florida 2002). Intangible assets in general and intellectual capital, knowledge and creativity in particular, represent new and different production factors that are relevant for the long-run development perspective, as compared with traditional tangible assets. Intangible assets are important because of their potential to generate increasing returns to scale and positive outcomes (in terms of a value added, new jobs and other expected effects relevant for the creative era).

One of the pioneers of the creative economy research field is Richard Florida. He has stressed since 2002 the importance of the creative economy, pointing out the concept of *creative class*. According to Richard Florida, creative class is a socio-professional class that includes two major types: the *super-creative core* and the *creative professionals*. Florida argued that a new *people-oriented climate* would overtake the already mainstream *business climate*. As a consequence, in other words, the long-term competitive advantage would belong to the cities and regions which invest more and more in increasing their attractiveness for creative people (Cojanu and Croitoru 2015). The way in which competition between cities such as Berlin, London or Helsinki has led to the creation of an attractive business climate is already clearly visible. Smart and competitive cities support both cultural and innovative activities while bringing together young entrepreneurs and artists from all over the world whose mostly important assets are their talent and creativity.

The importance of *CCE* as a prerequisite for prosperity and growth has been confirmed by a fairly large number of international organizations and forums. One of the organizations claiming the role of CCE as one of the main supporters of the cultural expression of diversity was UNESCO. Since the agreement on 20 October 2005, UNESCO has created a network of creative cities and communities. In 2015, UNESCO experts published an analytical report stressing the importance of the cultural and creative industries (CCI) at a global level. UNESCO has been actively involved in reaffirming the strategic role of these industries in generating 29.5 billion jobs globally and an output of 2.250 billion USD value added (UNESCO 2015).

The institutional developments aiming to support the growth of creative economies within the European Union had been acknowledged also through *the Europe 2020 Strategy* (European Commission 2010).

The main priorities are referring to the *smart, sustainable and inclusive growth* and *development* by creating a competitive knowledge-based economy and society with high employment that provides also social, cultural and economic cohesion. The EU's efforts in supporting the objectives established since 2010 have afterwards evolved in conducting programmes meant to improve the attractiveness of its member countries.

For instance, *Creative Europe* initiative is a 1.46 billion euros programme dedicated for the period 2014–2020. It aims to strengthen the competitiveness of cultural and creative sectors (CCS) in all the member countries, by offering funding to individuals and companies wishing to perform in CCS fields. In the last years, European countries started to create their own national programmes targeting the cultural and creative industries (De Voldere et al. 2017). *The EU legislation* is also favourable and supports the development of these sectors.

In Romania, the interest towards supporting cultural and creative industries is becoming more important because of their outcomes. Even though Romania's performance benchmarking tools used until 2014 did not target priorities areas such as developing cultural infrastructure or supporting the cultural-creative services, the importance of *the cultural-creative sectors* (*CCS*) was mentioned recently as a strategic objective by the national authorities, mostly by the Ministry of Culture and National Heritage (Cojanu and Croitoru 2015). At the local level, certain local communities in the counties of Cluj, Timis or Mureș are becoming more and more advanced in preparing a more proper, efficient and effective investment climate (Cojanu and Croitoru 2015). Moreover, *the Cultural Capital Cities* initiative had managed to create a new development pattern. According to this new perspective, smart cities have to exploit those opportunities effectively and efficiently, such as to assure the prerequisite for continuing to develop not only as tourist cities but also as culturally and economically oriented communities. It is clear that the cultural and creative industries (CCI) still have undiscovered issues, expected to be identified and explored properly, mostly within the regions with a lower development level.

Because of the way they are defined, cultural and creative industries (CCI) gather together almost everything that can be considered as a creative product designed and produced within the cultural sectors (Suciu 2008). Because of this broader vision of understanding, cultural and creative products gather a wide range of activities and services integrating both creative elements and components belonging to subdivisions of very different fields of activity. From this point of view, one important challenge for emergent countries such as Romania is to assess coherently the way in which public policies can interact in a synergetic way with the private initiatives in order to support the growth and development of the CCI sectors.

31.2 Alternative Benchmarking and Measurement Methods Used in the Context of the Creative and Cultural Economy

In the twenty-first century, the priorities of public economic policies are changing towards the development of a new economic model where the development of creative industries requires a new paradigmatic and conceptual framework for better understanding and facilitating a competitive development of the CCI activities.

In order to evaluate countries and their performance within a society and economy based on knowledge and innovation, new methods of benchmarking are now breaking the traditional establishment in the field of mainstream economic indicators.

31.2.1 Why Do We Need to Measure and Rank Performance and Competitiveness in a Different Way with Regard to the CCE?

Evaluating the current level of development for the cultural and creative industries (CCI) has become a key condition for the European countries committed to the fulfilment of *the Europe 2020 Strategy* (European Commission 2010). Furthermore, while the creative industries are growing stimulating an increase of the interdependence with other economic activities, the recent developments in this research field have determined new models of assessing and ranking countries, regions, sectors and organizations based on their performance that take into account mostly qualitative issues concerning creativity, innovation, intellectual capital and intangible assets (Correia and Costa 2014; Bobircă et al. 2009).

31.2.2 Global Creativity Index (GCI)

One of the most well-known indicators is *the Global Creativity Index* (*GCI*) (Florida et al. 2015) developed since 2011 by *the Martin Prosperity Institute* under Richard Florida supervision. GCI had been designed based on Richard Florida's assessment of GCI which is based on *the 3Ts model – talent*, *technology* and *tolerance*.

Table 31.1 The top six European countries and Romanian position according to the Global Creativity Index (2015)

Rank	Country	Technology	Talent	Tolerance	Global Creativity Index
5.	Denmark	10	6	13	0.917
5.	Finland	5	3	20	0.917
7.	Sweden	11	8	10	0.915
10.	Netherlands	20	11	6	0.889
12.	United Kingdom	15	20	5	0.881
13.	Ireland	23	21	7	0.845
68.	Romania	56	60	76	0.425

Talent Index is an aggregate index containing three other sub-indicators, namely, *the Creative Class Index (CCI)*, the percentage of population employed in creative activities computed based on *International Labour Organization* statistics regarding the structure of the labour market; the *Human Capital Index* (*HCI*), data collected by *Eurostat* regarding the number of individuals with an age between 25 and 64 years old with at least an university diploma; and *the Scientific Talent Index (STI)*, data collected by *Eurostat* representing the number of researchers employed in the scientific field per 1000 inhabitants.

Technology Index is an aggregate index based on three other sub-indicators, namely, *the Innovation Index (II)*, the number of patents per 1000 inhabitants; *Technology Innovation Index*, the number of patent requests for high technologies per 1 million inhabitants; and *R&D Index* (RDI), the percentage of GDP for expenses on research and development.

Tolerance Index (TOLI) is an aggregate index formed by other three sub-indicators: *Tourism Openness Index (TOI)*, the number of tourists arriving on national territory within a year; *Student Index (STI)*, the number of foreign students or nationals studying in foreign countries; and *Creative Trade Index* (*CTI*), international trade with creative products and services.

In Table 31.1 we illustrate the top six European countries plus Romania based on their respective positions according to *the Global Creativity Index*. We look at six countries, instead of five because Denmark and Finland are tied for the fifth place with a score of 0.917. There is something to be said about European positions in the index in general as there are no European countries in the top 3 and only 4 in the top 10. Globally the first three positions go to Australia, the United States and New Zealand. Additionally, it is worth mentioning that Sweden ranked first in the index in its previous 2011 edition.

Romania is ranked poorly compared to the top European countries with a score of 0.425 which is less than half of those of Denmark and Finland. The largest gap in Romania ranking is due to *the Tolerance Index*. Of the three components of this index, *the TOI sub-index* plays a deciding role as Romania scored lower than most European countries in terms of tourists arriving on its national territory in and before 2015. Romania's performance on *the STI sub-index* was also weak, as very few foreign students come to study in Romania (Florida et al. 2015). Many Romanian students did however study abroad. Based on *the CTI sub-index*, Romania performed better than many countries, thanks largely to its burgeoning ITC sector.

Insofar as *the Talent Index* is concerned, Romania fairs poorly due to both the relatively low number of researchers compared to the overall population and to the relatively low number of people working in creative industries (20.36%). Romania ranks 60th on both of these counts (Florida et al. 2015). We consider that this ranking isn't even lower due mostly to a fairly large number of people enrolled in tertiary education. Romania ranks 45th with an average of 53% (UNESCO Institute for Statistics 2017) which is still below the European average but quite high above the global average.

On *the technology side*, Romania ranks 48th and 49th, respectively, in terms of *R&D spending* and *number of patents relative to the overall population* (Florida et al. 2015). Unfortunately, the great majority of patents filed in Romania do not qualify for the "high technology" status which is why the ranking for the third sub-indicator in the Technology Index is a much lower 65th position.

31.2.3 European Innovation Scoreboard (EIS)

The European Innovation Scoreboard (EIS) provides other benchmarking method used for measuring and comparing progress and performance among European countries according to the general framework of a knowledge and innovation-based society (European Innovation Scoreboard 2017b). EIS compares the current status of innovation for particular EU countries to the EU average taken from the previous index. In the case of data presented in Fig. 31.1, the EU average in 2010 is used as a baseline, and each country is assessed relative to this baseline. We can thus primarily assess progress made by each country and get an idea of each country's current standing and even about its expected trends of evolution, at least in the near future.

As we can see in Fig. 31.1, again Denmark and Finland are at the forefront of innovation, although they are surpassed by Sweden which, according to EIS 2016, seems to preserve its dominance with respect mostly to the technological innovation. The data includes member countries of *the European Economic Area (EEA)* and Switzerland, as featured in Fig. 31.1, as well as other countries with strong connections to *the European Union*.

Based on *the EIS data* for 2016, Romania performs poorer than all other EU countries. Its poor performances might even show a quite regressive trend in innovation.

By diving into the data (European Innovation Scoreboard 2017a, b), we can get a sense of the underlying variables that lead to this severe underperformance. Romania scores lower than all other EU countries in almost all issues concerning innovation. Among these paradoxical rankings in which its scores aren't severely low are *medium and high-tech product exports* and *broadband penetration*.

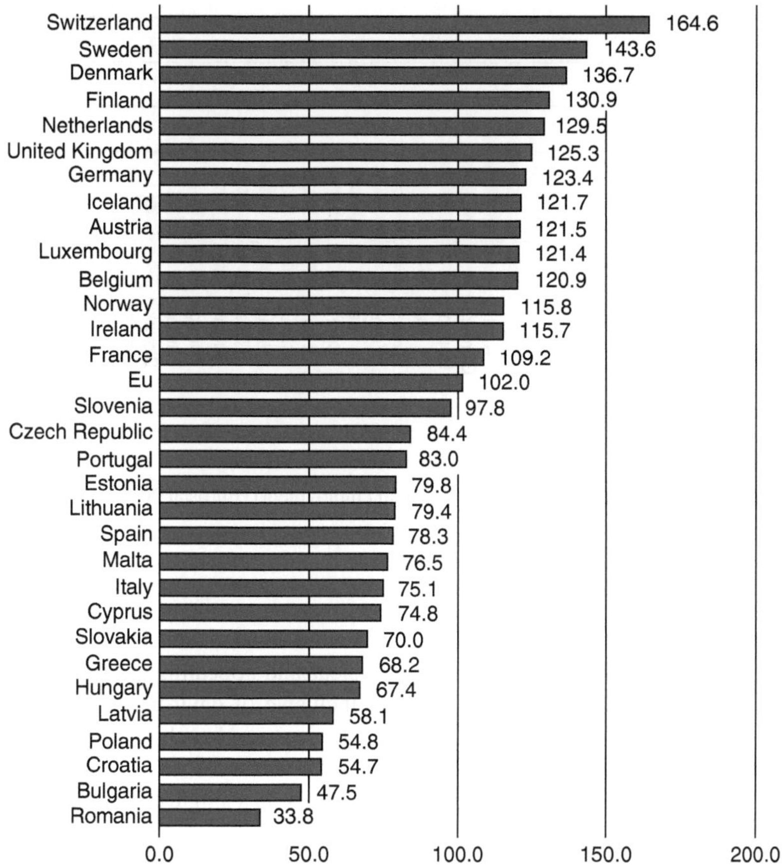

Fig. 31.1 European Innovation Scoreboard (EIS) 2016 – Relative performance as compared to EU in 2010 (European Innovation Scoreboard 2017a)

Somehow, despite lack of investment in R&D&I (Research & Development & Innovation), low rate of tertiary education completion, low science output, lack of innovative SMEs, etc., Romania ranks higher than 22 other countries in a dataset of 37 countries when it comes to the *medium and high-tech product exports*.

31.2.4 Cultural Employment Index (CEI)

A niche measurement that provides insight into the economic structure of particular countries is *the Cultural Employment Index* (Eurostat 2017) illustrated in Fig. 31.2.

The EU average for cultural employment is 2.9% (Eurostat 2017) whereas Romania is, again, last in the EU with a rate of 1.2%.

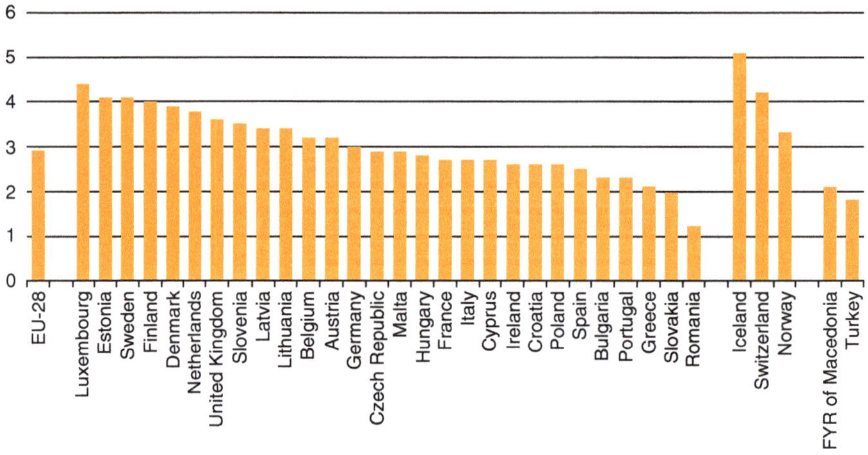

Fig. 31.2 Cultural Employment Index (% of total employment) (Eurostat 2017)

31.2.5 Beyond GDP

Beyond GDP is an initiative of the European Union aimed at developing new indicators and benchmarking methods that are as clear and appealing to economists and social scientists as GDP but that are more inclusive of environmental and social issues. A long list of some examples of these indices and benchmarking methods is available in the specific literature (Beyond GDP 2017).

To better understand this initiative, we will focus on a single example, *the Happy Planet Index (HPI).*

As stated in the index description, the Happy Planet Index (2016) wishes to measure what matters: sustainable well-being for all. It tells us how well nations are doing at achieving long, happy, sustainable lives (Fig. 31.3).

According to *the Happy Planet Index*, Romania is on the 55th position with a score of 28.8. This result is quite interesting both compared to GDP per capita (rank 82) (The World Fact Book 2017) and to the GINI coefficient (rank 10) (The Happy Planet Index 2016).

It provides some insights into additional issues by taking into account social issues concerning *the inclusive dimension of development* (such as equality of chances and inequalities) and correspondingly some ecological issues targeting mostly *the sustainability dimension of growth and development.*

31.3 Main Challenges of CCE

Most of the indicators measuring the potential impact of CCS provide a fairly big amount of information useful for understanding how these sectors and industries are evolving. However, relying mostly on data collected at a national level, the results

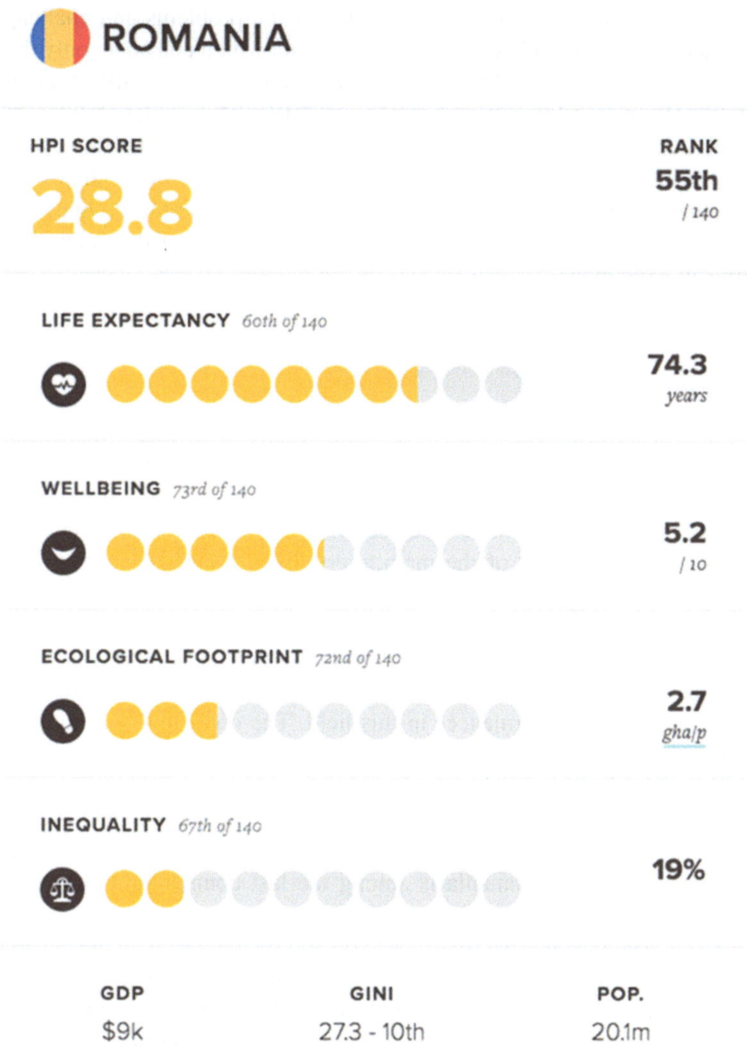

Fig. 31.3 Happy Planet Index (2016)

may not show always the entire picture. One of the problems and challenges we need to face is therefore related to the national data which considers only the traditional sectors, following *the NACE classification* and not necessarily a value chain perspective (European Innovation Scoreboard 2017a, b). In order to assess the real impact of CCS, the official statistics have to be complemented with new ways of gathering both qualitative and quantitative data within the value chains. Directly related to the lack of accurate data is the fact that there are not many qualitative and especially quantitative studies to argue for the importance of the cultural-creative industries in Romania.

31.4 Conclusions

The main aim of this paper was to assess from a micro- and macroeconomic perspective the importance of cultural and creative industries in promoting the Europe 2020 vision supporting a smart, sustainable and inclusive development. We have therefore focused on some of the main alternative ways of measuring economic performance, using new benchmarking methods to quantify creativity and the performance of the new economy, such as *the Global Creativity Index*, *the European Scoreboard Index*, *the Cultural Employment Index* and *the Beyond GDP* indicators. The comparison between Romania and the other EU countries revealed large discrepancies regarding performances in this field. The only subsector that seems to perform better is ITC. We consider that one of the most important reasons for that is related to the existence of a highly skilled and sometime quite cheap labour force activating within the CCI fields. Although there might be some discrepancies due to the way data is collected, empirical studies performed by scholars and international organizations show that Romania is among the last countries in Europe when it comes to enhancing and supporting creativity.

Therefore, we consider that, in order to overcome the delays in the development of the cultural-creative economy (including creative class, creative communities and creative and cultural sectors), a long-term vision is required, as well as the creation of policy instruments that might make Romania more attractive to young people, both for residents or non-residents. Furthermore, in order to fulfil the objectives set up by the *Europe 2020 Strategy*, Romania needs to improve its outcomes in education attainment by investing in the key strategic sectors of research and development.

References

Bobircă, A., Drăghici, A., Dumitrescu, S., Mihuț, O.: Măsurarea Economiei Creative – Studiu de caz România. The Romanian. Econ. J. **34**(4), 117–144 (2009)

Cojanu, V., Croitoru, C.: Introducere. In: Cojanu, V., Croitoru, C., Becuț, A. (eds.) Sectoarele culturale și creative în România. Importanța economică și contextul competitiv. Pro Universitaria, București (2015)

Correia, C.M., Costa, J.: Measuring creativity in the EU member states. Investigaciones Regionales. **30**, 7–26 (2014)
De Voldere, I., Romainville, J.F., Knotter, S., Durinck, E., Engin, E., Le Gail, A., Kern, P., Airaghi, E., Pletosu, T., Ranaivoson, H., Hoelck, K.: Mapping the Creative Value Chains: a Study on the Economy of Culture in the Digital Age. Publications Office of the European Union, Luxembourg (2017)
European Commission: Europe 2020: A Strategy for Smart, Sustainable and Inclusive Growth 2020 (2010)
European Commission: Beyond GDP – Individual Indices and Indicators. http://ec.europa.eu/environment/beyond_gdp/links_en.html (2017). Accessed 30 June 2017
European Innovation Scoreboard: Annex B (Performance per indicator), http://ec.europa.eu/docsroom/documents/23604 (2017a). Last accessed 30 May 2017
European Innovation Scoreboard: Publication Office of the European Union, Luxembourg. http://ec.europa.eu/growth/industry/innovation/facts-figures/scoreboards_en (2017b). Accessed on 30 June 2017
Eurostat: Culture Statistics – Cultural Employment. Publication Office of the European Union, Luxembourg. http://ec.europa.eu/eurostat/statistics-explained/index.php/Culture_statistics_-_cultural_employment (2017). Accessed 30 June 2015
Florida, R.: The Rise of the Creative Class. Basic Books, New York (2002)
Florida, R., Mellander, C., King, K.: The Global Creativity Index 2015. Martin Prosperity Institute, Toronto (2015)
Howkins, J.: How People Make Money from Ideas. Penguin Press, London (2001)
New Economics Foundation: Happy Planet Index. London. http://happyplanetindex.org/ (2016). Accessed 30 June 2017
Oxford Dictionaries: Entry creativity. http://en.oxforddictionries.com/ (2017) Accessed 29 June 2017
Smith, A.: An Inquiry into the Nature and Causes of the Wealth of Nations. Great Books of Western World, London (1990)
Suciu, M.C.: The creative economy. Lex ET Scientia. Int. J. **15**, 145–154 (2008)
The World Fact Book: Central Intelligence Agency https://www.cia.gov/library/publications/the-world-factbook/rankorder/2004rank.html (2017). Accessed 30 June 2017
UNESCO: Cultural times The first global map of cultural and creative industries. Ey, London (2015)
UNESCO: Gross Enrolment Ration, tertiary, both sexes. Institute for statistics. http://data.worldbank.org/indicator/SE.TER.ENRR?display=graph&locations=RO-DK (2017). Accessed 30 June 2017

Chapter 32
The Challenge of Managing Knowledge Workers and Their Skills

Ramona Todericiu and Alexandra Boantă

Abstract Knowledge workers are people with a high degree of expertise; education is the main purpose of their jobs, which includes the processes of creation, distribution, and application of knowledge. One of the major challenges for today's managers is to find the right tools to manage knowledge workers and measure their performance individually. The increased demand for employees who know how to use their professional skills and their talent to perform complex tasks within the organization has led to the emergence of opportunities, as well as challenges. The aim of this article is to identify and present what are the key skills of knowledge workers and what makes them so difficult to be managed by their superiors.

Keywords Knowledge • Skills • Knowledge worker

32.1 Introduction

It is a fact that the only constant of this century is change, a change that targets all areas of activity and all processes that take place in organizations. Change in today's organizations, say specialists, is a rule, rather than an exception. The new technologies and workforce diversity, as well as the processes of redesign and restructuring generate new pressures and expectations for all employees, regardless of hierarchical level, that require a positive, proactive approach toward change.

One of the most important and complex shifts concerns the nature of work in organizations, which has already changed fundamentally. In the knowledge-based organization, the employees are workers in the field of knowledge. Their ability to create and innovate and improve the way they manage and interact with other people in their organization is essential and decisive for the success of the organization.

R. Todericiu • A. Boantă (✉)
Lucian Blaga University of Sibiu, Sibiu, Romania
e-mail: alexandra.boanta@ulbsibiu.ro

S.C. Mărginean et al. (eds.), *Emerging Issues in the Global Economy*, Springer Proceedings in Business and Economics,
https://doi.org/10.1007/978-3-319-71876-7_32

Peter Drucker was the first to anticipate the shift toward the knowledge-based society in 1959, when in *Landmarks of Tomorrow* he first described the rise of "knowledge work," considering that this evolution is the dominant factor of the twenty-first century (Wartzman 2014).

Peter Drucker is the one who also predicted that information will soon become the reason of major changes in today's society. According to him, "knowledge workers" will become the largest and most desired working group, and that is because they have a high level of education, development, and training (Wartzman 2014).

Peter Drucker considers that knowledge workers are essential elements in the knowledge society chain, calling them assets, rare and valuable resources. He also believes that managers must help them continue their education and training program (Drucker 1999a).

In the knowledge-based society and economy, knowledge workers become important and valuable to organizations, primarily because of their ability to adapt quickly to a changing environment, to assimilate new knowledge, and to develop their skills. Specialists argue that the basic unit of the new economy – the knowledge-based economy – will no longer be the corporation but the individual. For organizations to thrive, knowledge workers need to learn, individually or interconnected, how to work together better and how to capitalize on their collective knowledge for the benefit of their organizations. Society has gone a long way since Peter Drucker first used the term "knowledge worker." "At that time, we were just starting to see a shift from manual work to jobs requiring a high level of expertise, education and experience" (Wartzman 2014). Now we are talking more and more about knowledge workers – this category comprises also employees who do mainly physical work but have jobs that are very intensive in knowledge. Anywhere between 25 and 50% of jobs nowadays require people to create, use, and share knowledge. This intensity of knowledge implies on the part of employees' essential and basic skills that aim at identifying, preserving, and disseminating information in the organization they are part of.

Thus, we are seeing an increase in the number of knowledge workers contributing to the development of learning organizations. These organizations are knowledge-based organizations, driven by workers who adapt and develop with the changes that take place in the environment in which they work. They are dynamic, customer-oriented organizations with a long-term business plan that knows the value of collaboration and innovation and maximizes the expertise of knowledge workers.

Hence, we can say that there are many new challenges that managers must take into account when they measure knowledge workers' performance and must use the right tools to evaluate their level of education and their ability of creating and sharing knowledge. The increased demand for employees who know how to use their professional skills and their talent to perform complex tasks in the organization has led to the emergence of opportunities, as well as challenges (Cochran and Ferrari 2009).

The aim of this article is to identify and present the key skills of knowledge workers and the reason for which they are so difficult to manage by their superiors.

32.2 About Knowledge Workers

Michelle LaBrosse, the founder and CEO of Cheetah Learning, thinks that "Today, of course, the term is half a century old, and in a world where 'Google' is a universal verb, being a knowledge worker is firmly part of our 'new normal'" (LaBrosse 2009).

We must agree that, nevertheless, there is still no universally agreed-upon definition of "knowledge work." Most of specialists agree that it requires nonroutine problem solving.

The term refers to those workers whose main capital is knowledge, for example, scientists, architects, engineers, etc., and whose work is out of the routine, being the result of a convergent, divergent, and creative combination of thinking.

Knowledge workers are the ones who analyze information; make connections between data; evaluate complex situations; establish causality relationships; interpret trends; respond to the latest developments in the "knowledge market"; adapt and use tools, applications, and technological solutions in their activity; are able to perform under various circumstances and under crisis situations; and are "creative, imaginative, and innovative people who can work with almost anyone, anytime, anywhere."

Knowledge workers are a new category of workforce – they are people who can very well interpret data from a particular field, being very well trained, and can come up with very good solutions to problems in a very short time (Huang 2009).

Knowledge workers are often the core of organizations. Therefore, we believe that it is necessary to define and understand the concept of knowledge workers and their role in ensuring and maintaining the competitive advantage in organizations. We will present some of the definitions that, in our opinion, best describe the concept of knowledge workers.

The term was first coined by Peter Drucker in *The Landmarks of Tomorrow* (1959), where the concept was named to be "the most valuable asset of a 21st-century…" (Drucker 1999b).

Toffler mentioned that the knowledge worker has to observe the creation procces and enhance their own knowledge. In some cases they would also need to manage the knowledge of their co-workers."

Nonaka (1991) observed a new characteristic of the knowledge worker, calling them "the fuel for innovation," and his main concern was about the fact that managers failed to support workers in creating and innovating.

The OECD stated in competencies for the knowledge economy (OECD 2000) that the term "knowledge worker" has been coined to describe those workers who are participating most effectively in the knowledge-based economy. If the definition

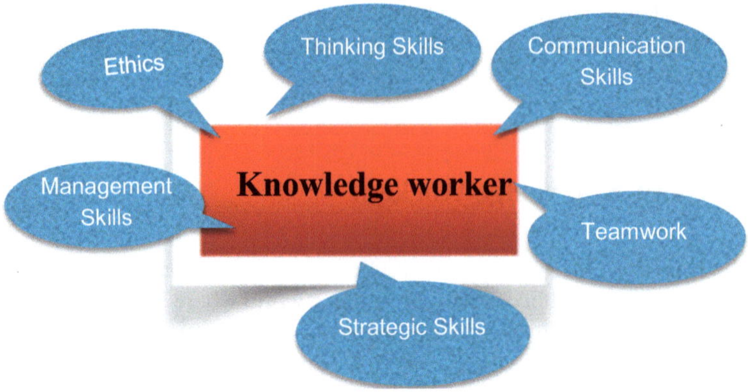

Fig. 32.1 Knowledge worker skills (T.F.P.L. 2000)

of the knowledge economy is challenging, so is that of the knowledge worker. It can refer to people who are working in knowledge-based sectors or workers who have specific skills and competencies. At the heart of all the suggested definitions lies the idea that knowledge workers are participating in the creation of knowledge.

Thomas Davenport defines knowledge workers to be people with high degrees of expertise, education, or experience (Davenport 2005a).

In the case of knowledge workers, the focus is on knowledge capital, and the main characteristic that differentiates knowledge workers from other types of workers is their ability to solve "nonroutine" problems by using their creative and innovative thinking. Thirty-eight percent of the knowledge workers' time is spent on searching for new, relevant information. Another feature is that they are detached from their managers, working in various departments or from remote sites, such as home offices.

One of the main characteristics of this kind of workers is that they can be extremely creative, which is one of the reasons for managers to encourage them to develop innovative thinking and to reward this behavior as much as possible.

Managers of knowledge-based organizations should understand that, in order to make the most of the creative potential of these workers, it is important that they are treated individually. As presented above, knowledge workers are usually responsible for creating new ideas, rather than implementing and managing existing processes. (Mind Tools 2017)

32.2.1 The Knowledge Management Skills Map: Knowledge Workers' Skills

Managing knowledge workers has never been an easy task, because these kinds of workers usually have a strategic role for their companies due to the fact that they own special skills, skills in which innovative companies are interested (Fig. 32.1).

TFPL 2000 is the global market leader in recruitment and consulting in the knowledge and information sector. As a result of a survey conducted by TFPL 2000 on more than 500 organizations, they created a map that shows the knowledge management skills. The result of this extensive research is presented by grouping the knowledge workers' features and skills according to six main domains, as the following (T.F.P.L. 2000):

Strategic and business skills: this category refers to business planning, strategic thinking, leadership, and organizational skills.
Management skills: is about having the skills to create business processes, people management, and process mapping.
Intellectual and learning skills: is about having the right skills to solve different kinds of problems, mentoring, and analytical skills.
Communication skills: including negotiation, marketing, team working.
Information management skills: IT processes.
IT skills: programming and management of databases.

Knowledge work is a complex type of work, which requires workers to be skilled and trained to perform certain tasks, as well as to have the abilities to improve their skills. Therefore, when referring to knowledge worker skills, we must point out that they are able to find and apply information and to share it with others if needed. Another important skill refers to their ability to properly use the information they obtain, creating good relations with customers, supervisors, and teammates.

32.2.2 The Roles of the Knowledge Worker

When analyzing the roles that a knowledge worker has in a knowledge-based organization, we can highlight, in general, the following: a knowledge worker can analyze data by assessing input, establishing new direct relationships, evaluating complex priorities, and making rapid connections by understanding the cause-effect relationship; they also have the ability to brainstorm and have a strategic thinking.

According to several authors, a classification of knowledge workers can be done based on the role they have in their organizations, as follows (Montana 2009):

- The controller – is the person that monitors, based on raw data, the performance of the organization
- The helper – whose prime job is to transfer information obtained to teach other co-workers
- The learner – who always improves personal skills and competences
- The linker – analyzing, disseminating, searching, and organizing information, in order to generate new information
- The networker – who creates, on a permanent basis, personal or project-related connections with co-workers, in order to establish important relationships
- The organizer – who is involved in personal or organizational planning of activities

- The retriever – searching and collecting information on a given topic
- The sharer – disseminating the information in their community
- The solver – finding or providing ways to deal with problems
- The tracker – monitoring and reacting on personal and organizational actions that have the potential of becoming problems

The roles of a knowledge worker are multiple and complex. They result from the challenges and opportunities that knowledge economy is creating for the innovative organizations who aim to increase their performance. Therefore, in this context, the role of a knowledge worker is to increase productivity, influencing success in today's competitive work economy. Knowledge workers must also analyze information and apply expertise in a variety of areas – to solve problems, generate ideas, or create new products and services.

32.3 The Management of Knowledge Workers

Most of the time, when it comes to knowledge workers and how they can be managed, managers have to understand that this is a rather difficult task, because they are not comfortable with the idea of being followed or having strict tasks to complete. That is why, most of the time, all those who manage knowledge-based workers are actually knowledge workers themselves or have held this status in the past.

Knowledge workers must be considered individuals and the projects that are designed to be carried out by them must achieve objectives that resonate with their own interests, so as not to affect the way in which the project is completed. That is why, most of the time, knowledge workers need to manage themselves, which is actually the biggest challenge, and managers are only a source of help when needed (Davenport and Prusak 2000).

Thomas Davenport, professor at Babson College, suggested, after concluding his study on more than 100 companies and 600 individual knowledge workers, the idea that people having this kind of skills must also be supervised by their managers, with the condition: "knowledge workers can't be managed in the traditional sense of the word, you can intervene, but you can't do it in a heavy-handed, hierarchical way" (Davenport 2005a).

A modern society must be instructive; its employees need to learn and reflect. Generating knowledge requires not only systematic work; much knowledge can be generated and transferred outside the formal environment. In order to achieve this, it is necessary to have a mentality in which knowledge is valued at its fair value.

Managers need to be aware that people are knowledgeable and they decide to create, use, and communicate their ideas. Knowledge management can only be applied where the true values are stimulated. Application and use of knowledge are complex activities that should respect the following conditions in order to be effective:

- The company must be convinced that it stimulates and rewards decisions and actions through which knowledge is used and communicated,
- New employees need to be hired only if they want to apply their knowledge and to train continuously,

Managers need to determine whether knowledge accumulated by employees during work can be disseminated in the form of certain information as part of the organization's intangible assets. Consequently, managers need to facilitate the transfer of knowledge by stimulating those who generate new knowledge and rewarding them properly.

32.4 Conclusions

The major changes faced by organizations force them to change the way they approach human capital and knowledge workers. While the industrial society focused on the material and financial resources, the knowledge-based society relies on knowledge, and the employees who manage it are the most important intangible assets of organizations.

However, although most organizations are aware that human capital is their most important asset, this resource is still treated as a cost, as a debt rather than an asset that creates value for the organization.

Changing this attitude toward human capital must become an aim of all organizations. Managers, regardless of their hierarchical level, must understand the importance of these intangible assets and the importance of creating a culture supportive of the development of human capital. Accordingly, it is important for all to change their mindset and see knowledge workers as assets. This, in turn, will change what the company does to find, develop, nurture, and retain those workers.

Jordan Cohen, a knowledge worker productivity specialist, thinks that the "Companies that consider both the organization's success and the knowledge workers' success when they design the organization, will make better use of their people. Most companies focus on setting objectives for departments, divisions or teams. This process generally works pretty well. However, there is a side-effect in that the company that is optimized for departmental performance is not necessarily optimized for the knowledge worker's performance. If the focus is on knowledge workers and the tools they need to be successful, then different objectives and solutions emerge." (Financial Times 2017)

Peter Drucker states very clearly the reason for which knowledge workers are important for organizations and their productivity is so important to the world economy (Davenport 2005b).

Certainly, when the management of an organization understands knowledge management processes and the importance of developing the necessary skills, knowledge workers will increase and improve worker productivity.

References

Cochran, G. R., Ferrari, T. M.: Preparing Youth for the 21st Century Knowledge Economy: Youth Programs and Workforce Preparation. After School Matters, Spring, http://www.niost.org/pdf/afterschoolmatters/asm_2009_8_spring/asm_ 2009_8_spring-2.pdf (2009). Accessed 14 Feb 2017

Davenport, T.: The Importance of Knowledge Workers in a Global Economy, November 02, 2005, http://www.babsonknowledge.org/2005/11/the_importance_of_knowledge_wo.htm (2005a). Accessed 18 Aug 2017

Davenport, T.: Thinking for a Living: How to Get Better Performance and Results from Knowledge Workers. Harvard Business School Press, Boston (2005b)

Davenport, T., Prusak, L.: Working Knowledge: How Organizations Manage What They Know. Harvard Business School Press, Boston (2000)

Drucker, P.: Knowledge-worker productivity: the biggest challenge. Calif. Manag. Rev. **41**(2), 79–94 (1999a)

Drucker, P.: Management Challenges for the 21st Century. Harper Collins, New York (1999b)

Financial Times Ltd.: Companies Must Treat Knowledge Workers as Assets, https://www.ft.com/content/5731c4e0-edcf-11e0-acc7-00144feab49a (2017). Accessed 23 Apr 2017

Huang, J.J.: The evolutionary perspective of knowledge creation – a mathematical representation. Knowl.-Based Syst. **22**(6), 430–438 (2009)

LaBrosse, M.: Knowledge Worker 2.0: The Skills You Need to Adapt, Nov. 16 http://www.computerworld.com/article/2521609/it-management/knowledge-worker-2-0--the-skills-you-need-to-adapt.html (2009). Accessed 2 Mar 2017

Mind Tools Ltd.: Managing Knowledge Workers, Getting the Most from Them, https://www.mindtools.com/pages/article/newTMM_45.htm (2017). Accessed 7 Feb 2017

Montana, G. C.: Knowledge Worker's Characteristics, Bharath University, School of Management Studies (2009)

Nanoka, I.: The knowledge-creating company. Harv. Bus. Rev. **69**(6), 96–104 (1991)

TFPL Ltd.: KM Skills Map, http://library.tmu.edu.tw/chiu/KMmap2000.pdf (2000). Accessed 12 Apr 2017

Wartzman, R.: What Peter Drucker Knew About 2020, October 16, *Harvard Business Review*, (2014)

Chapter 33
Brand Unhappiness on Social Media

Kumru Uyar, Esra Kahya Ozyirmidokuz, and Eduard Alexandru Stoica

Abstract Social media is one of the places where brands can communicate with their customers and potential customers easily and fast. Although there are lots of advantages to using social media including low cost, being able to measure customers' feelings, having fast and easy access to consumers, etc., it is very important for a firm not to make any mistakes on social media, because the online brand is lonely against to the crowd. Customers can easily give feedback about brands. Unhappy customers can share their opinion with the masses through social media and negatively affect the firm. It is important for firms to control and manage brand unhappiness. Firms should understand brand unhappiness factors in order to increase the happiness of their customers. This research aims to discover a better understanding of the brand unhappiness concept by examining the online social media feedback of customers. For this purpose, 17 different firms' Facebook customer comments are analyzed. Therefore, the brand unhappiness factors on social media are extracted.

Keywords Brand unhappiness • Customer feedback analysis • Social media analysis • Customer well-being

33.1 Introduction

With the recent popularity of social media (Stoica et al. 2013; Stoica et al. 2014), social media usage has exploded, and online platforms have become vital tools for marketing. With the advent of "big data," ways to acquire a user's opinion on a

---

K. Uyar
Nuh Naci Yazgan University, Kayseri, Turkey
e-mail: kuyar@nny.edu.tr

E.K. Ozyirmidokuz
Erciyes University, Kayseri, Turkey
e-mail: esrakahya@erciyes.edu.tr

E.A. Stoica (✉)
Lucian Blaga University of Sibiu, Sibiu, Romania
e-mail: eduard.stoica@ulbsibiu.ro

S.C. Mărginean et al. (eds.), *Emerging Issues in the Global Economy*, Springer Proceedings in Business and Economics,
https://doi.org/10.1007/978-3-319-71876-7_33

product or service have become diverse, such as social media and product review sites. These so-called user-generated contents are created and presented by the users themselves. Compared to the traditional in-depth interview techniques, these new sources allow researchers to easily access a wide range of data types from structured to unstructured formats such as text, image, and video (Kim et al. 2016).

Unsatisfied unhappy customers share their experiences on social media. The comments of an unhappy customer can spread among all consumers very quickly like viruses and affect all consumers negatively. Thus, it is important for firms to control and manage brand unhappiness. Customers can easily give feedback about the brands. To improve the satisfaction levels of customers, firms are trying to understand their customers' expectations including their emotions by directly interacting with them through social media. In the literature there are studies which mine customer feedback (Stoica and Kahya Ozyirmidokuz 2015). Moreover, in the brand and customer relationship management field, there are sentiment and opinion mining studies (Liu 2012; Ren and Quan 2012; Mostafa 2013; Yen et al. 2014; Gupta et al. 2013; Fang et al. 2011; Mogaji et al. 2016). Affective computing and sentiment analysis also have great potential as a subcomponent technology. They can enhance the capabilities of customer relationship management and recommendation systems, for example, to reveal which features customers enjoy or to exclude from the recommendations items that received negative feedback. Similarly, they can be exploited for affective tutoring and affective entertainment or for troll filtering and spam detection in online social communication (Cambria 2016).

The concept of happiness has been studied in psychology in behavioral economics (Kahneman et al. 2004), and in economics. But it has received limited attention in the marketing field. Happiness has also attracted the attention of the world of marketing and consumption. Firms need to understand their customers' happiness; if not, they won't be able to manage it in order to change the behaviors that they want to change. In addition, the emotions of online customers have a direct effect on what they will do next. Customer feelings also have an important role in adaptation. It is valuable for a firm to know how happy their customers are with their product for the purpose of customer satisfaction. Emotion has been shown to be an important factor affecting individual behavior and decision-making, but we know little about its effects on online bidding. Desmeules (2002) provides a theoretical framework for the study of the impacts of marketing strategies on general happiness. He presents a road map to establish a link between the constructs of consumer behavior and happiness. Hsieh et al. (2016) discover customers' in-role participation behavior and extra-role citizenship behavior to determine their influence on customers' happiness.

Today, consumer happiness is a new concept in marketing research. Recently, researchers have been able to form some ideas about what makes customers happy. However, this concept has been rarely examined by researchers in the field of marketing. In forming of a relationship with their customers, a company should consider creating a feeling of happiness, for that relationship to be successful and sustainable in order to retain them. Several studies have been conducted in the field of e-marketing, but none addresses consumer happiness online. Consumers don't want to be "satisfied," – they want to be happy. A product's long-term success depends on loftier goals and a broader array of design strategies that deliver emotional and social results for customers (Norton et al. 2010). In order to control customer happiness, firms should understand brand unhappiness factors.

Various researchers have sought to understand and measure happiness (Abdel-Khalek 2004; Lyubomirsky and Lepper 1999; Diener et al. 1985; Hills and Argyle 2002; Ura et al. 2012; Csikszentmihalyi 2005; Kahneman et al. 2004). Researchers measure online happiness in different languages from unstructured text data (Dodds and Danforth 2010). Understanding social happiness gives us a competitive advantage through continuous market monitoring at real time. If we measure the happiness as a key tool for making a decision on social networks, we can also generate improving strategies about the system to change perceptions that drive the behaviors of users. If we understand the crowd's happiness, we can control it and we can drive the crowd's behavior. Happiness will be manageable in social networks if we measure that emotional well-being in STS. In order to achieve this and to measure online brand unhappiness in Turkish, firstly, researchers must identify the factors of unhappiness from customer feedback data on social media. This research presents the unhappiness factors of a brand by using online customer feedback analysis.

The paper is organized as follows. Firstly, the main concepts of the methodology are given. Secondly, the results are presented followed by an analysis and discussion of the findings. We then present the conclusions and suggestions for future research directions.

33.2 Methodology

This research aims to develop a better understanding of the brand unhappiness concept by examining the online social media feedback of customers. Therefore, we analyze online customers' unstructured feedback about their experiences. We used text mining in order to reduce and group the feedback of the customers. After collecting data we are able to understand the formation and structure of the feedback. To analyze qualitative data, we have to understand the data. Understanding data starts with collecting them. In this research, we preferred to collect data from the firms' social media websites where firms use encouraging methodologies like gamification or persuasion techniques in order to collect customer feedback data. This is because some consumers actively give feedback while others may just want to observe the written stories. Purposeful sampling (Creswell 2007), which is a common technique in qualitative research (Almaliki et al. 2014), was used to collect data.

An empirical study of a single industry can reduce potential problems when sampling firms from diverse industries (Han et al. 1998). Thus, we investigated negative comments on Facebook of 158 Turkish customers related to 17 different firms. We selected the feedback in order to understand the factors of brand unhappiness. Thirty-six negative customer feedbacks are selected and coded in order to explore the factors related to brand unhappiness. After collecting customer comments' URLs, the online unstructured text is converted into numbers in order to understand the data by applying natural language processing techniques. The word vector of the documents is achieved. The similarity-based clustering approach is also used in order to detect and eliminate the outlier data in the feedback automatically. The data matrix was then used in the thematic analysis to extract the themes. Once you have gathered data, you need to put them into a format that is suitable for analysis. In most cases, you will find a way to transcribe interviews, capture online discussions, or otherwise put words and text into a useful format (Lichtman 2013). One of the first ways in which you can manipulate data is to assign codes to portions of the data (Lichtman 2013).

33.2.1 Natural Language Processing

Real data are generally incomplete, noisy, and inconsistent. In the preprocessing process, if it is necessary, we clean the data, integrate and transform them, and reduce it. Data reduction, which is one of the most important steps of the preprocessing phase, aims to select and reduce the volume but produces the same or similar analytical results. We applied text mining techniques in the study to reduce the data. Thus, we achieved more quality data for the modeling step, which is thematic analysis. We obtained reduced representation in volume with similar analytical results. We applied natural language processing techniques and data coding in this research. Before applying similarity analysis, we need to convert conversations to numbers automatically by using NLP techniques. We were able to establish groups, categories, and relations. The TF-IDF (term frequency-inverse document frequency) method was used in the NLP. This is a static numeric which is used in documents to measure the importance of documents and words. It is the most commonly used method in text analysis. Formulas (1) and (2) present the TF-IDF measures. In this study, we also employed a similarity-based model. We used a cosine similarity measure to understand the similarity of the documents.

$$t_f(t,d) = f(t,d) / \max\{f(t,d) : W \in d\} \tag{33.1}$$

$$idf(tD) = \log\left(\frac{|D|}{|\{d \in D : t \in d\}|}\right) \tag{33.2}$$

To get a better understanding of the text, a word list (a list of word frequencies) and a word vector (a cross-tabulation of word frequencies and documents) are examined. When we apply natural language processing techniques to comments, we obtain a word vector, which is a numeric matrix. Its rows represent documents and

Table 33.1 Document occurrences of the words in the word list

Word	English meaning	Total frequency	Document frequency
Marka	Brand	150	35
Müşteri	Customer	139	34
Taraf	Side	63	35
Kargo	Delivery	57	12
Hizmet	Service	51	12
Sikayet	Complaint	47	35
Garanti	Guarantee	43	10

Table 33.2 Similarity distances of some documents

Document id	Document id	Distance
1	2	1.394
1	24	1.410
15	35	1.337
23	27	1.411
33	35	1.356

its columns represent words. After mining the documents, we extracted 2 special attributes and 760 regular attributes with rules. Table 33.1 presents some of the words in the word list.

The feedback is now ready for the similarity-based approach. We employed a cosine similarity-based model to the documents after text processing. Table 33.2 shows some examples of the documents and the similarity values between them. Every word's distance in each document and the similarities between the documents are extracted. Additionally, all documents can be compared with each other according to the distances between them.

We mine online negative customer feedback. In addition, we used natural language processing techniques to improve the efficiency and ease of the analysis and we used similarity analysis in the preprocessing process to extract clusters and then understand the structure and the similarity of the documents.

33.2.2 *Thematic Analysis*

Thematic analysis is a widely used method of analysis in qualitative research (Braun and Clarke 2006). After reading the data while looking for the patterns in them, we generate codes which are then used to identify candidate themes. We applied the thematic coding qualitative research technique (Braun and Clarke 2006; Gibbs 2007) to the feedback data. Thematic analyses, as in the grounded theory and development of cultural models, require more involvement and interpretation from the researcher. They go beyond counting explicit words or phrases and focus on identifying and describing both implicit and explicit ideas within the data, that is, themes (Guest et al. 2012).

The thematic framework is used to classify and organize data according to key themes, concepts, and emergent categories. As such, each study has a distinct thematic framework comprising a series of main themes, subdivided by a succession of related subtopics. These evolve and are refined through familiarization with the raw data and cross-sectional labeling. Once it is judged to be comprehensive, each main theme is displayed or "charted" in its own matrix, where every respondent is allocated a row and each column denotes a separate subtopic. Data from each case are then synthesized within the appropriate part(s) of the thematic framework. These processes are described in more detail in the boxed illustrations. When "framework" was first developed, it was usual for charts to be drawn up manually on large A3 sheets of paper. However, most spreadsheet "worksheets" can be adapted in a matter of minutes to accommodate a thematic chart. Extra worksheets can be created within a spreadsheet file to store additional thematic charts, so that one file can host synthesized data for an entire study.

Counting the frequency of a word or a phrase in a given data set is often a good starting point for identifying repeated ideas within a large body of text and gives an idea of the prevalence of thematic responses across participants. Simple keyword searches or word counts within a data set can allow a quick comparison of the words used by different subpopulations within an analysis or can be useful in developing a thematic codebook. Therefore, depending on what is being counted, frequencies can be part of either content or thematic analyses. The example provided below illustrates the advantage of simple keyword quantification as a potentially effective way to make decisions about what to include in or how to structure thematic codebooks (Namey et al. 2008).

There is, of course, no guarantee that any analysis of a word co-occurrence matrix will be meaningful, and it is notoriously easy to read a pattern (and thus meaning) into any set of items (Ryan and Bernard 2003). We get an idea about the data by analyzing the language. Because of the lack of interpretation of the NLP results, the meaninglessness constraints of the figures which are achieved after NLP analysis, and the lack of summarization of the NLP in a text form, we prefer to use thematic analysis in this study.

The cause of consumer unhappiness might be attributed to external causes that are either uncontrollable ("The flight was delayed because of a blinding snowstorm") or controllable ("The personnel are poorly trained so that boarding takes forever") by the service or product company (Weiner 2000). We modeled expressions to achieve the relations between them. We obtained a list of expressions by coding and categorizing. After we had reviewed and updated the themes according to the previous studies (Mogaji et al. 2016), the feedback seemed to consist of five major themes, which are as follows: communication problem with customer services, timing issue, bad behavior to the customer, quality problem, and unjust gain. Table 33.3 shows the obtained themes and some examples of users' feedback and the codes of the data. Within each theme, some sub-themes were identified which are described in Table 33.4.

Table 33.3 Some data set examples after coding

Categories	Sub-categories	Sample coded phrases
Communication problem with customer services	Lack of feedback	"I sent an email but they didn't reply to it, they put me in an awkward position"
	Lack of information	"I have not told that the service would require payment"
Timing issue	Delay in delivery	"I haven't received the product yet"
	Service delay	"It is unacceptable that the process is so slow"
	Waiting for payment or information	"Operations are very slow. I waited 15 min for one product"
Bad behavior to the customer	Disrespectful behavior to the customer	"If I give value to the brand and buy a product, the firm should give the same value to the brand's customer"
	Threatening and argumentative behavior	"They behaved badly to me and said: If you do not pay, then you will have to pay with interest"
	Deception	"We buy the product to take part in a raffle, but we couldn't do so because there wasn't any password"
Quality problem	Product malfunction and broken product	"The product has a problem and it doesn't work now"
	Low quality	"I'm tired of the poor quality of product"
	Service problem	"Service with inexperienced, surly, disrespectful employees"
Unjust gain	Price inconsistency	"...Then I saw the same product somewhere else at a lower price"
	Unjust gain	"I do not accept this money outage without any justification"
	Not accepting returns	"They don't accept returns if the products don't have any defects"
	Warranty issue	"Although they gave 90 days guarantee they didn't contact with me"
Uncontrollable conditions	Firms can't control the situation	"The airline's flight was delayed as usual…"

Via an experimental approach, this research therefore seeks to examine the factors related to brand unhappiness which are post-sale issues and problems with the product.

33.3 Conclusions

Customers can easily give feedback about the brands. An unhappy customer can share their opinion with a large number of people through social media and negatively affect the firm. It is important for firms to control and manage brand

Table 33.4 Themes and sub-themes of the thematic model

Themes	Sub-themes	Description
Post-sale issues		Refers to problems which happen after sales. Customers are not happy because of the problems which come under the three sub-themes. The customer gives a warning and describes the negative reasons for unhappiness with the product after it has been purchased. The customer is unhappy because of post-sale issues
	Communication problem with customer services	Due to problems caused by lack of communication, customers have problems with customer services
	Bad behavior to the customer	Supporting the comments, bad behaviors is shown to the customer instead of good behavior
	Unjust gain	Refers to the brand's unjust gain
Problems with the product		The customer is unhappy because of problems with the product
	Timing issue	Refers to customers' unhappiness due to timing issues
	Quality problem	Customers are unhappy because of the low quality of the product
	Unjust gain	Refers to the brand's unjust gain

unhappiness. To improve the satisfaction levels of customers, firms are trying to better understand their customers' expectations including their negative emotions by directly interacting with them through social media. In this research, the brand unhappiness factors are determined in order to cluster customer negative feedback.

We investigated the factors of customers' brand unhappiness related to product quality in order to explore online customer behaviors. We also achieved some interesting information about customers' online behaviors. Based on the results, this study explored the factors related to brand unhappiness. Consequently, by understanding and predicting the factors related to brand unhappiness, in future work, we will easily understand, control, and model the customers' behaviors. In addition, a questionnaire with a larger sample of customers via a quantitative method is planned for our future work to help understanding the relations between the factors.

The limitations of the research are that the study adopted purposeful sampling to collect the research data and, secondly, the pre-sale unhappiness issues about the brand are ignored (i.e., communication problems with customer services before buying the product).

Understanding social happiness gives us a competitive advantage through continuous market monitoring at run time. If we measure happiness as a key tool for making a decision on social networks, we can also generate improving strategies concerning the system so as to change perceptions that drive behaviors of users. We need to use an adaptive, dynamic approach to measure the well-beings and happiness on social networks. Happiness will be manageable in social networks if we measure that emotional well-being in an STS. In future research we will investigate the happiness factors of the marketing environment and thus we will present the happy marketing STS which measures the happiness of online big data. We believe that the results of such a study will further help us form some hypotheses in order to understand concept of happiness in marketing.

Acknowledgment This research was supported by Erciyes University Research Fund under the title "Formalizing and Analyzing Users' Feedback to Evolve of STSs" project (Project id: FBA-2014-4850).

References

Abdel-Khalek, A.M.: Happiness among Kuwaiti college students. J. Happiness Stud. **5**(1), 93–97 (2004)

Almaliki, M. et al.: The design of adaptive acquisition of users feedback: an empirical study. In: The IEEE Eighth International Conference on Research Challenges in Information Science (RCIS 2014), Marrakesh, Morocco, 28–30 May 2014

Braun, V., Clarke, V.: Using thematic analysis in psychology. Qual. Res. Psychol. **3**(2), 77–101 (2006)

Cambria, E.: Affective computing and sentiment analysis. IEEE Intell. Syst. **31**, 102–107 (2016)

Creswell, J.W.: Qualitative Inquiry and Research Design: Choosing among five Approaches, 2nd edn. Sage Publications, Thousand Oaks (2007)

Csikszentmihalyi, M.: Akış: Mutluluk bilimi. HYB Yayınları, Ankara (2005)

Desmeules, R.: The impact of variety on consumer happiness: marketing and the tyranny of freedom. Acad. Mark. Sci. Rev. **1**, 1–18 (2002)

Diener, E., et al.: The satisfaction with life scale. J. Pers. Assess. **49**(1), 71–75 (1985)

Dodds, P.S., Danforth, C.M.: Measuring the happiness of large-scale written expression: songs, blogs and presidents. J. Happiness Stud. **11**(4), 441–456 (2010)

Fang, R.-Y. et al.: Emotion detection based on concept inference and spoken sentence analysis for customer service. In: Twelfth Annual Conference of the International Speech Communication Association (INTERSPEECH 2011), pp. 1409–1412, Florence, Italy, August 27–31 2011

Gibbs, G.R.: Thematic Coding and Categorizing. Analyzing Qualitative Data. Sage Publications, London (2007)

Guest, G., et al.: Applied Thematic Analysis. SAGE Publications, Los Angeles (2012)

Gupta, N., et al.: Emotion detection in email customer care. Comput. Intell. **29**(3), 10–16 (2013)

Han, J.K., et al.: Market orientation and organizational performance: is innovation a missing link? J. Mark. **62**, 30–45 (1998)

Hills, P., Argyle, M.: The Oxford happiness questionnaire: a compact scale for the measurement of psychological well-being. Personal. Individ. Differ. **33**, 1073–1082 (2002)

Hsieh, Y.-C., et al.: Does raising value co-creation increase all customers' happiness? J. Bus. Ethics., Springer. **1**, 1–15 (2016). https://doi.org/10.1007/s10551-016-3293-5

Kahneman, D., et al.: A survey method for characterizing daily life experience: the day reconstruction method. Science. **306**(5702), 1776–1780 (2004)

Kim, G. W. et al.: Understanding characteristics of user-generated content as a source of extracting user value. In: IEEE International Conference on Industrial Engineering and Engineering Management (IEEM), 4–7 Dec. 2016 pp. 1751–1755, Bali, Indonesia (2016) doi: https://doi.org/10.1109/IEEM.2016.7798178

Lichtman, M.V.: Qualitative Research in Education: a user's Guide, 3rd edn. Sage Publications, Los Angeles (2013)

Liu, B.: Sentiment analysis and opinion mining. Synth. Lect. Hum. Lang. Technol. **5**(1), 1–167 (2012)

Lyubomirsky, S., Lepper, H.S.: A measure of subjective happiness: preliminary reliability and construct validation. Soc. Indic. Res. **46**(2), 137–155 (1999)

Mogaji, E., et al.: Factors shaping attitudes towards UK bank brands: an exploratory analysis of social media data. Cogent Bus. Manag. **3**(1.):1223389), 1–15 (2016)

Namey, E., et al.: Data reduction techniques for large qualitative data sets. In: Guest, G., MacQueen, K.M. (eds.) Handbook for Team-Based Qualitative Research, pp. 137–163. Altamira Press, Lanham (2008)

Norton, D.W., et al.: Producing customer happiness: the job to do for brand innovation. Des. Manag. Rev. **21**(3), 6–15 (2010)

Ren, F., Quan, C.: Linguistic-based emotion analysis and recognition for measuring consumer satisfaction: an application of affective computing. Inf. Technol. Manag. **13**(4), 321–332 (2012)

Ryan, G.W., Bernard, H.R.: Techniques to identify themes. Field Methods. **15**(1), 85–109 (2003). https://doi.org/10.1177/1525822X02239569

Stoica, E.A., Kahya Ozyirmidokuz, E.: Mining customer feedback data. Int. J. Knowl. Eng. **1**(1), 68–71 (2015)

Stoica, E.A., et al.: A novel model for e-business and e-government processes on social media, proceedings of the international economic conference of Sibiu 2013 post crisis economy: challenges and opportunities, IECS 2013. Proc. Econ. Finan. **6**, 760–769 (2013)

Stoica, E.A., et al.: New media e-marketing campaign. Case study for a Romanian press trust. Proc. Econ. Finan. **16**, 635–640 (2014)

Ura, K. et al.: A Short Guide to Gross National Happiness Index. The Centre for Bhutan Studies, Thimphu, http://www.ophi.org.uk/wp-content/uploads/Ura-et-al-BhutanHappiness-Chapter.pdf?cda6c1 (2012.) Accessed 14 Feb 2016

Weiner, B.: Attributional thoughts about consumer behavior. J. Consum. Res. **27**(3), 382–387 (2000)

Yen, H., et al.: Emotional product design and perceived brand emotion. Int. J. Adv. Psychol. **3**(2), 59–66 (2014)

Chapter 34
Sustainable Growth Rate: An Analysis Regarding the Most Traded Companies on the Bucharest Stock Exchange

Diana Elena Vasiu and Livia Ilie

Abstract The concept of sustainable growth rate was originally developed by Robert C. Higgins. In the case of companies with given stable financial policies, it is considered to be the link between growth-return rate combinations that gives a *balanced growth* line. This indicates the possibilities for a company to grow without generating deficits or cash surpluses. Increased sales require more assets, which can be financed by new debt, external equity, and internal equity through retained earnings. The sustainable growth rate is the maximum rate at which company sales can increase without decreasing its financial resources. The aim of this paper is to determine if the last year most traded companies on the Bucharest Stock Exchange (BSE) have registered growth and if it was a sustainable one. Our research is based on two hypotheses: (1) the analyzed companies have a constant growth and the growth is sustainable and (2) the main factor that is influencing SGR is the retention rate. The results are only partially validating these hypotheses.

Keywords Sustainable growth rate • Financial performance

In the current economic context, dominated by globalization and IT technologies expansion, growth tends to become the absolute goal of any company: higher profit, higher turnover, more clients, and more diversified markets. Still there is a risk that the growth is exhausting the organization, regardless how strong it looks or at least will make it vulnerable in front of an economic crisis.

The question raised in this context is growth only for the sake of growth, or should a balanced, sustainable growth strategy be identified?

D.E. Vasiu (✉) • L. Ilie
Lucian Blaga University of Sibiu, Sibiu, Romania
e-mail: diana.vasiu@ulbsibiu.ro; livia.ilie@ulbsibiu.ro

S.C. Mărginean et al. (eds.), *Emerging Issues in the Global Economy*, Springer Proceedings in Business and Economics,
https://doi.org/10.1007/978-3-319-71876-7_34

34.1 Sustainable Growth Rate: Conceptual Framework and Literature Review

In the literature there are several development models of sustainable growth, proposed by de Higgins (1977) and Van Horne and Wachowicz (2008) and developed by them between 2001 and 2007, from an idea presented in an earlier paper (Van Horne and Wachowicz 2008).

Generally, two models of determination of sustainable growth rate are used: the first based on the aforementioned classical concepts developed by Higgins and the second, more recently, developed by Hamman (1996) and Churchill and Mullins (2001), based on a cash flow model, a synthesis of these models being presented by Rădăşanu (2015).

These models were also refined by other economists. Ashta suggested the use of opening total assets divided by opening equity (Ashta 2008). Fonseka studied Higgins and Van Horne models, finding that both are offering results that do not differ significantly, being equally preferred by researchers and managers (Fonseka et al. 2012). Chen is focusing on sustainable growth rate, optimal growth rate, and optimal payout ratio, developing a theoretical dynamic model considering both the investment and the financing decision (Chen et al. 2013). Varsha studied sustainable growth rate in case of Tata Motors and Maruti Suzuki, combining two sets of ratios of SGR equation, one containing retention ratio and leverage ratio and the second containing the asset turnover ratio and profitability ratio (Varsha 2013).

Regarding sustainable growth rate in the case of listed companies, Huang and Zhang studied listed companies on Chinese Growth Enterprise Market, identifying profitability as the most important factor affecting the sustainable growth ability of a listed company (Huang and Zhang 2015). Rahim and Saad studied the relationship between sustainable growth, capital structure, and firm performance in case of public listed companies in ASEAN countries (Rahim and Saad 2014). The relations between growth rate, liquidity, and firm performance in case of Iran Stock Exchange have been studied by Nasrollah Amouzesh, finding a significant association between the deviation of actual growth rate from sustainable growth rate and ROA and P/B ratios (Amouzesh 2011). Hartono and Utami made a comparison of sustainable growth rate, firm's performance, and value among some companies from Indonesia Stock Exchange (Utami and Hartono 2016).

The sustainable growth rate represents a balanced development direction of a company, indicating a way to grow without generating deficits or cash surpluses (Amouzesh 2011).

According to Higgins (1977) growth is not always representing a blessing for a company: a rapid growth can put high pressure over the company's resources and can even bring the company into bankruptcy. According to his model, an increase in sales requires an increase in assets which generates new financial needs.

The required funds can be raised either through debt or internal or external equity (retained earnings or issuing new shares). If the company is not willing to change the structure of ownership, increasing the retention rate remains the only equity solution. So, Higgins` opinion is that the growth rate of sales is in fact the growth rate of equity, which is considered a sustainable growth rate. The sustainable growth rate (SGR) is calculated multiplying the company's return on equity (ROE) by the proportion of its retained earnings (R):

$$\mathrm{SGR} = \frac{\text{change in equity}}{\text{Equity}_{\text{at the beginning-of-period}}} = \frac{R^{*}\text{Earnings}}{\text{Equity}_{\text{at the beginning-of-period}}} = R^{*}\mathrm{ROE}, \quad (34.1)$$

where R represents firm's retention rate or plow back ratio.

If ROE is decomposed based on the DuPont system (Halpern et al. 1994), SGR can be computed according to the following equation, known as PRAT model: $\mathrm{SGR} = P^*R^*A^*T$, where P is the profit margin, R is the retention rate, A is the asset turnover ratio, and T is the assets-to-equity ratio. Based on this model, SGR of a company will depend on four factors (Amouzesh 2011):

Profit margin. Increasing the profit margin is enabling the company to generate the necessary funds without using external sources and, therefore, fosters sustainable growth.

Asset turnover. An increase in the efficiency in using its assets determines an increase in sales. This is reducing the need to increase the asset base to sustain the increase in sales and thus contributes to the increase in the sustainable growth rate.

Capital structure. An increase in the debt-to-equity ratio (which determines an increase in T) is increasing the financial leverage of the company and consequently an increase in the sustainable growth rate due to available resources.

Dividend policy. A diminishing of the payout ratio determines an increase in the retention rate and implicitly an increase in the sustainable growth rate.

The model developed by Van Horne and Wachowicz is also taking into account four financial ratios: net profit margin, asset turnover, retention rate of return, and equity multiplier. The result depends on the performance on sales, financing capacity, and dividend policy. SGR is computed as follows (Varsha 2013):

$$\mathrm{SGR} = \frac{(R)*\left(\frac{\text{NetProfit Margin}}{\text{Sales}}\right)*\left(1+\frac{D}{E}\right)}{\left(\frac{A}{S}\right)-\left[R^{*}\left(\frac{\text{NetProfit Margin}}{\text{Sales}}\right)\left(1+\frac{D}{E}\right)\right]} \quad (34.2)$$

where R is retention rate, D/E is debt to equity, and A/S is total assets to sales.

34.2 Case Study

The listed companies on Bucharest Stock Exchange are those that have good financial performances in order to match the requirements of the regulated market. Growth is for most of them a must. But the question is: is this growth sustainable?

34.2.1 Methodology

The main aim of this paper is to determine if the analyzed companies have a sustainable growth model. Our research is based on two hypotheses: (1) *the analyzed companies have a constant growth and the growth is sustainable*, and (2) *the main factor that is influencing SGR is the retention rate.*

Out of the ten most traded companies on the Bucharest Stock Exchange, we selected for our analysis five companies, *Romgaz*, *OMV Petrom*, *Transgaz*, *Societatea Energetica Electrica*, and *Transelectrica*, considering the criteria of homogeneity of the corresponding industries. The other five companies out of the ten most traded are in the banking or investment industry and we considered to be less relevant to compare the growth rates. The selected companies have achieved together more than 66% of the value and 63% of the volume of all transactions on BSE during 2015–2016.

For computing the financial ratios and the SGR, we used the financial statements and financial information for each company publicly available on www.bvb.ro and www.tradville.eu. Considering the homogeneous criteria imposed for financial reporting of the listed companies starting 2012 (Order of the Minister of Public Finance no. 1286/2012), we decided to make the analysis for the timeframe 2012–2016.

For computing the sustainable growth rate, we decided to use the initial model developed by Higgins (2012): *SRG = P*R*A*T*, where:

$$\begin{aligned} \mathrm{SGR} &= \frac{\text{Net Profit}}{\text{Turnover}}^{*} R^{*} \frac{\text{Turnover}}{\text{Total Assets}}^{*} \frac{\text{Total Assets}}{\text{Equity}} \\ &= R^{*} \frac{\text{Net Profit}}{\text{Equity}} = R^{*}\mathrm{ROE} \end{aligned} \tag{34.3}$$

where ROE is the return on equity, computed according to the DuPont model (Halpern et al. 1994).

The growth rate (GR) is computed as the growth rate of sales (turnover), mainly the percentage change in the company's sales during the analyzed period vs. the previous period.

$$GR = \frac{\text{Turnover}_1 - \text{Turnover}_0}{\text{Turnover}_0} \tag{34.4}$$

In order to analyze the causes that have generated the SGR, the chain-based factorial substitution was applied, according to the theoretical model:

$$\Delta SGR = SGR_1 - SGR_0 \tag{34.5}$$

Factorial influences that can be explained from the quantitative perspective (by margin rates) and qualitative perspective (the turnovers and structure) were determinate according to:

- Factorial change due to net profit (P) change: $\Delta\ SGR_P = (P_1 - P_0)*R_0*A_0*T_0$
- Factorial change due to retention rate (R) change: $\Delta\ SGR_R = P_1*(R_1 - R_0)*A_0*T_0$
- Factorial change due to asset turnover (A) change: $\Delta\ SGR_A = P_1*R_1*(A_1 - A_0)*T_0$
- Factorial change due to assets-to-equity (T) change: $\Delta\ SGR_T = P_1*R_1*A_1*(T_1 - T_0)$

34.2.2 Data Analysis and Results

Based on the SGR and GR computed according to the abovementioned methodology, we can observe that the evolution of SGR is similar for the analyzed companies, except OMV Petrom. In the case of OMV Petrom, the year 2015 was a special one, hence the company has encountered losses, and consequently there were no dividend payments, and the financial ratios computed using net income was negative. Additionally, OMV Petrom has registered both the highest and the lowest values for SGR. The evolution of SGR for the five analyzed companies, for the period 2012–2016, is presented in Fig. 34.1.

The computation of the average SGR, for each company, over the period 2012–2016, was made using the annual value of SGR for each company. With a prudent interpretation of the results due to large variation of individual annual values of SGR, the highest average value was obtained by OMV Petrom despite the recorded loss in 2015. The lowest average value of SGR was obtained by Romgaz. The evidence of average values of SGR is presented in Fig. 34.2.

We made a comparative analysis of the SGR and GR values, and we observed that for most companies, over the period, the values of GR are lower as compared to SGR. Consequently, most companies are having a sustainable growth. Societatea Energetica Electrica is a special case in the sense that it has large variations in the turnover, from decreases of 0.5 times to increases of 22 times, which generates non-relevant data for the analysis. The evolution of GR for each company, over the period 2012–2016, is presented in Fig. 34.3.

The average GR for each company, computed based on individual annual values, is presented in Fig. 34.4. The highest values can be observed for Societatea

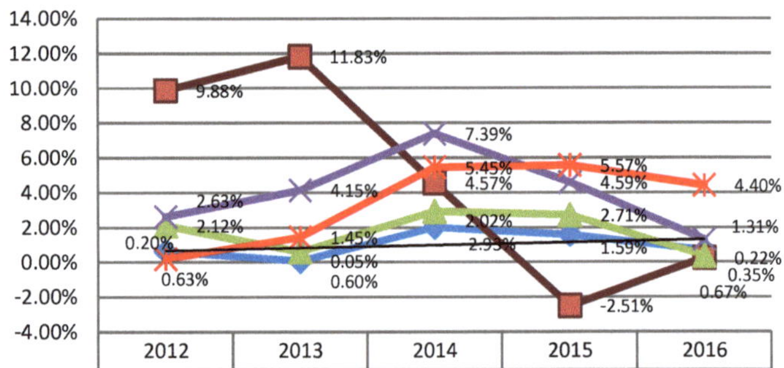

	2012	2013	2014	2015	2016
S.N.G.N. ROMGAZ S.A.	0.63%	0.05%	2.02%	1.59%	0.67%
OMV PETROM S.A.	9.88%	11.83%	4.57%	-2.51%	0.22%
SOCIETATEA ENERGETICA ELECTRICA S.A.	2.12%	0.60%	2.93%	2.71%	0.35%
S.N.T.G.N. TRANSGAZ S.A.	2.63%	4.15%	7.39%	4.59%	1.31%
C.N.T.E.E. TRANSELECTRICA	0.20%	1.45%	5.45%	5.57%	4.40%

Fig. 34.1 Evolution of SGR, 2012–2016

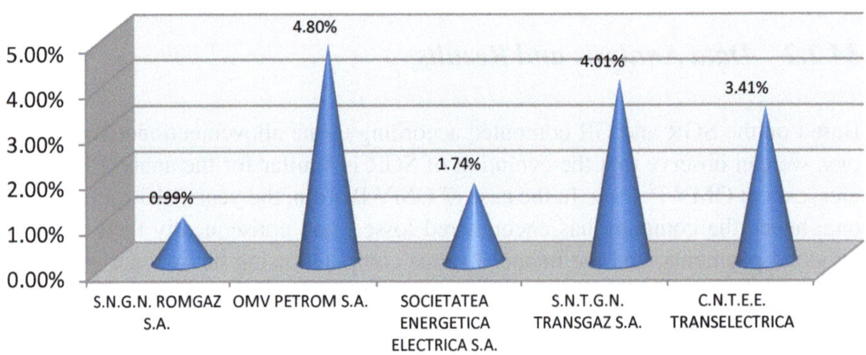

Fig. 34.2 SGR average values, 2012–2016

Energetica Electrica, one cause being the large change in turnover in 2016 as compared to 2015. Even if we eliminate this statistical irrational value, the average will be still the highest (18.17%) but homogenous as compared to the other companies.

Considering that the main aim of this paper is to identify the kind of growth the five companies out of top ten most transacted on BVB is facing, we analyzed the pairs SGR-GR for each company, determining $\Delta G = GR - SGR$. The results are presented in Fig. 34.5.

The smallest differences between GR and SGR can be identified for S.N.G.N., for which in 2012 there is only a 0.76 pp. difference and in 2012 a 6.24 pp. Still, due to higher differences in the other years, one cannot conclude that this company is close to a sustainable growth model. For all the other companies, the differences were significant for most of years. Taking into account the lack of homogeneity of

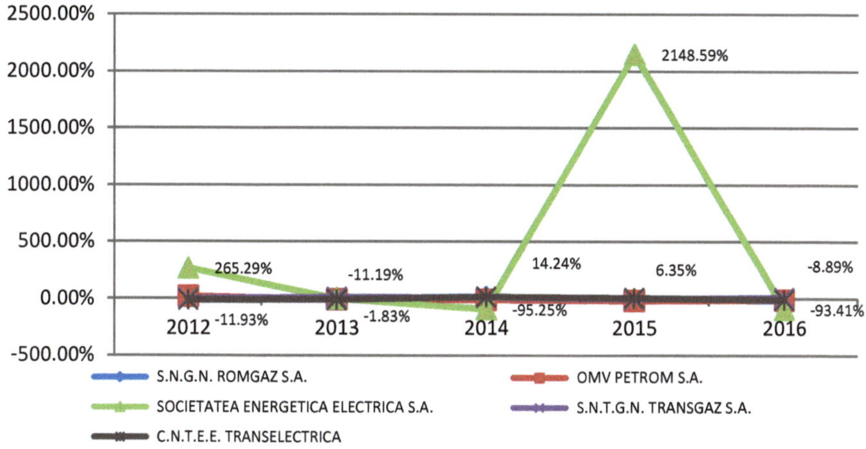

Fig. 34.3 Evolution of GR, 2012–2016

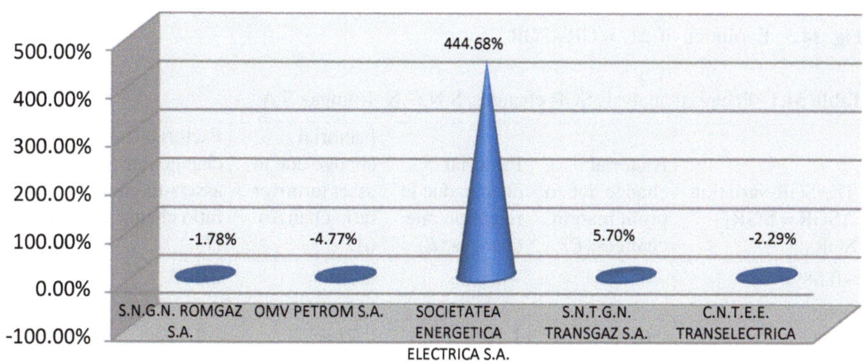

Fig. 34.4 Average GR, 2012–2016

results, the existence of statistical irrational data, and the individual behavior of the analyzed companies, there was no sustainable growth model developed. In this context, the growth model was analyzed for each company.

Factorial analysis based on the chain substitution method was performed for each company and for consecutive 2 years, t_0 and t_1, in the interval 2012–2016, in order to analyze the factors that cause the change in SGR. The results are presented in Tables 34.1, 34.2, 34.3, 34.4, and 34.5.

S.N.G.N. Romgaz S.A. A comparative evolution of SGR and GR for Romgaz is presented in Fig. 34.6. In 2013 and 2014, GR is higher than SGR. The growth in GR is observable in 2012–2014, while SGR growth only in 2013–2014. Over the entire period of time, the SGR increased in average 1.62% annually (0.01 pp. per year), while GR decreased in average 3.92 pp. per year.

The results of the factorial analysis are presented in Table 34.1 and are showing that in three out of the four consecutive periods, SGR records decreases between

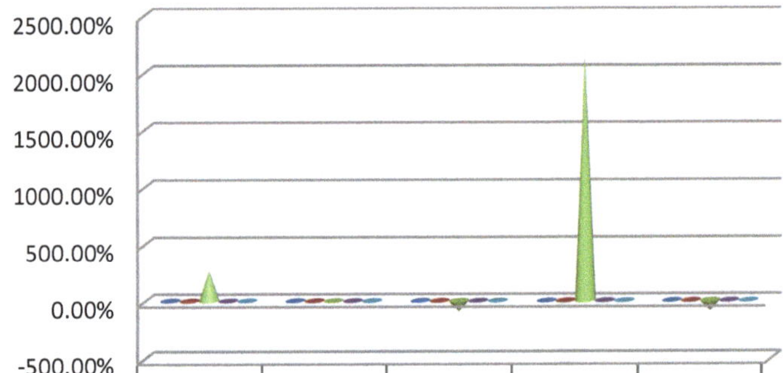

	2012	2013	2014	2015	2016
S.N.G.N. ROMGAZ S.A.	-0.76%	1.41%	13.37%	-11.39%	-16.49%
OMV PETROM S.A.	7.89%	-19.20%	-13.21%	-14.59%	-8.73%
SOCIETATEA ENERGETICA ELECTRICA S.A.	265.29%	-1.83%	-95.25%	2148.59%	-93.41%
S.N.T.G.N. TRANSGAZ S.A.	-3.30%	7.65%	1.59%	-6.85%	9.36%
C.N.T.E.E. TRANSELECTRICA	-12.13%	-12.64%	8.79%	0.78%	-13.30%

Fig. 34.5 Evolution of ΔG = GR−SGR

Table 34.1 Factorial analysis SGR changes, S.N.G.N. Romgaz S.A.

The SGR variation $\Delta SGR = SGR_1 - SGR_0$	Factorial change due to profit margin changes (*P*)	Factorial change due to retention rate changes (*R*)	Factorial change due to asset turnover ratio changes (*A*)	Factorial change due to assets-to-equity ratio changes (*T*)	Period $t_1 - t_0$
−0.58%	−0.08%	−0.50%	0.00%	0.00%	2013–2012
1.96%	0.01%	**1.76%**	0.21%	−0.02%	2014–2013
−0.43%	−0.12%	−0.14%	−0.15%	−0.02%	2015–2014
−0.91%	0.03%	**−0.82%**	−0.14%	0.02%	2016–2015

Source: Own processing

0.58 and 0.91 pp. The largest decrease is in 2016 as compared to 2015 and is of 0.91 pp. This decrease is mainly due to the variation of the retention rate factor (0.82 pp. out of 0.91 pp). The same factor had also the most significant positive influence, in the period 2014–2013, when out of a 1.96 pp. increase, 1.76 pp. is due to the variation in the retention rate.

OMV Petrom S.A. A comparative evolution SGR-GR for OMV Petrom is presented in Fig. 34.7. For each year over the period 2013–2016, SGR is higher than GR, especially due to negative values of GR. The company records decrease in turnover over the period 2012–2016 and an increase only for 2015–2016, while SGR is increasing only in 2012–2013. Over the entire period, SGR is decreasing in

Table 34.2 Factorial analysis SGR changes, OMV Petrom S.A.

The SGR variation $\Delta SGR = SGR_1 - SGR_0$	Factorial change due to profit margin changes (*P*)	Factorial change due to retention rate changes (*R*)	Factorial change due to asset turnover ratio changes (*A*)	Factorial change due to assets-to-equity ratio changes (*T*)	Period $t_1 - t_0$
1.94%	**3.53%**	1.17%	−1.59%	−1.16%	2013–2012
−7.26%	**−6.91%**	0.12%	−0.89%	0.43%	2014–2013
−4.57%	−4.57%	0.00%	0.00%	0.00%	2015–2014
0.22%	0.0000%	0.2535%	−0.0235%	−0.0062%	2016–2015

Source: Own processing

Table 34.3 Factorial analysis SGR changes, Societatea Energetica Electrica S.A.

The SGR variation $\Delta SGR = SGR_1 - SGR_0$	Factorial change due to profit margin changes (*P*)	Factorial change due to retention rate changes (*R*)	Factorial change due to asset turnover ratio changes (*A*)	Factorial change due to assets-to-equity ratio changes (*T*)	Period $t_1 - t_0$
−1.52%	−1.48%	0.00%	−0.03%	−0,01%	2013–2012
2.33%	**31.58%**	8.62%	**−35.83%**	−2.04%	2014–2013
−0.21%	−2.76%	0.03%	1.94%	0.58%	2015–2014
−2.36%	20.69%	−20.20%	−2.76%	−0.10%	2016–2015

Source: Own processing

average by 61.21% annually, meaning 2.42 pp. per year, while GR is decreasing in average by 6.57 pp. per year.

The above results are showing that, in the intervals 2014–2013 and 2015–2014, SGR is decreasing by 7.26, respectively 4.57 pp. The largest decrease of 7.26 is mainly due to the variation in the profit margin (6.91 pp). The same factor is having also the largest positive influence of 3.53 pp. over an overall 1.94 pp. increase, in the interval 2013–2012.

Societatea Energetica Electrica S.A. The comparative analysis SGR-GR for Societatea Energetica Electrica S.A. is presented in Fig. 34.8. In 2012 and 2015, GR is higher than SGR, while in 2013 the levels of the two rates are close. The company records the increase in turnover only in the interval 2014–2015, while SGR is increasing only in the interval 2013–2014. Over the period 2012–2016, SGR has an average decrease of 36.27% annually (0.44 pp. per year), while GR has an average decrease of 89.67 pp. per year.

Table 34.4 Factorial analysis SGR changes, S.N.T.G.N. Transgaz S.A.

The SGR variation $\Delta SGR = SGR_1 - SGR_0$	Factorial change due to profit margin changes (P)	Factorial change due to retention rate changes (R)	Factorial change due to asset turnover ratio changes (A)	Factorial change due to assets-to-equity ratio changes (T)	Period $t_1 - t_0$
1.52%	−0.24%	1.43%	0.42%	−0.09%	2013–2012
3.24%	1.57%	**1.62%**	−0.68%	0.73%	2014–2013
−2.80%	−0.04%	−2.32%	−0.34%	−0.11%	2015–2014
−3.28%	0.46%	**−3.78%**	0.03%	0.00%	2016–2015

Source: Own processing

Table 34.5 Factorial analysis SGR changes, C.N.T.E.E. Transelectrica

The SGR variation $\Delta SGR = SGR_1 - SGR_0$	Factorial change due to profit margin changes (P)	Factorial change due to retention rate changes (R)	Factorial change due to asset turnover ratio changes (A)	Factorial change due to assets-to-equity ratio changes (T)	Period $t_1 - t_0$
1,25%	1.12%	0.43%	−0.25%	−0.04%	2013–2012
4,00%	0.81%	**2.87%**	0.42%	−0.10%	2014–2013
0,12%	−0.29%	0.43%	0.59%	−0.60%	2015–2014
−1,17%	**−0.95%**	0.33%	−0.45%	−0.11%	2016–2015

Source: Own processing

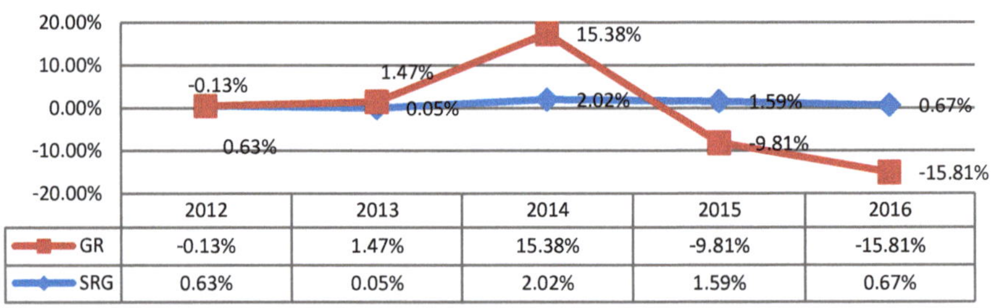

Fig. 34.6 Comparative evolution GR-SGR, S.N.G.N. Romgaz S.A.

According to the factorial analysis results, presented in Table 34.3, in three out of four consecutive intervals, SGR has registered decreases, between 0.21 and 2.36 percentage points. In the interval 2014–2013, we can observe the largest both positive (profit margin has a positive influence of 31.58 pp) and negative (asset turnover

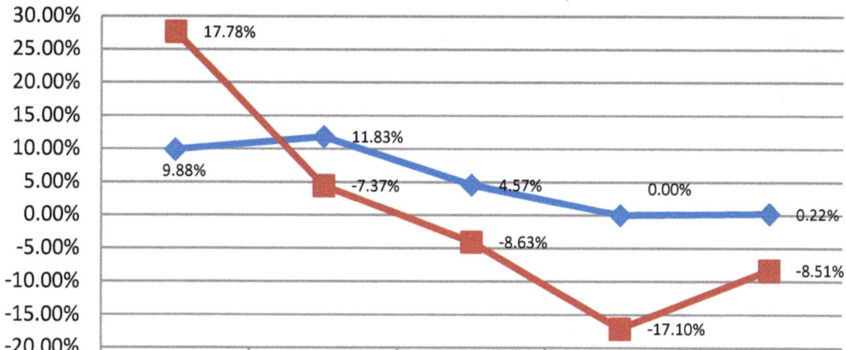

	2012	2013	2014	2015	2016
GR	17.78%	-7.37%	-8.63%	-17.10%	-8.51%
SGR	9.88%	11.83%	4.57%	0.00%	0.22%

Fig. 34.7 Comparative evolution GR-SGR, OMV Petrom S.A.

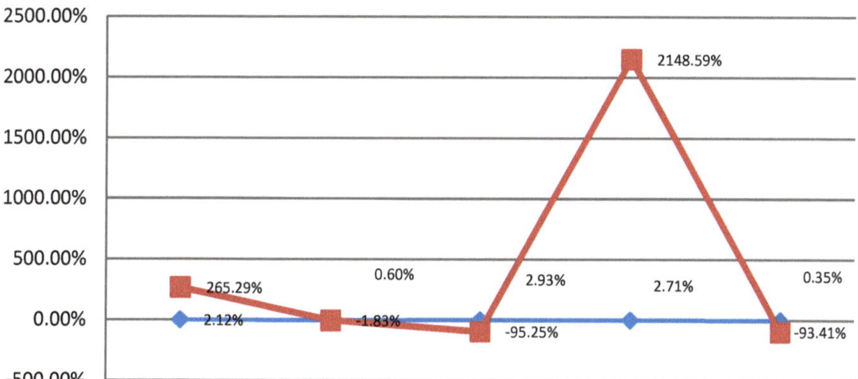

	2012	2013	2014	2015	2016
GR	265.29%	-1.83%	-95.25%	2148.59%	-93.41%
SGR	2.12%	0.60%	2.93%	2.71%	0.35%

Fig. 34.8 Comparative evolution GR-SGR, Societatea Energetica Electrica S.A.

has a negative influence of 35.83 pp) influences of the factors that determine the evolution of SGR and which almost cancel each other.

S.N.T.G.N. Transgaz S.A. The comparative evolution SGR-GR for S.N.T.G.N. Transgaz S.A. is presented in Fig. 34.9. Over the period 2012–2016, GR is higher than SGR, excepting 2015. The company's turnover is increasing only in the intervals 2012–2013 and 2015–2016, while SGR is increasing in two consecutive intervals, 2012–2014. SGR decreased in average by 16.33% annually (meaning a 0.33 pp. per year), while GR increased in average by meaning 2.84 pp. per year.

The results of the factorial analysis are presented in Table 34.4. SGR is increasing in two intervals, 2013–2012 and 2014–2013, and decreasing in the other two.

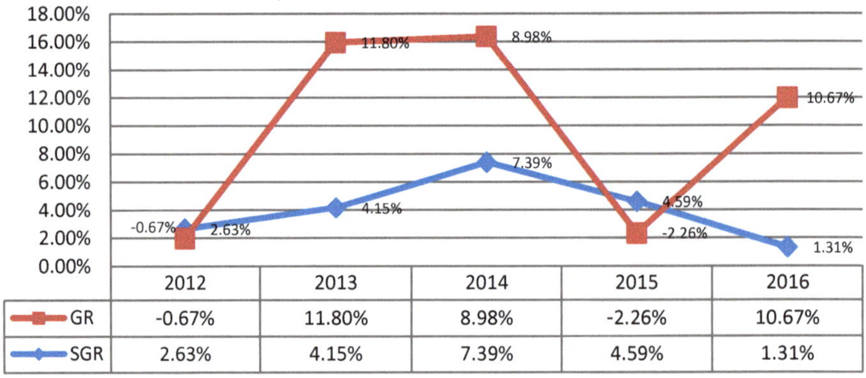

Fig. 34.9 Comparative evolution GR-SGR, S.N.T.G.N. Transgaz S.A.

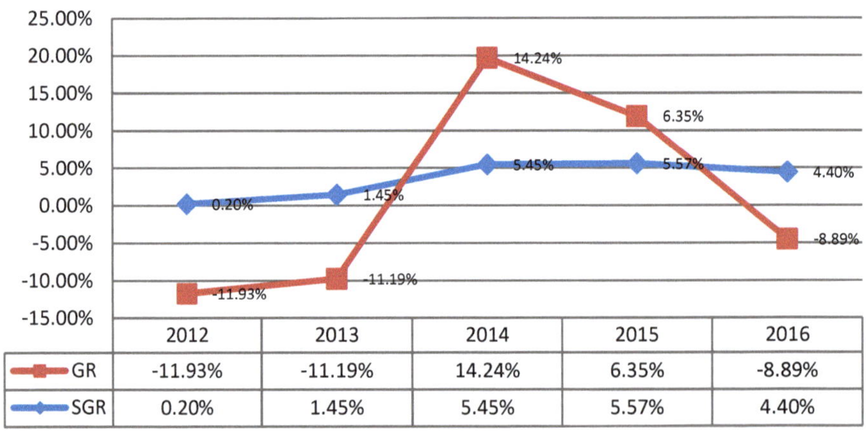

Fig. 34.10 Comparative evolution GR-SGR, C.N.T.E.E. Transelectrica

Retention rate factor has both the largest negative and positive influence. In the interval 2016–2015, the retention rate has a negative influence of 3.78 pp. on SGR, canceling the small positive influence of the other factors. In 2014–2013, the retention rate factor had a positive influence of 1.62 pp. out of the 3.24 pp. increase in SGR.

C.N.T.E.E. Transelectrica. The comparative evolution SGR-GR for C.N.T.E.E. Transelectrica is presented in Fig. 34.10.

Over the period 2014–2015, GR is higher than SGR, but without a significant difference between them. The company has increasing turnover in two consecutive intervals, 2012–2014, while SGR is increasing over three consecutive intervals, 2012–2015. Overall, SGR is decreasing in average by 116.47% annually (1.05 pp. per year), while GR is increasing in average by 7.08% annually (meaning 0.76 pp. per year).

The factorial analysis results show that SGR is increasing in three out of four intervals. The strongest negative influence is given by the profit margin factor, in the interval 2016–2016, contributing to the decrease in the SGR with a 0.95 pp. The highest positive influence is given by the retention rate factor, with a contribution of 2.87 pp. to the increase in SGR in the interval 2014–2013.

34.3 Conclusion

After processing the available data and analyzing the results, we conclude the following:

Comparing SGR and GR, in most cases, SGR is higher as GR, but this situation is due to the negative values of GR, recorded as sales declined. The difference between SGR and GR are between 0.76 pp. and 19 pp. The exception is the case of Societatea Energetica Electrica S.A., where the values of the differences are between 2 pp. and 2145 pp., due to statistically aberrant registered values. Transgaz is the company where the growth is closest to the sustainable model, with the average difference of 1.69 pp. between the two indicators. Three of five companies recorded growth of SGR during 2012–2015, while two of five companies recorded growth of GR in the same period. Even if in many cases there are decreases of GR, these are due mostly to economic, external factors and cannot be explained by convergence between the two rates. *The results we obtained are validating only in part the first research hypothesis: the analyzed companies have a constant growth and the growth is sustainable.*

In what concerns the influences of the factors that compose SGR, we observe that for three companies (S.N.G.N. Romgaz S.A., OMV Petrom S.A., and S.N.T.G.N. Transgaz S.A.), one factor had in different intervals the strongest both positive and negative influences. For two companies, this factor was retention rate and for one profit margin. It is also worth to mention that in no case the factor assets-to-equity ratio was not producing the strongest influence, neither positive nor negative. Without considering the strongest influences, in most cases SGR recorded increases due to the variation in the retention rate (12 cases, 60% out of the 20) and decreases due to the variation in assets-to-equity ratio (14 cases, 70% out of the 20). These results are partially confirming the second research hypothesis: *the main factor that is influencing SGR is the retention rate.* The confirmation of this hypothesis is in the sense that the retention rate is influencing the increase in SGR in the most analyzed cases.

References

Amouzesh, N.: Sustainable growth rate and firm performance: evidence from Iran stock exchange. Int. J. Bus. Soc. Sci. **2**(23), 249–255 (2011)

Ashta, A.: Sustainable growth rates: refining a measure. Published online in Wiley Inter Science, 207–214, (www.interscience.wiley.com) (2008). Accessed 5 May 2017

Chen, H., Gupta, M.C., Alice, C.L., Cheng-Few, L.: Sustainable growth rate, optimal growth rate, and optimal payout ratio: a joint optimization approach. J. Bank. Financ. **37**(4), 1205–1222 (2013)

Churchill, N.C., Mullins, J.W.: How fast can your company afford to grow. Harvard Business Review **79**(5), 135–143 (2001)

Fonseka, M.M., Ramos, C.G., Tian, G.: The most appropriate sustainable growth rate model for managers and researchers. J. Appl. Bus. Res. **28**(3), 481–500 (2012)

Halpern, P., Weston, J., Brigham, F.: Finanţe manageriale, traducere, p. 117. Economică, Bucureşti (1994)

Hamman W.D.: Sustainable growth: A cash flow model. Investment Analysts Journal, **43**, 57–61 (1996)

Higgins, R.: How much growth can a firm afford? Financ. Manag. **6**(3), 7–16 (1977)

Higgins, R.: Analysis for Financial Management, 10th edn. The McGraw-Hill, Irwin (2012)

Huang, X., Zhang, J.: Research on the financial sustainable growth of the listed companies on GEM. Int. Bus. Manag. **10**(2), 32–37 (2015)

Order of the Minister of Public Finance no.1286/2012

Rădăşanu, A.C.: Cash-flow sustainable growth rate models. J. Pub. Adm. Financ. Law. **7**, 62–70 (2015)

Rahim, N., Saad N.: Sustainable Growth Of Public Listed Companies (Plc) Using Capital Structure Choices And Firm Performance. In An Asean Market. Proceeding of the Global Summit on Education GSE 2014 (E- ISBN 978-967-11768-5-6) 4–5, Kuala Lumpur, Malaysia, 433–444 (2014)

Utami, S.R., Hartono, G.: The comparison of sustainable growth rate, Firm's performance and value among the firms in Sri Kehati index and Idx30 index in Indonesia stock exchange. International journal of advanced research in management and. Soc. Sci. **5**(5), 68–71 (2016)

Van Horne, J.C., Wachowicz J.M., Jr.: Fundamentals of Financial Management. Prentice-Hall. 13th edition, ISBN: 978-0-273-71363-0, 190–194 (2008)

Varsha, V.: Sustainable growth rate: refining a measure – a case study of Tata motors and Maruti Suzuki. Ind. J. Appl. Res. **3**(4), 317–319 (2013)

www.bvb.ro

www.tradeville.eu

Chapter 35
Comparative Assessment of the Income and Productivity Convergence of Albania and Western Balkans to the European Union

Ermelinda Xhaja and Ermelinda Meksi

Abstract This paper aims to look into the convergence model of Albania within the Western Balkans and toward the European Union. The Western Balkan countries are stuck in transition as their rate of economic growth has slowed substantially compared to the pre-global crisis period. Thus the economic convergence evidenced in the convergence of incomes and productivity is put into question. The variables that are used in the study are the income per capita, growth rate, and income per worker in the Western Balkan countries and EU. The data are measured for the period 1995–2015 in order to build a sound data series for trend analysis. In the paper, it is concluded that the Balkan countries are converging among themselves and toward the EU, but the speed of convergence is moderated with the hit of global crises, and the recovery seems still difficult to the rate of precrises. The main question remains on promoting productivity of their growth factors for sustainable growth and competitiveness in the wider European market. The region has a number of political and geographical advantages and unexploited potentials to stimulate further investments and thus growth.

Keywords Economic convergence • Economic growth • Structural convergence • Productivity

35.1 Introduction

The six Western Balkan countries, such as Albania, Bosnia and Herzegovina, Macedonia, Montenegro, Serbia, and Kosovo, have politically and economically committed to the EU membership process. The catching up to the EU will be a natural result of the integration process that has to be supported by the application of

E. Xhaja (✉) • E. Meksi
University of Tirana, Tirana, Albania
e-mail: ermegjika@outlook.com; e_meksi@yahoo.com

S.C. Mărginean et al. (eds.), *Emerging Issues in the Global Economy*, Springer Proceedings in Business and Economics,
https://doi.org/10.1007/978-3-319-71876-7_35

good governance principles within institutions and economic policies and sound macroeconomic and fiscal policies, leading to conducive investment climate. There is already a positive experience of the new EU members that have converged to some extent to the EU income. The aim of this paper is to empirically assess the convergence model for Albania and the Western Balkan region by calculating the speed of convergence of income through GDP per capita growth as well as the pace of convergence of productivity through GDP per employee growth. Additionally, it will assume the catching-up time gap based on forecasted figures of economic growth from the International Monetary Fund (IMF) projections. In this paper, it is provided also a comparison with the convergence speed of the 13 newest EU member countries to understand where the WB countries stand toward the EU level.

The discussion will be based on the classical approach of economic convergence for developing countries. Data used in this paper are subtracted by the World Bank Data and IMF World Economic Outlook. The countries included in the analysis are Albania, Bosnia and Herzegovina, Bulgaria, Croatia, Cyprus, Czech Republic, Estonia, Hungary, Latvia, Lithuania, Macedonia, Malta, Montenegro, Poland, Romania, Slovakia, Slovenia, and Serbia. For calculation purposes, the statistics for variables used are converted in natural logarithm.

35.2 Theoretical Approach

The convergence concept stands at the core of growth theories, from neoclassical to new growth theory. The convergence model looks into the income levels of the poorest countries of the world if they are getting closer to the richer countries. This has become a question of great importance for the prosperity of the world. Various debates, interpretations, and implications of the convergence encompass the convergence concept and absorptive capacities within the economic development theories. There are opinions that economic inequalities between nations are more likely increasing (Myrdal 1957). According to that, investments are more likely to take place in already advanced economies, and skilled workers are more likely to move from peripheral to core regions than the other way round. This thesis is supported also by Prebisch (1959) and Singer (1950) stating that the divergence among developed and developing countries will deteriorate over time. It is explained by the deterioration of production structure and trade between primary goods and manufactured products in the long run. The convergence notion comes as a derivation of the Solow model (1956). The main derivations supported by the diminishing returns of capital model are (i) a less developed economy (with a lower GDP per capita) tends to grow faster than a more developed one, (ii) the growth rate tends to diminish with the development of the economy, and (iii) if the economies share the same important features, the less developed economy will tend to converge its revenue to the developed ones. The convergence thesis incentives the developing countries to establish sound preconditions in terms of governance, institutions, macroeconomic stability, and investment climate, in order to accelerate their development pace and catch up with developed countries. In this light, South and Central East European countries would benefit from the combination of rapid technology diffusion and a major restructuring of the manufacturing sector. Increased investment in new forms, such as ICT capital, may have been a major source of accelerated productivity growth (Van Ark and Piatkowski 2004). According to Prof. Abramowitz (1950), the second way for increasing output in the economy is to use new ways of getting more output from the same number of inputs. Only about 15% of the actual growth in the output of the American economy was due to the measured growth of inputs (i.e., in capital and labor) for an 80-year period. The rest of 85% was unexplained residual, named total factor productivity (TFP), even in many other studies, including Robert Solow studies in 1960. The size of TFP represents by most economists' technological innovation as a major force in the growth of output in highly industrialized economies. The impact of a technological innovation will generally depend not only on its inventors, patents, and their protection but also on the creativity of the eventual users of the new technology.

Based on the Solow model and Cobb-Douglas production function, Barro and Sala-i-Martin (1990) have approximated the transitional growth process in the neoclassical model as in the following:

$$\left(\frac{1}{T}\right)\cdot\log\left(\frac{y_{it}}{y_{i,t-T}}\right)=x_i^*+\log\left(\frac{\hat{y}}{\hat{y}_{i,t-T}}\right)\cdot\frac{\left(1-e^{-\beta T}\right)}{T+\mu_{it}} \tag{35.1}$$

where i indexes the economy, t indexes time, y_{it} is the output per capita, x^* is the steady state per capita growth rate, $\hat{y}_{it}$ is output per effective worker, $\hat{y}_i^*$ is the steady-state level of output per worker, T represents time of observations, β is the rate of convergence, and σ_{it} is an error term. β indicates the pace at which $\hat{y}_{it}$ approaches to the steady state. Matkowski and Prochniak (2004) have simplified the evaluation of the value of β through a simplified equation of rate of growth:

$$g_y \approx \beta\left(\ln y^* - \ln y_t\right) \tag{35.2}$$

The coefficient β gives information on the speed of convergence or the pace at which the distance covered annually from the steady state. In addition to the β coefficient for defining the concept of convergence, the classical literature also presents another concept that is σ convergence. The σ convergence involves a decline over time in the cross-sectional dispersion of per capita income. The confirmation of the β convergence is a must to achieve σ convergence, but the vice versa is not always true. The concept of σ convergence means to assess if the dispersion of the real per capita GDP levels of a group of economies tends to decrease over time:

$$\sigma_{t+T} < \sigma_t \tag{35.3}$$

where σ_t is the time t standard deviation of the $\log\left(y_{i,t}\right)$ across countries i.

35.3 Comparative Assessment to Income Convergence Among Balkan Countries and New EU Members

The Balkan countries have a lot in common in terms of their economic and political context, whereas the most significant is their commitment to the EU integration process. In this sense, there are barriers that are falling between them in making their economies more connected, by converging among them and to the EU. This paper has started the collection of data from the year 1995 when the countries in the region and the CEE began their economic recovery and economic transformation from centralized to one market, following the postcommunist era. Bulgaria, Croatia, and Romania, already members of the EU, are also included in the group of countries in the Balkan region, with the aim of verifying the convergence in this region, the speed, and the extent to which the so-called emerging economies of the Balkan countries are converging to the economies of EU member states. Additionally, the paper is necessary to see any implication of the EU accession process to growth rates of these three countries. Bulgaria and Romania have accessed the EU in 2007 where the GDP per capita in PPP was 12,521 USD and 13,160 USD, respectively, consisting of 41% and 43% of the GDP per capita of the European Union in that year. For conducting a comparative assessment, the convergence indicators are estimated for the 13 newest EU members.

35.3.1 *Assessing Conditional Convergence*

The concept of β convergence relates to poor economies growing faster than rich ones. The neoclassical model predicts that each economy converges toward its steady state if the speed of convergence relates inversely with the distance from the initial condition. In other words, the model predicts conditional convergence in the sense that a smaller initial value of real per capita income tends to generate a higher rate of growth per capita. The higher the absolute value of β, the greater the responsiveness of the average growth rate to the gap between y^* and $y(0)$, so the more rapid the convergence to the steady state. A regression analysis is made for calculating the absolute convergence, where the dependent variable is the annual rate of growth of GDP per capita per each country for 1995–2015. Natural logarithm of GDP per capita per each country at the initial year (1995) is referred as an independent variable. Figures 35.1 and 35.2 show the scatter plot of the regression analyses for the WB and 13 newest EU members. Table 35.1 depicts the results of regression and validity, where β is also calculated through the Eq. (35.3).

The existence of conditional convergence is proved by the regression analyses for both datasets of countries, the negative value of $\alpha 1$. Thus, the inverse relationship between growth rate and initial level of income per capita is confirmed. The speed of convergence for WB is estimated approximately 7%, which is substantially higher than EU average growth rate and also WB region. It is calculated that the

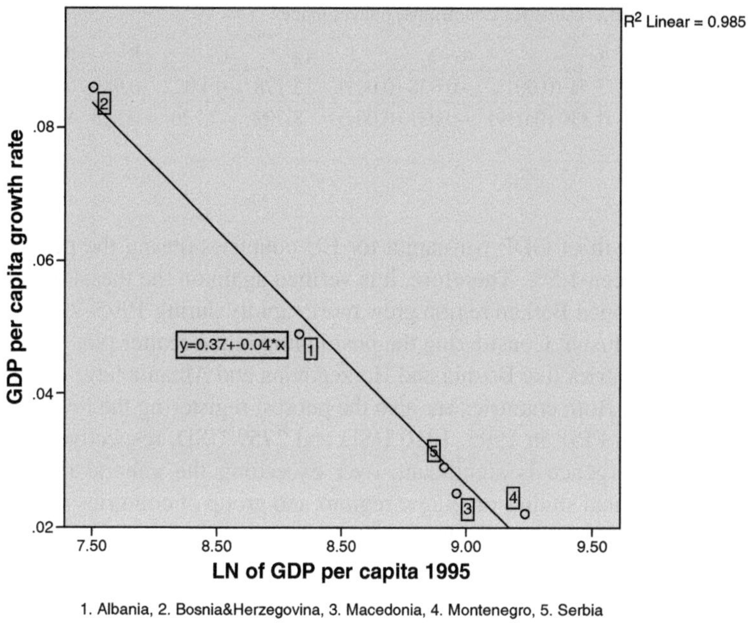

Fig. 35.1 Regression graph for the Western Balkan countries (Authors' calculations; Source: World Development Indicators)

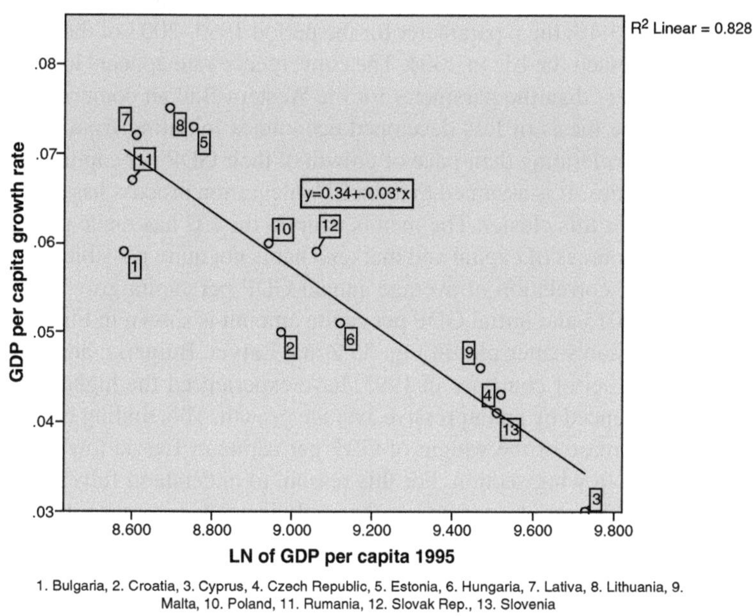

Fig. 35.2 Regression graph for 13 newest members of the EU (Authors' calculations; Source: World Development Indicators)

Table 35.1 Regression results for conditional convergence

Period	α_0	α_1	$t_{\alpha 0}$	$t_{\alpha 1}$	R^2	β-conv.	Beta
WB	3.71 (0.001)	−0.038 (0.001)	15.778	−14.022	0.980	Yes	0.071
13 newest EU members	0.339 (0.039)	−0.031 (0.004)	8.702	−7.276	0.828	Yes	0.048

mean annual growth of GDP per capita for EU countries during the period under observation has been 1.5%. Therefore, it is verified again on the thesis that in average the less developed Balkan region grew more rapidly during 1995–2015 than the EU average as a cluster. Considering the positioning in the scatter plot in Fig. 35.1, it is seen that countries like Bosnia and Herzegovina and Albania have experienced the major growth. Both countries are also the poorest registering the lowest level of GDP per capita in PPP[1] in 1995, 1810 USD and 2759 USD, respectively. The 7% speed of β convergence is significant, over exceeding the general trend of 2% reported by empirical studies on bigger regions and group of countries in Barro and Sala-i-Martin (1992). Following the *rule of 72* (it is used in finance and investment for calculating the time to double the initial capital), at suggested convergence speed, Albania would need approximately 10 years to double its 2015 GDP per capita.

For the newest members of the EU, the negative α1 confirms the existence of conditional convergence β. The indicator is calculated at about 4.8%, which is lower than 5.5%, estimated by Meksi and Xhaja (2015). Matkowski and Prochniak (2004) have calculated at 3.4% the β parameter for the period 1993–2003 of the eight CEE countries that accessed the EU in 2004. The convergence rate appears lower for the 13 last EU members than the parameter for the Western Balkan countries. Thus, it is again proved the thesis of less developed economies initiating from a very low GDP per capita accelerating their pace of growth of their GDP per capita more than developed economies. It is assumed that the EU integration process has sped up the catching-up rate for this cluster. The membership to the EU has made possible the opening of other sources of capital and markets that is not quite possible for Balkan region. A negative correlation of average annual GDP per capita growth rate over the period 1995–2015 and initial GDP per capita amount is shown in Fig. 35.2. It is seen in the regression scatter plot in Fig. 35.2 that Latvia, Bulgaria, and Romania, the poorest in this set of countries in 1995, have experienced the highest speed of convergence, evidenced by an impressive average growth. This finding is viewed by the substantial increase of the weight of GDP per capita of Latvia toward the EU, explained in the following section. For this reason, to understand fully the convergence situation of the set of countries in the study is needed to assess the absolute convergence parameter, σ. This assessment will give an insight if the conditional convergence is enough for Balkan countries to catch up the developed economy of the EU.

[1]Constant 2011 international $.

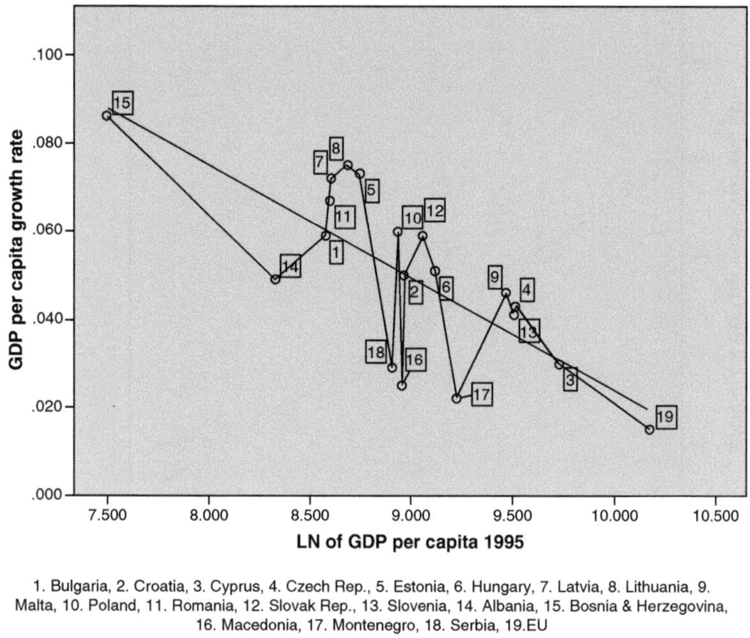

Fig. 35.3 Regression scatter plot 1995–2015 (Authors' calculations; Source: World Development Indicators)

35.3.2 Assessing Absolute Convergence

The conditional convergence among both set of countries, the Western Balkans and the 13 EU members is confirmed from the empirical analysis shown in Sect. 35.2. To understand if all 18 countries coming from communism regime despite their status in the EU have somehow converged with each other is assessed the conditional convergence of GDP per capita in PPP through the regression plot in Fig. 35.3. The graph provides insight on the differences in the development and the income per capita among the countries in the study. Again, the inverse interaction of initial level of income and growth rate is verified, but the rate is lower ($\beta = 3.4\%$). Although there are similarities in historical background, still countries are different in regard to their development stages. The growth has been higher for less developed economies in Europe, for the Western Balkans, and specifically for Bosnia and Herzegovina and Albania.

In order to estimate if their income per capita has really converged with other countries in the Balkans, meaning that the gap to the EU income is diminishing, absolute convergence is assessed through the parameter σ. The estimations are made by calculating the standard deviation for the logarithm of GDP per capita per each country toward the EU for the period 1995–2015. If the trend line of such regression scatter plot over time is negative, then absolute convergence exists. In such case, it

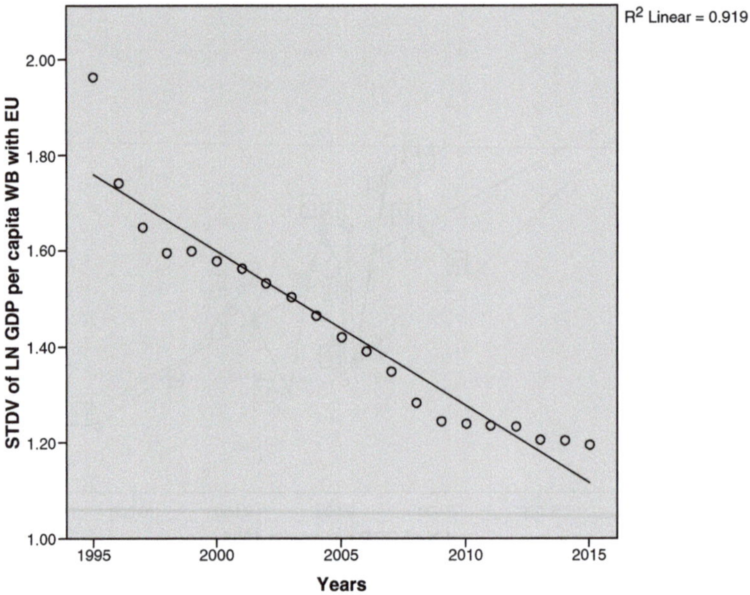

Fig. 35.4 Regression scatter plot of standard deviation of income per capita for WB, 1995–2015 (Authors' calculations; Source: World Development Indicators)

Fig. 35.5 Share of GDP per capita of the Balkans (Authors' calculations; Source: World Development Indicators)

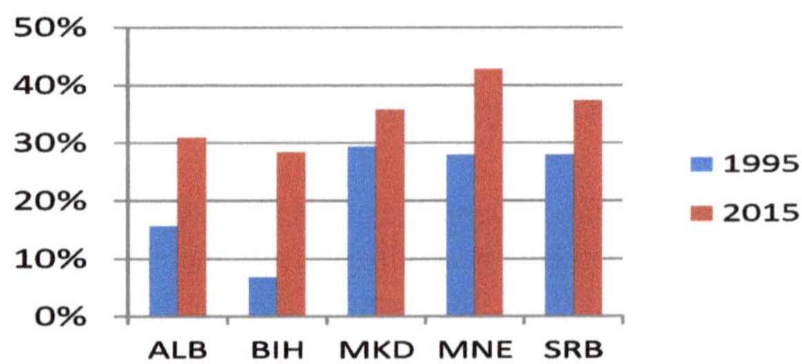

means that income dispersion tends to diminish. The regression results confirm a conditional convergence as the coefficient of the regression slope is negative, $\alpha 1 = -0.032$ (see Fig. 35.4).

Therefore, GDP per capita of the Western Balkans is diminishing the gap with GDP per capita of the EU. A picture of the catching up is given in Fig. 35.5 where two moments of the share of GDP per capita per each WB country versus the EU GDP per capita, at the initial year 1995 and the last year of study 2015, are provided.

The divergence of income per capita among countries in the Balkans with the EU is diminished. A substantial decrease of the gap is highlighted in the poorest countries of the region, such as Bosnia and Herzegovina and Albania, although they are still lagging far behind from the EU income per capita.

35.4 Convergence of Productivity in Western Balkans

To assess the convergence of productivity, the indicator of GDP per person employed is used throughout 1995–2015. Relevant data are generated by the World Development Indicators database for all the countries in the study. The entire WB region has experienced a growth in productivity during the transition path, appearing higher in some countries than the growth rate of income per capita. The country where the highest decrease of the gap of GDP per person employed with the EU is Bosnia and Herzegovina followed by Romania, Albania, and Montenegro. However, for the entire region, the average of GDP per person employed stands to about 50% than that of the EU. (see Fig. 35.6).

So far, we have analyzed the conditional and absolute convergence of income per capita variable. Herein, the same model will be used for calculating the conditional convergence of GDP per person employed, β parameter. The parameter will give information of the speed of convergence through β for the GDP per capita in PPP per WB countries toward the EU. The relevant regression equation will assess the relationship between the independent variable which is log GDP per employee for 1995 and the dependent variable which is the average annual growth rate of GDP per employee for 1995–2015. In case a sign of negative correlation is shown and the requirement for regression analyses is met, the existence of conditional convergence within productivity levels in the WB countries may be concluded.

The regression scatter plot for the convergence of productivity of WB countries toward the EU is depicted in Fig. 35.7. The relationship in the regression is given by the negative slope of regression line and the negative coefficient of the eq. A strong correlation among variables is also confirmed where R^2 equals 0.78. Again, the poorest countries in the region at their productivity level have grown more rapidly (Bosnia and Herzegovina, Albania, etc.) than the developed ones (EU).

Based on the regression results, it is calculated at 5,2% the parameter β convergence of GDP per person employed. Although there is the positive trend of convergence at productivity levels, it seems that it is not experiencing the same speed as the convergence of income per capita, calculated at 7% rate for WB countries. The core question remains on how the region can boost productivity and growth. The increase in productivity will make the WB more competitive for investors and European markets as well. The intensification of regional economic connections,

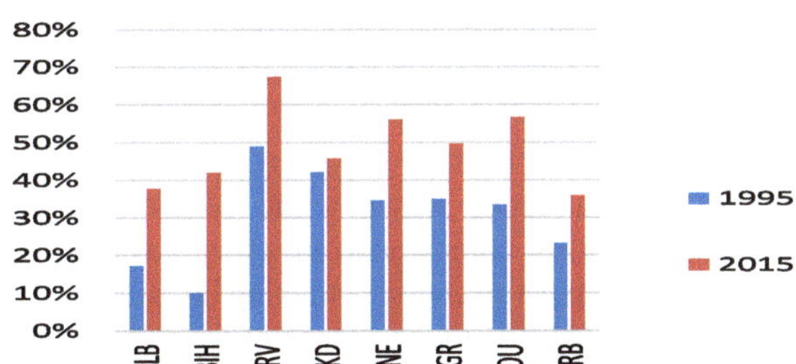

Fig. 35.6 Share of GDP per person employed toward countries to the EU GDP per capita EU (Authors' calculations; Source: World Development Indicators)

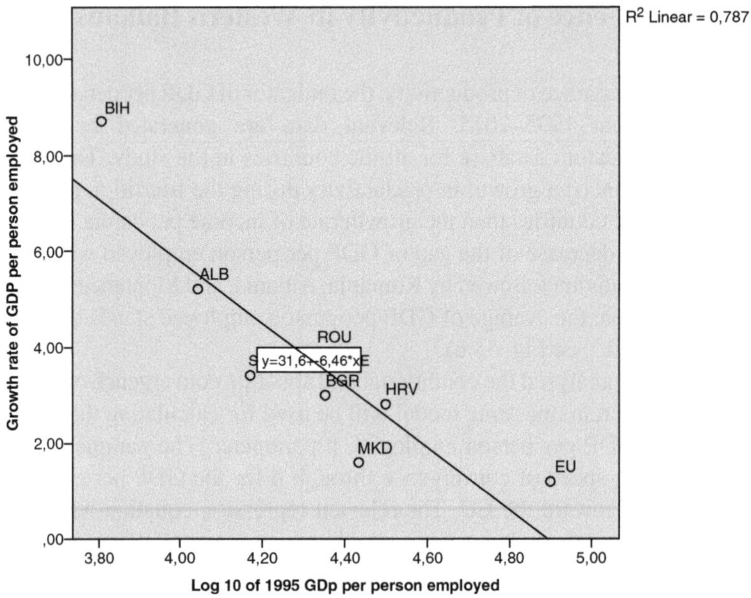

Fig. 35.7 Regression scatter plot of GDP per person employed (Authors' calculations; Source: World Development Indicators)

adherence to common supply chains, and attraction of innovative technologies are seen as priorities for the region in the context of European integration. The WB region has the potential for attracting foreign investments due to low labor costs combined with relatively well-educated people as well as geographic location to EU markets. Thus incentivizing innovation to the economy and investing in human resources are key factors for competitiveness and productivity. According to the Global Competitiveness Reports of World Economic Forum, the WB is still ranked low in a set of competitiveness indicators in particular on innovation pillar where concrete measures are immediate to speed up the process.

35.5 Conclusions

Although Balkan countries have experienced higher growth rates, still it has not been enough for reducing the gap with the EU in comparison with the newest EU member countries. The WB region continues to feel the aftershock of global crisis reflected in lower rates of growth after 2009. To that extent, the catching up is slowed down affecting somehow the membership process. The countries need to explore better their comparative advantages as a region to improve their productivity and thus competitiveness. Attracting investments that bring innovation, technology, and high skills is the challenge of the region. Thus, efforts have to be focused on creating a conducive environment for investments and technology. The contribution of FDIs in innovation and technology is still limited although the countries are moderately converging in terms of GDP per capita and GDP per person employed.

References

Abramovitz, M.: Inventories and Business Cycles with Special References to Manufacturer's Inventories, NBER, 40–74 (1950)

Barro, R.J., Sala-i-Martin, X.: Economic Growth and Convergence accross the United States, NBER Working Paper 3419 (1990)

Barro, R.J., Sala-i-Martin, X.: Convergence. J. Polit. Econ. **100**(2), 223–251 (1992)

Matkowski, Z., Prochniak, M.: Real economic convergence in the EU accession countries. Int. J. Appl. Econ. Quant. Stud. **1–3**, (2004)

Meksi, E., Xhaja, E.: On economic convergence of Albania and other Balkan countries with EU. Int. J. Sci. Inno. New Technol. **1**(13), 9–19 (2015)

Myrdal, G.: Economic Theory and Underdeveloped Regions, published by Gerald Duckworth & co Ltd., (1957)

Prebisch, R.: Commercial policy in the underdeveloped countries. The American Economic Review, Vol. 49, No. 2, Papers and Proceedings of the Seventy – First Annual Meeting of the American Economic Association (1959)

Singer, H.W.: The distribution of gains between investing and borrowing countries. The American Economic Review Vol. 40, No. 2, Papers and Proceedings of the Sixty-Second Annual Meeting of the American Economic Association (1950)

Solow, R.: A contribution to the theory of economic growth. Q. J. Econ. **70**(1), 65–94 (1956)

Van Ark, B., Piatkowski, M.: Productivity, Innovation and ICT in Old and New Europe Research Memorandum GD-69. Groningen Growth and Development Centre, Groningen (2004)

Chapter 36
Strategic Analysis and Evaluation of a Research University's Performance

Oksana Zhylinska and Maksim Sitnitskiy

Abstract The article analyzes and compares the main rating systems of research universities' performance at the world level. It also suggests a system of relevant criteria designed to conduct strategic analysis and evaluation of a research university's performance. The criteria allow objectivizing the results of the evaluation while minimizing the level of a subjective component within a set of consolidated results.

Keywords Research university • Activity evaluation • Evaluation criteria • Strategic analysis • Assessment rankings • Evaluation methodology

36.1 Introduction

According to the concept of research development in the countries of the European Union, as well as other European countries, national governments are responsible for their education and training systems. On the other hand, universities form and implement their own research programs. At the same time, the problems faced by research universities in all EU countries are similar. Above all, this addresses concerns about the objectivity that universities must meet the challenges of the future. As a result, an objective assessment of their own potential creates the basis for future planning. It does this along with the development of existing research programs and the expected results of educational and research activities. According to the Education and Training Program of the Strategy for 2020 (ET2020), the EU sets five key priorities for higher education. Those priorities are (1) increasing the number of graduates of higher education institutions; (2) improving the quality and relevance of teaching and learning; (3) facilitating student and teacher mobility and

---

O. Zhylinska (✉) • M. Sitnitskiy
Taras Shevchenko National University of Kyiv, Kyiv, Ukraine
e-mail: zhylinska@ukr.net; maksim.sitnitskiy@ukr.net

S.C. Mărginean et al. (eds.), *Emerging Issues in the Global Economy*, Springer Proceedings in Business and Economics,
https://doi.org/10.1007/978-3-319-71876-7_36

cross-border cooperation; (4) strengthening of the "knowledge triangle," linking the areas of education, research and development (R & D), and innovation; and (5) creating effective mechanisms for management and financing of higher education. Up to 40% of young Europeans with a higher education should direct their efforts toward the implementation of these priorities. This should be done in order to satisfy the needs of today's Europe for economic growth and prosperity. Creation of new jobs will ensure the realization of high-quality human capital. It is through the comprehensive potential of research universities that the current issues of society have to be addressed and resolved.

36.2 Literature Review

Historically, the first classification of universities took place in the United States in the Carnegie's book *Carnegie Classification* (1973). In subsequent years it was consistently reprinted (1976, 1987, 1994, 2000, 2005) by its Foundation, The Carnegie Foundation for the Advancement of Teaching (2017). The main purpose of the classification was to create the conditions for improving the level of teaching at universities. The system of evaluation was based on the principle of university competitiveness, that is to say, for universities of research on an open competitive basis.

At the same time, only the most prestigious universities were included in the classification. Others could not reach this level because of the high bar of the evaluation criteria. In fact, the necessity for objectivity of evaluation criteria arose when the first version of the rating was published. The last classification (2005) was substantially revised. In 2014, the Carnegie Foundation transferred the responsibility for the Carnegie Classification of Higher Education Institutions to the Center for Advanced Studies at the Indiana University School of Education.

US News & World Report (1983) published its own rating, based on the principle of a clear definition of the criteria for evaluating the performance of research universities. This provided a far greater objectivity in the results. Among the main criteria they put forward for universities were the following: (a) the administration assessment of competitive universities, (b) the ratio of the number of graduates and the number of freshmen, (c) the results of entrance examinations, (d) the proportion between the number of submitted applications and the number of enrolled students, (e) the quality of teaching staff and their wages, (f) average training expenses per student, and (g) assessment and feedback from graduates on the quality of study at the university.

The current world ranking of universities was developed by the Chinese University of Shanghai (2003). It is called the Academic Ranking of World Universities or the "Shanghai Ranking" in short.

In 2004, the British Rating from the publication, Times Higher Education, "QS World University Rankings" was published for the first time. At the same time as the British Ranking (2004), the Spanish National Research Council (CSIC) issued the Webometrics Ranking of World Universities. It reflected the extent of the presence of a research university on the Internet. The peculiarities of approaches to assess research universities' performance are analyzed in more detail further on.

The works of such scholars as Babansky (2000) and Gorelov et al. (2002) deserve special attention as they contributed a lot to the issue on the development of research universities' ranking system and their effective management. Their works focus on the justification of evaluation criteria for higher educational institutions of the research type and the authors' approach to the methodology.

Wedlin (2004, 2007), analyzing the system of evaluation of business education at a research university, created the author's development of ratings of research universities and education management in them, while a scientometric specialist, Leydesdorff (2008), noted a growing focus on university rankings as a method of assessing their role in the global community.

Kalenyuk (2007, 2008) in his studies emphasizes the importance of the human resource component when developing objectivity of the assessment criteria for the institutions that provide educational services. It is the high education and leadership qualities of education staff which play a decisive role in shaping the competitiveness crucial to the process of Ukraine's integration into European realm of science and education.

In the series of scientific works, the Ukrainian scientist Kurbatov (2008, 2011, 2015a, 2015b, 2016) studies the process of formation of university ratings in Ukraine and abroad. The author highlights the possibilities for objectivity of rating indicators. He also shows the British innovation approaches in the development of international university rankings. He researches the influence of university ratings on the development of modern academic politics and provides justification for theoretical and methodological principles of development of international university ratings.

Antonyuk and Satsyk (2009) study in detail the issues of international competitiveness management of research universities and summarize the experience of their management within the leaders of the global market for educational services.

Zhylinska in her scientific publications (2010–2016) discloses the economic nature of educational services from the standpoint of the institutional approach, according to which the educational service is a trustworthy blessing with high transaction costs of measuring quality and identifying alternatives. Attention is focused on the accelerated development of globalization processes in the field of higher education. This provided the needs for a new information product: university rankings designed to reduce the information asymmetry on the world markets. Based on the application of analytical apparatus, it was determined that the system of rating assessment of universities' effectiveness is based on the economic criteria of their performance and in the field. Whereas, the expert assessment of research and innovation activities of universities in ranking becomes a socially significant assessment as economic agents from the point of view of scientific ethics. The latter is intended to minimize the transaction costs of choosing alternatives on the markets with a high level of information asymmetry based on the institute's reputation. A modern entrant connects his expectations of higher education with the level of future income. The decision to choose a university and obtain a degree is based on certain benchmarks, the ratings that reduce the information asymmetry on the market of educational services. The abovementioned research emphasizes the importance of objectivity in assessment criteria to evaluate scientific results of research universities and the relevance of the continuation of scientific research in this direction to single out balanced indicators and minimize the subjective approach.

Scientific literature has already addressed the problem of manipulating the ratings of universities. In their work, Balatsky and Yekymova (2012) note such issues as the conjectural nature of publication activity indicators and the index of quotes.

(A) The problem of a 2-year window when evaluating the impact factor of a magazine
(B) Status manipulation of foreign students and professors
(C) The prestige effect of professors' replacement (Shanghai Rating)
(D) The effect of excessive trust to a university when collecting information for the rating assessment
(E) The "anchor effect" in reputational surveys when a university with a high reputation score in the previous year improves its position
(F) The need to increase the "cognitive distance" between the expert and the object of evaluation
(G) The strong nucleus syndrome – in the reputation rating of the powerful core of the top 6 and the blurred "tail" of 94 universities

The focus of the scientific work of Pavlenko and Antonyuk (2014) lies in the systemizing of methodological principles of competitiveness. It also entails the generalization of establishment experience of the world-class universities along with determination of their role and significance in economic growth of their countries. There is some discussion of the research of tendencies in high school development regarding the formation mechanisms of competitive advantages. Moreover, the work analyzes the competitive situation of Ukrainian higher educational establishments and defines strategic directions for creation and development of the world-class research universities in Ukraine.

The scholar Ilnytskyi (2015) report in depth the subject of methodological aspects and tools for assessing the international competitiveness of research universities, referred to by the author as the world-class universities. In this context, he disclose the methodical foundations for assessing the competitive positions of universities. The research also highlights the features of rating methodologies for research universities and business schools compared with the Ukrainian methodological approaches to ranking universities.

Sheremetieva (2014) in her research investigates the legal status and features of a research university in contemporary Ukrainian conditions in the context of best practices of world research universities. The scholar makes an expert review of the new Law of Ukraine "On Higher Education" and proposes measures to improve certain provisions of this legal act.

In this context, we plan to analyze the qualities that form successful management practices of research universities' development and the leaders of the global educational services market, based on their strategic flexibility.

A significant contribution to the development of methodological foundations was made by scientists Zong and Wang (2017). They developed their own approach to assessing research capacity, investigated on the basis of scientific and technical work criterion. The researchers rated four university alliances from North America, Great Britain, Australia, and China. Each was selected as subjects of thematic research on evaluation. In the process of evaluation, a hierarchical structure was created to show the impact factors on research potential. The results were compared and discussed in an expert environment to check the effectiveness and feasibility of the study.

36.3 Goals of the Article

The purpose of this article is to show ways to improve the effectiveness of a research university evaluation through objectivity in a criteria system for an evaluation procedure. The strategic analysis issues are considered in a broad and nonspecific context. This will allow readers to consider the diversity of relevant criteria. This will also give these criteria a different weight in accordance with their contribution and the level of impact on the development of a research university.

36.4 Methodology and Empirical Results

The evaluation criteria for determining the rating are an extremely important component. Their subjectivity must be minimal. Nowadays, there are three recognizable ranking systems: (1) the Shanghai Ranking "Academic Ranking of World Universities," (2) the British Ranking "QS World University Rankings," and (3) the Spanish "Webometrics Ranking of World Universities." The indicated rating systems make it possible to evaluate the performance of a university by comparing it to other research-based educational institutions. Table 36.1 lists and analyzes the criteria for evaluating these rating systems.

The authors' articles substantiate the thesis about the necessity to determine the relevant assessment criteria that most fully correspond to the essence and the main purpose of a research university. This helps to avoid subjectivity in the process of evaluation and criticism of the rating results obtained.

The mission of the modern institution is to create a system for generating scientific and technical knowledge. It is there for a subsequent knowledge transfer through a provision of educational services. The net result is the creation of new generations of researchers and generators of new knowledge. Another aspect is the economic implementation through commercialization or creation of new innovation participants: start-up companies. The effective implementation of this mission is also based on creation of a mechanism to encourage the development of these activities. It is also capable of intensifying their interaction on both internal university

Table 36.1 Criteria for assessing research universities by the leading rating systems of the world (Source: Developed by authors based on Shanghai Ranking Academic Ranking of World Universities (2017), QS World University Rankings (2017), Webometrics Ranking of World Universities (2017))

No.	Rating system	Criteria	Fraction (%)
1.	Academic ranking of world universities	1. Nobel prize or fields medals laureates among alumni	10
		2. Nobel prize or fields medals laureates among staff	20
		3. "Highly cited researchers in 21 categories"	20
		4. Articles published in nature or science journals	20
		5. Natural sciences and humanities citation index by the Institute of Scientific Information (ISI), science citation index and social sciences citation index, as well as indexes of the leading journals, arts and humanities citation index	20
		6. University size	10
2.	QS world university rankings	1. Reputation in the academic environment	40
		2. Citation of scientific publications of the university representatives	20
		3. The ratio of the number of teachers and students	20
		4. Attitudes of employers to the graduates	10
		5. Relative number of foreign teachers and students	5
3.	Webometrics ranking of world universities	1. The number of pages of all formats present on the university site and indexed by Google's search engine	20
		2. The combination of the number of external hyperlinks to the university's domain (external inlinks) and the number of domains these links come from (referring domains) two providers, majestic SEO and Ahrefs, is used to increase the validity of data. Thus, the resulting values of external inlinks and referring domains are selected as the maximum of these two sources. According to the authors, the number of such links indicates the visibility of the university and the importance of published materials (most of these links serve the same way as a citation in the bibliography)	50
		3. The number of adobe acrobat (.pdf), Microsoft word (.doc, .docx), and Microsoft PowerPoint (.ppt) files on the university site indexed by the academic search engine: Google scholar	15
		4. Scientific articles published by the authors of the university in journals indexed in SCOPUS, the international science and technology base, and being the 10% part of the articles most cited in their scientific fields, according to the Scimago Group	15

level and on the level of partnerships with business, academic, and governmental institutions. In accordance with this purpose, we will attempt to single out our own system of criteria. These will be the most relevant from the economic and managerial points of view, providing an objective assessment of performance (Fig. 36.1).

Figure 36.1 shows ten relevant criteria for assessing university performance with an appropriate percentage of the total result of the university assessment rating. Further, each of them is characterized separately and in detail.

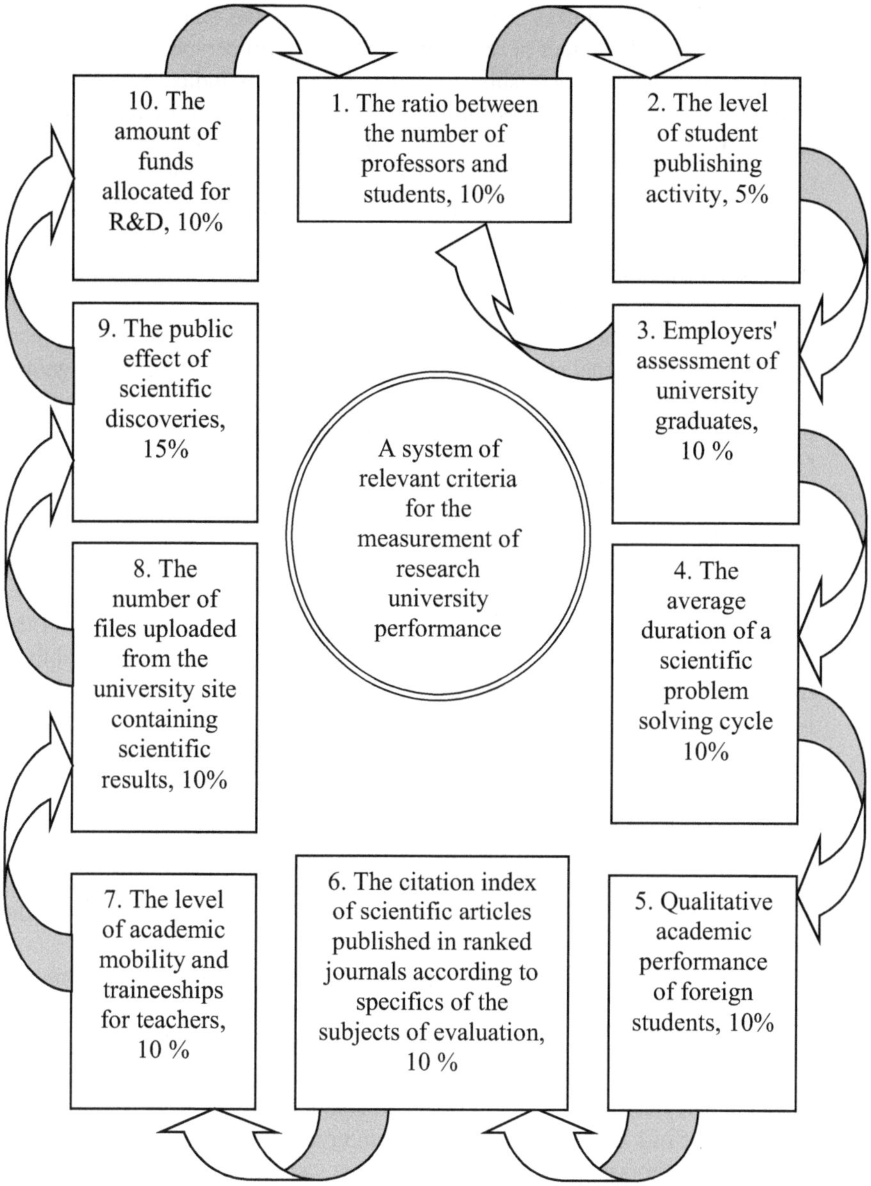

Fig. 36.1 A system of relevant criteria for the measurement of research university performance (Source: Developed by authors)

1. The ratio between the number of professors and students (10%) – In this criterion, we consider it necessary to compare not the total number of teachers and students, as done previously, but the number of scientific and pedagogical workers of higher education as represented by professors. This assessment

demonstrates the readiness of a university to ensure the quality of the educational process and conduct of research in the long-term perspective.

2. The level of students' publishing activity (5%) – This indicator is not sufficiently relevant given the possibility of insufficient quality of research conducted by students. Nevertheless, it should be taken into account in the consolidated result of the rating. It reflects the level of research competence of new researchers and realizes the strategic direction of evaluation. The continuity of scientific research subjects forms a solid systemic structure in the strategic perspective which guards against the emergence of "human resource-hunger" and preserves "institutional memory."
3. Employers' assessment of university graduates (10%) – This indicator reflects the universities external image in the context of professional competence gained by graduates in relation to their success in the labor market. Despite its importance, this criterion applies only to the university ranking system "QS World University Rankings".
4. The average duration of a scientific problem-solving cycle (10%) – In our opinion, the application of this criterion enables the identification of the quality of university's scientific and pedagogical composition. This means that existing assessment systems use static assessment indicators. It does not fully assess the effectiveness of R&D. The assessment of a university's performance and the quality of its results should, first of all, be manifested at the level of its ability/readiness to perform scientific tasks for a limited period of time and with limited resources in hand.
5. Qualitative academic performance of foreign students (10%) – Here we take under consideration quantitative parameters that are not currently used in performance rating. These do not objectively reflect the level of acquired competencies by foreign students but, first of all, qualitative parameters of their academic success. This criterion shows the ability of a university to attract a foreign student and prepare him as a research specialist to be competitive in the labor market.
6. Citation index of scientific articles published in ranked journals according to specifics of the subjects of evaluation (10%) – This criterion is considered to be the most discussed in scientific circles. It happens because the quality R&D results done by researchers are not fully taken into account by existing rating systems. They only measure the quantitative index of published works in a certain range of journals, belonging to the international science-computer databases. The authors of the article argue against such restrictions. They propose taking into account the level of scientific influence and public resonance of journals included in other scientometric databases when evaluating the quality of scientific work.
7. The level of academic mobility and traineeships for teachers (10%) – The processes of experience exchange, approval of research results, and providing additional competencies for scientists and teachers should receive high priority

in assessment of university performance. The promotion of international coauthorship becomes a top priority when assessing the quality of results. It is specifically seen in the editorial policy of scientific journals that are part of international science-computer databases. Strengthening this component of the criteria defines a necessary condition for its inclusion in those databases. It relates to the ethnic diversity of editorial board members and authors of scientific publications. The international composition of authors and the presence of foreign authors are welcomed. Scientific publications where the authors of one scientific organization or university are not included in the Scopus database are not internationally productive. The impact of cooperation and the high quality of scientific results of international authors' groups were confirmed by the results of the OECD survey, in 2003–2011. In all countries with the highest levels of scientific and technical knowledge generation, the share of scientific articles with a high citation index is a result of international cooperation. In the total number of the most cited articles, they significantly exceed the proportion of articles produced in cooperation with national authors. For example, in the United States, it is 1.2 times; in Japan and China, it is 1.8 times; in Great Britain it is 3.8 times; and in France it is 34 times. The high quality of results is seen further in the following areas: (1) in the total number of scientific articles in the Scopus database and (2) the share of articles with a high citation index of international teams of authors which is many times higher than the share of similar articles by the leading national authors. This is an indicator ranging from 14.5% in China to 25% in the United States and South Korea and up to over 50% in Austria and Sweden.

8. The number of files uploaded from a university site containing scientific results (10%) – This indicator shows the level of interest and online mobility of the users of scientific and technical information. Quantitative download tells about innovation and timeliness of a disclosure of scientific and technical information to the public.
9. The public effect of scientific discoveries (15%) – According to our belief, the criterion should embrace the university's reputation an academic environment. This should embrace the number of graduates along with any Nobel Prize or Fields Medals Laureates among university staff. However, we should not evaluate the number of awards, medals, and titles received, but the level of results behind these awards. It means encouraging universities to conduct research to solve socially significant problems ensuring strategic orientation in any future rating assessment.
10. The number of funds allocated for R&D (10%) – The criterion of the level of resources directed to R&D indicates the level of interest of business environment representatives, State, other public entities, and private investors, in the efficiency of university results. It gives a real picture of university's level of self-sufficiency.

36.5 Conclusions

A detailed analysis of the existing global rating systems has made it possible to compare their criteria and their share in the consolidated rating result. Based on the revealed reserves, we propose an optimized system of relevant criteria. This will minimize the subjective approach to the process of strategic analysis and performance evaluation. Its application will reduce the level of tension and criticism of rating subjects in relation to its results. This will be a consolidated representation for each university and its research results. At the same time, the system of rating assessment should provide the possibility of adjusting the presented evaluation criteria. This should be done within the context of the latest scientific and technological achievements and socioeconomic development of society.

Therefore, in further research we consider it necessary to develop our own methodology for the process of strategic analysis evaluation and when measuring each university's research performance. The methodology will be based on the elimination of weaknesses and strengthening reserves of the existing world rating systems.

References

Antonyuk, L., Satsyk, V.: Tendencje i perspektywy jakościowego wzrostu gospodarczego Ukrainy, Konwergencja modeli ekonomicznych. Polska i Ukraina, Część 3.4, pp. 394–409. Fundacja Uniwersytetu Ekonomicznego w Krakowie, Kraków (2009)

Babansky, M.: Classical universities: modernity and prospects. Univ. Manag. Pract. Anal. **2**(13), 20–21 (2000)

Balatsky, E., Yekymova, N.: Global university ratings: the problem of manipulation. J. New Econ. Assoc. **1**(13), 126–148 (2012)

Carnegie Foundation for the Advancement of Teaching. https://www.carnegiefoundation.org (2017). Accessed 18 June 2017

Gorelov, B., Karmazinskii, A., Klygina, I.: Technique for rating assessment of a technical university. Scientific session, vol.6 Actual problems of humanities. Problems of university education. Economics and Management, pp. 118–120. MEPHI (2002)

Ilnytskyi, D.: Universities in the global knowledge economy: an eclectic paradigm. Int. Econ. Policy. **1**(22), 123–155 (2015)

Kalenyuk, I.: The development of European integration in educational sphere. Shared European environment: harmonization of megaregional contradictions [Monograph]. In: Lukyanenko, D., Chuzhikova, V., 456–464. KNEU, Kyiv (2007)

Kalenyuk, I.: Educational imperative to ensure competitiveness of national economy. Compet. Monit. **1-2**, 74–76 (2008)

Kurbatov, S.: University rankings as education indicators. Philosophy of Education: Scientific Journal "Chasopys", No. 1–2 (7). Institute of Higher Education of the Academy of Pedagogical Sciences of Ukraine, National Pedagogical University named after M.P. Drahomanov, Ukranian Academy of Political Sciences, 309–317. Publishing House of the NPU named after M.P. Drahomanov, Kyiv (2008)

Kurbatov, S.: A university of the world class as a materialization of the idea of an elite educational institution. Manag. Soc. Syst. Phil. Psychol. Pedag. Soc. **3**, 11–18 (2011)

Kurbatov, S.: Theoretical and methodological perspectives of international university ratings development. High. Educ. Ukraine. **1**, 34–39 (2015a)
Kurbatov, S.: University rankings and their influence on contemporary academic policy. Ann. Sci. Polit. **4**(2), 75–79 (2015b)
Kurbatov, S.: Modern British innovations in the development of international university rankings. High. Educ. Ukraine. **1**, 65–73 (2016)
Leydesdorff, L.: Caveats for the use of citation indicators in research and journals evaluation. J. Am. Soc. Inform. Sci. Technol. **59**(2), 278–287 (2008)
Pavlenko, A., Antonyuk, L., (Eds): Research Universities: world experience and development prospects in Ukraine: Monograph. Ministry of Education and Science of Ukraine, Kyiv. National Economic University named after Vadym Hetman, Institute of higher education, 350 p. KNEU, Kyiv (2014)
QS World University Rankings. https://www.topuniversities.com (2017). Accessed 18 June 2017
Shanghai Ranking Academic Ranking of World Universities (ARWU). http://www.shanghairanking.com. (2017). Accessed 18 June 2017
Sheremetieva, O.: Legal status and features of a research university in modern conditions (in the context of the law of Ukraine "on higher education"). Legal Regul. Econ. **14**, 29–40 (2014)
Webometrics Ranking of World Universities. http://www.webometrics.info (2017). Accessed 18 June 2017
Wedlin, L.: Playing the Ranking Game. Field Formation and Boundary-work in European Management Education. University of Uppsala, 242 p. (2004)
Wedlin, L.: The role of ranking in codifying a business school template: classification, diffusion and mediated isomorphism in organizational fields. Eur. Manag. Rev. **4**, 24–39 (2007)
Zhylinska, O.: Research universities in commercialization of R&D results. Modern science and technology: from fundamental research to commercialization of R & D results. Materials of the International Scientific and Practical Conference, pp. 171–173. Phoenix, Kyiv (2010)
Zhylinska, O.: Complementary effects in development activation of scientific and technological activities in information society. Bulletin of the Taras Shevchenko Kiev National University. Series: Economics. **9**(186), 6–15 (2016). doi.org/10.17721/1728-2667.2015/172-7/1
Zong, F., Wang, L.: Evaluation of university scientific research ability based on the output of sci-tech papers: a D-AHP approach. PLoS One. **12**(2), (2017.) https://doi.org/10.1371/journal.pone.0171437. Accessed 17 June 2017

MIX
Papier aus verantwortungsvollen Quellen
Paper from responsible sources
FSC® C105338

FSC
www.fsc.org

If you have any concerns about our products,
you can contact us on
ProductSafety@springernature.com

In case Publisher is established outside the EU,
the EU authorized representative is:
Springer Nature Customer Service Center GmbH
Europaplatz 3, 69115 Heidelberg, Germany

Printed by Libri Plureos GmbH
in Hamburg, Germany